WOMEN IN COMBAT

Selected Titles in ABC-CLIO's
CONTEMPORARY WORLD ISSUES
Series

For a complete list of titles in this series, please visit
www.abc-clio.com

Books in the Contemporary World Issues series address vital issues in today's society, such as genetic engineering, pollution, and biodiversity. Written by professional writers, scholars, and nonacademic experts, these books are authoritative, clearly written, up-to-date, and objective. They provide a good starting point for research by high school and college students, scholars, and general readers as well as by legislators, businesspeople, activists, and others.

Each book, carefully organized and easy to use, contains an overview of the subject, a detailed chronology, biographical sketches, facts and data and/or documents and other primary source material, a directory of organizations and agencies, annotated lists of print and nonprint resources, and an index.

Readers of books in the Contemporary World Issues series will find the information they need to have a better understanding of the social, political, environmental, and economic issues facing the world today.

WOMEN IN COMBAT

A Reference Handbook

Rosemarie Skaine

CONTEMPORARY WORLD ISSUES

 ABC-CLIO

Santa Barbara, California • Denver, Colorado • Oxford, England

Library of Congress Cataloging-in-Publication Data

Skaine, Rosemarie.
    Women in combat : a reference handbook / Rosemarie Skaine.
      p. cm. — (Contemporary world issues)
    Includes bibliographical references and index.
      ISBN 978–1–59884–459–7 (alk. paper) — ISBN 978–1–59884–460–3 (e-book)
1. Women in combat—United States. 2. Women in combat—
Government policy—United States. 3. United States—Armed Forces—
Women. 4. United States—Armed Forces—Women—Biography.
5. Women soldiers—United States—Biography. 6. Women sailors—United
States—Biography. I. Title.
UB418.W65S563   2011
355.4082′0973—dc22   2010039859

ISBN: 978–1–59884–459–7
EISBN: 978–1–59884–460–3

15 14 13 12 11   1 2 3 4 5

This book is also available on the World Wide Web as an eBook.
Visit www.abc-clio.com for details.

ABC-CLIO, LLC
130 Cremona Drive, P.O. Box 1911
Santa Barbara, California 93116-1911

This book is printed on acid-free paper ∞

Manufactured in the United States of America

Contents

List of Tables and Figures

Preface

From ancient times, women have fought their country's enemies. They fought sometimes as queens, sometimes as gener-
als, sometimes as admirals, sometimes as foot soldiers. Not
all societies, however, admitted women into the military. Some
women were permitted to join the military but not permitted to
serve in combat. In the United States today, women comprise
more than 15 percent of the military, but society remains divided
as to whether women should be legally allowed to serve in
combat.

Defining combat is basic to understanding what drives the
controversy. In the 1990s, change took place in two types of combat: allowing women to fly aircraft and to be assigned to ships at
sea. In ground combat, the third aspect of combat, policy, not
law states women are not to be assigned. Despite the policy,
women serve in ground combat in Operation Iraqi Freedom and
Operation Enduring Freedom in Afghanistan. On what basis do
women serve in ground combat? Are women permitted to defend
themselves, but not to engage the enemy? In the type of wars the
United States is involved in today where there is no front line, is it
possible to not attack the enemy? When women are placed in
combat, how is it justified? Chapter 1 seeks to outline the issues
of ground combat by framing the controversy in the context of
history, law, and policy.

Women who serve in combat zones face specific challenges.
Women face sexual issues: pregnancies, harassment, assault, rape,
and consensual relationships including same sex. Suicide and
murder are also potential problems. Balancing family life and work
is a challenge as is, for some, reconciling serving in combat with
their religious beliefs. After their service is completed, women
have readjustment issues. Post-traumatic stress disorder (PTSD)

and suicide have increased as women return to civilian life. Chapter 2 examines these challenges and presents both sides of the issues. The controversy on whether women should serve in combat is intense. Proposed solutions to the issue range from reinstating rigid exclusion provisions to repealing the remaining exclusion provisions.

Worldwide, countries are opening military service to women. Countries that already have women in their armed forces are expanding military occupations open to women. Despite this growth in numbers, most countries are disinclined to place women in combat. This reluctance is found even in countries that require women to serve in the military. Chapter 3 surveys women in military combat worldwide and assesses women serving in countries' state-based or government-run military. It examines as well women who are actively involved in revolutionary movements whether state-based or independent of the state. In the context of these movements, the chapter examines female suicide bombing as a component of modern warfare.

Women have served in warfare since ancient times, and women in the United States have served the military since the Revolutionary War (1775–1783). Chapter 4 presents a chronology of the evolution of U.S. military women's status from active supporter to clandestine combatant to overt warrior and of the issues that defined change such as, whether women are needed to win the war and whether there is a cultural lag present in American society that affects change?

Voices supporting and opposing women in combat are found in the biographies in Chapter 5. Included are women who have performed exceptionally in military duty or have had an effect on the issues of women in the military and combat. The biographies selected are representative of how women serve. Some of the women are on active duty, others are retired. Women in the wars in Iraq and Afghanistan are serving in ground combat and are receiving and returning fire. Two of the biographies that demonstrate that women served in combat and did so with honor are Veronica Alfaro and Monica L. Brown. Specialist (Spc.) Veronica Alfaro, U.S. Army, was granted the military's fourth-highest combat award, the Bronze Star Medal for Valor, in Iraq in 2008; and Private First Class (Pfc.) Monica L. Brown, U.S. Army, is a combat medic from the 782nd Brigade Support Battalion, 4th Brigade Combat Team, 82nd Airborne Division, who did not take cover but went through gunfire to assist comrades. On March 20, 2008, she became the second female Silver Star recipient since World War II.

Biographies of those opposed to allowing women in combat include Elaine Donnelly, founder and president of the Center for Military Readiness, and Dr. Peter A. Lillback, president, Westminster Theological Seminary. The people and their differing views represent the fabric of our larger society and its divergent views.

Chapter 6 supports Chapters 1 through 5 with data and documents. The data identifies the active duty women service members, how they serve, how many women serve and in what capacity, for example, by race, by service and by enlisted or officer status. Other data include the number of deaths in current wars and the number of servicewomen in specific wars. Documents pertaining to policy and law are included. The separation of powers parts of the U.S. Constitution are included. The section on the Policy Concerning Homosexuality in The Armed Forces has the language of the law when passed and testimony from a member opposed to repeal. A major feature of this chapter is a table entitled, "Selected Military Awards." This table serves as a valuable addendum to Chapter 5 Biographies. It provides information for approximately 50 awards on the award's authorizing source, description, and requirements. Awards include: the Purple Heart, Silver Star, Bronze Star, North Atlantic Treaty Organization (NATO) Medal, and awards for specific conflicts.

Chapter 7 Directory of Organizations and Chapter 8 Resources provide places to look for information on topics covered in the book. The directory offers a wide variety of groups that have an interest in women in combat. Some groups support women in combat while others oppose. The groups are governmental, nongovernmental (NGOs), and private. Some organizations offer online resources including bibliographies, chronologies, Internet links, and articles. The Resources chapter contains print and nonprint works. Nonprint works include DVDs, videotapes, films, databases, and Internet sites.

Acknowledgments

The quality of this book has been greatly enhanced through the efforts of my editor, Maxine Taylor, Military History. Her expertise and encouragement are invaluable. I am grateful to Bhuvaneswari Rathinam, production editor, and to Marcia

Youngman and others of the production staff. Appreciation for guidance, resources, and interviews, is extended to: Brigadier General Wilma L. Vaught, USAF (Ret.), President of Women In Military Service For America Memorial Foundation, Inc., Arlington, Virginia; Lieutenant Colonel Marilla Cushman, USA (Ret.), Director of Development and Public Relations also at the Women's Memorial; Captain Lory Manning, USN (Ret.), Director of the Women in the Military Project at the Women's Research and Education Institute (WREI) in Washington, D.C.; Dr. Jennifer Mathers, Department of International Politics, Aberystwyth University, Aberystwyth, United Kingdom; Dr. Peter A. Lillback, president, Westminster Theological Seminary, Glenside, Pennsylvania; and Captain Robert H. Miller, Hope for America. Finally, I am grateful for the support and assistance from my husband, James C. Skaine, and to family members, Richard L. and Nancy L. Craft Kuehner and William V. and Carolyn E. Guenther Kuehner, and to my friend, Cass Paley, for lasting inspiration.

1

Background and History

Women have served in the military and in combat in the wars and armed conflicts of the United States. Chapter 1 seeks to understand the history of the legal definition of combat and its relationship to the controversy about women serving in combat. It also outlines the relationship between history, combat, and culture.

The examination of the legal definition of combat shows how the status of women is affected by policy. Evolution of law demonstrates that combat exclusion was challenged as women continued to perform as pilots and crew members of aircraft. This challenge peaked during Operation Desert Shield and Desert Storm, the 1990–1991 war against Iraq, because it exposed 41,000 servicewomen to hostile fire. However, the most controversial aspect of combat remains the policy that provides the legal definition of direct ground combat. The policy is executed through the Direct Combat Probability Coding (DCPC) which assigns all military positions a code. The wars in Iraq and Afghanistan challenge the implementation of this policy because the military has a need to have a ready force as the battlefield has changed. The role and influence of Congress, through its oversight responsibility and its "intent," are important aspects of the existing policy.

The connection between history and women in combat is that women serving in military combat are found not only in the history of the United States, but in history in general. Ending the draft, the beginning of the all volunteer force, significant legal cases, and armed conflicts contributed to more opportunities opening for women in the 1970s. The most noteworthy changes came in the 1990s during and after the Persian Gulf War.

The nature of the battlefield changed, public opinion shifted, and women serving in combat became increasingly accepted. The 1990s saw the repeal of the combat exclusion laws in the Air Force and Navy and the opening of more positions in the Army, even with the ground combat restriction in the 1994 policy. The first decade of the twenty-first century has produced more change for women in the military because of the military's need to be ready. Women are participating in ground combat out of necessity.

The Link between the History of the Definition of Combat and the Controversy

The interrelationship between the context of the definition of combat over time and the pro and con arguments about women serving in combat is basic to our understanding of this issue. Brig. Gen. Wilma L. Vaught, USAF (Ret.), and president of the board of directors of the Women In Military Service For America Memorial Foundation, Inc., is a proponent of women serving in combat. In an interview with the author, she stressed this interrelationship that is fundamental to the controversy. She said:

> I think the arguments that come forth, begin with the probably totally unrealistic and one that we shouldn't even think about any longer, but there are still probably a few people who believe this and that's beginning with women shouldn't be in the military and then you move from that to "it's okay for them to be in the military," but there are things they shouldn't do and the major thing is combat. When you think about combat, the first thing you need to think about, and most people don't, is "what do you really mean when you say combat?" What is your definition of "combat?" That's been argued now, probably in the early '80s as we have gotten more precise about trying to define what it was and try to put in writing what it was. I suspect that, looking back, the same people who came up with the words that are in the policy, probably if they were to read those words today, it would be interesting to hear what they would say about what they thought was the solution back then,

if they would still see that as the solution today or how they would want to rewrite it.

So as you think about the definition of combat, we have so many different aspects to combat. One of those, you think about the women flying aircraft; that is a type of combat. Then you look at ground combat and that is different. Then you can look at those women who are assigned to ships at sea and that is a third aspect of combat. Then you can look at it from the aspect of the offensive point of view or the defensive point of view. Is it okay to be in combat if what you are doing is defending yourself or defending your unit? Or is it okay to do that and in addition to be able to play a combat role with the same weapons, or maybe different weapons, in an offensive kind of situation. That you can engage the mission. That you can engage the enemy. What they have tried to say is, that women should not be assigned to units whose primary mission is to engage or destroy the enemy. That is clearly an offensive mission. Another aspect is that our whole concept of warfare has changed. (Vaught 2009)

Brig. Gen. Vaught stressed the historical importance of the vanishing frontline as an aspect of combat. She traced how the whole concept of warfare has changed:

When you go back to World War I, there are great discussions about the front line. That endured through World War II. The front line. It became less clear in the Korean War because the front line kept shifting very rapidly. Perhaps more so than it did in the latter part of World War II. Then, in Vietnam, we had something that was more like what we are confronted with today, but not quite as much because there were areas that were reasonably safe. But when you think about what we have gone through in Iraq and even more so in Afghanistan, you can't say that there is any place that's truly safe, where you can say, I am here, I am safe, I don't need to worry about anything. And so, if you're there, in one sense of the word, you are truly in a combat zone and you certainly may be called upon to defend yourself. You may have to go into an offensive role if you are soldiers serving there. (Vaught 2009)

Legal Definition of Combat

No laws restrict women from serving in combat positions (Alliance for National Defense 2009, 2), but the Army's written exclusion policy and Congressional intent and oversight restricts women from serving in ground combat (Aspin 1994, 2). Since each service engages the enemy in different ways, and at the same time, overlap exists among the services; no single operational definition of combat prevails (Alliance for National Defense 2009, 2). The role of women in combat (and many have served) is determined by the combination of law, policy, and practice. Internal legal military opinions have also been a part of the evolution of law and policy (Skaine 1999, 89).

The Status of Women Is Affected by Policy

In 2008, the Executive Summary of the White House Project *Benchmarking Women's Leadership* reported the following breakdown of the number of women in the military:

- Since 1950, women have grown from 2 percent of all military personnel to 14 percent today. (*See Chapter 6, Figure 6.1 Active Duty Military: 1.4 Million People.*)
- Women are 15 percent of officers (commensurate with their proportion of military personnel overall), but are only 4 percent of top military leadership positions. (*See Chapter 6, Figure 6.2 Women as Percent of Officers by Service Branch.*)
- The percentage of women varies across military branches, but no single arm is comprised of less than 80 percent men. The Air Force has the largest proportion of women (20 percent), while the Marines Corps has the smallest (6 percent) (White House Project 2008, 3). (*See Chapter 6, Figure 6.3 Women as Percent of Enlisted Personnel by Service Branch.*)

A more detailed documentation of enlisted and officer personnel appears in Chapter 6. A thorough account of demographics for each of the services also appears in Tables 6.1 through 6.4.

The White House Project predicts, "it will be halfway through the twenty-first century before women are half of all top level military leaders, as the rate of change is slowest here of all the sectors profiled in this report" (White House Project 2008, 4). While there are several contributing factors to the slow entry, one not listed in this report but pointed out by a Harvard University panel member, Judith Stiehm, is that women are officially prohibited from engaging in ground combat. Certain jobs in the military are not open to the soldier who has not been a combat officer (Stiehm n.d., Panel 1). The exclusion laws have been repealed, but the policy of exclusion from ground combat in the Army and Marines and certain positions in the Navy is the last to change. Gen. Vaught adds, "When the Congress has discussed this issue, more often than not, it has been in hearings. There are opinions expressed in the course of those hearings, but they didn't end up in legislation" (Vaught 2009).

Evolution of the Law

Background

After the declaration of War in 1941, the Army looked for ways to bring women into the service. In 1942, public law established the Women's Army Auxiliary Corps (WAAC) and by eliminating the word "auxiliary" established the Women's Army Corps (WAC). The WAC law did not exclude women from combatant roles and gave women equal status, benefits, pay, and disciplinary code, but Army regulations did exclude women (Lindon 2008, 38).

The remarkable service of women in World War II (1941–1945) gave impetus to the passage after the war of the Women's Armed Services Integration Act of 1948 (Pub. L. No. 80-625, 62 Stat. 356 1948). The act gave women permanent status in the military. Before the act was passed, except for nurses, the military formed and dissolved special all women auxiliary corps such as the Women's Army Corps (WACS) according to personnel needs.

Provisions of the act excluded women from combat, specifically in the Navy, Marine Corps, and Air Force. Women could not be assigned to ships or aircraft engaged in combat missions. The law did not address the assignment of Army women. The Army based its policy on the perceived intent of Congress (Skaine 1999, 89). In addition, this act placed a 2 percent limit on the number of women who could serve and limited positions available to them. President Lyndon Johnson lifted the cap in 1967 when the U.S. was engaged in the Vietnam War (Keenan 2008, 21). Women are denied spousal benefits for their husbands unless husbands depend on their wives for more than 50 percent of their support. Women are prohibited from having command authority over men (WREI 2003, 1).

The original combat exclusion provisions in the 1948 Act became codified in 1956 (USC 10 (1956), § 6015). The law directly affected the Navy, but in 1978, § 6015 was amended to permit the temporary assignment of women to combat vessels (Skaine 1999, 96). (*See Chapter 6, Document 6.2 Combat Exclusion Law, Title 10 Armed Forces (USC), Subt. C, § 6015 (1956).*) Congress prevented Air Force women from being assigned on combat aircraft. The law did allow medical personnel, judge advocate and chaplain positions to serve on combat aircraft (USC 10 § 8549). (*See Chapter 6, Document 6.1.*)

The 1988 Risk Rule required the services to compare the risk of exposure to direct combat, hostile fire, or capture present in noncombat units associated with combat units. (*See Chapter 6 Document 6.6 1988 Risk Rule.*) If such risks were equal to or greater than that experienced by combat units in the same theater of operations, those units and positions would be closed to women (U.S. House 1994, 83–84). The law governing the Army states that "the Secretary of the Army may ... (1) assign, detail and prescribe the duties of members of the Army ... and (3) prescribe regulations to carry out his functions, powers, duties under this title" (USC 10 § 3013[g] [1988]). (*See Chapter 6, Document 6.3 USC 10§ 3013[g].*) This law and the interpretation of the Navy and Air Force laws signified congressional intent to prohibit women from serving in all combat. In 1988, the Secretary of the Army issued a combat exclusion policy also known as the Risk Rule. Women could not serve in the following units: Infantry, Armor, Cannon Field Artillery, Combat Engineer, or Low Altitude Air Defense Artillery units of Battalion/Squadron or smaller size (Skaine 1999, 100).

The U.S. Presidential Commission (1993) reinforced the attempt to standardize combat exclusion of women across the services: "[because] the line between direct combat and support units is sometimes blurred, the [1988] Risk Rule provides the best mechanism available for maintaining consistency in assignment policies and integrity of the relationship between support and direct land combat units" (Presidential Commission, 1993, 36). Maj. Mary Finch, USA, a commissioner, wrote that a sharp division existed in society over women serving in combat, "The fact that the Commission could not come to the same conclusion as the Congress and Secretary of Defense is disturbing and gives some indication as to why it was so controversial" (Finch 1993). The hearings of 1994 also attested to sharp conflict and resistance (Skaine 1999, 101).

Repeal of Combat Exclusion Laws

Combat exclusion was challenged as women continued to perform as pilots and crew members of aircraft (Skaine 1999, 86–199). The 1990 build up during Operation Desert Shield and the 1991 war against Iraq in Desert Storm exposed 41,000 service-women to hostile fire and capture. According to Capt. Georgia Clark Sadler, USN (Ret.), women were directly exposed to the dangers of war while they performed their duties on or near the battlefield: flying troops to the front lines, refueling fighter aircraft, driving trucks, guarding captured Iraqi soldiers, and shooting down SCUD missiles. Thirteen women were killed, five in action, and two were captured. The line between combat and noncombat was not very clear (Sadler 1997, 80). As a result of women's service in the first Gulf War, combat aviation (USC 10 § 8549) was opened to women and the combat ship exclusion (USC 10 § 6015) was repealed (Alliance for National Defense 2009, 2).

Legal Definition of Direct Ground Combat through Policy

In 1994, the Department of Defense (DoD) rescinded the 1988 risk rule. (*See Chapter 6, Document 6.7 DoD Assignment Policy, 2010: Direct Ground Combat Definition and Assignment Rule, 1994 [rescinding 1988 Risk Rule.*) A new assignment policy for women opened almost all positions, units and assignments for which they were qualified. Units below brigade level were not opened because their primary mission was direct ground combat. The new policy defined ground combat as:

> Engaging the enemy on the ground with individual or crew-served weapons, while being exposed to hostile fire and to a high probability of direct physical contact with the hostile force's personnel. Direct ground combat takes place well forward on the battlefield while locating and closing with the enemy to defeat them by fire,

maneuver, or shock effect. (U.S. House Committee
October 6, 1994, 84)

Services may close positions to women if (1) they are
required to physically collocate and remain with direct ground
combat units, (2) the cost of providing appropriate living
arrangements for women is prohibitive, (3) the units are engaged
in special operations forces' missions or long-range reconnaissance,
or (4) job related physical requirements would exclude the majority
of women. The military services may propose additional exceptions
(GAO 1998, 3).

The policy that includes this definition of direct ground combat
remains in 2010 as it was set forth by the Department of Defense
(DoD) in 1994. Direct ground combat is the most controversial part
of the policy since the definition is based on 20th century Cold War
perceptions rather than the reality of the wars of Afghanistan and
Iraq (Alliance 2009, 2). An Army document states, "Today, women
play a much more substantive and sophisticated role in the Army
and enjoy greater equality with their male counterparts then they
have in previous generations. . . . Female Soldiers are assigned to
units and positions that may necessitate combat actions—
actions for which they are fully prepared to respond to and to
succeed, as they have in operations in Iraq and Afghanistan.
Female Soldiers may find themselves in hostile actions regardless of their unit's mission and will remain with their assigned
units, perform their assigned duties, and fight as a team alongside male Soldiers" (Jones 2010, Women in the Army). As a
result of the wars in Afghanistan and Iraq, an unprecedented
number of positions for women have been opened (Keenan
2008, 22). The Women's Research and Education Institute
(WREI) reported 32,700 Army positions and 48,000 Marine
Corps positions were opened (WREI 2008, 8).

In 2007, the RAND National Defense Research Institute, a
nonprofit research organization, issued a report that emphasizes
two points. One, the Army did not revise its policy when Congress
repealed the legal restrictions against women serving in combat
aircraft and on combatant ships nor when Aspin revised the DoD
policy in 1994. Army policy for assigning women, Army Regulation
(AR) 600-13, was in effect before the 1994 DoD policy for assigning
military women (Harrell et al. 2007, xii, xiii). The Army Regulation
states:

The Army's assignment policy for female soldiers allows women to serve in any officer or enlisted specialty or position except in those specialties, positions, or units (battalion size or smaller) which are assigned a routine mission to engage in direct combat, or which collocate routinely with units assigned a direct combat mission. (Army 1992)

Two, the RAND study also points out that Army policy defines direct combat differently than DoD (Harrell et al. 2007, xii):

Engaging an enemy with individual or crew served weapons while being exposed to direct enemy fire, a high probability of direct physical contact with the enemy's personnel and a substantial risk of capture. Direct combat takes place while closing with the enemy by fire, maneuver, and shock effect in order to destroy or capture the enemy, *or while repelling the enemy's assault by fire, close combat, or counterattack.* [Emphasis RAND] (Army 1992, 5)

The RAND study emphasizes that part of the Army assignment policy states women should be prohibited from serving in units that have a routine mission of direct combat, "repelling the enemy's assault by fire, close combat, or counterattack." The policy is unclear "whether level I self-defense is included in 'repelling the enemy's assault,' as another interpretation of this phrase of the policy is that it intentionally refers to the documented core mission of maneuver units, which is to 'close with the enemy by means of fire and maneuver to destroy or capture enemy forces, or to repel their attacks by fire, close combat, and counterattack' " (Harrell et al. 2007, xvi). (*See Chapter 6, Document 6.5 Army Policy for the Assignment of Female Soldiers, 1992 [Major Relevant Parts].*)

In an interview with the author, Brig. Gen.Wilma L. Vaught, USAF (Ret.), who is founder and president of the board of directors of the Women in Military Service for America Memorial Foundation, Inc., Arlington, Virginia, explains this unclear phrase in Army policy.

As you think about the definition of combat, we have so many different aspects to combat. One of those, [is] you can look at it from the aspect of the offensive point of view or the defensive point of view. Is it okay to be in combat if what you are doing is defending yourself or defending your unit? Or is it okay to do that and in addition to be able to play a combat role with the same weapons, or maybe different weapons, in an offensive kind of situation? That you can engage the mission. That you can engage the enemy. What they have tried to say is, that women should not be assigned to units whose primary mission is to engage or destroy the enemy. That is clearly an offensive mission. (Vaught 2009)

Significant differences do exist between the Army and DoD policies' definition of combat and on the assignment of women, according to RAND (Harrell et al. 2007, xiii):

Definition of combat:
Army: definition of direct combat includes a requirement that there be a risk of capture, but also includes "repelling the enemy's assault."
Assignment of women:
DoD: restricts to units whose primary mission is direct ground combat.
Army: restricts to units that have a routine mission of direct combat and also restricts assignment to units that collocate with direct combat units.

The Marine Corps defines "direct combat operations" as "seeking out, reconnoitering, or engaging in *offensive* action." Women, therefore, could be assigned to combat support and combat service support units in a designated hostile fire area that might involve a *"defensive"* combat action (Skaine 1999, 51).

Implementation

Congress and various interested groups expressed concern whether the roles of Army women in Iraq were consistent with existing policies. These concerns arose primarily from the Army's recent modularization as defined by then Secretary of Defense Donald H. Rumsfeld. Rumsfeld advocated not just adding more divisions, but focusing on creating smaller, self-contained, interchangeable brigades that would be available to work for any division anywhere. The Iraq war was fought in the context of the Global War on Terror and was void of the linear battlefields of past wars. These concerns gave impetus for Public Law 109-163, which "requires the Secretary of Defense to submit a report on the current and future implementation of DoD policy for assigning military women (Harrell et al. 2007, xiii; Rumsfeld 2004). The assignment of women within Brigade Combat Teams that resulted from the Army's reorganization into a modular force continues to be an issue (Keenan 2008, 22).

An important aspect of Army policy is the Direct Combat Probability Coding (DCPC) system first designed during the Reagan administration. DCPC is the classification of positions according to the probability of direct combat (Skaine 1999, 62, 112). According to Michele M. Putko, this system implements the combat exclusion policy. It assigns all positions a code. Army Regulation 600-13 assigns a P1 code to positions closed to women and a P2 to positions open (Putko, Michele M. 2008, 29; U.S. Army Policy, 1992, 2-2 b(1)). (*See Chapter 6, Document 6.4 Army Direct Combat Probability Coding [DCPC] System, 1992 and Table 6.10 Army Position Coding and Decision Chart, 1992.*)

In an interview with the author, Lt. Col. Marilla Cushman, USA (Ret.), director of development and public relations at the Women In Military Service For America Memorial Foundation, Inc., explained that the origination of the DCPC followed an immense discussion in the early 1980s concerning where women would serve. She said,

> The Army's first sweep closed around 70 percent to women. DACOWITS got wind of this and demanded a review. I thought to the relief of a lot of people in the Army, not just women but a lot of men too, that another look would be taken at the closing of these positions. Where they are today is that the combat arms are basically closed to women, all of armor, infantry, and most artillery. (Cushman 2009)

Cushman explained how the DCPC classification affected her position in the military:

> There are not some positions that are open in the corps themselves. One cannot be an armor officer. I couldn't go to the armor basic course or the infantry basic course

because of my gender. Now those are closed, the combat arms, what they call the combat arms. There are some combat support jobs that are closed to women as well because of what soldiers do on the battlefield and that is combat engineers. Most artillery are closed, depending on where soldiers are on the battlefield. On the enlisted side of the house, there are some MOS [Military Occupational Specialty] that are closed. That also speaks to the combat arms. On top of that, every unit and every job in that unit is reviewed for where it serves on the battlefield. Essentially, I could serve with an armor unit in a support job from brigade up because I'm not going to go out into the fight, I would support the fight. If I am a mechanic, a logistic officer, somewhere on the logistic side of the house and a tank needs repairing, they have integral mechanics who know how to do repairs to keep themselves moving on the battlefield, but let say it's a bigger thing, so I could go from the brigade level, go out and fix the tank and go back. So it's not a continual position on the battlefield, but I could go in and support it. It's all very intricate, but it permits them to use the people to the extent that they possibly can without violating policy. So when you hear this [foolishness] about, well, they are not really in combat, . . . you [must] look at the strict definition that the primary mission is to engage with and destroy the enemy offensively, that's combat. Then these people who are on a convoy taking [supplies] out to them and they get it and they have to assume an offensive, actually it is a defensive position, but they are operating in an offensive manner. (Cushman 2009)

Gen. Vaught clarified that in the cases Cushman describes, "they are not violating policy" (Vaught 2009). What follows is a short discussion between the two that helps shed light on the DCPC classification system and direct ground combat:

C: So it's all very tricky. That is not to say that, in the heat of war if your best qualified person as in Monica Lin Brown, the medic, or the only one available happens to be of the other gender, a woman, and you need that person to go save something. . . .

V: Or fix something.

C: Or fix something. Whether it be a machine or people, that's who you are going to send.

V: And it's okay. The Army is doing that and they go in and do it. They do a really good job. You can't say, "You did such a good job, we are going to keep you here." No, you got to go back.

C: So, it is all very tricky, sticky, tricky. The point is: What is the definition of combat? We talked a little earlier about if you are safe on the battlefield. Well, I think in the old days, when I was on active duty, in the early days when I was on active duty, that was an issue. Was I safe? That isn't an issue anymore. You don't hear that in the discussions of [combat] that women, are they in a safe place. Are they in harms way, yes or no. So I think that [issue] has evolved. (Cushman and Vaught 2009)

In May 2004, the Army distributed an unclassified paper, "Combat Exclusion Quick Look Options" (Center for Military Readiness [CMR] June 1, 2005). This paper illustrates the intricacies in assignment of women that Cushman and Vaught were discussing. According to Krystyna M. Cloutier, the paper stated several ways to circumvent policy that prevents the assignment of women to direct combat units. First, without approval of the secretary of defense or notification to Congress, the Army assigned women to 24 direct combat positions (Cloutier 2008, 1550–1551). To meet its mission of readiness, the Army advocated adding these positions in forward support units of the Third Infantry Division due to a shortage of males. The limited number of available male soldiers is attributed to U.S. involvement in two wars (Bender 2005). This action on the part of the Army demonstrates the use of recoding unit assignments to meet its mission of readiness. War is erratic and as Lt. Col. John S. Westwood, U.S. Army, Chief Leadership Division explained, figures only reflect a "snapshot in time," that they could be higher or lower on any given day (Skaine 1999, 117). Putko stated that as combat operations began in Iraq, DCPC codes went unnoticed and unchallenged. In March 2003, women along with men went into Iraq. The almost three day old ground war saw the 507th Maintenance Company attacked. Casualties resulted for both men and women. Women were taken as prisoners of war. Putko noted that neither Congress nor the public became outraged at the loss of women soldiers (Putko 2008, 29). She concluded that no matter how the policy is viewed, it is a source of confusion for leaders and soldiers (Putko 2008, 32).

The RAND study also evaluated whether the Army was complying with the assignment policy. The study found that the Army was complying with the DoD policy, but it may not be complying with its separate Army policy. In addition it found, "a lack of common understanding of the 'letter' of the policy," but not of the "spirit" (Harrell et al. 2007, xiv). In the Iraq war, RAND revealed a specific example of this inconsistency in that "women assigned to support units are in relationships with maneuver units that differ very slightly from the actuality of being assigned to those maneuver units, and that, in some circumstances, members of such a support unit have a closer relationship with the maneuver unit than with the unit in their assigned chain of command" (Harrell et al. 2007, xv). Further, substantial evidence indicates "that support units are collocated with direct combat units if the definition is based purely on proximity. However, if the definition of collocation is based on interdependency and proximity, the evidence is inconclusive" because it is conceivable that a maneuver unit might succeed in its mission on its own (Harrell et al. 2007, xvii). The study concludes that the existing policy for assigning military women is not well suited to the type of operations taking place in Iraq (Harrell et al. 2007, xix).

Putko points out that within the confusion, contradictions also exist within the assignment policies. As preparation for combat, every soldier learns the Soldier's Creed. Included in the Creed are the following words: "I stand ready to deploy, engage, and destroy the enemies of the United States of America in close combat" (army.mil 2008). (*See Chapter 6, Document 6.8 Soldier's Creed.*) Putko maintains these words challenge the Combat Exclusion Policy. She asks, "If Army leadership fully expects female soldiers to deploy and engage in 'close combat,' then what is the policy excluding females from? . . . How does one rationalize the more than 50 combat deaths [mid-2006] of female soldiers in Iraq and Afghanistan and maintain the validity of the Combat Exclusion Policy?" (Putko 2008, 32). Putko poses more questions, such as how can the Army support the exclusion policy when it trains 50,000 women soldiers for combat? Is the policy relevant in a modern security environment? Why does official recognition through awards and decorations not signal women soldiers are capable of engaging in direct combat?

The Role and Influence of Congress

Civilian Control

The framers of the U.S. Constitution placed responsibility for the military with the civilian sector, specifically with Congress and the President in Articles I and II. Article I, Section 8 of the Constitution gives Congress the power "to raise and support Armies ... " and "to provide and maintain a Navy." Also "Congress has the power to declare war and to make the rules for governing the military." The Congress has civilian control of the military. Article II, Section 2 states, "The President shall be the Commander in Chief of the Army and Navy of the United States, and of the Militia of the several States when called into the actual Service of the United States" (Garamone 2001). (*See Chapter 6, Document 6.9 U.S. Constitution, Articles I The Legislative Branch and Article II The Executive Branch; Article I, Section 8–to Article II, Section 2.*)

Oversight Responsibility and Intent

In addition to its constitutional power, Congress has implied authority that derives from public laws and House and Senate rules. To fulfill its implied role, Congress must exercise oversight responsibility. This oversight function is an integral part of the United States government's system of checks and balances that is in effect to protect the institution. In addressing oversight responsibilities, Congressional intent is also a factor. Kaiser stated that Congress could not reasonably or responsibly carry out its power unless it knows "what the executive is doing; how programs are being administered, by whom, and at what cost; and whether officials are obeying the law and complying with legislative intent" (Kaiser 2006, 1, 3). In a controversial congressional hearing, William A. Woodruff observed that lack of oversight in the area of defense concerning women in combat "risks compromising our nation's ability to defend its vital interests" (U.S. House Committee October 6, 1994, 83).

Hunter/McHugh Amendment

Captain Pat Gormley, Judge Advocate General Corps (JAGC), USN (Ret.), the president of the Alliance for National Defense (AND), remarked at the WREI/AND Conference in 2009 that, over the last 10 years and two wars, there is an increasing use of women in ground combat. Women have made significant contributions and the scope of their work brings into focus womanpower and manpower. One significant occurrence was a limiting amendment that failed (Gormley 2009). Congressmen Duncan Hunter (R-CA), House Armed Services Committee chairman and John McHugh (R-NY), Personnel Subcommittee chairman, proposed what became known as the Hunter/McHugh amendment to the National Defense Authorization Act of 2006. This amendment was limited, but it was a significant jumping off point, Gormley reported. On May 23, 2005, the House Armed Services Committee approved the amendment, which codified Department of Defense regulations exempting women from involuntary assignments in or near land combat units (Solaro 2006, 231–232).

Cloutier and Solaro viewed the Hunter/McHugh amendment to the 2006 Defense Authorization Act as Congress's intent through their oversight responsibility to exclude women from serving in combat. Cloutier believed it sent a clear message that military services may not change personnel policies without congressional oversight and approval (Cloutier 2008, 1551–1552; Solaro 2006, 233). Elaine Donnelly, Center for Military Readiness, believed the amendment was necessary to comply with the law:

> The Hunter/McHugh amendment reasserts civilian control of the military, and affirms congressional intent that women should not be placed in land combat units, or in support units that collocate with them. It is entirely appropriate for Congress to codify current DoD regulations, and to remind Pentagon officials that they are expected to comply with the law requiring formal notice in advance of proposed changes. (CMR May 23, 2005, 1)

Congresswoman Rosa L. DeLauro (D-CT) believed that some provisions in this bill were unfortunate and not in the best interests of the American people or national security. She said:

> First, over the objections of the Joint Chiefs of Staff, it restricts the role of women in combat. Congress ought to charge the military with the responsibility to move people into jobs and positions based on merit. But

excluding women from combat effectively creates two classes of servicemember, which is both bad for morale and may ultimately limit the ability of women to receive promotions in the future. Regrettably, the military already suffers from a case of not having enough women in senior positions, and this bill threatens to make that problem worse, not better. (National Defense Authorization 2006, 1134)

Cloutier concluded that Congress, as it had when it enacted Title 10 USC § 652, with the amendment, acted to reassert civilian control over the Armed Services and make certain that women were not positioned in direct combat or collocated with units that engaged in direct combat (Cloutier 2008, 1552). In the end, according to Andrew Feickert, the Hunter/McHugh amendment failed to make it into the FY2006 Defense Authorization Act (P.L. 109–163) and these restrictions on women in combat did not make it into law (Feickert 2006, 14).

Congress made very clear the requirement of DoD to notify Congress within 30 days when women were going to be assigned to or collocated with ground combat units. Congress also directed that DoD conduct a review on how the Army deployed women (Keenan 2008, 23). Lieutenant Cushman explains, "If [the Army is] going to assign women down wherever in this particular unit or you wanted to make women combat medics, because we are really, really short of combat medics and you wanted to put them in units whose primary missions are to engage the enemy, then you have to go back to Congress and say, 'We need to do this.' " (Cushman 2009).

Can you in the midst of battle take the time to go back to Congress? Cushman believes that in one respect commanders can do this because, "Commanders watch; they know what their numbers are with respect to these MOSs (Military Occupational Specialty), and if they are short combat medics, for example, they will come up on the net and say, 'They are losing them because they are not reenlisting or [other reasons].' And they know this is pretty far out that you could go to the Hill and feasibly say, 'Look, we're not going to be able to send these units out because we don't have combat medics. We've gotta' use women' " (Cushman 2009). The commanders need to supplement their existing troops with women and are able to know 30 days ahead of time because they project numbers as they evaluate shortages. Gen. Vaught puts this policy in perspective:

> I think to a greater degree [the commander projects numbers] than I've seen in my association with the military. I think there is a greater appreciation of the fact that a commander should be able to use the resources at hand to do the mission. And there isn't time to be standing out there and saying, "Wait a minute, quick bring me this policy so I can read it so I know what to do with these people over here and these people over here." You got to act. And that's a good thing. It's the way it always should have been.
>
> I've always been very appreciative of one person's registration. During Desert Storm, one commander, maybe even never had read the policy, sent this women, a Lt. Col. intelligence officer, across the line, this was before the war started, into Iraq. So they asked him, "Why did you do that?" He said, "Because she was the best intelligence officer I had." According to the policy, he probably shouldn't have done that. (Vaught 2009)

In 2009, at his nomination hearings for secretary of the Army, John McHugh said he supported keeping women in combat support roles and that the policy in effect since 1994 was working. If his earlier amendment had passed, it would have removed women from such service. McHugh's hearing statement is significant. "Women in uniform today are not just invaluable, they're irreplaceable," said Gormley (Senate Committee on *Defense Department Nominations* July 30, 2009).

History, Combat, and Culture

The issue of women serving in combat continues to be debated as the military struggles to meet its mission of readiness. Congress works to fulfill its oversight responsibilities. The Defense Department Advisory Committee on Women in the Services (DACOWITS), established in 1951 by then Secretary of Defense George C. Marshall, is one organization that monitors and reports on combat and culture. In 2002, the Office of the Secretary of Defense allowed the DACOWITS' charter to expire and in 2003, the new charter reduced the members by over half (WREI 2008, 9). The DACOWITS' mission states in part, "The Committee is composed of civilian women and men who are appointed by the Secretary of Defense to provide advice and recommendations on matters and policies relating to . . . [military women]" (DACOWITS 2009). At the time of the reduction in numbers, family issues were added to its purpose. One of its main areas of study and recommendation centers on examining the career barriers that women service members experience and how have they changed over time.

History and Women in Combat

Women serving in military combat are found early in history. The Old Testament portrayed women as warriors. During the time of Deborah's rule between the years 1209 and 1169 BC, the Canaanites had controlled the nation of Israel for 20 years. Israel asked God for deliverance. God's prophecy given General Barak was that his army would win. Barak agreed to battle only if Deborah accompanied him. She agreed and together they led the army and defeated the Canaanites (*Judges* 4:3, 6–9, 16). The most well-known woman warrior of the Middle Ages is Jeanne La Pucelle or Joan of Arc who had near overwhelming military successes. She recaptured much of French territory from the English and was taken prisoner (Peters Winter 2004, 355).

Women have taken up and fought often in the guise of men (Skaine 1999, 46). Women served as men in the Crusades of the twelfth century. During the Second Crusade, Queen Eleanor of Aquitaine led an entire army of women dressed as men. Angola's Queen Jinga (Jinga Mbandi) led her people as a male in guerrilla warfare against Portuguese occupiers (Hall 1993, xii).

United States History

From our country's very early conflict, the Revolutionary War (1775–1783), to our current day wars in Afghanistan and Iraq, women have served in combat. In the Revolutionary War, the most well known women combatants were Molly Pitcher, Margaret Corbin, and Debra Sampson. Mary Ludwig Hayes, who became known as Molly Pitcher, fought for seven years.

During the battle, she brought pitchers of water to her husband John Hays, and fellow soldiers at the front line, thus earning the title Molly Pitcher. When her husband was wounded, she operated his cannon and fought against the British (Lockhart and Pergande Summer 2001, 154).

As the wife of soldier John Corbin, Margaret Corbin accompanied him to the Continental forces. She most likely served as a nurse, cook, or washwoman until her husband was mortally wounded at Fort Washington in Upper Manhattan. She took over loading and firing his cannon until she was wounded by British fire. She lost the use of her arm. In July 1779, Congress awarded her a pension for her military service and disability. Corbin was the first woman to receive the award (Hirsch 2005, 365).

Debra Sampson served disguised as a man named Private Robert Shirtliff in the Massachusetts Regiment of the Continental Army. She treated her own wounds the first two times. At the time of her third wound, a physician treated her and discovered her gender. The Women in Military Service for America Memorial Foundation (WIMSA) believe there were many women like Pitcher, Corbin, and Sampson that are not written into history books (Skaine 1999, 49).

The research of Kathryn Sheldon indicates that women who served as women did so not only in the Revolutionary War, but also during the War of 1812. Their service is not well documented, but an examination of records, journals, and diaries indicates women served. In the ship log of the *United States* were the names of two nurses, Mary Allen and Mary Marshall (Sheldon in Skaine 1999, 50).

Women served as women and as men in the Civil War (1861–1865), but exact numbers are unknown. Dr. Mary Walker was a doctor with the Union Army at the First Battle of Bull Run (Manassas). Her involvement in three major engagements, as a prisoner of war captured in April 1864, and performing her duty as a doctor were the basis for Congress awarding her the Medal of Honor, the nation's highest award for military valor. She holds the distinction of being the only woman to win the medal in United States history. However, in 1916, a special Medal of Honor commission revoked her medal and the medal of over 900 others. In 1977, Walker's medal was reinstated (Blumber 1999, 20).

Clara Barton, a medical aid, who founded the Red Cross, served in the Civil War. Many other women served in support roles. Black women served in these ways as well. In 1862, five black nurses and four Sisters of the Holy Cross were documented as serving on the Navy's first hospital ship, USS *Red Rover* (WREI 2008, 3).

Belle Boyd was a nurse who served as a spy by befriending Union officers and passing on military secrets to the Confederacy. She is known for her 30 mile ride to bring information to Confederate General Stonewall Jackson. Boyd was commissioned as a captain. She reported as a spy about 30 times, was arrested about a half dozen times, and imprisoned twice (Massey; Hart in Skaine 1999, 51).

The Civil War had women who served as men: Sarah Emma Edmonds as Private Franklin Thompson; Loreta James Velazquez as Harry T. Buford; two sisters Mary and Molly Bell as Tom Parker and Bob Martin; Sara Rosetta as Private Lyons Wakeman; and Cathay Williams, a black woman, as William Cathey. The discovery of their gender varied and, in some cases, their identity became known only after the war or was not discovered at all. Research to further identify women who served as men is ongoing (Skaine 1999, 50).

Nurses comprised most of the 1,500 women who served in the Spanish-American War (1898–1899). In 1901, the Nurse Corps became a permanent part of the Medical Department, but it was not until 1947 that the Army and Navy Nurse Corps became permanent staff of the regular Army and in 1949, the Air Force Nurse Corps was established. In World War I (1917–1918), 35,000 women served as nurses and in the reserves in the Navy and Marine Corps, but were discharged once the war was over. During the war nurses served near the front lines and became wounded or were gassed. Three nurses were awarded the Distinguished Service Cross. In World War II (1941–1945), 400,000 women served, 200 nurses died, and 543 women died overall. Sixteen died from enemy fire, and 90 were prisoners of war. In the Korean War (1950–1953), 1,000 women served and 17 of 57 nurses died. The Vietnam War (1956–1973) saw 8 women die with one from hostile fire (Lindon 2008, 37–38; WREI 2008, 3–4). In theater, 7,500 women served. During the war, about 11,000 women were stationed in Vietnam and approximately 265,000 military women served their country in various parts of the world. In Vietnam, nearly 90 percent were nurses serving in the Army, Navy, and Air Force. Others served in various capacities, such as medical personnel, communications, intelligence, and clerks. Almost all volunteered (Vietnam Women's Memorial 2010, VWMF; Women in Military Service For America

Memorial Foundation 2010, No. of Women; and No. of POWs). (*See Chapter 6, Table 6.7 Number of Women in Individual Military Conflicts and Table 6.8 Number of Military Women Held as Prisoners of War During Individual Military Conflicts.*)

The changes in the Selective Service Act in 1973 ended the draft and provided for the All-Volunteer Force (WREI 2008, 6). The period 1968–1981 brought about an increase in female enlisted personnel six times greater than before. According to Mark R. Lindon, public opinion in 1979 was mixed as to whether women should be required to participate in the draft if reinstated. Results were similar when those who favored women being drafted responded to the question should women be eligible for combat roles (Lindon 2008, 38).

Changes that took place for women in the military in the 1970s included allowing the assignment of women to noncombatant aviation and ships and the opening of service academies and the Reserve Officer Training Corps (ROTC) to women. According to WREI, important court cases played a part in the progression of women's rights within the military during this same period. In 1972, a significant Supreme Court case, *Frontiero v. Richardson*, ruled that "military women with a spouse could receive the same entitlements as those offered to military men with a spouse without the requirement that the woman prove dependency of their spouse" (Skaine 1999, 59). Also in 1973, women became eligible to command men except in combat and tactical units and in 1973 flight training opened to women in the Army and Navy.

In 1978, *Owens v. Brown* in U.S. District Court for the District of Columbia ruled that 10 USC Section 6015 was unconstitutional when it did not allow the permanent assignment of women to naval vessels except for hospital and transport ships. This clause was amended as part of the FY-79 Defense Authorizations Act. In 1981, the Supreme Court case *Rostker v. Goldberg* ruled that excluding women from the draft and Selective Service registration was constitutionally based (WREI 2008, 6–7).

Women served in three conflicts during the 1980s. They were a part of the Lebanese Peace Keeping Force in 1982–1984. Air Force women in tanker crews took part in a raid on Libya in 1983 and 170 women participated in Operation Urgent Fury, the invasion of Grenada. Air Force women served in air transport crews. In 1989, 770 women deployed to Operation Just Cause, the invasion of Panama. According to WREI, women flew Black Hawk helicopters that came under fire and one woman military police

(MP) commanded troops in a "ground combat-like operation" (WREI 2008, 7; Cassiopaean Experiment 1994–2008).

An important milestone in the 1980s was the 1988 DoD Risk Rule. Units supporting ground combat remained closed to women.

The Persian Gulf War, Desert Storm (1990–1991), was a watershed because it had the largest single deployment of women in history; about 41,000 women soldiers or 7 percent of the forces were deployed. Although women were not "officially" in combat, because of long-range artillery and surface-to-surface missiles, the lines became blurred. According to Jeanne M. Holm, the "unisex weapons" did not distinguish between combat and support troops (Holm 1992, 445–6 in Skaine 1999, 64). WREI reported that 15 women were killed in-theater and two were taken prisoners of war (WREI 2008, 3). Mark R. Lindon observed that public opinion changed dramatically and was reflected in Gallup's 1992 poll with 55 percent favoring and 42 percent not favoring women serving in combat roles. The percentage in favor more than doubled in 12 years (Lindon 2008, 39). Since Desert Storm, there have been two significant Army policy shifts affecting the types of positions and units where women can serve. These policy shifts resulted in approximately 30,000 positions being opened to women (Jones 2010, Women in the Army).

Despite the blurring of battle lines in the Gulf War, the debate on whether women should serve in combat continued with the Presidential Commission on the Assignment of Women in the Armed Forces. Other incidences took place that spoke to changing women's assignments. In 1991, the Kennedy-Roth Amendment to the FY 1992–1993 Defense Authorization Act repealed provisions of Title 10 USC 8549 than banned women from serving on combat aircraft engaged in combat missions. In 1993, the secretary of defense ordered all services to open combat aviation to women and the Navy to draft legislation for repealing combat ship exclusion, Title 10 USC 6015, and the Army and Marine Corps to study opening more positions to women (WREI 2008, 8).

The 1990s was a decade of progress for women in the military with the rescinding of the 1988 DoD Risk Rule. This change opened 32,700 Army positions and 48,000 Marine Corps positions. The repeal of Title 10 USC 6015 opened most combatant ships to women. The Marine Corp selected a woman for aviation training. Women continued to serve in the conflicts in Bosnia-Kosovo (1992–1994) numbering 1,000 and in 1999 in Kosovo, women aviators were included in combat in air warfare; Haiti (1995) with 1,200;

and in Operation Desert Fox by enforcing the no-fly zone in Iraq (1991–2003). For the first time women flew combat aircraft on combat missions (WREI 2008, 8–9; Quantum Future Group 2009). (*See Chapter 6, Table 6.9 Evolution of Statutory and Policy Combat Restrictions.*)

After the repeal of combat exclusion provisions, policy still restricted women from serving in specific combat units. In 1999, James C. Skaine and I conducted a survey of 889 college students in six universities and colleges in the midwestern and eastern United States. We found:

> In responses to the statement "Congress should lift all restrictions on women serving in combat," 46.4 percent of the survey respondents agreed and 28.3 percent disagreed. They were even stronger in their response to "women should be allowed only in noncombatant military positions." Only 22.6 percent agreed but 51 percent disagreed. (James C. Skaine and Rosemarie Skaine in Skaine 1999, 128)

The decade of the 1990s brought about much change in the battleground environment that began with Operation Desert Shield and Desert Storm and continued with a shift in public opinion. Paul L. Grosskruger wrote, "These operations [Provide Comfort, Iraq; Macedonia; Bosnia; Kosovo; for example] revealed the changing nature of war from a clearly defined, linear, and static engagement, to operating in a complex and noncontiguous environment while confronting an all-encompassing threat" (Grosskruger 2008, 44).

Grosskruger points out that as missions and environment changed so did his unit's formations. There were more female leaders. The increase was a result of the exclusion policy that allowed certain engineer units to receive women. In Grosskruger's command the number of women officers was disproportionate. Because only support units could integrate women leaders, women's opportunity to develop was limited as were the combat units' ability to benefit from their talents and professionalism (Grosskruger 2008, 45).

The wars in Iraq and Afghanistan produced change. These wars in the context of the Global War on Terror have constructed a noncontiguous and unclear environment. Grosskruger believed that a more subtle change also was occurring, and that was the steady increase in female contributions to the Army's mission that was critical to the success of operations (Grosskruger 2008, 51). In 2000, terrorists attacked the destroyer USS *Cole*. Among the 17 killed were 2 women. In 2001, 6 military women were killed in the September 11th attack on the Pentagon. On October 7, 2001, Operation Enduring Freedom began in Afghanistan and goes on today; and Operation Iraqi Freedom began March 19, 2003, and on August 31, 2010, the United States officially ended combat operations (WREI 2008, 9; Bazinet and Defrank 2010, News).

In 2007, the RAND organization issued a report. Commissioned by the Department of Defense on *Assessing the Assignment Policy for Army Women* was released after the Hunter/McHugh amendment had been defeated (Harrell et al. 2007). This study put forth nine recommendations. All are related to the first, which suggested that the assignment policy for women be recrafted to conform to the nature of warfare today and to review the policy periodically (Harrell et al. 2007, xx).

Efforts continue to gauge public opinion. In 2009, the *New York Times* reported on a poll conducted by *CBS News* that asked respondents about their support for women on the battlefield. The poll asked, "Do you favor allowing women in the military to serve in combat zones as support for ground troops?" Of all respondents, 83 percent favored women in combat zones as support and 14 percent opposed. To the question: "Would you favor allowing women in the military to join combat units?," of all respondents, 53 percent favored and 43 percent opposed. On this question, men and women responded nearly identically with men showing 53 percent in favor and 45 percent opposed and women, 53 percent in favor and 42 percent opposed. People under the age 65 showed that 56 percent were in favor and 40 percent were opposed while those people over 65, 36 percent favored with 58 percent opposed (*New York Times* 2009).

Change

Women have been warriors since very early times. In the United States women have fought since the Revolutionary War. In the last 10 years, the military has increasingly used women on the ground because of their significant contributions. According to WREI, evidence demonstrates that women have performed well under fire (WREI 2008, 10).

A discussion between Lt. Col. Cushman and Brig. Gen. Vaught reveals the great change from a linear battlefield of previous wars to the asymmetric battlefield of 2010 and the importance of winning ground warfare:

C: The asymmetric battlefield [demonstrates that] warfare has evolved so much since Desert Storm. It is about technology today, but I recall from quotes by an Iraqi armor colonel who said, "We could deal with all of the air strikes, but when the tanks started coming at us, then the whole equation changed." And you will always hear when they're talking about combat, it can never be totally technical. If you want to hold ground, you gotta' be on the ground.

V: You don't win the war until you have taken control of the ground.

C: And I guess you see that with Afghanistan today. How much more advanced could any warfare be than what we are using there today?

V: There's an aspect to Iraq and Afghanistan that you cannot escape and that is the aspect of Afghan and Iraqi women. They are part of the equation because some of them are strapping weapons to themselves and going out and committing suicide to try to have some effect on this whole thing. And, you can't assign men to go deal with this problem of Iraqi and Afghan women primarily for cultural and religious reasons. You can't do it. If you're going to deal with that, then you have to have women there to deal with the women. And that's an aspect that I can't think of a single war that we've been involved with that that ever was an aspect that you had to pay attention to.

C: And I think probably, I don't know that I want to call it a breakthrough, but if you look at this war, this war in Iraq, the thing that sort of tipped things over for women was when they started taking them out on patrols because they were critical in searching [Iraqi] women. If soldiers are going to go into households, or into neighborhoods, and they don't want to get people too mad at them, then they have to honor some of the customs. That was the tipping point in my opinion for women. It was need. It's always about need. And they needed women soldiers. First, they started assigning Army women because Army women have been weapons training since the early 1970s. And that training has become more serious because it needed to be.

V: There's another aspect to this. We've had so many women who were assigned as drivers and where in other conflicts, you could be a driver of a convoy and you were relatively safe. That has changed because of the type of weapons that have been used in these conflicts, explosive devices and things of that type; and the attacks on convoys are much greater then I think in World War II, for example.

C: Are you saying that we have more casualties because of that, general?

V: Women are being used in that capacity and they were not being used in that capacity normally as drivers in convoys to the degree that they are today.

C: Well, on the Army side, they have. Women have been in the transportation positions.

V: They've been in the transportation side, but I don't recall in Vietnam that they were out driving.

C: But that was different then; it was a different kind of war. If you look at Desert Storm. . . .

V: But the thing with Desert Storm, it only lasted five days.

C: But general, they were there and would have done it.

V: They were there and would have done it if called upon, but it only lasted five days. Where this time, they did and they're there and the danger is everywhere.

C: If I can recommend that you see one thing, watch *Lioness*. It's the story of four of the first women who served with the Marine Corps, joining soldiers in the house-to-house searches and what happened. It is a very powerful piece, but what it tells you is what is expected of these women. The military has learned a lot. If women are going to do this, then the military has to train them properly. It will give you a kind of like you were there feeling on the ground. (Cushman and Vaught 2009)

Some of the pictures of women who were serving were featured in the *New York Times* series in 2009 and some women are presented on the Women Memorial's Web site. These featured soldiers demonstrate women are serving in a changed warfare and on the ground. It also illustrates the wonderment of how anyone can stay alive. The danger is everywhere. In September 2010, Defense Secretary Robert Gates said he foresaw a day when the military would lift its ban on women serving in elite special forces. Although military rules prohibit women from ground combat, the wars in Iraq and Afghanistan have pushed female troops into firefights and forced commanders to review the policy (AFP 2010). Special forces are those U.S. forces organized, trained, and equipped to conduct special operations with an emphasis on unconventional warfare capabilities. An example of a special force is the Navy SEAL (sea, land, and air) teams.

Capt. Pat Gormley remarked at the 2009 WREI/AND Conference that, "as we look back over the last 10 years and analyze two wars, there is an increasing use of women in ground combat and select women have earned recognition for their service" (Gormley 2009). The military has appointed Lt. Gen. Ann E. Dunwoody as the first Army four-star general; promoted Command Sgt. Maj. Teresa L. King to commandant of Fort Jackson's South Carolina drill sergeant school; and awarded two silver stars to Army combat medic Spc. Monica Lin Brown, Afghanistan, and Sgt. Leigh Ann Hester, Iraq. In addition, the Navy allows women to serve on submarines (WREI 2008, 10; Dao 2009; Raddatz and Gorman 2009; McMichael and Scutro 2009).

Lt. Col. Cushman reminds us that in all of these years of conflict, women serving has been "about need" (Cushman 2009). Brig. Gen. Vaught says we have come to the point of need again, "And our advancements have come because of need and they've had to use women to fulfill the need and we get a new level of things that we could do. That's where we are again. When the Army heard about the Hunter/McHugh amendment, within two hours this is what I heard, they were over there saying 'You can't pass this legislation, because if you do, we can't perform our mission. We'd have to pull those women out in Iraq' " (Vaught 2009).

References

AFP. 2010. "Gates Predicts Women Will Serve in Special Forces." *AFP American Ed*. September 30. www.thefreelibrary.com (accessed September 30, 2009).

Alliance for National Defense (AND). 2009. "Issue: Women in Combat, AND Positions." *AND*. www.4militarywomen.org (accessed September 1, 2009).

Aspin, Les, Secretary of Defense (SECDEF). 1994. Memorandum for Secretary of the Army, Navy, and Air Force, Chairman, Joint Chiefs of Staff, Assistant SECDEF (Personnel and Readiness), and Assistant SECDEF (Reserve Affairs), "Direct Ground Combat Definition and Assignment Rule." January 13, 2.

Bazinet, Kenneth R. and Thomas M. Defrank. 2010. "Obama Declares End to Iraq War, Pledging It's 'Time to Turn the Page' and Focus on Economy." *Daily News*. August 31. www.nydailynews.com (accessed September 28, 2010).

Bender, Bryan. 2005. "US Women Get Closer to Combat Some Say Move Imperils Units, Violates Law." *Boston Globe*, January 26, National/Foreign section. 3rd ed.

Blumberg, John. October 1999. "Only Female Medal of Honor Recipient." *American History*. 34 (4): 20.

Cassiopaean Experiment. 1994–2008. "American Wars." Quantum Future Group. http://cassiopaea.org (accessed October 31, 2009).

Center for Military Readiness. 2005. "Hunter Admonishes Army on Women in Land Combat." June 1. http://cmrlink.org (accessed September 11, 2009).

Center for Military Readiness. 2005. "Policy Analysis—Frequently Asked Questions: The Hunter/McHugh Amendment to H.R. 1815 Codification of DoD Regulations Re: Women in Land Combat." May 23. http://cmrlink.org (accessed September 15, 2009).

Cloutier, Krystyna M. 2008. "Note: Marching Toward War: Reconnoitering the Use of All Female Platoons." *Connecticut Law Review* 40 (July): 1531–1579.

Cushman, Marilla. Interview by Rosemarie Skaine. Tape recording. Arlington, VA: Women In Military Service For America Memorial Foundation, Inc. September 23, 2009.

Defense Advisory Committee on Women in the Services (DACOWITS). 2009. "About DACOWITS." http://dacowits.defense.gov (accessed October 30, 2009).

Feickert, Andrew. 2006. "U.S. Army's Modular Redesign: Issues for Congress." *Congressional Research Service*. http://fpc.state.gov (accessed September 17, 2009).

Finch, Mimi. USA. 1993. "Women in Combat: One Commissioner Reports." Paper presented at the Military Manpower Conference: A Military of Volunteers. September 17, at the U.S. Naval Academy in Skaine, 1999, 101.

Garamone, Jim. 2001. "Why Civilian Control of the Military?" *American Forces Press Service*, U.S. Department of Defense. www.defenselink.mil (accessed September 14, 2009).

General Accounting Office (GAO). 1998. *Gender Issues: Information on DoD's Assignment Policy and Direct Ground Combat Definition*. Report to the Ranking Minority Member Subcommittee on Readiness, Committee on Armed Services, U.S. Senate. GAO/MSOAD-99-7. October. www.gao.gov (accessed December 5, 2009).

Grosskruger, Paul L. 2008. "Women Leaders in Combat: One Commander's Perspective." In *Women in Combat Compendium*, ed. Michele M. Putko and Douglas V. Johnson II, 43–52. Carlisle, PA: Strategic Studies Institute U.S. Army War College.

Hall, Richard. 1993. *Patriots in Disguise: Women Warriors of the Civil War*. 1st ed. New York: Paragon House.

Harrell, Margaret C., et al. 2007. *Assessing The Assignment Policy for Army Women*. Santa Monica, CA: RAND National Defense Research Institute. www.rand.org (accessed September 20, 2009).

Hart, Roxine C. 1991. "Women in Combat." Family Service Center, Port Hueneme, CA, Research Division, Defense Equal Opportunity Defense Management Institute, Patrick AFB, Florida. February 1–23.

Hirsch, Alison Duncan. 2005. Corbin [nee Cochran], Margaret (C). *Encyclopedia of New York State*: 395.

Holm, Jeanne, USAF (Ret.) 1992. *Women in the Military: An Unfinished Revolution*. Rev. ed. Novato, CA: Presidio.

Jones, Philip H. CIV USA OCPA. 2010 "Women in the Army Talking Points: What Positions Are Closed to Women?" E-mail to Rosemarie Skaine, July 23.

Kaiser, Frederick M. 2006. "Congressional Oversight. Congressional Research Service." www.fas.org (accessed September 15, 2009).

Keenan, Jimmie O. 2008. "In the Combat Exclusion Policy in the Modern Security Environment." In *Women in Combat Compendium*, ed. Michele M. Putko and Douglas V. Johnson II, 31–25. Carlisle, PA: Strategic Studies Institute U.S. Army War College.

Lindon, Mark R. 2008. "Impact of Revising the Army's Female Assignment Policy." In *Women in Combat Compendium*, ed. Michele M. Putko and Douglas V. Johnson II, 37–42. Carlisle, PA: Strategic Studies Institute U.S. Army War College.

Lockhart, Nikki and Jenna Pergande. 2001. "Women Who Answered the Call: World War II as a Turning Point for Women in the Workforce." *Journal of Women's History* 13(2): 154.

Massey, Mary Elizabeth. 1966. *Bonnet Brigades*. New York: Alfred A. Knopf, Inc.

McMichael, William H., and Andrew Scutro. 2009. "SecNav, CNO: Women Should Serve on Subs." *Navy Times*. September 27, News. www.navytimes.com (accessed October 30, 2009).

National Defense Authorization Act for Fiscal Year 2006. "Speech of Hon. Rosa L. DeLauro." *Congressional Record* 151:72. Section: Extension of Remarks 1133. 109th Congress, 1st Session, May 26, 2005.

New York Times. 2009. "Support for Women on the Battlefield." *CBS News Poll*. August 16. www.nytimes.com (accessed October 30, 2009).

Peters, Julie Stone. 2004. "Joan of Arc Internationale: Shaw, Brecht, and the Law of Nations." *Comparative Drama* 38(4): 355–78.

Putko, Michele M. 2008. "The Combat Exclusion Policy in the Modern Security Environment." In *Women in Combat Compendium*, eds. Michele M. Putko and Douglas V. Johnson II, 27–36. Carlisle, PA: Strategic Studies Institute U.S. Army War College.

Raddatz, Martha and Elizabeth Gorman. 2009. "Female Warriors Engage in Combat in Iraq, Afghanistan." *ABC*, October 25, World News. http://abcnews.go.com/WN (accessed Oct. 30, 2009).

Rumsfeld, Donald H. 2004. "Rumsfeld on Creating a 'Modular Army' for the 21st Century." *Wall Street Journal*. February 4, Op-ed.

Sadler, Georgia Clark. 1997. "Women in Combat: The U.S. Military and the Impact of the Persian Gulf War." In *Women in the Military in U.S. and Canada*, ed. Laurie Weinstein and Christie C. White, 79–97. Westport, CT: Bergin and Garvey. www.strategicstudiesinstitute.army.mil (accessed September 13, 2009).

Sheldon, Kathryn. 1996. "American Military Women at War." Washington, D.C.: Women in the Military Service for America Foundation, Inc., (WIMSA), 8 pp.

Skaine, James C. and Rosemarie Skaine. 1999. "The American Public." In *Women at War: Gender Issues of Americans in Combat*. Rosemarie Skaine. Jefferson, NC: McFarland & Co. Inc. 119–131.

Skaine, Rosemarie. 1999. *Women at War: Gender Issues of Americans in Combat*. Jefferson, NC: McFarland & Co. Inc.

Solaro, Erin. 2006. *Women in the Line of Fire: What You Should Know about Women in the Military*. Emeryville, CA: Seal Press.

Stiehm, Judith. n.d. "Panel 1–Rights." Conference Notes. www.law.harvard.edu/students/orgs (accessed October 12, 2009).

U.S. Army. "Soldier's Creed." 2008. www.army.mil (accessed September 15, 2009).

U.S. Congress. House of Representatives. 1994. Military Forces and Personnel Subcommittee of the Committee on Armed Services. *Assignment of Army and Marine Corps Women under the New Definition of Ground Combat*. 103rd Cong., 2nd sess. October 6. H.A.S.C. 103–50. U.S. Government Printing Office. 1995.

U.S. Congress. Senate. 2009. Armed Services Committee. *Subject: Defense Department Nominations*. 111th Cong., 1st sess. July 30.

U.S. Department of the Army. 1992. Headquarters. Army Regulation 600-13. *Army Policy for the Assignment of Female Soldiers*. March 27.

U.S. Presidential Commission on the Assignment of Women in the Armed Forces. 1993. *Report to the President: Women in Combat*. Washington: Brassey's.

Vaught, Wilma L. Interview by Rosemarie Skaine. Tape recording. Women In Military Service For America Memorial Foundation, Inc., Arlington, Virginia, September 23, 2009.

Vietnam Women's Memorial Foundation. 2010. "VWMF." www.vietnamwomensmemorial.org (accessed April 30, 2010).

White House Project. 2008. *Benchmarking Women's Leadership*. Executive summary. 1–5. http://womenscollege.du.edu (accessed October 12, 2009).

Women in Military Service For America Memorial Foundation, Inc. 2010. "Number of Women in Individual Military Conflicts," *Statistics on Women in the Military*. Revised February 17. www.womensmemorial.org (accessed May 27, 2010).

Women's Armed Services Integration Act. 1948. Public Law 80-625, 62 Stat. 356-75 (1948), codified at U.S. Code 10 (1956), § 6015.

Women's Research and Education Institute (WREI). 2003. "Chronology of Significant Legal & Policy Changes Affecting Women in the Military: 1947–2003." www.wrei.org (accessed June 17, 2010).

Women's Research and Education Institute (WREI). 2008. *Women in the Military: Where They Stand*. 6th ed. Arlington, VA: WREI.

2

Problems, Controversies, and Solutions

Problems

Women serving in combat face specific challenges. Heading the list are policy problems that affect women. At the base of many issues lie the differences in opinion as to whether women should serve in combat. Women face other issues as well. Sexual issues that arise include consensual relationships, both heterosexual and homosexual, pregnancies, sexual harassment, assault, and rape. Military women find balance issues in deployment, family life, and work. For some, a balance issue relates to their religious beliefs. After service is completed, men and women alike face readjustment issues. Readapting to civilian life has brought an increasing number of cases of post-traumatic stress disorder (PTSD) and suicide.

Policy

Cultural Lag or Cultural Dissonance?

Policy, like law, is both a social product and a social force. It takes time to effect social change. One way to demonstrate the need for a strong policy is to observe what occurs when no policy exists or the policy is weak (Skaine 1996, 377). Or when the Army policy and DoD policy are inconsistent. Or a lack of understanding of the letter of policy, but not the spirit prevails (Harrell et al. xiii, xv). Law must be understood as part of the social order

33

simultaneously reflecting society and influencing it (Mariske et al. 46, in Skaine 1996, 110). Operation Desert Storm (1991) demonstrated that women were not only essential to military readiness, but they were needed in combat. This prompted Congress to repeal the Air Force and Navy exclusion laws. In this case, the repealing of the laws was a social product. The Army and the Marines retention of their exclusion policy regarding direct ground combat, was a social force.

Proponents advocate women serve in combat and believe that a cultural lag exists: the change in policy has not kept up with the change on the battlefield and with what's happening to women in combat. It is not whether women should be in combat, they already are. The Alliance for National Defense (AND), a nonprofit, tax-exempt educational organization comprised of veterans and concerned civilians, states, "Current doctrine and policy concerning the assignment of military women have outlived past usefulness, and it is time for their revision, if not elimination to reflect actual practices that are essential to wage this type of war" (AND 2009, 3).

Opponents of women serving in ground combat believe existing policy is appropriate and the laws that were repealed should be reinstated. A long time opponent, Elaine Donnelly, founder and president of the Center for Military Readiness, an independent public policy organization that specializes in military personnel issues, testified that a cultural dissonance sets in with the concept of violence against women in armed combat (Donnelly in Congress 1993, 112). (*See Chapter 6, Document 6.10 Excerpt from Elaine Donnelly's Congressional Testimony, 1993.*)

Cultural lag and cultural dissonance form much of the basis for proponents and opponents on all primary issues, but especially in the ground combat exclusion rule and the collocation policy. AND maintains that unlike in past wars, today the battle lines are blurred because there are no front lines and direct ground combat is no longer isolated to a position of *well forward on the battlefield* [emphasis AND's]. Today's battles are asymmetrical in Iraq and Afghanistan. It is precisely the ground combat exclusion rule that controls "that women may not occupy any assignment (in any capacity) to a unit below brigade level which has the primary mission of engaging in direct ground combat" (AND 2009, 3). Through this regulation, the Army and Marine Corps keep their current policies excluding women from the Infantry and Armor. The Marine Corps also excludes women from Field Artillery, but the Army does not. The Army does not permit women to serve in Special Forces including aviation. Women also may not serve in Navy Seals.

In addition to the Direct Ground Combat Exclusion rule, the Army and Marine Corps Collocation Policy impacts military women. According to AND, this policy refers to the placement of the positions of combat support and combat service support relative to direct ground combat. The RAND study reported the existence of two definitions of collocation. One definition is based on proximity and the other is based on proximity and interdependence (Harrell et al. 2007, xvii). AND explains that the Army policy does not allow *"routine* collation with a unit whose *primary* mission is to engage in direct ground combat" (AND 2009, 3). Adding the word *routine* further complicates a term that does not have a common definition, stated AND. In addition, the Army collocation policy does not allow women to serve in the Army Combat Engineers and portions of the Field Artillery.

Sergeant First Class Monica Lin Brown, who was awarded the Silver Star on March 20, 2008, exemplifies that the definition of some units fluctuates (Skaine 1999, 117). On April 25, 2007, Brown, an 18 year-old medic, not assigned to combat, was sent on a combat mission in Afghanistan because no other medic was available to assign. While on patrol, one of the vehicles struck an improvised explosive device (IED). Brown got off her vehicle amid intense enemy fire and moved to the burning vehicle to treat her comrades. Despite this act of bravery, President George W. Bush and the Army removed Brown from combat duty and offered her an assignment at the White House (Adair 2008, News).

Issues That Present Challenges to Women

Policy

The case of Sergeant First Class Monica Lin Brown exemplifies how policy affects women in military service by limiting where and how they serve. Adair reported that the removal of Brown from combat was against Brown's wishes. Her strong performance in Afghanistan is parallel to Sgt. Leigh Ann Hester, also a Silver Star recipient, the first awarded to a woman for direct combat action. In 2005, in Iraq, Hester, a 23-year-old military policewoman responded to an insurgent attack on a convoy by firing grenades. According to Sgt. Sara Wood, Hester killed three insurgents with her rifle, and in total the attack left 27 insurgents dead, 6 wounded, and 1 captured. Hester responded, "It really doesn't have anything to do with being a female. It's about the duties I performed that day as a soldier" (Wood 2005, News). When the Army Women's Museum at Ft. Lee, Virginia, unveiled its Global War on Terrorism Exhibit, Hester's comments provide insight into the performance of women as well as men:

> "There are a lot of soldiers [who] are doing this job right now," she says. "Right this minute, right now, they're doing now what we were doing then, and they're not getting the credit they deserve. Look at the big picture. We did great one day, but there are people doing that every day. Don't lose sight of that." (WIMSA 2008, Voices of Valor)

Brown and Hester served in exemplary ways but in ways that policy prohibits. As Hester reminded, serving in combat is not a matter of gender. Soldiers serve every day as they did.

Women assigned to noncombatant units, but who perform in combat, have promotional opportunities only as a noncombatant. These women cannot realize their leadership potential when they are not allowed to enter career track or combat positions that lead to the top ranks of command officers. Men who serve in noncombatant units can enter combatant units if they are qualified. In addition, when gender requirements change for certain jobs such as in Field Artillery and Air Defense Artillery, women lose opportunities to serve in positions which may be required later to progress in their career. They may not be permitted to hold a command position in these units (Skaine 1999, 26).

The Iraq and Afghanistan Veteran's of America reported on three studies that indicated career progression remains a barrier for women. DACOWITS reported women are underrepresented in the higher ranks of the military, and have lower promotion rates than their male counterparts (DACOWITS in IAVA 2009, 3). The RAND study reported that the Army's exclusion policy on assigning women in direct ground combat may be one major factor affecting opportunities for promotions and selection for command (Harrell et al. in IAVA, 2009, 3). A 2008 DoD survey found many women doubted their opportunities for career advancement (DACOWITS in IAVA 2009, 3).

The inconsistent enforcement of policy enables women to serve in combat due to the changing nature of warfare. They serve at the order of commanders who must meet readiness requirements but without rank and career benefits commensurate with their performance and the great risk. Col. Kelly Hamilton, USAF (Ret.), who flew combat support missions in the Gulf War in 1990–1991, stated that the definition of combat had nothing to do with risk when only fighters, bombers, and attack aircraft may log actual combat time. Combat is defined as the ability to inflict damage on the enemy. When an aircraft is sent to an expanded forward location, Hamilton asked, "How does the military know for sure when it is in a combat zone?" (Hamilton in Skaine 1999, 26–27). Does not shooting make combat a gray area? Melissa Embser-Herbert wrote that, since it is known that women are serving in combat, the real issue is whether their vital role will be acknowledged and "the country will make more occupational categories and assignments available to women" (Clemmitt 2009, 973).

Elaine Donnelly points out that even though today's wars do not have front lines, the missions of close combat remain the same. All deployed soldiers are in danger, but that is not the same as direct combat which is "closing with and destroying the enemy with deliberate *offensive* action under fire." Additionally, Donnelly maintains that because current policy requires DoD to notify Congress in advance of proposed changes affecting women, Army officials "have redefined regulations unilaterally, without authorization." She concluded, the flawed policy encourages all sorts of problems. Congress needs to fulfill its oversight responsibility and hold DoD officials accountable (Clemmitt 2009, 973).

Gender and Sexual Issues

Some challenges women face are gender related. Gender and sexual issues include logistics; consensual sexual relationships including same sex; pregnancies; gender and sexual discrimination, sexual harassment, assault, and rape.

Logistics

The opening of submarine positions to women on September 24, 2009, represents Navy efforts to address crewing policies that include the lack of privacy and the cost of reconfiguring (McMichael and Scutro 2009). According to Capt. Lory Manning, USN (Ret.), director of the Women in the Military Project, WREI, the significance of the Navy's move is that submarines are the last of the warfare units to integrate. Integration will have a significant impact on deployment and how deployed women are used. Manning observed that it was in 1990 that DACOWITS recommended that submarines be integrated (Manning 2009). In April of 2010, the Navy announced that the first women allowed to serve aboard submarines will report for duty by 2012 (*AP* 2010, *Chicago*).

Warhorse, the forward operating base in Iraq, demonstrates how the Army has transformed facilities for women soldiers. At the beginning of the war in 2003, the initial invasion force included women, but the military was unprepared to address logistical issues such as privacy and health. As the bases became more permanent and the Army adjusted to war with mixed forces, many of the initial problems decreased. According to Steven Lee Myers, women have their own living quarters, bathrooms, and showers. Married couples live together. Feminine urinary directors have made elimination easier because women can urinate standing up without pulling their pants down (Myers 2009).

Consensual Sexual Relationships

A gender-integrated unit might address three types of consensual sexual relationships: (1) one partner is married; (2) one partner is superior in rank or position; and (3) between single service members of similar rank. Behavior when one partner is married is considered adultery and is punishable under Article 134, UCMJ. Misconduct when one partner is a superior in rank is prohibited by service regulations. The UCMJ condemns "all unprofessional relationships that degrade good order and discipline—whether between individuals of the same gender or opposite sex" (McSally 2007, Cohesion). McSally believed that relationships of service members of similar rank is a leadership issue. Commanders set the climate for the good order and discipline which is about dignity and respect. Commanders also must enforce that tone. Maj. Mary Finch, USA, believed that any kind of attraction between service members, homosexual or heterosexual activity, innuendo, and gaming are contrary to good order and discipline. Since regulations exist to support the commander, it is only when good, strong leadership fails, units will have problems. She concluded, "A strong commander makes all the difference" (Finch in Skaine 1999, 190–191).

Consensual Same Sex Relationships

From the early part of the twentieth century consensual same sex relationships referred to as bisexual, homosexual (gay or lesbian) have been against military policy. In 1982, the Department of Defense Directive 1332.14, stated, "homosexuality is incompatible with military service" and if service members either stated they were homosexual or engaged in homosexual acts, policy dictated discharge. In the 1980s and 1990s, the public scrutinized the policy (Robert Crown Law Library 1999, #2). In 1993, Congress passed the law known as, DADT or "Don't Ask, Don't Tell." This law mandates the discharge of openly gay, lesbian, or bisexual service members. Over 13,500 service members have been discharged under the law since 1994. Since 2001, however, discharges have declined by almost half and during every major military conflict the number of discharges has dropped (Service members Legal Defense Network 2010, About DADT). (*See Chapter 6, Document 6.12 Policy Concerning Homosexuality in The Armed Forces: Title 10.*)

On May 27, 2010, the House approved a proposal to repeal the 1993 law that allowed gays to serve in the military on the condition that they don't disclose their sexual orientation. It is scheduled to become law in December 2010 when the DoD working group is expected to produce its findings and recommendations in an implementation plan (Davis 2010, AP; DoD 2010, Update).

The debate on Don't Ask, Don't Tell has been long and intense. Over time, views on this policy have differed. In 2008, the Service members Legal Defense Network (SLDN) executive director Aubrey Sarvis reported, "Women make up 15 percent of the armed forces, so to find they represent nearly 50 percent of Army and Air Force discharges under 'Don't Ask, Don't Tell' is shocking. . . . 'Don't Ask, Don't Tell' is often used as a weapon of vengeance against service members. Women in particular have been caught in the crosshairs of this counterproductive law" (SLDN 2008, Newsroom).

SLDN reported that in FY 2007, women represented 14 percent of the Army's active duty force and made up 46 percent of DADT discharges, compared to FY 2006 when women were 17 percent of the Army and 35 percent of DADT discharges. FYs 2006 and 2007 data from the Air Force shows women are 20 percent of the force but made up 49 percent of DADT discharges (SLDN 2008, Newsroom).

Part of the movement to end the current law is the Military Readiness Enhancement Act (H.R. 1283) of 2009. Current policies on good conduct would remain, but members previously discharged on the basis of sexual orientation would be eligible to reapply (Burrelli 2009, Summary).

The DADT policy again is under scrutiny. In 2008 and 2010, the U.S. House held two hearings, first on a "Repeal Plan," and the second on a "Review" (House Committee on Armed Services, Military Personnel Subcommittee, *Don't Ask, Don't Tell Repeal Plan: Hearing* 111th Cong., 2nd sess., 2010; *Don't Ask, Don't Tell Review Hearing* 110th Cong., 2nd sess., 2008). In 2010, the U.S. Senate held a hearing to examine policy (Senate Committee on Armed Services, *Don't Ask, Don't Tell Policy Hearing*. 111th Cong., 2nd sess., 2010). Until Congress acts on a repeal, the military is required to follow the law first enacted in 1993. During the Senate hearing, Secretary of Defense Robert Gates testified he fully supported President Barack Obama's announcement made during the State of the Union Address. The president said he would work with Congress in 2010 to repeal the law known as "don't ask, don't tell." Gates subsequently directed the Department of Defense to begin the preparations necessary for a repeal of the current law and policy. Adm. Michael G. Mullen, chairman, Joint Chiefs of Staff, DoD, then stated that the Chiefs of Staff and he were in complete support of the approach that Secretary Gates had outlined.

On March 25, 2010, Secretary of Defense Robert Gates announced adjustments in the way the military applies the Don't Ask, Don't Tell policy, but these measures do not overturn or nullify portions of it. The level of officers is raised that are authorized to initiate and conduct inquiries into allegations of sexual orientation. Third parties that might be motivated to harm a homosexual will be scrutinized and in some cases privacy rights will be respected when homosexual orientation is revealed, such as a priest or medical professional (Dwyer 2010, Politics). In the meantime, the Pentagon is conducting a complete review of the policy and its impact if repealed. This report is likely to be completed by December 1, 2010 (AND *Advocate* 2010, 2).

Other indicators signify a change in attitudes towards service members of homosexual orientation, for example, public opinion polls measuring attitudes in the larger society and in the military. In 2009, a Gallup poll found "Americans are 6 percentage points more likely than they were four years ago to favor allowing openly gay men and lesbian women to serve in the military, 69 percent to 63 percent. While liberals and Democrats remain the most supportive, the biggest increase in support has been among conservatives and weekly churchgoers—up 12 and 11 percentage points, respectively" (Morales 2009, Gallup). In 2010, The Center for American Progress, a liberal think tank, found a similar result. Of Americans polled, 54 percent said the 17-year-old Don't Ask, Don't Tell law should be reversed (Lubold 2010, USA). In 2006, Zogby International found that military attitudes are also favorable, with 73 percent of military personnel comfortable with members who have a homosexual orientation. In addition, the poll found one in four U.S. troops who served in Afghanistan or Iraq knows a member of their unit who is gay (SLDN 2010, About DADT). In May 2010, a Gallup poll revealed that two-thirds of Americans are in favor of allowing gays to serve openly in the military (AND *Advocate* 2010, 2).

According to the Government Accountability Office (GAO), an increasing concern is that separation of homosexuals from the service costs money. In the post-September 11th environment, a concern is the effect of the separation of service members who have critical occupations or important foreign language skills, for example, Arabic, Farsi, or Korean. About 757 (8 percent) of the 9,488 service members separated for homosexual conduct held critical occupations. GAO estimated that over the 10-year period, 1994 to 2003, it could have cost the DoD about $95 million for replacements for service members separated under the policy (GAO 2005, What GAO Found).

In spite of these indicators, Don't Ask, Don't Tell casualties continue, for example, Army Medic Sgt. Lacye Presley, who in 2006 was awarded a Bronze Star for saving lives in Iraq. When she reported a superior commander for suspected drug dealing, she was discharged for having a girlfriend (who was also discharged). Under the military's revised policy, Lacye Presley and her girlfriend most likely would not have been discharged (Dozier 2010, Sunday Morning).

Opponents say that the Don't Ask, Don't Tell law should not be repealed. Some opponents contend homosexual acts violate religious convictions. David R. Carlin, Jr. argues that the liberal left "doesn't get it" and asks that it consider why some oppose homosexuality. He suggests that approval of homosexual behaviors also means "approval of 'unnatural' forms of vice that will lead to further approval of already flourishing 'natural' forms" (Carlin 1993, 1). Some people fear that approving homosexuality will open the door wider to lying, stealing, cheating, violence, and other forms of sexual misconduct. They see the issue as but one item on a much larger gay rights agenda. They believe the ultimate goal is to get full social approval of homosexuality not just tolerance. Another religious reason is that the homosexual movement is a secularist assault on religion with the aim of wearing away and eventual destruction of religion.

Christine E. Gudorf suggests that the military debate is not about legitimizing homosexual activity, but about supporting the rights of people with a same sex orientation to serve. There always have been and always will be gays in the military. She contends the objections to gays serving in the military are frequently contradictory and reflect a sexual insecurity. She says, "Discussions about homosexuality frequently reflect more of the projected fears and anxieties of heterosexuals than they do any elements of homosexual reality. Social scientists have reported that high homophobia levels correlate directly with insecurity about sexual identity and rigid male-female sex role stereotypes" (Gudorf 1993, 1).

In 2008, witnesses testified before Congress voicing arguments for and against the Don't Ask, Don't Tell policy. Sgt. Maj. Brian Jones (Ret.), USA, a former Ranger, testified that he finds it difficult to understand why, during wartime, the issue of Don't Ask, Don't Tell takes a priority. He maintains that to disregard the fact that, in the military, soldiers share intimate living quarters is a great risk. He believes that one of the greatest challenges a commander faces is dealing with inappropriate relationships and sexual harassment and that having to do so takes away from other critical duties related to the mission.

As a Ranger, Jones speaks to actions soldiers must take to survive, for example, on missions where it is so cold that soldiers must keep from freezing at night. Ranger units are composed of all males. The only way "was to get as close as possible for body heat—which means skin to skin" (House Committee on Armed Services, Military Personnel Subcommittee, *Don't Ask, Don't Tell Review Hearing* 110th Cong., 2nd sess., 2008). The presence of openly gay men would elevate tensions and would affect morale and unit cohesion. During the course of his career, Jones had witnessed several incidences of lesbian soldiers in acts of severe homosexual bullying, threatening, and groping of heterosexual women. He believes that allowing open homosexuality among women will also cause unnecessary sexual tension and disruption of good order, morale, discipline, and unit cohesion.

Elaine Donnelly, president of the Center for Military Readiness, testified that repeal of the law would impose new and unneeded burdens of sexual tension on soldiers serving in high-pressure working conditions far from home. She argues, "Inappropriate passive/aggressive actions common in the homosexual community, short of physical touching and assault, will be permitted in all military communities" (House Committee on Armed Services, Military Personnel Subcommittee, *Don't Ask, Don't Tell Review Hearing* 110th Cong., 2nd sess., 2008). She contends repeal and forced cohabitation will negatively affect morale and discipline and commanders will be powerless to act as soldiers leave or avoid the service. The same result will occur for those whose religious convictions dictate disapproval of homosexual orientation. She suggests that civil rights and reporting of homosexual misconduct is fraught with problems, such as inadequate reports and risk of abuse.

Health issues, primarily HIV infection, concern Donnelly: "Given the officially recognized correlation between homosexual conduct and HIV infection, it is reasonable to expect that repeal of the law could increase the number of troops who require medical benefits for many years but cannot be deployed. At a time when multiple deployments are putting great stress on the volunteer force, Congress should not make a major change in policy that could increase the number of nondeployable personnel" (House Committee on Armed Services, Military Personnel Subcommittee, *Don't Ask, Don't Tell Review Hearing* 110th Cong., 2nd sess., 2008).

Donnelly argues that any soldier who expresses concerns about professed homosexuals in the military, for any reason, will be looked upon as intolerant, and suspected of harassment, homophobia, bullying, or bigotry. These attitudes and behavior are not tolerated and penalties and career-ending denials of promotions would be a consequence of treating homosexuals as a civil rights issue. She questions whether evidence of problems will be reported to Congress or the public. Donnelley also argues that having recruiting quotas for gays is fraught with problems, for example, whether the efforts will require the military to ask a person's sexual orientation (House Committee on Armed Services, Military Personnel Subcommittee, *Don't Ask, Don't Tell Review Hearing* 110th Cong., 2nd sess., 2008).

Donnelly refutes each argument posed in favor of repealing the law. She maintains that poll results, such as Zogby, are skewed and that the GAO report can be refuted by evidence to the contrary. Hers is a detailed case for opposing repeal of Don't Ask, Don't Tell. At the 2008 hearing, Maj. Gen. Vance Coleman (Ret.), a former artillery officer and division commander, argued for repeal. He spoke of a parallel between the issues of race and homosexuality.

> I served in segregated units in both the United States and Europe before being selected to attend an integrated Leadership Academy and then Officers Candidate School. After Officers Candidate School, I was assigned to a combat arms unit. When I reported for duty, however, I was promptly reassigned to a service unit that was all-black. The message was clear: It did not matter that I was a qualified Field Artillery Officer who was qualified to serve in the all- white combat arms unit. It only mattered that I was black. (House Committee on Armed Services, Military Personnel Subcommittee, *Don't Ask, Don't Tell Review Hearing* 110th Cong., 2nd sess., 2008)

Later, because of his experience in integrated units, Coleman testified, that the military has demonstrated it can blend people together from different backgrounds and beliefs to put the mission first. Repealing the law, he maintained, would allow the military the best and the brightest regardless of sexual orientation. In the Korean conflict combat situation, troops are not concerned about who soldiers are or what they believe, but whether they can perform. Soldiers with homosexual orientation are needed to meet readiness. He added that a parent of a soldier may not care that a lesbian soldier saved his life. S.Sgt. Eric F. Alva (Ret.), USMC served 13 years in the Marines and was wounded in the Iraq War. He served in Somalia during Operation Restore Hope. On March 21, 2003, the first day of the ground war in Iraq, he triggered a land mine that caused the loss of one leg and permanent damage to one arm. He testified that his being gay elicited a response, "So what?" from fellow soldiers. He testified that response, "[W]as a very powerful thing for me, that I still had their trust, because the supporters of 'Don't Ask, Don't Tell' are right about one thing—unit cohesion is essential. What my experience proves is that they're wrong about how to achieve it. My being gay, and even many of my colleagues knowing about it, didn't damage unit cohesion. They still put their lives in my hands, and when I was injured they risked those lives to save mine" (House Committee on Armed Services, Military Personnel Subcommittee, *Don't Ask, Don't Tell Review Hearing* 110th Cong., 2nd sess., 2008). Alva maintained that Don't Ask, Don't Tell by imposing secrecy, undermined unit cohesion, and that discharging gays and lesbians is at the expense of the military readiness of the United States.

Pregnancies

Pregnancy has always been a "hot button" issue, according to AND. From 1940 to the mid 1970s, pregnant women were automatically discharged. Unmarried pregnant women received dishonorable discharges. The advent of the all volunteer force underscored the need for women to serve in the military, but attitudes did not change and the military was properly concerned for the operational and deploying units. Extensive policies that are in place reflect the Navy and Marine Corps policy addressing pregnancy that stress "By itself, pregnancy should not restrict tasks normally assigned to servicewomen . . . and that it is the servicewoman's responsibility to try to plan her pregnancies with regards to her military duties [around operational necessities] . . . (AND 2010, Issue Paper). AND maintains that since the majority of women are in their prime childbearing years, it is critical that the military encourage them to plan their pregnancies around their operational duties. AND recommends, "Pregnancy prevention training *must* include information on 'emergency contraception.' Training should emphasize the partner's mutual responsibility to pregnancy prevention and the transmission of diseases."

An unplanned pregnancy is challenging. Soldiers who become involved in a pregnancy are faced with a dilemma. If a military woman gets the care she needs or she takes leave, either way her career is in jeopardy. Some turn to abortion as a way to deal with the pregnancy. Amy, a Marine military journalist serving in Fallujah, discovered she was pregnant. Faced with the reporting dilemma, Amy self-aborted. Twice she used her sanitized rifle cleaning rod and a laundry pin to manually dislodge the fetus while lying on the bathroom floor. Amy lost a lot of blood after her first try. Increasingly sick, she continued working for five weeks until she realized she was still pregnant. She aborted after the second attempt (Joyce 2009, 1).

Adding to the pregnant soldier's difficulties are the laws that prohibit the Defense Department from providing medical care overseas. Starting in 1979, Defense Department appropriations bills have been used to restrict or prohibit the use of federal funds for all military health coverage including for abortion services at overseas military hospitals. In 1992, Congress passed an amendment to make abortions available at overseas installation, but President H. W. Bush vetoed it. In 1993, President Bill Clinton modified the military policy on providing abortions, thus overturning a former interpretation of the law that barred availability of services for abortion. Under the change, military medical facilities were allowed to perform abortions provided they were privately funded (Burrelli 2002, Summary). Requiring a woman to pay for an abortion began as a funding ban, but in 1995, due to anti-abortion forces in Congress, military hospitals are prohibited to provide abortion services, except in cases of life endangerment, rape, or incest (and for the latter two reasons, the patient pays for the service). The prohibition is still in effect. In 2005 and 2006, Representative Susan Davis (D-CA), tried unsuccessfully to repeal the ban or bring it compatible with current Medicaid standards to allow abortion funding in rape and incest cases. She argued that "servicewomen do not receive the protection of the Constitution they defend" (Joyce 2009, 1). Representative Jim Ryan (R-KS) opposed the repeal, saying it would bring about abortion clinics.

Abortion remains problematic, but there is a possibility that will change. The quality of care for abortion in local hospitals is uneven at best. Military women may be stationed in countries where abortion is illegal or unavailable. Even women who can conveniently access a clinic, "if they can't afford the care they need, they don't have access to service either" (Joyce 2009, 2). A little noticed amendment appears within the 852-page Pentagon policy bill that if passed should make abortion easier for military women in war zones because it allows privately financed abortions at military hospitals and bases (Bumiller 2010, Politics).

According to the Government Accountability Office (GAO), in 2002, about 10 percent of women in the military became pregnant each year (GAO 2002, 10). Donnelly maintains that in a two-year period, pregnancy rates have increased from 12 to 19 percent. In addition, she holds the position that experts have identified health risks specific to the embryo in the beginning weeks before a woman knows she is pregnant (Clemmitt 2009, 973). Opponents argue that pregnancy requires the woman to be flown out of her assignment within two weeks, causing personnel disruptions in units. Donnelly suggests that having submarines with pregnant women on board may require the Navy to evacuate a woman from the middle of the ocean and compromise its mission (Clemmitt 2009, 973). At the Warhorse base, pregnancy is relatively rare and has had little effect on overall readiness. The First Stryker Brigade, composed of thousands of soldiers, has sent only three women home due to pregnancy in 10 months in Iraq (Myers 2009).

Pregnancy and Readiness

Each service has its pregnancy policy based on DoD guidance. President Harry Truman authorized the Services to involuntarily discharge women due to pregnancy in 1951. Before the early 1970s, Services routinely discharged women involuntarily for pregnancy or adoption of minor children. When the All-Volunteer Force was established in 1972 the DoD authorized the Services to retain uniformed women parents on a case by case basis and in 1975, the DoD mandated the end of involuntary separations due to pregnancy or parenthood. Thus, the Army has no policy that prohibits or restricts the pregnancy of soldiers (U.S. Army n.d., Slide 1). In 2010, the DoD announced that the morning-after pill will be available at all of its hospitals and health clinics including overseas (AND *Advocate* 2010, 4).

Nonetheless, commanders are faced with readiness issues. To meet readiness in Iraq in 2009, Maj. Gen. Anthony Cucolo created a rule that outlined possible punishments for pregnancy. It prohibited "becoming nondeployable for reasons within the control of the soldier," including "becoming pregnant or impregnating a soldier . . . resulting in the redeployment of the pregnant soldier" (CNN 2009). The rule affected 22,000 people including 1,682 women under his command in northern Iraq. Although Cucolo was attempting to get his soldiers to think and to protect combat readiness, the military said that any unit must get the permission of the commander of U.S. Forces-Iraq before creating new rules restricting the activity of troops. The policy came under criticism from four U.S. senators who wrote to the secretary of the Army to ask that the policy be rescinded. New, Iraq-wide guidelines took effect beginning January 1 that lifted the rules enacted by the Cucolo (Abbas 2009).

AND points out that studies such as the U. S. Navy Work Loss Studies-NPRDC, "have shown that pregnant military women lose no more work time than military men . . . , who lose more time due to sports injuries and disciplinary reasons" (AND 2010, Issue Paper). Thus, men who lose time would also pose readiness issues. In addition, Department of Defense statistics show that the numbers of women released from active duty before completing their obligations had remained the same from 2004 to 2007 (average of 5 percent), as had the number released for the reason of pregnancy (average of 1.25 percent).

Motherhood

Over 100,000 women who served in the wars are mothers or not quite half (40 percent) of those women have been deployed. Most are primary caregivers and one-third are single mothers. The military's challenge is to help soldiers understand that they do not have to choose between family and career (Alvarez 2009). According to GAO, "Family satisfaction with military life can influence a service member's decision whether to remain in the military" (GAO 2002, 7). In addition, DoD surveys revealed that a larger percentage of female soldiers gave as the most important reason for leaving the military the amount of time separated from family. Long, multiple, and too frequent deployments affect family life (Mulhall 2009, 4).

Although single parents are not allowed to enlist in active duty, they can, if they become single after enlistment and present a family care plan. In 2008, single women numbered about 12 percent of the Army and single men represented 4 percent (Alvarez 2009).

The military faces a need for soldiers and without the return of the draft, the need for women soldiers will continue. The Army has instituted some policy changes to address the challenges mothers face. In 2008, the Army extended deployment deferment time for a new mother from four to six months. The base commander at the Landstuhl Regional Medical Center in Germany followed the Navy's lead and increased the time to a year to accommodate breast feeding (Alvarez 2009).

Other Army improvements include: allowing families to go with a deploying soldier in some cases, building more day care centers, allowing families to stay in one place longer, and approving a 10-day paternity leave for new fathers. The Navy allows more sailors to work from home on computers and permits a three-year sabbatical (Alvarez 2009).

In spite of the military's efforts, problems remain. According to Capt. Lory Manning, the military needs to provide child care around the clock (Manning in Alvarez 2009). In addition, the military might deem it necessary to deploy couples to war simultaneously. Alvarez reports that the effects of deployments on children concerns parents. About two million children belong to families who have gone to war. Afghanistan and Iraq wars have produced approximately 25 casualties of mothers out of a total of 121 women.

Gender and Sexual Discrimination: Sexual Harassment, Assault, and Rape

Sexism, gender discrimination, and sexual harassment are related. Gender harassment has no sexual aspect, but it is directed against one sex. Skaine defined sexism as "the pattern of institutional and societal responses which determines an individual's roles and status on the basis of gender. It sets up artificial patterns to which a person is pressured to conform. Sexism produces sexual harassment when a person, usually a woman, is harassed for behaving contrary to the expectations of society or particular individuals" (Skaine 1996, 16). These forms of discrimination may be used to perpetuate status as a subordinate, especially if the one being discriminated against is fearful of consequences.

The Defense Manpower Center's *2006 Gender Relations Survey of Active Duty Members* is a significant report because it presents a trend analysis across survey years 1995, 2002, and 2006. (*See Chapter 6, Table 6.11.*) The report defined sexist behaviors as involving "unwanted actions that refer to an individual's gender and are directed toward all persons of that gender. Experiences of sexist behavior include verbal and/or nonverbal behaviors that convey insulting, offensive, or condescending attitudes based on the gender of the respondent." The trend analysis found:

- In 2006, 54 percent of women and 22 percent of men indicated experiencing sexist behavior
- 2006 incident rate for women was lower than the 1995 incident rate (54 percent vs. 63 percent), but was higher than the 2002 incident rate (54 percent vs. 50 percent); 2006 incident rate for men was higher than the 1995 (22 percent vs. 15 percent) and the 2002 (22 percent vs. 17 percent) incident rates. (Lipari et al. 2008, ix–x)

Related to the Defense Manpower's measurements of sexist behavior were the results of responses to the "unwanted gender-related experiences in one situation" question. Those results were higher than the incidence of sexism:

- 81 percent of women and 60 percent of men indicated that some or all of the behaviors in the one situation occurred at a military installation, 24 percent of women and 22 percent of men indicated the behaviors occurred in living quarters or barracks, 29 percent of women and 24 percent of men indicated the behaviors occurred in the local community around an installation, and 73 percent of women and 54 percent of men indicated the behaviors occurred at their permanent duty station. (Lipari et al. 2008, x)

DoD defines sexual harassment as "a form of sex discrimination that involves unwelcome sexual advances" (Department of Defense, 1995 in Lipari et al. 2008, viii). The trend analysis found

- In 2006, 34 percent of women and 6 percent of men indicated experiencing sexual harassment
- For both women and men, the sexual harassment incident rate in 2006 was lower than the 1995 rate (46 percent for women and 8 percent for men) but higher than the 2002 rate (24 percent for women and 3 percent for men). (Lipari et al. 2008, viii)

It is difficult to accurately gauge the number of women who experience sexual harassment, assault or rape. It is also difficult to measure the severity of these acts. Because what is heard (or not heard) from women who experience sexual harassment, assault, or rape is only the tip of the iceberg; actual incidence may be much higher (Skaine 1996, 198, 307–308, 398). The Iraq and Afghanistan Veterans of America (IAVA) reported that in the military, "women have been coping with significant and underreported sexual assault and harassment for decades" (IAVA 2009, 6).

In assault, the number of cases reported appears to have increased in the fiscal year 2008. The DoD reported 2,908 total reports of sexual assault (*see Chapter 6, Table 6.12*). These reports represent an 8 percent increase from 2007. Of the 2,908 reports, 251 reports occurred in combat areas (Bahrain, Iraq, Jordan, Lebanon, Syria, Yemen, Egypt, Kuwait, Oman, Qatar, Saudi Arabia,

United Arab Emirates, Iran, Pakistan, and Afghanistan) while 163
(65 percent) took place in Iraq and Afghanistan. Sexual Assault
Response Coordinators (SARCs) and Victim Advocates (VAs)
are in place in combat areas. Larger field hospitals are equipped
with Sexual Assault Forensic Exam or SAFE kits for evidence
collection (DoD 2009, 33, 41). In 2009, reports of sexual assault
increased by 11 percent to 3,230 or overall two reports per thousand
service members. The Army rate was 2.6 per thousand; the
Navy, 1.6; the Air Force, 1.4; and the Marine Corps, 1.3. The director
of DoD's Sexual Abuse Prevention and Response Office said that
she would like to conclude that the increase is due to the emphasis
DoD is placing on prevention and education about the program
(AND *Advocate* 2010, 5).

Sexual assault in the military includes a broad range of sex
crimes from rape or nonconsensual sodomy to indecent assault,
as well as attempts to commit these offenses. It is important to
remember that sexual assault is a crime. The DoD defines sexual
assault as

> intentional sexual contact, characterized by use of
> force, physical threat or abuse of authority or when the
> victim does not or cannot consent. It includes rape,
> nonconsensual sodomy (oral or anal sex), indecent assault
> (unwanted, inappropriate sexual contact or fondling), or
> attempts to commit these acts. Sexual assault can occur
> without regard to gender or spousal relationship or age
> of victim. "Consent" shall not be deemed or construed to
> mean the failure by the victim to offer physical resistance.
> Consent is not given when a person uses force, threat of
> force, coercion, or when the victim is asleep, incapacitated,
> or unconscious. (DoD 2009, 9)

The U.S. military and civilian society are well aware of the
problem of rape and sexual violence. According to Elizabeth L.
Hillman, commanders, members of Congress, legal reformers,
educators, media coverage, and political response are significant
resources dedicated to eradicating this violence (Hillman 2009,
102). Hillman contended these efforts have been unsuccessful
because military institutions resist cultural change. In addition,
the cases upon which the reforms were built operate with the
view of women "as vulnerable yet dangerous, soldiers as male
and overpowering, and accountability as a slippery slope rather

than a clear-cut principle" (Hillman 2009, 119). Hillman believed the military justice system has helped to sustain a legal culture that reinforces the relationship between sexual violence and authentic soldiering (Hillman 2009, 101).

Melissa Rathbun-Nealy and Rhonda Cornum were two U.S. servicewoman taken prisoner by the Iraqis in the 1991 Persian Gulf War against Iraq. Rhonda Cornum's experience demonstrated that female soldiers can serve in expanded roles in wartime. In her 1993 book, *She Went to War: The Rhonda Cornum Story,* she wrote about her eight days as a prisoner of war (POW). She told the *Washington Post*'s Henry Allen: "So then you have to organize the bad things that can happen to you in some other hierarchy. My hierarchy was, is it going to make me stay here longer, is it life-threatening, is it disabling or is it excruciating. If it's none of those things, then it took on a fairly low level of significance" (Allen *Washington Post* in *World Book Encyclopedia* 2006).

Cornum believes women in the military should be evaluated on their own talents. She dismissed those who would use her experience as an argument to prevent women from serving on the front lines. "Every 15 seconds in America, some woman is assaulted. Why are they worried about a woman getting assaulted once every 10 years in a war overseas? It's ridiculous," she told Cathy Booth Thomas of *Time.* "Clearly it's an emotional argument they use . . . because they can't think of a rational one. . . . " (*Time* 2003 in *World Book Encyclopedia* 2006).

Opponents of women serving in combat hold the position that a threat exists of female prisoners being raped or tortured could negatively affect the way that a captured male reacts to interrogation (International Debate Education Association 2006, Con). According to Embser-Herbert, one of the arguments against women serving in combat is that men are predisposed to protect women, therefore women would be a distraction. The services would not have had to establish sexual harassment programs if men were so inclined to protect women (Clemmitt 2009, 973).

AND stated that sexual assault is not only criminal, it hinders military readiness. It impinges on physical and mental health, restricts ability to perform missions, and can affect ability to lead productive civilian lives after military service. Sexual assault affects recruitment and retention of women. IAVA reported that half of all sexual assaults go unreported and prosecution rates were alarmingly low (IAVA 2009, 7). (*See Chapter 6, Table 6.13 Barriers to Reporting Sexual Assault.*) As part of the Defense Authorization

Act for 2005, Congress established the Defense Task Force on Sexual Assault in the Military Services (AND 2009).

In 2009, the task force reported that DoD had made significant progress in improving response to victims' needs and that there was more success when commanders took an active role. The task force stressed the need for institutional change to more effectively prevent sexual assault. Doing so was essential to military readiness (DoD 2009, ES-6).

Balance Issues

Both men and women hold family issues important. Women often are primary caretakers for their children. Balancing a military career and a family can be especially challenging. About 40 percent of active duty women have children, compared to 44 percent of active duty men. Approximately 11 percent of women are single mothers compared to 4 percent of men as single fathers. Women are five times (10 percent vs. 2 percent) more likely to be in dual military marriages, with both partners eligible for deployment (U.S. Congress 2007, 2).

Mothers in the military face longer deployments, which increased from 12 to 15 months or longer and an increase in the number of redeployments. Problems that mothers might face include dual parent deployments, child care access, adequacy of medical leave, and access to appropriate health care services. Despite progress in increasing child care access and lowering cost, need still exists. This need affects readiness (U.S. Congress 2007, 4, 5). IAVA reported the emergence of "a very troubling pattern" when divorce data compares the genders. Marriages of active duty women are failing almost three times the rate of men. More study is needed to assess the stressors such as multiple deployments, mental health injuries, dual-military marriages, gaps in family support programs especially for women and veterans, and access to health care relating to issues specific to women (IAVA 2009, 4, 5, 6).

Mental Health Care

In 2009, hospitalization for mental disorders surpassed hospital stays for injuries or pregnancies for the first time in 15 years of the Pentagon's *Medical Surveillance Monthly Report*. In 2009, 17,538 service members required hospitalization for mental health problems compared to 17,354 for pregnancy and childbirth issues and 11,156 for injury and poisoning reasons. In 2007, mental health disorders ranked second compared to pregnancy and childbirth that ranked first. In 2005, mental health ranked third with pregnancy and childbirth ranking first. However, hospitalization for mental health reasons has steadily increased from 2005, showing 11,335 service members to 13,703 in 2007, and 17,538 in 2009. The same five mental disorders were the leading causes of mental health hospitalizations for both men and women. The disorders, adjustment reactions including post-traumatic stress disorder (PTSD) and episodic mood disorders, accounted for 14 percent and 17 percent of all hospitalizations (other than pregnancy or childbirth-related issues) of males and females, respectively (Armed Forces Health 2010, 3, 5). (*See Chapter 6, Table 6.14 Hospitalizations Mental Disorders, Pregnancy and Childbirth, and Injury and Poisoning, Active Component, U.S. Armed Forces, 2005, 2007, and 2009.*) An Army report from January 1, 2005, to March 9, 2010, indicated 39,311 individual cases of PTSD. An 8 percent decrease of new cases from 2008 to 2009 was reported. A DoD report recorded 39,365 PTSD cases from 2003 to 2007 (Fischer 2010, 1).

Brig. Gen. Rhonda Cornum, Medical Corps, U.S. Army, said at the 2009 WREI Conference that the nation is asking a lot from the young men and women in the military. Not only must they "be prepared for 'full spectrum' warfare (from peacekeeping through high intensity conflict), but must engage in offense, defense, and 'nation building,' simultaneously. Our soldiers, often led by junior leaders in small groups, must continue to show trust, respect and compassion towards members of local populations, even when their loyalties and actions are suspect" (Cornum 2009, Power Point).

The increased rate of "stress symptoms" such as PTSD, depression, suicides, risk-taking behaviors, family violence, and drug and alcohol use following deployments, especially among junior soldiers is no surprise, Cornum explained. The stress is a reflection of the fact that the military asks its soldiers to do things which are very challenging, often dangerous, and that soldiers and their families are inconsistently prepared to cope successfully with significant challenge. The Army concluded that how a soldier comes out of an experience is in great measure determined by how that soldier went into it. In 2008, the Army established the Directorate of Comprehensive Soldier Fitness. The Army's commitment is to increase the baseline resilience of a soldier before she or he is placed in the most difficult and challenging experiences. In so doing, the Army applies the same resources to ensure psychological fitness as it has historically applied to physical and technical excellence (Cornum 2009, Power Point).

Significantly, this new program, Comprehensive Soldier Fitness, emphasizes psychological strength as well as physical fitness training. "Physical fitness is not achieved by a single visit to the gym, and psychological strength is not achieved by a single class or lecture" (Cornum 2009, Power Point). Comprehensive Soldier Fitness is a long term strategy with five dimensions: physical, social, family, emotional, and spiritual. Evaluation of a soldier's comprehensive fitness is modeled after the Army's approach to physical and technical fitness and proficiency. The first of four steps involves an assessment, using a Global Assessment Tool (GAT) and reassessment at appropriate intervals. It begins at accession and follows the soldier throughout her or his entire career. The scores help the Army determine the training needed. Scores between men and women were relatively equal (Cornum 2009, Power Point). In the mean results, women were even a little higher (3.74 to 3.68). In the maximum results, men were a little higher (5.0 to 4.9). (*See Chapter 6, Table 6.15 Emotional Fitness Results, 2009.*) As soldiers receive this comprehensive fitness training, the Army hopes they will become more resilient, better able to overcome challenges, more mature, and able to bounce back from adversity.

Suicide

Statistics on suicide are difficult to get, but the wars in Iraq and Afghanistan have taken toll on men and women soldiers in the largest numbers since the beginning of record keeping in 1980. In 2008, 128 Army personnel were confirmed suicides and 41 marines. In February 2009, another 15 Army deaths were still under investigation. In 2008, an estimated 30 percent of soldiers took their own lives while on deployment and 35 percent did so after returning from a tour of duty (Cogan 2009). During the first six months of 2010, 65 members of the Guard and Reserve committed suicide compared with 42 for the same period in 2009 (Military.com 2010, News). Almost twice as many women serving in the wars committed suicide compared to women not sent to war. The Army said causes of suicide include occupational/operational issues, failed relationships, and legal and financial issues. The Army did not speculate on the morale of U.S. combat (Doyle 2007, News).

In some cases, whether suicide or murder is the cause of death, is not clear and may not ever be clear. In some cases cause of death is ruled as a noncombat related incident (DoD 2009, Release No. 597-09). An example of an unclear case of suicide is that of U.S. Army Staff Sgt. Amy Seyboth-Tirador, 29, who was killed in Iraq by a gunshot wound to the back of her head. She was an interrogator and a recipient of a Bronze Star (Staff Sgt. 2010).

After the War, the Veterans

Veterans, men and women, face major issues including post-traumatic stress, lack of acceptance, access to health care, employment, and homelessness. DoD early studies indicate that mental health issues are proportionately about the same for each gender. Damien Cave reported that post-traumatic stress affected 8,454 women as of June 2008. This number excludes troops still enlisted or those who have not used the V.A. system (Cave 2009). As commanders quietly sidestepped exclusion regulations because they needed resources, women fight "on dusty roads and darkened outposts in ways that were never imagined by their parents or publicly authorized by Congress," Cave wrote. They have distinguished themselves and are emerging as equals.

Controversies Surrounding Women in Combat and in the Military

On May 31, 2010, 255,136 soldiers—of which 26,961 were women—deployed in support of Operation Iraqi Freedom and Operation Enduring Freedom in Afghanistan (DoD 2010, Memo). As of August 31, 2010, deaths for Operation Iraqi Freedom totaled 4,408 with 110 or 2.50 percent being women. In Operation Enduring Freedom in Afghanistan, 1,262 soldiers died with 20 or 1.58 being women as of September 4, 2010 (DoD 2010, OIF; DoD 2010, OEF). (*See Chapter 6, Tables 6.5 and 6.6.*) Approximately 153 women have received the Purple Heart in recent wars (WIMSA 2006). In 2005, Sgt. Leigh Ann Hester became one of only 14 women in U.S. military history to receive the Silver Star. Retired Air Force Brig. Gen. Wilma L. Vaught, president of the Women's Memorial, explained the significance of Hester's award, "This is the first time in history that a woman has been decorated for direct actions against an enemy force" (WIMSA 2008, *Voices of Valor*).

Women in Direct Ground Combat

Women soldiers continue to demonstrate their abilities. A recent series in the *New York Times* on "Women at Arms" laid bare the roles of risk military women have and the success with which they perform. Gervasio Sanchez reported, "Their success, widely known in the military, remains largely hidden from public view. In part, this is because their most challenging work is often the result of a quiet circumvention of military policy" (Sanchez 2009). Sanchez explained that for the commanders to meet readiness needs, they justify using women by describing their order as "women have been 'attached' to a combat unit rather than 'assigned'" (Sanchez 2009). Many women are trained to search Iraqi women at checkpoints because of local cultural sensitivities. This assignment places them at risk as much as male soldiers (Myers 2009).

When Elaine Donnelly responded to the question: "Doesn't the experience of female soldiers in Iraq prove that they are ready for anything, including direct ground combat?" she wrote that women have served well and bravely their unprecedented duties. But, she added:

> Nothing that has happened in Iraq, however, changes the fact that in direct ground combat units, where women have not yet been assigned, physical differences and other factors could detract from mission accomplishment and other factors necessary to prepare for close combat. The Presidential Commission confirmed that during the first Gulf War, servicewomen were three to four times as non-deployable than the men, primarily due to pregnancy and related family issues. (Brower and Donnelly 2005, CON)

During the Vietnam War, some men used the tactic of a significant other's pregnancy to avoid service. Opponents argue that when women face active duty call-up some will do the same (International Debate Education Association 2006).

According to Donnelly's Center for Military Readiness, most of the issues raised in the 1992 Presidential Commission on the Assignment of Women in the Armed Forces remain valid today (CMR 2004). On the other hand, in an e-mail message to the author on August 12, 2009, Capt. Lory Manning, USN (Ret.), director of the Women in the Military Project of the WREI, stated her research found, "Most of the arguments against women in combat now comes in the form of mothers leaving children or religious convictions on God-given roles for each of the sexes."

Even though women serve in combat and even though we have learned much about women's abilities since 2001, controversy continues as to whether women should serve in combat, and, in some cases, serve in the military. Controversies and positions of proponents and opponents of inclusion of women in combat follow.

Physical Abilities

Proponents believe that the military should adopt physical requirements for each military specialty and assign soldiers to each specialty based on their ability to meet requirements apart from their gender (Cloutier 2008, 1533). In an interview with the author, Brig. Gen. Wilma L. Vaught, founder and president of the Women In Military Service For America Memorial Foundation, Inc., Arlington, Virginia, said:

> If you are not able to perform the duties that are required in a specific specialty you shouldn't be assigned to that. I mean, if it requires heavy lifting and you can't do that, you shouldn't be assigned to that. So I would certainly favor testing some of these things, as some countries have done. Notably Denmark has. Norway has. Canada is pretty much open to assignment any place. I don't know whether you would say they have tested it or not, but you can be assigned any place. I would always have felt much better if we had really conducted some evaluations of what women can do and what can't they do. And I think there are some aspects of what shouldn't they do and that needs to be looked at very carefully. Just as in the present conflicts in Iraq and Afghanistan, we now have a different aspect that we are forced to come to grips with. It was there in times past but we didn't have to come to grips with it. And that's the cultural aspect of the treatment of women. As so really you look at this whole thing, it becomes a question of what women should be permitted to do with respect to combat or anything else. What does the job require and not what women can do. (Vaught 2009)

Major Lillian A. Pfluke, U.S. Army (Ret.) from personal experience found the women's assignment policy in the Army "extraordinarily disheartening and deeply personally disappointing" (Pfluke in Haley 2004, 60). (*See Chapter 6, Document 6.11 Profile of a Soldier.*) Less qualified males were selected over more qualified women for key leadership positions in part because of "deeply entrenched and dated ideas." As she approached consideration for lieutenant colonel, she realized that although she was qualified for positions in the Airborne Rangers and Infantry battalion commander, her goal was unrealizable. Thus, she retired in 1995.

In 2009, Capt. Ervin R. Stone, USMC, prepared a report, *Women in Combat: Standardize the Physical Fitness Test.* He held, "Allowing women who meet the mental and physical combat requirements of the Marine Corps to serve in any military occupational specialty will ensure the military of the future fulfills the expectations of our nation" (Stone 2009, 1). The Marine Corps should establish one standard for all regardless of gender. The starting point for gender integration is to address the disparity of physical ability.

Stone points out that the 1992 Presidential Commission reported several findings concerning physical strength. First, "the average female Army recruit is 4.8 inches shorter, weighs 31.7 pounds less, and has 37.4 pounds less muscle mass and 5.7 pounds more fat mass." Second, "women have 55 percent of the upper torso, 72 percent of the lower torso and 64 percent of the trunk isometric strength [taking place against resistance] of men." Third, muscle building hormones or androgens are at higher levels in males. Males develop larger muscles, but in training, women develop the same amount of strength but in smaller muscles (*Presidential Commission* 1992, C-3 in Stone 2009, 6).

Stone proposes the gender overlap area is where the Corps needs to focus. This area consists of women who perform equal to, or better than, some of their male counterparts. These women can perform combat duties with a unified combat standard and proper training. He believes, "The Marine Corps needs to establish what this level of performance is and do away with separate physical standards for men and women" (Stone 2009, 7, 8). Anyone who meets the standard, should be allowed to serve in all fields.

In an interview with the author, Jennifer G. Mathers, Department of International Politics, Aberystwyth University, Aberystwyth, United Kingdom, said that one of the arguments made against women serving in combat falls into the category of "the relative capabilities of women and men to cope with the physical and emotional demands of combat situations." She explained the argument, "often boils down to whether or not women could carry heavy loads for long distances, whether women would be able to win a hand-to-hand fight against an enemy male soldier and also whether a woman would be able to cope with the emotional and mental strain of being under attack, returning fire, being responsible for killing (this, of course, assumes that men cope well with these strains or that the male way of coping is the benchmark for judging women's responses)" (Mathers 2010, Interview).

Mathers finds interesting that this argument, almost never refers to actual examples, historical or contemporary, of women's performances in de facto combat situations. She explains,

> While it is undeniable that most men are stronger and have greater upper body strength than most women, we also know from historical cases that women have, in wartime and combat situations, carried extremely heavy loads and met the physical and other requirements of the circumstances. For example, during the Second World War Soviet women served in a variety of combat roles and there are numerous cases of Soviet women actually rescuing wounded male comrades, including carrying much heavier men away from the battlefield. Similarly, Vietnamese women carried heavy burdens up and down the Ho Chi Minh trail during the conflict in that country and some of the Vietnamese women who participated in combat missions (the "long-haired warriors" or "long-haired army") became famous for their fighting spirit, bravery and ability to endure hardship and even torture after being captured by South Vietnamese forces (Taylor 1999). (However, note that the women soldiers who joined the North Vietnamese state military, the People's Liberation Armed Forces, were phased out of combat roles as the war progressed due to the attitudes of the male soldiers, who did not approve of women in such nontraditional roles.) (Mathers 2010, Interview)

Opponents hold that women's physical abilities are not best suited to combat (Cloutier 2008, 1533, 1547). The 1992 commission issued 17 findings. Key was the commission's recommendation that "women should be excluded from direct land combat units and positions." The commission reasoned that the physiological differences between men and women placed women at a disadvantage. Women who could meet the physical standards for ground combat, were few (*Presidential Commission* 1993, i, 24). The Secretary of Defense and Congress, however, came to a different conclusion with the repeal of exclusion laws in the Air Force and Navy (Skaine 1999, 101). Donnelly believes that coed training sets different physical standards of achievement for men and women. The lower standard assures success for women, but on the battlefield there is no gender norming (Donnelly 2005 in Clemmitt 2009, 959).

The *Washington Post* reported that accounts by men who have fought alongside women suggest that "what's true for women generally may not be as true for women who join the military" (Henderson 2008). Further, Henderson maintained surveys by the U.S. Army Research Institute indicate that while some civilians continue to argue over whether women have the physical strength, stamina and mental toughness for combat, most soldiers have already concluded that women do have these qualities to be effective. The surveys show that about 14 percent of male and female soldiers say they'd change their career plans if women were to start fighting alongside men in direct ground combat. Henderson concludes in about a decade, military attitudes have done an about-face (Henderson 2008).

So if these favorable military attitudes exist and when in 2005, the military leadership in the Department of Defense objected to the Hunter/McHugh Amendment, Henderson asks the pivotal question: "if the military society gets it why does not society?" Part of the reason lies in the philosophies of the 60s and advocated by people such as Elaine Donnelly and Phyllis Schlafly that mothers should not kill when there are able-bodied males available. A primary reason more women are now in the military is that from the mid-60s on, women could control their fertility through birth control, according to Lori Manning of WREI (Henderson 2008).

From a mental health perspective, killing is not the only way to receive psychological injury. Researchers have found that what matters more is the number of times soldiers believed they and their fellow soldiers were going to die. Military mental health surveys don't just ask returning soldiers if they killed anyone;

they're quizzed on whether they were shot at, handled dead bodies, or knew someone who was killed (Henderson 2008).

Exposure to Danger

Mathers believes a category of arguments surrounding the issue of whether women should serve in combat is, "Women should not be in combat because it is unacceptable to place women in danger of being wounded, killed or, if they became prisoners of war, raped by their captors" (Mathers 2010, Interview). Mathers said that this category of arguments supports the belief that

> it is not acceptable to place women in the sort of danger which is posed by combat missions, ignores the fact that women's health and lives are placed in danger by wars all the time, whether they are wearing the uniform of a state military or not. But while this concern is expressed for the safety of women soldiers, it appears to be acceptable to place some categories of women in danger of injury, death and enemy capture—nurses, for example. Women spies are another example. During the Second World War there were numerous cases of women being sent by the Allies into occupied France to undertake work for the resistance. These women were in very great danger and many were captured and held in concentration camps and very few of them survived.
>
> It is also illustrative to look at some historical examples to see how lines have been drawn between combat and noncombat roles for men and women and how this has worked in practice. In Britain during the Second World War, women were used very successfully in anti-aircraft batteries, for example in London during the Blitz. Women were trained to and did perform every element of the roles except for one—they were not allowed to pull the trigger. (Campbell 1993 in Mathers 2010, Interview)

Women's Effect on Unit Cohesion

Unit cohesion is how well soldiers function or work together (Skaine 1999, 167). The commission placed much emphasis on that the presence of women in ground combat units adversely affected unit cohesion (*Presidential Commission*, 1993, i, 25). At the time of the Presidential Commission report, all cohesion research had been limited to all-male combat units (Finch 1993, 11–13 in Skaine 1999, 167). Stone points out that the commission's objections, except for the first, can be readily resolved by strong leadership. Primarily, those issues were the ability of women of perform physically, forced intimacy and privacy, men will protect women, sexual misconduct and pregnancy (Stone 2009, 9; Commission 1992, 25). Opponents held that these issues and unit bonding issues would affect negatively the ability of soldiers to work together. Mathers believes another category of arguments that are made against women serving in combat is, "the possible/likely responses to women in combat from their fellow male soldiers. For example, it is often argued that if men and women served together in combat units, in an actual combat situation the men would seek to protect the women soldiers and would therefore be distracted from their professional duties, thereby endangering the mission and, perhaps, the safety of the entire unit. A variation on this theme presents the distraction posed by women as sexual and suggests that the male soldiers would compete with each other for the romantic or sexual interests of the women and that this would undermine the cohesion of the unit" (Mathers 2010, Interview).

Mathers believes this argument about the presence of women eroding unit cohesiveness and triggering protective instincts in male soldiers is also based on hypothetical situations. She explains:

> This is precisely the argument that was made to justify the 2002 decision against opening up ground combat positions to women in the British army—that it was simply too risky to introduce gender integration into combat units because of concerns about what might happen and there was no way to test this realistically outside of combat conditions (Great Britain Ministry of Defence 2002, Nos. 13, 17, 18). And yet in the many historical and contemporary cases I have read about involving women and men in combat situations, I have yet to come across one which states that the presence of women DID distract the men, undermine the cohesion and effectiveness of the unit and endanger the mission. For a discussion of the actual effects of women's presence on mixed units in the Soviet Union during the

Second World War, see Reina Pennington's, *Wings,
Women and War: Soviet Airwomen in World War II Combat.*
(Pennington 2001, 162–165 In Mathers 2010, Interview)

In 2009, Steven Lee Myers wrote that in the wars in Iraq and
Afghanistan, tens of thousands of American military women
have lived, worked, and fought with men for prolonged periods
and "have done so without the disruption of discipline and unit
cohesion that some feared would unfold." Myers relayed the
comment of Brig. Gen. Heidi V. Brown, one of the two highest
ranking women in Iraq at the start of the war, who recalled, "Here
we are six years later, and you don't hear about it. You shouldn't
hear about it" (Myers 2009).

The military is gender blind in a war zone. That does not
mean the problems that could affect cohesion do not occur such
as sexual harassment and assault. The means to deal with them
are improvised, for example, women are advised to travel in
pairs. Some carry folding knives and flashlights. The issues of
harassment, bias, hardship, and sexual relations are a matter of
discipline, maturity, and professionalism not as arguments for
separating the sexes (Myers 2009).

In addition to the commission's reasons for lack of cohesion,
McSally lists reasons such as "double standard issues such as
gender-segregated basic training, separate standards for men and
women in basic training, lack of uniformity in military uniforms,
policies that demean or degrade servicewomen, women's
exemption from selective service registration and poorly timed
pregnancies" (McSally 2007, Cohesion). All other causes of reduced
cohesion fall into the category of behavior called "prejudicial to
good order and discipline." Sexual misconduct arises from gender
integration and can be militarily defined misconduct in consensual
relationships. Donnelly believes that not only do women weaken
overall standards, the addition to women in ground combat also
has "sown seeds of discord among the ranks" (Clemmitt 2009,
959). In addition, favoring women's career paths affects readiness.
Another point in this position is that men, particularly those who
enlist, uphold traditional gender roles. Therefore, men might act
foolishly to protect women in combat units (International Debate
Association, Con).

In 1999, Skaine maintained "the process of attaining a cohesive
unit is fraught with cultural biases," and that "biases center
primarily around the issues of gender, ability, sexual behaviors,

and opportunity. Readiness hinges on how well the cohesion issues are addressed by force command" (Skaine 1999, 134).

Women's Effect on Readiness

Readiness is the "ability of units and joint forces to fight and meet the demands of the national security strategy" (GAO 2009, 4). Several broad components measure readiness, including budget, that is, funding to maintain and modernize the forces. Whether or not women affect readiness because of their physical abilities, their gender, and the nature of their effect on unit cohesion is a point of controversy (Skaine 1999, 153).

Mady Segal wrote that when the need to defend our society exists, women are not defined in a societally constructed gender role and if they are, such an assigned role will be overridden to help the war effort. When there are not enough men, women will be called upon (Segal 1995, 760–762 in Skaine 1999, 154).

Readiness and increased roles for women in the military are mutually reinforcing, wrote McSally. To have the most capable force, "a policy that excludes the majority of the population from even being considered to serve in over 200,000 military positions is inefficient and only decreases military flexibility" (McSally 2007, Conclusion).

Jill A. Rough, Navy Reserve Intelligence Officer, maintains that regardless of the ongoing debate, "we are at war and it may not matter what your assignment is" (Rough 2009). At the WREI Women in the Military Conference, Rough asked "Is gender an issue?" The items that matter are genderless: rank (which is established), quest (mission), and uniform. These items establish competence that translates into acceptance.

Rough listed four ways the military targets women for assignment: (1) as a member of the Lioness teams which accompany the male soldiers on house-to-house searches to search the women, (2) as a member of the Human Train Team, (3) to use their attribute of a calming presence, and (4) as a member of the Civil Affairs Teams. Rough concluded that the evidence doesn't support the theories that women negatively impact unit cohesion or readiness (Rough 2009).

Marcia Clemmitt maintains evidence is lacking that demonstrates military readiness has suffered with the growth of women in numbers and in rank. Clemmitt outlined some of the arguments that affect readiness: women get injured trying to keep up with men, women do not have the upper body strength equal to men's, men compete with women affecting cohesiveness necessary for readiness, women get pregnant to avoid deployment or escape difficult jobs thus affecting morale, and women join for a career while men join to fight (Clemmitt 2009, 961–962).

Opponents believe that women serving in combat will drastically affect readiness. Reasons include that women have particular health needs, the increased risk of sexual encounters, and the negative effect on unit cohesion (Cloutier 2008, 1547). Phyllis Schlafly contends that historically, evidence does not support "the proposition that the assignment of women to military combat jobs is the way to advance women's rights, promote national security, improve combat readiness, or win wars." The many World War II books have not said that "Hitler or the Japanese should have solved their manpower shortage problem by using women in combat." Further, she believes that women serving in combat is a death wish for "our species" (Schlafly 2003).

The Issue of Equality

Proponents maintain that prohibiting women from serving in combat violates the Equal Protection Clause of the Fourteenth Amendment, denies women's rights as full citizens, and affects their promotional opportunities

Opponents believe that the military must focus on winning the war and make decisions that best affect military readiness, cohesion, and morale (Cloutier 2008, 1533, 1547). In an interview with the author, Dr. Peter A. Lillback, president, Westminster Theological Seminary, Glenside, Pennsylvania, said that he believes that while men and women have equal rights, each has a unique, different mission ordained by the Creator: the male, to lead and protect the woman, and the woman, to give birth to and nurture the next generation (Lillback 2009). Dr. Lillback served as chairman of the Ad Interim Study Committee on Women in the Military for the General Assembly Actions and Position Papers of the Presbyterian Church in America (PCA 2002).

The Issue of Motherhood

Dr. Lillback studied the issue of motherhood from the Biblical perspective. He explained, "It is very clear that men and women are both made in the image of God, both have great dignity and value, that the legal requirements of persons extend to both, and therefore, any discussion of the roles of men and women does not in any way impugn the full equality of each of the genders before the Creator. Having said that, it is also clear that the Biblical account recognizes the unique calling of women as the progenitors of infants in a way that men can never be" (Lillback 2009).

In an interview with the author, Brig. Gen.Wilma L. Vaught introduced one aspect of the issue of combat that has been important to some who "object to women being in combat, using that in its broadest sense, that is the aspect of women being mothers. What should their role be? Should they be permitted to leave their children? Should they be prohibited from leaving their children and being deployed?" These questions are the focus of those who support and those who oppose women in combat. Vaught believes women should be deployed and be deployed in combat zones. She believes that the nature of the mission should determine how women are used.

> Then you get into the aspect of assignment versus utilization. You can be assigned to some unit, well then how are you going to be used in that unit? Maybe what you are assigned to is a specialty that would say, "Oh, it is all right for this person to be assigned there because this specialty says, they are not going to be involved in combat, so it's okay for them to go" and yet, in the reality of the place where they are and what's going around there, they have to be utilized in a different capacity. So that's among the many aspects you have to think about when you look at this whole thing.
>
> Just from a very simplistic way of looking at it and what is my personal feeling about this and it has always been: (1) the commander should be able to utilize his or her troops however he or she needs to do that, given whatever the situation is. To be writing rules to say you can't do this or you can't do that, that just might not apply given the type of situation a commander may be confronted with; (2) with respect to women, I have always felt that women should be able to serve wherever they can make a contribution. (Vaught 2009)

Dr. Lillback expands on women's unique role as mothers:

The uniqueness of motherhood and the responsibilities of the nurturing function of the home and other duties that particularly in a pre-modern civilization were incredibly serious because the need to have so many children with infantile deaths and other problems, the culture made that task extremely important. We tend to be oblivious about that today because of the advances of medical science and population control theories, etc., but it is very clear that there was a Biblical concern that women would be free to do what only they could do and that is give forth life to the next generation. In that sense then, Biblical revelation recognized that there is a sense in which the woman has a greater glory than man does. Man has a leadership role that is clearly defined within a Christian world view, but there is a glory that is uniquely inherent to the feminine gender and that is in the role of advancing the next generation of both men and women, being their nurturers, trainers, educators, etc. That function was very important.

In conjunction with the function of advancing the next generation, in regard to the issue of combat, Dr. Lillback maintains, that from a moral position, one of the questions that has to be asked is:

Can there be a moral engagement of the enemy by a woman as a combatant if there is no clarity and protection of bringing a noncombatant into the battle because if she is killed, there are two people being killed from a Biblical viewpoint. Within the womb, personhood is extended to the child or the fetus or the product of conception. Within the Biblical revelation, an unborn child is an image bearer of God carrying on the uniqueness of humanity. Of course, that's been buttressed again and again by all the studies of biological science that what's within the womb is clearly human. It is nothing else. It is a human reality bearing the chromosome structure of life. (Lillback 2009)

Because they are life givers and there is the possibility of the presence of an unborn child, women should not serve in combat, according to Lillback.

Women in Combat and Societal Expectations

Culture is not monolithic. In an e-mail to the author, Maj. Lillian A. Pfluke, USA (Ret.), was hesitant to say we are addressing a cultural value when we discuss readiness. "Culture holds diverse opinions. There is no one element to a culture" (Pfluke in Skaine 1999, 166). If society is considered a composite of its institutions including the military, the public, and Congress, societal expectations in these groups have begun to modify concerning assigning women to combat. In the ongoing wars, the military's use of servicewomen to the fullest extent possible under current military regulations may be testing regulatory boundaries. Hasday contends that the evidence points to a noticeable positive shift in congressional, executive, military, and popular support for women's military service, including in combat. Survey data indicates that popular support for women's military service and combat, has also increased since *Rostker*. Growing popular support and women actually serving in combat may influence Congress (Hasday 2008, 146, 147, 150).

A 2005 CNN/USA Today/Gallup poll indicated a shift in societal expectations of women serving in the military and in ground combat. Seventy-two percent supported women serving in Iraq and 44 percent supported women serving in "ground troops who are doing most of the fighting" (Putko 2008, 28). There was no societal or congressional outrage over female casualties and prisoners of war in March 2003 and neither the Iraq nor Afghanistan wars reopened debate on women in direct combat, according to Putko.

Opponents hold a different view. Societally constructed gender roles for women includes that women should be protected from harm and that women should not kill (Putko 2008, 27; Sagawa and Campbell 1992, 3). Western societal biases tend to favor women not killing. In Tracy L. Conn's review of Belinda Morrissey's book, *When Women Kill: Questions of Agency and Subjectivity*, Conn noted that Morrissey maintained that "the media's efforts [is] to rewrite women's violent acts as life-givers, whereas the purposeful termination of life is more commonly attributed to men. This difference was based mainly on the fact that women are seen so" (Conn 2004, 285 in Skaine 2006, 31). Morrissey advises that we need to be aware of media and legal sources that sustain the concept that women do not kill (Morrisey 2003, 24 in Skaine 2006, 31), and the myth persists in spite of existing information otherwise (Kruger 2005, Abstract in Skaine 2006, 31).

Religious Conviction and Women in Combat

Religiously based ideas often overlap with societally constructed views, particularly of women's roles is demonstrated in Dr. Lillback's position on women in combat. He said his position "is divided between a Christian moral duty and what I call a general equity or universal moral duty and thirdly, a recognition that there is a pragmatic sociological and legal reality" (Lillback 2009). From a Christian perspective Dr. Lillback believes,

> The Biblical account recognizes the unique calling of women as the progenitors of infants in a way that men can never be. The uniqueness of motherhood and the responsibilities of the nurturing function of the home and other duties. . . . Man has a leadership role that is clearly defined within a Christian world view, but there is a glory that is uniquely inherent to the feminine gender and that is in the role of advancing the next generation of both men and women, being their nurturers, trainers, educators, etc. That function was very important. Even in a modern or post-modern world, for Christians, that pattern that God has given should not be set aside. We need to say as believers in the revelation of God that that pattern of men seeking to protect women has a moral duty that is upon us as Christian leaders and family men. That has a couple of practical realities.

The practical realities Dr. Lillback discusses center around universal moral or ethical concerns of "just worth" and "just war." Lillback contends that in the just worth theory,

> One of the foundational principles that every combatant and non-combatant needs to think about is the protecting of people who have not taken on the military task. A just war has combatants fighting combatants and non-combatants need to be protected and recognize that they are not part of the military engagement. A woman, by very nature of being a life giver, always has the potential, particularly in a more openly sexual environment that we live in today of actually bringing into combat a non-combatant within her womb. The possibility of that is heightened by a very general acceptance of

pre-marital and extra-marital sexuality and that becomes even more possible in a military gender-normed into just soldiers without regard to maleness and femaleness. So, from a moral position, one of the questions that has to be asked is: Can there be a moral engagement of the enemy by a woman as a combatant if there is no clarity and protection of bringing a non-combatant into the battle because if she is killed, there are two people being killed from a Biblical viewpoint.

Lillback's second point of a just war "is the duty to protect someone who is more vulnerable to harm and hurt by those who are stronger. Generally speaking, in a just war, you do not put your most vulnerable, most unskilled, those most at risk of harm in the place of danger. You put your most well-prepared, strongest and wisest and developed defenders in the place of battle. . . . " An area that needs to be given more thought is the subject of rape for which women are at greater risk. The moral question becomes is it appropriate to position women as a combatant, to defend men knowing women are more vulnerable to enemy abuse and atrocity.

Lillback's last point is that we are in a sociological environment where pragmatically to meet quotas so that we don't have to go to a draft, we make enticements for women to come into the military. He does not object to a woman entering the military to support her family, especially in the case of single mothers. But if able bodied men are available, mothers should not be required to leave her children to protect those men who are not entering the military. Lillback said the question that has to be asked is:

If that pragmatic decision to fill the quotas of the military by women serving is something that we can say is just when it is leaving behind women's most important function, the young children. Even in the courts of our land, in this post-modern world, when there's a debate about custody of young children, the judge often favors the mother. It takes some heinous struggles in a mother's life for her to lose the right to protect her children because of the unique nurturing role that is recognized worldwide between a mother and her children. Yet, pragmatically, we have determined as a culture that it's alright to take a woman and deploy her for months, put her in harm's way, leaving in effect her children behind as orphans and, perhaps, because of combat making them orphans in fact. That pragmatic reality should be judged and questioned by the whole issue is this just, is it just for the children, is it just to the mother, is it just perhaps even to the unborn child that the woman may be carrying with her into harm's way. These are huge moral questions. I think they should be asked and answered. I think they have been sidestepped by and large by our secular government.

Solutions

The debate on whether women should serve in combat is intense. Proposed solutions to the issue range from reinstating rigid exclusion provisions to having all female platoons to repealing remaining exclusion provisions.

Facsimile to Reinstating the Risk Rule

Kinglsey Brown put forth a collection of ideas at the extreme end of the continuum of opposition to women serving in combat. He proposed that "something like the risk rule should be reinstated" (Browne 2007, 296). In so doing, the rule would exclude women not only from combat, but from positions that present considerable risk of combat or capture. He reasoned that the number of positions open to women in Iraq would be substantially reduced. Second, reinstate the exclusion of women from combat aviation because when aircraft go down, aviators end up fighting on the ground. If the aircraft is hit by fire, physical strength is a factor. Third, bar women from warships because of pregnancies and sexual activity. Women threaten cohesion. They also lack physical strength needed for damage control putting the entire ship in danger (Browne 2007, 297).

All-Female Platoons

Krystyna M. Cloutier advocates implementing all-female platoons. Women would have a real opportunity to serve in combat and the fundamental nature of the military and its primary mission of winning wars would be fulfilled. She reasoned that because women lack physical strength equal to men, they contribute to the lack of cohesion. The adoption of gender-neutral physical requirements will not succeed in giving women access to combat positions; rather, it will effectively keep women out of combat positions. All-female platoons would prohibit women from being barred from combat because platoons would be designed around women's strengths (Cloutier 2008, 1534–1535).

Eliminate Policy Prohibitions and Establish Gender-Neutral Performance-Based Requirements

Proponents believe policy prohibitions of women serving in combat should be eliminated, specifically, "policies limiting assignment of women regardless of their qualifications, such as the Direct Combat Probability Coding and the 'risk rule,' which closes even noncombat positions to women." Congress should do its part in lifting the restriction. Additionally, the Secretary should order the establishment of "fair, gender-neutral perfor-mance based job standards for all positions, which would enable any individual who can meet these qualifications to be eligible for the assignment" (Sagawa and Campbell 1992, 7).

Permitting men and women to compete for all military occu-pational specialties is not an equal rights issue, but a matter of military effectiveness. If the United States is to remain a most capable and most powerful military power worldwide, it needs to have the best person in each job, regardless of their gender (Willens 1996, Women in the Military). Capt. Rosemary Mariner, USN (Ret.) believes that the services should match people with jobs. "A soldier is a soldier," she stated (Mariner in Skaine 1999, *Women at War*, 11).

References

Abbas, Mohammed. 2009. "Military to Scrap Pregnancy Punishment." *Reuters*. U.S., December 24. www.reuters.com/article (accessed April 25, 2010).

Adair, Aly. 2008. "Women in Combat: Should They Fight for Freedom?" May 1. *Associated Content*. News. www.associatedcontent.com (accessed November 1, 2009).

Alliance for National Defense (AND). 2010. "DoD 'Don't Ask, Don't Tell' Review Due Soon." *Advocate* 12: 1, 2.

Alliance for National Defense (AND). 2010. "Issue Paper: Pregnancy and Military Operations." *AND*. www.4militarywomen.org (accessed April 27, 2010).

Alliance for National Defense (AND). 2009. "Issue: Women in Combat, AND Positions." *AND*. www.4militarywomen.org (accessed September 1, 2009).

Alliance for National Defense (AND). 2008. "Eliminating Sexual Assault Should Be a Top Priority of the Department of Defense." December 3. www.4militarywomen.org (accessed November 7, 2009).

Alvarez, Lizette. 2009. "Wartime Soldier, Conflicted Mom." *New York Times*. Women at Arms Series. September 27. www.nytimes.com (accessed November 12, 2009).

AP. 2010. "Women to Serve on U.S. Submarines Starting in 2012." *Chicago Sun-Times*. Nation, April 30. www.suntimes.com (accessed April 30, 2010).

Armed Forces Health Surveillance Center. 2010. *Medical Surveillance Monthly Report* 17:04, April. 1–39. www.afhsc.mil (accessed May 19, 2010).

Booth Thomas, Cathy. 2003. *Time*, March 28. In *Encyclopedia of World Biography*. 2006. "Rhonda Cornum." A-Ec. www.notablebiographies.com (accessed April 13, 2010).

Brower, J. Michael, and Elaine Donnelly. 2005. "Examining the Pros and Cons of Women in Combat." *The Officer* 81.2: 38+.

Browne, Kingsley. *Co-ed Combat: The New Evidence that Women Shouldn't Fight the Nation's Wars*. New York: Penguin. 2007.

Bumiller, Elisabeth. 2010. "Plan Would Allow Abortions at Military Hospitals." *New York Times*, Politics. www.nytimes.com (accessed July 13, 2010).

Burrelli, David F. 2009. " 'Don't Ask, Don't Tell:' the Law and Military Policy on Same-Sex Behavior." *Congressional Research Service (CRS) Reports and Issue Briefs. Academic OneFile*, August 14. http://find.galegroup.com.proxy.lib.uni.edu (accessed April 20, 2010).

Burrelli, David F. 2002. "Abortion Services and Military Medical Facilities." *Congressional Research Service (CRS)*, April 24. www.policyarchive.org (accessed April 26, 2010).

Campbell, D'Ann. 1993. "Women in Combat: The World War II Experience in the United States, Great Britain, Germany and the Soviet Union." *Journal of Military History* 57, April. In Mathers, Jennifer G. 2010. Interview by Rosemarie Skaine. E-mail, May 26, 2010.

Carlin, David R., Jr. 1993. "They Call Themselves Liberals." *Commonweal* 120.4: 8+, February 26. *Academic OneFile.*

Cave, Damien. 2009. "A Combat Role, and Anguish, Too." *New York Times.* Women at Arms Series. October 31. www.nytimes.com (accessed November 12, 2009).

Center for Military Readiness (CMR). 2004. "Frequently Asked Questions: Women in Combat." November 22. www.cmrlink.org (accessed November 10, 2009).

Clemmitt, Marcia. 2009. "Women in the Military." *CQ Researcher*: 19.40, 957–980, November 13.

Cloutier, Krystyna M. 2008. "Note: Marching Toward War: Reconnoitering the Use of All Female Platoons." *Connecticut Law Review* 40 (July): 1531–1579.

CNN. 2009. "U.S. Military Drops Ban on Soldiers Getting Pregnant." World. December 25. www.cnn.com (accessed April 16, 2010).

Cogan, James. 2009. "US Military Suicide Rate at Record High." *World Socialist Website.* International Committee of the Fourth International, February 4. www.wsws.org (accessed June 14, 2010).

Conn, Tracy L. 2004. "Book Review: When Women Kill: Questions of Agency and Subjectivity by Belinda Morrissey. 2003 [London: Routledge. pp. 213]." 27 *Harvard Women's Law Journal* 285, Spring. In Rosemarie Skaine. 2006. *Female Suicide Bombers.* Jefferson, NC: McFarland Publishers, 31.

Cornum, Rhonda. 2009. "Comprehensive Soldier Fitness: Strong Minds, Strong Bodies. [10/9/2009 12:21 PM Army G-3/5/7 Unclassified/FOUO DAMO-CSF America's Army: The Strength of the Nation] Keynote Address. Power Point Presentation. Women in the Military Conference. Women's Research and Education Institute (WREI). Arlington, Virginia. September 25. www.4militarywomen.org (accessed April 15, 2010).

Davis, Julie Hirschfeld. 2010. "House Approves Repeal of Gay Ban in Military." *AP. Las Vegas Sun*, June 3. www.lasvegassun.com (accessed June 3, 2010).

Defense Department Advisory Committee on Women in the Services (DACOWITS). 2008. Report, Second draft, November 14. p. 4–5, 7. In Erin Mulhall. 2009. "Women Warriors Supporting She 'Who Has Borne the Battle.' " *Iraq and Afghanistan Veterans of America.* Issue report. October. http://media.iava.org (accessed October 17, 2009).

Department of Defense (DoD). 2009. "DoD Identifies Army Casualty Staff Sgt. Tara J. Smith." Release No. 597-09, August 10. www.trackpads.com (accessed June 14, 2010).

Department of Defense (DoD). 2010. Office of the Assistant Secretary of Defense (Public Affairs). Defense Press Office, MAJ April D.

Cunningham, OSD PA Memo to the author, July 6.

Department of Defense (DoD). 2010. "Operation Iraqi Freedom—Military Deaths," August 31. http://siadapp.dmdc.osd.mil (accessed September 29, 2010).

Department of Defense (DoD). 2010. "Operation Enduring Freedom—Military Deaths," September 4. http://siadapp.dmdc.osd.mil (accessed September 29, 2010).

Department of Defense (DoD). 2010. "Update on the 'Don't Ask, Don't Tell' Policy." General Questions Issues and Policies. http://erms.dma.mil/Scripts (accessed June 3, 2010).

Department of Defense (DoD). 2009. *Report of the Defense Task Force on Sexual Assault in the Military Services*, December. www.dtic.mil (accessed May 21, 2010).

Department of Defense (DoD). 2009. *FY08 Report On Sexual Assault in the Military.* March 15. www.sapr.mil (accessed November 6, 2009).

Department of Defense (DoD). 2009. "U.S. Casualty Status." *DefenseLink.* November 6. www.defenselink.mil (accessed November 9, 2009).

Donnelly, Elaine. 2005. "The Army's Gender War." *National Review Online.* Jan. 7. www.nationalreview.com. In Marcia Clemmitt. 2009. Women in the military. *CQ Researcher*: 19.40, 959.

Doyle, Leonard. 2007. "Suicide Rate in US Army at Highest in 26 Years." The Independent. World News, August 17. www.independent.co.uk (accessed June 14, 2010).

Dozier, Kimberly. 2010. "Casualties of 'Don't Ask, Don't Tell.'" *CBS.* Sunday Morning, March 28. www.cbsnews.com (accessed April 18, 2010).

Dwyer, Devin, Luis Martinez, and Martha Raddatz. 2010. "A 'More Humane' Don't Ask, Don't Tell? Military Adjusts Approach to Outing Gays: Pentagon Announces New Measures to Soften Policy on Military Gays." *ABC News/Politics*, March 25. http://abcnews.go.com (accessed April 18, 2010).

Finch, Mimi. E-mail message to author, August 15, 1996 In Rosemarie Skaine. 1999. *Women at War: Gender Issues of Americans in Combat.* Jefferson, NC: McFarland Publishers, 190–191.

Finch, Mimi. USA. 1993. "Women in Combat: One Commissioner Reports." Paper presented at the Military Manpower Conference: A Military of Volunteers. September 17, at the U.S. Naval Academy. In Rosemarie Skaine. 1999. *Women at War: Gender Issues of Americans in Combat.* Jefferson, NC: McFarland & Co. Inc., 167.

Fischer, Hannah. 2010. "United States Military Casualty Statistics: Operation Iraqi Freedom and Operation Enduring Freedom." *Congressional Research Service (CRS)*, May 4.

Government Accountability Office (GAO). 2002. *Military Personnel: Active Duty Benefits Reflect Changing Demographics, but Opportunities Exist to Improve.* September, 7. GAO-02-935. www.gao.gov (accessed November 14, 2009).

Government Accountability Office (GAO). 2005. *"Military Personnel: Financial Cost and Loss of Critical Skills Due to DoD's Homosexual Conduct Policy Cannot Be Completely Estimated."* February 23. GAO-05-299. www.gao.gov (accessed April 21, 2010).

Government Accountability Office (GAO). 2009. *Military Readiness: DoD Needs to Strengthen Management and Oversight of the Defense Readiness Reporting System.* September. GAO-09-518. www.gao.gov (accessed November 20, 2009).

Great Britain Ministry of Defence. 2002. "Women In the Armed Forces." Directorate of Service Personnel Policy Service Conditions, May. www.mod.uk (accessed June 12, 2010). In Mathers, Jennifer G. 2010. Interview by Rosemarie Skaine. E-mail, May 26, 2010.

Gudorf, Christine E. 1993. "Gays in The Military: Homosexual Stereotypes." *The Christian Century* 110.17: 540+. Academic OneFile.

Hamilton, Col. Kelly. 1991. Letter home. January 23. In Rosemarie Skaine. 1999. *Women at War: Gender Issues of Americans in Combat.* Jefferson, NC: McFarland & Co. Inc., 26–27.

Harrell, Margaret C., et al. 2007. *Assessing the Assignment Policy for Army Women.* Santa Monica, CA: RAND National Defense Research Institute. www.rand.org (accessed September 20, 2009).

Hasday, Jill Elaine. 2008. "Article: Fighting Women: The Military, Sex, and Extrajudicial Constitutional Change." 93 *Minnesota Law Review* 96. November.

Henderson, Kristin. 2008. "Ready to Kill." *Washington Post*, February 24. www.washingtonpost.com (accessed April 13, 2010).

Hillman, Elizabeth L. 2009. "Front and Center: Sexual Violence in U.S. Military Law." *Politics and Society* 37.1: 101–130. March. DOI: 10.1177/0032329208329753. Thousand Oaks, CA: Sage.http://pas.sagepub.com (accessed October 11, 2009).

Joyce, Kathryn. 2009. "Military Abortion Ban: Female Soldiers Not Protected by Constitution They Defend." *Religion Dispatches.* December 15. www.religiondispatches.org (accessed April 25, 2010).

Kruger, Lisa. 2005. *Gender and Terrorism: Motivations of Female Terrorists.* Master of Science, Strategic Intelligence (MSSI) Thesis, Joint Military Intelligence College. July.

Lillback, Dr. Peter A. Interview by Rosemarie Skaine. Tape recording by telephone. November 7, 2009.

Lipari, Rachel N., Paul J. Cook, Lindsay M. Rock, and Kenneth Matos. 2008. *2006 Gender Relations Survey of Active Duty Members*. Defense Manpower Data Center (DMDC) Report No. 2007-022. March. www.sapr.mil/media (accessed July 15, 2010).

Lubold, Gordon. 2010. "Americans Support 'Don't Ask, Don't Tell' Repeal, New Poll Finds." *Christian Science Monitor*. February 17. www.csmonitor.com (accessed April 18, 2010).

Manning, Lory. E-mail message to author, August 12, 2009.

Manning, Lory. 2009. "Opening Remarks." 2009. Women in the Military Conference. Women's Research and Education Institute (WREI). Arlington, Virginia. September 25.

Mariner, Capt. Rosemary Bryant, USN, telephone interview, February 27, 1996 In Skaine, *Women at War*, 11. *See also:* Mariner. 1993–1994. "A Soldier Is a Soldier." *Joint Force Quarterly* 3 (Winter): 54–61.

Mariske, Charles E., Steven Vagi and Arlene Taick. 1980. "Combating Sexual Harassment: A New Awareness." *USA Today*. March, 46. In Rosemarie Skaine. 1996. *Power and Gender: Issues in Sexual Dominance and Harassment*. Jefferson, NC: McFarland Publishers. 110.

Mathers, Jennifer G. 2010. Interview by Rosemarie Skaine. E-mail, May 26, 2010.

McMichael, William H. and Andrew Scutro. 2009. "SecNav, CNO: Women Should Serve on Subs." *Military Times*. News. September 27. www.militarytimes.com/news/2009/09/navy_roughead_subs_092409w/ (accessed October 2, 2009).

McSally, Martha. 2007. "Women in Combat: Is the Current Policy Obsolete?" *Duke Journal of Gender Law & Policy* 14.2: 1011+.

Military.com. 2010. "Guard and Reserve Suicide Rates Climbing." *Knight Ridder*. News, July 26. www.military.com (accessed July 30, 2010).

Morales, Lymari. 2009. "Conservatives Shift in Favor of Openly Gay Service Members: Weekly Churchgoers also Show Double-Digit Increase in Support from 2004." Gallup. Politics, June 5, www.gallup.com (accessed April 18, 2009).

Morrissey, Belinda. 2003. *When Women Kill: Questions of Agency and Subjectivity*. London: Routledge,

Mulhall, Erin. 2009. "Women Warriors Supporting She 'Who has Borne the Battle.' " *Iraq and Afghanistan Veterans of America*. Issue report. October. http://media.iava.org (accessed October 17, 2009).

Myers, Steven Lee. 2009. "Living and Fighting Alongside Men, and Fitting In." Women at Arms Series. *New York Times*. August 17. www.nytimes.com (accessed August 17, 2009).

Patterson, Drew. 2006. "Women in Combat." International Debate Education Association. Con, July 24. www.idebate.org (accessed April 13, 2009).

Pennington, Reina. 2001. *Wings, Women and War: Soviet Airwomen in World War II Combat*. Lawrence: University Press of Kansas, 162–165. In Mathers, Jennifer G. 2010. Interview by Rosemarie Skaine. E-mail, May 26, 2010.

Pfluke, Lillian A. "The Best Soldier for the Job: A Personal Perspective." *Women in the Military*, ed. James Haley. San Diego: Greenhaven Press, 2004, 57–61.

Pfluke, Maj. Lillian A., USA (Ret.). E-mail message to the author July 29, 1996. In Rosemarie Skaine. 1999. *Women at War: Gender Issues of Americans in Combat*. Jefferson, NC: McFarland & Co. Inc., 166.

Presbyterian Church in America (PCA). 2002. "Historical Center. General Assembly Actions and Position Papers." Ad Interim Study Committee on Women in the Military. www.pcahistory.org (accessed November 27, 2009).

Putko, Michele M. 2008. "The Combat Exclusion Policy in the Modern Security Environment." In *Women in Combat Compendium*, ed. Michele M. Putko and Douglas V. Johnson II, 27–36. Carlisle, PA: Strategic Studies Institute U.S. Army War College.

Robert Crown Law Library. 1999. "Don't Ask Don't Tell Don't Pursue." Digital Law Project. Stanford Law School, September 7. http://dont.stanford.edu (accessed April 18, 2010).

Rough, Jill A. 2009. "Women in the U.S. Military: Showing the Way or Blocking the Road?" Women in the Military Conference, WREI. Arlington, Virginia. September 25.

Sagawa, Shirley, and Nancy Duff Campbell. 1992. *Women in the Military Issue Paper: Women in Combat*. National Women's Law Center, Washington, D.C. October 30. www.nwlc.org (accessed August 23, 2009).

Sanchez, Gervasio. 2009. "G.I. Jane Breaks the Combat Barrier as War Evolves." *New York Times*, Women at Arms Series. August 15. www.nytimes.com (accessed August 16, 2009).

Schlafly, Phyllis. 2003. "Women Should not Serve in Military Combat." *Women in Combat*. www.bible-researcher.com (accessed July 12, 2010).

Segal, Mady Wechsler. 1995. "Women's Military Roles Cross-Nationally: Past, Present, and Future." *Gender & Society* 9:6. December, 757–775.

Servicemembers Legal Defense Network. 2010. "About 'Don't Ask, Don't Tell.' " www.sldn.org (accessed April 18, 2010).

Servicemembers Legal Defense Network. 2008. "Women in Uniform Disproportionately Affected by 'Don't Ask, Don't Tell' Law." Newsroom, June 23. www.sldn.org (accessed April 22, 2010).

Skaine, Rosemarie. 2006. *Female Suicide Bombers*. Jefferson, NC: McFarland Publishers.

Skaine, Rosemarie. 1996. *Power and Gender: Issues in Sexual Dominance and Harassment*. Jefferson, NC: McFarland Publishers.

Skaine, Rosemarie. 1999. *Women at War: Gender Issues of Americans in Combat*. Jefferson, NC: McFarland & Co. Inc.

"Staff Sgt. Amy Seyboth-Tirador Death Ruled A Suicide." 2010. My American Iraq Life Blog, March 11. http://myamericaniraqlife.blogspot.com (accessed June 14, 2010).

Stone, Ervin R. 2009. *Women in Combat: Standardize the Physical Fitness Test*. USMC. Command and Staff College. Marine Corps Combat Dev. Marine Corps University. Quantico, March 9. www.dtic.mil (accessed April 29, 2010).

U.S. Army. n.d. "The Army's Pregnancy Policies": Historical Overview. [This source lists specific Army regulations] www.dtic.mil/dacowits/agendadoc/ppts/Army_Pregnancy (accessed May 21, 2010.)

U.S. Congress. 2007. Joint Economic Committee. "Helping Military Moms Balance Family and Longer Deployments." May 11. http://jec.senate.gov/archive (accessed November 8, 2009).

U.S. Congress. 2010. House. Committee on Armed Services, Military Personnel Subcommittee. *Don't Ask, Don't Tell Repeal Plan: Hearing*. 111th Cong., 2nd sess., March 3,

U.S. Congress. 2008. House. Committee on Armed Services, Military Personnel Subcommittee. *Don't Ask, Don't Tell Review Hearing*. 110th Cong., 2nd sess., July 23.

U.S. Congress. 1993. House. Committee on Armed Services. Military Forces and Personnel Subcommittee. *Women in Combat: Hearing*. 103rd Congress, 1st session. May 11.

U.S. Congress. Senate. 2010. Committee on Armed Services. *Don't Ask, Don't Tell Policy Hearing*. 111th Cong., 2nd sess., February 2.

Presidential Commission on the Assignment of Women in the Armed Forces. 1992. *Report to the President: Women in Combat November 15, 1992*, Washington, D.C.: The Commission.

U.S. Presidential Commission on the Assignment of Women in the Armed Forces. 1993. *Report to the President: Women in Combat*. Washington: Brassey's (U.S.).

Taylor, Sandra C. 1999. *Vietnamese Women at War: Fighting for Ho Chi Minh and the Revolution*. Lawrence, KS: University Press of Kansas. In Mathers, Jennifer G. 2010. Interview by Rosemarie Skaine. E-mail, May 26, 2010.

Vaught, Wilma L. Interview by Rosemarie Skaine. Tape recording. Women In Military Service For America Memorial Foundation, Inc., Arlington, VA, September 23, 2009.

Willens, Jake. 1996. "Women in the Military: Combat Roles Considered." *Center for Defense Information*, August 7. www.cdi.org (accessed July 29, 2010).

Women In Military Service For America Memorial Foundation, Inc (WIMSA). 2006. "Women Purple Heart Recipients Located to Date." News and Events. May 8. www.womensmemorial.org (accessed November 10, 2009).

Women In Military Service For America Memorial Foundation, Inc (WIMSA). 2008. "SGT Leigh Ann Hester US Army Silver Star Operation Iraqi Freedom. 2005." *Voices of Valor Women's History Month Kit*. www.womensmemorial.org (accessed August 14, 2009).

Wood, Sara. 2005. "Woman Soldier Receives Silver Star for Valor in Iraq." *U.S. Department of Defense*. News. June 16. www.defenselink.mil (accessed November 3, 2009).

3

Worldwide Perspective

An examination of women in military combat worldwide assesses women serving in countries' state based or government run military and surveys women actively involved in revolutionary movements whether state based or independent of the state. An increasing number of countries are opening military service to women and more countries that already have women in their armed forces are expanding military occupations open to women (WREI 2008, 33). Although most countries have women in their military, "there is a general disinclination to placing women in combat roles even in countries that make it mandatory for women to serve" (CBC 2006). Some countries including Chili and Egypt do not allow women to serve in the military (Nystrom 2002, 4).

In 2010, some countries consent to have women in certain aspects of the military, such as aviation, but prohibit women from serving in combat aviation. Examples are China, Israel, India, and Pakistan. Israel introduced its first women fighter pilots in 2001, but remains hesitant to place them in a combat zone. In Pakistan and China, women fighter pilots have never faced direct combat. Although the Soviet Union had three successful regiments of women combat pilots, in 2010, Russia had no woman fighter pilots. The Indian Air Force has a good number of women military aviators who fly helicopters and transport aircraft, but its few fighter pilots have not engaged the enemy in combat (Sharma 2009). For India, the issue of inducting women fighter pilots is under study (*Women Fighter Pilots* 2010, India). In 1937, Sabiha Gokcen, an adopted daughter of Turkey's founder, took part in an operation against clans of Kurdish Alevis. She was Turkey's first female fighter pilot (Seibert 2009, World). Turkey admitted women with some restrictions into the military in 1957 (see Table 3.1).

Women as Combatants in State-Based Military

International Framework

The United Nations is the primary advocate for the development of gender mainstreaming through its international peace operations, according to Inger Skjelsbæk and Torunn L. Tryggestad. In 2000, through Resolution 1325, the Security Council for the first time in its history demonstrated the importance of gender issues to international peace and security. The resolution called for member states to increase the number of women in the armed forces and to provide gendersensitive training to all military staff (UN Security Council 2000, 1325 in Skjelsbæk and Tryggestad 2009, 38–39). The resolution stressed the need to view women as actors in conflicts rather than solely as victims, and when women serve in the military, they have international protections. Women have rights in war, and violence against women and women in armed conflict are monitored (Adams 2009, 4).

At the time of the adoption of Resolution 1325, arguments were based on gender equality, write Skjelsbæk and Tryggestad. Women had a right to be in UN peace operations, represented, and pursue a career. In 2007, the Department of Peacekeeping Operations encouraged member states to send more women to operations and to double the number of women in their own forces over the next five years. In 2009, the number of women in peace operations depended on resources and operational efficiency. Yet in spite of the growth of UN peacekeeping operations and the resulting need for qualified personnel, women as a resource remain basically untapped. Skjelsbæk and Tryggestad found that, in operations, women were present in the following proportions: 2 out of 18 were heads of ongoing UN peace operations; 1 percent of the military personnel; 4 percent of the police personnel; and 30 percent of international civilian personnel, but only 10 percent when leadership positions are considered.

An important aspect of UN peacekeeping operations is that the United Nations is dependent on contributions from member states (Skjelsbæk and Tryggestad 2009, 39, 40).

Incidence

North Atlantic Treaty Association (NATO) countries represent a range of dates the law indicated that services were officially opened to women. Table 3.1 includes the date of the actual first entry of

TABLE 3.1

Admittance of Women in NATO Countries' Armed Forces and Subsequent Changes, Situation in 2003

Country	Year of Legal Admittance	Actual Entry with Some Restrictions	Most Recent Restriction Modifications
US	1948	1973	1993
UK	1949	1991	1992
Canada	1951	1968	2002*
Turkey	1955	1957	–
Denmark	1962	1971–1974	*1988*
France	1972	1973	*1998*
Romania	1973	–	2001
Belgium	1975	1977	*1981*
Germany	1975	1975	*2000*
Norway	1977	–	*1985*
Greece	1979	1979	–
Netherlands	1979	1979	1981
Czech Republic	1980 (early)	1980 (early)	*2002*
Slovakia	1980 (early)	1980 (early)	1993
Luxemburg	1980	1987	*1997*
Poland	1988	–	2003
Spain	1988	1988	*1999*
Latvia	1991	1991	1991
Lithuania	1991	1991	1991
Slovenia	1991	1991	*2002*
Portugal	1992	1992	1992
Bulgaria	1995	1995	*2001*
Hungary	1996	1996	*1996*
Italy	1999	2000	*2000*

*The years in italics in the last column signify the abolition of any restriction for women, i.e., their full integration into the Armed Forces.

Source: Adapted from NATO Forces, 2003, Office on Women, Women in the Armed Forces, Table 2–3, www.nato.int/issues/women_nato (accessed November 23, 2009).

women in the armed forces with restrictions and the date of the most recent reduction or elimination of assignment restrictions. Canada, United Kingdom (UK), and the United States admitted women the earliest, 1951, 1949, and 1948, respectively. Each country waited several years to permit women to enter some posts, 1968, 1991, and 1973. The most recent change in assignment restrictions occurred even later, 2002, 1992, and 1993.

Other NATO countries that by law admitted women later than Canada, UK, and the US, also waited a shorter period of time to actually have women enter and to modify assignment restrictions. Italy, for example, admitted women in 1999, but actually entered women into some posts and modified restrictions in 2000.

In 2008, although women made up 14.3 percent of the United States military (WREI 2008, 12), the percentages of female soldiers in four of the NATO countries in 2007 were higher than the United States. Latvia ranks highest with 23 percent followed by Canada and Hungary at 17.3 percent and Slovenia, 15.3 (NATO 2007).

WREI surveyed 19 countries where women serve in the military but do not necessarily serve in combat. WREI noted there are more countries with women serving than those included in their sample. Most recently, Botswana and Mexico have opened military service to women. The following are reasons for the inclusion of women in the services:

(1) the growing recognition that women can do most jobs as well as men, (2) an ongoing need for service members, (3) ending of the draft in most countries, (4) more reliance on technology, (5) passage of equal rights laws, (6) wish to keep up with the civilian sector, and (7) court decisions opening military service, as in Germany, or admitting women into occupations previously closed, as in Israel (WREI 2008, 33).

Most nations increase women's military roles when shortages of qualified men exist, particularly during times of national emergency (Segal 1995, 760). Usually countries draft women only during emergencies. The United States considered drafting women during the invasion of Japan and again when President Carter proposed registration for women and men, but Congress enacted legislation for males only. In World War II, Britain and the former Soviet Union conscripted women. In 2002, Sweden considered conscription. In 2006, eight countries drafted women, China, Eritrea, Israel, Libya, Malaysia, North Korea, Peru, and Taiwan (CBC 2006; *Time* 1980).

TABLE 3.2
Percentages of Female Soldiers in NATO Nations' Armed Forces, 2007

Country	2007
Belgium	8.25
Bulgaria	–
Canada	17.3
Czech Republic	–
Denmark	5.4
France	14.0
Germany	7.5
Greece	5.6
Hungary	17.3
Italy	2.6
Latvia	23.0
Lithuania	12.0
Luxembourg	–
The Netherlands	9.0
Norway	7.1
Poland	1.0
Portugal	13.0
Romania	6.37
Slovenia	15.3
Slovakia	8.65
Spain	12.0
Turkey	–
United Kingdom	9.3
United States	*14.3

*Women's Research and Education Institute (WREI), 2008, *Women in the Military: Where They Stand*. Arlington, VA: WREI, 12.
Source: NATO Forces, 2007, Office on Women, Women in the Armed Forces, www.nato.int/issues/women_nato (accessed November 26, 2009).

In some, countries, women participate in combat, but usually, they have their noncombat functions increased (Segal 1995, 760). When the conflict is over, women are not retained in the military in some countries. Women occupy combat oriented positions in ground combat and on aircraft, combat ships, and submarines. Table 3.4 shows the positions open to women in selected countries. The services allowed in the countries range from Canada, Spain, and Sweden that permit women to serve in all combat-oriented positions to Hungary that permits women to serve only in ground combat to Tunisia that places limits on women who serve on combat ships to Taiwan that limits them to military aircraft.

TABLE 3.3
Selected Examples of Countries in Which Women Serve in the Military, 2007

Country	Percentage Women
Australia	13.4
Austria	1.6
Bangladesh	.4
Brazil	3.5
Ghana	8.7
Nepal	3.8
New Zealand	29.9
Peru	4.7

Source: Based on, in part, WREI, 2008, *Women in The Military: Where They Stand,* Arlington, VA: WREI, 34.

African countries involve women in the military. In Ghana, 8.7 percent of the military are women (Table 3.3). Women in Morocco fly military aircraft. In South Africa, they serve in all areas except submarines, and in Tunisia they serve aboard combat ships (Table 3.4). In 2006, Senegal opened military and paramilitary bodies to women in the Gendarmerie and the Customs (Senegal 2006, 10). In Libya, the women's unit is Colonel Kadaffi's personal bodyguard and is known as the Green Nuns and The Amazonian Guard. The unit of 200 members is referred to as The Revolutionary Nuns (*New World Encyclopedia* 2008, Libya). According to the countries' *Solemn Declaration on Gender Equality,* the African countries that promoted women's participation in decision-making structures relating to conflict resolution and peace building are South Africa, Mauritius, and Namibia (Declarations in Africa Union 2006, 15, 6, 17).

Table 3.4 lists countries that allow women in one or more of the four types of combat (military aircraft, combat ships, ground combat, submarines). The category of ground combat includes Belgium, Canada, Denmark, France, Germany, Hungary, Israel (some), the Netherlands (except the marines), New Zealand, Norway, Portugal (except marines and combat divers), Spain, South Africa, South Korea, and Sweden. Countries outside this survey include China and Sudan, which allow women in some areas of combat. Women serving in ground combat remains a source of controversy in the United States.

Dr. Jennifer Mathers, Department of International Politics, Aberystwyth University, Aberystwyth, United Kingdom, said in

TABLE 3.4
Military Occupations in Which Women in Other Countries Serve

Occupation	Countries
Military aircraft	Australia, Belgium, Brazil, Canada, Denmark, France, Germany, Israel, India, Japan, Morocco, the Netherlands, New Zealand, Pakistan, Portugal, Russia, Singapore, South Africa, South Korea, Spain, Sri Lanka, Sweden, Taiwan, Turkey, United Kingdom
Combat ships	Australia, Belgium, Canada, Chile, Denmark, France, Germany, Israel, Italy, the Netherlands, New Zealand, Norway, Portugal, Singapore, South Africa, Spain, Sweden, Tunisia, Turkey, United Kingdom
Ground combat	Belgium, Canada, Denmark, France, Germany, Hungary, Israel (some), the Netherlands (except the marines), New Zealand, Norway, Portugal (except marines and combat divers), Spain, South Africa, South Korea, and Sweden. Other nations allow female soldiers to serve in certain Combat Arms positions, such as the United Kingdom, which allows women to serve in Artillery roles, while still excluding them from units with a dedicated Infantry
Submarines	Australia, Canada, Norway, Spain, Sweden

an interview with the author that it is a challenge to identify countries that currently permit women to serve in combat roles, but WREI's efforts are authoritative (see Table 3.4). She believes, "it is surprisingly difficult to be confident of having a comprehensive list," She explains further,

> It can also be challenging to determine how many or what proportion of women in these countries are actually serving in combat roles, but I am aware of published work on several of the ones in the ground combat list [in Table 3.4] that indicate several trends: women are not rushing to serve in combat roles in large numbers; some core elements of combat roles are sometimes still retained for men even where others are opened to women; and attitudes within the countries concerned in civilian society and the military remain ambivalent at best and sometimes actively hostile towards women in combat roles and even to women in the military. (Mathers 2010, Interview)

Examples that help to illustrate these points are found in the countries of Israel, Scandinavia, Sweden, Norway, and Canada.

Examples of Military Roles in Some Countries

Israel

Unlike the United States and most western countries, the military service in Israel is compulsory. Israel has conscripted women by law since 1949. Married women and mothers are exempt (Sasson-Levy 2003, 456; Sasson-Levy 2007, 482, 484, 485). Women serve for a shorter time than men do, generally two years, which limits what positions they can fill (Sandhoff 2009, WREI). Orna Sasson-Levy found women represent 32 percent of the regular army but are generally excluded from combat roles. These differences not only limit the roles to which women may be assigned, but they also are a barrier to women's advancement (Sasson-Levy 2003, 445).

Mathers explains the original philosophical basis for Israel's military and how women are perceived. Israel is often held up as a model of equality since both men and women are conscripted. She explained how the founders of the Israeli state envision the military as an instrument of nation-building:

> [I]n other words [they foresaw the military] as a place where the diverse communities who came together to populate the new state could create a new common national identity and loyalty and so it was important in principle for all citizens to have this experience of service. However, at the very same time Israeli women were called upon to fulfill the role of becoming mothers and raising a new generation of Israelis and this domestic role was explicitly elevated above any civic role that women might play or wish to play. As a result, it has always been much easier and more socially acceptable for women to get exemptions from military service (for example, for religious reasons) than for men. Those women who do serve also have a shorter period of military service than men (2 years in comparison with men's three years) and a shorter period in the reserves after they are discharged from the military—men serve in the reserves until they are 51 years old while women serve in the reserves until they are 24 years old or become mothers. (Mathers 2010, Interview)

Only 20 percent of the Israeli military consists of combat soldiers. The Israeli military is gradually integrating women into positions previously open only to men, according to Sasson-Levy. This integration has followed a pattern similar to the American military, short-term inclusion of women in combat roles followed by long term exclusion and then by another short-term inclusion. A significant change after the 1973 war occurred. A shortage in human power existed and civilian feminist groups exerted pressure that contributed to women filling nontraditional roles such as infantry and tank instructors, basic training commanders, and aircraft mechanics. They did not serve in combat roles, however. In 1995, the military allowed women to serve in a few select combat roles and some training courses were integrated (Sasson-Levy 2003, 445–446, 457).

An Israeli law passed in January 2000 specified the acceptance of women in any military job. Mather's explained its results:

> Until 2001 all women Israeli soldiers belonged to the Women's Corps whose acronym CHEN means charm in Hebrew, which says a lot about the way that women soldiers' service was perceived by the armed forces. Although the women's corps has now been disbanded and the Knesset passed a law in 2000 opening all military jobs to women, the law also stipulates that combat roles are only for women who volunteer for them and then only on the basis of military need. The most recent reports I have seen indicate that only 2.5% of women soldiers serve in combat roles and that women are still banned from the infantry, armour and reconnaissance units, which are considered the core of combat.
>
> A further twist is added by the presence of very conservative and religious male soldiers, who object to serving in units with women. Special single sex companies have been created to cater for this group and although, in principle, it is an option that is available for both men and women, in practice, very few highly-religious women choose to serve in the military so the effect has been to create a number of all male units and there is a suggestion that secular male soldiers are pleading religious conviction in order to join all-male units and have a military experience which is exclusively male.

In addition, the fact that only men serve in the reserves for many years after their initial military service gives men opportunities for networking and bonding when they go on their annual training which reinforces the divide between men as defenders of the nation and women as keeping the home fires burning. Distinguished military service and high rank is also a significant advantage in civilian life—especially politics but also in business. (Mathers 2010, Interview)

Orna Sasson-Levy and Sarit Amram-Katz believe that despite integration in the military, it has led to a process of "degendering and regendering." This process is best explained by example. Before 1948 all women in the Women's Corps and those trained for battle were transferred to female-dominated positions, for example, social work, nursing, or teaching. The transfer is regendering. The conscription of women based on women's right to contribute and to become soldiers is also an example. Conscription was accompanied by regendering when it stipulated that married women and mothers were exempted from the draft (Sasson-Levy and Amram-Katz 2007, 106).

When military women have a positive military experience, it does not transmit into civilian life. They are not given the economic privileges, political voice, and power that combat soldiers have. Society does not accord them recognition and respect. It is the Jewish male who serves in combat roles and is looked upon as a good citizen. Women's power is limited to the time she is in the service. Sasson-Levy explains how these dynamics affects equality for women:

Thus, the link between military service and equal citizenship exists only for Jewish men in Israel (albeit not for all Jewish men). The breach between women's military and civic identities indicates that, though women's military service is mandatory, it is not considered a "civic virtue": general conscription does not lead to civic equality for Israeli women. (Sasson-Levy 2003, 460)

Although Israel drafts women, conscription has not been without challenges. On November 23, 2009, the Knesset Legislative Committee approved a bill that prevents young women from avoiding being drafted into the Israeli Defense Force (DF) by falsely declaring they are religiously observant. The bill also states the IDF would carry out surveillance to confirm the declarations. At the time the IDF caught 80 young women who had falsely declared themselves in the 2009, 570 women confessed they made false declarations regarding religious observance to avoid military service. IDF drafted all of these women. Draft dodging had increase by 25 percent over the past two decades. In 2009, 44 percent of young women who qualified to enlist did not join and 26 percent of men evaded enlistment. (Slobodkin 2009)

Norway
Norway has some interesting aspects to its military, according to Mathers.

> Since 1984 all military posts in the Norwegian armed forces have been open to women and, in general, Norway is very proud of its record in promoting gender equality through the actions of the state since the 1970s. One might expect from that to find a high rate of women soldiers serving in combat positions but this is not the case at all. Overall military service is not a popular career choice for women (about 8% of the Norwegian military is composed of women which is on the low side for a NATO country) and this may be linked to the fact that Norway operates a system of male-only conscription and the authors of an article by Inger Skjelsbaek and Torunn Tryggestad published in *Minerva* recently argued that the country's military culture is defined largely by its culture of male conscription. (Mathers 2010, Interview)

Skjelsbæk and Tryggestad would agree that Norwegian women are underrepresented in the military and in 2007, accounted for 7.1 percent of the forces, slightly less than 8 percent in 2010. Nonetheless, 7.1 percent was an increase from about 4.5 percent in the mid-1990s (Skjelsbæk and Tryggestad 2009, 34, 41; NATO 2007). From 2006 to 2008, debate on compulsory service increased, but in 2008, the Norwegian government withdrew a proposal for compulsory military service for women. Skjelsbæk and Tryggestad noted that, although Norwegian society sees itself promoting gender equality, the military is lacking. Most NATO countries have a higher percentage women participating in the military. (See Table 3.2.)

In 1977, Norway admitted women to its military, and to combat roles in 1984. In 1995, Norway became the first country to assign women to submarines. Australia followed in 1998 and Canada did so in 2000 (CBC 2006; Skjelsbæk and Tryggestad 2009, 41). In March 1999, Norway appointed its first female Minister of Defense, and in November 1999, its first female colonel. Women serve in integrated units of all types under the same rules and regulations as men. Training standards, performance levels, and discipline are equal to those of men (NATO 2002, Norway).

Although Norway allows women to serve in combat roles, military service is compulsory for men only. Since the percentage growth of women in the military is about 3 percent, the government has said it hopes to raise women's level of participation to 20 percent by the end of 2020. As the first step, in 2007, the government invited all women born in 1989 to voluntary assessment sessions. Out of the 30,000 women invited, 7,277 responded positively. By January 2008, almost 4,000 had actually attended the sessions. Although the government withdrew the second step, compulsory service for women, it instituted compulsory military assessment sessions beginning January 1, 2010 (Skjelsbæk and Tryggestad 2009, 41).

From 2006 to 2007, debates on diversity and gender equality took place in Norway. Two arguments offered were that, first, the armed forces needed to be more in tune with society at large and second, increasing the number of women is related to security issues. War is more diverse and complex in international operations and requires new skills. Skjelsbæk and Tryggestad write that in military language that means the operations are asymmetrical. Weaponry is unconventional, for example, suicide bombing, and managed either by nonstate groups such as a terrorist group or by state militaries (Skjelsbæk and Tryggestad 2009, 47).

Sweden
Sweden also operates a system of male conscription although it has decided to move to an all-volunteer force soon, according to Mathers. She elaborates:

> I have not found any statistics on the numbers or proportions of Swedish women serving in combat roles but

I understand that about 5 percent of Sweden's armed forces are composed of women and I suspect that very few would be in combat posts. In 2000, there was a national debate about whether conscription should be extended to women and some Swedish scholars conducted a study of attitudes towards the proposed change, including among male conscripted soldiers—the following remark is very telling: "Everything would fall apart if women joined. . . . It would be enough to see a woman, to destroy the masculine games going on around here. The mere presence of women would make it all break." (Kronsell and Svedberg 2001, 163 in Mathers 2010, Interview)

Canada

Canada is often presented or presents itself as a leader in equal opportunities for women in the military, according to Mathers. She presents her findings:

All occupations including combat roles were opened to women in 1989 (except service on submarines and that was opened up in 2000). About 15 percent of Canadian military personnel are women, which is comparable with the U.S., but although women have had access to combat roles for more than 20 years, only 2 percent of Canada's regular force combat troops are women. Putting that together with media publicity and academic work on sexual harassment of women soldiers by their male colleagues in the Canadian armed forces suggests that there is a prevailing culture of masculinity and that few women feel comfortable choosing a traditionally male role such as combat instead of military roles that have been gendered female such as military medicine, administration, etc. (Mathers 2010, Interview)

Other countries in which women are allowed to serve in ground combat, according to WREI's research (see Table 3.4), include Australia, Belgium, South Africa, and South Korea.

Australia

As states limit military roles for women, countries are faced also with the issue of attracting women to serve in the military. Women compose 13.4 percent of the 50,000 defense personnel in Australia. Women service members are greatly needed. The Australian Defense Force conducted a study to discover why women are reluctant to join the military and why so many enlisted soldiers don't stay. Balance issues challenge women who want to have children. Flexibility in working arrangements is needed so that these women can take leave without jeopardizing their careers and then return to duty with proper support. Women also sought mentoring and improved communications. The Defense Force rejects the reason women do not join is because they do not serve in direct combat (Nicholson 2009, National).

Belgium

Historically, the Belgian Army serving in the United Kingdom had a detachment of nurses who first served in World War I. Unlike the women who served in the Auxiliary Territorial Service (ATS) and the Women Auxiliary Air Force (WAAF) in World War II, the British made the nurses an official part of the Belgian Army. The ATS and the WAAF numbered around a few dozen women volunteers. These women were from the Belgian refugee community in the United Kingdom. Their duties consisted primarily of administrative and logistical functions and their units ceased to exist after 1946 (Units of the Belgian Armed Forces, Short History).

In 2010, men and women who are 18 years of age are eligible for voluntary military service. In 2008, Belgium suspended conscription (CIA 2009, "Belgium"). Women may serve in occupations in air, ground, and sea, but not on submarines (WREI 2008, 33). Belgium's national report to NATO for 2010 indicates that the first servicewomen were enrolled in the Belgian Armed Forces in 1975. In 2010, all functions are open to both women and men, but the report concludes that the representation of women has not increased in the last four years. The primary reasons are the "restrictions on recruitment and the limitation of soldier's vacancies to combat functions." The fact that a law exists that ensures the implementation of gender mainstreaming in all government policies and the publication of a national action plan is certainly a factor of success (Belgium 2010, 1, 4).

As of January 2009, 2,859 servicewomen represented 8.02 percent of the total strength. Two hundred eighteen women deployed in military operations, or about half of the total number of servicewomen. The report indicates the number of women deployed is remarkable given between 1992 and 2004, only 2.3 percent were women. Most women serve in the Navy (11.1 percent), followed by the Air Force (8.5 percent), and the lowest number in the Army (6.3 percent). For men the percentages except for the Air Force (91.5 percent) reverse with most men serving in the Army (93.7 percent) and the least number serve in the Navy (88.9 percent). Since 1999, women officers have increased from 4.14 percent to 8.89 percent in 2009 (Belgium 2010, 1, 2, 3).

South Africa
In the 1980's, South Africa went through an intense period of militarization, mobilized the resources for war, and made its Defense Force (SADF) central to state decision making. White women "turned their heads" from the SADF and supported traditional gender roles. Yet many women were also capable of brutality and also supported the brutality of men, wrote Jacklyn Cock (Cock 1994, 154).

South Africa's experience demonstrates four points in relation to women and militarization, according to Cock. First, women are active contributors to and are not marginalized from militarization. Second, the position of women is similar in conventional and guerrilla armies. Third, women's gains during war do not withstand patriarchy. Last, the debate is sharpened concerning the relationship between equal rights and the participation of women in the military, and she concludes there is none (Cock 1994, 152–153).

Cock's second point is relevant. The armies of the SADF and the African National Congress (ANC) increasingly included women, but excluded them from combat roles. The exclusion may account for the underrepresentation of women in positions of leadership. Men justified exclusion advocating women were not suited for killing. Women's role is to give and preserve life. They also justified excluding women because menstruation made women less able to serve and male chivalry (Cock 1994, 155–156). The SADF assigned women auxiliary roles in World War I and World War II, and to active, noncombat duties after 1970. In 1970, the SADF started to accept women volunteers into the Permanent Force, but it did not train women for combat nor did it assign women to duties that presented a high risk of capture. Women also served in military elements of liberation militias in the 1970s and the 1980s, and the ANC's military wing, Umkhonto we Sizwe (or MK), translated Spear of the Nation, accepted women throughout the antiapartheid struggle (Country Data 1996, *Women in the Military*). In the late 1970s and 1980s, women were active in civil defense organizations. They were trained as part of the country's general mobilization against possible terrorist attacks (Mongabay.com 1996).

In the 1990s, South Africa made the transition to democracy from authoritarian rule, and faced the restructuring of its military (Cock 1995, Conclusion). During this transition, debate flourished on whether women should serve in combat, according to Lindy Heinecken. Debate differed from the liberal feminism of Western societies to a feminist position linked to the revolutionary struggle in South Africa. This connection was militarist and stressed the equal right of women to take up arms with men. No active women's rights movement existed that lobbied for or against women serving in the armed forces, as found in the United States and some European countries. In the past, the gender struggle, particularly for black women, had been subordinate to the liberation struggle. In the late 1990s, women began to criticize the idea of triple repression. Black women suffered because they were black, because they were women, and because they were chiefly working class (Heinecken 2000, 5.1).

In 1995, the South African National Defense Force (SANDF) incorporated women of all races (Mongabay.com 1996). The SANDF expanded roles for women largely because of pressure from the campaign for equal opportunity for women in employment, the all volunteer force, and cultural considerations. White and black women had suffered discrimination, but white women had access to the economic, social, and political power of white men; were educated equal to that of men; and had higher status and better paying jobs. Even though legislation may have removed discrimination, culture did not. As of 2000, the SANDF was culturally diverse and its challenge was to meet membership diversification (Heinecken 2000, 5.2). No provisions limit the career path of women and the SANDF is among the most progressive defense forces. In 2000, Heinecken pointed out, "Despite the formal provisions stipulating that women can serve in any position, opinion is almost evenly divided, both within society and the military, on whether women should be allowed to serve in combatant positions" (Heinecken 2000, 5.3).

In 2008, South Africa led the continent, with women representing 22 percent of its National Defense Force. South Africa's

Unkhonto we Sizwe gave women the same training as men, and involved them in combat to comply with the ANC's policy of nonsexism (Juma and Makima 2008). According to WREI, in 2010, South Africa is one of several countries that assigns women to ground combat. (See Table 3.4.)

South Korea

In 1990, South Korea expended 30 percent of its Gross National Product for the military, because of the threat of North Korean aggression. The country spent only 10 percent on social programs. For every one percent in reduction of military spending, five times as many infant centers could be built, according to the Young Korean Movement of Europe. Because militarization in society affects women the most, women's organizations took up the issues of peace and demilitarization. Their movement worked against the construction of new atomic energy plants and U.S. military spending. They were active in the National Coalition of Anti-Nuclear Peace Groups formed in March 1991 (Young Korean 1995, Women in the Peace Movement).

Although women have been in the South Korean military service since the Korean War (1950 to 1953), constitutional and cultural restraints have limited their roles. South Korea abolished the separate Women's Army Corps in the early 1990s, and integrated women into the various branches of the armed forces. They are admitted to the service branches, including infantry, but are excluded from artillery, armor, anti-aircraft, and chaplaincy corps. In 2009, approximately 4,000 women served as commissioned and noncommissioned officers and represent about 2.3 percent of all officers. The South Korean armed forces plan to recruit women to a level of 5 percent of the total officers and noncommissioned officers in the three services by 2020. Military service is compulsory for all South Korean males with conscription at 18 years of age. Men serve 26 months in the army and 30 in the navy and air force (CIA 2010, S. Korea; Library of Congress 2005, 20).

Women do excel in the military. In 2007, Capt. Park Jie-yeon, 28, became the South Korean Air Force's first woman flight leader. Park has been the first woman in other positions. She was the school's first female student at the Korea Air Force Academy in 1997 when the school opened its doors to women and was the air force's first female pilot in 2002 (BBC 2007, S. Korean).

Progress toward Gender Equality in Women in Combat Roles

Are women making progress in combat roles? A difficult but not impossible question to answer, Mathers believes,

> In terms of which countries are making the most progress towards gender equality in combat roles, I find that a very difficult question. I don't see a great deal of progress happening in this area because, as I have indicated, even where combat roles are in theory open to women, only a very small number enter them and when we have the detailed information that allows us to learn more about their experiences and circumstances, we tend to see further barriers put in their path. For example, in the Israeli case the combat roles open to women have a lesser status than those still preserved for men. (Mathers 2010, Interview)

Mathers finds persuasive the arguments made by Cynthia Enloe concerning the link between military service, masculinity, and the privileging of male over female experiences and attributes in civilian society. It also helps explain why so little progress has been made towards genuine gender equality in combat roles. Mathers observes:

> There is a paradox at the heart of the relationship between women and war, in that wars and militaries depend on women's actions and beliefs for their existence and functioning but at the same time the belief that it is unnatural for women to be involved in militaries and wars but natural for men is very widespread—in fact, for militaries to continue to function as they do, it is necessary for men and women to hold and act on this belief. The belief that there is something special and very important (military service/combat) that is naturally male and that only men can do (or only men can do right) both supports and is supported by the gender hierarchy in civilian society. Enloe argues that "Women may serve the military, but they can never be permitted to be the military." (Enloe, 1988, 15 in Mathers 2010, Interview)

In other words, there needs to be some element of military service that is kept just for men. If women were permitted to enter this all-male space and were acknowledged to perform well as women (and not just as exceptional individuals) then it would have wider implications for all kinds of hierarchies. This argument helps to make sense of the ferocity behind the debates about women in combat as well as the way that the definition of combat keeps shifting around and can be so different from one country to another.

One of my favorite examples of this is the experiment that the Singapore armed forces conducted in 2004 with assigning women to lead motor platoons in infantry units. In many countries infantry is regarded as a combat arm but in Singapore the Air Force and the Navy are the elite arms and the ones that would are assumed to be in the forefront of any military operations. In neither service have women been permitted to fly combat aircraft! The infantry, on the other hand, has struggled to recruit enough men to fill essential roles (Walsh 2007, 277 in Mathers 2010, Interview).

Selected Countries Allowing Women in Occupations Flying Aircraft or Aboard Combat Ships

To totally evaluate progress, examining countries which allow women in some combat roles is helpful. Russia, for example, has not utilized women in combat roles to the extent that the Soviet Union did. Yet Russia allows women in some of those roles.

Russia: Airborne Positions

Women played a larger role in the Soviet Union during World War II than they did when Russia became a separate nation in the 1980s. According to D'Ann Campbell, the Soviets mobilized their women beyond the auxiliary stage. Approximately 800,000 women served in the Soviet Army in the war. Over half served on the front line. They held positions such as partisans (members of a resistance movement which fought a guerrilla war), snipers, and tank drivers. Women comprised three regiments of pilots, fighter pilots, bombers, and the very effective Night Bombers. Women combatants represented eight percent of the combatants. The Soviet Union decorated between 100,000 and 150,000 women and awarded 91 its highest award for valor, the Hero of the Soviet Union medal (Campbell 1993, 318–329). Soviet military records from World War II verify that women can be as effective front line soldiers as men. Women snipers killed over 11,000 German soldiers. The Soviets knew to select the best qualified, male or female. After the war, they demobilized women. Having women out of the military to give birth appeared more critical than having women in the military as career officers (*USA Today Magazine* 2006, 3–4).

The Soviet Union collapsed in 1991 and Russia created a military in 1992. Russia has a crisis of identity and a painful and long transition from the collapse of the Soviet Union, according to Mathers. The Russian armed forces slowly disintegrated and the two wars waged against Chechnya have contributed to young women steadily volunteering, from the 1990s to 2007. Young men have not been willing to be conscripted, but women have been willing to join the forces (Mathers 2006, 207). The number of military women have increased since early 1990 to about 10 percent of the total armed forces. This percentage compares with a range of 5 percent such as in Denmark, Norway, China, and the United Kingdom to 14 percent such as in Australia, New Zealand, and the United States (Mathers 2007, 8; Mathers 2006, 208). Mathers writes, "the position of women in the Russian armed forces is extremely fragile and is vulnerable to erosion and even to elimination at fairly short notice" (Mathers 2007, 9). Russian women are needed to meet recruiting quotas, but state groups are not at ease with large numbers of women serving for long periods. Women have no advocate for more open positions or removal of obstacles to promotions.

As it did in the United States, ending conscription caused the Russian military to need to recruit more troops. The advent of voluntary service helped meet the shortage. The difference in the two countries' approach lay in their approach to the shortage, the United States taking a political and policy approach while in Russia women were not part of the Defense Ministry's agenda for addressing the personnel crisis (Mathers 2007, 11).

Within the military, Russian women soldiers serve in mixed gender units and hypothetically have the same rights and privileges as males serving on contract, such as wages, material benefits, and pensions. Women and men are subject to the same disciplinary procedures. Women tend to work in female-dominated positions, but they are included in the airborne and special forces. Women's roles and duties are restricted. They do not carry personal arms and perform guard duty only in all-female barracks. They do not serve in combat nor on submarines or surface ships except for hospital vessels (Mathers 2006, 210–211).

In Russia's tentative economic period, many young women volunteer for the military for economic opportunities not found in civilian life. Social pressures, however, influence them to become wives and mothers rather than compete with men in the civilian sector. Mathers writes, "There is little enthusiasm in Russian society or among many Russian women for the notion that women's employment opportunities should be equal to those of men. . . . The language of equality, which was extensively employed by the Soviet regime, has been replaced by the language of essentialism" (Mathers 2007, 15). Mathers concludes that the Russian women soldiers are a success story that the military and society do not want to hear. Women soldiers represent a temporary solution to short-term problems, rather than a mechanism for institutional and personal change.

Women as Combatants in Nonstate-Based Revolutionary and Guerilla Military

As combatants and noncombatants, women have served in partisan and guerrilla operations in Algeria, China, Nicaragua, Rhodesia, Russia, Vietnam, and Yugoslavia (Segal 1995, 761). The anticolonial wars for independence in Africa involved revolutionary and guerilla warfare. Liberation wars provided an important way for the colonized to regain their dignity and their agency, or the capacity to shape events. Women had active military roles that provided agency in the Algerian Revolutionary War (1954 to 1962), but only a select group of women felt empowered by the war for independence from France after it was over. This lack of empowerment was due to the contradictions between the values of democratic revolution and militarism. Women felt postwar pressure to censor reports of their nontraditional roles and gendered tortures and to resume traditional female roles. Official accounts of the war tended to discount the service of women even though they played important roles (White 2007, 859, 880, 885).

Female suicide bombers have been used as active combatants in area conflicts beginning in 1985 with the Syrian Socialist

National Party (SSNP/PPS). Women have been active combatants as female suicide bombers during the War on Terror against al-Qaeda which first used women in Iraq in 2003 and continued to use them in 2010 (Skaine 2006, 26, 77; Suicide Sisterhood 2010, Special Reports).

There seem to be more opportunities for women to perform nontraditional roles in those nonstate militaries that are less structured, according to Mathers. She has found, "The more organized a nonstate military is (in other words, the more it looks like a state military in the way that it operates and the way that its members regard it), the fewer women we usually see in de facto combat roles" (Mathers 2010, Interview). Some examples useful to note are the Spanish Civil War and South Africa during the apartheid era. Nicaragua is an exception to the patterns in Spain and South Africa. Mathers explains,

> In the early months of the Spanish Civil War, a small group (perhaps a few hundred) young women enrolled in the militia to defend the Republic against the Fascists. They became known as milicianas, but the presence of women at the front was very short-lived—as the militias became better organized and Spanish society readjusted itself to its new circumstances, there was widespread acceptance of the slogan "men to the war front, women to the home front." (Nash 1993)
>
> In South Africa during the apartheid era, the African National Congress had an ideological commitment to equality between men and women and it did train some women to become part of its the armed wing (Unkhonto we Siswe or MK) but in practice the vast majority of the women who served in it were assigned supporting roles (Cock 1994). A woman who was a member of the MK and was one of the few women to participate in its operations was a guest speaker in my department last year and her comments about her experience revealed that the ideological commitment to equality by the ANC as an institution did not really penetrate to the level of individual male soldiers in training or in operations. She had to fight hard to get trained and be assigned to active service and then repeatedly prove herself at every stage. She did not go into much detail about sexual harassment but it was clear that most of the men she met in the MK thought

she was there for their entertainment—in other words, there was a great deal in common with the experiences of women soldiers in state militaries. (Mathers 2010, Interview)

Nicaragua may be an interesting exception to this pattern, in that the military forces of the Sandinistas had a large proportion of women as fighters—some estimates suggest that as many as one third of the combat soldiers were women. The Sandinistas had a strong women's organization in their political movement which made it more attractive to women and it also had an ideological commitment to gender equality, and in this case it seemed to be more successful than the MK in turning that commitment into practice. Women fighters were praised by the Sandinista leadership for being in the forefront of the fighting and many achieved high ranks. After the Sandinista victory in 1979, however, most women were demobilized from the military and in post-revolutionary collective memories the emphasis seems to be placed on commemorating women's roles in more traditional activities such as enduring suffering, making sacrifices for the cause and nurturing male soldiers. (Mathers 2010, Interview)

Afghanistan is of special interest because, in spite of patriarchal traditions, some women have found opportunity to serve in conflicts. The Revolutionary Association of the Women of Afghanistan (RAWA) exemplifies women breaking from societal roles to help that very society in its struggle to be free.

Afghanistan and the Revolutionary Association of the Women of Afghanistan

In recent times, Afghanistan has had to endure conflict. Soviet aid helped establish the communist regime in Afghanistan in 1978. To preserve the regime, the Soviet Union invaded Afghanistan in 1979. The Soviets did not withdraw until 1989. After the Soviets withdrew, Afghanistan was plunged into civil wars. The two strongest factions were the Northern Alliance and the Taliban. The Taliban faction of Afghanistan with the aid of Pakistan captured their first city, Kandahar, in 1994. Under the Taliban's brutal leadership, women endured extreme hardship because of extreme restrictions of all kinds which led to a new government. But because Afghanistan provided safe haven for Osama bin Laden, known terrorist leader of al Qaeda, the United States and its allies launched a massive attack in the country at alleged terrorist networks. The United States and its allies remain in Afghanistan in 2010 (Skaine 2002, 8, 45, 47).

Through the 30 some years of conflict, the Revolutionary Association of the Women of Afghanistan (RAWA) has been working for women's rights and to establish an independent, free, democratic, and secular Afghanistan. It is the oldest political/ social organization of Afghan women, having its beginning in 1977. After the Soviet Occupation, RAWA became involved in the war of resistance advocating secularism and democracy. Its work extended to the Afghan refugees in Pakistan through establishing schools, hostels and hospitals (RAWA 2010, About).

Hafizullah Emadi wrote of RAWA's resistance activities, "Women's role in the national liberation struggle was not restricted to rallies, protest demonstrations, noncooperation with the enemy, etc. They participated in organized struggles such as abduction, assassination and bombing of the enemy positions" (Emadi 1991, 239 in Skaine 2002, 19). Emadi reported that one leading woman fighter, Tajwar Kalwar (Sultan), was beaten and tortured in prison.

Because RAWA held demonstrations against the war crimes of the Soviets, they soon became marked for annihilation. Because they were against Islamic fundamentalists, they were subject to their wrath as well. The greatest example of that wrath was the martyrdom of their founding leader, Meena, and a large number of key activists. Agents of KHAD (Afghanistan branch of KGB) and their fundamentalist accomplices in Quetta, Pakistan, assassinated Meena on February 4, 1987 (RAWA 2010, About; RAWA 2010, Martyred Meena).

In answer to a set of questions that I submitted to RAWA in 2000, I learned that RAWA's work continued to be a threat to the Taliban and the Jehadis. In an open ended discussion, Shabana, an activist, volunteered some of the consequences, death threats, imprisonment in Pakistan, persecution, pressure not to make "propaganda against the Jehadis and Taliban," and the kidnapping of one of RAWA's technical aids (at the time, under urgent action from Amnesty International) (Skaine 2002, 81). Some members were hit with sticks, arrested, and put in prison. RAWA's coping tactics included using pseudonyms in travel, underground home-based classes, and not caring for their own safety to perform their mission.

In 2010, RAWA credits the United States for removing the Taliban regime in October 2001, but says, "it has not removed religious fundamentalism, which is the main cause of all our miseries. In fact, by reinstalling the warlords in power in Afghanistan, the U.S. administration is replacing one fundamentalist regime with another" (RAWA 2010, About).

Female Suicide Bombers

Suicide bombing is a tactic of war whether it is used in the war on terror or in civil conflicts. Sometimes civil conflicts spill over into global territory as in the cases where the bombers and their organizations object to foreign "occupation." An example is the insurgency in Iraq.

War on Terror and the al Qaeda Network

Like the United States, the international community is challenged by its policy role in the problematic twenty-first century security environment of complexity, connectivity, and rapid change. According to Phil Williams, "Security and stability in the twenty-first century have little to do with traditional power politics, military conflict between states, and issues of grand strategy. Instead, they revolve around governance, public safety, inequality, urbanization, violent nonstate actors, and the disruptive consequences of globalization" (Williams, Phil 2008, ix).

According to Rear Adm. D. M Williams, Jr. USN (Ret.), former Commander, Naval Investigative Service Command, the War on Terror has no one location. The enemy "does not abide by rules of warfare that have evolved over centuries in terms of what constitutes legitimate targets and what does not." He explains state-based military and suicide bombers further:

> The military functions as part of a state. The state is taking action. In the case of terrorists, for the most part, that frequently is not the case. They may be acting independently or if they are acting on behalf of some state, that is difficult if not impossible to prove. Having said that, the military functions on a body of rules that relates to targeting discretion. You are only allowed to attack

military objectives. You don't attack churches. You don't attack hospitals. You don't attack civilians. If you look at the object of terrorist attacks, they are precisely the opposite of that. Indiscriminate killing is their touchstone and hallmark. Innocent civilians, children are killed. They don't really care. You can cite any number of examples of that from international wars; the bombing of airliners, the bombing of the World Trade Center, the IRA killing of Lord Mountbatten. All of those involved incidents of where the people being attacked are civilians that have no connection to combat. (Williams, D. M. in Skaine 2006, 70)

The al Qaeda network is an adversary of those nations waging the War on Terror. The network began in 1988 to unite Muslims, overthrow non-Muslim regimes, and rid existence of non-Muslims. Their ultimate goal is to establish Islamic leadership and governments worldwide. In 2003, al Qaeda realized the value of women combatants and used its first female suicide bomber in Iraq (Skaine 2006, 22, 26).

According to Ali and Dow, divergent views of women exist within al Qaeda. The older generation believes women hold traditional roles and that men only should be recruited. The younger generation believes women are nurturers, but they are also defenders of the faith. Women should be recruited, be active, and that women are expendable (Ali and Dow 2006, Slides 13, 14).

Syrian Socialist National Party, Lebanon and the PKK, Turkey

Secular organizations that utilize bombings with women attackers do so often and include the Kurdistan Workers Party (PKK) in Turkey, the Syrian Socialist National Party, the Chechen rebels, and the Tamil Tigers. The first suicide attacks conducted by women were organized by the Syrian Socialist National Party (the SSNP/PPS), in Lebanon in 1985. Women represented 45 percent of the attackers. Of the suicide bombings conducted by the PKK in Turkey, 76 percent of the attacks were carried out by women (Skaine 2006 50; O'Rourke 2008, Op-Ed).

Since then other groups have utilized women as suicide bombers in the spirit of nationalism. In 2002, women represented five percent of the suicide bombings in conflict between Palestine and Israel, 16 percent of suicide bombers of the Lebanese Hezbollah.

In 2010, in two forceful groups, The Liberation Tigers of Tamil Eelam, LTTE, a Sri Lankan rebel group and the Chechen Rebels who sought independence from Russia, women represented 25 percent and 66 percent, respectively. Both of these groups existed in an effort to gain independence for their country (Skaine 2006, 26; O'Rourke 2008, Op-Ed).

Palestinian and Israeli Conflict

Each society relies on communal support, but the reasons for support differ (Skaine 2006, 21). The Palestinians, for instance, combine a sense of historical injustice with personal loss and humiliation of Israeli occupation while the al Qaeda and Jemaah Islamiyah (Egyptian Islamic Jihad) are more ideologically driven (Skaine 2006, 132). The following passage demonstrates how one leader, Yasser Arafat, significantly led his society to accept an equal role for women in order to strengthen his own military position, according to Barbara Victor. On January 27, 2002, Arafat spoke to over one thousand Palestinian women at his compound in Ramallah. He said, "Women and men are equal. You are my army of roses that will crush Israeli tanks" (Victor 2003, 19 in Skaine 2006, 132). Arafat's use of the phrase, "*Shahida* all the way to Jerusalem" was more important (Victor 2003, 20 in Skaine 2006, 132). Before this speech, no feminized version of the masculine form of the Arab word for martyr, *shahide*, existed. Victor describes this persuasive speech,

> [Arafat] repeated it [*shahida*] over and over again until the crowd, with raised fists, took the cue and chanted along with him: "*Shahida, Shahida* ... until Jerusalem. We will give our blood and soul to you, Abu Amar [Arafat's nom de guerre], and to Palestine."
>
> "You," he continued, his arm sweeping across the group of women and young girls, "are the hope of Palestine. You will liberate your husbands, fathers, and sons from oppression. You will sacrifice the way you, women, have always sacrificed for your family". (Victor 2003, 20 in Skaine 2006, 132)

Arafat gave his speech in the morning. In the afternoon that same day, 26-year-old Wafa Idris exploded in a downtown Jerusalem shopping mall.

Liberation Tigers of Tamil Eelam, Sri Lanka

In 1983, the Liberation Tigers of Tamil Eelam (LTTE) began fighting for a separate Tamil homeland. In 2009, the Sri Lankan government declared victory over the group. The LTTE women represented about a quarter of the Tamil Tigers. In addition to suicide bombing, women comprised LTTE front line units. They were more known for their ability to target and kill important political representatives using suicide bombings. One of the most famous and successful of these attacks was committed by the woman who murdered India's former Prime Minister, Rajiv Gandhi. Dhanu, a young Tamil woman, exploded herself during a political rally held by Rajiv Gandhi just before the Indian elections on May 20, 1991. She was a member of the Black Tigresses who prepared members for suicide terrorism. Women participated in about 30 to 40 percent of overall suicide activities. The LTTE is credited with suicide bombings numbering close to 200. One source reports that the organization had nearly 4,000 women, but all of them were not suicide bombers. This group was quiescent for a period, but resurfaces from time to time (Bloom 2006, Slide 13; O'Rourke 2008, Op-Ed; Tamil Tigers 2010, Times Topics; Skaine 2006, 88, 93–95).

The Tamil Tigers wreaked havoc during their struggle for independence. The Tigresses were carefully selected and much was expected of them. The Tigers required a number of steps women must take to join the suicide squad. The first step required that women be highly motivated to perform their mission. Mental stability was valued over tactical military skill. Second, attackers were taught in special training camps only for suicide missions. Each day members took part in physical exercises, arms training, and political classes that stress results. Third, attackers conducted dress rehearsals near the intended location of an attack and studied past operations through films of actual suicide missions (Pape 2005, 45 in Skaine 2006, 20).

Chechen Rebels and Russia

When the Soviet Union collapsed in 1991, Chechnya declared its independence. President Boris Yeltsin rebuffed the declaration and went into Chechnya with troops in 1994, which marked the first conflict with Russia. In 2003, the women in the Chechen Rebels, the Black Widows, had been responsible for about half of the suicide bombings. It is difficult to estimate their numbers because the Russian government does not return bodies of bombers because it does not want honor given to bombers, but

O'Rourke reports women represent 66 percent of the attackers. In October 2002, the Chechen rebels held the distinction of having killed the largest number, 170 in Moscow, when with a high percentage of women they held hostages in the Theater Center. The police killed 129 captives and 41 rebels in a rescue effort. Many of the women in the Moscow Theater Center siege of 700 hostages remain unknown, but estimates are that 18 women were known participants. Two deadly events occurred in 2004; on August 24, two passenger planes crashed almost simultaneously after leaving Moscow, killing a total of about 90 people on board, and on September 1, a school was siezed in Beslan, killing about 326 children and adults (Skaine 2006, 97, 100, 108, 110).

The Women Who Bomb

Much has been written about the motives of female suicide bombers. Some experts say that females bomb for many of the same reasons that men do (Rajan 2004, 13 in Skaine 2006, 38–40; Kruger 2005, 84 in Skaine 2006, 35; O'Rourke 2008, Op-Ed); and that it is important to recognize that: "(L)ike other soldiers, suicide bombers are following orders, participating in a warfare campaign intended to overwhelm an enemy and rack up military victories" (Friedman 2005, 7–8). Thus, the acts of the suicide bombers are not random or mindless, but a tactic of war. Only a small minority of female suicide bombers are psychologically disturbed and therefore, coerced into their attacks, and when they are coerced, claims are exaggerated, according to Lindsey O'Rourke.

Contrary to some media reports, women have strategic appeal, according to O'Rourke. Many are from countries that view women as second class, thus these women are better able to explode without arousing suspicion. Female attackers provide more media interest in their own countries and in foreign countries. Women bombers have overcome the gender barriers, but, according to my own research and that of O'Rourke's, little evidence of uniquely feminine motivations underlies attacks.

In 2010, the U.S. Customs Office of Intelligence and Operations Coordination found the following patterns in female suicide bombers:

- The majority of female suicide bombers are young, primarily between the ages of 17 and 24, however; the overall range in age for female suicide bombers is from 15 to 64.

- Female suicide bombers come from various educational, religious, social, and personal backgrounds.
- Education plays a role, with the "more educated" females such as lawyers, paramedics, or students accounting for the greatest percentage of suicide attacks.
- Most tend to be of average economic status and are rarely impoverished.
- Some may be dishonored through sexual indiscretion, or unable to produce children.
- Some appear motivated by revenge or grief of losing husbands or children, as in the woman who killed 15 people in Diyala province on December 7, 2008. Her two sons joined al-Qaeda in Iraq and were killed by security forces. (U.S. Customs 2010, 11)

Since 1985, U.S. Customs found that reporting shows there have been over 262 women suicide bombers and their attacks have resulted in higher casualties than the same number of attacks by male suicide bombers. The reason for more casualties is that women can get closer to their target (U.S. Customs 2010, 12).

So regardless of the conflicting ways women are perceived within their organizations or from without, women combatants are highly successful at their assigned task, suicide bombing. Men alone cannot win the war and since this phenomenon is war, the men and women who recruit women, are highly aware of women's ability to meet the organization's need in combat (Ali and Dow 2006, Slides 13, 14, 15).

References

Adams, Karen. 2009. "Topic 2: Examining the Role of Women in Military Conflict." *General Assembly Third Committee Topic Background Guide*. Teton County Model UN. High School Conference. October 24. www.cas.umt.edu (accessed November 20, 2009).

African Union. 2006. *Implementation of the Solemn Declaration on Gender Equality in Africa: First Report by All AU Member States, for Consideration at the January 2007, Addis Ababa, Ethiopia*. Index. South Africa, Mauritius, and Namibia, 15, 6, 17. www.africa-union.org (accessed November 20, 2009).

Ali, Farhana and Jennie Dow. 2006. "Examining the Role and Contribution of Muslim Women to the Global Jihadi Movement." Ali

Dow Power Point Presentation Link. Female Suicide Bombing and Europe Counter-Terrorism Series Conference. The International Institute for Strategic Studies, March 6. www.iiss.org (accessed June 8, 2010).

BBC Monitoring International Reports. 2007. "South Korean Air Force Gets First Woman Flight Leader," February 22.

Belgian National Report. 2010. NATO Unclassified Releasable For Internet Transmission, 1-4. Download: National Reports 2010. www.nato.int (accessed June 13, 2010).

Bloom, Mia. 2006. "Engendering Suicide Terror." Mia Bloom Power Point Presentation Link. Female Suicide Bombing and Europe Counter-Terrorism Series Conference. The International Institute for Strategic Studies, March 6. www.iiss.org (accessed June 8, 2010).

Campbell, D'Ann. 1993. "Women in Combat: The World War II Experiences in the United States, Great Britain, Germany and the Soviet Union." *Journal of Military History*: 57: 301–323.

CBC News Online. 2006. "Women in the Military—International." *The National*. May 30. www.cbc.ca (accessed July 13, 2010).

Central Intelligence Agency (CIA). 2009. *World Factbook*. Belgium. www.cia.gov (accessed November 21, 2009).

Central Intelligence Agency (CIA). 2010. "Military service age and obligation: South Korea." www.cia.gov (accessed May 18, 2010).

Cock, Jacklyn. 1994. "Women and the Military: Implications for Demilitarization in the 1990s in South Africa." *Gender and Society*: 8:2, June 152–169.

Cock, Jacklyn. 1995. "Forging a New Army Out of Old Enemies: Women in the South African Military." *Women's Studies Quarterly*: 23: 97–111, Fall/Winter.

Country Data. 1996. "Homeland Militaries." *South Africa—A Country Study*, May. www.country-data.com (accessed May 16, 2010).

Emadi, Hafizullah. 1991. "State, Modernization and the Women's Movement in Afghanistan*." Review of Radical Political Economics* 23:3–4. Fall-Winter, 227–228. In Rosemarie Skaine. 2002. The Women of Afghanistan under the Taliban. Jefferson, NC: McFarland Publishers, 19.

Enloe, Cynthia. 1988. *Does Khaki Become You? The Militarization of Women's Lives*. London:Pandora Press. In Mathers, Jennifer G. 2010. Interview by Rosemarie Skaine. E-mail, May 26, 2010.

Friedman, Lauri S., ed. 2005. *What Motivates Suicide Bombers?* San Diego: Greenhaven Press.

Heinecken, Lindy. 2000. "Securing South Africa's Future: Putting Women in the Frontline." *Strategic Review for Southern Africa* 22:2: 76+.

Juma, Monica and Anesu Makina. 2008. "Africa at Large: Too Few Women in Armed Forces." *Monitor* (Uganda), September 11. www.afrika.no (accessed May 16, 2010).

Kronsell, Annica and Erika Svedberg. 2001. "The Duty to Protect: Gender in the Swedish Practice of Conscription." *Cooperation and Conflict* 36:2, 163. In Mathers, Jennifer G. 2010. Interview by Rosemarie Skaine. E-mail, May 26, 2010.

Kruger, Lisa. 2005. *Gender and Terrorism: Motivations of Female Terrorists*, MS Thesis. Strategic Intelligence (MSSI). Joint Military Intelligence College, July 20.

Library of Congress. 2005. "Country Profile: South Korea." Federal Research Division, May. http://memory.loc.gov (accessed May 18, 2010).

Mathers, Jennifer G. 2006. "Women, Society and the Military: Women Soldiers in Post-Soviet Russia." *Military and Society in Post-Soviet Russia*. Stephen L. Webber and Jennifer G. Mathers, eds. Manchester, UK: Manchester University Press.

Mathers, Jennifer G. 2007. "Russia's Women Soldiers in the Twenty-First Century." *Minerva Journal of Women and War*. 1:1: 8–18, Spring.

Mathers, Jennifer G. 2010. Interview by Rosemarie Skaine. E-mail, May 26, 2010.

Mongabay.com. 1996. "South Africa—Women in the Military Homeland Militaries." May. www.mongabay.com (accessed May 17, 2010).

Nash, Mary. 1993. "Women in War: Milicianas and Armed Combat in Revolutionary Spain 1936–1939." *The International History Review* 15:2, 269–282. In Mathers, Jennifer G. 2010. Interview by Rosemarie Skaine. E-mail, May 26, 2010.

"Nation: No draft Without Women Too." 1980. *Time*. July 28. www.time.com (accessed November 18, 2009).

NATO Forces. 2002. Office on Women. *Women in the Armed Forces*. "International Military Staff: Norway," March 26. www.nato.int (accessed May 14, 2010).

NATO Forces. 2003. Office on Women. *Women in the Armed Forces*. "Table 2–3." and "Women Admittance in the NATO Countries Armed Forces and Subsequent Changes." www.nato.int (accessed November 23, 2009).

NATO Forces. 2007. Office on Women. *Women in the Armed Forces*. "Percentages of Female Soldiers in NATO Nations' Armed Forces." www.nato.int (accessed November 26, 2009).

New World Encyclopedia. 2008. "Women in the Military." Libya. www.newworldencyclopedia.org (accessed November 11, 2009).

Nicholson, Brendan. 2009. "Women Reluctant to Join Military." National, November 20. www.theage.com.au (accessed April 29, 2010).

Nystrom Division of Herff Jones, Inc. 2002. *Serving the Country: Military Service around the World*. January 1. 1–4. www.worldatlases.com (accessed November 23, 2009).

O'Rourke, Lindsey. 2008. "Behind the Woman Behind the Bomb." *New York Times*. Op-Ed, August 2. www.nytimes.com (accessed June 6, 2010).

Pape, Robert A. 2005. "A Nationalism." In Lauri S. Friedman, ed. 2005. *What Motivates Suicide Bombers?* San Diego: Greenhaven Press, 44–49.

Rajan, V. G. Julie. 2004. "A Essay: Subversive Visibility and Political Agency: The Case of Palestinian Female Suicide Bombers." *To Kill, To Die: Feminist Contestations on Gender and Political Violence*, March. In Skaine. 2006, 38–40).

Revolutionary Association of the Women of Afghanistan. 2010. "About RAWA." www.rawa.org (accessed June 11, 2010).

Revolutionary Association of the Women of Afghanistan. 2010. "Martyred Meena." www.rawa.org (accessed June 11, 2010).

Sandhoff, Michelle. 2009. "Women's Participation in the Military: Placing Israel in a Transnational Perspective." Panel Participant: International Issues, September 25.

Sasson-Levy, Orna. 2003. "Feminism and Military Gender Practices: Israeli Women Soldiers in 'Masculine' Roles." *Sociological Inquiry* 73: 3, August, 440–465.

Sasson-Levy, Orna. 2007. "Contradictory Consequences of Mandatory Conscription: The Case of Women Secretaries in the Israeli Military." *Gender and Society* 21: 4, August, 481–508.

Sasson-Levy, Orna and Sarit Amram-Katz. 2007. "Gender Integration in Israeli Officer Training: Degendering and Regendering the Military." *Signs* 33: 1, 105–133.

Segal, Mady Wechsler. 1995. Women's Military Roles Cross-Nationally: Past, Present, and Future. *Gender & Society* 9:6, December, 757–775.

Seibert, Thomas. 2009. "Turkey Confronts Its Past with Review of 1930s Operation Against Kurds." *The National*. World, December 11. www.thenational.ae (accessed April 28, 2010).

Senegal, Republic of. 2006. Ministry of Women and Family and Social Development. *National Report. Senegal Report on the Implementation of the Solemn Declaration of the Heads of State and Government on Gender Equality in Africa*. www.africa-union.org (accessed November 20, 2009).

"Sharp-Shooting Women Best Soviet Snipers." 2006. *USA Today Magazine*. The World at War. Newsview, December: 3–4.

Sharma, Ritu. 2009. " 'Night Witches' or Mere Symbols? India Debates Induction of Women Fighter Pilots." *Prokerala.com*, December 17. www.prokerala.com (accessed April 28, 2010).

Skaine, Rosemarie. 2002. *The Women of Afghanistan Under the Taliban*. Jefferson, NC: McFarland Publishers.

Skaine, Rosemarie. 2006. *Female Suicide Bombers*. Jefferson, NC: McFarland Publishers.

Skjelsbæk, Inger, and Torunn L. Tryggestad. 2009. "Women in the Norwegian Armed Forces: Gender Equality or Operational Imperative?" *Minerva Journal of Women and War* 3:2: 34–51, Fall.

Slobodkin, B. 2009. "Jerusalem–Knesset Bill Threatens to Restrict IDF Exemptions for Girls." *Vos Iz Neias*, November 24. www.vosizneias.com (accessed May 13, 2010).

"Suicide Sisterhood: Al-Qaida's Female Bombers." 2010. *UPI.com*. Special Reports, February 2. www.upi.com (accessed June 18, 2010).

"Tamil Tigers." 2010. *New York Times*. Times Topics, June 6. http://topics.nytimes.com (accessed June 6, 2010).

United Nations Security Council. 2000. "Resolution 1325." October 31. www.un.org (accessed May 6, 2010).

Units of the Belgian Armed Forces. n.d. "Belgian Women in Uniform ATS and WAAF Army Nurses 1940–1946." Short history. www.be4046.eu (accessed November 21, 2009).

U.S. Customs. 2010. Office of Intelligence and Operations Coordination. *Threat Assessment: Female Suicide Bombers*, March. http://info.publicintelligence.net (accessed June 7, 2010).

Victor, Barbara. 2003. *Army of Roses: Inside the World of Palestinian Women Suicide Bombers*. Emmaus, PA: Rodale.

Walsh, Sean P. 2007. "The Roar of the Lion City: Gender and Culture in the Singapore Armed Forces" *Armed Forces and Society* 33:2, 277. In Mathers, Jennifer G. 2010. Interview by Rosemarie Skaine. E-mail, May 26, 2010.

White, Aaronette M. 2007. "All the Men are Fighting for Freedom, All the Women are Mourning Their Men, But Some of Us Carried Guns: A Raced-Gendered Analysis of Fanon's Psychological Perspectives on War." *Signs: Journal of Women in Culture and Society* 32.4: 857–884, Summer.

Williams, Jr., Rear Adm. D. M., USN (Ret.). Former Commander, Naval Investigative Service Command. Interview by Rosemarie Skaine. Tape recording by telephone. May 16, 2005. In Rosemarie Skaine. 2006. *Female Suicide Bombers*. Jefferson, NC: McFarland Publishers, 70.

Williams, Phil. 2008. "From the New Middle Ages to a New Dark Age: The Decline of the State and U.S. Strategy." Carlisle, PA: Strategic Studies Institute, U.S. Army War College, June. www.strategicstudiesinstitute.army .mil/pubs (accessed May 19, 2010).

"Women Fighter Pilots? Not Soon, Says Air Force Chief." 2010. NDTV. India, March 9. www.ndtv.com (accessed April 29, 2010).

Women's Research and Education Institute (WREI). 2008. *Women in the Military: Where They Stand*. 6th ed. Arlington, VA: WREI.

Young Korean Movement of Europe. 1995. "Women Taking the Initiative: The Women's Movement in South Korea," March 9. www.hartford-hwp .com (accessed May 18, 2010).

4

Chronology

Women have served the military or have served in the military since the Revolutionary War. Women's involvement has changed and grown over the centuries. This chronology reflects the change in military women's status from active supporter to clandestine combatant to overt warrior and in the issues that defined change such as whether women are needed to win the war, and whether a cultural lag is present in American society that affects change.

Significant Highlights of Women in Military History 1775–2010

1775–1783 Revolutionary War Continental Army combatants Molly Pitcher, Margaret Corbin, and Debra Sampson alias Private Robert Shirtliff serve.

1812 Mary Allen and Mary Marshall serve as nurses on USS *United States* in the War of 1812.

1846–1848 Elizabeth Newcom enlists in the Missouri Volunteer Infantry as Bill Newcom in the Mexican War. She marches 600 miles to winter camp in Colorado before being discovered and discharged.

1861–1865 Civil War is waged. Dr. Mary Walker, soldier, physician, and prisoner of war, becomes the first female

119

1861–1865
(cont.) Congressional Medal of Honor recipient. Women are combatants and serve disguised as men, including: Sarah Emma Edmonds as Private Franklin Thompson; Loreta James Velazquez as Harry T. Buford; two sisters Mary and Molly Bell as Tom Parker and Bob Martin; Sara Rosetta as Private Lyons Wakeman; and Cathay Williams, a black woman, as William Cathey. Other women serve in noncombat capacities. Belle Boyd, a nurse, serves as a spy. She befriends Union officers and passes on military secrets to the Confederate Army.

1861 In April, Clara Barton, known as the Angel of the Battlefield, begins aid to servicemen. On May 21, Barton founds the American Red Cross.

1862 Five black nurses and four Sisters of the Holy Cross serve on the Navy's first hospital ship, USS *Red Rover*.

1898–1899 Spanish-American War deploys 1,500 women, most of whom are nurses. An explosion on the U.S. battleship *Maine* off the coast of Cuba causes the United States to go to war against Spain. Cuba's independence from Spain was intertwined with naval operations in the Philippines and the annexation of Hawaii, the Philippine Islands, and Puerto Rico. Of the 263,000 troops, 379 die in combat. Pneumonia, typhoid, malaria, and yellow fever claim 5,000. The Army hires 80 African American professional nurses; 33 are hired because the Army believes they are immune to yellow fever, but three die (WIMSA).

1901 The Army Nurse Corps becomes a permanent part of the Medical Department.

1908 Congress establishes the Navy Nurse Corps.

1917–1918 Over 10,000 nurses serve in World War I. Three nurses receive Distinguished Service Crosses. Only nurses serve in the Army. For the first time, women who do not serve as nurses enlist in the Navy and Marine Corps. Marines number 305 enlisted women and the Navy numbers approximately 12,000 as

1917–1918   Yeomen. The Army hires about 200 civilian women
(cont.)   who speak English and French to serve as telephone
operators. Women number 350,000 during the war.
More than 400 nurses die in the line of duty. Four navy
nurses earn the Navy Cross, the highest Navy decoration. Lenah S. Higbee is the second superintendent of
the corps from 1911 to 1923. Marie Louise Hidell,
Lillian M. Murphy, and Edna S. Pierce are awarded
the Navy Cross posthumously. In January 1945, for
the first time, a destroyer, USS *Higbee*, is named after
a woman, Lenah S. Higbee.

1920   Army Reorganization Act provision grants military
nurses officers status with "relative rank" from
second lieutenant to major (but not full rights and
privileges).

1941–1945   World War II nurses receive 1,619 medals, citations, and
commendations. Sixteen women are awarded the
Purple Heart for injury due to enemy action. For
outstanding performance, 1st Lt. Annie G. Fox, Army
Nurse Corps, is awarded the Purple Heart for duty at
Pearl Harbor at the time of the attack. Fox is awarded
the Bronze Star as well. The Bronze Star is awarded to
565 women for meritorious service overseas. American
women do cryptography and clerical duties; 432 are
killed, and 88 are taken prisoner of war.

1942   On May 15, Public Law 77-554 establishes the
Women's Army Auxiliary Corps (WAAC) as the
women's auxiliary branch of the Army. It is not an
official part of the Army. Women do not receive full
benefits.

1942   On July 30, Public Law 689 establishes WAVES,
Women Accepted for Voluntary Emergency Service
and the Women Marines, Marine Corps Women's
Reserve, as an official part of the services. Women
receive full benefits.

1942   In September, The Women's Auxiliary Ferrying
Squadron (WAFS) is formed.

1942	On November 23, Coast Guard Women's Reserve (SPAR) is formed. SPAR represents the first four letters of the Coast Guard's motto—Semper Paratus, Always Ready. Over 11,000 SPARs serve in World War II.
1943	Women's Army Corps (WAC) consists of the first women other than nurses to officially serve within the ranks of the U.S. Army. The WAAC is converted into WAC. WAC women receive full benefits.
1943	Women Air Force Service Pilots (WASP) is formed to fly military aircraft under the direction of the U.S. Army Air Forces during World War II. The group has no official status.
1944	WASP no longer functions.
1946	SPAR disbands.
1947	Public Law 36-80C, the Army–Navy Nurse Act, forms the Women's Medical Specialist Corps, making the Army and Navy Nurse Corps permanent staff of the regular services.
1948	Women's Armed Services Integration Act provides permanent positions for women. It includes ceiling and promotion caps. A provision excludes women from combat. Women cannot be assigned to ships or aircraft engaged in combat missions. The law did not address the assignment of Army women. The original combat exclusion provisions in the 1948 Act became codified in 1956 (USC 10 (1956), § 6015).
1948	Women in the Air Force (WAF) is established.
1949	Air Force Nurse Corps forms.
1950–1953	Korean War. Numbers 120,000 women on active duty as nurses and in support positions. Of 540 Army nurses who serve in Korea, only one dies, Genevieve Smith. She is not considered a casualty of war. Active duty Navy nurses number 3,081 and reserve Navy

1950–1953 (*cont.*)	nurses number 1,702. No records of female casualties exist in any service.
1950	The *Uniform Code of Military Justice* is enacted. It is found at 10 U.S.C. §§ 801-946.
1951	Defense Advisory Committee on Women in the Services (DACOWITS) is created with an initial mission to help the military meet recruiting goals.
1951	Executive Order 10240 authorizes all services to discharge any woman who becomes pregnant or a parent by adoption, or who has a minor child/stepchild at home at least 30 days per year.
1953	The Regular Army commissions its first woman physician as a medical officer.
1953	The Navy assigns Navy Hospital Corps women to positions aboard Military Sea Transportation Service (MSTS) ships for the first time.
1955	Army and Air Force Nurse Corps open to men.
1958	Military nurses are assigned to the hospitals which deploy during the Lebanon Crisis to support over 10,000 troops.
1961	The Marine Corps promotes its first woman, Bertha Peters Billeb, to Sergeant Major.
1965–1975	Vietnam War. About 10,000 women are often in the line of fire from rockets and mortars, mainly during the Tet offensive with the Viet Cong attacks on Saigon. The Tet offensive is a military campaign that began on January 31, 1968, Têt Nguyên Ðán, the first day of the year on a traditional lunar calendar and the most important Vietnamese holiday. Vietnamese communist guerilla fighters and the North Vietnamese Army launches a surprise attack on U.S. forces in South Vietnam. It is one of the most dangerous time periods to be in Vietnam. Approximately

1965–1975 7,000 American military women, mostly nurses,
(cont.) serve in Southeast Asia. An Army nurse is the only
woman to die from enemy fire in Vietnam. An Air
Force flight nurse dies aboard a C-5A Galaxy transport evacuating Vietnamese orphans when it
crashes on takeoff. Six additional women die in the
line of duty.

1965–1973 Jeanne M. Holm served as director of Women in the
Air Force (WAF).

1965 The Marine Corps assigns its first woman to attaché
duty. Later, she becomes the first woman Marine to
serve under hostile fire.

1965 Navy Nurse Corps open to men.

1967 Women become eligible for promotion to Admiral/
General. Women are eligible for promotion to flag/
general officer.

1967 Public Law 90-30 eliminates the ceiling and promotion cap, and thus repeals parts of the Integration
Act of 1948.

1968 The Air National Guard (ANG) swears in its first Air
Force woman because of the passage of Public Law
90-130, which allows the ANG to enlist women.

1969 Air Force Reserve Officers Training Corps (AFROTC)
opens to women.

1969 Joint Armed Forces Staff College admits women.

1970 Army promotes first women to Brigadier (one star)
General, Anna Mae Hays, Army Nurse Corps chief,
and Elizabeth Hoisington, WAC director.

1971 Air Force is the first service to change recruiting rules
to allow enlistment of mothers. It also allows
pregnant women to request a waiver of the automatic
discharge policy.

1971	The Air Force promotes its first woman to brigadier general.
1971	An Air Force woman completes Aircraft Maintenance Officer's School. She is the first woman aircraft maintenance officer.
1971	The Air Force and the Air Force Reserve assign the first woman as a flight surgeon.
1971	The Air Force Reserve assigns a staff sergeant as the first female technician.
1972	Navy and Army open Reserve Officer Training Corps (ROTC) to women.
1972	Equal Rights Amendment (ERA) passes Congress. It is signed by the President and sent to the states to be ratified.
1972	Chief of Naval Operations, Admiral Elmo R. Zumwalt, publishes Z-116, which states the Navy's commitment to equal rights and opportunities for women.
1972	The first naval vessel, the Hospital Ship USS *Sanctuary*, sails with a mixed gender crew.
1972	The Navy promotes the first woman to rear admiral, director of the Navy Nurse Corps.
1972	Supreme Court case *Frontiero v. Richardson* rules that military women with a spouse can receive the same entitlements as military men with a spouse.
1973	Air Force promotes first woman to Major (two star) General, Jeanne M. Holm. It is also the first time in history that the Armed Forces promotes a woman to major general. In 1982, Holm publishes her book, *Women in the Military: An Unfinished Revolution*. She publishes a revised edition in 1992.

1973	Selective Service Act ends the draft and provides for the All-Volunteer Force.
1973	The All-Volunteer Force becomes effective, and DoD authorizes provisions to permit services to retain uniformed women parents on a case-by-case basis.
1973	Navy opens aviation in noncombat aircraft to women.
1973	The Navy assigns the first woman chaplain.
1974	Army opens aviation in noncombat aircraft to women.
1974	Women enter the Merchant Marine.
1974	Six women earn wings as naval aviators. These women are the first women pilots in any branch of the services.
1974	Army's first woman receives her wings.
1975	DoD reverses policies that give pregnant women the option of electing discharge or remaining on active duty. Previous policies (1951) required women be discharged upon pregnancy or the adoption of children.
1975	The Air Force places its first woman on operational crew status.
1975	Coast Guard Academy enrolls women.
1976	Public Law 94-106 allows women to enter the Service Academies. One hundred nineteen women enter West Point; 81 enter the U.S. Naval Academy; and 157 enter the U.S. Air Force Academy.
1976	Second Circuit Court rules in *Crawford v. Cushman* that Marine Corps regulations requiring the discharge of pregnant Marines is a violation of the due process clause of the Fifth Amendment to the Constitution.

1976   The Navy promotes its first woman line officer to rear admiral.

1976   The Air Force selects its first woman reservist for the undergraduate pilot training program.

1976–78   Full integration of women into the services occurs with the abolishment of the following service groups as separate entities for women: The services then integrated women into their regular respective branches. Women in the Air Force (WAF), Women's Army Corps (WAC), Navy, Women Accepted for Voluntary Emergency Service (WAVES), Coast Guard, Semper Paratus, Always Ready (SPAR), and Women Marines.

1977   The Coast Guard assigns its first women to sea duty as crew members aboard the *Morgenthau* and *Gallatin*.

1977   Military veteran status is granted to the Women Air Force Service Pilots (WASP) who flew during WWII.

1977   Army policy opens additional occupations, including some aviation assignments, but formally closes combat positions to women.

1977   Air Force opens positions to women to serve on noncombat aircraft. The Coast Guard assigns women to shipboard duty.

1978   The Marine Corps promotes its first woman to brigadier general.

1978   The Army promotes its first woman to two-star general, Maj. Gen. Mary Elizabeth Clarke. She is also the first woman officer to command a major military installation when she takes command at Fort McClellan, Alabama.

1978   The Air Force Strategic Air Command assigns the first woman aircrew member to alert duty.

1978	Congress amends the 1948 Integration Act to allow women to serve on additional types of noncombat ships.
1978	Coast Guard removes gender restrictions on all assignments.
1978	FY-79 Defense Authorizations Act, 10 USC 6015 amendment, allows permanent assignment of women to noncombatant ships and temporary assignment to ships not having a combat mission.
1978	In *Owens v. Brown*, U.S. District Court for the District of Columbia rules that 10 USC Section 6015 is unconstitutional when it did not allow the permanent assignment of women to naval vessels except for hospital and transport ships.
1979	Navy opens Surface Warfare and Special Operations diving and salvage communities to women officers.
1979	First African American female in history, Hazel Johnson-Brown, is promoted to brigadier general.
1979	The first woman to command a military vessel takes command of the Coast Guard Cutter *Cape Newagen*.
1979	The first woman naval aviator obtains carrier qualification.
1979	The Marine Corps assigns women as embassy guards.
1980	Defense Officer Manpower Personnel Management Act (DOPMA) passes laws abolishing separate procedures for women officers in the Army, Navy and Marine Corps. The Air Force, founded in 1947, continues to operate under laws from its beginning that provide the same personnel system for male and female officers. The Act also requires that women in the three services be selected as opposed to appointed

1980 (*cont.*)	to flag/general officer rank. This requirement means that women must compete with men for promotion.
1980	The first women graduate from the service academies.
1980	The first woman is assigned to command a Naval Training Command.
1981	In *Rostker v. Goldberg*, the Supreme Court case rules that excluding women from the draft and Selective Service registration is constitutionally based.
1982	Women in the Army Policy Review Group (WITA) is established to review issues and formulate policy. WITA establishes physical strength requirements for each Military Occupation Specialty (MOS).
1982	The Air Force selects its first woman aviator for Test Pilot School.
1982	The Marine Corps prohibits women from serving as embassy guards.
1982–1984	Women are part of the Peace Keeping Force in Lebanon.
1983	Air Force women as members of refueling tanker crews take part in a raid on Libya.
1983	Operation Urgent Fury, the invasion of Grenada, deploys about 200 Army and Air Force women. Air Force women serve in air transport crews. Women also serve as military police.
1983	The first Navy woman completes Test Pilot School.
1983	The first woman in any reserve component, an Air Force Reserve officer, is promoted to brigadier general.
1984	Sexual harassment provision becomes part of the *Manual for Courts-Martial*.

1984	The Naval Academy's top graduate is a woman for the first time in history.
1984	A Coast Guard officer is the first woman to serve as a Presidential Military Aide.
1985	The Coast Guard Academy's top graduate is a woman for the first time in history.
1985	The Air Force Reserve promotes its first nurse to brigadier general.
1986	Six Air Force women serve as pilots, copilots, and boom operators on the KC-135 and KC-10 tankers that refuel FB-111s all through the raid on Libya.
1986	The Air Force Academy's top graduate is a woman for the first time in history.
1986	A Navy woman becomes the first female jet test pilot in any service.
1986	The Coast Guard's rescue swimmer program graduates its first woman.
1987	September, Defense Secretary Caspar W. Weinberger establishes the Task Force on Women in the Military to review women's roles after several women's groups charge that women face widespread sexual harassment and limited career opportunities.
1987	The Navy assigns its first woman Force Master Chief and Independent Duty Corpsman to serve at sea.
1987	The Coast Guard assigns its first enlisted woman as Officer-in-Charge aboard a Coast Guard vessel.
1988	DoD adopts the Risk Rule, which sets a single standard for evaluating the positions and units from which the military service can exclude women. Units supporting ground combat remain closed, but 30,000 new positions are opened to women.

1988   July 20, Secretary of Defense (SECDEF) Memorandum defines sexual harassment and makes committing sexual harassment an offense punishable under the Uniform Code of Military Justice (UCMJ). This regulation is the first instance of criminalizing conduct as per se sexual harassment. It is found in the UCMJ, Article 2 (1988).

1988   NASA selects its first Navy woman as an astronaut.

1988   The Coast Guard's "Chief Warrant Officer to Lieutenant" program promotes its first woman.

1988   Marines again assign women as embassy guards.

1988 and 1989   The Secretary of Defense (SECDEF) Task Force recommends a DOD survey on sexual harassment, which is conducted worldwide.

1989   September, Navy-wide survey on sexual harassment is administered.

1989   Operation Just Cause, the invasion of Panama, deploys 770 women. Women fly Black Hawk helicopters under fire and one military policewoman (MP) commands troops in a ground combat-like operation. Two women command Army companies and three women Army pilots are nominated for Air Medals. Two receive the Air Medal with "V" device for participation in a combat mission.

1989   The Military Academy at West Point names a woman as its Brigade Commander and First Captain for the first time in history.

1989   NASA selects its first Army woman to be an astronaut.

1989   The Navy assigns its first woman, Janice Ayers, as Command Master Chief at sea.

1989   The Coast Guard selects a woman as the first person trained for a new specialty, Coast Guard Flight

1989 (*cont.*)	Officer. These officers are in charge of tactical coordination of the drug interdiction efforts aboard Coast Guard aircraft.
1990–1991	Persian Gulf War, Operation Desert Shield/Desert Storm, sends the largest single deployment of women in history, 40,782 soldiers or 7 percent of the forces. Two Army women become prisoners of war and 15 are killed.
1990	The Navy assigns its first women, Capt. Marsha Evans, to command a Naval Station and Cmdr. Rosemary Mariner to command an aviation squadron.
1990	The first Navy woman, Lt. Cmdr. Darlene Iskra, SPECOPS officer, takes command of a ship.
1991	Kennedy-Roth Amendment repeals provisions of Title 10 USC 8549 that ban women from serving on combat aircraft that engage in combat missions.
1991	The Air Force Reserve selects its first woman senior enlisted advisor.
1991	The Naval Academy names a woman Brigade Commander for the first time in history.
1991	July 12, Memorandum from Dick Cheney, Secretary of Defense, directs all major parts of the DoD to implement a zero-tolerance policy for sexual harassment.
1991	September 7, a group of naval officers allegedly physically and indecently assault Navy helicopter pilot, Lieut Paula Coughlin, while attending the Tailhook Symposium at the Las Vegas Hilton. Soon she complains to Rear Adm. John Snyder, Commander, Naval Air Test Center.
1991	September 8–12, the Navy's Tailhook Association holds the 35th Annual Symposium.

1991	October 11, the Naval Investigative Service (NIS) opens investigation into assault on Lt. Coughlin.
1991	October 29, the Naval Inspector General (NIG) begins the investigation of non-criminal violations associated with the Tailhook Association and its September 1991 symposium.
1991	November 5, the Navy relieves Rear Adm. John Snyder of command for his improper handling of Lt. Coughlin's complaint.
1991	Tailhook Association loses Navy support after reports of misconduct.
1992–1993	National Defense Authorization Act repeals the prohibition on the assignment of women to combat aircraft in the Air Force, the Navy, and the Marines Corps.
1992	Presidential Commission on the Assignment of Women in the Armed Forces report recommends retaining the direct ground combat exclusion for women. Women may serve in combat aircraft.
1992	April 15, NIS completes its investigation into criminal violations.
1992	April 29, NIG releases its investigation results.
1992	May 13, NIS releases a supplemental report.
1992	June 11, NIS releases its *Supplement Report* which places Secretary of the Navy (Sec. Nav.) Garrett at Tailhook in a suite on the third floor of the Las Vegas Hilton.
1992	June 26, Sec. Nav. Garrett resigns in response to the NIS *Supplemental Report*.
1992	July 29–30, the House Armed Service Committee conducts a hearing on gender discrimination in the military.

1992	September 25, the Department of Defense Inspector General (DoDIG) releases its first report, *Tailhook '91, Part 1—Review of the Navy Investigations.*
1992	September, Roper Organization, Inc. conducts for the Commission on the Assignment of Women in the Armed Forces, *Attitudes Regarding the Assignment of Women in the Armed Forces: The Military Perspective.*
1992	November 15, the Presidential Commission on the Assignment of Women in the Armed Forces issues its *Report to the President.*
1992	The Coast Guard promotes its first active duty woman officer to captain.
1992–1994	Bosnia-Kosovo deploys 1,000 women.
1993	Sheila Widnall becomes the first secretary of a service as head of the Air Force.
1993	January 6, a regulation implementing a new sexual harassment policy for the naval services is published. It defines sexual harassment and makes violation of its prohibition of sexual harassment a punitive offense punishable under the Uniform Code of Military Justice (UCMJ). This regulation is the first to criminalize conduct as sexual harassment.
1993	February, DoDIG releases its second report, *Tailhook '91, Part Two: Events at the 35th Annual Tailhook Symposium.*
1993	April, Secretary of Defense directs the services to open more specialties and assignments to women. The Army and the Marine Corps are directed to study the possibility of opening more assignments to women, but direct ground combat positions are to remain closed.
1993	May, the Air Force opens all aircraft to women.

1993	November, Congress repeals naval combat ship exclusions and requires DoD to notify Congress prior to opening additional combat positions to women. Women deploy with the USS *Fox*.
1993	The Navy's first woman aviator, Lt. Cmdr. Kathryn Hire, USNR, serves with a combat squadron.
1993	The Navy's first woman, Rear Adm. Louise Wilmot, takes command of a base.
1993	The Marine Corps opens pilot positions to women.
1993	The Army selects a woman "Drill Sergeant of the Year" for the first time in the 24-year history of this competition.
1993	The Army assigns its first woman combat pilot.
1993	The Air Force assigns its first woman to command an Intercontinental Ballistic Missile unit.
1993	The first woman in any reserve component is promoted to major general.
1993	The Air Force assigns its first woman to command an air refueling unit.
1993	The Coast Guard promotes its first active duty woman to master chief.
1993	The Coast Guard assigns its first woman as Chief Judge.
1994	February 7, Lt. Coughlin submits her resignation from the Navy.
1994	March, the Navy assigns the first women (63) aboard a combat ship, USS *Eisenhower*.
1994	Lt. Carey D. Lohrenz and Lt. Kara Hultgreen are the first Navy female pilots to complete F-14

1994 (*cont.*)	training and to be assigned to squadrons on the west coast.
1994	Lt. Kara Hultgreen becomes the first Navy woman fighter pilot to be killed when her F-14 crashes into the sea during flight operation off the USS *Abraham Lincoln*.
1994	May, the first Air Force Reserve woman completes combat pilot training.
1994	The first woman assumes command of a Naval Air Station.
1994	The first woman, an Air Force major, copilots the Space Shuttle.
1994	October 1, Lt. Coughlin settles out-of-court her suit against the Tailhook Association for $400,000.
1994	October 28 and 31, a Nevada jury awards Lt. Coughlin $6.7 million in her suit against the Las Vegas Hilton.
1994	Risk Rule of 1988 is repealed. A new DoD direct ground combat assignment rule allows all service members to be assigned to all positions for which they qualify, but excludes women from assignment to units below the brigade level whose primary mission is direct ground combat.
1994	Congress repeals Title 10 USC 6015 which opens to women Navy combatant ships except for submarines and some smaller ships.
1994–1995	Haiti Operation Uphold Democracy deploys 1,200 women.
1995	The first female Marine pilot pins on naval flight wings.
1995	First female Navy aviator lifts off in Space Shuttle *Endeavor*.

1995   An Air Force lieutenant colonel becomes the first woman Space Shuttle pilot.

1995   The Air Force promotes its first African American female officer to major general.

1995   April, the Navy's USS *Eisenhower* completes a deployment with the distinction of being the first combat ship to deploy with a mixed gender crew and the first to launch women aviators on a combat mission.

1995   Navy institutes military's first policy on pregnancy as a natural event and not a presumed medical incapacity. Pregnancy and parenthood are compatible with naval career.

1995   DoD Sexual Harassment Study is a highly detailed summary of a 1995 DoD second sexual harassment survey. This survey documents a significant decline in sexual harassment complaints.

1995   The DoD Task Force on Discrimination and Sexual Harassment convenes.

1996   March, the first woman, Army Sgt. Heather Johnson, is assigned to guard the Tomb of the Unknown Soldier.

1996   The first woman commands the Army's Old Guard Fife and Drum Corps.

1996   The first women in the history of the armed forces are promoted to three-star rank, Carol Mutter, Marine Corps, and Patricia Tracey, Navy.

1996   A Navy woman, Lt. Erica Niedermeier, is one of two officers supervising the strike team, firing eight Tomahawk cruise missiles at Iraq from USS *Laboon*. The missile strikes are the first time female sailors take part in combat operations since the Navy opened warship assignments to women in 1994.

1996	A Navy woman commands an operational flying wing for the first time.
1996	Bosnia peacekeeping begins. Over 12,000 women deploy.
1997	October 18, Women In Military Service For America Memorial in Arlington National Cemetery is dedicated after approximately 11 years in the making. It is the only major national memorial honoring women who have defended the nation during all eras and in all services. Brig. Gen. Wilma L. Vaught, USAF (Ret.) is the founder.
1997	November, the U.S. Army brings charges of rape and sexual harassment against military trainers at the Army Ordnance Center at Aberdeen Proving Ground, Maryland.
1997	December, the Federal Advisory Committee on Gender-Integrated Training and Related Issues publishes a report in response to the incidents at Aberdeen.
1997	The Army promotes its first woman to lieutenant general.
1997	The Army assigns the first woman and the first nondoctor to command an Army hospital.
1997	The first woman in history is appointed state adjutant general, Vermont Air National Guard Lt. Col. Martha T. Rainville.
1998–1999	Women take part in combat in air war in the Kosovo conflict. Over 8,000 women serve.
1998	Operation Desert Fox, the enforcement of the no-fly zone in Iraq begins. For the first time, women fly combat aircraft on combat missions. Lt. Kendra Williams, USN, F/A-18 pilot becomes the first female pilot to launch missiles in combat.

1998	The Air National Guard promotes its first woman to major general.
1999	The Congressional Commission on Military Training and Gender-Related Issues releases its review of the sexual misconduct incidents at Aberdeen.
1999	First woman, Col. Eileen Collins, USAF, commands a Space Shuttle.
1999	Nancy Ruth Mace is the first woman to graduate from the Citadel, the formerly all-male military school in South Carolina.
1999	The Virginia Military Institute graduates its first woman.
1999	The Air Force promotes its first woman, Leslie F. Kenne, to lieutenant general.
1999	The first woman and first African American, Evelyn Fields, commands the National Oceanic and Atmospheric Administration Corps.
1999	The Navy selects its first African American woman, Cmdr. Michelle Howard, to command a surface combatant ship, the USS *Rushmore*.
2000	The Air Force promotes their first woman pilot, Betty Mullis, to brigadier general.
2000	The first Coast Guard women are promoted to flag officer rank, admiral.
2000	The National Guard names its first female major general.
2000	Terrorists attack destroyer USS *Cole*, killing 17 including two women.
2000	Lt. Gen. Claudia Kennedy, deputy chief of staff for intelligence, charges Maj. Gen. Larry Smith of sexual

2000 (*cont.*)	misconduct after he is nominated as the Deputy Inspector of the Army. The incidents occurred when Smith visited her office in 1996. Kennedy was a major general and assistant deputy chief for intelligence at the time. After an investigation, Defense officials confirm Smith sexually harassed Kennedy.
2000	Navy reestablishes official ties with the Tailhook Association.
2000	The Navy assigns its first woman, Capt. Kathleen McGrath, to command a warship in the Persian Gulf.
2000	The Army National Guard promotes its first woman to major general.
2001	September 11, terrorist attack on the Pentagon kills six military women.
2001	October 7, Operation Enduring Freedom begins in Afghanistan. As the war progresses, women, like men, often serve more than one tour of duty.
2001	The Army promotes the first woman, Col. Coral Wong Pietsch, USAR, to brigadier general in the Judge Advocate General's Corps. She is also the first Asian Pacific American woman promoted to brigadier general.
2001	The Air National Guard security force appoints its first woman to complete the counter-sniper course, the only military sniper program open to women.
2001	The U.S. Army Women's Museum opens at Ft. Lee, Virginia.
2002	Office of the Secretary of Defense permits the DACOWITS charter to expire. New Charter reduces the number committee members by over half and alters its mission. Family matters are added to its mission.

2002	On December 2, Congress prohibits the military from requiring military women to wear abayas, a large, black cloak, worn either loose and flowing or wrapped around the entire body (Pub. L. No. 107-314). The FY 2003 Defense Authorization Act forbids commanders from requiring or strongly suggesting that women serving in Saudi Arabia wear the abaya.
2002	A woman Marine, Sgt. Jeannette L. Winters, is the first U.S. servicewoman to die in the war on terrorism.
2002	The Army National Guard promotes an African American woman, Julia Cleckley, to the rank of brigadier general for the first time.
2002	The Army Reserves selects a woman, Michele S. Jones, as its top enlisted advisor as a command sergeant major. This selection is the first time in any of the military services.
2003	Over 25,400 women deploy in Operation Iraqi Freedom. One woman is killed and two are prisoners of war.
2003	January 2, an anonymous e-mail is sent to the Secretary of the Air Force, the Chief of Staff of the Air Force, Senator Wayne Allard, Senator Ben Nighthorse Campbell, other U.S. congressmen, and media representatives. The e-mail claims a significant sexual assault problem exists at the U.S. Air Force Academy and the academy's leadership is ignoring it.
2003	Mary Walker, general counsel and chair of a Working Group, issues *The Report of the Working Group Committee Concerning the Deterrence and Response to Incidents of Sexual Assault at the U.S. Air Force Academy.*
2003	Tillie Fowler, chair of the House and Senate Armed Services Committee's independent panel to investigate Air Force Academy sexual misconduct, holds hearings and issues a report.

2003	The first Native American servicewoman is killed in combat. She is one of three women who became prisoners of war during the first days of the war in Iraq.
2003	The Army forms a group of 25 women soldiers, Team Lioness. The soldiers represent a variety of military occupational specialties (MOS) and accompany infantry units on search missions and raids.
2004	Congressional hearings on charges of U.S. servicemen committing sexual assault on U.S. servicewomen in Iraq.
2004	Secretary of Defense Donald Rumsfeld directs undersecretary of defense for personnel and readiness to review sexual assault policies and programs and to make necessary recommendations that will increase prevention, reporting, quality of support to victims and accountability of offenders.
2004	April, the Task Force issues its report on *Care for Victims of Sexual Assault.*
2004	Congress orders Department of Defense to review *UCMJ* and the *Manual for Courts-Martial* to recommend changes in addressing sexual offenses.
2004	The Department of Defense assembles a Care for Victims of Sexual Assault Conference to address policy.
2004	Joint Task Force on Sexual Assault Prevention is established.
2004	Defense Task Force on Sexual Harassment and Violence at the Military Service Academies is established
2004	By the end of the year, 19 servicewomen are killed as a result of hostile action since the war in Iraq began in 2003. This is the largest number of servicewomen to die as a result of hostile action in any war.

2004   The Air Force selects its first woman, Col. Linda
            McTague, to command a fighter squadron.

2005   January, DoD announces in sexual assault policy
            changes: definition, more support for victims, training
            standards for members and a commitment to develop
            policy for confidential reporting.

2005   *Report on the Service Academy Sexual Assault and
            Leadership Survey* is released. Two hundred sixty-two
            female participants out of 1,906 report 302 incidents
            and 54 male participants out of 3,107 report
            55 incidents.

2005   Provisions for confidentiality to victims of sexual
            assault are announced.

2005   The Task Force on Sexual Assault Prevention and
            Response becomes the permanent Sexual Assault
            and Prevention Response Office within the Office of
            the Secretary of Defense.

2005   Hunter/McHugh amendment to exempt women
            from involuntary assignments in or near land combat
            units fails and is not included in the National Defense
            Authorization Act of 2006.

2005   June 16, Sgt. Leigh Ann Hester, Iraq, vehicle
            commander, 617th Military Police Company,
            Richmond, Kentucky, is awarded the Silver Star. Sgt.
            Hester was the first woman soldier since World War II
            to receive the Silver Star.

2005   The Air Force selects a woman as the Academy's
            Commandant of Cadets, the No. 2 position at the
            nation's service academies. She is the first woman at
            any of the academies to be appointed to this position.

2005   The USAF Air Demonstration Squadron "Thunder-
            birds" chooses its first woman member and is the first
            woman to perform on any U.S. military high profile
            jet team.

2006   PL 109-163, Section 541, requires the Secretary of Defense notify Congress 30 days ahead of making any change in the ground combat exclusion policy or of any military career designator to women.

2006   Defense Manpower Center's *2006 Gender Relations Survey of Active Duty Members* is released.

2006   The Coast Guard appoints its first woman vice commandant of the Coast Guard. She is also the first woman to serve as a deputy service chief in any of the US Armed Forces.

2006   The Marine Corps assigns its first woman to command a Recruit Depot.

2006   The Coast Guard selects Vice Adm. Vivien S. Crea as the first woman ever to serve as a deputy service chief in any of the armed forces.

2007   The Navy selects its first woman, Sara Joyner, to command a fighter squadron.

2007   RAND issues a report, *Assessing the Assignment Policy for Army Women.*

2007   April, Army awards silver star to combat medic Specialist Monica Brown, Afghanistan, of the 782nd Brigade Support Battalion, 4th Brigade Combat Team, 82nd Airborne Division.

2007   October 1, the updated UCMJ, Article 120, goes into effect. One update changes the title of the Article from "Rape and Carnal Knowledge" to "Rape, Sexual Assault and Sexual Misconduct" and includes 14 offenses.

2008   The Army appoints the first woman, Lt. Gen. Ann E. Dunwoody, to four-star general rank, the first woman military officer to attain the rank.

2008   The Army establishes the Directorate of Comprehensive Soldier Fitness to correct the observed gaps in capability due to the nature of war, because how

2008 (*cont.*)	soldiers come out of an experience is in great measure determined by how they went in to it. The program is a holistic fitness program for soldiers, families, and Army civilians designed to enhance performance and build resilience.
2008	Spc. Tiffany Knotts becomes the Army's first woman Stryker Armored Vehicle driver.
2009	Army promotes first woman, Command Sgt. Maj. Teresa L. King, to commandant of Fort Jackson's (SC) drill sergeant school.
2009	Navy opens submarines to women.
2010	Army selects Brig. Gen. Colleen L. McGuire as its first woman provost marshal general. She also takes command of the U.S. Army Criminal Investigation Command.
2010	Army selects first female commandant; the 369th Adjutant General Battalion's Command Sgt. Maj. Teresa King, to lead Drill Sergeant School.
2003–2010	In Operation Iraqi Freedom in Iraq and Operation Enduring Freedom in Afghanistan, women perform combat roles on land, at sea, and in the air.
2010	August 31, end of combat operations in Operation Iraqi Freedom; 4,408 U.S. military service members died in Iraq; 110 of that number were women. At the war's peak in 2007, more than 170,000 troops were in the country; only around 50,000 troops remain on this date.

References

Colonial Williamsburg Foundation. 2008. "Time Line: Women in the U.S. Military." www.history.org/History/teaching/enewsletter/volume7/images/nov/women_military_timeline.pdf (accessed June 16, 2010).

Hasday, Jill Elaine. 2008. "Article: Fighting Women: The Military, Sex, and Extrajudicial Constitutional Change." 93 *Minnesota Law Review* 96. November.

Manual for Courts-Martial. 1984. Sexual harassment provision. United States, pt. IV para. 16b(3)(b).

National Archives and Records Administration. n.d. "Women Who Serve: Annie G. Fox." *A People at War.* www.archives.gov/exhibits (accessed June 17, 2010).

National Archives and Records Administration. n.d. "Records of Nurse Casualties in the Korean War." Electronic and Special Media Records Services Division Reference Report, Research. www.archives.gov (accessed June 17, 2010).

"Nurses in World War I." 2001. Encyclopedia.com, January www.encyclopedia.com (accessed June 17, 2010).

Oracle ThinkQuest Foundation. "A Timeline of the History of Women in Aviation." Projects by Students for Students. http://library.thinkquest.org (accessed June 29, 2010).

Parrish, Deanie. 2008. "TimeLine of WASP History." Women Airforce Service Pilots (WASP). http://publishing.yudu.com (accessed June 29, 2010).

Skaine, Rosemarie. 1996. *Power and Gender: Issues in Sexual Dominance and Harassment.* Jefferson, NC: McFarland & Co. Inc.

Skaine, Rosemarie. 1999. *Women at War: Gender Issues of Americans in Combat.* Jefferson, NC: McFarland & Co. Inc.

U.S. Department of Homeland Security and U.S. Coast Guard. 2009. "Women and the U.S. Coast Guard: Moments in History." www.uscg.mil (accessed July 12, 2010)

U.S. Navy. 2007. "History and Firsts." Office of Women's Policy. Bureau of Navy Personnel. www.npc.navy.mil (accessed June 21, 2010).

Wilson, USAF (Ret.), Capt. Barbara A. 1996–2010. "Women Medal Recipients—Military and Civilian." *Military Women Veterans: Yesterday, Today, Tomorrow.* http://userpages.aug.com (accessed June 17, 2010).

Women in Military Service For America Memorial Foundation, Inc. 1775–2008. "Highlights in the History of Military Women." www.womensmemorial.org (accessed June 17, 2010).

Women Marines Association. 2010. "Women Marine Milestones." History of the Women Marines. www.womenmarines.org (accessed June 29, 2010).

Women's Research and Education Institute. 2003. "Chronology of Significant Legal & Policy Changes Affecting Women in the Military: 1947–2003." www.wrei.org (accessed June 17, 2010).

WREI. 2008. *Women in the Military: Where They Stand.* 6th ed. Arlington, VA: WREI.

5

Biographical Sketches

The individuals included in this chapter have performed exceptionally in military duty or have had an effect on the issues of women in the military and combat. Some women are on active duty, others are retired. The biographies selected are representative of how women serve. Voices supporting and opposing women in combat are included. Elaine Donnelly, founder and president of the Center for Military Readiness, and Dr. Peter A. Lillback, president, Westminster Theological Seminary, are among those opposed to allowing women in combat. Together the people and their views represent the fabric of our larger society and its divergent views. Many servicewomen have received awards; some, numerous times. For an explanation of these awards see Chapter 6, Table 6.16, Selected Military Awards.

Specialist Veronica Alfaro, U.S. Army (1985–)

Specialist (Spc.) Veronica Alfaro, U.S. Army, was granted the military's fourth-highest combat award, the Bronze Star Medal for Valor, in Iraq in 2008. She was a combat medic and convoy vehicle driver, Bravo Company, 297th Support Battalion. She was driving a light medium tactical vehicle gun truck, escorting a convoy of third country nationals on the main U.S. supply route from Baghdad to Balad, Iraq. She met heavily armed insurgents and turned into the line of enemy fire to protect the civilian drivers and to allow her gunner the ability to return fire. Spc. Alfaro ran through gunfire

50 yards away to save the lives of two injured civilian convoy drivers who were ahead of her. The driver was injured and she used her body as a shield. He died later, but she helped save the life of another wounded civilian driver. Spc. Alfaro's commander said that her courage under fire is exceptional and that she helps make the hostile environment a little safer.

In 2005, Spc. Alfaro joined with the California Army National Guard and in 2007 she applied to be transferred to the Alaska Guard because she wanted to serve in Iraq. She was originally from Modesto, California.

Sources

"United States Bronze Star." 2009. *Orders, Decorations and Medals*. Medals by Country. November 11. www.jeanpaulleblanc.com (accessed February 4, 2010).

U.S. Army Pacific. 2008. "Alaska Army Guard Soldier Earns Bronze Star with Valor in Iraq: Spc. Veronica Alfaro Helps Save A Man's Life while Coming under Enemy Fire." April 28. www.usarpac.army.mil/news (accessed February 4, 2010).

Colonel Ruby Bradley, U.S. Army (December 19, 1907–May 28, 2002)

Colonel (Col.) Ruby Bradley, U.S. Army, survived two wars, a prison camp and near starvation. She is one of the most decorated women in U.S. military history. She was born in Spencer, West Virginia. She entered the Army Nurse Corps in 1934. In 1941, Col. Bradley served at Camp John Hay in the Philippines when the Japanese attacked Pearl Harbor. In 1943, she was captured by the Japanese and transferred to the Santo Tomas Internment Camp in Manila. While there, she lost weight partly because she gave her food to starving children. The weight loss made room in her uniform to smuggle surgical equipment into the camp. She was a captive until the U.S. troops liberated the prisoners in 1945.Col. Bradley served in the Korean War as Chief Nurse for the 171st Evacuation Hospital. In 1951, she became the Chief Nurse for the Eighth Army. At her scheduled departure, 100,000 Chinese soldiers surrounded her. She refused to leave until she had loaded the sick and wounded onto a plane, nearly escaping death. When she did board the plane, her ambulance exploded from an enemy shell. Col. Bradley retired from the Army in 1963. In 1999 at 91 years of age, she received more than a dozen military awards to replace those she had lost over the years. These awards included the Legion of Merit medals, the Bronze Star, two Presidential Emblems, the Meritorious Unit Emblem, The American Defense Service Medal, the American Campaign Medal, the Asiatic-Pacific Campaign Medal, the World War II Victory Medal, the Army Occupational Medal with Japan clasp, three Korean Service medals, the Philippine Liberation Medal, the Philippine Independence Ribbon, and the United Nations Service Medal.

Sources

Arlington National Cemetery Web site. 2006. www.arlingtoncemetery.net (accessed February 4, 2010).

Norman, Elizabeth and Sharon Elfried. 2007. "The Angels of Bataan." *Journal of Nursing Scholarship* 25:2. October 2, 121–126. www3. interscience.wiley.com (accessed January 14, 2010).

Specialist Monica L. Brown, U.S. Army (1989–)

Spc. Monica L. Brown, U.S. Army, is a combat medic from the 782nd Brigade Support Battalion, 4th Brigade Combat Team, 82nd Airborne Division, who did not take cover but went through gunfire to assist comrades. On March 20, 2008, she became the second female Silver Star recipient since World War II and then the Army removed her from combat. On April 25, 2007, her heroic act involved her opening the door of her Humvee in the Jani Khail district of Paktika Province in Afghanistan. Taliban fighters were shooting, but she did not take cover. She seized her medical bag and ran through gunfire toward soldiers in a burning vehicle. The Army reasoned the restrictions on women in combat barred her from such missions, but a platoon leader with Charlie Troop, 4th Squadron, 73rd Cavalry Regiment, whose men Brown saved, said there was no other medic and that she was doing everything the others were doing. Spc. Brown was born in Lake Jackson, Texas. In November 2005, she and her brother, Justin, joined the Army together, he joined the infantry and she enlisted as a medic.

They deployed to Afghanistan in 2007. Sgt. Lee Ann Hester, a military policewoman in Iraq, is the only other female Silver Star recipient in the past 60 years. The Silver Star is America's third highest combat medal awarded for heroic bravery.

Sources

Adair Aly. 2008. "Women in Combat: Should They Fight for Freedom?" Associated Content. May 1. www.associatedcontent.com (accessed January 16, 2010).

Tyson, Ann Scott. 2008. "Woman Gains Silver Star—and Removal from Combat: Case Shows Contradictions of Army Rules." Washington Post. May 1. www.washingtonpost.com (accessed January 16, 2010).

Major Kim Campbell, U.S. Air Force (June 6, 1975–)

Major (Maj.) Kim Campbell, U.S. Air Force, safely landed an A-10 Warthog hit by enemy fire in a close support mission over Baghdad, Iraq, on April 7, 2003. She was on a support mission to aid troops with the 3rd Infantry Division who were under attack. She was a captain at the time. Maj. Campbell had first deployed from the 75th Fighter Squadron at Pope Air Force Base, NC, then she became a part of the 332nd Air Expeditionary Wing. Prior to the aircraft being hit, it had gone through bad weather and a dust storm to reach the troops' location before they fired on enemy positions with the Warthog's 30 mm, seven-barrel Gatling gun and anti-tank missiles. When enemy fire hit the Warthog, it caused a loss of hydraulics, there were no brakes or steering. Maj. Campbell decided to change to manual inversion rather than risk capture by ejecting over Bagdad. Few pilots succeeded in a manual landing of a Warthog so badly damaged.

Maj. Campbell has had three deployments in support of Operations Enduring Freedom serving in Afghanistan and Operation Iraqi Freedom serving in Iraq. During her second deployment in 2003, she earned the Distinguished Flying Cross. She has been awarded the Air Medal with one Silver and two Bronze Oak Leaf Clusters (OLC) and the Aerial Achievement Medal with two Bronze OLCs. She has flown more than 400 hours in the A-10, including 120 combat hours during the Global War on Terror. Maj. Campbell was born in Honolulu, Hawaii. She graduated from the U.S. Air Force Academy in 1997. She ranked number one in military merit. She joined the Air Force in 1997.

Sources

Aircraft Resource Center. 2010. "Gulf War 2 Battle Damaged A-10." www.aircraftresourcecenter.com (accessed January 18, 2010).

Stephens Media. 2010. "Saluting American Valor." www.americanvalor.net (accessed January 18, 2010).

WIMSA. 2008. "Voices of Valor: Capt. Kim Campbell." www.womensmemorial.org (accessed January 18, 2010).

Colonel Eileen M. Collins, U.S. Air Force (Ret.) and Former NASA Astronaut (November 19, 1956–)

Colonel (Col.) Eileen Collins, U.S. Air Force (Ret.) is NASA's first female Space Shuttle pilot and commander. She is also a former Air Force flight instructor and test pilot. She was selected for the astronaut program while attending the Air Force Test Pilot School at Edwards Air Force Base, California, from which she graduated in 1990. She became an astronaut in 1991. She logged over 6,751 hours in 30 different types of aircraft. She retired from the Air Force in January 2005. Col. Collins flew on four Space Shuttle flights: the STS-63 Discovery from February 3 to 11, 1995, serving as a pilot, the STS-84 Atlantis from May 15 to 24, 1997, serving as a pilot, and served as the commander on STS-93 from July 22 to 27, 1999, and the STS-114 from July 26 to August 9, 2005. Col. Collins logged over 872 hours in space. She retired from NASA in May 2006.

Col. Collins was born in Elmira, New York. In 1974, Col. Collins graduated from Elmira Free Academy, Elmira, New York. In 1976, she earned an associate in science degree in mathematics and science from Corning Community College. In 1978 she received a B.A. degree in mathematics and economics from Syracuse University. In 1986, she graduated with an M.S. degree in operations research from Stanford University, and in 1989 she earned a M.A. degree in space systems management from Webster University.

Col. Collins was awarded honors that included the Defense Superior Service Medal, the Distinguished Flying Cross, the Defense Meritorious Service Medal, the Air Force Meritorious Service Medal with one oak leaf cluster, the Air Force Commendation Medal with one oak leaf cluster, the Armed Forces Expeditionary Medal for service in Grenada (Operation Urgent Fury, October 1983), the French Legion of Honor, the NASA Outstanding Leadership Medal, the NASA Space Flight Medals, the Free Spirit Award, and the National Space Trophy.

Source

NASA Advisory Council. 2009. Biography. March 18. www.nasa.gov (accessed February 6, 2010).

Brigadier General Rhonda Cornum, Ph.D., M.D., U.S. Army (1955–)

Brigadier General (Brig. Gen.) Rhonda Cornum is the Director of Comprehensive Soldier Fitness in the Army. She was commissioned into the Army in 1978. As an Army flight surgeon she became one of two American servicewomen taken prisoner in the 1991 Persian Gulf War against Iraq. Her experience demonstrates that female soldiers can serve in expanded roles in wartime. Gen. Cornum's helicopter was shot down in an effort to rescue a downed fighter pilot. Five of the eight crew members died. In her 1993 book, *She Went to War: The Rhonda Cornum Story,* she wrote about her eight days as a prisoner of war (POW). At the time of capture, she asked herself, whether it is life-threatening, disabling, or excruciating. She believed that if not, then it took on a fairly low level of significance. Gen. Cornum believes her experience should not be a reason for not assigning women to combat, but that they should be evaluated on their own abilities.

Gen. Cornum was born in Dayton, Ohio. She earned a Ph.D. in biochemistry and nutrition in 1978 from Cornell University. She earned an M.D. at the Uniformed Services University of the Health Sciences in 1986; and studied at the National War College in 2003.

In addition to senior flight surgeon wings, Gen. Cornum wears the airborne, air assault, and the expert field medic badges. Decorations include the Legion of Merit (with two oak leaf clusters), Distinguished Flying Cross, Bronze Star, Meritorious Service Medal (with four oak leaf clusters), Purple Heart, Air Medal, and POW Medal.

Sources

Brigadier General Rhonda L. Cornum, Ph.D., M.D., Director, Comprehensive Soldier Fitness. HQDA, DCS G-3/5/7. http://usacac.army.mil (accessed January 9, 2010).

Brigadier General Rhonda L. Cornum, Ph.D., M.D. as a Soldier and Physician. http://spotlight.vitals.com (accessed January 9, 2010).

Encyclopedia of World Biography. www.notablebiographies.com (accessed January 9, 2010).

Lieutenant Mary (Missy) L. Cummings, U.S. Navy (1966–)

Lieutenant (Lt.) Mary (Missy) L. Cummings, U.S. Navy, received her B.S. in Mathematics from the United States Naval Academy in 1988, her M.S. in space systems engineering from the Naval Postgraduate School in 1994, and her Ph.D. in systems engineering from the University of Virginia in 2003. As a naval officer and military pilot from 1988–1999, flying the A-4, F/A-18, and F-14 Tomcat, she was one of the Navy's first female fighter pilots. In 2010, she is an associate professor in the Aeronautics and Astronautics Department at the Massachusetts Institute of Technology and is the director of the Humans and Automation Laboratory (http://halab.mit.edu). Her previous teaching experience includes instructing for the U.S. Navy at Pennsylvania State University and as an assistant professor for the Virginia Tech Engineering Fundamentals Division. Her research interests include human supervisory control, human-unmanned vehicle interaction, bounded collaborative human-computer decision making, direct perception decision support, information complexity in displays, and the ethical and social impact of technology.

Lt. Cumming's book, *Hornet's Nest: The Experiences of One of the Navy's First Female Fighter Pilots*, is a clear, sometimes humorous, but always a riveting description of her experience as one of the first women combat aviators. Her book gives society valuable knowledge of her breaking ground in an area that previously was off-limits to women. Lt. Cummings describes her Naval Academy days and her service in the Philippines as well. She was born in Camp Zama, Japan.

Sources

Cummings, Mary L. (Missy). 2000. *Hornet's Nest: The Experiences of One of the Navy's First Female Fighter Pilots.* Bloomington, IN: Universe.com.

Elaine Donnelly (NA–)

Elaine Donnelly is the founder and president of the Center for Military Readiness (CMR), an independent public policy organization that specializes in military personnel issues. Since its beginning in 1993, "CMR advocates high, single standards in training, and sound priorities in military/social policies" (CMR 2001–2010, Bio). From 1984 to 1986, Mrs. Donnelly was a member of DACO-WITS. In 1992, she served on the Presidential Commission on the Assignment of Women in the Armed Forces. As a member of these bodies, she visited many military bases on fact-finding missions. In 1997, she became the first woman to receive the Admiral John Henry Towers award from the New York Naval Aviation Commandery. In 2002, she received the American Conservative Union's Ronald Reagan Award.

Mrs. Donnelly believes military women to be courageous and their accomplishments impressive, but that unsound policies should not be adopted that would encourage social problems affecting discipline, deployability, morale, and readiness. Mrs. Donnelly held the alternative view in the Presidential Commission and in 1993, she testified in congressional hearings reiterating her position not favoring women serving in combat. She attended Schoolcraft College and the University of Detroit.

Sources

Center for Military Readiness. 2009. "Combat Realities and Respect for Law." http://cmrlink.org (accessed February 3, 2010).

Center for Military Readiness. 2001–2010. "Elaine Donnelly's Bio." http://cmrlink.org (accessed February 1, 2010).

Donnelly, Elaine. 1993. Testimony. *Women in Combat: Hearing*. House Committee on Armed Services. Military Forces and Personnel Subcommittee, 103rd Congress, First Session, May 12, 61.

Major L. Tammy Duckworth, U.S. Army (March 12, 1968–)

Major (Maj.) L. Tammy Duckworth, U.S. Army, is an Iraq War veteran and former Army aviator. She served as an Assistant Operations Officer with the Unit 106th Aviation Regiment. She flew combat missions as a Black Hawk helicopter pilot. In 2004, north of Bagdad, Iraqi insurgents fired a rocket propelled grenade that struck the aircraft that she was copiloting. Her combat wounds caused her to lose both of her legs and damaged her right arm. Maj. Duckworth's awards include the Purple Heart, the Air Medal, and the Army Commendation Medal.

Since her recovery at Walter Reed, Maj. Duckworth has advocated for disability rights and veterans. She has testified before Congress regarding medical care and employment for veterans. In 2006, she ran for the U.S. House of Representatives and lost by less than 2 percent of the vote. In 2008, despite having two artificial legs and sometimes being in a wheelchair, she completed the Chicago marathon on a hand-cranked bicycle in 2 hours, 26 minutes, and 31 seconds.

From 2006 to 2008, Maj. Duckworth was the director of the Illinois Department of Veterans Affairs. She continues to serve in the Illinois Army National Guard. In 2009, she became the Assistant Secretary for Public and Intergovernmental Affairs for the U.S. Department of Veterans Affairs.

Born in Bangkok, Thailand, Maj. Duckworth earned a bachelor's degree from the University of Hawaii in 1989. She joined the Reserve Officers' Training Corps (ROTC) as a graduate student at George Washington University in 1990, and in 1992 she became a commissioned officer in the U.S. Army Reserve. She then went to flight school, and in 1996, she joined the Illinois National Guard. In 2004 she was enrolled in a Ph.D. program in political science at Northern Illinois University when she deployed to Iraq.

Sources

Duckworth, Tammy. 2006. Bio. www.duckworthforcongress.com (accessed January 20, 2010).

"L. Tammy Duckworth." 2010. Times Topics. People. *New York Times.* http://topics.nytimes.com (accessed January 20, 2010).

Shane III, Leo. 2005. "The Pedals Were Gone, and So Were My Legs." *Stars and Stripes.* June 14. www.stripes.com (accessed January 20, 2010).

U.S. Department of Veterans Affairs. 2009. Official Biography. www1.va.gov (accessed January 20, 2010).

General Ann E. Dunwoody, U.S. Army (1953–)

General (Gen.) Ann E. Dunwoody, U.S. Army, is the first woman to reach four star rank in the U.S. military. In 2008, the Senate confirmed her rank and assignment as commanding general, U.S. Army Materiel Command, headquartered at Fort Belvoir, Virginia. Prior to her recent appointment as deputy commanding general and chief of staff of Army Material Command (AMC), Gen. Dunwoody served as the first woman deputy chief of staff, G-4, United States Army in Washington, D.C.

In 1975, Gen. Dunwoody joined the Army after graduating from the State University of New York at Cortland. She served as a platoon leader with the 226th Maintenance Company, 100th Supply and Services Battalion, Fort Sill, Oklahoma. She remained in the Army for 33 years serving as the commander for the 5th Quartermaster Detachment, 66th Maintenance Battalion, 29th Area Support Group, Germany; the commander of the Division Support Command, 10th Mountain Division, Fort Drum, New York; and the commanding general, United States Army Combined Arms Support Command, Fort Lee, Virginia.

Born at Fort Belvoir, Virginia, Gen. Dunwoody earned an M.S. Degree in logistics management from the Florida Institute of Technology in 1988. She earned an M.S. in national resource strategy from the Industrial College of the Armed Forces in 1995.

She is the recipient of the Distinguished Service Medal, with oak leaf cluster; the Defense Superior Service Medal; the Legion of Merit, with two oak leaf clusters; the Defense Meritorious Service Medal; the Meritorious Service Medal, with five oak leaf clusters; and the Army Commendation Medal. The general has also earned the master parachutist badge and the parachutist rigger badge.

Sources

Hames, Jacqueline M. 2008. "Army Promotes First Woman to Four-Star General." U.S. Army. Nov 14. www.army.mil (accessed January 20, 2010).

U.S. Army. 2008. "Dunwoody Confirmed As First Female Four-Star." *Army News Service*. July 24. www.army.mil (accessed January 20, 2010).

Sergeant Theresa Lynn Flannery, U.S. Army (1978–)

Sergeant (Sgt.) Theresa Lynn Flannery, U.S. Army Reserve, was a driver to a deputy commander in Iraq with the 350th Civil Affairs Command. For her bravery in battle, she received the nation's fourth highest military honor, the Bronze Star with a "V" for valor, and a Purple Heart for receiving injury under fire. Her actions broke the ground combat barrier. She received enemy fire, returned fire, and treated her wounded comrades. Sgt. Flannery volunteered to go with a group of coalition military observers in Najaf. Nearly a million Shiite Muslims were participating in an annual religious pilgrimage. On April 4, 2004, insurgents attacked Sgt. Flannery's unit. Their goal was to kill or capture a member of U.S. Ambassador Paul Bremer's staff in Najaf. Sgt. Flannery jumped to the ground to take cover, fracturing her hand. For nearly 2 hours, she fired her rifle. She was the only woman in a group of about 20 Americans who with Spanish soldiers warded off the attack by about 1,000 insurgents. When Sgt. Flannery joined the military in 2000, she became a combat engineer and served in Germany and other places. She joined the Army Reserve after her enlistment ended.

Sources

Captain Barbara A. Wilson, USAF (Ret.). 2009. "Military Women Veterans." http://userpages.aug.com (accessed January 21, 2010).

"Kentucky Soldier Recommended for Bronze Star. 2004. *Army Times* (AP). April 30. www.armytimes.com (accessed January 21, 2010).

"Spec. Theresa Lynn Flannery." 2007. *Army Times*. In *America's North Shore Journal*. October 17. http://northshorejournal.org (accessed January 21, 2010).

Captain Dawn Halfaker, U.S. Army (Ret.) (July 26, 1979–)

Captain (Capt.) Dawn Halfaker, U.S. Army (Ret.), was a platoon leader and first lieutenant of the 293rd Military Police, 3rd Infantry Division. On a reconnaissance patrol in Baquba, Iraq, Diyala Province, on June 19, 2004, the enemy shot a rocket propelled grenade into their armored Humvee. Capt. Halfaker was badly injured, losing her right arm. Six days later she was one of five American military women at Walter Reed Hospital who had limbs lost from combat injuries in Iraq. She also suffered lung damage and five broken ribs from shrapnel. She was in a coma over a week and spent one year at the hospital. She earned a Purple Heart and Bronze Star. After retiring from the military, Capt. Halfaker served as a military liaison to the House Armed Services Committee. In 2005, she worked with the Defense Advanced Research Projects Agency. She served on the Veterans Affairs Committee for Operation Iraqi Freedom and/or Operation Enduring Freedom soldiers and families. In 2007, she became the Vice President of the Wounded Warrior Project. In 2009, the Secretary of Labor appointed her to the Advisory Committee on Veterans' Employment, Training, and Employer Outreach. Capt. Halfaker earned a B.S. degree from the United States Military Academy at West Point in 2001, and an M.S. in security studies from Georgetown University in Washington, D.C. She grew up in Rancho Bernardo, California.

Sources

American Wounded Heroes. 2005/2010. http://ultimatesacrificememorialsupportcenter.com (accessed January 22, 2010).

Halfaker Associates, Inc. 2010. "Dawn Halfaker: Chief Executive Officer." www.halfakerandassociates.com (accessed January 23, 2010).

Wounded Warrior Project. 2010. "Dawn Halfaker: Vice President, Board of Directors." www.woundedwarriorproject.org (accessed January 22, 2010).

Colonel Kelly Hamilton, U.S. Air Force (Ret.) (October 16, 1949–)

Colonel (Col.) Kelly Hamilton, U.S. Air Force (Ret.), was the senior woman pilot to fly in the first Gulf War, 1990–1991. In 1973, she joined the Air Force in Oakland, California, training as one of five women in the aircraft avionics maintenance career field. When the Air Force opened pilot training to women in 1976, she was one of 20 selected. During her career she flew T-37, T-38, and KC-135 aircraft and taught flying at the Air Force Academy. As a KC-135 commander, certified in combat operations, her main missions included providing global air refueling for fighters, bombers, transport and reconnaissance aircraft; which sometimes included going into high threat areas. After the Gulf War, Col. Hamilton served in Honolulu, Hawaii, as the Pacific Command's Chief of Southeast Asia Policy. Her final assignment, in 1997, was Assistant Director of Operations for Strategic Planning, Air Mobility Command, Scott Air Force Base, Illinois.

Col. Hamilton's honors include the Defense Superior Service Medal, Legion of Merit, Meritorious Service Medals, Aerial Achievement Medals, Commendation Medals, Achievement Medals, Combat Readiness Medals, Southwest Asia Service Medal for Kuwait and Saudi Arabia, National Defense Service Medals, Humanitarian Service Medal, and Kuwait Liberation Medal. Col. Hamilton was born in Scott Field, Illinois.

Source

Hamilton, Kelly. Interview by Rosemarie Skaine. E-mail, February 4, 2010.

Sergeant Leigh Ann Hester, U.S. Army (1982–)

Sergeant (Sgt.) Leigh Ann Hester of the 617th Military Police Company, a National Guard unit out of Richmond, Kentucky, was a military policewoman in Operation Iraqi Freedom in 2005 who responded to an insurgent ambush on a U.S. supply convoy. Anti-Iraqi fighters ambushed the convoy while Sgt. Hester's squad was shadowing it. Her squad cut off their escape route.

"Hester led her team through the "kill zone" and into a flanking position, where she assaulted a trench line with grenades and M203 grenade-launcher rounds" (Wood 2005). When she and her squad leader cleared two trenches, she killed three insurgents with her rifle. In all, 27 insurgents were dead, six were wounded, and one was captured, Sgt. Hester was awarded the Silver Star. She is the first female soldier since World War II to receive the medal. Her award is significant because it "is the first time in history that a woman has been decorated for direct actions against an enemy force" (Vaught 2008; WIMSA). Sgt. Hester is the recipient of the National Defense Service Medal, Global War on Terrorism Expeditionary Medal, and the Army Service Ribbon. She was born in Bowling Green, Kentucky.

Sources

Shane III, Leo. 2005. "Female Soldier Awarded Silver Star." *Stars and Stripes European ed*. June 17. www.military.com/ (accessed January 23, 2010).

Vaught, Wilma. In Military Service For America Memorial Foundation, Inc (WIMSA). 2008. "SGT Leigh Ann Hester US Army Silver Star Operation Iraqi Freedom. 2005." *Voices of Valor Women's History Month Kit*. www.womensmemorial.org (accessed January 23, 2010).

Wood, Sara. 2005. "Woman Soldier Receives Silver Star for Valor in Iraq." *American Forces Press Service*. DOD. June 16. www.defense.gov (accessed January 23, 2010).

Major General Jeanne M. Holm U.S. Air Force (Ret.) (June 23, 1921–February 15, 2010)

Major General (Maj. Gen.) Jeanne M. Holm USAF (Ret.) was the first female one-star general of the United States Air Force (1971) and the first female two-star general in the Air Force and Department of Defense (1973). She enlisted in the Army in 1943 and entered the Women's Army Air Corps in 1943. She began as an Army truck driver. She became a commissioned third officer.

When Gen. Holm served in World War II, she was assigned to the Women's Army Corps Training Center at Fort Oglethorpe, Georgia. She commanded a basic training company and a training regiment. At the end of the war, she commanded the 106th WAC Hospital Company at Newton D. Baker General Hospital, West

Virginia. She retired from active military duty in 1946. She attended Lewis and Clark College for two years. She returned in 1956 and earned a B.A. degree.

In October 1948 during the Berlin crisis, she was recalled to active duty with the Army. She served as a company commander at Camp Lee, Virginia. She served as a company commander within the Women's Army Corps Training Center. The following year she transferred to the Air Force and was sent to Erding Air Depot, Germany. There she served as assistant director of plans and operations for the 7200th Air Force Depot Wing, and later was War Plans Officer for the 85th Air Depot Wing. She was the first woman to attend the Air Command and Staff School, Maxwell Air Force Base, Alabama, in 1952.

Gen. Holm served in two conflicts, World War II and the Korean War. She served in a variety of personnel assignments, including director of Women in the Air Force from 1965 to 1973. She was an advocate for women's equality. In 1973 she was appointed as Secretary of the Air Force Personnel Council. She retired in 1975. Gen. Holm served three presidential administrations: special assistant on women for President Gerald Ford, policy consultant for President Jimmy Carter and first chairperson of the Veterans Administration's Committee on Women Veterans for President Ronald Reagan. She wrote two books on women in the military, *Women in the Military: An Unfinished Revolution* published in 1982 and revised in 1994. In 1998, she wrote *In Defense of a Nation: Servicewomen in World War II.*

General Holm was born in Portland, Oregon. Prior to entering military service, she was a professional silversmith. General Holm was a snow and water skier, a student of ancient history, scuba diver, and skipper of her own power cruiser.

Sources

Department of Defense. 2010. "Face of Defense: Military Community Loses Pioneer." American Forces Press Service. News. February 18, 2010. www.defense.gov (accessed July 20, 2010).

Jeanne Holm Collection (AFC/2001/001/4293), Veterans History Project, American Folklife Center, Library of Congress. www.google.com (accessed July 20, 2010).

Major General Jeanne M. Holm. 1973. (United States Air Force) (Biography). *U.S. Air Force Military Biographies*. 2004. *HighBeam Research*. Aug. 15. www.highbeam.com (accessed July 20, 2010).

Captain Kathleen Christine Horner, U.S. Marine Corps (November 16, 1988–)

Captain (Capt.) Kathleen Christine Horner, USMC, finished flight school in July 2004. She learned to fly the AH-1W Super Cobra attack helicopter at Marine Corps Base Camp Pendleton. She served two tours in Iraq. As a Cobra pilot, Capt. Horner's hand rests on the controls of a three-barrel 20 mm turreted cannon that sticks out from the aircraft's nose. Under both wings just behind the cockpit are rockets or missiles. In 2007, over Anbar Province, she unleashed fire power on the enemy to assist a Marine ground patrol taking fire. Capt. Horner was the president of her senior class and vice president of the Student Advisory at Park Center High School in Brooklyn Park, Minnesota. She was a National Honor Society member who majored in history. From high school she went to Dartmouth (class of 2000) where she was a varsity hockey player and a member of the Student Athletic Advisory Committee. She belonged to Kappa Kappa Gamma Fraternity for Women. She took part in a mentorship with the Minnesota Twins.

Sources

Dartmouth College. 2004. "Class of 2000." November/December. www.dartmouth2000.org (accessed February 7, 2010).

Henderson, Kristin. 2008. "Ready to Kill." *Washington Post Magazine*. February 24. www.washingtonpost.com (accessed January 24, 2010).

Women's Hockey. 1997–1998. "Katie Horner." Dartmouth Varsity Athletics. http://dartmouthsports.com (accessed February 7, 2010).

Rear Admiral Michelle Howard, U.S. Navy (April 30, 1960–)

Rear Admiral (Rear Adm.) Michelle Howard, U.S. Navy, a two-star admiral, commanded the U.S. 5th Fleet task forces, including CTF 151, that rescued the Merchant Marine captain who was held as a captive by the Somali pirates in early 2009. Admiral Howard was the first African American woman to command a Navy combat vessel, USS *Rushmore* (LSD 47) in 1999. Adm. Howard became the senior military assistant to the Secretary of the Navy from

2007 to 2009. In 2010, she serves as Commander, Expeditionary Strike Group 2. She was the Commander of Amphibious Squadron 7 from 2004 to 2005. She deployed with Expeditionary Strike Group 5. Operations included tsunami relief efforts in Indonesia and maritime security in the North Persian Gulf.

In 1978, Adm. Howard graduated from Gateway High School in Aurora, Colorado. She then graduated in one of the first classes to include women from the U.S. Naval Academy in 1982. She graduated from the Army's Command and General Staff College in 1998 with a master's degree in military arts and sciences. Her awards include Secretary of the Navy/Navy League Captain; Winifred Collins Award, 1987; Navy Commendation Medal (four awards); Navy Achievement Medal; National Defense Medal; Armed Forces Service Medal; NATO Medal; Kuwaiti Liberation Medal; and Saudi Arabia Defense Medal.

Sources

Answers.com. 2010. "Black Biography: Michelle Howard." www.answers .com (accessed January 25, 2010).

U.S. Naval Academy. 2009. "Pirates Feel the Might (Michelle J. Howard '82)." Alumni Association and Foundation, News Room April 20, https://www.usna.com (accessed January 25, 2010).

U.S. Navy. 2009. "Bio: Rear Admiral Michelle Howard, Commander, Expeditionary Strike Group 2." September 3. www.navy.mil/navydata/ bios (accessed January 25, 2010).

Lieutenant Kara Hultgreen, U.S. Navy (October 5, 1965–October 25, 1994)

Lieutenant (Lt.) Kara Hultgreen, the first female carrier-based Navy F-14 fighter pilot, died in a training exercise crash off the California coast on October 25, 1994. As she approached the USS *Abraham Lincoln*, the aircraft overshot the centerline. Lieutenant Hultgreen's attempted correction demonstrated a weakness in the F-14 engines in that they were old, unreliable, and should have been replaced. Some believed her flight training was compromised because of her gender. Official records indicate that she was qualified, and that no special exceptions were made.

The controversy surrounding her aircraft mishap reflected her personal battle to succeed where women had not previously had an opportunity to succeed, carrier aviation. The F-14A's engine problems serve as a reminder that history illustrates male aviators have been on the edge of the sword, lived and died as did Lt. Hultgreen and, as she did, have performed their missions. Ten male pilots from Lt. Hultgreen's squadron died in this aircraft before her appointment.

Standard practice in fatal mishaps requires that separate Judge Advocate General (JAG) and Naval Safety Center Mishap investigations are conducted. The JAG report cited mechanical malfunction as the primary cause, and this became the official Navy position to the public. The Mishap Investigation Report (MIR) came to a different conclusion and cited pilot error as the primary factor.

Commander Jay P. Yakeley, Carrier Group THREE, explained Lt. Hultgreen's narrow margin was dependent on four seconds that were critical to the outcome of the mishap, starting at time when the left engine stalled and overshooting occurred to ending time when the starboard engine is in afterburner, left wing down, excessive left yaw rate, angle of attack not advantageous. In the case of Lt. Hultgreen's mishap, the tasks at hand to correct the situation were reduced to time in terms of a very few seconds, and had ejection occurred just four-tenths of a second earlier, she might have survived.

Lt. Hultgreen was born in Greenwich, Connecticut, and was a graduate of Alamo Heights High School, where she played basketball and tennis. In 1987, she graduated from the University of Texas at Austin with a major in aerospace engineering. She then entered Aviation Officer Candidate School, Pensacola, Florida before ending up taking a year of training in the F-14 fighter at Miramar Naval Air Station in San Diego, California.

Sources

Accident Mishap Board. 1995. *F-14A Mishap Investigation Report* (*MIR*). March. www.panix.com (accessed January 14, 2010).

Arlington National Cemetery Web site. 2006. "Kara Spears Hultgreen." April 7. www.arlingtoncemetery.net (accessed February 7, 2010).

Skaine, Rosemarie. 1999. *Women at War: Gender Issues of Americans in Combat*. Jefferson, NC: McFarland & Co. Inc.

Yakeley, Cmdr. Jay B. 1995. Carrier Group THREE. Memo to Office of the JAG. February 19, 34–35. In Skaine, Rosemarie. 1999. *Women at War: Gender Issues of Americans in Combat*. Jefferson, NC: McFarland & Co. Inc., 39.

Specialist Shoshana Johnson, U.S. Army (Ret.) (January 18, 1973–)

Specialist (Spc.) Shoshana Johnson, U.S. Army, is the first African American female prisoner of war (POW), captured after the 507th Maintenance Company, 5/52 ADA BN, 11th ADA Brigade, Third Infantry Division, was ambushed at An Nasiriyah on March 23, 2003, during Operation Iraqi Freedom. Her company provided maintenance support to the 5th Battalion, 52nd Air Defense Artillery, based at Fort Bliss, Texas. Specialist Johnson was part of a convoy to Baghdad on Highway 1, Iraq's main north-south artery. Her convoy made a wrong turn and was alone and defenseless when the ambush occurred. She returned fire from under a truck, but her gun jammed. Three soldiers were captured including one other woman, Private (Pfc.) Jessica Dawn Lynch, who was at a different location. Nine soldiers died in the ambush. Before she was captured, Spc. Johnson suffered bullet wounds to both of her ankles from a gun fight. On April 13, 2003, the Marines rescued her. In 2010, Simon & Schuster published her book, *I'm Still Standing: From Captive U. S. Soldier to Free Citizen—My Journey Home.*

Specialist Johnson's awards include the U.S. Army's Service Ribbon, Army Commendation Ribbon, Good Conduct Medal, Bronze Star Medal, Purple Heart Medal, and the Prisoner of War Medal. Specialist Johnson served in the Army from 1998 to 2004 to earn tuition money to enroll at a culinary arts school. She attended the University of Texas at El Paso before joining the military. She was born in Panama. In 1991, she was in the JROTC program at Andress High School in El Paso.

Sources

Brief Biographies. 2010. "Shoshana Johnson Biography." *Encyclopedia.* http://biography.jrank.org (accessed January 25, 2010).

Indiana University Northwest. 2006. "Mommy has to Go to War: First African American Female POW to Speak." Office of Marketing and Communications. January 26. www.iun.edu (accessed January 25, 2010).

U.S. Army Quartermaster Corps. "Quartermaster Corps in the Media: Shoshana Johnson." *Encyclopedia.* www.absoluteastronomy.co. (accessed January 25, 2010).

First Lieutenant Cheryl Lamoureux, U.S. Air Force (1972 Circa–)

First Lieutenant (1st Lt.) Cheryl Lamoureux, U.S. Air Force, served with the 20th Bomber Squadron of the 2nd Bomber Wing at Barksdale Air Force Base, Louisiana. She was the first woman to fly on a B-52 combat mission, breaking the fixed-wing combat barrier. In 1998, Iraq's repeated refusal to cooperate with UN weapons inspectors brought about the strike missions in Operation Desert Fox, the four-day air war against Iraq. It was the first time women dropped bombs and fired missiles in combat. In a 14-hour mission, Lieutenant Lamoureux's plane launched eight cruise missiles over the Persian Gulf toward targets in Baghdad from the U.S. base on the Indian Ocean island of Diego Garcia.

Sources

Times-Picayune. 1999. In "1st Lt. Cheryl Lamoureux." The Pioneers. January 4. www.ctie.monash.edu.au (accessed January 30, 2010).

Sisk, Richard. 1998. "Five Female Pilots Launch First Aerial Combat Missions Women Fly into History." *New York Daily News*. Washington Bureau. December 22. www.nydailynews.com (accessed January 30, 2010).

Dr. Peter A. Lillback, President, Westminster Theological Seminary (June 9, 1952–)

Dr. Peter A. Lillback is the president of Westminster Theological Seminary, Glenside, Pennsylvania, since 1995. He is a professor of historical theology. He has served at Westminster since 1986. He has authored books and many articles. Dr. Lillback believes that, while men and women have equal rights, each has a unique, different mission ordained by the Creator: the male, to lead and protect the woman and the woman, to give birth to and nurture the next generation (Lillback 2009). He opposes women in combat and women in support positions in combat zones.

From 1982, Dr. Lillback served in pastoral ministry in Delaware and Pennsylvania, including Proclamation Presbyterian Church. From 1995 to 1999; Dr. Lillback was a professor at the Philadelphia Theological Seminary. Since 1999, he has been the president of The Providence Forum. He served as chairman of the Ad Interim Study Committee on Women in the Military for the General Assembly Actions and Position Papers of the Presbyterian Church in America (PCA 2002). Dr. Lillback graduated with a B.A. from Cedarville College in 1974, a Th.M. from Dallas Theological Seminary in 1978, and a Ph.D. from Westminster Theological Seminary in 1985. He was born in Painesville, Ohio.

Sources

Lillback, Dr. Peter A 2007/2008. Faculty Profile. Westminster Theological Seminary. www.wts.edu (accessed February 4, 2010).

Lillback, Dr. Peter A. Interview by Rosemarie Skaine. Tape recording by telephone. November 7, 2009.

Presbyterian Church in America (PCA). 2002. *Historical Center. General Assembly Actions and Position Papers*. Ad Interim Study Committee on Women in the Military. www.pcahistory.org (accessed November 27, 2009).

Captain Rosemary Bryant Mariner, U.S. Navy (Ret.) (April 2, 1953–)

Captain (Capt.) Rosemary Bryant Mariner, U.S. Navy (Ret.), was among the first of eight women to earn aviator gold wings in 1974. She became the first woman naval aviator to fly tactical jet aircraft, the A-4E Skyhawk, in 1975 and the frontline attack aircraft, A-7E Corsair II, in 1976. She was first to command an operational squadron. During Desert Storm she commanded the Tactical Electronic Warfare Squadron 34. In 24 years of military service, Capt. Mariner logged over 3,500 flight hours in 15 different aircraft and made 17 carrier landings.

Capt. Mariner retired from the National War College in 1997 as the Chairman of the Joint Chiefs of Staff Professor of Military Studies. In 2010, she is on the staff at the Center for the Study of

War and Society in the Department of History at the University of Tennessee at Knoxville.

A long time advocate of women serving in combat, Capt. Mariner believes that the services should match people with jobs. "A soldier is a soldier" is Capt. Mariner's philosophy. She explains that "it is the common identity of being a soldier first that transcends the differences of gender and unites highly competitive people to serve under a common purpose. Participation based upon individual ability also insures the strongest possible national defense . . . the support of all the people is fundamental to victory" (Mariner 1993–1994, 61, in Skaine 1999, 11).

Capt. Mariner grew up in San Diego, California. She began flying at 15 and washed airplanes to pay for flight time. At 17, she earned a private pilot license. In 1970, she entered Purdue University as a geophysics major. The next spring, she was the first woman to enter their aviation degree program. Within a year, Mariner earned her commercial license with instrument and multiengine ratings and was a certified flight instructor.

Sources

Holden, Henry M. with Captain Lori Griffith. 1991. *Ladybirds—The Untold Story of Women Pilots in America*. Black Hawk Publishing Co. In Women in Aviation Resource Center. "Rosemary Mariner." www.women-in-aviation.com (accessed February 6, 2010).

Holm, Maj. Gen. Jeanne, USAF (Ret.). 1992. *Women in the Military: An Unfinished Revolution*. Rev. ed. Novato, CA: Presidio.

Mariner, Rosemary Bryant. 1993–1994. "A Soldier Is a Soldier," *Joint Force Quarterly*, 3, Winter, 54–61. In Skaine, Rosemarie. 1999. *Women at War: Gender Issues of Americans in Combat*. Jefferson, NC: McFarland & Co.

University of Tennessee. 2006. *Rosemary Bryant Mariner. Study of War and Society Personnel*. https://my.tennessee.edu/portal/ (accessed February 6, 2010).

Sergeant April Pashley, U.S. Army Reserves (1983–)

Sergeant (Sgt.) April Pashley, U.S. Army Reserves, from Egg Harbor Township, New Jersey, was the first woman to receive the Army's new Combat Action Badge for her bravery in 2005 during Operation Iraqi Freedom. Sergeant Pashley served with the Guard/Reserve unit, 404th Civil Affairs Battalion (Special Operations), Fort Dix, New Jersey, as a Team Sergeant for a Civil Affairs Team. In 2003, she was in the first wave of soldiers deployed to Iraq in 2003. In 2005, Sgt. Pashley was on guard duty on the rooftop of a building housing Coalition Forces when armed insurgents attacked using 106 mm rockets. She returned fire without hesitation as rounds landed within 100–150 meters of her position. Sergeant Pashley awards include: Army Commendation Medal, Armed Forces Reserve Medal with Mobilization Appurtenance, National Defense Service Medal, Global War on Terrorism Expeditionary Medal, and the Global War on Terrorism Service Medal.

Sources

Boujnida, Cheryl. 2005. "Soldiers Receive Combat Action Badge." *The Signal*. Army News Service. July 8. www.gordon.army.mil (accessed January 27, 2010).

U.S. Army, Combat Action Badge. "Soldiers Biographies." SGT April Pashley—Army Reserves. www.army.mil (accessed January 27, 2010).

Major Lillian Pfluke, U.S. Army (Ret.) (February 21, 1959–)

Major (Maj.) Lillian Pfluke, U.S. Army (Ret.), originally from Palo Alto, California, served from 1976 to 1995. She is a member of the first class of women to graduate from the United States Military Academy at West Point in 1980. She majored in weapons systems engineering, and graduated first in her class in physical education. Upon leaving West Point, she wanted to serve in the infantry, but her request for an exception to the combat exclusion policy was denied by the Secretary of the Army. Instead, she served in the Ordnance Corps, but remained an outspoken supporter of combat roles for women through media appearance and by writing numerous articles and opinion pieces. In 1989, Maj. Pfluke received an M.S. degree in mechanical engineering from George Washington University.

In 1992, Maj. Pfluke testified before the Presidential Commission that her attitudes, matured and refined by experience, and her desire to serve in the infantry were stronger than ever, as was her conviction that that is where her talents could best be utilized. She testified that she was the current national military triathlon champion, two-time national military cycling champion, two-time European interservice ski champion. She earned a varsity letter in ski jumping on the men's ski team at West Point and captained the women's lacrosse team. She played rugby. She achieved a maximum score on every PT test taken in 12 years of service. She retired in 1995 when no further progress had been made on opening combat roles to women.

In 2008, Maj. Pfluke founded the nonprofit organization American War Memorials Overseas, Inc., which documents, promotes, and preserves America's overseas wartime (uswarmemorials .org). Her passion is bicycle racing and she is the current Masters World Hour Record holder at 41.2397 kms. She lives in Paris, France, with her husband and two sons.

Sources

Pfluke Maj. Lillian A. 1992. U.S. Army, Testimony, Presidential Commission on the Assignment of Women in the Armed Forces. Sept. 12. Washington, D.C. Referred to in *Report to the President, Women in Combat: Presidential Commission on the Assignment of Women in the Armed Forces* 1993. Washington: Brassey's. Appendices F-18.

Pfluke Maj. Lillian A. 2004. "The Best Soldier for the Job: A Personal Perspective." *Women in the Military.* James Haley, ed. San Diego: Greenhaven Press.

Pfluke Maj. Lillian A. 2010. "Profile." Facebook. www.facebook.com/ wildwoman (accessed February 6, 2010).

Pfluke Maj. Lillian A. 2010. "Profile." Linkedin www.linkedin.com/pub/ lillian-pfluke/5/a20/6b3 (accessed February 6, 2010).

Private Lori Piestewa, U.S. Army (December 14, 1980–March 23, 2003)

Private (Pfc.) Lori Piestewa, U.S. Army, was the first American woman killed in Operation Iraqi Freedom and the first Native American woman to die in combat while serving with the U.S. military. She was a member of Fort Bliss' 507th Maintenance Company. The unit conducted repairs and other support services for the 5-52 Battalion of the 11th Air Defense, consisting of five Patriot missile batteries. In the Middle East, the company was attached to 3rd Infantry Division.

Iraqi military forces and irregulars ambushed an 18 vehicle convoy near Nasiriyah, Iraq, on March 20, 2003. Private Piestewa was killed. She was the driver in one of the vehicles in Group 3 of the convoy. Two other women who were taken as prisoners of war were in this convoy. Private Jessica Lynch was a passenger in the rear of Pfc. Piestewa's vehicle, and Specialist Shoshana Johnson was a passenger in a different vehicle of the same convoy. The convoy missed a turn and were ordered to turn around. One of the vehicles was then hit by fire and crashed at a high rate of speed into the rear of a stopped tractor-trailer, still occupied by Spc. Johnson and another soldier. Private Piestewa survived, but was seriously injured and died in captivity. The U.S. Army said the error had tragic results because it placed the soldiers in a torrent of fire from an adaptive enemy employing asymmetrical tactics.

The Army awarded Pfc. Piestewa the Purple Heart and Prisoner of War Medal, and posthumously promoted her to specialist. Private Piestewa was a single mother raising a 4-year-old boy and a 3-year-old girl, enlisted in the Army in 2001, and had served as a commanding officer of Junior ROTC in high school. She was born and raised in Tuba City, Arizona.

Sources

Militarycity.com. "Army Pfc. Lori Ann Piestewa." *AP*. www.militarycity .com (accessed January 27, 2010).

U.S. Army. "Attack on the 507th Maintenance Company 23 March 2003 An Nasiriyah, Iraq." Executive Summary. www.army.mil/features (accessed January 28, 2010).

Command Sergeant Major Cynthia A. Pritchett, U.S. Army (May 11, 1955–)

Command Sergeant Major (Com. Sgt. Maj.) Cynthia A. Pritchett, U.S. Army, served two years (2004 to 2006) in Afghanistan as Combined Forces Command Afghanistan's Command Sergeant Major, the Army's first and only female to ever serve in such a position for a four-star combatant commander. She led over 27,000 coalition forces in this position. After that, she was assigned to the United

States Central Command (USCENTCOM). In March 2010, she retired. When Com. Sgt. Maj. Pritchett entered the service on July 2, 1973, it was in the Women's Army Corps. She never dreamed that she would serve as the command sergeant major of a subunified command during wartime.

Com. Sgt. Maj. Pritchett's duty assignments over the years have included: supply specialist; drill sergeant; platoon sergeant; Commandant, Basic Leadership Course, 1st Corps Support Command, Fort Bragg, North Carolina; Instructor, U.S. Army Sergeants Major Academy, Battalion Command Sergeant Major, 561st Corps Support Battalion, Fort Campbell, Kentucky and Mogadishu, Somalia; Command Sergeant Major Combined Arms Center Fort Leavenworth, Fort Leavenworth, Kansas and Command Sergeant Major Combined Forces Command, Afghanistan.

Com. Sgt. Maj. Pritchett has earned many decorations and awards, including the Defense Superior Service Medal, three awards of the Legion of Merit, the Bronze Star Medal, three awards of the Meritorious Service Medal, five awards of the Army Commendation Medal, two awards of the Army Achievement Medal, the Armed Forces Expeditionary Medal, the United Nations Medal (Somalia), the Afghanistan Campaign Medal, and Drill Sergeant and Army Recruiter Badges.

Com. Sgt. Maj. Pritchett was born in Concord, New Hampshire. Later, she attended Excelsior College, where she took courses in liberal arts with a concentration in homeland security.

Sources

"Cynthia A. Pritchett's Biography." 2007–2010. *Who's Who*. Cambridge University. www.cambridgewhoswho.com (accessed February 10, 2010).

Obermeyer, Jessica. 2008. "Ground-Breaking Senior NCO Shares Her Experiences." November 3. www.army.mil (accessed January 28, 2010).

U.S. Army. "Command Sergeant Major Cynthia A. Pritchett." Accessions Newsroom. www.armyaccessionsnewsroom.com (accessed January 27, 2010).

Phyllis Schlafly (August 15, 1924–)

Phyllis Schlafly has been a national leader of the conservative movement since she wrote her 1964 book, *A Choice Not An Echo*. She believes that military women serve admirably, but they should not be assigned to military combat or to combat support where risk of capture is built in. In 1972, Mrs. Schlafly became a leader of the profamily movement, and started the national volunteer organization Eagle Forum. Over a period of 10 years, she led the movement to victory in its goal of helping to defeat the Equal Rights Amendment. The *Ladies' Home Journal* named her one of the 100 most important women of the twentieth century, 1977–1990. The World Almanac named her one of the 25 Most Influential Women in America during the years 1978–1985. In 2003, she published her book, *Feminist Fantasies*. Mrs. Schlafly was born in Saint Louis, Missouri. She is an attorney who is licensed to practice law in Illinois, Missouri, the District of Columbia, and before the U.S. Supreme Court. Mrs. Schlafly is a 1944 Phi Beta Kappa A.B. graduate of Washington University, St. Louis. She earned an M.S. degree in government from Radcliffe College, in Cambridge, Massachusetts, in 1945. She earned her J.D. from Washington University Law School, St. Louis, in 1978. In 2008, Washington University awarded her an honorary Doctor of Humane Letters.

Sources

"Phyllis Schlafly." *Eagle Forum.* www.eagleforum.org (accessed February 3, 2010).

"Schlafly, Phyllis." 1995. *Microsoft(R) Encarta.* Microsoft Corporation. In *Distinguished Women of Past and Present.* www.distinguishedwomen.com (accessed February 10, 2010).

Schlafly, Phyllis. 2003. "Women Should not Serve in Military Combat." Women in Combat. Womanhood. *Bible Research.* www.bible -researcher.com/women (accessed February 3, 2010).

Corporal Ramona M. Valdez, U.S. Marine Corps (June 26, 1984–June 23, 2005)

Corporal (Cpl.) Ramona M. Valdez, U.S. Marine Corps, was killed in action by a suicide bomber, at Camp Fallujah, Iraq in 2005. She was traveling in a convoy when a suicide, vehicle-borne, improvised explosive device attack occurred. She was assigned to Headquarters Battalion, 2nd Marine Division, II Marine Expeditionary Force, Camp LeJeune, North Carolina. In 2007, the Marine

Corps dedicated its new II MEF Communications Training Center at the Marine Corps Base Camp LeJeune, North Carolina, as the "Valdez Training Facility." Cpl. Valdez had served over three and a half years, from January 15, 2002, to June 23, 2005. After recruit training, she participated in Marine Combat Training. In 2003, she graduated from the Marine Corps Electronics Communications School in Twentynine Palms, California. She then was transferred to Camp LeJeune. She served as a field radio operator until her assignment in Operation Iraqi Freedom in 2005.

Cpl. Valdez's duties included providing communications support to help make certain that Iraq elections went well. Later, she and other servicewomen became a part of the Female Search Force to search Iraqi women and children for explosive devices at checkpoints. The United States created the all-female search forces to alleviate Iraqi concerns that male soldiers might search Islamic women, which would be contrary to their cultural customs. The Female Search Force's truck became an inferno at the end of the day of a checkpoint mission. Cpl. Valdez and Lt. Cpl. Holly Charette, also a member of the Search Force, were the first two women Marines killed in Iraq. Cpl. Valdez's awards include: the Purple Heart, Navy Achievement Medal, and Marine Corps Good Conduct Medal with Oak Leaf Cluster. She was born in the Dominican Republic, but joined her family in the Bronx, New York City, at the age of six.

Sources

Lee, Jennifer 8. 2005. "Out of the Bronx, to Iraq, and Never to Come Home." *New York Times*. June 29. http://topics.nytimes.com (accessed February 10, 2010).

WIMSA. "CPL Ramona M. Valdez, USMC." Education. www .womensmemorial.org (accessed January 30, 2010).

WIMSA. 2008. "Voices of Valor Cpl Ramona M. Valdez." www .womensmemorial.org (accessed January 30, 2010).

Brigadier General Wilma L. Vaught, USAF (Ret.) (March 15, 1930–)

Brigadier General (Brig. Gen.) Wilma L. Vaught, USAF (Ret.) is the president of the board of directors of the Women In Military Service For America Memorial Foundation, Inc. in Arlington,

Virginia. Under her leadership, the nonprofit foundation built and operates the $22.5 million Memorial. The Women's Memorial is the nation's only major memorial to pay tribute to the over 2.5 million women who have served in the nation's defense, beginning with the American Revolution.

Gen. Vaught's military career spans nearly 29 years. She served in the United States and overseas, including Vietnam and Spain. She is one of the nation's most highly decorated military women. In 1980, she became the first woman and remained for nearly 22 years the only woman promoted to brigadier general from the comptroller field.

Gen. Vaught served as chairperson of the NATO Women in the Allied Forces Committee from 1983 to 1985 and was the senior woman military representative to the DACOWITS from 1982 to 1985.

Gen. Vaught's distinctive achievements include being the first woman to head a board of directors of a major credit union (1976–1982); the first to command a unit receiving the Joint Meritorious Unit Award, which is the nation's highest peacetime unit award (1985); and the first to deploy with a Strategic Air Command bombardment wing on an operational deployment (1966–1967). In 2008, the General Federation of Women's Clubs recognized General Vaught as their History Month Honoree. In 2010, the U.S. Army Women's Foundation inducted her into their Hall of Fame.

Her numerous military decorations and awards include the Defense and Air Force Distinguished Service Medals, the Air Force Legion of Merit, the Bronze Star Medal, the Meritorious Service Medal, the Joint Service Commendation Medal, the Air Force Commendation Medal with Oak Leaf Cluster, the Joint Meritorious Unit Award, the Vietnam Service Medal with four service stars, the Republic of Vietnam Gallantry Cross with palm, the Republic of Vietnam Campaign Medal, the Legion of Honor Bronze Medallion Award (2003), the Chapel of Four Chaplains, and the U.S. Air Force Woman of Distinction Merit Award (2007).

General Vaught is a native of Scottland, Illinois. She earned a B.S. degree from the University of Illinois, Champaign-Urbana in 1952; an M.B.A. from the University of Alabama, Tuscaloosa; and an Honorary Doctorate of Public Affairs from Columbia College, South Carolina. She is the first Air Force woman graduate of the Industrial College of the Armed Forces.

Source

Biographies: Women's Memorial, and U.S. Air Force.

Lieutenant (Lt.) Kendra Williams, U.S. Navy (July 22, 1972–)

Lieutenant (Lt.) Kendra Williams, U.S. Navy, an F/A-18 pilot, is recognized as the first female pilot to launch missiles in combat. She served in Operation Desert Fox in 1998 in Iraq from the USS *Enterprise* in the Arabian Gulf. Lieutenant Williams flew in the first wave of strikes which consisted of 30 fighter aircraft. The mission lasted two hours.

A 1994 graduate of the Naval Academy, Lt. Williams was among the first group of women allowed to train for fighter duty. She graduated from jet training at the Naval Air Station in Kingsville, Texas, in 1997.

Sources

"Female Pilots Dropped Bombs in Iraq Mission." 1998. Los Angeles Times. December 23. http://articles.latimes.com (accessed January 31, 2010).

Cava, Marco R. della. 1998. "Alaskan Is First Female Pilot in Combat." *USA Today*. In *The Pioneers*. 1999–2002. www.ctie.monash.edu.au (accessed January 31, 2010).

U.S. Navy. Personnel Command. 2008. "History and Firsts." June 13. www.npc.navy.mil.

Captain Elizabeth (Betsy) G. Wylie, U.S. Navy (Ret.) (March 4, 1939–)

In the Vietnam War, 7,000 women served and eight died in the line of duty, one died from hostile fire. Captain (Capt.) Elizabeth (Betsy) G. Wylie served in this war and became the first female unrestricted line officer (URL) assigned to Vietnam. She is the first woman to serve in the position: as Commanding Officer of a Military Sealift Command Office (1978–1980) in Seattle, Washington; as Commander Military Sealift Command Area Commander

(1983–1986) in Bayonne, New Jersey; as Commander Military Sealift Command Atlantic; and as Dean of Academics at the Naval War College (1988–1991). She served on the staff of the Joint Chiefs of Staff in Washington, D.C., and participated in the J5 Strategic Arms Limitation Talks (SALT) that took place from 1977 to 1979 and in the Law of the Sea Talks from 1975 to 1978.

Capt. Wylie served in the Navy from June 1961 to September 1991. She received many decorations and awards. She is a five time recipient of The Legion of Merit, 1980, 1983, 1986, 1988, and 1991. She received the Defense Meritorious Medal 1978, the Meritorious Service Medal, the Navy Commendation Medal 1968, the Navy Achievement Medal 1971, and the National Defense Service Medal 1961. From 1967 to 1968, Capt. Wylie received the following Vietnam campaign honors: the Republic Of Vietnam Service Medal, the Vietnam Service Medal, the Navy Unit Commendation Ribbon, and the Vietnam Campaign Ribbon. Overseeing and acquiring accreditation for the masters' degree program for the Naval War College Wylie considers a distinctive achievement. The program was initiated in 1988, and was completed and started awarding degrees in 1991.

Capt. Wylie was born in San Diego, California. She earned a B.A. in history and philosophy from Dickinson College in Carlisle, Pennsylvania, in 1961. The Navy sent her to graduate school at The Fletcher School of Law and Diplomacy in Medford, Massachusetts, where she earned a masters degree, a M.A. degree in law and diplomacy, and a Ph.D. in International Relations, graduating in 1975.

Service in the Navy is Capt. Wylie's heritage. Her father served from 1932 to 1974. Her brother served for about 25 years as a JAG officer. Wylie states that she joined the Navy because the pay was better than that she was offered to teach history.

Source

Wylie, Elizabeth (Betsy) G. Interview by Rosemarie Skaine. Telephone and e-mail, December 20, 2009.

6

Data and Documents

This chapter presents data primarily from government sources that indicate demographic characteristics of the United States military. Information pertaining to emotional health and the issues of sexual harassment and assault are addressed. This data supplements the discussions in Chapters 1 and 2. One set of data is a composite listing of the requirements to earn the medals awarded to service members whose biographies appear in Chapter 5. The second part of the chapter contains documents or relevant parts of them. These selections illustrate the legal evolution of women in combat. They include the Risk Rule policy and combat exclusion law and policy. The Direct Combat Probability Code system is demonstrated. A section is given to documents that guide actions in civilian and military sectors, the Constitutional powers of Congress and the executive branch and the Soldier's Creed. Testimony for and against women serving in combat is provided. The Don't Ask, Don't Tell law as it will stand when repealed is included.

Data Overview of the Women in the Military

Who are the active duty women service members and how do they serve? These are some of the questions the *White House Project Report: Benchmarking Women's Leadership* helps answer. For example, active duty service members numbered 1.4 million as of September 2008. Women represent 14.3 percent of the

179

forces. Data in this report represents the Army, Navy, Marine Corps and Air Force (WH Project 2009, 66). The project's results are demonstrated in Figures 6.1 through 6.7. In 2010, each branch of the military reports its individual data that demonstrates the division's demographics, how women serve, and assignments closed to women. The services' results are demonstrated in Tables 6.1 through 6.4.

FIGURE 6.1
Active Duty Military: 1.4 Million People

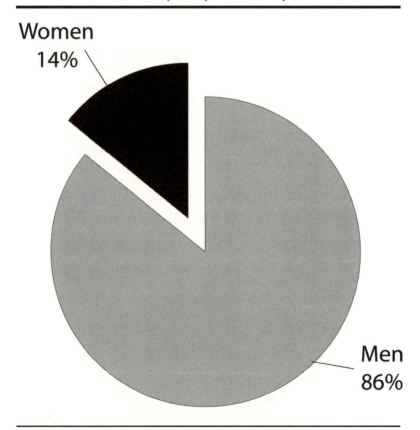

Source: White House Project, 2009, "The Status of Women in Leadership in Individual Sectors: Military." *Report: Benchmarking Women's Leadership,* November, 66, www.thewhitehouseproject.org (accessed May 23, 2010).

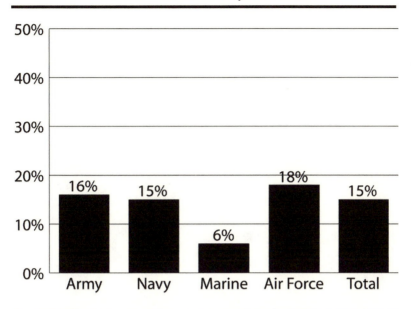

FIGURE 6.2
Women as Percent of Officers by Service Branch

Source: White House Project, 2009, "The Status of Women in Leadership in Individual Sectors: Military," *Report: Benchmarking Women's Leadership,* November, 67, www.thewhitehouseproject.org (accessed May 23, 2010).

FIGURE 6.3
Women as Percent of Enlisted Personnel by Service Branch

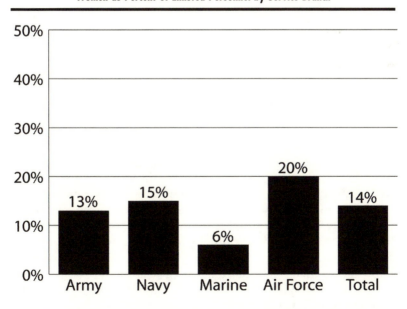

Source: White House Project, 2009, "The Status of Women in Leadership in Individual Sectors: Military," *Report: Benchmarking Women's Leadership,* November, 67, www.thewhitehouseproject.org (accessed May 23, 2010).

FIGURE 6.4
Women Enlisted Personnel as Percent of Total Enlisted Personnel

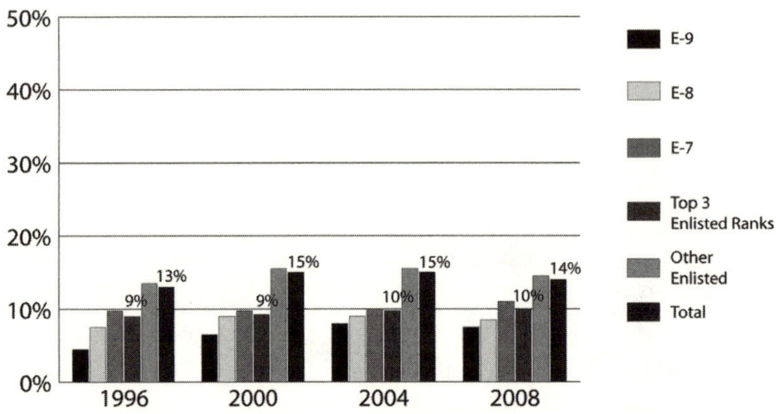

Source: White House Project, 2009, "The Status of Women in Leadership in Individual Sectors: Military," *Report: Benchmarking Women's Leadership,* November, 68, www.thewhitehouseproject.org (accessed May 23, 2010).

Women play an important role in the military of 2010. Their presence makes total military readiness possible. One way to get a sense of women's contributions is to examine their strength in numbers, their level of leadership as officers, and where they serve as enlisted personnel. Women represent 15 percent of all officers and 14 percent of all enlisted personnel.

A more detailed examination of enlisted personnel and women officers provides a picture of women's presence in the military. The graph below (Figure 6.4) shows that the total enlisted personnel declined by 5 percent overall between 1996 and 2008, but the number of enlisted women dropped by less than 1 percent. The top three grades of enlisted personnel, E-7, E-8, and E-9 are ranks achieved through time and merit. The number in these grades declined by 8 percent, but, the number of women in these grades increased in absolute numbers by 4 percent. Women represent 10 percent of the top three enlisted grades, compared with 9 percent in 1996. Between 1996 and 2008, the number of enlisted women decreased by 1.5 percent, or 2,603, but in the top three enlisted grades, the number increased by 3.8 percent, or 904 women.

Between 1996 and 2008, the total number of officers declined by 4 percent, but the number of female officers increased by

FIGURE 6.5
Women Officers as Percent of Total Officers

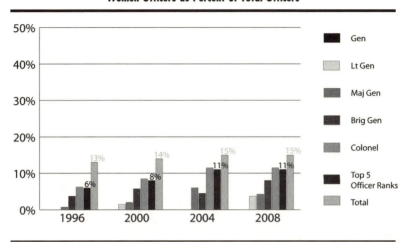

Source: White House Project, 2009, "The Status of Women in Leadership in Individual Sectors: Military," *Report: Benchmarking Women's Leadership,* November, 69, www.thewhitehouseproject.org (accessed May 23, 2010).

FIGURE 6.6
Enlisted Women by Race

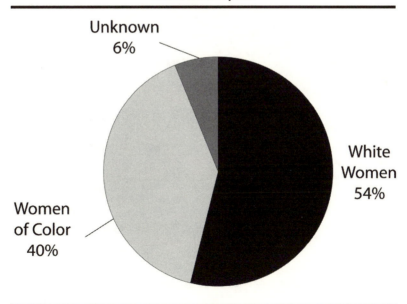

Source: White House Project, 2009, "The Status of Women in Leadership in Individual Sectors: Military," *Report: Benchmarking Women's Leadership,* November, 71, www.thewhitehouseproject.org (accessed May 23, 2010).

10 percent. Women increased their numbers in the top five officer ranks from 6 percent to 11 percent, but the total number of female officers in these ranks remained the same. Since a set amount of time is required in a previous rank for all service members to advance, an increase will occur in the numbers of women in the top levels of the military officer ranks in the future.

Among active duty enlisted service members, 29 percent of men identify themselves as nonwhite compared with 46 percent of women. Among officers, 18 percent of male officers compared with 32 percent of female officers identify themselves as non-white.

In 2010, two years after the White House *Benchmark* project gathered its data, the service branches report data in Tables 6.1 through 6.4. The Air Force demographics and positions that are open and closed as of March 31, 2010, are presented in Table 6.1.

The most controversy surrounds whether or not women should be assigned to direct ground combat. All services have a

FIGURE 6.7
Female Officers by Race

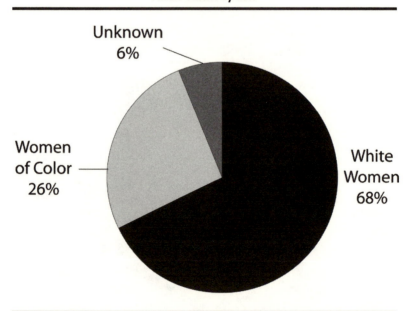

Source: White House Project, 2009, "The Status of Women in Leadership in Individual Sectors: Military," *Report: Benchmarking Women's Leadership,* November, 71, www.thewhitehouseproject.org (accessed May 23, 2010).

TABLE 6.1
Air Force Demographics and Positions Open and Closed to Women, March 31, 2010

| | Total Active Duty Force | | | |
	Female	Male	Total	Percent Female
Total	64,199	267,287	331,486	19.4

Ways Air Force Women Serve

Active Duty Officers
- 56.6 percent of the female officers are line officers; 43 percent are nonline
- 85.1 percent of the male officers are line officers; 15 percent are nonline

Women first entered pilot training in 1976, navigator training in 1977, and fighter pilot training in 1993. In 2010, women make up the following proportion in these categories.
- Pilots number 643 (4.4%)
- Navigators 283 (6.3%)
- Air battle managers 176 (12.2%)

92% of specialties are open to women, which presents no limitation for promotion.

Personnel Assignment Policy*

When units engage in ground combat, the DoD policy guiding the assignment of women is in effect.

Closed to Women*

Combat control
Pararescue

*White House Project, 2009, *White House Project Report: Benchmarking Women's Leadership*, Military, 70, November. www.thewhitehouseproject.org/ (accessed July 7, 2010).
Note: Number of Women in Occupational Fields not available.
Sources: Air Force Personnel Center, 2010, Air Force Demographics, U.S. Air Force, Quarterly Snapshot, March 31, www.afpc.randolph.af.mil (accessed July 19, 2010).

percentage of personnel dedicated to direct ground combat. Nowhere is the percentage as large as it is in the Army and the Marine Corps. The Army demographics and in what positions women do and do not serve are illustrated in Table 6.2.

Although there has been no change in the Army assignment policy since 1994, "since Desert Storm, there have been two significant policy shifts affecting the types of positions and units where women can serve. These policy shifts resulted in approximately 30,000 positions being opened to women. Today's woman soldier, regardless of specialty, who is deployed in support of the Global War on Terrorism, may find herself in combat as part of a unit's mission" (Jones 2010, e-mail).

TABLE 6.2
Army Demographics and Positions Open and Closed to Women, July 23, 2010

| | Number of Women Active Duty Force, May 2010 | | | |
	Female	Male	Total	Percent Female
Total	175,645	1,131,005	1,306,650	15.53

Ways Army Women Serve

- Women are authorized to serve in 93.4 percent of military occupations.
- Currently, 90% of the enlisted military occupational specialties (MOS), 98% of the warrant officer military occupational specialties (MOS), and 98% of the officer Army occupational specialties (AOC) are open to women.
- Women may serve in any officer or enlisted specialty or position, except those specialties, positions or units, battalion size or smaller, assigned a routine mission to engage in direct combat. Women are prohibited from serving in specialties, positions or units that collocate routinely with units assigned a direct combat mission.
- Female soldiers are assigned to units and positions that may necessitate combat actions—actions for which they are fully prepared to respond to and to succeed, as they have in operations in Iraq and Afghanistan. Female soldiers may find themselves in hostile actions regardless of their unit's mission and will remain with their assigned units, perform their assigned duties, and fight as a team alongside male soldiers.

Positions Open to Women, February 2010*		Military Occupations Open to Women, April 13, 2010**	
Active Army	325,129 (69.4%)	Enlisted	185 of 210 (88.1%)
Reserves	248,702 (71.4%)	Warrant Officer	70 of 71 (98.5%)
Army National Guard	179,646 (97.1 2%)	Commissioned Officer	186 of 19 (97.3%)

Personnel Assignment Policy

Positions Closed to Women	Enlisted Military Occupational Specialties (MOS) Closed to Women	
Infantry	11B	Infantryman
Armor	11C	Indirect Fire Infantryman
Combat Engineer	11Z	Infantry Senior Sergeant
Special Forces	13B	Cannon Crewmember
Some Field Artillery	13C	Tactical Automated Fire Control Systems Specialist
Some unit-type specific positions such as supply specialist in an Infantry company.	13D	Field Artillery Automated Tactical Data System Specialist
	13E	Cannon Fire Direction Specialist
	13F	Fire Support Specialist
	13M	Multiple Launch System (MLRS)/High mobility Artillery Rocket System (HIMARS) Crewmember
	13P	Multiple Launch Rocket System (MLRS) Operational Fire Direction Specialist
	13R	Field Artillery Firefinder Radar Operator
	14R	Bradley Linebacker Crewmember
	18B	Special Forces Weapons Sergeant
	18C	Special Forces Engineer Sergeant

Personnel Assignment Policy	
Positions Closed to Women	Enlisted Military Occupational Specialties (MOS) Closed to Women
	18D Special Forces Medical Sergeant
	18E Special Forces Communications Sergeant
	18F Special Forces Assistant Operations and Intelligence Sergeant
	18Z Special Forces Senior Sergeant
	18D Cavalry Scout
	19K M1 Armor Crewman
	19Z Armor Senior Sergeant
	21B Combat Engineer
	63A M1 Abrams Tank System Maintainer
	63D Artillery Mechanic
	63M Bradley Fighting Vehicle System Maintainer
	96R Ground Surveillance Systems Operator

*DAPE-PRP
**DAPE- PRP & HRC
Note: Number of Women in Occupational Fields not available.
Source: Jones, Philip H., CIV USA OCPA, 2010 "Women in the Army Talking Points: What Positions are Closed to Women?" and "Women in the Army: Positions Open to Women," e-mail to Rosemarie Skaine, July 23.

Female Marines are authorized to serve in 67 percent of the T/O (Table of Organization; see Table 6.3 Note for further explanation) billets within the Marine Corps, in all but the ground combat arms occupational fields (infantry, artillery, tank/assault amphibian vehicle) and some specific military occupational specialties. A detailed assignment policy for women is contained in the following table.

TABLE 6.3
Marine Corps Demographics and Positions Open and Closed to Women, July 15, 2010

	Total Active Duty Force			
	Female	Male	Total	Percent Female
Total	13,329	187,584	200,913	6.6
Ways Marine Corps Women Serve				

Female Marines are authorized to serve in 67 percent of the T/O* billets within the Marine Corps.

(continued)

TABLE 6.3 (CONTINUED)

Marine Corps Demographics and Positions Open and Closed to Women, July 15, 2010

Personnel Assignment Policy

Occupational Fields Closed to Women	Military Occupational Specialty (MOS) Closed to Women
03 (infantry)	0203, Ground Intelligence Officer
08 (artillery)	0251, Interrogation Specialist
18 (tank/assault amphibian vehicle)	2110, Ordnance Vehicle Maintenance Officer
	2131, Towed Artillery Systems Technician
	2141, Assault Amphibian Repairer/Tech
	2146, Main Battle Tank Repairer/Tech
	2147, Light Armored Vehicle Repairer/Tech
	7207, Forward Air Controller/Air Officer
	7206, Low Altitude Anti-Air Warfare Officer
	8152, Marine Corps Security Forces Guard
	8154, Mobile Cryptologic Support Facility (MCSF)
	Close Quarter Battle Team Member

Number of Women in Occupational Fields

Occupational Field	Number of Women
01 Personnel Administration and Retention	2054
02 Intelligence	436
03 Infantry	0
04 Logistics	682
05 MAGTF Plans	36
06 Communications	1352
08 Artillery	0
09 Training	0
11 Utilities	253
13 Engineer, Construction, Facilities, and Equipment	310
18 Tank and Assault Amphibious Vehicle	0
21 Ground Ordnance Maintenance	68
23 Ammunition and Explosive Ordnance Disposal	211
26 Signals Intelligence/Ground Electronic Warfare	359
27 Linguist	0
28 Ground Electronics Maintenance	133
30 Supply Administration and Operations	1588
31 Traffic Management	128
33 Food Service	364
34 Financial Management	275
35 Motor Transport	620
41 Marine Corps Community Services	16
43 Public Affairs	163
44 Legal Services	198
46 Combat Camera	116
48 Recruiting	72
55 Music	172

Number of Women in Occupational Fields

Occupational Field	Number of Women
57 Chemical, Biological, Radiological, Nuclear Defense	65
58 Military Police and Corrections	395
59 Electronics Maintenance	111
60 Aircraft Maintenance	467
61 Aircraft Maintenance	215
62 Aircraft Maintenance	122
63 Avionics	310
64 Avionics	225
65 Aviation Ordnance	167
66 Aviation Logistics	443
68 Meteorology and Oceanography (METOC)	29
70 Airfield Services	212
72 Air Control/Air Support/Anti-Air Warfare/Air Traffic Control	146
73 Navigation Officer and Enlisted Flight Crews	16
75 Pilots/Naval Flight Officers	175
80 Miscellaneous Requirements	356
84 Miscellaneous Requirements	12
89 Miscellaneous Requirements	84

*The Table of Organization (T/O) is the Marine Corps source document for all Navy manpower requirements. The T/O section denotes every authorized billet within a unit by rank and Military Occupational Specialty required to fulfill the necessary duties.

Source: Haney, Maj. Shawn, USMC. Public Affairs Officer, 2010, "Demographics and Closed Positions," Manpower and Reserve Affairs, E-mail to Rosemarie Skaine, July 15; Vick, Kathleen, Public Affairs Office Student Intern, 2010, "Female Occupational Fields and Count," Manpower and Reserve Affairs, e-mail to Rosemarie Skaine, July 26.

Ninety-five percent of Navy billets are open to women. Closed billets are those associated with SEALS and Marine Corps support in compliance with the direct ground combat rule The term SEALS stands for Sea, Air, and Land and is the name given to a United States Navy military special forces team member. A detailed look at women in the Navy is provided in Table 6.4.

TABLE 6.4
Navy*Demographics and Positions Open and Closed to Women, June 2010

	Total Active Duty Force (Includes TAR)**			
	Female	Male	Total	Percent Female
Total	53,374	283,409	336,783	15.85
Officers	8378	46187	54565	15.35
Enlisted	44996	237222	282218	15.94

(*continued*)

TABLE 6.4 (CONTINUED)
Navy* Demographics and Positions Open and Closed to Women, June 2010

Ways Navy Women Serve

Ninety-five percent of Navy billets are open to women. Closed billets are those associated with SEALS and Marine Corps support in compliance with the direct ground combat rule.

Active Duty Female Officers

Active Duty Enlisted Females
- 10,554 female enlisted are serving on combatants.

	Technical Ratings, 2009		Traditional, 2009	
• Unrestricted Line total is 2,016 (7.8%) Navy female officers	Construction	945	Administrative	4,946
	Crypto/Intel	2,469	Supply	4,593
• Restricted Line total is 1,123 (18.8%) Navy female officers	Engineering	3,911	Medical	5,432
	Operations	7,120	Total	14,971
• Staff Corps total is 4,308 (5.5%) Navy female officers	Aviation	8,497	Unrated	3,866
• LDO (Limited Duty Officer) total is 233 (5.5%) Navy female officers	Combat Systems	2,135		
• CWO (Chief Warrant Officer) total is 84 (5.0%) Navy female officers	Total	25,077		

Aviation:
- 317 pilots (4.2%) of total Navy pilots
- 228 Naval Flight Officers (6.9%) of total NFOs

Sea Duty:
- 1,049 female officers are serving on combatants; total of 1,833 female officers serving sea duty

Personnel Assignment Policy

Officer Designators (4 out of 102) Are Closed to Women

- 113X Special Warfare (SEAL/UDT)
- 615X Limited Duty Officer (Line) in Special Warfare Technician Specialty
- 715X Warrant Officer (Line) in Special Warfare Technician specialty
- 717X Warrant Officer (Line) in Naval Special Warfare Combatant-Craft Crewman

There Are 66 Enlisted Ratings of which Five Submarine and Seal Ratings (7.5%) Are Closed to Women

- MT/Missile Technician
- FT/Fire Control Technician
- STS/Sonar Technician Submarine
- Special Warfare Operator
- SB/Special Warfare Boat Operator

Enlisted women may not be assigned to the following Navy Enlisted Classification (NEC) coded billets:
- Special Operations Basic Combatant Swimmer
- SEAL Delivery Vehicle (SDV) Pilot/Navigator/Dry Deck Shelter Operator
- Special Warfare Operator
- Naval Special Warfare hospital Corpsman
- Special Warfare Combat Craft Crewman

*Excluding Marine Corps
**TAR Training and Administration of the Reserve
Notes: Active Duty Officer Data from R4 & R55
Active Duty Enlisted Data from R1, R2/R3

Source: Cole, Lt. Justin, 2010, Navy Office of Information (CHINFO), News Desk Action Officer, e-mail to Rosemarie Skaine, July 15.

The casualties in the wars, Operation Enduring Freedom (OEF) in Afghanistan and Operation Iraqi Freedom (OIF), are a solemn reminder that death does not discriminate. Table 6.5 shows that women accounted for 20 or 1.85 percent of 1,079 total deaths in Operation Enduring Freedom. Table 6.6 demonstrates that women represent 108 or 2.46 percent of 4,394 total deaths in Operation Iraqi Freedom.

TABLE 6.5

Operation Enduring Freedom in Afghanistan, Republic of the Philippines, and Southwest Asia, Gender Distribution of Deaths, October 7, 2001, through September 4, 2010

Gender	Military Deaths	Percent of Total Deaths
Male	1,242	98.42
Female	20	1.58
Total	1,262	100.0

Source: DoD, 2010, "Operation Enduring Freedom—Military Deaths," September 4, http://siadapp.dmdc.osd.mil/personnel/CASUALTY/oefdeaths.pdf (accessed September 30, 2010).

TABLE 6.6

Operation Iraqi Freedom Gender Distribution of Deaths, March 19, 2003, through August 31, 2010

Gender	Military Deaths	Percent of Total Deaths
Male	4.298	97.50
Female	110	2.50
Total	4,408	100.0

Source: DoD, 2010, "Operation Iraqi Freedom—Military Deaths," August 31, http://siadapp.dmdc.osd.mil/personnel/CASUALTY/oif-deaths-total.pdf (accessed September 30, 2010).

Women have always served in conflicts. Although the exact number of women who served in the War of 1812, the Revolutionary War (1775–1783) and the Civil War (1861–1865) is not known, evidence demonstrates that women played important roles, in some cases, a combat role. More is known about how many women served in later conflicts and how many served as POWs. Tables 6.7 and 6.8 provide data on how many women served in conflicts over time and how many women were POWs.

TABLE 6.7
Number of Women in Individual Military Conflicts

Military Conflict	Number
Civil War (total estimate)	650
Confederate (estimate)	250
Union (estimate)	400
Spanish-American War	1,500
World War I	35,000
World War II (era)	400,000
Korea (in theater)	1,000
Vietnam (in theater)	7,500
Grenada (deployed)	170
Panama (deployed)	770
Desert Storm (in theater)	41,000
Haiti	1,200
Somalia	1,000
Operation Iraqi Freedom and Operation Enduring Freedom (as of May 31, 2010)	26,961

Sources: Blanton, DeAnne, 1993, "Women Soldiers of the Civil War," *Prologue Magazine* 25:1, Spring in National Archives, www.archives.gov (accessed June 1, 2010); WREI, 2008, *Women in the Military: Where They Stand,* 6th ed. Arlington, VA: WREI, 8, 9; Women in Military Service For America Memorial Foundation, Inc., "Number of Women in Individual Military Conflicts," *Statistics on Women in the Military,* Revised February 17, 2010, www.womensmemorial.org (accessed May 27, 2010); and Cunningham OSD PA, Maj. April D, Department of Defense, Office of the Assistant Secretary of Defense (Public Affairs), Defense Press Office, e-mail to Rosemarie Skaine, July 6, 2010.

TABLE 6.8
Number of Military Women Held as Prisoners of War During Individual Conflicts

Military Conflict	Number of Women Prisoners of War
Civil War	1
World War II	90
Desert Storm	2
Operation Iraqi Freedom	3

Source: Women in Military Service For America Memorial Foundation, Inc., "Number of Military Women Held as Prisoners of War in Individual Military Conflicts," *Statistics on Women in the Military,* Revised February 17, 2010, www.womensmemorial.org (accessed May 27, 2010).

Even though women served in combat in most U.S. military conflicts, prior to 1991, law and policy in all services excluded them from engaging in combat. The Army based its combat exclusion policies on to Title 10 U.S. Code § 3012, and excluded women are excluded from most combat roles. The Air Force combat exclusion law was codified in Title 10 U.S. Code § 8549 in 1956 and was repealed after the Persian Gulf War in 1991. In 1956, the Navy and Marine Corps exclusion law was codified in § 6015 of Title 10, *United States Code.* It was repealed in 1993. The evolution of restrictions is demonstrated in Table 6.9.

TABLE 6.9
Evolution of Statutory and Policy Combat Restrictions

Law and Policy	Service	Repealed or Rescinded
Women's Armed Services Integration Act, 1948	Navy and Air Force	Combat exclusion provisions became codified in 1956, Title 10 U.S. Code § 6015
Risk Rule 1988		1994 rescinded
Title 10 U.S.Code § 6015, 1956	Navy and Marine Corps	1993 repealed
Title 10 U.S.Code § 8549, 1956	Air Force	1991 repealed
Policy combat exclusion, according January 13, 1994 Les Aspin Memo: Direct Ground Combat Definition and Assignment Rule	Army	2010 remains in effect
Policy, Submarines exclusion	Navy	2009 rescinded

Source: Adapted and updated from Becraft, Carolyn, "Women in the U.S. Armed Services: The War in the Persian Gulf," Washington, D.C.: WREI, March 1991, in Skaine, Rosemarie, 1999, *Women at War: Gender Issues of Americans in Combat,* Jefferson, NC: McFarland Publishers, 67.

The Direct Combat Probability Code (DCPC) is a system for how units or specialties are assigned. Procedures are in place for applying the codes to positions. The procedures are explained in the Army's Position Coding Decision chart in Table 6.10. First, an identifying question is asked, for example, whether the position engages in combat. Second, if the identifying answer in this case is "yes," then the position is assigned the position code of P1. Since women cannot be assigned any position with a P1 code, the answer to the question of the last column, "Can a woman be assigned in considered position?" has to be a "no."

TABLE 6.10
Army Position Coding Decision Chart (PCDC), 1992

Legend:
P1 positions are those to which women may not be assigned
P2 positions are open to women and are used for all other positions that do not meet the criteria of a closed (P1) position

(continued)

TABLE 6.10 (CONTINUED)
Army Position Coding Decision Chart (PCDC), 1992

Identifying Question	Identifying Answer	Resulting Position Code	Can a Woman be Assigned in Considered Position?
Does specialty/position require routine engagement in direct combat?	Yes	P1	No
Is position in a unit with a mission of routine engagement in direct combat?	Yes	P1	No
Is position in a unit which routinely collocates with a unit whose mission is to engage in direct combat?	Yes	P1	No
Is position in a part of a unit that routinely collocates with a unit whose mission is to engage in direct combat?	Yes	P1	No P2 Unit—battalion or smaller unit

Source: U.S. Department of the Army, Army Regulation 600-13, *Army Policy for the Assignment of Female Soldiers,* March 27, 1992, 3, www.aschq.army.mil (accessed June 1, 2010).

Servicewomen face several problems. Some women face sexism and sexual harassment. The Defense Manpower Center's *2006 Gender Relations Survey of Active Duty Members* is significant because it presents a trend analysis for the years 1995, 2002, and 2006. These trends are presented in Table 6.11. Sexist behaviors involve unwanted actions that refer to a person's gender and are directed toward all people of that gender. Sexual harassment can include sexist behaviors and involves unwelcome sexual advances.

TABLE 6.11
Incidence of Sexism and Sexual Harassment in the Military, 1995, 2002, 2006

Behavior	1995		2002		2006	
	Percent Women	Percent Men	Percent Women	Percent Men	Percent Women	Percent Men
Sexist	63	15	50	17	54	22
Sexual Harassment	46	8	24	3	34	6

Source: Lipari, Rachel N., et al., 2008, *2006 Gender Relations Survey of Active Duty Members,* Defense Manpower Data Center (DMDC) Report No. 2007-022, March, vii, ix–x, www.sapr.mil (accessed July 15, 2010).

In 2009, the Department of Defense Task Force issued a report, *Sexual Assault in the Military Services*. It found that restricted and unrestricted reports of sexual assault are less frequent than anonymous survey responses. The number of sexual assaults reported has increased, but the task force found that restricted and unrestricted reports continue to underestimate the prevalence of sexual assault in the military. The total number of cases for calendar years (CY) 2004 through 2006 and fiscal years (FY) 2007 through 2008 is summarized in Table 6.12. The task force attributes reason for the increase in the number of cases to increased reporting to the addition of the restricted reporting option and improved trust in reporting the process (DoD 2009, 19).

TABLE 6.12
Official Reports of Sexual Assault in the Military Services from DoD Annual Reports 2004 to 2008

	CY 2004	CY 2005	CY 2006	FY 2007*	FY 2008
Total Reports	1700	2374	2947	2688	2908
Unrestricted	1700	2047	2277	2085	2265
Restricted**	N/A	327	670	603	643
% Converted from Restricted to Unrestricted	N/A	25%	11%	14%	15%

*The department's annual report changed from calendar years (CY) to fiscal years (FY) in 2007. For further clarification of the data overlap, see the Sexual Assault Prevention and Response Office's (SAPRO's) annual report. **The numbers listed in this table have been adjusted to include only those reports that remain restricted. Those reports that became unrestricted are counted as unrestricted reports. Restricted reporting was made available midcalendar year 2005, so that number, 327, does not reflect 12 full months of restricted reporting. Restricted reporting is a process used by a service member to report or disclose that he or she is the victim of a sexual assault to specified officials on a requested confidential basis. Under these circumstances, the victim's report and any details provided to health care personnel, the Sexual Assault Response Coordinator, Surveillance and Reconnaissance Center (SARC), or a VA will not be reported to law enforcement to initiate the official investigative process unless the victim consents or an established exception is exercised under this Directive (DoD 6495.01).

Source: DoD, 2009, *Report of the Defense Task Force on Sexual Assault in the Military Services*, December, Table 1, 19, B-1, www.dtic.mil/dtfsams (accessed May 21, 2010).

Senior leaders and chaplains in the military believe that reporting would increase if victims trusted the reporting system more and if they had more control over the reporting process. While these concerns are very important, other personal concerns are powerful. Those concerns include establishing and maintaining a strong identity and making meaningful connections with others. Table 6.13 lists five categories of barriers to reporting.

TABLE 6.13
Barriers to Reporting Sexual Assault Described by Focus Group Participants

Theme and Description	Subcategories	Percent of Focus Group that Mentioned (Top 5)
1. Personal Identity is Threatened	Shame/embarrassment	56 (1)
	Self-blame	24 (4)
	Threats to manhood	15
	Pride	13
2. Social Consequences	Stigmatized	45 (2)
	Won't be believed	17
	Will be blamed	14
3. Fear of Reprisal or Punishment	Fear of reprisal	33 (3)
	Punishment for own actions	21
	Career impact	16
4. Mistrust of the Process	Poor outcome	21 (5)
	General lack of trust	16
	Revictimization	14
5. Perpetrator Characteristics	Family/friend/coworker	16
	Higher rank	14

Source: Adapted from the DoD, 2009, *Report of the Defense Task Force on Sexual Assault in the Military Services,* December, Table 4, 31, www.dtic.mil (accessed May 21, 2010).

Service members are subject to injury and illness. Well health treatment is required for pregnancy and childbirth. Table 6.14 shows the incidence, distribution, and trends of illnesses and injuries and pregnancy and childbirth.

Service members are required to perform at a high level. Aside from injury and illness, war takes its toll on their emotional and mental processes. Mental disorders sometimes force a soldier to leave the Army. The Army introduced a plan, "Comprehensive Soldier Fitness: Strong Minds, Strong Bodies," to meet that challenge to train soldiers on the emotional, mental, and physical level. Table 6.15 shows the differences were minor between the men and women's emotional fitness results.

The Military Awards Program is explained in DoD Instruction Number 1348.33, July 1, 2004, at www.dtic.mil, "It is DoD

TABLE 6.14

Hospitalizations: Mental Disorders, Pregnancy and Childbirth, and Injury and Poisoning, Active Component (Men and Women), U.S. Armed Forces, 2005, 2007, and 2009

Diagnostic Category	2005			2007			2009		
	No.	Rate[a]	Rank	No.	Rate[a]	Rank	No.	Rate[a]	Rank
Mental Disorders (Male and Female)	11,335	8.01	(3)	13,703	9.78	(2)	17,538	12.13	(1)
Pregnancy and Birth[b] (Female Only)	18,465	13.04 (89.78)	(1)	18,201	12.99 (90.80)	(1)	17,354	12.01 (84.46)	(2)
Injury and Poisoning (Male and Female)	12,358	8.73	(2)	12,531	8.95	(3)	11,156	7.72	(3)

[a]Rate per 1,000 person-years of service

[b]Rate of pregnancy and childbirth-related hospitalizations among females only (in parentheses)

Source: Adapted from Armed Forces Health Surveillance Center, 2010, *Medical Surveillance Monthly Report* 17:04 3, April 3, www.afhsc.mil (accessed May 19, 2010).

TABLE 6.15
Army Comprehensive Soldier Emotional Fitness Results, 2009

	Mean	Minimum	Maximum
Females	3.74	1.6	4.9
Males	3.68	1.1	5.0

Source: Cornum, Rhonda, 2009, "Comprehensive Soldier Fitness: Strong Minds, Strong Bodies," [10/9/2009 12:21 PM Army G-3/5/7 Unclassified/FOUO DAMO-CSF America's Army: The Strength of the Nation] Keynote Address. Power Point Presentation. Women in the Military Conference, WREI, Arlington, VA, September 25, www.4militarywomen.org (accessed April 15, 2010).

policy to provide, through the DoD Military Awards Program, tangible recognition for acts of valor, exceptional service or achievement, and acts of heroism not involving actual combat. Such recognition fosters morale, incentive, and esprit de corps." However, some women profiled in Chapter 5, Biographies, did serve in actual combat in current wars and were recognized with awards. The military awards in Table 6.16 were selected on the basis of the military women profiled in Chapter 5.

TABLE 6.16
Selected Military Awards

	Afghanistan Campaign Medal
Authorizing Source	Public Law 108-234, May 28, 2004 and President George W. Bush Executive Order 13363, November 29, 2004.
Description	Awarded to any soldier who has served as part of Operation Enduring Freedom.
Requirements	Meet designated time requirements or
	(a) Be engaged in actual combat involving grave danger of death or serious bodily injury from enemy action.
	(b) Require medical evacuation
	(c) While participating as a regularly assigned air crew member flying sorties.
	Aerial Achievement Medal
Authorizing Source	Secretary of the Air Force, February 3, 1988.
Description	Awarded to U.S. military and civilian personnel.
Requirements	Sustained meritorious achievement while participating in aerial flight. The achievements must be accomplished with distinction above and beyond that normally expected of professional airmen.
	Air Force Commendation Medal
Authorizing Source	Secretary of the Air Force, March 28, 1958.
Description	Awarded to U.S. members of the armed forces who served in any capacity with the Air Force after March 24, 1958.

| **Requirements** | Meritorious achievement and service. The degree of merit must be distinctive, though it need not be unique. |

Air Force Meritorious Service Medal

Authorizing Source	President Lyndon Baines Johnson, Executive Order 11448, January 16, 1969.
Description	Awarded to any member of the U.S. Armed Outstanding achievement or meritorious service to the United States.
Requirements	Meritorious noncombat service.

Air Medal

Authorizing Source	President Franklin Delano Roosevelt, Executive Order 9158, May 11, 1942, as amended by Executive Order 9242, September 11, 1942.
Description	Awarded to U.S. military and civilian personnel for single acts of heroism or meritorious achievements while participating in aerial flight and foreign military personnel in actual combat in support of operations.
Requirements	Accomplished with distinction above and beyond that expected of professional airmen. It is not awarded for peace time sustained operational activities and flights.

American Campaign Medal

Authorizing Source	President Franklin Delano Roosevelt, Executive Order 9265, November 6, 1942.
Description	Awarded to personnel for service within the American Theater between December 7, 1941 and March 2, 1946.
Requirements	Performed one year of duty within the continental borders of the U.S., or duty outside its borders but within the American Theater of Operations or in active combat and was awarded a combat decoration.

American Defense Service Medal

Authorizing Source	President Franklin Delano Roosevelt, Executive Order 8808, June 28, 1941.
Description	Recognized service before America's entry into the Second World War but during the early years of the European conflict.
Requirements	Performed active duty between September 8, 1939 and December 7, 1941.

Armed Forces Expeditionary Medal

Authorizing Source	President John Fitzgerald Kennedy, Executive Order 10977, December 4, 1961.
Description	Awarded for participation or anticipated participation in imminent hostile action by foreign armed forces for operations on or after July 1, 1958.
Requirements	Participate as members of any U.S. military units in a U.S. military operation in which service members participate in significant numbers and encounter foreign armed opposition, or hostile action by foreign armed forces was imminent even though it does not materialize. Be engaged in actual combat, or duty which is equally as hazardous as combat, during the operation with armed opposition, regardless of time in the area.

Armed Forces Reserve Medal

Authorizing Source	President Harry S. Truman, Executive Order 10163, September 25, 1950 and amended by President Harry S. Truman in 1953 and President William Jefferson Clinton in 1996.
Description	Awarded to anyone who completes or has completed a total of ten years of honorable service in one or more of such reserve components, including annual active-duty and inactive-duty training. Service shall not include that in a regular component of the armed forces.
Requirements	Honorable and satisfactory service within time designations.

(continued)

TABLE 6.16 (CONTINUED)
Selected Military Awards

Armed Forces Service Medal

Authorizing Source President William Jefferson Clinton, Executive Order 12985, January 11, 1996.

Description A theater service award that is given for service after June 1, 1992, for actions through which no foreign armed opposition or imminent threat of hostile action was encountered, for example, peacekeeping or humanitarian operations.

Requirements Honorable, significant activity for which no other campaign or service medal is authorized.

Army Achievement Medal

Authorizing Source Secretary of the Army, April 10, 1981.

Description Awarded to any member of the armed forces of the U. S., or to any member of the armed forces of a friendly foreign nation, who served in any capacity with the Army in a non-combat area.

Requirements Meritorious service or achievement of a lesser degree than required for award of the Army Commendation Medal. This medal is not awarded to general officers.

Army Commendation Medal

Authorizing Source War Department Circular 377, December 18, 1945 and amended in Department of the Army General Officer 10, March 31, 1960.

Description Awarded to any members of the U.S. Armed Forces while serving in any capacity with the Army or member of friendly foreign nation whose actions in combat do not qualify for a Bronze Star or for noncombat service.

Requirements Heroism, extraordinary achievement or meritorious service.

Army of Occupation Medal

Authorizing Source War Department Circular 102, April 5, 1946.

Description Awarded for military service of thirty or more consecutive days of duty in one of the occupied territories after World War II (Austria, Berlin, Germany, Japan, Korea, and Italy).

Requirements Designations according to occupied territory.

Army Service Ribbon

Authorizing Source Secretary of the Army, April 10, 1981.

Description A onetime award to soldiers of the Army, Army Reserve, and Army National Guard.

Requirements Successful completion of initial-entry training.

Asiatic-Pacific Campaign Medal

Authorizing Source President Franklin Delano Roosevelt, Executive Order 9265, November 6, 1942 and amended by President Harry S. Truman, Executive Order 9706, March 15, 1947.

Description A service decoration of the Second World War. Awarded to any service member who served in the Asiatic-Pacific Theater (the forces of Japan against those of the United States, the British Empire, the Netherlands and France).

Requirements Active combat against the enemy and was awarded a combat decoration.

Bronze Star Medal

Authorizing Source President Franklin Delano Roosevelt, first established by Executive Order No. 9419, February 4, 1944. Provisions found in Executive Order 11046, August 24, 1962.

200

Description	Awarded to any service member who while serving in any capacity in or with the U.S. Army, not involving participation in aerial flight while engaged in action against the opposition where the U.S. is the belligerent party or while serving with friendly foreign forces engaged in an armed conflict against an opposing armed force in which the United States is not a belligerent party.
Requirements	Heroic or meritorious achievement or service.

Captain Winifred Quick Collins Award

Authorizing Source	Secretary of the Navy/Navy League, 1973.
Description	Award named for the former Assistant Chief of Naval Personnel and given to one woman officer a year.
Requirements	Provide inspirational leadership and perform demanding duties in an exemplary and highly professional manner.

Combat Action Badge

Authorizing Source	Chief of Staff, Army, May 2, 2005.
Description	Award to all soldiers who serve in a combat zone or imminent danger area. Special recognition to any soldiers who personally engage the enemy, or are engaged by the enemy during combat operations. Can be issued from September 18, 2001, to a date to be determined.
Requirements	(a) Perform duties in an area where hostile fire pay or imminent danger pay is authorized.
	(b) Personally present and actively engaging or being engaged by the enemy, and performing satisfactorily in accordance with the prescribed rules of engagement.
	(c) Assigned/attached to a unit that would qualify the soldier for the badge.

Combat Readiness Medal

Authorizing Source	Secretary of the Air Force on March 9, 1964, and amended August 28, 1967.
Description	Award for sustained individual combat or mission readiness or preparedness for direct weapon-system employment.
Requirements	Complete an aggregate 24 months of sustained professional performance as a member of U.S. Air Force combat or mission-ready units subject. The term "Combat Ready" is to be professionally and technically qualified in an aircraft crew position in an aircraft that can be used in combat.

Defense Distinguished Service Medal

Authorizing Source	President Richard Milhous Nixon, Executive Order 11545 of July 9, 1970.
Description	Awarded to officers of the U.S. Armed Forces.
Requirements	Exceptional meritorious service in a duty of great responsibility.

Defense Meritorious Service Medal

Authorizing Source	President James (Jimmy) Earl Carter, Jr., Executive Order 12019, November 3, 1977.
Description	Department of Defense award to any member of the Armed Forces of the U.S.
Requirements	Outstanding noncombat meritorious achievement or service.

Defense Superior Service Medal

Authorizing Source	President Gerald R. Ford, Executive Order 11904 of February 6, 1976.
Description	Awarded to any member of the Armed Forces of the U.S.
Requirements	Superior meritorious service in a position of significant responsibility.

(continued)

TABLE 6.16 (CONTINUED)
Selected Military Awards

Distinguished Flying Cross

Authorizing Source	President Calvin Coolidge, Executive Order 4601, March 1, 1927 and was further amended by President Franklin Delano Roosevelt, Executive Order 7962, August 22, 1938, to provide for the award of the decoration to a certain member of the U.S. Coast Guard.
Description	Awarded to any US Armed Forces service member.
Requirements	Voluntary heroism or extraordinary achievement that sets her or him apart while participating in aerial flight.

French Legion of Honor

Authorizing Source	French order established by Napoleon Bonaparte, First Consul of the First Republic, on May 19, 1802. The Order is the highest decoration in France and is divided into five various degrees.
Description	Awarded to U.S. veterans who helped in the liberation of France during World War II could be eligible to receive this Medal.
Requirements	Excellent civil or military conduct delivered, upon official investigation

Global War on Terrorism Expeditionary Medal

Authorizing Source	President George W. Bush, Executive Order 13289, March 12, 2003.
Description	Awarded for qualifying service on or after September 11, 2001. Must have been deployed abroad for service in the Global War on Terrorism operations on or after September 11, 2001, and to a future date to be determined.
Requirements	Engaged in actual combat against the enemy and under circumstances involving grave danger or death or serious bodily injury from enemy action, regardless of time served in these wars or have been killed or wounded.

Global War on Terrorism Service Medal

Authorizing Source	President George W. Bush, Executive Order 13289, March 12, 2003.
Description	Awarded to U.S. soldiers who have participated in or served in support of Global War on Terrorism Operations outside the designated areas of eligibility for the Global War on Terrorism Expeditionary Medal, on or after September 11, 2001 to a date to be determined.
Requirements	Initial award of the Global War on Terrorism Service Medal will be limited to airport security operations (from September 27, 2001 through May 31, 2002) and soldiers who supported Operations Noble Eagle, Enduring Freedom and Iraqi Freedom.

Good Conduct Medal

Authorizing Source	President Franklin Delano Roosevelt, Executive Order 8809, June 28, 1941 and amendments, President Harry S. Truman, Executive Order 10444, April 10, 1953.
Description	Awarded for enlisted men of U.S. Army and Air Force.
Requirements	Exemplary behavior, efficiency, and fidelity.

Korean Service Medal

Authorizing Source	President Harry S. Truman, Executive Order 10179, November 8, 1950.
Description	Awarded to service members who served within the area or areas of military operations in the Korean theater.
Requirements	In active combat against the enemy in conditions of support of the troops.

Kuwait Liberation Medal (Kuwait)

Authorizing Source	Kuwaiti government and authorized by the DoD on August 7, 1995.
Description	Awarded to members of the U.S. military who participated in operations Desert Shield, Desert Storm, and the Liberation of Kuwait.

Requirements	Attached to or regularly supporting military operations involving ground/shore, aboard a naval vessel, or actually participating as a crew member in one or more aerial flights.

Kuwait Liberation Medal (Saudi Arabia)

Authorizing Source	Government of Saudi Arabia and authorized by DoD on January 3, 1992.
Description	Awarded to members of the U.S. Armed Forces who participated in Operation Desert Storm between January 17, 1991, and February 28, 1991, in one or more specific areas including the Persian Gulf, Red Sea, Gulf of Oman, Iraq, Kuwait, Saudi Arabia, Oman, Bahrain, Qatar, and the United Arab Emirates.
Requirements	Attached to or regularly serving ground or shore operations or aboard a naval vessel directly supporting military operations or participate as a crew member in one or more aerial flights supporting military operations in the designated areas.

Legion of Merit

Authorizing Source	President Franklin Delano Roosevelt, Executive Order 9260, October 29, 1942.
Description	Awarded to members of the U.S. armed forces and members of the armed forces of friendly foreign nations after the proclamation of an emergency by the President on September 8, 1939.
Requirements	Distinguish themselves by exceptionally meritorious conduct in the performance of outstanding services.

Medal of Honor

Authorizing Source	President Abraham Lincoln signed S.J.R. No. 82 on July 12, 1862, the Army Medal of Honor was born. Joint Resolution of Congress, July 12, 1962 (amended by Act of July 9, 1918 and Act of July 25, 1963).
Description	Also referred to as the Congressional Medal of Honor. A soldier is nominated by a superior officer or Congress member and the medal is given by the President.
Requirements	Personal bravery or self-sacrifice so conspicuous as to clearly distinguish it from comrades and gallantry that is at the risk of his or her life above and beyond the call of duty while engaged in action against the enemy. It is often awarded posthumously.

Meritorious Service Medal

Authorizing Source	President Lyndon Baines Johnson, Executive Order 11448, January 16, 1969. Amendments, President Ronald Wilson Reagan, Executive Order 12312 of July 2, 1981.
Description	Awarded to any member of the armed forces of the U.S., or to any member of the armed forces of a friendly foreign nation.
Requirements	Distinguished him or herself by outstanding meritorious achievement or service.

Meritorious Unit Commendation Emblem

Authorizing Source	Deputy Chief of Staff
Description	Awarded to service units larger than brigade after January 1, 1944. It has been awarded in conflicts that have occurred since World War II.
Requirements	Six months of exceptionally meritorious conduct in support of military operations.

NASA Outstanding Leadership Medal

Authorizing Source	Approved by the Administrator.
Description	Awarded for sustained contributions of a leader's effectiveness in advancing the Agency's quality result and building the organization's capacity for future performance while exemplifying NASA values in the work environment.

(continued)

TABLE 6.16 (CONTINUED)
Selected Military Awards

Requirements	Demonstrate outstanding leadership that has a pronounced effect upon NASA technical or administrative programs.

NASA Space Flight Medals

Authorizing Source	Approved by the Administrator.
Description	Awarded for participation in initial flight. The NASA Space Flight Cluster is awarded for subsequent flight(s).
Requirements	Space Transportation System (STS) flight crewmembers (civil and military astronauts, mission specialists, payload specialists, and civilians) to be recognized for individual participation in an STS flight mission.

National Defense Service Medal

Authorizing Source	President Dwight D. Eisenhower Executive Order 10448, April 22, 1953.
Description	Awarded as a member of the Armed Forces during the Korean War, Vietnam War, Iraq War in the Persian Gulf, and the War on Terrorism.
Requirements	Perform honorable active service.

National Space Trophy

Authorizing Source	Rotary National Award for Space Achievement Foundation. Award founded by the Space Center Rotary Club of Houston, Texas in 1985.
Description	Awarded to a civilian or military American.
Requirements	Outstanding and have made major contributions to the space program.

North Atlantic Treaty Organization (NATO) Medal

Authorizing Source	North Atlantic Treaty Organization (NATO).
Description	International military award given to various militaries of the world. Ten versions of the Medal are in existence.
Requirements	Service in one of the NATO designated areas such as Yugoslavia, the Republic of Macedonia, Balkans, Kosovo.

Navy Achievement Medal

Authorizing Source	Secretary of the Navy, May 1, 1961. After several name changes, on April 8, 1994 Secretary of the Navy John H. Dalton named it the Navy and Marine Corps Achievement Medal.
Description	Lowest medal for meritorious service in the Navy and Marine Corps and is awarded to enlisted personnel and junior officers.
Requirements	Achievement or meritorious service in either a combat or noncombat situation. Demonstrate sustained and extraordinary conduct or have performed a specific achievement.

Navy Commendation Medal

Authorizing Source	Secretary of the Navy Frank Knox, November 1, 1943 first designated as a ribbon. After several name changes, Secretary of the Navy John H. Dalton on September 23, 1994, announced that the name had been changed to The Navy and Marine Corps Commendation Medal.
Description	Awarded to members of the Navy and Marine Corps, or other members of the Armed Forces serving with these branches. First of the commendation awards.
Requirements	Heroism, outstanding achievement or meritorious service.

Navy Unit Commendation Ribbon

Authorizing Source	Secretary of the Navy James V. Forrestal, December 19, 1944.
Description	A deserved honor and distinction given to any organization, detachment, installation, ship, aircraft, or other unit.
Requirements	Outstanding performance in action against the enemy.

Philippine Independence Ribbon

Authorizing Source	Department of the Army, Circular 59, 1948.
Description	Awarded to for service in the Philippines.
Requirements	Recipient of both the Philippine Defense and Philippine Liberation ribbons.

Philippine Liberation Medal

Authorizing Source	Department of the Army, Circular 59, March 8, 1948.
Description	Awarded for service in the liberation of the Philippines from October 17, 1944, to September 3, 1945.
Requirements	Participated in initial landing operations on Leyte or in combat action against the enemy.

Presidential Unit Emblem

Authorizing Source	President Dwight David Eisenhower, Executive Order 10694 of Jan. 10, 1957, superseding President Franklin Delano Roosevelt, xecutive Orders No. 9050 of February 6, 1942, and No. 9396 of November 22, 1943.
Description	Awarded to unit of the Armed Forces of the United States and cobelligerent nations on or after December 7, 1941.
Requirements	Extraordinary heroism in action against an armed enemy, gallantry, determination, and esprit de corps in accomplishing unit mission under extremely difficult and hazardous conditions as to set it apart from and above other units participating in the same campaign.

Prisoner of War (POW) Medal

Authorizing Source	Public Law 99–145, 10 U.S.C. 1128, November 8, 1985, as amended by 10 U.S.C. 1128, November 29, 1989.
Description	Awarded to any person who, while serving in any capacity with the U.S. Armed Forces, was taken prisoner and held captive after April 5, 1917.
Requirements	Taken prisoner and held captive while engaged in an action against an enemy of the U.S. or military operations involving conflict with an opposing foreign force or while serving with friendly forces engaged in an armed conflict against an opposing force in which the U.S. is not a belligerent party or by foreign armed forces that are hostile to the U.S.

Purple Heart

Authorizing Source	General George Washington, Order, 1782, and reinstituted in 1932 for the bicentennial of Washington's birth. President John Fitzgerald Kennedy, Executive Order 11016, April 25, 1962.
Description	Award generally for service members wounded in action.
Description	Award generally for service members wounded in action.
Requirements	Wounded in action. Also awarded for any singular meritorious act of extraordinary fidelity or essential service. Later in the war, the requirements were limited to wounds received as a result of enemy action.

Republic of Vietnam Campaign Medal

Authorizing Source	Republic of Vietnam to members of the U.S. Armed Forces and authorized by DoD 1348.33–M.
Description	Award eligibility limited to service in the Republic of Vietnam during the period from March 1, 1961 to March 2, 1973.

(continued)

TABLE 6.16 (CONTINUED)
Selected Military Awards

Requirements	One of these requirements: (1) Served in the Republic of Vietnam for 6 months during designated period. (2) Served outside the geographical limits of the Republic of Vietnam and contributed direct combat support to the Republic of Vietnam and Armed Forces for 6 months. Such individuals must meet the criteria established for the Armed Forces Expeditionary Medal (Vietnam) or the Vietnam Service Medal, during the period of service required to qualify for the Republic of Vietnam Campaign Medal. (3) Served for less than 6 months and have been wounded by hostile forces, captured by hostile forces, but later escaped, was rescued or released or killed in action or otherwise in line of duty.

Silver Star

Authorizing Source	Act of Congress July 9, 1918 and amended by Act of July 25, 1963, 10 U.S.C. 3746.
Description	Award for distinctive bravery and gallantry in combat.
Requirements	Performed gallantry with marked distinction. Served in any capacity with the U.S. Army in action against an enemy while engaged in military operations involving conflict with an opposing foreign force, or while serving with friendly foreign forces engaged in an armed conflict against an opposing armed force in which the U.S. is not a belligerent party.

United Nations Medal

Authorizing Source	Secretary General of the United Nations and Executive Order 11139, January 7, 1964.
Description	U.S. service members who are or have been in the service of the United Nations in designated operations by the Secretary of Defense may accept this medal.
Requirements	Serve under the operational or tactical control in the service of the United Nations in designated missions/operations.

World War II Victory Medal

Authorizing Source	Act of Congress July 6, 1945 (59 Stat. 461).
Description	Awarded to any U.S. service member including members of the armed forces of the Government of the Philippine Islands.
Requirements	Serve on active duty, or as a reservist, between December 7, 1941 and December 31, 1946.

Sources: Congressional Medal of Honor Society, "History," 2010, www.cmohs.org/medal-history.php (accessed March 4, 2010); Foxfall Medals, March 1, 2010, www.foxfall.com/index.htm (accessed March 3, 2010); Grunt, "Military Factsheets," 2010, www.gruntsmilitary.com/factsheets.shtml (accessed March 3, 2010); Justica, U.S. Laws, *Code of Federal Regulations*, Title 32 National Defense, Chapter V—Department of the Army, Part 578 Decorations, Medals, Ribbons, and Similar Devices, http://law.justia.com/us/cfr/title32/32cfr578_main_02.html (accessed March 4, 2010); National Aeronautics and Space Administration (NASA), NASA People, "Agency Honor Awards," July 29, 2009, http://nasapeople.nasa.gov/awards/nasamedals.htm (accessed March 4, 2010); National Archives and Records Administration, "Codification of Presidential Proclamations and Executive Orders," *Federal Register*, Codification, April 13, 1945, through January 20, 1989, www.archives.gov (accessed March 3, 2010); U.S. Army, "Combat Action Badge Information," n.d., www.army.mil (accessed March 3, 2010); U.S. Army, Office of the Secretary, "Military Decorations and Service Medals," Institute to Heraldry. Ft. Belvoir, VA, updated weekly, www.tioh.hqda.pentagon.mil/Awards/dec_awards_military.aspx (accessed March 1, 2010).

Documents and Testimony Overview

The selections in this section show the legal evolution of women in combat. They include the repealed combat exclusion law and remaining combat policy. The Direct Combat Probability Code system is explained. A section is given to documents that guide actions in civilian and military sectors, the Constitutional powers of Congress and the executive branch and the Soldier's Creed. Testimony for and against women serving in combat is provided. The Don't Ask, Don't Tell law as it will stand when repealed is included.

In 1991, the Air Force combat exclusion law that had governed the assignment of women was repealed. This law prohibited the assignment of female members, except those designated under section 8067, to duty in aircraft engaged in combat missions. It read:

Combat Exclusion Law, Air Force, Title 10 Armed Forces (USC), Subt. C, § 8549 (1976)—Repealed 1991

Females of the Air Force, except those designated under section 8067 of this title, or appointed with a view to designation that section, may not be assigned to duty in aircraft engaged in combat missions. Section 8067 of Title 10 refers to the appointment of officers who serve in medical, dental, veterinary, medical service, nursing, medical specialist, judge advocate, and chaplain functions.

Source: Skaine, Rosemarie. 1999. *Women at War: Gender Issues of Americans in Combat.* Jefferson, NC: McFarland Publishers, Inc., 100.

Following the repeal of the law governing the Air Force was the repeal of the law in 1993 that prohibited women from being assigned to combat positions in the Navy and Marine Corp.

Combat Exclusion Law, Navy and Marine Corps, Title 10 Armed Forces (USC), Subt. C, § 6015 (1956)—Repealed: 1993

The Secretary of the Navy may prescribe the manner in which women officers appointed under section 5590 of this title, women warrant officers, and enlisted women members of the Regular Navy and the Regular Marine Corps shall be trained and qualified for military duty. The secretary may prescribe the kind of military duty to which such women members may be assigned and the military authority which they may exercise. However, women may not be assigned to duty in aircraft that are engaged in combat missions nor may they be assigned to duty on vessels of the Navy other than hospital ships, transports, and vessels of a similar classification not expected to be assigned combat missions.

Source: U.S. Code Annotated. 1959. "Title 10 Armed Forces (USC), Subt. C, § 6015." St. Paul, MN: West Publishing Co. and Edward Thompson Co., 336. (As amended by National Defense Authorization Act for Fiscal Years 1992 and 1993, P.L. No. 102-190, § 531[a], 105 Stat. 1290, 1365 [1991].)

By law the Secretary of the Army has the responsibility for personnel assignments. That part of the law remains in effect in 2010. It follows.

The Secretary of the Army, U.S. Code. Title 10 Subtitle B, Part I § 3013(g)

(g) The Secretary of the Army may—

(1) assign, detail, and prescribe the duties of members of the Army and civilian personnel of the Department of the Army;
(2) change the title of any officer or activity of the Department of the Army not prescribed by law; and
(3) prescribe regulations to carry out his functions, powers, and duties under this title.

Source: U.S. Code. Title 10 Subtitle B, Part I § 3013(g).

In 1982, the Army study. "Women in the Army Policy Review," provided a plan for every position in the Army for determining the probability of the participation of women in direct combat. The plan was the Direct Combat Position Coding (DCPC) system. The DCPC system included seven codes, PI through P7, with P1 representing the highest probability of engaging in direct combat and P7 the lowest. The Army applied one of these codes to each position. Coding each required the consideration of four criteria-unit mission, MOS duties, doctrine, and location on the battlefield. For example, soldiers who served in P 1 positions were required to be routinely located forward of the brigade rear boundary. Position coding is updated at least once a year to meet the Army's needs (U.S. Army 1983, 60-61). Title 10, USC 3013(g) authorizes the Secretary of the Army to determine policy. The DCPC system is intricately outlined in the Army's policy of 1992; relevant parts listed include the process, the classifications, and procedures for closed and open positions.

Army Direct Combat Probability Coding (DCPC) System, 1992

2–1. Coding process

a. The DCPC system implements Army policy for assigning women in both the Active Army and Reserve Component.

b. The DCPC system will use the following three dimensions to classify each position within a TOE:

(1) Duties of the position and area of concentration or military occupational specialty.

(2) Unit mission.

(3) Routine collocation.

2–2. Coding classifications

a. All TOE [tables of organization and equipment] positions will be evaluated during the formulation process and be assigned an appropriate DCPC code.

b. The following two codes will be used to classify positions:

(1) P1 will indicate those positions to which women may not be assigned. MTOEs will be coded with the identity code (officer/warrant officer/enlisted) equivalent to the P1 designation per AR 310–49.

(2) P2 (open to women) will be used for all other positions.

2–3. Coding procedures for closed (P1) and open (P2) positions

a. Procedures for applying the DCPC codes are found in this regulation and are included in AR 71–31. Establishment and change of identity codes in the MTOE [modification table of organization and equipment] are addressed in AR 310–49 and AR 570–4.

b. Procedures for classifying positions under DCPC will be accomplished as follows.

(1) Positions will be coded closed (P1) (See Table 6.10) only if—

(a) The specialty or position requires routine engagement in direct combat.

(b) The position is in a battalion or smaller size unit that has a mission of routine engagement in direct combat.

(c) The position is in a unit that routinely collocates with battalion or smaller size units assigned a mission to engage in direct combat. (See Section II, Terms, Collocation.)

(d) The position is in a portion of a unit that routinely collocates with a battalion or smaller size unit having a direct combat mission.

(2) Positions will be coded open (P2) if they do not meet the criteria of a closed (P1) position as defined above.

2–4. Coding of tables of distribution and allowance (TDA) [tables of distribution and allowances]

a. TDA positions will be gender neutral.

b. MACOM [major Army command] must submit requests for exception to policy to HQDA(DAPE–HR–S), WASH DC 20310–0300, before gender coding a TDA position. Requests for exception will be considered on a case-by-case basis. All requests must clearly justify the rationale and provide a detailed job or duty description. Any civil or military regulations or guidance involving job performance must be included. Sound logic must be evident in the request to justify an exception and permit gender coding. Factors affecting overall combat effectiveness such as readiness, health, welfare, and discipline and order may be justifiable reasons for ODCSPER [Office of the Deputy Chief of Staff for Personnel] granting an exception.

c. All such requests will be processed according to AR 570–4."

Source: U.S. Department of the Army, Army Regulation 600-13, *Army Policy for the Assignment of Female Soldiers,* March 27, 1992, 2. www.aschq.army.mil (accessed June 1, 2010).

The March 27, 1992 Army policy predates the DoD policy of 1994. The Army did not revise its policy when the 1994 policy rescinded the 1988 rule, both represented a significant departure from previous policy. The Army 1992 policy and the DoD 1994 policy are similar, but they also differ.

Army Policy for the Assignment of Female Soldiers, 1992 (Major Relevant Parts)

Section III Policy

1–12. Overall policy for the female soldier

a. The Army's assignment policy for female soldiers allows women to serve in any officer or enlisted specialty or position except in those specialties, positions, or units (battalion size or smaller) which are assigned a routine mission to engage in direct combat, or which collocate routinely with units assigned a direct combat mission.

b. The DCPC system implements the Army policy for the coding of positions in organization documents and the related assignment of all soldiers to these positions. Once properly assigned, female soldiers are subject to the same utilization policies as their male counterparts. In event of hostilities, female soldiers will remain with their assigned units and continue to perform their assigned duties.

c. Female soldiers will be provided full and equal opportunity to pursue careers in the military and will be assigned to all skills and positions according to the above policy.

d. All commanders and heads of agencies will ensure compliance with the provisions of this regulation and that subordinate commanders and staff are aware of their responsibilities.

Section II Terms
Collocation

Occurs when the position or unit routinely physically locates and remains with a military unit assigned a doctrinal mission to routinely engage in direct combat. Specifically, positions in units or sub-units which routinely collocate with units assigned a direct combat mission are closed to women. An entire unit will not be closed because a subunit routinely collocates with a unit assigned a direct combat mission. The sub-unit will be closed to women.

Direct Combat

Engaging an enemy with individual or crew served weapons while being exposed to direct enemy fire, a high probability of direct physical contact with the enemy's personnel and a substantial risk of capture. Direct combat takes place while closing with the enemy by fire, maneuver, and shock effect in order to destroy or capture the enemy, or while repelling the enemy's assault by fire, close combat, or counterattack.

Source: Headquarters, U.S. Department of the Army, Army Regulation 600-13, *Army Policy for the Assignment of Female Soldiers,* March 27, 1992, 1, 5. www.aschq.army.mil (accessed May 31, 2010).

The DoD policies of 1988 and 1994, were designed to limit the assignment of women into combat positions. The goal of the Risk Rule of 1988 was to standardize positions that were closed to women. It read:

Document 6.6. 1988 Risk Rule

The risk of direct combat, exposure to hostile fire or capture are proper criteria for closing positions to women. If the type, degree, and, to a lesser extent, duration of risk are equal to or greater than direct combat units (infantry/ armor), then units or positions may be closed to women.

Source: Carolyn Becraft. 1991. *"Women in the U.S. Armed Services: The War in the Persian Gulf.* Washington, D.C.: WREI, March. In Rosemarie Skaine. 1999. *Women at War: Gender Issues of Americans in Combat. Jefferson*, NC: McFarland Publishers, 231.

The 2010 U.S. Department of Defense (DoD) policy for assigning women was put forth in the following 1994 memorandum from Secretary of Defense Les Aspin:

DoD Assignment Policy, 2010: Direct Ground Combat Definition and Assignment Rule, 1994 (Rescinding 1988 Risk Rule)

THE SECRETARY OF DEFENSE
WASHINGTON, D.C. 20301-1000
January 13, 1994
MEMORANDUM FOR THE SECRETARY OF THE ARMY
SECRETARY OF THE NAVY
SECRETARY OF THE AIR FORCE
CHAIRMAN, JOINT CHIEFS OF STAFF
ASSISTANT SECRETARY OF DEFENSE
(PERSONNEL AND READINESS)
ASSISTANT SECRETARY OF DEFENSE
(RESERVE AFFAIRS)
SUBJECT: DIRECT GROUND COMBAT DEFINITION AND ASSIGNMENT RULE

References:

    (a) SECDEF memo, April 28, 1993
    (b) SECDEF memo, February 2, 1988
    (c) FY94 National Defense Authorization Act

My memorandum dated April 28, 1993, directed the Military Services to open more specialties and assignments to women and established an Implementation Committee to ensure that those policies are applied consistently. I also charged the Committee to review and make recommendations on several specific implementation issues.

The Committee has completed its first such review, that of the "appropriateness of the Risk Rule," reference (b), and concluded that, as written, the risk rule is no longer appropriate. Accordingly, effective October 1, 1994, reference (b) is rescinded.

My memorandum restricted women from direct combat on the ground. The Committee studied this and recommended that a ground combat rule be established for assignment of women in the Armed Forces. Accordingly, the following direct ground combat assignment rule, and accompanying definition of "direct ground combat," are adopted effective October 1, 1994 and will remain in effect until further notice.

> A. *Rule.* Service members are eligible to be assigned to all positions for which they are qualified, except that women shall be excluded from assignment to units below the brigade level whose primary mission is to engage in direct combat on the ground as defined below:
>
> B. *Definition.* Direct ground combat is engaging an enemy on the ground with individual or crew served weapons, while being exposed to hostile fire and to a high probability of direct physical contact with the hostile force's personnel. Direct ground combat takes place well forward on the battle field while locating and closing with the enemy to defeat them by fire, maneuver, or shock effect.

The Services will use this guidance to expand opportunities for women. No units or positions previously open to women will be closed under these instructions.

The Services will provide the Assistant Secretary of Defense (Personnel and Readiness), not later than May 1, 1994, with lists of all units and positions closed to women and their proposed status based on implementation of this policy. These lists will be arrayed in three columns: jobs currently closed that are proposed to be opened, jobs currently closed that that are proposed to remain closed, and a column justifying each entry. The proposed changes will be reviewed by the Implementation Committee and the Assistant Secretary of Defense (Personnel and Readiness). The Services will then coordinate approved implementing policies and regulations with the Assistant Secretary of Defense (Personnel and Readiness) prior to their issuance. These policies and regulations may include the following restrictions on the assignment of women:

> – where the Service Secretary attests that the costs of appropriate berthing and privacy arrangements are prohibitive;

- where units and positions are doctrinally required to physically collocate and remain with direct ground combat units that are closed to women;
- where units are engaged in long range reconnaissance operations and Special Operations Forces missions; and
- where job related physical requirements would necessarily exclude the vast majority of women Service members.

The Services may propose additional exceptions, together with the justification to the Assistant Secretary of Defense (Personnel and Readiness). The process described above will enable the Department to proceed with expanding opportunities for women in the military as well as comply with the reporting requirements contained in Section 542 of reference (c).

[signed] Les Aspin

Source: Harrell, Margaret C., et al. 2007. *Assessing The Assignment Policy for Army Women.* Santa Monica, CA: RAND National Defense Research Institute, 72, 73. www.rand.org (accessed May 30, 2010).

The U.S. Soldier's Creed is a standard that all Army personnel are to follow. All Army enlisted personnel are taught the Creed. It makes no gender distinctions which makes it relevant to women serving in combat. The significant line reads, "I stand ready to deploy, engage, and destroy the enemies of the United States of America in close combat."

Soldier's Creed

I am an American Soldier
I am a Warrior and member of a team. I serve the people of the United States and live the Army Values.
I will always place the mission first.
I will never accept defeat.
I will never quit.
I will never leave a fallen comrade.
I am disciplined, physically and mentally tough, trained and proficient in my warrior tasks and drills. I always maintain my arms, my equipment and myself.
I am an expert and I am a professional.
I stand ready to deploy, engage, and destroy the enemies of the United States of America in close combat.
I am guardian of freedom and the American way of life.
I am an American Soldier.

Source: Office of the Chief of Transportation. n.d. "Guardians of the Corps." "ENLISTED PROPONENCY." www.eustis.army .mil/OCOT (accessed May 21, 2010).

The civilian part of the U.S. society is responsible for the military. This responsibility is carried out through the President and the Congress. The President is the Commander-In-Chief of the military and Congress makes rules for the military along with its power to declare war. Articles I and II of the Constitution outline the powers of the President and Congress.

U.S. Constitution, Articles I—The Legislative Branch and Article II—The Executive Branch (Article I, Section 8 to Article II, Section 2)

Article I–The Legislative Branch

Section 8–Powers of Congress

[1] The Congress shall have power to lay and collect taxes, duties, imposts and excises, to pay the debts and provide for the common defense and general welfare of the United States; but all duties, imposts and excises shall be uniform throughout the United States;

[2] To borrow money on the credit of the United States;

[3] To regulate commerce with foreign nations, and among the several states, and with the Indian tribes;

[4] To establish a uniform rule of naturalization, and uniform laws on the subject of bankruptcies throughout the United States;

[5] To coin money, regulate the value thereof, and of foreign coin, and fix the standard of weights and measures;

[6] To provide for the punishment of counterfeiting the securities and current coin of the United States;

[7] To establish post offices and post roads;

[8] To promote the progress of science and useful arts, by securing for limited times to authors and inventors the exclusive right to their respective writings and discoveries;

[9] To constitute tribunals inferior to the Supreme Court;

[10] To define and punish piracies and felonies committed on the high seas, and offenses against the law of nations;

[11] To declare war, grant letters of marque and reprisal, and make rules concerning captures on land and water;

[12] To raise and support armies, but no appropriation of money to that use shall be for a longer term than two years;

[13] To provide and maintain a navy;

[14] To make rules for the government and regulation of the land and naval forces;

[15] To provide for calling forth the militia to execute the laws of the union, suppress insurrections and repel invasions;

[16] To provide for organizing, arming, and disciplining, the militia, and for governing such part of them as may be employed in the service of the United States, reserving to the states respectively, the appointment of the officers, and the authority of training the militia according to the discipline prescribed by Congress;

[17] To exercise exclusive legislation in all cases whatsoever, over such District (not exceeding ten miles square) as may, by cession of particular states, and the acceptance of Congress, become the seat of the government of the United States, and to exercise like authority over all places purchased by the consent of the legislature of the state in which the same shall be, for the erection of forts, magazines, arsenals, dockyards, and other needful buildings;—And [18] To make all laws which shall be necessary and proper for carrying into execution the foregoing powers, and all other powers vested by this Constitution in the government of the United States, or in any department or officer thereof.

Section 9. Limits on Congress

[1] The migration or importation of such persons as any of the states now existing shall think proper to admit, shall not be prohibited by the Congress prior to the year one thousand eight hundred and eight, but a tax or duty may be imposed on such importation, not exceeding ten dollars for each person.

[2] The privilege of the writ of habeas corpus shall not be suspended, unless when in cases of rebellion or invasion the public safety may require it.

[3] No bill of attainder or ex post facto Law shall be passed.

[4] No capitation, or other direct, tax shall be laid, unless in proportion to the census or enumeration herein before directed to be taken.

[5] No tax or duty shall be laid on articles exported from any state.

[6] No preference shall be given by any regulation of commerce or revenue to the ports of one state over those of another: nor shall vessels bound to, or from, one state, be obliged to enter, clear or pay duties in another.

[7] No money shall be drawn from the treasury, but in consequence of appropriations made by law; and a regular statement and account of receipts and expenditures of all public money shall be published from time to time.

[8] No title of nobility shall be granted by the United States: and no person holding any office of profit or trust under them, shall, without the consent of the Congress, accept of any present, emolument, office, or title, of any kind whatever, from any king, prince, or foreign state.

Section 10. Powers Prohibited of States

[1] No state shall enter into any treaty, alliance, or confederation; grant letters of marque and reprisal; coin money; emit bills of credit; make anything but gold and silver coin a tender in payment of debts; pass any bill of attainder, ex post facto law, or law impairing the obligation of contracts, or grant any title of nobility.

[2] No state shall, without the consent of the Congress, lay any imposts or duties on imports or exports, except what may be absolutely necessary for executing its inspection laws: and the net produce of all duties and imposts, laid by any state on imports or exports, shall be for the use of the treasury of the United States; and all such laws shall be subject to the revision and control of the Congress.

[3] No state shall, without the consent of Congress, lay any duty of tonnage, keep troops, or ships of war in time of peace, enter into any agreement or compact with another state, or with a foreign power, or engage in war, unless actually invaded, or in such imminent danger as will not admit of delay.

Article II–The Executive Branch

Section 1. The President

[1] The executive power shall be vested in a President of the United States of America. He shall hold his office during the term of four years, and, together with the Vice President, chosen for the same term, be elected, as follows:

[2] Each state shall appoint, in such manner as the Legislature thereof may direct, a number of electors, equal to the whole number of Senators and Representatives to which the State may be entitled in the Congress: but no Senator or Representative, or person holding an office of trust or profit under the United States, shall be appointed an elector.

[3] The electors shall meet in their respective states, and vote by ballot for two persons, of whom one at least shall not be an inhabitant of the same state with themselves. And they shall make a list of all the persons voted for, and of the number of votes for each; which list they shall sign and certify, and transmit sealed to

the seat of the government of the United States, directed to the President of the Senate. The President of the Senate shall, in the presence of the Senate and House of Representatives, open all the certificates, and the votes shall then be counted. The person having the greatest number of votes shall be the President, if such number be a majority of the whole number of electors appointed; and if there be more than one who have such majority, and have an equal number of votes, then the House of Representatives shall immediately choose by ballot one of them for President; and if no person have a majority, then from the five highest on the list the said House shall in like manner choose the President. But in choosing the President, the votes shall be taken by States, the representation from each state having one vote; A quorum for this purpose shall consist of a member or members from two thirds of the states, and a majority of all the states shall be necessary to a choice. In every case, after the choice of the President, the person having the greatest number of votes of the electors shall be the Vice President. But if there should remain two or more who have equal votes, the Senate shall choose from them by ballot the Vice President.

[4] The Congress may determine the time of choosing the electors, and the day on which they shall give their votes; which day shall be the same throughout the United States.

[5] No person except a natural born citizen, or a citizen of the United States, at the time of the adoption of this Constitution, shall be eligible to the office of President; neither shall any person be eligible to that office who shall not have attained to the age of thirty five years, and been fourteen Years a resident within the United States.

[6] In case of the removal of the President from office, or of his death, resignation, or inability to discharge the powers and duties of the said office, the same shall devolve on the Vice President, and the Congress may by law provide for the case of removal, death, resignation or inability, both of the President and Vice President, declaring what officer shall then act as President, and such officer shall act accordingly, until the disability be removed, or a President shall be elected.

[7] The President shall, at stated times, receive for his services, a compensation, which shall neither be increased nor diminished during the period for which he shall have been elected, and he shall not receive within that period any other emolument from the United States, or any of them.

[8] Before he enter on the execution of his office, he shall take the following oath or affirmation:—"I do solemnly swear (or affirm) that I will faithfully execute the office of President of the United States, and will to the best of my ability, preserve, protect and defend the Constitution of the United States."

Section 2. Civilian Power over Military, Cabinet, Pardon Power, Appointments

[1] The President shall be commander in chief of the Army and Navy of the United States, and of the militia of the several states, when called into the actual service of the United States; he may require the opinion, in writing, of the principal officer in each of the executive departments, upon any subject relating to the duties of their respective offices, and he shall have power to grant reprieves and pardons for offenses against the United States, except in cases of impeachment.

[2] He shall have power, by and with the advice and consent of the Senate, to make treaties, provided two thirds of the Senators present concur; and he shall nominate, and by and with the advice and consent of the Senate, shall appoint ambassadors, other public ministers and consuls, judges of the Supreme Court, and all other officers of the United States, whose appointments are not herein otherwise provided for, and which shall be established by law: but the Congress may by law vest the appointment of such inferior officers, as they think proper, in the President alone, in the courts of law, or in the heads of departments.

[3] The President shall have power to fill up all vacancies that may happen during the recess of the Senate, by granting commissions which shall expire at the end of their next session.

Source: Air University. 2010. "U.S. Constitution Literacy Reader, from OPM." *Military Law and Legal Links.* Jan. 4. www.au.af.mil/au/ (accessed May 26, 2010).

The subject of women in combat is controversial. After the Gulf War, the United States Congress held several hearings on the subject. Testimony of Elaine Donnelly, Center of Military Readiness, expresses her opposition to women serving in combat.

Excerpt from Elaine Donnelly's Congressional Testimony, 1993

We had "Take-our-daughters-to-work" day last week. Are we going to take our daughters to work in the rape fields of Bosnia in some future war? Do we have to do this? No, we don't have to do it.

If we do, how will that affect the Nation and how will it affect national security if the President has to end the conflict immediately because the Nation won't stand for it. This is an important cultural issue. At SERE [Survival Evasion Resistance Escape] camp, I watched men interrogating men, and I was also interrogated a little bit just to see what that was like. I kind of went along with the spirit of the thing and it didn't trouble me quite so much until I saw a man interrogating a woman. At that point, a cultural dissonance set in. It was hard to imagine a woman totally at the mercy of enemy interrogators in a combat situation. The SERE trainers told us that men react differently when they know what is happening to the women. I didn't make this up. This is what we were told in official testimony before the Commission [Presidential Commission on the Assignment of Women in the Armed Forces, 1992].

Source: U.S. Congress. 1993. House of Representatives. Subcommittee on Military Forces and Personnel Subcommittee, Committee on Armed Services. *Women in Combat: Hearing.* 103rd Congress, 1st session. May 11, 112.

The following is the testimony of Maj. Lillian Pfluke, U.S. Army, to the Presidential Commission on the Assignment of Women in the Armed Forces in 1992. Qualified for ground combat, she was not allowed to serve because of the exclusion policy. She supports women serving in ground combat.

Profile of a Soldier

I am a physically fit and mentally tough leader of soldiers. I am the current national military triathlon champion, two-time national military cycling champion, two-time European interservice ski champion. I earned a varsity letter in ski jumping on the men's ski team at West Point and captained the women's lacrosse team. I play rugby. I have achieved a maximum score on every PT test taken in 12 years of service. I am physical, aggressive, and very competitive. I am a leader who can inspire people to their own personal bests by providing a powerful example and through my genuine and infectious enthusiasm for adventure and challenge. Men will follow me, will bond with me, will respect me, and we will fight as a team. They have done so in all the infantry training I have been exposed to, including the jungle operations training course in Panama, Airborne training at Fort Benning, as an instructor during recondo training at West Point, and throughout my troop leading experience in the field at Ft. Bragg, Germany, and Ft. Lewis.

But I still have not addressed a fundamental question: do I have what it takes to ram my bayonet through my enemies' chest? First of all, very few deaths in modern combat are the result of bayonet wounds. Secondly, no man can answer that question with certainty until faced with that situation. Most importantly, though, that is a question I have had to think about already. [Women soldiers] are issued bayonets and we are trained to use them.

The real question, then, is am I comfortable with a vocation whose primary purpose is to close with and destroy the enemy? Once one comes to terms with using force to impose our nation's will on others by killing people and by risking one's own life (which every soldier, sailor, airman, and Marine must come to terms with), the only question that remains is how one wants to contribute to that mission. Is it by flying airplanes or steaming ships or fixing trucks or flipping hamburgers? My choice is to engage in the direct physical confrontation of the infantry, to close with and kill or capture the enemy, to hold the high ground. In my view, the essence of conflict.

I can do it. I want to do it. I should be given the chance to do it. *Source:* Maj. Lillian Pfluke, U.S. Army, Testimony, to the Presidential Commission on the Assignment of Women in the Armed Forces. September 12, 1992, Washington, D.C. referred to in *Report to the President, Women in Combat: Presidential Commission on the Assignment of Women in the Armed Forces,* Washington: Brassey's, 1993, Appendices F-18.

Another controversial issue is whether service members with homosexual orientations may serve openly declaring their sexuality. In 1993, President Bill Clinton introduced the policy, "Don't Ask, Don't Tell," banning military personnel with homosexual orientations from serving openly. Although the military is reviewing the possible effects of the proposed law, the following is that policy which was repealed in 2010.

Policy Concerning Homosexuality in the Armed Forces: Federal Law Pub.L. 103-160 (10 U.S.C. § 654). U.S. House Repealed May 27, 2010 to Take Effect December 1, 2010

(a) Findings.—Congress makes the following findings:

(1) Section 8 of article I of the Constitution of the United States commits exclusively to the Congress the powers to raise and support armies, provide and maintain a Navy, and make rules

for the government and regulation of the land and naval forces.
(2) There is no constitutional right to serve in the armed forces.
(3) Pursuant to the powers conferred by section 8 of article I of
the Constitution of the United States, it lies within the discretion
of the Congress to establish qualifications for and conditions of
service in the armed forces.
(4) The primary purpose of the armed forces is to prepare for
and to prevail in combat should the need arise.
(5) The conduct of military operations requires members of the
armed forces to make extraordinary sacrifices, including the
ultimate sacrifice, in order to provide for the common defense.
(6) Success in combat requires military units that are
characterized by high morale, good order and discipline, and
unit cohesion.
(7) One of the most critical elements in combat capability is unit
cohesion, that is, the bonds of trust among individual service
members that make the combat effectiveness of a military unit
greater than the sum of the combat effectiveness of the
individual unit members.
(8) Military life is fundamentally different from civilian life
in that—

> (A) the extraordinary responsibilities of the armed forces, the
> unique conditions of military service, and the critical role of
> unit cohesion, require that the military community, while
> subject to civilian control, exist as a specialized society; and
> (B) the military society is characterized by its own laws,
> rules, customs, and traditions, including numerous
> restrictions on personal behavior, that would not be
> acceptable in civilian society.

(9) The standards of conduct for members of the armed forces
regulate a member's life for 24 hours each day beginning at the
moment the member enters military status and not ending until
that person is discharged or otherwise separated from the
armed forces.
(10) Those standards of conduct, including the Uniform Code of
Military Justice, apply to a member of the armed forces at all
times that the member has a military status, whether the
member is on base or off base, and whether the member is on
duty or off duty.
(11) The pervasive application of the standards of conduct is
necessary because members of the armed forces must be ready
at all times for worldwide deployment to a combat
environment.
(12) The worldwide deployment of United States military
forces, the international responsibilities of the United States,

and the potential for involvement of the armed forces in actual combat routinely make it necessary for members of the armed forces involuntarily to accept living conditions and working conditions that are often spartan, primitive, and characterized by forced intimacy with little or no privacy.

(13) The prohibition against homosexual conduct is a longstanding element of military law that continues to be necessary in the unique circumstances of military service.

(14) The armed forces must maintain personnel policies that exclude persons whose presence in the armed forces would create an unacceptable risk to the armed forces' high standards of morale, good order and discipline, and unit cohesion that are the essence of military capability.

(15) The presence in the armed forces of persons who demonstrate a propensity or intent to engage in homosexual acts would create an unacceptable risk to the high standards of morale, good order and discipline, and unit cohesion that are the essence of military capability.

(b) Policy.—A member of the armed forces shall be separated from the armed forces under regulations prescribed by the Secretary of Defense if one or more of the following findings is made and approved in accordance with procedures set forth in such regulations:

(1) That the member has engaged in, attempted to engage in, or solicited another to engage in a homosexual act or acts unless there are further findings, made and approved in accordance with procedures set forth in such regulations, that the member has demonstrated that—

(A) such conduct is a departure from the member's usual and customary behavior;
(B) such conduct, under all the circumstances, is unlikely to recur;
(C) such conduct was not accomplished by use of force, coercion, or intimidation;
(D) under the particular circumstances of the case, the member's continued presence in the armed forces is consistent with the interests of the armed forces in proper discipline, good order, and morale; and
(E) the member does not have a propensity or intent to engage in homosexual acts.

(2) That the member has stated that he or she is a homosexual or bisexual, or words to that effect, unless there is a further finding, made and approved in accordance with procedures set forth in the regulations, that the member has demonstrated that he or she is not a person who engages in, attempts to engage in, has a propensity to engage in, or intends to engage in homosexual acts.

(3) That the member has married or attempted to marry a person known to be of the same biological sex.

(c) Entry Standards and Documents.—

(1) The Secretary of Defense shall ensure that the standards for enlistment and appointment of members of the armed forces reflect the policies set forth in subsection (b).

(2) The documents used to effectuate the enlistment or appointment of a person as a member of the armed forces shall set forth the provisions of subsection (b).

(d) Required Briefings.—The briefings that members of the armed forces receive upon entry into the armed forces and periodically thereafter under section 937 of this title (article 137 of the Uniform Code of Military Justice) shall include a detailed explanation of the applicable laws and regulations governing sexual conduct by members of the armed forces, including the policies prescribed under subsection (b).

(e) Rule of Construction.—Nothing in subsection (b) shall be construed to require that a member of the armed forces be processed for separation from the armed forces when a determination is made in accordance with regulations prescribed by the Secretary of Defense that—

(1) the member engaged in conduct or made statements for the purpose of avoiding or terminating military service; and

(2) separation of the member would not be in the best interest of the armed forces.

(f) Definitions.—In this section:

(1) The term "homosexual" means a person, regardless of sex, who engages in, attempts to engage in, has a propensity to engage in, or intends to engage in homosexual acts, and includes the terms "gay" and "lesbian."

(2) The term "bisexual" means a person who engages in, attempts to engage in, has a propensity to engage in, or intends to engage in homosexual and heterosexual acts.

(3) The term "homosexual act" means—

(A) any bodily contact, actively undertaken or passively permitted, between members of the same sex for the purpose of satisfying sexual desires; and

(B) any bodily contact which a reasonable person would understand to demonstrate a propensity or intent to engage in an act described in subparagraph

Source: U.S. Code Online via GPO Access (www.gpoaccess.gov, laws in effect as of January 3, 2007, CITE: 10USC654, 298–300.).

7

Directory of Organizations

The directory of organizations lists associations pertinent to the issue of women serving in combat. A wide variety of groups have a shared interest in women in combat. The groups are governmental, nongovernmental (NGOs), and private. Some organizations offer online resources including bibliographies, chronologies, Internet links, and articles.

Government Organizations

Center for Naval Analyses
www.cna.org
custerc@cna.org

The Center for Naval Analyses began in the early 1940s when its scientists deployed with Navy forces to assist the Navy in addressing the German U-boat threat. In 2010, 350 researchers and 45 analysts are employed. The Center conducts research and offers analyses for policy makers. It concentrates on issues involving technology, national security, international affairs and the public.

Center for Women Veterans: Department of Veterans Affairs
www1.va.gov/womenvet
Va.media.relations@va.gov

The United States has the most comprehensive system of assistance for veterans in the world. The extensive benefits system had its beginning in 1636 when the Pilgrims of Plymouth Colony and the Pequot Indians were at war. The Pilgrims passed a law which required the colony to support disabled soldiers. The Continental Congress of 1776 offered pensions to disabled soldiers to encourage enlistments for the Revolutionary War. After the Civil War, many State veterans homes with medical benefits were established. In 1917, during World War I, Congress established a system of benefits. Since 1930, when the Veterans Administration was formed, the VA health care system has grown from 54 hospitals to 171 medical centers; has more than 350 out-patient, community, and outreach clinics; 126 nursing home care units; and 35 homes where care is given. In 1989, the Department of Veterans Affairs became a cabinet level position.

This site provides links and documents relevant to women veterans. The latest relevant news is posted. A special project is the "Her Story" campaign. This effort recognizes the important contributions of women veterans to our lives and to the success of the United States. Each week a different story is posted. The best way to use this site is to search the term "women," or access the link for the site map. After searching for women, a link is provided for "A Historical Bibliography." Sections include articles and books and government publications. The link to veteran women's health with an emphasis on HIV/AIDS is located at www.hiv.va.gov/vahiv?page=pcm-301_womenCoast Guard. www.uscg.mil.

Defense Department (DoD) Advisory Committee on Women in the Services (DACOWITS)
http://dacowits.defense.gov
dacowits@osd.mil

DACOWITS advises the Department of Defense on the general well-being of military women. Secretary of Defense George C. Marshall established the Committee in 1951. It is authorized under the Federal Advisory Committee Act, Public Law 92-463. Its purpose is to make recommendations on policy regarding the recruitment and retention, treatment, employment, integration, and welfare of highly qualified professional women in the services. The committee's charter is reviewed every two years. Its members are not to exceed 35 and they must have experience with the military or with women's workforce issues. Although the "Reports" section is up-to-date ending in 2009, some sections need to be updated or are under construction.

**Defense Department (DoD) Deployment Health
Clinical Center**
www.pdhealth.mil
E-mail: Use the contact link.

The Deployment Health Clinical Center is located at Walter Reed
Army Medical Center. In 1994, its first title was the Gulf War
Health Center. Approximately 700,000 servicemembers, who
had deployed for the 1991 Gulf War, experienced unclear symptoms such as excessive fatigue and memory and concentration
problems. In 2001, the Gulf War Health Center was renamed the
Deployment Health Clinical Center and the organization
launched its Web site.

The purpose of the Deployment Health Clinical Center is to
improve deployment-related health through assistance and advocacy for military personnel and their families. The Center operates
as a part of the Defense Centers of Excellence for Psychological
Health and Traumatic Brain Injury. The Web site gives information
on all deployments and deployment support; specific diseases and
emerging health concerns; provider and patient education materials; news and information. The "Theater of War" link is directed
at increasing awareness of post-deployment psychological health
issues, reducing stigma, and fostering hope and optimism. Since
servicemembers often deploy more than one time, the site uses
dramatic readings as a catalyst for discussion of the impact and
effects of prolonged conflicts.

Defense Department (DoD) List of Web sites
www.defense.gov/RegisteredSites/RegisteredSites.aspx?s=A
E-mail: Use contact link.

This Department of Defense (DoD) site is a valuable resource to
gather information from all DoD Web sites. It is complete with
links to all of the featured Web sites. Since this is an extensive site,
searching for the term "women" is the most helpful way to use
the site. Many links to DACOWITS' reports are found. A most
useful link goes to *The Report to the White House Council on Women
and Girls*, September 1, 2009.

Defense (DoD) Manpower Data Center
www.dmdc.osd.mil/appj/dwp/index.jsp or www.dmdc.osd.mil
webmaster@osd.pentagon.mil

This site is a secure site and primarily contains extensive information for military personnel, but it has a page of useful links that includes Combat-Related Special Compensation.

Defense (DoD) Prisoner of War/Missing Personnel Office (DPMO)
www.dtic.mil/dpmo
E-mail: none listed.

The overall purpose of the Defense POW/Missing Personnel Office (DPMO) is to create and supervise policies on the rescue of living Americans and the recovery of the remains of the missing in action from foreign battlefields. The DPMO makes every effort to account for persons missing in past conflicts, and prepare to account for those individuals who remain missing following current and future conflicts. This site has many excellent links for more information. One such link is found at www.dtic.mil/dtic, which takes you to the Web site of The Defense Technical Information Center. Although the site provides information to the defense community, it also provides information to the public through searchable databases. In addition, each of the services' official links relative to POWs are listed and data can be found under the various links to wars at the top of the page.

House Committee on Veteran Affairs: "Eliminating the Gaps: Examining Women Veterans' Issues."
http://veterans.house.gov/hearings/hearing.aspx?NewsID=441
E-mail: None listed; inquirer must write to the committee

This page provides links to testimony given at the July 16, 2009, hearing before the Subcommittee on Disability Assistance and Memorial Affairs. A multimedia link and .pdf file are provided. The About the Committee link is most valuable because links it provides are extensive, including hearings, legislation, publications, documents, and resources for veterans.

Joint Chiefs of Staff
www.jcs.mil
E-mail: none listed

Established in 1947, the staff has no authority to operate or organize the overall armed forces general staff. Thus, the joint staff has no executive authority over combatant forces. In the command structure, the responsibilities of the members of the Joint Chiefs of Staff take precedence over duties as the Chiefs of Military Services. The staff is composed of equal numbers of officers from the Army, Navy and Marine Corps, and Air Force. The Marines make up about 20 percent of the number assigned to the Navy. The site gives an overview of the activities of the Joint Chiefs along with providing links, photos, biographies, speeches, interviews and imagery collections.

Lioness Program, Marine Corps
www.marines.com/rmi
E-mail: use the dialogue box at the Web address to submit a query to the Marine Corps about the Lioness Program

The Lioness program is a Marine Corps all-female Search Team. It was formed to support a culturally sensitive approach to search female Muslim and Iraqi women for potentially concealed weapons. The program was created because it is not culturally possible for men to search females of the Iraqi population. As the need for searching citizens at security checkpoints increases, the need for female search team members increases.

National Guard
www.ng.mil
E-mail: oncall.pao@ng.army.mil

The organization's areas of responsibility include the California wildfires, Homeland Defense, disaster preparedness, southwest border support, and troop support. This site has links to the Army and Air National Guard.

NATO Committee on Gender Perspectives
www.nato.int/cps/en/natolive/topics_50327.htm
E-mail: dialogue box at www.nato.int/cps/en/SID-CE8EC97F-C99529F4/natolive/contact.htm

In the 1960s and 1970s, the efforts of senior national military women in the North Atlantic Treaty Organization (NATO) led to ad hoc conferences. In 1973, a committee formed and made the first terms of reference. In 1976, the Committee on Women in the NATO Forces became official. In 2009, the Committee was renamed to the NATO Committee on Gender Perspectives. Its mandate was extended to support the integration of a gender perspective into military operations specifically to support the implementation of U.N. Security Council Resolutions (UNSCR) 1325 and 1820 and future security council resolutions. The committee has an advisory role to the military committee on gender-related policies for the armed forces of the alliance. It promotes gender mainstreaming. The committee consists of senior military officers or the civilian equivalent of each NATO nation. The site has a resource pdf file library.

Naval Historical Center
www.history.navy.mil
E-mail: Depends on which division; go to www.history.navy.mil/about/operation_hours.html for contact information

This organization's site is an excellent resource for navy history. It provides links to the U.S. Navy's 12 museums, resources, education programs, and services. "Women in the Navy" is featured extensively at www.history.navy.mil/special20highlights/women/Women-index.htm. The "Ships" link lists 14 ships named after women, the first a YT-266, a harbor tug commissioned in 1942 and named for Pocahontas. The "Interesting Reads" link ranges from the establishment of the Navy Nurse Corps in 1908 to "Women to serve on Ohio-class submarines" in 2010. Galleries and oral histories are presented along with links on Navy uniforms.

Naval Personnel Research, Studies and Technology (NPRST)
www.nprst.navy.mil
E-mail: nprstpao@navy.mil

NPRST began in1946 in the Navy Yard as the Personnel Research Detachment. It develops new technologies and techniques to improve the readiness, performance, retention, and quality of life of sailors and marines from initial service to retirement.

Office of Women's Policy, U.S. Navy
www.npc.navy.mil/AboutUs/BUPERS/WomensPolicy
E-mail: stephanie.p.miller@navy.mil; jean.m.sullivan@navy.mil; jessica.myers@navy.mil

This office interprets and influences policies on the assignment of women and on pregnancy. It monitors gender trends including but not limited to recruiting, assignments, promotions, career development, family care and pregnancy issues. Links available include history, current events, facts and statistics, and policy.

Detailed information on the Navy's pregnancy policy is outlined in friendly questions that female soldiers have presented to the link "FAQs-Women's Policy."

The "History and Firsts" link presents contributions beginning in 1776 when the first armed ship was named *Lady Washington* for a woman, Martha Washington. New York state built the ship to defend the Hudson River.

United States Army Women's Museum
www.awm.lee.army.mil/
leeeAWMWeb@conus.army.mil

The museum opened in 1955 at Fort McClellan, Alabama as the Women's Army Corps (WAC) Museum. When Fort McClellan closed in 1999, the Museum moved to Fort Lee, Virginia and given a new name, the U.S. Army Women's Museum. The groundbreaking for the current museum was held on April 9, 1999 and construction was completed in October 2000. This was followed by the installation of new exhibits and the dedication of the museum on May 11, 2001. The biennial Army Women's Reunion was held in conjunction with the dedication. The permanent exhibits feature the history of women in the Army. Other exhibits reflect current day activities. In 2007, the museum opened a new gallery on the Global War on Terrorism. It features Raven 42 and SGT Leigh Ann Hester, the first woman to receive the Silver Star for direct combat action since World War II. Other exhibits in the making include Army women Warrant Officers, Native American Women, and women at West Point in the past 30 years.

The Museum is a repository for artifacts and archival material pertaining to the service of women across all branches and organizations of the U.S. Army from the beginning to the present day. It is a valuable resource for military and civilian individuals.

U.S. Army, "Demographics"
www.armyg1.army.mil/HR/demographics.asp
E-mail: g1wita@conus.army.mil (for issues related to women in the army) or go to the link www.armyg1.army.mil/contactus.asp #women (to ascertain which office to contact)

The Demographics Division of the U.S. Army develops, manages, and executes all manpower and personnel plans, programs, and policies across all parts of the Army. Its main responsibility is to provide analytical and policy recommendations to support senior-level decisions that have to do with readiness and human resources policies and programs that will effect active-duty, reserve, and guard personnel, retirees, family members, veterans, and Army civilians. Their Web site has many specific reports; the "The Changing Army Profile," December 2008, offers a comparison. A special section, "Women in the Army," is featured.

U.S. Army Research Institute (ARI), Army Personnel Survey Office
www.hqda.army.mil/ari/index.shtml
RI_ARLINGTON_APSO@conus.army.mil

The Army Research Institute began in 1917 at a meeting of experimental psychologists at Harvard University. The Institute's heritage includes the preparation for WWII and the establishment of the Committee on Selection and Classification of Military Personnel. In 1939, what is known as the U.S. Army Personnel Research Office was set up and is the predecessor of ARI. Through the decades, research emphasis shifted until, in 2010, it focused on leader development, training, and soldier selection, assignment, and performance. The purpose of this Institute is to develop to the fullest each person's and unit's performance and readiness to meet the full range of Army operations. The site offers "Women in the Army: An Annotated Bibliography," library, research, and publications.

U.S. Army, "Women in the Army" (WITA)
www.armyg1.army.mil/HR/wita
wita@conus.army.mil

WITA's beginning is indeed historically significant and remains so today. The number of women in service increased during President Jimmy Carter's administration, but came to a pause under President Ronald Reagan's administration. Since no law existed regulating the percentage of women, the Army froze its percentage at approximately 9 percent. The Women in the Army (WITA) Policy Review group was established during the Reagan administration. They concluded that Army policy did not exclude women from combat, but it limited job opportunities without providing women with protection from danger (Hart 1991, 14, in Skaine 1999, 62).

The result of the Army's 1978 definition was that women could not serve in assignments responsible for killing the enemy, but they could serve in assignments that exposed them to an equal opportunity of being killed. WITA's efforts created the Direct Combat Probability Coding (DCPC). Direct combat became interchangeable with close combat, and the definition in effect as we know it today was formed (Hart 1991, 14, in Skaine 1999, 62).

The Army site Women in the Army (WITA) has abundant resources including downloads, links, and galleries. It goes beyond the normal resources by offering a Heroes Corner, a Celebrating Women in the Army column, and a What's New section. Most valuable is the Reference section which includes the Official Department of the Army Administrative Publications. This section includes regulations governing the assignment of women.

NGOs (Nongovernmental Organizations)

AcademyWomen
www.academywomen.org
feland@academywomen.org

Women military officers created AcademyWomen in 2003 for support, mentorship, and personal and professional development. Besides advocacy for military women to reach their potential as leaders, this group supports veterans. AcademyWomen members consist of outstanding leaders from all over the world. These members include officers, astronauts, pilots, combat leaders, ship commanding officers, business executives, diplomats, civic leaders, entrepreneurs, and homemakers. The organization offers programs such as a cross-service eMentorship Leadership Program.

Air Force Women Officers Associated
www.afwoa.org
AFWOA@afwoa.org

Retired Air Force women officers formed this organization in 1975. They wanted to keep the friendships that they had made while on active service. Membership now exceeds 1000, including active duty women, and retired and separated women officers of the regular Air Force and its reserve.

AlbertMohr.com
www.albertmohler.com
E-mail: use the dialogue box under the contact link

Dr. R. Albert Mohler, Jr. is the president of Southern Baptist Theological Seminary. He develops the argument against women serving in combat with the basic thesis: "If we truly believe that God created men and women for different but complementary roles and shows his glory in the faithfulness of men as primary protectors and women as primary nurturers, the entry of women into combat roles is an open rejection of God's purpose." His full report is located at www. albertmohler.com/2009/08/20/a-quiet -circumvention-of-morality-women-in-combat.

Alliance for National Defense (AND)

www.4militarywomen.org/
and @4militarywomen.org

The Alliance for National Defense is an educational foundation that is a positive voice for women in the military. It collects facts, figures, and information on U.S. military women and provides them to scholars, the media, national decision makers and the public. It also posts news and reports pertaining to military women. Its aim is to encourage and promote the vital role of military women in our nation's defense.

All Navy Women's National Alliance

www.www.anwna.com/
anwna@aol.com

This organization began in 1995. Its purpose is to honor the accomplishments and history of the women of the sea services and to "Sharing the Legacy." The alliance serves over 400,000 active duty, reserve, retired, and veteran women of the Navy, Coast Guard, and Marines, servicewomen in other branches of the Department of Defense, those women who serve in NATO forces, and civilian women serving the Department of Defense. Two of their services are a recommended reading list and a museum.

It believes that the joint venture between women and men strengthens the military, that readiness and mission accomplishment are vitally important, and that excellence in performance is required from all regardless of gender.

American Legion

www.legion.org
E-mail: use contact dialogue box

Congress chartered and incorporated the American Legion in 1919 as a patriotic veterans' organization dedicated to mutual helpfulness. Members number 2.6 million in 14,000 posts organized into 55 departments: one each for the 50 states, the District of Columbia, Puerto Rico, France, Mexico, and the Philippines. It is the nation's largest veterans' service organization. Grassroots organization makes the Legion different from other veterans' organizations. Local programs contribute to making this organization a powerful source for promoting patriotism, honor, strong national security, and ongoing loyalty to servicemembers and veterans.

Some of the American Legion's activities include American Legion Baseball, which is one of the most successful programs in recreational athletics; founding Boys Nation; the Heroes to Hometowns program, which is the only nationwide reintegration assistance service for wounded veterans from Iraq and Afghanistan; donations to veterans and their families in times of grief; and scholarships to help youth succeed. A timeline of the American Legion's relevant activities is found by clicking "History" located under "Who We Are" menu across the top. The timeline covers events from its inception in 1919 to June 30, 2008, when President George W. Bush signed into law the Post 9/11 Veterans Educational Assistance Act, a new GI Bill strongly supported by the Legion. The bill provides veterans with significantly improved education benefits. The Post 9/11 GI Bill took effect August 1, 2009 and sent a record number of veterans to college.

American Veterans (AMVETS)
www.amvets.org
amvets@amvets.org

The American Veterans organization sponsors programs that assist veterans and their families, such as providing advice and prompt action on compensation claims at no charge to the veteran, advocating on policy issues, and serving the hospitalized and homeless. Membership is open to anyone who currently serves or who has honorably served in the U.S. Armed Forces from World War II to the present. This requirement includes the National Guard and Reserves.

On December 10, 1944, 18 veterans representing 9 veterans clubs, met in Kansas City, Missouri, and founded the American Veterans of World War II. On July 23, 1947, President Harry S. Truman signed Public Law 216, which made AMVETS the first World War II organization to be chartered by Congress.

AMVETS began training national service officers (NSOs) in 1948 to help veterans of World War II to obtain the benefits promised by the federal government. NSO is a highly visible program accredited by the Department of Veterans Affairs. Officers are available in about 40 states to advise and prompt action on compensation claims. The NSOs do so at no charge to veterans. They have processed more than 24,000 claims in recent years that have resulted in veterans receiving about $400 million in compensation.

The AMVETS has many branch organizations. Pertinent to women's concerns is the AMVETS Ladies Auxiliary. In 1946, members from 13 states who were present at the National AMVETS Auxiliary organizational pre-convention meeting in Pittsburgh are its founding members. Members are themselves veterans or relatives of AMVETS. Their services include support to veterans, communities, and other nonprofit organizations such as Paws With a Cause, the John Tracy Clinic, and Freedoms Foundation. Their Web site is www.amvetsaux.org. Women also participate in Sackettes to raise funds for nurses' scholarships. Sackettes is the ladies auxiliary counterpart to the Sad Sacks, who also provide scholarships for nurses.

Army Nurse Corps Association
http://e-anca.org
mail@e-anca.org

The Army Nurse Corps officers formed this organization in 1977 as the Retired Army Nurse Corps Association. They meet in San Antonio and wanted to continue in retirement the friendship and close ties of the Army Nurse Corps. They also sought to establish communication by, for, and about Army Nurse Corps retirees. Other purposes are to bring army nurses together in a social setting and to support the goals of the corps, preserve its history, award scholarships to established baccalaureate nursing school programs. The 2010 scholarships are being awarded in memory of captain Gussie M. Jones, Army Nurse, who died of nonbattle related causes in Iraq. She was the first African American Army Nurse to die while assigned in a theater of operations.

Army Women's Foundation
www.awfdn.org
info@awfdn.org

The foundation was established in 1969. It is a national network for army women that provides education and preservation of history. Its goals are accomplished, for example, through scholarships, research, and a museum expansion project at Fort Lee, Virginia. The foundation honors those women who gave their lives in Afghanistan and Iraq with the link "Faces of the Fallen."

Business and Professional Women's Foundation
www.bpwfoundation.org
foundation@bpwfoundation.org

Business and Professional Women began in 1919. Its purpose has remained constant, a successful workplace for women, families, and employers; one that practices and believes in work–life balance, equity, and diversity. This organization provides programs and resources for women veterans when they return to civilian life, including a timeline of women and war from 2003 to present day. The foundation advocates that policy makers examine a number of factors to craft programs and service that more fully support women veterans who move into the civilian workforce. Two areas of legislative concerns are immediate and long-term health needs, particularly of women who served in Iraq and Afghanistan, and protection for soldiers and their families from domestic violence and sexual assault. Other issues the foundation advocates are located on www.bpwfoundation.org/i4a/pages/index.cfm?pageid=5673.

Center for Military Readiness (CMR)
www.cmrlink.org
info@cmrlink.org

CMR was founded in 1993 as an educational public policy organization that deals with military social issues. The center does not support women serving in ground combat or the law that would allow homosexuals to serve openly. A complete review of CMR's position on issues is located by accessing the link "About our issues." CMR's board of advisors consists of retired military personnel and civilians. Elaine Donnelly, president of CMR, served as a member of the Pentagon's DACOWITS from 1984 to 1986.

She served on the 1992 presidential commission on the assignment of women in the armed services.

Concerned Women for America
www.cwfa.org

E-mail: use the "feedback/questions" link at the bottom of the page
The purpose of Concerned Women for America is to protect and promote biblical values among all people. To reverse a perceived decline in moral values, the organization uses the avenues of: prayer, education, and influence. Areas of concern include sanctity of life, religious liberty, family, pornography, education, and national sovereignty. The organization holds that the Don't Ask, Don't Tell law, which may be repealed, is a reasonable law that ensures the military is ready and able to meet its primary purpose.

Eagle Forum
www.eagleforum.org
eagle@eagleforum.org

The Eagle Forum supports American sovereignty and identity, the U.S. Constitution, and traditional education. It opposes what it terms the "radical" feminist agenda by supporting marriage between a man and a woman and fulltime homemakers. It opposes the Equal Right Amendment. It opposes "the feminist goals" of stereotyping men as a constant danger to women yet pushing women into military combat.

Phyllis Schlafly started the Eagle Forum in 1972 as a leader of the profamily movement. In 2010, she is president of the organization. Her weekly radio talk show on education called "Eagle Forum Live" is heard on 75 stations and on the Internet.

The GI Rights Hotline
www.girightshotline.org
girights@girightshotline.org

A network of nonprofit, nongovernmental organizations that offer information to service members concerning military discharges, grievance and complaint procedures, and other civil rights. Services are free and confidential.

Hope for America
405 Easton Rd., Willow Grove, PA 19090-2514
Phone: (215) 659-0564

Hope for America is a private company categorized under Educational Cooperative Organizations. Established in 1993, it is located in Willow Grove, Pennsylvania. The organization maintains that there are moral issues not considered in some discussions on allowing women in the military and women in combat.

Hope for America Coalition
www.hopeforamericacoalition.org
info@hopeforamericacoalition.org

The purpose of the Hope for America Coalition is promoting individual rights and freedom for all. It proposes individuals should be free from burdensome taxation, oppressive bureaucratic regulation, and the interference and infringement of what it describes as an increasingly large, complex, and unaccountable federal government. It bases its belief on the Constitution of the United States. The coalition acts on these tenets through education, advocacy, and political action.

Independent Women's Forum
www.iwf.org
info@iwf.org

The issues of this forum center attention on mainstream women, men, and families. In so doing, it strives to build a stronger society through progress in economic liberty, personal responsibility, and political freedom. One of its efforts is to support powerful and effective national defense and foreign policy.

From 2004 to 2006, the organization undertook a project that involved working with Iraqi women. The U.S. State Department supported the project. The result of that project appears in its policy paper, "Advancing Women's Rights: Two Years in Iraq" available in digital form or downloadable on its Web site. This organization does not support women serving in combat roles. To read its positions, use the search terms "women combat roles" in the site's search box. My search revealed that some positions include putting military readiness before social engineering and denouncing DACOWITS' initiatives to allow women to serve in combat units. One IWF scholar believes that the times require turning attention away "from sexual harassment, date rape, the impractical notion of placing women in combat, and from the endless feminist myths that have invaded the public consciousness."

MilitaryWoman.org
www.militarywoman.org/forums
E-mail: use the Contact link at the bottom of the page. A dialogue box will appear.

MilitaryWoman.org has been online since 1996. Its purpose is to encourage the exchange of information between past, current, and future military women and keep up-to-date on current women's issues in the armed forces. Sections discusses issues pertaining to disabled women veterans; harassment, discrimination, and domestic violence; joining the military at the age of 30+; military life in the preseventies; single parents; why women leave the military; why women stay in the military; women's hair issues; and health issues.

MINERVA Center
www.minervacenter.com
depauw@minervacenter.com

The Minerva Center is an educational foundation devoted to promoting the study of women and the military and women in war. The center is affiliated with H-Minerva (www.h-net.org/~minerva/), which began in 1995. H-Minerva is affiliated with H-Net Network which is a discussion network dedicated to the study of women and war and women in the military, worldwide and in all historical areas. The center also publishes a scholarly journal, *Minerva Journal of Women and War* (www.minerva center.com/minerva-journal), which examines the roles of women in war and the ways that conflict affects women's lives.

Dr. Linda Grant DePauw, professor emeritus of history, The George Washington University, is founder and president of the Minerva Center since its establishment in 1983.

The Minerva Center addresses the question, "Who is Minerva?" in its Web site's "Frequently Asked Questions." In part, the site describes Minerva as follows: "Helmeted, golden-haired Minerva was the Roman goddess of war and wisdom. Her presence on a battlefield meant that the contest would be decided by sound strategy, cool courage, and military skill rather than by sheer animal strength and blood lust, the qualities represented by Mars, the god of battle."

National Association of Black Military Women
http://nabmw.com
Nabmw@aol.com

The Association began in July 1976 when 21 women got together in Hampton, Virginia. The women had served in the Women's Army Auxiliary Corps and Women's Army Corps during World War II and the Korean and Vietnam Wars. The women decided to invite other former servicewomen to a first reunion that was held in 1978 in Dallas, Texas.

Women at the first reunion realized that the contributions of black military women did not appear in the history books and were not shown in war movies. No one was preserving black military women's history. The reunion women recognized that black military women should record and tell their own story. The organization consisted mainly of Army women. In 1998, the structure was changed to include all the services. In 2010, the group works to preserve the history of black military women who have served and who are currently serving in the United States Armed Forces.

National Native American Veterans Association
www.nnava.org
info@nnava.org

The organization assists Native Americans with their business with the Department of Veterans Affairs. Their Web site contains links on veteran's benefits. Native Americans are the smallest ethnic group in the United States, but, per capita, they provide more members to the armed forces than any other population sector. Native American veterans use their benefits the least of any sector. The reason for lack of use is that over 500 federally recognized tribes exist, each with their own government and programs to assist each tribes' veterans. The National Native American Veterans Association fills the gap with a national-level organization. The national level can inform veterans, who are often unaware, of their benefits. Some veterans are turned off by government structures and the National Native American Veterans Association facilitates the veterans' efforts through the established tribal and nation programs. This assists the veterans in actually receiving their benefits and being informed on the changes dictated by Congress.

National Women Veterans United (NWVU)
www.nwvu.org
ladyvets2@yahoo.com

The group researches state and federal legislation pertinent to women veterans. It then holds meetings throughout the United States to keep the membership informed of its rights and entitlements. A link, "Women Veterans Benefit Information," contains up-to-date information on those benefits. NWVU hosts an annual "Salute to Women in Defense of our Nation." The association recognizes significant contributions and accomplishments of women in the armed forces during National Women's History Month to make certain they are included in history.

Services include making available critical information and assistance with VA claim filing, making referrals to the county, assisting homeless women veterans find emergency housing and food, and maintaining a strong network with professionals in the federal, state, county, and local VA organizations, agencies, and healthcare system.

National Women's History Museum
www.nwhm.org
info@nwhm.org

Karen Staser founded The National Women's History Museum in 1996. The organization realizes women are under written into history. It believes rather than rewriting current exhibitions at other history museums or omitted elsewhere in order to fit it into women's history, the National Women's History Museum places women's history alongside current historical exhibitions. Its method expands rather than rewrites history. Educational programs, outreach, and exhibits include ways the Museum realizes its mission. The institution is private and does not yet have a physical site. When one is completed, the Museum plans to apply to the Smithsonian for an affiliation. In 2009, the Museum revised its mission statement, "The National Women's History Museum affirms the value of knowing Women's History, illuminates the role of women in transforming society and encourages all people, women and men, to participate in democratic dialogue about our future." The organization's site has an online exhibit that includes women spies and women in World War II.

National Women's History Project
www.nwhp.org
nwhp@nwhp.org

In 1980, Molly Murphy MacGregor, Mary Ruthsdotter, Maria Cuevas, Paula Hammett and Bette Morgan founded the project in Santa Rosa, California. The organization led a campaign that successfully lobbied Congress to authorize March as National Women's History Month, now observed throughout the United States. This project recognizes and celebrates the accomplishments of multicultural women. It provides information and educational materials and programs. In 2010, the project's theme is writing women back into American history. One of their events is, "Honor Women on Memorial Day."

National Women's Law Center, Women in the Military
www.nwlc.org/display.cfm?section=military
Info@nwlc.org

The Center began in 1972 to increase opportunities for women and girls through the law including getting laws into the books, enforcement, and litigation. Its emphasis includes finding ways to make the law work for women through its program areas. These areas are, education, employment, family economic security, and reproductive rights.

The Center addresses "Women in the Military" as one of their many issues. Links to their issue papers are available. Papers include "Military Women Should Have Full Access to Reproductive Health Care" (December 2008), "Eliminating Sexual Assault. Should Be a Top Priority of the Department of Defense" (December 2008), and "Military Women Should Be Allowed to Serve in All Units and Occupations for Which They Qualify" (December 2008).

Navy Memorial
www.navymemorial.org/Home/tabid/36/Default.aspx
library@navymemorial.org

The Navy Memorial was dedicated in 1987 to recognize and honor the service and sacrifices of men and women in uniform and their families. The Memorial has an education department that includes programs and internships, exhibits and artifacts and a library and media resource Center. The Memorial is a nonprofit organization designed to honor sea services.

Navy Nurse Corps Association
www.nnca.org
president@nnca.org

The Association began in 1987 to make an effort to bring together Navy nurses, retired or active duty. It also works to preserve history and collects memorabilia. Part of its mission is to develop locator files and personnel information pertaining to current and past members of the Navy Nurse Corps. The group strives to identify needs of members and eligible non-members. It works to encourage individuals to choose a career in the Corps. For those nurses interested a forum is offered where new friends are made and old friends become reacquainted. Prospective members can also post to gain career information for example. Likely members may also get information by clicking on the link, "A Career in the Navy Nurse Corps."

Presbyterian Church in America (PCA) Historical Center
www.pcahistory.org/pca
wsparkman@pcanet.org

The Historical Center of the Presbyterian Church in America (PCA) is the official archive of the PCA. Its primary duty is to collect and preserve the records of this denomination. Making the record is accomplished by training church historians, producing relevant literature and serving the historical preservation and research needs of the Church and its committees and agencies and the churches of the denomination. Not only is it their goal to preserve records, but also to make them available.

Of special importance, is the "General Assembly Actions and Position Papers," Ad Interim Study Committee on Women in the Military. The report goes into detail, but in brief, the PCA's conclusion is, "that it is the teaching of Scripture that men are duty-bound to defend women and children, both born and unborn. Our Lord gave Himself up for His Bride, the Church, and we are to follow

Him by loving our brides as He loved His Bride, proving our love by giving up our lives for them. While it is true that women, also, are to care for the weak and defenseless, Scripture lays the man under a special obligation to follow Christ in this duty."

Revolutionary Association of the Women of Afghanistan (RAWA)

www.rawa.org
rawa@rawa.org

In 1977, RAWA's martyred leader, Meena, and Afghan women intellectuals founded the Association in Kabul, Afghanistan. RAWA was established as an independent political and social organization fighting for human rights and social justice in Afghanistan. Soon RAWA became involved in education, health, fund raising, and political agitation. RAWA limited its activities to campaigning for women's rights and democracy until the Soviet occupation in 1979. The Association then became directly involved in the war of resistance promoting democracy and secularism. One of its projects was working with refugees in the Pakistan camps by establishing hospitals for refugee Afghan women and children in Quetta, conducting nursing courses, literacy courses and vocational training courses for women. Meena was martyred on February 4, 1987.

After the Soviet occupation ended in 1992, RAWA has turned its attention against the fundamentalists' and the ultra-fundamentalist Taliban's criminal policies and atrocities. RAWA believes that although the US War on terrorism removed the Taliban regime in October 2001, it has not removed religious fundamentalism. Today RAWA's mission for women's rights continues as RAWA works for establishment of an independent, free, democratic and secular Afghanistan.

Servicemember's Legal Defense Network (SLDN)

www.sldn.org
sldn@sldn.org

SLDN refers to its organization as a "watchdog" and policy association whose goal is to end discrimination against and harassment of military personnel affected by "Don't Ask, Don't Tell" (DADT). Free confidential legal service is available. The Web site covers the issue of homosexuality in the military in detail.

The organization states its vision succinctly, "Freedom to Serve." Its goals include: lift the ban preventing homosexuals and bisexuals from serving openly and honestly in the military, provide them free legal services, protect them from harassment based on perceived sexual orientation or gender identity, advocate policies and practices to improve their lives, support service member and veteran pride as homosexual, bisexual or transgender persons, and strengthen organizational capacity to assure the freedom to serve.

Society of Air Force Nurses
www.safn.org
safn10@aol.com

Organized in 1986, this veterans' organization provides support and social opportunities for its 2000 members. The members include retired, active duty and reserve status Air Force nurses, as well as those nurses transferred to the Biomedical Science Corps, honorably discharged Corps members, and U.S. Army Air Corps nurses who were honorably discharged.

Survivors Take Action Against Abuse by Military Personnel (STAMP)
www.nsvrc.org/organizations/108
resources@nsvrc.org

Survivors Take Action Against Abuse by Military Personnel or STAMP is a national advocacy group for victims of abuse committed by members of the military. Resources and support for victims include: domestic violence, rape and sexual assault, child abuse, gay bashing, and sexual harassment.

Tragedy Assistance Program for Survivors (TAPS)
www.taps.org
info@taps.org

The Tragedy Assistance Program for Survivors (TAPS) started in 1994 and cares for the families of the fallen. The organization provides assistance to surviving loved ones through National Military Survivor Seminars and Good Grief Camps. It has assisted over 25,000 family members, casualty officers, and caregivers. The Iraqi Women's Program offers support for widows of servicemen who died in Iraq. It also provides programs for women to sustain themselves financially.

United Nations Association of the United States of America (UNA-USA)
www.ngo.org/index2.htm
unahq@unausa.org

The United Nations Association of the United States of America is a nonprofit organization. Its purpose is to build understanding of and support among the American people for the United Nations' ideals and work. In 1943, the UNA-USA was first the League of Nations Association. In 1951, First Lady Eleanor Roosevelt, had completed her term as U.S. representative to the United Nations. She volunteered to work in the Association and created its first office and became its first chair in 1961. In 1964, the Association merged with the United States Committee for the United Nations creating the organization UNA-USA.

Global issues such as peace and security are among the group's many areas of policy research. The organization has almost 20,000 members nationwide. It makes an effort to educate Americans and build a constituency. It responds to individuals worldwide who wish to be heard in Washington, D.C.

Vietnam Women's Memorial Foundation
www.vietnamwomensmemorial.org
vwmfdc@gmail.com

The Vietnam Women's Memorial Foundation established in 2002, was previously, The Vietnam Women's Memorial Project. The Project was incorporated in 1984 as a non-profit organization located in Washington, D.C. The mission of the Vietnam Women's Memorial Project is to promote the healing of Vietnam women veterans, to identify the military and civilian women who served during the Vietnam War; to educate the public about their role; and to facilitate research on the issues related to their service. The Vietnam Women's Memorial was dedicated in 1993 as part of the Vietnam Veterans Memorial.

The Foundation honors women who served, but it also provides information for the families who lost loved ones in the war, so they would know about the women who served. They provide stories of women who served to preserve for history as well as a bibliography.

Women Airforce Service Pilots (WASP)
http://wingsacrossamerica.us/wasp
at6flyer@comcast.net

The Women's Auxiliary Ferrying Squadron (WAFS) formed in 1942 preceded the formation of the Women Airforce Service Pilots (WASP) the name officially designated in 1943. That the WAFS ferried light aircraft and women pilots began flying larger planes was a factor in the formation of the WASP. On June 21, 1944, the house defeated a bill to militarize WASP. The House recommended the WASP Training program except for those currently in training, be discontinued. On June 26, 1944, the WASP was ordered to discontinue and on October 2, deactivation of the WASP was ordered to take place on December 20, 1949. The WASP dissolved with no honors, benefits or veteran status. The official WASP records were sealed, marked classified, and sent to the government archives. It wasn't until 1977 that former WASP members began their campaign to unseal the records and in that same year, Public Law 95-202 gave WASP veteran status. In 1979, the Air Force officially recognized them.

The "WASP on the Web" site began in 1996 to emphasize the history of the Women Airforce Service Pilots of World War II and their stories. Its "Interactive Gallery" presents a detailed timeline of WASP history.

Women Accepted for Volunteer Emergency Services (WAVES) National
www.womenofthewaves.com
Dassa@att.net

Women Accepted for Volunteer Emergency Services (WAVES) was officially established in 1948. WAVES served in a far wider range of occupations than had the Yeomen who preceded them. Although traditionally female clerical jobs were a large portion of WAVES, thousands performed previously atypical duties in the aviation community including, Judge Advocate General Corps, medical professions, communications, intelligence, science and technology. At the end of World War II, female officers numbered over 8,000, about ten times the number of enlisted WAVES. They represented about 2.5 percent of the Navy. Naval History and Heritage presents an overview of WAVES at www.history.navy.mil/photos/prs-tpic/females/wave-ww2.htm.

WAVES National is an organization for women who have served or are serving in the sea services.

Women In Military Service For America Memorial (Women's Memorial)
www.womensmemorial.org
hq@womensmemorial.org

On June 22, 1995, under the leadership of Air Force Brigadier General Wilma L. Vaught, the Foundation broke ground for the Women's Memorial at Arlington National Cemetery, and on October 18, 1997, the memorial was dedicated. It is the first and only major national memorial honoring all women in the military in all wars and in all periods, during conflict or peace. The memorial features a collective history of nearly two million women who have served in defense of our nation and the individual stories of registered servicewomen. The foundation is a non-profit organization established to build the memorial. It now continues with fund raising to manage and maintain the Memorial Education Center.

The Memorial's Register, an accessible computerized database about the women who are registered, is central to its purpose. Photographs, military histories, and individual stories of registrants are available to visitors. Not only is the database a valuable resource, it also preserves history as it adds new registrants. The foundation's ongoing goal is to register as many veterans, active duty, National Guard and Reserve servicewomen as possible. Women from service organizations who served overseas during time of war, as well as Cadet Nurses, are also eligible. About 250,000 of the two million women eligible are registered thus far.

Women Marines Association
www.womenmarines.org
wma@WOMENMARINES.ORG

In 1960, the Women Marines Association was established in Denver, Colorado, to preserve their history from World War I to the present. Their work includes charitable and educational programs, assistance to veterans and active duty members in need, providing entertainment and assistance to hospitalized veterans, participation in patriotic events and preserve comradeship within its members.

This association is comprised of women who have served or are serving honorably in the United States Marine Corps regular or reserve components. Program includes professional development, scholarships, and volunteer service. It features a chronology of "Women Marine Milestones."

Women Military Aviators
www.womenmilitaryaviators.org
E-mail: use dialogue box on the Web site

Women Military Aviators formed in 1978 and now has about 800 members. Because a small percentage of the military aviation is female, the organization believes it is especially important to get to know, network with, and mentor other women military aviators. The Aviators' charter is to promote and preserve women's roles in military aviation. The group annually awards a scholarship to a woman pursuing an aviation degree of license.

Women Veterans of America
www.wvanational.org
Nationalcommander@womenveteransofamerica.org

A support group consisting of four women veterans and their leader, Claudia Mitzeliotis, Brooklyn Veterans Administration, on September 19, 1990 formed the Women Veterans of America. The other founding members are Katherine Mussen, Vietnam veteran; June Panzeri, World War II veteran; Mildred Cipolla, Korean War veteran; and Colleen Mussolino, Vietnam veteran. The group requested that issues pertinent to women veterans needed to be addressed. These issues ranged from privacy matters, well health such as mammograms, to special needs of women veterans. Their goal is the best possible medical care at VA Medical Centers. These women are advocates for all women veterans and women currently serving in the forces.

Women's Action for New Directions (WAND)
www.ngo.org/index2.htm
peace@wand.org

Dr. Helen Caldicott, a physician from Australia and expert on nuclear disarmament, organized Women's Action for Nuclear Disarmament in 1982. At the end of the cold war, the group became the Women's Action for New Directions. It works to redirect federal budget priorities away from the military and toward human needs. Although Women's Action for New Directions has various projects, it makes efforts with women to act politically to reduce violence and militarism, and to redirect unnecessary military resources to the needs of people and the environment that are unmet. WAND has teamed with organizations that work to stop the war in Iraq.

Women's Army Corps (WAC) Veterans' Association
www.armywomen.org
info@armywomen.org

Active members and veterans of the Women's Army Corps were sponsored by the WAC Mothers Association in January 1946 when they met in the Chicago area to discuss the prospect of organizing a Women's Army Corps Veterans' Association. In June 1946, the Association was formed in Illinois. Similar groups met in other cities and, in 1947, the group held its first national meeting in Chicago. In 1951, it was incorporated in the District of Columbia. On October 30, 1984, President Ronald Reagan signed into a law that granted the Association a Federal Charter. President Reagan declared the first National Women Veterans Recognition Week to begin on November 11, 1984. In 2005, the Association had approximately 4,500 active members.

The WAC Veteran's Association emphasizes Veterans Administration Hospital volunteer work and community service in the local and national community. It also makes monetary donations to charity organizations and collections of all types, and sponsors scholarships for relatives of Army servicewomen.

Women's Federation for World Peace
www.wfwp.org/wfwpi/index.cfm
WFWPIntl1@aol.com

The Women's Federation for World Peace International is a nonprofit, nongovernmental, organization in General Consultative Status of the Economic and Social Council (ECOSOC) and in association with the United Nations Department of Public Information.

The federation realizes its goal for a peaceful global family through two main worldwide projects. The poverty eradication project targets the empowerment of women and children. The peace-building "Bridge of Peace" sisterhood project works to end the cycle of conflict by gaining a new perspective to achieve world peace. The Federation works to accomplish this outlook through the Bridge of Peace Ceremony. Women who participate in the Ceremony meet a peer from a former enemy nation, a different faith, culture or race and commit themselves to bridge the gaps between them. They try to resolve their collective hurt to move beyond the pain of conflict. According to the Web site, "This stops the cycle of conflict, cuts chains of resentment and anger, and frees the newfound sisters to experience a new beginning." The project began in 1994 under the leadership of Dr. Hak Ja Han Moon. The first ceremonies were between the women of Japan and Korea, and at the end of World War II, the ceremonies began in the United States. The organization works to build partnerships for peace through cooperation of women.

Women's Overseas Service League
www.wosl.org
carolhabgood@sbcglobal.net

Women's Overseas Service League is a registered NGO (non-governmental organization) with the United Nations. Representatives regularly attend briefings and meetings held at the UN for nongovernmental organizations. When servicewomen returned home after World War I, most had no assistance or benefits that were given male soldiers. In May of 1921, the Women's Overseas Service League formed to continue friendships and patriotic spirit, and to provide financial and other types of aid to the women who were coming home. One of its major accomplishments was assisting the veterans gain admittance to veterans' hospitals.

The league has projects that include: supporting the Cathedral of the Pines, an all wars memorial with its Bell Tower honoring women's service; the Hospitalized Veterans Writers Program; the Freedom Foundation Youth Leadership Seminars; scholarships for women pursuing studies emphasizing public service; and grants to members with special needs. This national organization consists of women who have served overseas in or with the Armed Forces.

Women's Research and Education Institute (WREI)
www.wrei.org
WREI@WREI.org

The Women's Research and Education Institute (WREI) began in1977. It shared its research about the status of American women with their first organization, 18 congresswomen. Through time, the number of Congresswomen increased to 90 women serving in the House and Senate plus state officials, local governments, women's advocates, corporate policymakers, the media, teachers, and students. WREI continues to provide members of Congress with nonpartisan information and policy analysis on women's equity issues.

Advances in women's rights increased WREI's responsibilities to include the area of national defense. One of their major projects is women in the military which includes the publication of *Women in the Military: Where They Stand*, in its fifth edition in 2010. The Women in the Military project was established in 1990 to supply information and policy analysis on issues important to military. Downloadable files on pertinent military data is available on the Web site. These files pertain to military history, statistics, bibliographies, and collections.

Wounded Warrior Project
www.woundedwarriorproject.org
1120 G Street NW, Suite 700 Washington, D.C. 20005
(202)-558-4302

Wounded Warrior Project is a nonprofit organization formed by a group of veterans. The group was watching the evening news and were moved by the stories they heard of the first wounded service members returning home from Afghanistan and Iraq. They decided provide tangible support for the severely wounded and help them heal. The Wounded Warriors deliver backpacks to the bedside of wounded warriors. Other programs include: advocacy, benefits counseling, caregivers retreats, coping/family services, peer mentoring, and warriors to work.

The project's mission has three parts: To raise awareness and enlist the public's aid; to help the severely injured and aid in assisting each other; and to provide programs and services to meet the needs of severely the injured.

References

Hart, Roxine C. 1991. *Women in Combat*. Family Service Center. Port Hueneme, California. The Research Division, Defense Equal Opportunity Defense Management Institute, Patrick Air Force Base, Florida, February, 1–23.

Skaine, Rosemarie. 1999. *Women at War: Gender Issues of Americans in Combat*. Jefferson, N.C.: McFarland & Co.

8

Resources

The resources available to research women in combat, its context, and its issues are extensive. The most relevant print and nonprint resources have been selected for inclusion in this chapter. The Print Resources section is organized by books; articles, journals, and journal articles; hearings and reports; legal cases; papers, proceedings, and memorandums; and theses and dissertations. The Nonprint Resources are organized by bibliographies, databases, DVDs/videotapes, film/multimedia, and Internet sites.

Print Resources

Books

Bailey, Beth. *America's Army: Making the All-Volunteer Force.* **Cambridge, MA: Harvard, 2009. 352 pp.**

This book gives a detailed account of the ending of the draft after combat troops were withdrawn from Vietnam. It discusses difficult issues such as: does a volunteer force offer young men and women an opportunity to improve their lives and serve their country or is it a duty expected of every citizen? Is serving in the military worth all of the pain and sacrifice?

Barkalow, Carol, with Andrea Raab. *In the Men's House*. New York, NY: Poseidon Press, 1990. 283 pp.

The author is a member of the first class of women admitted to West Point. She portrays life at the academy and as an army officer. She describes the demanding physical training, the controlled social life, and hazing she experienced.

Benedict, Helen. *The Lonely Soldier: The Private War of Women Serving in Iraq*. Boston, MA: Beacon Press, 2009. 280 pp.

The author relates stories of five women of different ethnicities and backgrounds who served in Iraq between 2003 and 2006. Through them, she tells of the private war of female soldiers against their comrades in a military culture hostile to women.

Bigler, Philip. *Hostile Fire: The Life and Death of First Lieutenant Sharon Lane*. Falls Church, VA: Vandamere Press, 1996. 192 pp.

Lt. Sharon Lane was the only American servicewoman to die in the Vietnam War as a result of hostile fire. Lane was a 25-year old nurse at the U.S. 312th Evacuation Hospital in Chu Lai, Vietnam that came under enemy fire. Bigler's book is a tribute to Lane.

Blanton, DeAnne. "Cathay Williams: Black Woman Soldier, 1866–68." In *Buffalo Soldiers in the West: A Black Soldier's Anthology*, Bruce A. Glasrud and Michael N. Searles, eds. College Station, TX: Texas A&M University Press, 2007. 101–113.

Deanne Blanton writes about Cathay Williams. On November 15, 1866, Cathay Williams enlisted in the U.S. Regular Army under the name William Cathay. She is the only documented African American woman to serve in the U.S. Army before the official introduction of women.

Blanton, DeAnne, and Lauren Cook. *They Fought Like Demons: Women Soldiers in the American Civil War*. Baton Rouge, LA: Louisiana State University Press, 2007. 277 pp.

The authors demonstrate that many women took male names, disguised themselves in men's uniforms, and went into battle as Union and Confederate soldiers. This book tells of the controversy and of the issues surrounding their service.

Bragg, Rick. *I Am a Solder, Too: The Jessica Lynch Story.* **New York, NY: Knopf, 2003. 256 pp.**

The author is a Pulitzer Prize-winning reporter who worked with *The New York Times.* The narrative is told in Jessica Lynch's own words. She tells of her capture during an ambush in Iraq and of her rescue from a hospital there. He also presents how Lynch coped with all of the controversy surrounding her rescue.

Breuer, William B. *War and American Women: Heroism, Deeds, and Controversy.* **Westport, CT: Praeger Security International, 1997. 280 pp.**

The book tells of military women's achievements starting in World War I and continuing through the Gulf War of 1991. It also discusses the controversy over sending women into combat. The author claims the dispute contributed to the suicide of Admiral Jeremy Boorda in 1996.

Browne, Kingsley. *Co-Ed Combat: The New Evidence That Women Shouldn't Fight the Nation's Wars.* **New York, NY: Sentinel HC, 2007. 368 pp.**

Kingsley holds the position that women are not physically and psychologically suited for combat. He proposes that women should not be assigned in forward support units. He claims women's presence on the front lines endangers the military.

Burgess, Lauren Cook. *An Uncommon Soldier: Civil War Letters of Sarah Rosetta Wakeman, Alias Lyons Wakeman, 153rd Regiment, New York State Volunteers.* **Pasadena, MD: The Minerva Center, 1994. 128 pp.**

This book is a collection of letters of Sara Wakeman, who served as a Union soldier as Lyons Wakeman during the Red River campaign. The letters are about her experiences from her enlistment to shortly before her death in 1863.

Camp, LaVonne Telshaw. *Lingering Fever: A World War II Nurse's Memoir.* **Jefferson, NC: McFarland & Company, 1997. 184 pp.**

The author describes nursing soldiers in 1945 in the monsoon-drenched jungles of Assam, in the China-Burma-India theater of

World War II. Her nurse's training did not prepare her for the tropical diseases or the bad conditions in the hospital. Her romance with her future husband kept her going. She relates the events in letters she wrote to her parents.

Cardoza, Thomas. *Intrepid Women: Cantinières and Vivandières of the French Army.* **Bloomington, Indiana: Indiana University Press, 2010. 312 pp.**

The book describes the daring actions of women noncombatants in the French military from 1793 to the eve of World War I. Although the women were noncombatant spouses of active-duty soldiers, they fought in all wars in this time period. For a detailed explanation about the book, visit the author's Web site at www.cantinieres.com.

Carreiras, Helena. *Gender and the Military: Women in the Armed Forces of Western Democracies.* **New York, NY: Routledge, 2006. 288 pp.**

The book presents a comparative, cross-national study of the participation of women in the armed forces of NATO countries. The Netherlands and Portugal are presented as case studies. Chapters 4–7 and the conclusion are of particular value.

Claghorn, Charles. *Women Patriots of the American Revolution: A Biographical Dictionary.* **Metuchen, NJ: Scarecrow Press, 1994. 519 pp.**

Brief biographies of 600 women who performed patriotic acts in all roles.

Cooke, O. A. *The Canadian Military Experience, 1867–1995: A Bibliography.* **3rd ed. Canada: Department of National Defence, Directorate of History, 1997. 151 pp.**

The book is divided into sections: Army, Navy, and Air Force. Each service is divided into year groupings: before World War I, World War I, and World War II. The book includes an index.

Cornum, Rhonda, with Peter F. Copeland. *She Went to War: The Rhonda Cornum Story.* **Novato, CA: Presidio Press, 1992. 256 pp.**

During the Gulf War, a U.S. Army helicopter on a medical rescue mission inside Iraq was shot down. Five of the eight Americans were killed instantly. Saddam Hussein's elite Republican Guard captured the three survivors. One of the survivors was Maj. Rhonda Cornum. This book is about her experience based on her diary.

Cummings, Missy. *Hornet's Nest: The Experiences of One of the Navy's First Female Fighter Pilots.* **Lincoln, NE: Writer's Showcase Press, 2000. 416 pp.**

Cummings tells her story as one of the first women in Navy fighter squadrons in 1993. She does so in a clear, sometimes humorous, but always riveting, manner. Her book gives society valuable knowledge of voices yet unheard.

D'Amico, Francine and Laurie Weinstein, editors. *Gender Camouflage: Women and the U.S. Military.* **New York, NY: New York University Press, 1999. 320 pp.**

The editors have assembled a strong group of contributors including Connie Reeves, Georgia Clark Sadler, Gwyn Kirk, and Joan Furey. These women experienced and understand the U.S. military. Topics include women who are nurses, servicemembers, military academy students, veterans, lesbians, military wives, DoD employees, and civilian military instructors. Women not in the military are also covered, peace workers and comfort women near U.S. bases, for example.

DeGroot, Gerard and Corinna Peniston-Bird, eds. *A Soldier and a Woman: Sexual Integration in the Military.* **White Plains, NY: Pearson/ Longman, 2000. 448 pp.**

The book covers the experiences of women in the military from the late mediaeval period to 2000. The wars addressed include: The Thirty Years War, the French and Indian Wars in northern America, the Anglo-Boer War, the First and Second World Wars, the Long March in China, and the Vietnam War. Terrorism studies and contemporary military service are also covered. Chapters 4, 9, 10, 12, 14, 15 are especially relevant to militaries worldwide.

De Pauw, Linda Grant. *Battle Cries and Lullabies: Women in War from Prehistory to the Present.* **Norman, OK: University of Oklahoma Press, 1998. 432 pp.**

The author presents women in all of the roles assumed during war. These roles include those as: victims, warriors; nurses, spies, sex workers, wives, mothers, warrior queens who lead armies into battle, and baggage carriers marching in the rear. De Pauw demonstrates that women have been present on and near the battlefield since ancient times.

Disher, Sharon. *First Class: Women Join the Ranks of the Naval Academy.* Annapolis, MD: Naval Institute Press, 1998. 264 pp.

The author was one of 81 in the first class of women admitted to the Naval Academy. She describes the mental and physical challenges of the academy routine and the psychological isolation of being a woman in what had been a man's world. Disher writes of the prejudice and abuse frequently met and which was for the most part unreported and unpunished. She wrote the book to document history.

Ebbert, Jean and Marie-Beth Hall. *Cross Currents: Navy Women from World War I to Tailhook.* Washington, D.C.: Brassey's, 1993. 357 pp.

The book presents a balanced history of how women have struggled for acceptance in the U.S. Navy from World War I through the Gulf War and the 1991 Tailhook scandal.

Ebbert, Jean and Marie-Beth Hall. *The First, the Few and the Forgotten: Navy and Marine Corps Women in World War I.* Annapolis, MD: Naval Institute Press, 2002. 189 pp.

The book covers women who served during World War I. The authors address the misconception that women's military role in the war was limited to nursing. From 1917 to 1920, about 12,000 enlisted women served in the U.S. Naval Reserve and 305 in the U.S. Marine Corps Reserve.

Eisenstein, Zillah. "Resexing the Wars of/on Terror." *Sexual Decoys: Gender, Race, and War in Imperial Democracy,* 17–48 pp. London, England: Zed Books, 2007. 256 pp.

The author presents the most recent militarist and masculine configurations through discussions of the wars in Afghanistan and Iraq, violations at Guantánamo and Abu Ghraib. She believes that women's rights rhetoric is being maneuvered as a tactic for global dominance and a misogynistic capture of democratic discourse.

Enloe, Cynthia. *Does Khaki Become You?* Boston, MA: South End Press, 1983. 2nd ed. 1993. 224 pp.

The book is considered a classic. Topics include: the military needs camp followers, militarization of prostitution, keeping the home fires burning, military wives, nursing the military, women in liberation armies, and feminism and militarism.

Fenner, Lorry M., and Marie de Young. *Women in Combat: Civic Duty or Military Liability.* Washington, D.C.: Georgetown University Press, 2001. 192 pp.

Opposing views about whether American service women should be assigned to combat roles, ground combat in particular, is the focus of this book.

Francke, Linda Bird. *Ground Zero: The Gender Wars in the Military.* New York, NY: Simon & Schuster, 1997. 304 pp.

The book portrays the lives of men and women in the context of the debate on women in combat. The author discusses both sides in the gender struggle. She concludes that the military's internal gender war will never be over.

Holm, Jeanne M. *In Defense of a Nation: Servicewomen in World War II.* Arlington, VA: Military Women's Press, 1998. 192 pp.

Holm presents a history of American servicewomen in World War II. The book contains photographs that demonstrate what servicewomen did.

Holm, Jeanne M. *Women in the Military: An Unfinished Revolution.* Rev. ed. Novato, CA: Presidio Press, 1993. 560 pp.

The book is considered a classic in that it comprehensively addresses fundamental issues for women in the service. First published in 1982, Jeanne M. Holm adds information on the role of military women in the Grenada, Panama and Persian Gulf conflicts in this edition. She also updates the discussion of the ongoing debate over the combat exclusion laws and draft policies relating to women.

Holmstedt, Kirsten. *Band of Sisters: American Women at War in Iraq.* **Mechanicsburg, PA: Stackpole Books, 2007. 384 pp.**

Band of Sisters tells the stories of twelve of American women in the frontlines. These stories include: the first female pilot to be shot down and survive, the first black female combat pilot, a turret gunner who defends a convoy, two military policewomen in a firefight, and a nurse who works to save lives.

Hunter, Mic. *Honor Betrayed: Sexual Abuse in America's Military.* **Fort Lee, NJ: Barricade Books, 2007. 355 pp.**

The author describes the hostile, dehumanizing sexual environment in the military. Most vulnerable to sexual abuse are minorities, women and homosexuals. Tacit acceptance of the abuse includes prisoner abuse.

Johnson, Shoshana (Author). M. L. Doyle (Contributor), *I'm Still Standing: From Captive U.S. Soldier to Free Citizen—My Journey Home.* **New York, NY: Simon & Schuster Adult, 2010. 276 pp.**

Shoshana Johnson is America's first black female prisoner of war. She was a cook in the Army hoping to earn money to support her young child. She tells how she was sent with a convoy and experienced combat. She was taken as a prisoner of war. Her book provides information on the black military experience and the Iraq War. The book is in hardcover, audio CD and cassette, MP3 CD, and can be downloaded from Amazon.com as an e-book.

Karney, Benjamin R., and John S. Crown. *Families Under Stress: An Assessment of Data, Theory, and Research on Marriage and Divorce in the Military.* **Santa Monica, CA: RAND, 2007. 206 pp. (UB403. K36 2007). www.rand.org/pubs/monographs/2007.**

This report evaluates the effects of stress on military marriages in order to develop good programs and policies. Most military members are married. The state of their marriage affects performance and retention and has significant implications for national security.

Kennedy, Claudia, and Malcolm McConnell. *Generally Speaking.* **New York, NY: Warner Books, 2001. 352 pp.**

A subtitle was added in later editions and the audio and e-book versions: "A Memoir by the First Woman Promoted to Three-Star General in the U.S. Army." General Claudia Kennedy was the highest-ranking female officer of her time. She served as Deputy Chief of Staff for Intelligence and managed 45,000 soldiers worldwide.

Mathers, Jennifer. "Women, Society and the Military: Women Soldiers in Post-Soviet Russia." Part III, Ch. 8, 208–227. In *Military and Society in Post-Soviet Russia.* **Stephen L. Webber and Jennifer G. Mathers, eds. Manchester, UK: Manchester University Press, 2006. 296 pp.**

The book gives an overview of the nature of the relationship between the military and society in post-Soviet Russia. Mather's chapter focuses on women soldiers in post-Soviet Russia.

Mitchell, Brian. *Weak Link: The Feminization of the American Military.* **Washington, D.C.: Regnery Publishing, Inc., An Eagle Publishing Company, 1989. 160 pp.**

The author is an established opponent of women serving in combat. The book presents the arguments against women in the military.

Mitchell, Brian. *Women in the Military: Flirting with Disaster.* **Washington, D.C. Regnery Publishing, Inc., An Eagle Publishing Company, 1998. 344 pp.**

The book offers the position that the integration of women into the military has proved a national security disaster. The author examines sexual harassment and assault scandals including those at Aberdeen and Tailhook '91.

Monahan, Evelyn M., and Rosemary Neidel-Greenlee. *A Few Good Women: America's Military Women From World War I to the War in Iraq and Afghanistan.* **New York, NY: Knopf Doubleday Publishing Group, 2010. 496 pp.**

The book is an account of the U.S. women's military corps that fought for the right to defend their country by serving in our armed forces with full military rank and benefits. The account includes the struggle of women to serve in combat. Newspaper and personal stories help the reader through dates and events.

Morden, Bettie J. *The Women's Army Corps, 1945–1978.* **Washington, D. C.: Center of Military History, 1990. 563 pp.**

A presentation of 33 years of the Women's Army Corp (WAC) from V-J Day 1945 to October 20, 1978, when the Women's Army Corps was abolished. WAC officers were assimilated into the other branches of the Army except combat arms.

Norman, Elizabeth. *Women at War: The Story of 50 Military Nurses Who Served in Vietnam.* **Philadelphia, PA: University of Pennsylvania Press, 1990. 238 pp.**

Fifty members of the Army, Navy, and Air Force Nurse Corps tell of their service working in military hospitals, aboard ships, and air evacuation squadrons during the Vietnam War.

Norman, Elizabeth. *We Band of Angels: The Untold Story of American Nurses Trapped in Bataan by the Japanese.* **New York, NY: Random House, 1999. 384 pp.**

This book tells of American nurses who provide their courage under combat conditions. During three years of captivity under the Japanese, they demonstrated their ability to survive.

Oliver, Kelly. *Women as Weapons of War: Iraq, Sex, and the Media.* **New York, NY: Columbia University Press, 2007. 224 pp.**

Kelly Oliver demonstrates how the media and the George W. Bush administration used images of weaponry to describe women and female sexuality to create a link between vulnerability and violence. To illustrate, she includes discussions of female soldiers of Abu Ghraib prison.

Pape, Robert A. *Dying to Win: The Strategic Logic of Suicide Terrorism.* **New York, NY: Random House Publishing Group, 2006. 368 pp.**

The author has an extensive database covering every suicide terrorist attack in the world from 1980 until the present time. In

Dying to Win, Pape provides a demographic profile of the modern suicide terrorist.

Pennington, Reina, and Robin Higham, eds. *Amazons to Fighter Pilots: A Biographical Dictionary of Military Women.* **2 Volumes. West Port, CT: Greenwood Press, 2003. Vol. 1, 848 pp. Vol. II (r–z). 760 pp.**

The book is a history of women in the military emphasizing women who fight. Over 300 women are profiled. Groups covered include: the Amazons, women in the Spanish Civil War, and Native Americans.

Pfluke, Lillian A. "The Best Soldier for the Job: A Personal Perspective." 57–61. In *Women in the Military.* **James Haley, ed. San Diego, CA: Greenhaven Press, 2004. 94 pp.**

Major Pfluke provides an intellectual outline of the reasons she was qualified to be a ground combat soldier. Her thesis is that a soldier should be assigned to a job on the basis of ability.

Ruff, Cheryl Lynn, and K. Sue Roper. *Ruff's War: A Navy Nurse on the Frontline on Iraq.* **Annapolis, MD: Naval Institute Press, 2005. 209 pp.**

Ruff is a surgical nurse serving in Iraq in 2003. She explains why she wanted to serve and her readjustment to civilian life.

Sadler, Georgia. "Women in Combat: The U.S. Military and the Impact of the Persian Gulf War," In Laurie Weinstein and Christie White. *Wives and Warriors: Women and the Military in the United States and Canada.* **Westport, CT: Bergin & Garvey, April 1997. 272 pp.**

A wide range of scholars examine how the military in Canada and the U.S. constructs gender to exclude women from being valued as equals to men. Sadler focuses on the impact of the Persian Gulf War on women's roles.

Schneider, Dorothy and Carl J. Schneider. *Into the Breach: American Women Overseas in World War I.* **New York, NY: Viking Press, 1991. 384 pp.**

The authors address how 25,000 women served in World War I. They found that the women served various needs of the military, civilians and refugees by working overseas in relief organizations.

Sherrow, Victoria. *Women and the Military: An Encyclopedia.* **Santa Barbara, CA: ABC-CLIO, 1996. 304 pp.**

The book addresses significant contributions and roles of military women throughout history. Covered are the accomplishments and struggles of military women.

Sjoberg, Laura. *Gender, Justice, and the Wars in Iraq: A Feminist Reformulation of Just War Theory.* **Lanham, MD: Lexington Books, 2006. 278 pp. Paperback.**

The author draws upon feminist just war theory to analyze the conflicts since the end of the Cold War.

Skaine, Rosemarie. *Female Suicide Bombers.* **Jefferson, NC: McFarland & Co. Inc., 2006. 225 pp.**

Overview of the phenomenon of suicide bombing and the U.S. policy approach. Detailed chronology of female bombers is included and is illustrated with photos of actual bombers.

Skaine, Rosemarie. *Power and Gender: Issues in Sexual Dominance and Harassment.* **Jefferson, NC: McFarland & Co. Inc., 1996. 460 pp.**

Chapter 9 presents an overview of sexual harassment in the military including issues and history. The U.S. Navy's Tailhook '91 scandal is presented in great detail including the results of three investigations, one little-known Admirals Responses, and the Navy Consolidated Disposition Authority results of the fate of the aviators.

Skaine, Rosemarie. *Women at War: Gender Issues of Americans in Combat.* **Jefferson, NC: McFarland & Co. Inc., 1999. 299 pp.**

The book traces the history of women in war, but its primary emphasis is the detailed legal efforts to allow women in combat.

Solaro, Erin. *Women in the Line of Fire: What You Should Know About Women in the Military.* Emeryville, CA: Seal Press, 2006. 411 pp.

In 2004, the author went to Iraq and in 2005, to Afghanistan. She spent time embedded with combat troops. Solaro believes in removing all limits on women's service. She says it is time to drop all remaining restrictions on women serving in combat.

Stabe, Mary E. *Diary From the Desert.* Bedford, Ind.: JoNa Books, 2003. 196 pp.

Mary E. Stabe's story is of an Iowa farm girl who joins the Army and serves in the Gulf War (1990–1991). She writes about her feelings of isolation as the only woman among 300 troops and of her fears of war.

Sterner, Doris. *In and Out of Harm's Way: History of the Navy Nurse Corps.* Seattle, WA: Peanut Butter Publishing, 1997. 390 pp. Paperback.

The author, a retired Navy captain, presents a history of the Navy Nurse Corps.

Stiehm, Judith Hicks. Ed. *Women and Men's Wars: Special Issue of Women's Studies International Forum.* Oxford, England: Pergamon. 1983.

This work was previously published as a special issue of *Women's Studies International Forum* 5: 3–4. It addresses subjects such as women's attitudes and war.

Stremlow, Mary V. U.S. Marine Corps Reserve. *A History of the Women Marines, 1946–1977.* Washington, D.C.: U.S. Marine Corps, 1986. 250 pp.

Contents include: Postwar Women's Reserve Board, Volunteer Women's Reserve, Women's Armed Forces legislation Public Law 625, the pioneers, first black women Marines, the Korean War, and the first seven Women's Reserve Platoons. It has black and white photos.

Taylor, Susie King. *A Black Woman's Civil War Memoirs: Reminiscences of My Life in Camp with the 33rd U.S Colored Troops, Late 1st South Carolina Volunteers.* Princeton, NJ: Marcus Wiener Publishing, 1988. 152 pp.

The author Taylor was born a slave. She gained her freedom early in the Civil War and served as a nurse for the first black regiment of the Union Army.

Treadwell, Mattie E. *The United States Army in World War II, Special Studies: The Women's Army Corps.* Washington, D. C.: Office of the Chief of Military History, Department of the Army, 1991. 841 pp.

The book is a major record and study of the Women's Army Corps (WAC). Treadwell was at one time the director of WAC.

Wise, James E., Jr., and Scott Baron. *Women at War: Iraq, Afghanistan, and Other Conflicts.* Annapolis, MD: Naval Institute Press, 2006. 234 pp.

The authors contend that insurgency war with no rear or front lines has made the debate regarding women in combat irrelevant. In this kind of war zone, anyone can be killed or injured at any time. The authors present stories of the courageous women who serve.

Witt, Linda, Judith Bellafaire, Britta Gradrud, and Mary Jo Binker. *A Defense Weapon Known to Be of Value: Servicewomen during the Korean War Era.* Lebanon, NH: University Press of New England, 2005. 336 pp.

The book looks at the multiple roles of women in the U.S. military and the auxiliary civilian component from 1945 to 1953.

Zeigler, Sara L., and Gregory G. Gunderson. *Moving beyond G.I. Jane: Women and the U.S. Military.* Lanham, MD: University Press of America, 2005. 204 pp.

The authors offer analyses of the debates over integrating women into combat roles and the appropriate approach to confronting sexual harassment within the ranks. Each chapter provides recommendations on how the services should handle these personnel problems.

Articles, Journals, and Journal Articles

Brooks, Bradley, and Russ Bynum. "Husband-Wife Soldiers Get to Share Quarters." *USA Today*, April 1, 2008, 10. www.usatoday.com.

The Army is allowing husband-and-wife soldiers to live and sleep together in the war zone, representing a historic change in policy. The policy hopes to preserve marriages.

Brower, J. Michael. "PRO: Expanding Roles for Women Warriors." *Officer* 81 (March 2005): 38, 42–45. Donnelly, Elaine. "CON: Women in Combat." 39–42. ProQuest and http://goliath.ecnext.com/coms2/gi_0199-4139768/Examining-the-pros-and-cons.html.

Michael Brower outlines arguments that support women serving in combat. Elaine Donnelly provides the case for not supporting women serving in combat.

Burstein, Janet. "Reviews." *Minerva Journal of Women and War* 3: 2 (Fall 2009), 103. www.mcfarlandpub.com/minervaback.html.

The article reviews a number of films made by Israeli women that address the issues of men's and women's military service.

Campbell, D'Ann. "Women in Combat: The World War II Experiences in the United States, Great Britain, Germany and the Soviet Union." *Journal of Military History*: 57 (1993): 301–323.

In World War II. most of the combatant nations did not allow the assignment of females to a direct combat role, but women were often exposed to combat. Only the USSR had allowed women in front-line combat units. Germany and the United Kingdom assigned women to operate crew-served weapons such as anti-aircraft batteries. Only the U.S. did not allow any large-scale mobilization of women for possible combat duty.

CBC News Online. "Women in the Military—International." *The National*. May 30, 2006. www.cbc.ca (accessed July 13, 2010).

This article provides NATO data on the year of legal admittance of female soldiers for seven countries. It also provides the countries that draft (conscript) women into the armed forces and a brief comparison of the militaries of the United Kingdom and the United States.

Center for Military Readiness. "Background and Facts: Women In or Near Land Combat." June 16, 2006. www.cmrlink.org.

The Center for Military Readiness is a nonprofit organization that has long held the position that women should not serve in combat.

Center for Military Readiness. "Grim Toll of Military Women Killed in War: 105 Women Killed in War on Terror." March 22, 2010. www.cmrlink.org (accessed July 7, 2010).

The article maintains "there is no military necessity to send young women and mothers to fight in close combat areas where they do not have an equal opportunity to survive, or to help fellow soldiers survive." An updated list of the names of female casualties is provided.

Center for Military Readiness. "Rules for Women in Combat." http:/cmrlink.org (accessed July 7, 2010).

The article provides a list of documents that give factual information and historic context on the issue of military women serving in or near direct ground combat.

Center for Military Readiness. 2005. "Policy Analysis— Frequently Asked Questions: The Hunter/McHugh Amendment to H.R. 1815 Codification of DoD Regulations Re: Women in Land Combat." May 23. http:/cmrlink.org (accessed July 7, 2010).

The article discusses the amendment to the 2006 Defense Authorization Bill, co-sponsored by House Armed Services Committee Chairman Duncan Hunter (R-CA) and Military Personnel Subcommittee Chairman John McHugh (R-NY), which would have, had it passed, codified current Department of Defense (DoD) regulations governing the assignment of female soldiers.

Cock, Jacklyn. "Women and the Military: Implications for Demilitarization in the 1990s in South Africa." *Gender and Society*: 8: 2 (June 1994): 152–169.

The article illustrates the relationship between gender and militarization, but concludes that there is no necessary relationship.

Corbett, Sara. "The Women's War." *New York Times Magazine,* **March 18, 2007, 40–55, 62, 71–72. ProQuest and www.nytimes .com/2007/03/18/magazine/18cover.html.**

The article addresses the role of women soldiers in the Iraq war and the toll it is taking on them. It also addresses sexual harassment and Post Traumatic Stress Disorder (PTSD).

Donnelly, Elaine. "Constructing the Co-ed Military." *Duke Journal of Gender Law and Policy* **14: 815 (2007). www.law.duke.edu/ shell/cite.pl?14+Duke+J.+Gender+L.+&+Pol'y+815#FA0 (accessed July 7, 2010).**

Donnelly maintains there has not been an official, comprehensive analysis of social policies involving women in the military since 1992. She calls for an objective analysis.

Forgey, Mary Ann, and Lee Badger. "Patterns of Intimate Partner Violence among Married Women in the Military: Type, Level, Directionality and Consequences." *Journal of Family Violence* **21 (August 2006): 369–380. ProQuest and EBSCO host Academic Search Elite.**

The authors discover that the majority of military violence reported was perpetrated by both spouses and was equal in terms of type and level of severity. Enlisted women were more than three times as likely to be victims of unilateral severe violence as their male civilian spouses.

Frank, Nathaniel. "Gays and Lesbians at War: Military Service in Iraq and Afghanistan Under 'Don't Ask, Don't Tell.'" UC Santa Barbara: Center for the Study of Sexual Minorities in the Military, 2004. 52 pp. www.escholarship.org/uc/item/51d2b60d (accessed July 9, 2010).

The article discusses Don't Ask–Don't Tell, the military policy for soldiers with same sex orientation in the framework of the wars in Afghanistan and Iraq. It includes an excellent bibliography with several cross-cultural references.

"Gender, Sexuality & the Military." *Duke Journal of Gender Law & Policy* 14 (May 2007): entire issue. www.law.duke.edu/journals/djglp/gentoc14n2.

The issue is devoted to issues such as homosexuality, integration, consensual sex, combat and law. Links give direct access to articles.

Geren, Pete, and George Casey. "A Sacred Trust." *Army.mil/News*, September 16, 2008. www.army.mil/-news/2008/09/16/12462-a-sacred-trust (accessed July 9, 2010).

The authors emphasize the importance of the Army's plan to eliminate the incidence of the crime of sexual assault and the offense of sexual harassment.

Harman, Jane. "Rapists in the Ranks: Sexual Assaults Are Frequent, and Frequently Ignored, in the Armed Services." *Los Angeles Times*, March 31, 2008, sec. A, p. 15. http:/articles.latimes.com/2008/mar/31/opinion/oe-harman31 (accessed July 8, 2010).

The article presents examples, statistics of rape in the military and responses of responsible government bodies.

Hasday, Jill Elaine. "Article: Fighting Women: The Military, Sex, and Extrajudicial Constitutional Change." 93 *Minnesota Law Review* 96 (November 2008): 96–164.

The author focuses on the record of women's legal status in the military. One of her points is that the record of women's legal military status is significant counterevidence to the widespread assumption that sex equality already exists.

Hoge, Charles W., Julie C. Clark, and Carl A. Castro. "Commentary: Women in Combat and the Risk of Post-Traumatic Stress Disorder and Depression." *International Journal of Epidemiology* 36 (April 2007): 327–329. ProQuest.

This article addresses how women who serve in combat are at risk of PTSD and/or depression.

Kronsell, Annica, and Erika Svedberg. "The Duty to Protect: Gender in the Swedish Practice of Conscription." *Cooperation and Conflict* 36:2 (2001): 163.

Swedish scholars conducted a study of attitudes towards the proposed change of extending conscription to women, including attitudes among male conscripted soldiers.

Marine Corps Gazette

All *Marine Corps Gazette* articles can be found through the databases Proquest or EBSCO. *Leatherneck* articles can be found in Proquest. The articles listed are examples of the writings on the issue of women in combat.

Mariner, Rosemary Bryant. "A Soldier Is a Soldier." *Joint Force Quarterly* 3 (Winter 1993–1994): 54–61.

The author supports the position that the services should match soldiers' abilities, not their gender, to the position.

Mathers, Jennifer. "Russia's Women Soldiers in the Twenty-First Century." *Minerva Journal of Women and War.* (Spring 2007): 8–18

The author examines the influx of women into the Russian military since the early 1990s. She compares the experience of women in the Russian military with that of women in the U.S. military. She argues that the integration of women is partial and that their position is susceptible to erosion.

Anonymous. "Regarding Women in Combat." *Marine Corps Gazette.* Quantico 82: 2 (February 1998): 29. 2 pp.

Anonymous. Women in Combat? Insights Worth Repeating." *Marine Corps Gazette.* Quantico 81: 11 (November 1997): 73. 1 p.

Florian, Timothy A. "Women Should Have the Same PLC Options As Men." *Marine Corps Gazette.* Quantico 81: 9 (September 1997): 31. 3 pp.

Karcher, Mary D. "Female Marines Put Training to the Test." *Leatherneck.* Quantico 88: 2 (February 2005): 44. 4 pp.

Lisbon, William M. "Corps Testing Push-Ups for Female Marine PFT." *Leatherneck.* Quantico 81: 9 (September 1998): 41. 1 p.

Luddy II, John F. "Role for Women in Combat Expands." *Marine Corps Gazette*. Quantico 78: 12 (December 1994): 55. 1 p. 2008, sec. C, p. 1.

McDougall. Walter. "Selected Responses to HB#15—Women in Combat." *Marine Corps Gazette*. Quantico 84: 7 (July 2000): 18. 1 p.

Riggs. William W. "The Shibboleth of Women in Combat." *Marine Corps Gazette*. Quantico 87: 3 (March 2003): 61. 2 pp.

Sherman. Julie W. "Combat Duty for Women? One Woman's Point of View." *Marine Corps Gazette*. Quantico 85: 2 (February 2001): 41. 2 pp.

Walker, Karen M. "Women Leading Men." *Marine Corps Gazette*. Quantico 93: 5 (May 2009): 41. 4 pp.

McLaughlin, Matthew. "Dual-military Couples Share Deployment." *American Forces Press Service News Articles,* **January 26, 2005. www.defenselink.mil/news/newsarticle.aspx?id=24263 (accessed July 8, 2010).**

The articles takes a look at a married couple who believes that separating family life from the professional work environment is one of several issues that make deployment difficult. for soldiers.

Milko, James D. "Beyond the Persian Gulf Crisis: Expanding the Role of the Servicewomen in the United States Military." *American University Law Review* **41 (Summer 1992): 1302–1337.**

The article presents the legalities of the combat exclusion laws in understandable terms.

Minerva Journal of Women and War. **(print and online at www.mcfarlandpub.com/minervaback.html).**

Some journals and magazines devote their content to military issues. A strong journal to that end is the *Minerva Journal of Women and War*. Extensive information about the journal can be found on the Minerva web site located at www.minervacenter.com/minerva-journal. Links with complete table of contents for the Spring and Fall 2007 and Spring 2008 issues are available. For 20 years, the Minerva Center, Inc, a nonprofit, tax exempt educational organization, published the journal. The early journals were titled, *MINERVA: Quarterly Report on Women and the Military.* Beginning in 2007, the journal is published by McFarland and Company in Jefferson, NC See www.mcfarlandpub.com/minerva for more information

Minerva Journal of Women and War 3: 2 (Fall 2009): 103. (print and online at www.mcfarlandpub.com/minervaback.html).

The Fall 2009 issue is devoted to women in militaries of other countries.

Moss, Michael. "Hard Look at Mission That Ended in Inferno for 3 Women." *New York Times*, **December 20, 2005, sec. A, p. 1. ProQuest and http://query.nytimes.com/gst/fullpage.html? res=9804EFD71730F933A15751C1A9639C8B63&sec=&spon=& pagewanted=1.**

Three women Marines die from a suicide bomber. The title, "Hard Look at Mission That Ended in Inferno for 3 Women." is a fitting description of the article.

PBS. "Fact Check: Military Sexual Trauma." *NOW*, **September 7, 2007. www.pbs.org/now/shows/336/fact-check-military-sexual-trauma.html (accessed July 8, 2010).**

Definitions, sources, and statistics about military sexual trauma.

Putko, Michele M., and Douglas V. Johnson, II. Editors. *Women in Combat Compendium.* **Carlisle Barracks: U.S. Army War College, Strategic Studies Institute, January 2008. 75pp. www.strategicstudiesinstitute.army.mil/pdffiles/pub830.pdf (accessed July 7, 2010).**

This *Compendium* is strongly pro women serving in combat.

Quenqua, Douglas. "Sending in the Marines (To Recruit Women)." *New York Times*, **April 21, 2008.**

An overview of Marine recruiting methods to attract women to the Corps because of recruitment shortages due to the long and difficult wars.

Sasson-Levy, Orna. "Feminism and Military Gender Practices: Israeli Women Soldiers in 'Masculine' Roles." *Sociological Inquiry* 73: 3 (August 2003): 440–465.

The article explains the role of Israeli women soldiers and how the pattern of Israel's integration of women follows that of the United States.

Sasson-Levy, Orna, and Sarit Amram-Katz. "Gender Integration in Israeli Officer Training: Degendering and Regendering the Military." *Signs* 33: 1 (2007): 105–133.

The article explains that although women are admitted to the military (degendering), they are assigned to female roles (regendering).

Schlafly, Phyllis. 2003. "Women Should Not Serve in Military Combat." *Women in Combat*. www.bible-researcher.com/women/schlafly3.html (accessed July 12, 2010).

The author maintains that women serving in combat is unnatural.

Segal, Mady Wechsler. "Military Family Research." In *Psychology in the Service of National Security*, ed. A. David Mangelsdorff, 225–234. Washington, D.C.: American Psychological Association, 2006. 9 pp.

The author is a longtime expert in the military family research and is considered authoritative.

Segal, Mady Wechsler. "Women's Military Roles Cross-Nationally: Past, Present, and Future." *Gender & Society* 9: 6, (Dec. 1995): 757–775. 18 pp.

The article provides an overview of cross-cultural military women's roles.

Stone, Andrea. "Mental Toll of War Hitting Female Service-members." *USA Today*, January 7, 2008. www.usatoday.com/news/nation/2008-01-01-womenvets_N.htm (accessed July 7, 2010).

The article discusses the psychological risks of war for women soldiers.

Walsh, Sean P. "The Roar of the Lion City: Gender and Culture in the Singapore Armed Forces." *Armed Forces and Society* 33: 2 (2007): 277.

The article discusses the Singapore armed forces experiment conducted in 2004 with assigning women to lead motor platoons in infantry units.

Women at Arms Series. *New York Times.* **August 16 and 17, 2009, November 1, 2009, and December 28, 2009. http://topics .nytimes.com (accessed July 12, 2010).**

The series explores how the Iraq and Afghanistan wars have redefined the role of women in the military. Series includes sexual abuse in the ranks, post-traumatic stress disorder, unit cohesion, and breaking the ground combat barrier.

Hearings and Reports

The first part of this section lists important Congressional hearings relevant to women in the military and combat. The second section lists reports relevant to government and the military. Digitalized copies of recent hearings are available at the GPO access page for hearings 1995 to the present www.gpoaccess.gov/chearings/index.html. Key hearings follow.

Hearings

U.S. Congress. House. Committee on Armed Services. *Assignment of Army and Marine Corps Women under the New Definition of Ground Combat: Hearings before the Military Forces and Personnel Subcommittee.* 103rd Cong., 2nd sess., October 6, 1994. 107 pp.

The hearing discusses how the new definition of ground combat affects the assignment of Army and Marine Corps women.

U.S. Congress. House. Committee on Armed Services. *Gender Discrimination in the Military: Hearings before the Military Personnel and Compensation Subcommittee and the Defense Policy Panel.* 102nd Cong., 2nd sess., July 29 and 30, 1992. 128 pp. www.dtic.mil/dtfs/doc_research/p18_3.pdf (accessed July 7, 2010).

The hearings address sexual harassment and discrimination in the military.

U.S. Congress. House. Committee on Armed Services. *Don't Ask, Don't Tell Repeal Plan Hearing before the Military Personnel Subcommittee.* **CIS-NO: Not Yet Assigned, 111th Cong., 2nd sess., March 3, 2010. CIS/Index.**

The hearing, when published by GPO, can be found on Lexis-Nexis. The hearing includes: requirements to implement repeal of "Don't Ask, Don't Tell" policy regarding homosexuals in the military. Testimony includes: the Co-Chairs Don't Ask, Don't Tell Working Group, U.S. European Command and Counsel, Co-Chairs Don't Ask, Don't Tell Working Group, DoD. In total the House held three hearings and the Senate held one on this subject. Lexis-Nexis offers retrievable selected transcripts.

U.S. Congress. House. Committee on Armed Services. *Don't Ask, Don't Tell Review: Hearing before the Military Personnel Subcommittee.* **110th Cong., 2nd sess., July 23, 2008. CIS-NO: Not Yet Assigned, CIS/Index. July 23, 2008.**

The hearing examines and reviews the "Don't Ask, Don't Tell" policy on homosexuals. It includes a discussion or the arguments against the policy, with personal experiences; objections to the policy, and need for elaboration of perspectives. Contains testimony from Elaine Donnelly Center for Military Readiness as well as four military witnesses. Lexis-Nexis offers retrievable full text of testimony.

U.S. Congress. House. Committee on Armed Services. *Implementation of the Repeal of the Combat Exclusion on Female Aviators: Hearing before the Military Personnel and Compensation Subcommittee of the Committee.* **102nd Cong., 2nd sess., January 29, 1992. 40 pp.**

The hearing addresses the implementation of the repeal of combat exclusion for female aviators.

U.S. Congress. House. Committee on Armed Services. *Women in Combat: Hearing before the Military Forces and Personnel Subcommittee.* **103rd Cong., 2nd sess., May 12, 1993. 179 pp.**

The hearing examines how the services planned to implement the recent decision to allow women to compete for assignments on combat aircraft, and to consider the DoD's request that the statutory exclusion for combatant ships be repealed.

U.S. Congress. House. Committee on Armed Services. *Women in the Military: Hearing before the Military Personnel and Compensation Subcommittee.* 101st Cong., 2nd sess., March 20, 1990. 93 pp.

The hearing provides an update to three hearings held two years previous. At that time, the DoD, Navy, and Marine Corps each established task forces on women that resulted in opening more noncombat positions to women and strengthening procedures to deal with sexual harassment.

U.S. Congress. House. Committee on Oversight and Government Reform. *Sexual Assault in the Military: Hearing before the National Security and Foreign Affairs Subcommittee.* 110th Cong., 2nd sess., July 31, 2008. 140 pp. www.gpoaccess.gov/congress and www.oversight.house.gov (accessed July 8, 2010).

The hearing assesses the military's efforts to improve training, education, and care. Specifically, it focused on exploring what more can be done to prevent sexual assaults from happening in the first place; to provide support, dignity, and services to victims; and to quickly and vigorously punish those committing the crimes.

U.S. Congress. House. Committee on Oversight and Government Reform. *Sexual Assault in the Military Part II: Hearing before the National Security and Foreign Affairs Subcommittee.* 110th Cong., 2nd sess., September 10, 2008. 86 pp. www.gpoaccess.gov/congress and www.oversight.house.gov (accessed July 8, 2010).

The hearing's goal was to empower sexual assault victims to come forward, seek justice, receive help, and ensure a climate in the military where sexual assault is in no way either officially or unofficially condoned, ignored, or tolerated.

U.S. Congress. House. Committee on Oversight and Government Reform. *Sexual Assault in the Military Part Three: Context and Causes: Hearing before the National Security and Foreign Affairs Subcommittee.* 111th Cong., 1st sess., June 25, 2009. 52 pp.

www.gpoaccess.gov/congress/index.html and www.house.gov/reform (accessed July 8, 2010).

The hearing examined the underlying dynamics of sexual assault crime.

U.S. Congress. House. Committee on Government Reform. *Sexual Assault and Violence Against Women in the Military and at the Academies: Hearing before the National Security, Emerging Threats, and International Relations Subcommittee.* **109th Cong., 2nd sess., June 27, 2006. 283+ pp. www.gpoaccess.gov/congress/index.html and www.house.gov/reform.**

The hearing addresses the concern about the DoD's commitment to aggressively respond to sexual assault incidents and to work to prevent them. Specifically, it asks whether the 2005 Defense Task Force on Sexual Assault in the Military Services recommendations had been put into effect, Second, it addresses when the task force will become operational and when its recommendations will be presented to the public.

U.S. Congress. Senate. Committee on Armed Services. *Don't Ask, Don't Tell Policy Hearing.* **111th Cong., 2nd sess., February 2, 2010. CIS-NO: Not Yet Assigned. CIS/Index.**

The hearing examines the "Don't Ask, Don't Tell" policy. Witnesses include the Secretary of DoD, Robert M. Gates, and the Chairman of the Joint Chiefs of Staff, DoD, Adm. Michael G. Mullen. Lexis-Nexis offers retrievable selected transcripts.

U.S. Congress. Senate. Committee on Foreign Relations. International Operations and Organizations, Democracy. *Closing Legal Loopholes: Prosecuting Sexual Assaults and Other Violent Crimes Committed Overseas by American Civilians in a Combat Environment: Hearing before the Human Rights Subcommittee.* **110th Cong., 2nd sess., April 9, 2008. 70 pp. www.gpoaccess.gov/congress/index.html (accessed July 8, 2010).**

The hearing evaluated victimization of women overseas by American soldiers and contractors. It examines effectiveness of legal recourse including the Justice Department.

Reports

Burrelli, David F., and Jody Feder. "Homosexuals and U.S. Military Policy: Current Issues." *CRS Report for Congress*, July 22, 2009. 33 pp. www.fas.org/sgp/crs/natsec/RL30113.pdf (accessed July 9, 2010).

This *CRS Report* is an update from 2008. Reports are updated as events warrant. Background information, legal challenges recruiting, discharge statistics and homosexual marriages in the U.S. are addressed along with a section on foreign militaries.

Clemmitt, Marcia. "Women in the Military." *CQ Researcher* 19:40, (November 13, 2009): 957–980. www.cqpress.com/product/Researcher-Women-in-the-Military-v19.html.

The author covers all issues and all positions related to women serving in the military and in combat. She also provides historical context.

Defense Task Force on Sexual Assault in the Military Services. *Report of the Defense Task Force on Sexual Assault in the Military Services*, December 2009, 176 pp., and *Annex to the Report of the Defense Task Force on Sexual Assault in the Military Services*. December 2009. 130 pp. Both reports downloadable at www.dtic.mil/dtfsams/reports.html (accessed July 8, 2010).

The first report gives the results of fact-finding and analysis of installations in 16 states and nine countries including six in theatre and six with service members returning from Afghanistan and Iraq. The *Annex* is the appendix to the report.

Government Accountability Office (GAO). *Defense Force Management: DoD's Policy on Homosexuality.* NSIAD-92-98, June 12, 1992. 79 pp. http:/archive.gao.gov/d33t10/146980.pdf (accessed July 9, 2010).

The report gives good background material along with cost to the Department of Defense for separation.

Government Accountability Office (GAO). *Military Personnel: Financial Cost and Loss of Critical Skills Due to DoD's Homosexual Conduct Policy Cannot Be Completely Estimated.*

GAO-05-299, February 23, 2005. 44 pp. www.gao.gov/new.items/ d05299.pdf (accessed July 9, 2010).

The report makes the case that not only does separation of homosexuals cost money, but in the post-September 11 environment the separation of servicemembers with critical occupations or important foreign language skills, for example, Arabic, is a cause for concern.

Harrell, Margaret C., et al. *Assessing the Assignment Policy for Army Women.* Santa Monica, CA: RAND, 2007. 157 pp. www .rand.org/pubs/monographs/2007/RAND_MG590-1.pdf.

The publication offers a balanced view of the Department of Defense and the Army's combat exclusion policies. It discusses interpretations of policies.

Lipari, Rachel N., et al. 2008. *2006 Gender Relations Survey of Active Duty Members.* Defense Manpower Data Center (DMDC) Report No. 2007-022, March. 246 pp. www.sapr.mil/ media/pdf/research/WGRA_OverviewReport.pdf.

The results of the 2006 Workplace and Gender Relations Survey of Active Duty Members are compared to results from the 1995 Sexual Harassment Survey and the 2002 Workplace and Gender Relations Survey. Behaviors examined include: unwanted sexual contact, unwanted gender-related experiences, sexual harassment, sexual assault, sexist behavior, and sex discrimination.

Stone, Ervin R. *Women in Combat: Standardize the Physical Fitness Test.* USMC. Command and Staff College. Marine Corps Combat Dev. Marine Corps University. Quantico, March 9 2009. 12 pp. www.dtic.mil (accessed April 29, 2010).

The author's main point is to allow women who meet the mental and physical combat requirements of the Marine Corps to serve in any military occupational specialty because doing so will guarantee the military will meet expectations of the country.

U.S. Department of the Army. *Combat Exclusion: Quick Look Options*, Version 4.0. Washington, D.C.: U.S. Department of the Army, May 10, 2004. 22 pp. http://cmrlink.org (accessed July 7, 2010).

One of the helpful features of the document is that the Combat Exclusion law in Title 10 of the USC appears at the conclusion on pages 21 and 22.

U.S. Department of Defense. *Defense Department Advisory Committee on Women in the Services. DACOWITS 2008 Report.* **Washington, D.C.: Defense Department Advisory Committee on Women in the Services, December 3, 2008. 182 pp. www .defenselink.mil/dacowits (accessed July 7, 2010).**

The report addresses the findings of DACOWITS regarding the background: success strategies for female service members and the background: educational opportunities for military children.

U.S. Department of Defense. *FY09 Report on Sexual Assault in the Military.* **Washington, D.C.: U.S., March 2010. 24 pp. www.sapr.mil/media/pdf/reports/fy09_annual_report.pdf. If the link doesn't work, go to the DoD Sexual Assault Prevention and Response Program Web page at www.sapr.mil/index.php/ annual-reports to follow their link for this report and/or other reports.**

The report documents what the Department of Defense calls the considerable advances made in sexual assault prevention, response, and program oversight from October 1, 2008, through September 30, 2009.

U.S. Department of Defense. *Report to the White House Council on Women and Girls,* **September 1, 2009. 53 pp. www.defense.gov (accessed July 8, 2010).**

DoD prepared this report to illustrate its efforts to support women in uniform, the DoD civilian work force, and their families. Areas included are policies on the assignment of military women, on deployment deferment following the birth of a child, and the leave program. Other areas such as health, human rights, and sexual assault are also included.

U.S. Department of Defense. *Women in the Combat Zone.* **www .defenselink.mil/home/features/2007/women_serve/ (accessed July 7, 2010).**

This is an index page to news stories about women serving in combat.

U.S. General Accountability Office (GAO). *Gender Issues: Information on DoD's Assignment Policy and Direct Ground Combat Definition*. Washington, D.C.: U.S. GAO, October 1998. 21 pp. www.gao.gov/archive/1999/ns99007.pdf (accessed July 9, 2010).

The report evaluates the policy that excludes women from direct ground combat and its definition of direct ground combat. It includes the numbers and types of positions that are closed to women and the justifications for closure; DoD's current basis for excluding women from direct ground combat; and the relationship of DoD's definition of direct ground combat to current military operations. The report did not evaluate the appropriateness of DoD's direct ground combat exclusion rationale.

U.S. General Accountability Office (GAO). *Women in the Military: Deployment in the Persian Gulf War*. GAO/NSIAD 93–93, July 1993. 58 pp. http://archive.gao.gov/t2pbat5/149552.pdf (accessed July 8, 2010).

The report discusses the deployment of women in the military to the Persian Gulf during *Operations Desert Shield* and *Desert Storm*. The deployment renewed debate about the restrictions that prohibit the assignment of women to combat positions. The report addresses women's roles and performance, ability to endure deployment conditions, effect on unit cohesion, and effect on a unit's ability to deploy.

U.S. Presidential Commission on the Assignment of Women in the Armed Forces. *Report to the President: Women in Combat*. Herndon, VA.: Brassey's, 1993. 413 pp.

The question: "Should women serve in American Combat Units?" is addressed. Their report is a key resource for anyone who seeks to know all the pros and cons.

White House Project. 2009. *White House Project Report: Benchmarking Women's Leadership*. Military. 66–74, November. 130 pp. www.thewhitehouseproject.org (accessed July 7, 2010).

The report is a survey of the current state of women's leadership in 10 different fields: Academia, Business, Film & Television Entertainment, Journalism, Law, Military, Nonprofit, Politics, Religion, and Sports.

Women's Research and Education Institute (WREI). *Women in the Military: Where They Stand.* **6th ed. Arlington, Virginia: WREI, 2008. 39 pp.**

Published every other year, the report provides Congress with compact data and key findings on the status of women in the armed forces.

Legal Cases

Legal cases played a significant part in the evolution of women's roles in the military. To find the text of a Supreme Court case, FindLaw at www.findlaw.com/casecode/supreme.html has a searchable database of decisions since 1893. FindLaw's Cases and Codes section at www.findlaw.com/casecode/ has resources and links for state and federal laws. Resources pertaining to constitutions, statutes, and cases are included.

Campbell v. Beaughler, **519 F.2d 1307, 1308 (9th Cir. 1975), cert. denied, 423 U.S. 1073 (1976).**

This case involved hair length regulations. The court held that Marine Corps' regulations setting different standards for men and women's hairstyles does not offend equal protection law. Enlisted Marine Reservists challenged this concept saying that women could wear hairpieces, but men could not, and this stipulation interfered with uniformity of combat units. The military argued that the hairpieces were a safety hazard with gas masks and earphones in mine detecting units. Furthermore, due to combat exclusion rules, female Marines do not wear gas masks or operate mine detectors.

Chandler v. Callaway, **No. C-74-1249 (N.D.Cal. Nov. 4, 1974).**

Chandler involved a challenge to an Army enlistment policy that required female enlistees to have a High School Diploma (HSD) or General Educational Development (GED) and be at least age eighteen. At the time, men could enlist at age 17 and did not have to be HSD graduates or GED holders. The basis for the difference was the policy excluding women from combat. The court found the distinction "reasonable and lawful." It concluded that admission standards could be set higher for women than men since the Army's need for women enlistees was not as great.

Crawford v. Cushman, 531 F.2d 1114 (2D Cir. 1976).

The court held that women have the right to remain in service after bearing children. The court reversed the judgment that upheld the United States Marine Corps' rule requiring the discharge of the woman because she was pregnant, because the rule was not constitutionally tailored to promote the Marine Corps' interest in insuring the general mobility and readiness of its personnel.

Frontiero Et Vir v. Richardson, Secretary of Defense, et al. No. 71-1694, 411 U.S. 677; 93 S. Ct. 1764; 36 L. Ed. 2d 583; (1973 U.S.).

The court held that "military women with a spouse could receive the same entitlements as those offered to military men with a spouse without the requirement that the woman prove dependency of their spouse."

Goldman v. Weinberger, 475 U.S. 503; 106 S. Ct. 1310; 89 L. Ed. 2d 478; (1986 U.S.), affirmed.

The court upheld the Air Force regulation that it did not violate the petitioners First Amendment religious exercise rights when it prohibited a soldier from wearing a yarmulke (skullcap). The explanation was that the regulation sensibly and fairly regulated dress in the interest of the military's perceived need for uniformity and discipline. First Amendment right to free exercise of religion held not been violated by applying Air Force regulation, the prohibiting of wearing headgear while indoors, to the Orthodox Jew's wearing of yarmulke.

Hill v. Berkman, 635 F. Supp. 1228; U.S. Dist.1238 (E.D.N.Y. 1986).

A female enlistee in the United States Army filed suit against the Chief of Army Reserve, the Secretary of the Army, the Secretary of Defense, and some federal officials, alleging violation of her right to be free from discrimination on the basis of sex. After her enlistment, the position that she sought was closed to women on the justification that persons with this specialty would likely be exposed to combat. The court found no challenge to exclusionary statutes in reported case law. The court held that because combat risk was an occupational qualification mandated by federal statute, it was an appropriate legitimate occupational qualification exception to Title VII. The classification was valid.

Kovach V. Middendorf, 424 F. Supp. 72 (D. Del. 1976).

The case entailed allocation of military scholarships. The district court reasoned that Navy policy setting stricter requirements for women and granting a higher number of Navy Reserve Officer Training Corps (NROTC) scholarships to men was based on the greater need for males than females due to the exclusion law. The court upheld the constitutionality of exclusion because it was necessary to maintain the Navy, therefore, a "legitimate government purpose." It held "that disparate classifications of men and women mandated by section 6015 do not violate female plaintiff's equal protections rights."

Lewis v. U.S. Army, 697 F. Supp. 1385 (E.D. Pa. 1988).

A woman enlistee challenged the enlistment policy of the Army and the National Guard. She alleged the policy showed favoritism to men over women in that she was not permitted to enlist because she was not a high school diploma graduate. She contended the policy, which permitted men who had not graduated from high school but who had obtained a GED certificate to enlist but prohibited women from so doing, was unconstitutional on its face and as applied to her and women in general because it violated equal protection principles. The court upheld that the Army setting higher service entrance requirements for female enlistees does not violate due process or equal protection on the basis that men and women are not "similarly situated" because of the exclusion policy. Gender discrimination in the military is subject to judicial review under the Constitution's Fifth Amendment Due Process clause.

Owens v. Brown, 455 F. Supp. 291 (1978 U.S. Dist. D.C.).

The court ruled that 10 USC Section 6015 was unconstitutional when it did not allow the permanent assignment of women to naval vessels except for hospital and transport ships. The section was amended as part of the FY-79 Defense Authorizations Act.

Roper v. Department of the Army, 832 F. 2d 247 (2nd Cir. 1987).

The court held that Title VII of the *Civil Rights Act of 1964* that prohibits sex discrimination in employment did not apply to uniformed military members.

Rostker v. Goldberg, 453 U.S. 57; 101 S. Ct. 2646; 69 L. Ed. 2d 478 (1981).

The court ruled that excluding women from the draft and Selective Service registration was constitutionally based. The court reasoned that the purpose of the draft is to prepare for combat and women were not eligible for combat, therefore, due process had not been violated.

Schlesinger v. Ballard, 419 U.S. 498; 95 S. Ct. 572; 42 L. Ed. 2d 610; (1975 U.S.).

The court upheld a discriminatory mandatory discharge statute, 10 U.S.C. S 6382(a), which requires that male officers who have not been promoted in nine years be discharged from service. The Navy lieutenant said that if he had been female, he would have been entitled to 13 years before discharge. He alleged that he was discriminated against on the basis of his gender. The court reasoned that because females were restricted from compiling similar sea duty, and the longer period is consistent with the goal of providing women fair opportunity for promotion, the law was fair.

Solorio v. U.S. 483 U.S. 435; 107 S. Ct. 2924; 97 L. Ed. 2d 364 (1987 U.S.).

It was noted that any action by Congress to ease the exclusion increased the Navy's litigation risk because the Supreme Court in cases such as this one had relied upon Congress's "plenary" power under the Constitution to regulate land and naval forces.

U.S. v. Oscar Ellsworth Clinton, 310 F. Supp. 333 (E.D. La. New Orleans Division 1970).

The court used the "rational basis" test. Gender-based discrimination, the court stated, "may be unconstitutionally arbitrary in some contexts, congressional chivalry in drafting men only to comprise an army has a sufficiently rational basis to avoid constitutional condemnation as mere chauvinism." Some classification is permissible. The art is in determining the line between permissible and prohibited classifications for which the Courts have traditionally "sustained a government classification if it is reasonable rather than arbitrary."

U.S. v. Cook, 311 F. Supp. 618 (W.D. Pa. 1970).

The case addresses women lacking physical strength for close combat. Therefore, the United States will be compelled to establish and maintain armed forces of males which may at least physically be equal to the armed forces of other nations, likewise composed of males, with which it must compete.

U.S. v. Dorris, 319 F. Supp. 1306, 1308 (W.D. Pa. 1970).

The sole issue before the court was whether the Military Selective Service Act deprived the defendant of his life and liberty without due process of law, contrary to the mandate of the Fifth Amendment by the use of gender and age based classifications. The court found that the gender-based classification did not violate due process because it was justified by government's interest to provide for defense.

U.S. v. St. Clair, 291 F. Supp. 122 (S.D.N.Y. 1968).

The case addresses providing for involuntary service for men and voluntary service for women, Congress followed the teachings of history. If a nation is to survive, men must provide the first line of defense while women "keep the home fires burning." Moreover, Congress recognized that in modern times there are certain duties in the Armed Forces which may be performed by women volunteers. For these reasons, the distinction between men and women with respect to service in the Armed Forces is not arbitrary, unreasonable or capricious.

United States v. Virginia, No. 94-1941, S. Ct., 518 U.S. 515; 116 S. Ct. 2264; 135 L. Ed. 2d 735 (1996 U.S.).

The case involved a challenge to the policy denying women admission to a publicly funded university, Virginia Military

Institute. The court ruled the policy violated the Equal Protection Clause of the 14th Amendment of the U.S. Constitution.

U.S. v. Yingling, 368 F. Supp. 379; 1973 U.S. (W.D. Pa. 1973).

The case addresses women lacking physical strength for close combat. It held, "While each of the sexes has its own innate characteristics, for the most part physical strength is a male characteristic, and so long as this is so, the United States will be compelled to establish and maintain armed forces of males which may at least physically be equal to the armed forces of other nations, likewise composed of males, with which it must compete."

Papers, Proceedings, and Memoranda

Alliance for National Defense (AND). 2009. "Issue: Women in Combat, AND Positions." *AND.* 4 pp. www.4militarywomen .org/WIC_%20Jan_2009.pdf (accessed July 7, 2010).

A position paper in favor of women serving in combat.

Aspin, Len. "Direct Ground Combat Definition and Assignment Rule." Memorandum for Secretaries of the Military Departments. Washington, D.C., January 13, 1994. http:/cmrlink .org/CMRNotes/LesAspin%20DGC%20DefAssign%20Rule% 20011394.pdf.

The memorandum that outlined the ground combat policy, still in effect in 2010.

Cornum, Rhonda. "Comprehensive Soldier Fitness: Strong Minds, Strong Bodies." October 9, 2009. Army G-3/5/7 Unclassified/FOUO DAMO-CSF America's Army: The Strength of the Nation. Keynote Address. Power Point Presentation. Women in the Military Conference. Women's Research and Education Institute (WREI). Arlington, VA. September 25. www.4militarywomen.org/WIM09Presentations/Cornum.pdf (accessed April 15, 2010).

The Army's most recent effort to reduce the stress of combat is based on the key belief that the total soldier must be fit in mind and body.

U.S. Naval Institute Proceedings

All U.S. Naval Institute Proceedings are from the Cumulative Index 1874–1977. These representative articles provide a contemporary look at the issue of women in combat. The articles listed are samples of the writings on the issue of women in combat.

Burgess, J.E. "The Female Naval Aviator: A Free Ride?" (Shipman) (C&D). *U S. Naval Institute Proceedings*: 874. 75.

Burnett, D.R. "The Sexually-Integrated Warship." (NAMB). *U.S. Naval Institute Proceedings*: 890. 90.

Drag. Joellen M. "The Female Naval Aviator: A Free Ride?" (Shipman) (C&D). *U. S. Naval Institute Proceedings*: 876. 76.

Kaufman. E. M. "The Sexually-Integrated Warship." (Burnett) (C&D). *U.S. Naval Institute Proceedings*: 894. 63.

Wellershoff, 1.M. "The Sexually-Integrated Warship." (Burnett) (C&D). *U.S. Naval Institute Proceedings*: 897. 77.

Theses and Dissertations

Andrews, Heather A. *Veiled Jihad: The Threat of Female Islamic Suicide Terrorists*. Master of Science, Strategic Intelligence (MSSI) Unpublished Thesis. Joint Military Intelligence College, July 2005.

The author's primary focus is female Islamic suicide bombers from Palestine and Chechnya. For comparison, she includes the Liberation Tigers of Tamil Eelam (LTTE) females in her case studies "to illustrate that females living under traditional, patriarchal societies are subject to the same problems, which drives them to commit these acts."

Baker, Henderson, II. *Women in Combat, a Culture Issue?* Strategy Research Project. Master of Strategic Studies Degree. Carlisle Barracks, U.S. Army War College, March 14, 2006. 15 pp. http://handle.dtic.mil/100.2/ADA449305 (accessed July 9, 2010).

The paper examines the role of women in combat from an Army prospective.

Burba, Kathryn A. *Leveraging the Army Vision to Amend the Combat Exclusion Law.* **Strategy Research Project. Master of Strategic Studies Degree. Carlisle Barracks: U.S. Army War College, March 30, 2007. 14 pp. http://handle.dtic.mil/100.2/ ADA469395 (accessed July 9, 2010).**

The paper proposes that the Army position on women in combat needs to be reevaluated.

Burnes, Thresa. *Contributions of Women to U.S. Combat Operations.* **Strategy Research Project. Master of Strategic Studies Degree. Carlisle Barracks: U.S. Army War College, March 24, 2008. 20 pp. http://handle.dtic.mil/100.2/ADA479020 (accessed July 9, 2010).**

The paper recommends that the Department of Defense rescind the combat exclusion policy. Two reasons are: all service members are exposed to combat conditions on the modern asymmetric battlefield and the historical contributions of women to combat warrant it.

Gould, Jennifer Margaret. "The Women's Corps: The Establishment of Women's Military Services in Britain." Unpublished Dissertation. University College London (University of London), 1988. Free to download via http://ethos.bl.uk (accessed July 9, 2010).

Topics covered are the history of the British Armed forces, national security, and camouflage.

Kruger, Lisa. *Gender and Terrorism: Motivations of Female Terrorists.* **Master of Science, Strategic Intelligence (MSSI) Unpublished Thesis. Joint Military Intelligence College, July 2005.**

The author finds the motivation of women terrorists are not unlike the reasons men give.

Whitman, Gailyn F. *Female Captive Stories in the United States from the Colonial Era to Present: A Study in the Pervasive*

Elements of the Traditional Narrative. Manhattan, KS: Kansas State University, Unpublished Masters Thesis, 2005. 106 pp. http:/handle.dtic.mil/100.2/ADA443942 (accessed July 9, 2010).

The author argues that women warriors are now into a revised female captivity narrative rather than incorporated into American war stories. She believes the common narrative has revolved around three recurrent and fundamental elements that together comprise the American female captivity: the female is white European with a captor of color; the female is both a heroine and a victim, and the captives and American cultural perceptions.

Nonprint Resources

Nonprint resources are grouped into the following categories: bibliographies; databases; DVD/videotapes; films/multimedia; and Internet sites.

Bibliographies

All Navy Women's National Alliance (ANWNA). "Suggested Reading List." www.www.anwna.com/reading.html (accessed July 9, 2010).

ANWNA provides a selection of books of Navy women's history.

Alliance for National Defense (AND). "A Starter Reading List on Military Women." www.4militarywomen.org/Reading_ List.htm (accessed July 9, 2010).

This list of books is an introduction to a variety of military events and issues including women in combat.

Andrusyszyn, Greta H. *Women in the Military A Selected Bibliography.* Army War College. Carlisle, Pennsylvania, August 2009. 26 pp. www.dtic.mil/cgi-bin/GetTRDoc?AD=ADA506391& Location=U2&doc=GetTRDoc.pdf (accessed July 28, 2010).

With certain exceptions, the materials in the college's 2009 bibliography are dated from 2005 to the present. Prior to 2005, the following reference, Jacqueline S. Bey, should be used. These bibliographies and others are available online through the War

College Library's home page at www.carlisle.army.mil/library/bibliographies.htm.

Bey, Jacqueline S. *Women in the Military: A Selected Bibliography.* Carlisle Barracks: U.S. Army War College Library, January 2005. 28 pp. www.carlisle.army.mil/library/bibs/women05.htm (accessed July 28, 2010).

Most of the books, documents, and periodical articles cited were published since 2000.

Ike Skelton Library. *Women, Then and Now Bibliography.* Norfolk: U.S. Joint Forces. March 2008. www.jfsc.ndu.edu/library/publications/bibliography/women_then_and_now.asp (accessed July 28, 2010).

The bibliography is the library's most recent. In addition to a sizable selection of links about women, other topical links are available. They include: books and documents, periodicals, multimedia, and electronic resources.

Ike Skelton Library. *Women in the Armed Services Bibliography.* Norfolk: U.S. Joint Forces. March 2005. www.jfsc.ndu.edu/library/publications/bibliography/women_armed_services.asp (accessed July 28, 2010).

The site is an earlier bibliography that also includes many links to information on women. Other links include: books and documents, periodicals, media, and Web sites.

Lomio, J. Paul. "Annotated Select Bibliography." Robert Crown Law Library. Stanford University, Stanford, CA. July 16, 2003. http:/dont.stanford.edu/commentary/ann.bib.html (accessed July 9, 2010).

The sources relate to the issue of gay people in the armed forces. It includes monographs and articles.

Navy Women's Bibliography. www.history.navy.mil/faqs/faq48-2.htm.

This bibliography presents sources from World War I through Operation Iraqi Freedom. It also lists general reading and unpublished archival readings.

Rostker, Bernard D. *I Want You! The Evolution of the All-Volunteer Force*. RAND Corporation, 2006. 832 pp. Hard Cover with or without DVD. Or e-version. Full document at www.rand.org/pubs/monographs/MG265/ (accessed July 7, 2010).

The author evaluates U.S. forces from 1960 through the first part of the Iraqi War. The accompanying DVD consists of over 1,700 primary-source documents, government and Presidential memos, and letters, staff papers, and reports that are linked directly from citations in the electronic version of the book.

U.S. Army Research Institute for the Behavioral and Social Science. *Women in the U.S. Army: An Annotated Bibliography*. May 2002. 51 pp. www.hqda.army.mil/ari/pdf/WomenInTheArmy -DrHarris.pdf (accessed July 7, 2010).

The annotated bibliography of research and studies conducted over the last 5 to 10 years prior to 2002 is at the end of a special report on important issues pertaining to women in the military.

Databases

Anna Ella Carroll, Civil War Strategist. www.usd.edu/~acjones/ index.html.

The site contains transcripts from the Congressional hearings concerning Carroll's part in authoring "The Tennessee War Plan" of 1861–1862. It is presented as a stage play.

Duke University. "Civil War Women: Primary Sources." Sallie Bingham Center for Women's History and Culture. http:// library.duke.edu/specialcollections/bingham/guides/ cwdocs.html.

Annotated links are provided including diaries, letters, documents, photographs, prints, and a bibliography. These collections contain images and transcriptions of three women, Rose O'Neal Greenhow, Alice Williamson, and Sarah Thompson.

Global Issues Resource Center. *An Annotated Bibliography of Conflict Resolution Resources: Books, Curricula, Videotapes, Simulations, Games*. www.creducation.org/resources/conference/ GIRC_International_Bib_Jan_08.pdf.

The bibliography of January 25, 2008 is an award winning product of the Center at Cuyahoga Community College in Cleveland located at www.tri-c.edu/community/girc.htm.

Government Printing Office (GPO). www.gpoaccess.gov/chearings/index.html.

This helpful site provides digital copies of hearings, but a shortfall of the site is that it only has very recent hearings.

Library of Congress. Law Library. www.loc.gov/law/find/ databases.php (accessed July 9, 2010).

The Internet Congressional Record Database contains the official record of the proceedings and debates of the United States Congress from Volume 140 (1994) to the present.

Navy Department Library. www.history.navy.mil/library/ index.htm (accessed July 9, 2010).

This Navy site has a lot to offer including: special collections, bibliographies, links and wars and conflicts. The civilian related links include Congress, Supreme Court decisions, and U.S. Code. Military links include the Uniform Code of Military Justice (UCMJ).

Texas Woman's University Libraries. *Digital Collections.* **http:/ twudigital.cdmhost.com/index.php.**

The collection includes a woman's digital collection, and collections on women Air Force service pilots and women in aviation.

U.S. Army Museum. "Common Research Topics." www.awm.lee.army.mil/awm_research_topics.html (accessed July 9, 2010).

Digital collection has links to bibliographies and to women's history and notable women.

Vietnam's Women's Memorial Foundation. "Women in Vietnam: A Bibliography." www.vietnamwomensmemorial.org/bibliog .php (accessed July 9, 2010).

The bibliography contains books, film, and biographies.

DVDs/Videotapes

The section represents a select group of video opportunities. News media on their Web sites offer extensive multimedia libraries. Media Web sites include those of CNN, MSNBC, and the *New York Times* and the service branches, Air Force, Army, Navy, and Marine Corps.

An American Nurse at War. DVD Price: $14.95. Available at the National Women's History Project. http:/store.nexternal.com/ shared/StoreFront/default.asp?CS=nwhp&StoreType=BtoC& Count1=688991725&Count2=606132149&ProductID=5022&Target =products.

The DVD tells the story of Marion McCune Rice, a World War I Red Cross nurse.

Called to Serve: A History of America's Military Women. DVD. Women in Military Service for America Memorial Foundation (WIMSA), Educational Film Center, Arlington, VA: WIMSA, 2007. Run time: 15 minutes. Price: $10.00. http:/ womensmemorialstore.com.

The DVD reviews the history of military women.

Lioness. DVD. Directed by Meg McLagan and Daria Sommers. New York: Room 11 Productions, 2008. Run time: 82 minutes. Price: $26.95. Amazon.com.

Lioness tells the story of four of the first women to serve in the Marine Corps when they accompanied the men in the house-to-house searches. The story tells what is expected of these women. They served in direct ground combat.

Michelle Obama: Speech Honoring Women in the Military. Authenticated text, audio, audioXE, and video. Washington, D.C.: White House East Room, November 18, 2009. It is available on demand at www.americanrhetoric.com/speeches/ michelleobamacelebratingmilitarywomen.

The speech is a tribute to women in the military, past and present.

Women in Military: Willing, Able, Essential. DVD. Pennsylvania Veterans Museum, 2009. Run time: 59 minutes. Price: $15.00. http:/paveteransmuseum.org/home/education-women.php.

The DVD depicts how women have served this country since it was founded. Women were uncommon soldiers who disguised themselves to fight, nurses that faced horrific wounds and those who wear the uniform today. Their story is of war and peace, a pursuit for status and recognition, a patriotic journey to protect the freedom.

Films/Multimedia

History Channel. *Military History.* **http:/military.history.com/**

The Military History Store offers purchase of videos, but online features include international and American military history. ROTC is also featured.

Kobre's Guide to the Web's Best Videojournalism. **"Women at Arms."** *New York Times.* **www.kobreguide.com/content/ Women_at_Arms.**

This guide lists all links to videos on the *New York Times* series, "Women at Arms." It also lists videos from other sources on a variety of topics.

MSNBC. *Investigating the Role of Women in Combat.* **June 14, 2010. This video is free and is 4.24 minutes long. http:/ video.tvguide.com/MSNBC/Investigating+the+role+of+women +in+combat.**

MSNBC military analyst Col. Jack Jacobs discusses that the number of women serving on the frontlines being injured is increasing. The video is a brief but thorough look at war in 2010 and at women in combat.

New York Times.com. *Women at Arms: In Their Own Words.* **Multimedia Feature. www.nytimes.com/interactive/2009/08/16/ us/20090816_women_feature.html#.**

Ground combat was rare for female soldiers before 2001. In Iraq and Afghanistan, this is no longer true. Three women were commended for their performance in combat and discuss their experiences.

U.S. Congress. Committee on Veterans Affairs. http:/veterans .house.gov/multimedia/index.shtml.

The site provides live and archived broadcasts of selected hearings and events.

U.S. Department of Defense (DoD) "Multimedia/Photos." www.defense.gov/multimedia/multimedia.aspx.

The site contains all forms of still, motion, and multimedia imagery from across the DoD. It includes imagery of operations and activities.

U.S. Department of the Navy. "Media Resources." www .navy.mil/swf/index.asp.

The site contains multimedia sources including photo and video galleries, television archive, podcasts and RSS feeds, and radio archives.

U.S. Department of Veterans Affairs. *Women Who Served in Our Military: Insights for Interventions: For Veterans and Families.* **41 min. Washington, D.C.: National Center for Posttraumatic Stress Disorder Web site. Windows Media Player video files. www.ptsd.va.gov/public/videos/women-served-military.asp.**

The video examines how women's deployment to war zones can lead to stress. Women veterans testify and offer proof that treatment does make a difference and can help the return to normal life. It also describes the significant contributions of women in the military.

U.S. Navy Memorial Library and Media Resource Center. www.navymemorial.org/HistoryEducation/LibraryandMedia ResourceCenter.

The Center has nearly 1,000 books and periodical titles, 30,000 photographs, 1,500 voices entries, and an assortment of multimedia items.

Vietnam's Women's Memorial Foundation. "The Vietnam War in Film." www.vietnamwomensmemorial.org/bibliog.php.

The section "The Vietnam War in Film" follows the bibliography of printed material.

WASP on the Web. Audio and Video. http:/wingsacrossamerica .us/wasp/video/index.htm.

Multimedia topics include history, President Franklin Roosevelt's speech on the day of the D DAY Invasion, June 6, 1944, sounds of aircraft, and accounts of flights.

Internet Sites

In this section, Web sites for branches of the military are not listed, but should be considered vital sources of information. Those sites are listed on the U.S. Army Center for Military History site at www.history.army.mil/websites.html. Those sites listed include not only the branches, Air Force, Army, Army National Guard, Coast Guard, Defense Department, Marine Corps, Navy, but also a variety of nongovernment collections. You may have to search a site for the term "women."

Alliance for National Defense (AND). www.4militarywomen.org.

The Alliance is a nonprofit educational site composed of veterans that presents a positive voice for American military women.

Arlington National Cemetery. Prominent Women Buried at Arlington National Cemetery. www.arlingtoncemetery.org/ historical_information/prominent_women.html.

The Arlington National Cemetery site provides biographical information.

Armstrong, Glenda, comp. *Gender Issues in Physical Fitness Standards: OTS Current Military Topics*. Maxwell Air Force Base: Air University Library, August 2005. www.au.af.mil/au/ aul/school/ots/genderissues.htm.

The site features entries on health and fitness.

Army Nurse Corps History. www.army.mil/cmh-pg/anc/ anchhome.html.

History is presented in pictures and biographies. The site covers the period from the war with Spain through the Korean War.

Bible Research. Womanhood. "Women in Combat." www.bible-researcher.com/women/women-in-combat.html.

The bibliography is divided into online articles on the Iraqi prisoner abuse scandal, organizations opposed to women serving in combat and those promoting it; books about women in the military; and online bibliographies, selected articles, and government documents.

Center for Military Readiness. http:/cmrlink.org.

The center, an independent, nonpartisan educational organization, seeks sound military personnel policies in the armed forces. The site's founder, Elaine Donnelly, opposes women serving in combat roles and lesbian and gay servicemembers serving openly.

Coast Guard Compass, **the Official Blog of the U.S. Coast Guard: Its People and Missions. http:/coastguard.dodlive.mil.**

The site offers information on the activity of women servicemembers including combating modern day piracy and responding to the Haiti earthquake.

Combat Studies Institute (CSI). http:/usacac.army.mil/cac2/csi/index.asp.

The site has relevant historical studies for use by current U.S. Army leaders and planners. CSI publications are available in a variety of formats. All wars are covered.

Congressional Research Service (CRS) Reports on General National Security Topics. www.fas.org/sgp/crs/natsec/index.html.

The site provides links to the latest reports by CRS. It is an excellent site for well researched information on topics such as Afghanistan casualties: military forces and civilians, Iraq war, legislation, and historical background.

Defense Advisory Committee on Women in the Services (DACOWITS). http:/dacowits.defense.gov.

DACOWITS provides research documents about policies that relate to recruitment and retention, treatment, employment, integration, and well-being of women in the Armed Forces and to family issues.

Defense Task Force on Sexual Assault in the Military Services. www.dtic.mil/dtfsams.

The site provides general information on the Task Force and contains its report completed December 1, 2009.

Defense Technical Information Center. www.dtic.mil/dtic/search/tr/str/guided-tr.html.

The Technical Center is a searchable database for Department of Defense Collections.

DoD Dictionary of Military Terms. www.dtic.mil/doctrine/dod_dictionary.

The DOD Dictionary and the Joint Acronyms and Abbreviations master data base is also published in hard copy as amended to April 2010. A .PDF version is available for download.

DoD Pentagon Library, Washington, D.C. www.whs.mil/library.

The Pentagon Library provides information from seven collections. Some links, such as the Library Intranet collection, require that the user be a member of the Department of Defense, but many are open access databases that include electronic journals and Department of Defense National Defense-Authorization Laws, and are important in getting information on women in combat.

DoD Sexual Assault Prevention and Response Program. www.sapr.mil/index.php/annual-reports.

The site has links to DoD Annual Reports, Annual Report on Sexual Harassment and Violence at the U.S. Military Service Academies, a resource guide, and fact sheet.

DoD Web sites. www.defense.gov/RegisteredSites/RegisteredSites .aspx.

The site is an extensive listing of all the Web sites for the Department of Defense. Its purpose is to help find U.S. military information online.

Library of Congress. *Experiencing War: Women at War; Stories from the Veterans History Project.* **www.loc.gov/vets/stories/ex-war-womenatwar.html.**

The project has a searchable database that spans four wars. Many of the women included are nurses, but also include is a code breaker, Ann Caracrist; a welder, Meda Brendall; and a flight surgeon, Rhonda Cornum. It included as well two women who rose through the ranks to make history, Jeanne Holm, who served for 33 years, and in 1971 became the first woman general in the Air Force and Darlene Iskra who became the first woman to command a U.S. Navy ship December 1990.

Minerva Center. www.minervacenter.com.

The center is a nonpartisan and educational organization that studies and provides information on women in the military and war. The site has information on its publications and on scholarly societies. Through H-Net, Minerva has a discussion group on women and war.

National Archives. www.archives.gov.

The archives holds the records of the United States federal government. They represent a small part of the archives' actual data, but records available on war and the military are a tremendous amount. A user can link to other databases, which makes this site extremely useful to researchers.

NATO (North Atlantic Treaty Organization). *The Committee on Women in the NATO Forces.* **www.nato.int/issues/women_nato/index.html.**

The NATO Committee on Gender Perspectives is an advisory body to the Military Committee on policies related to gender for the Armed Forces of the Alliance. Gender mainstreaming is a fundamental goal. Several PDF files are downloadable including, recommendations on the implementation of UNSCR 1325, training and education related to gender or UNSCR 1325 and 1820 at the national level, new terms of reference: committee on gender perspectives, improving the gender balance, guidance for NATO gender mainstreaming, recruiting and retention of military personnel, and national reports.

Noonie Fortin, Author and Speaker. www.nooniefortin.com.

Noonie Fortin, 1st Sgt., USAR (Ret.) has constructed the site to provide a wide range of informational links that include in memory, Iraq, Afghanistan, the Pentagon, Desert Storm, Vietnam, earlier wars, buddy search, awards, POW-MIA, photos, Colonie Veterans Memorial, and excerpts and reviews include those related to POW and War.

Presbyterian Church in America (PCA). "Historical Center. General Assembly Actions and Position Papers." Ad Interim Study Committee on Women in the Military. www.pcahistory .org/pca/aiscwim.html#2.

The Interim Study Committee of the Presbyterian Church in America provides a religious basis for women not serving in combat roles.

RAND Corporation. Reports and Bookstore. www.rand.org/ pubs.

Reports and Bookstore is RAND's document archive, and as a public service, their unrestricted work published since 1998 is available free as downloadable documents in PDF format. RAND has a number of Public Use Databases available at www.rand.org /about/tools/. Core research areas include international affairs, national security and terrorism, and homeland security at www.rand.org/research_areas.

U.S. Army Center of Military History. www.history.army.mil/ index.html.

The Center is a service of the U.S. Army Center of Military History featuring the role of women in the Army. A strong feature is the history of the Army Nurse Corps.

U.S. Department of the Army, Deputy Chief of Staff, Army G-1, Office of Army Demographics. *Demographics.* **20 February 2009. www.armyg1.army.mil/HR/demographics.asp.**

The Web site provides documents with statistical data about women Army members.

U.S. Department of the Navy, Navy Personnel Command, Bureau of Naval Personnel. *Office of Women's Policy.* www .npc.navy.mil/AboutUs/BUPERS/WomensPolicy.

The site offers links about women in the Navy, including women's health, facts and statistics, FAQs on women's policy, history and firsts, news stories, policies and instructions, and research and studies.

U.S. Department of Veterans Affairs. *Center for Women Veterans Home Page.* www1.va.gov/womenvet.

The Center provides history and up-to-date information relevant to women veterans. It was established in 1994 to monitor and coordinate VA benefits for women.

U.S. Government Accountability Office (GAO). www.gao.gov.

GAO is the investigative arm of Congress and monitors any Congressional activity on women in the military.

U.S. Navy. "History and Firsts." Personnel Command. June 13, 2008. www.npc.navy.mil.

The Personnel Command not only provides a chronology of women who first achieved in the Navy, but it also gives brief descriptions of the records from 1700 to the present. A link is provided to view records in their entirety at the Naval Historical Center-Women's Policy.

University of Wisconsin-Milwaukee Libraries. Lesbian, Gay, Bisexual and Transgender People—Archives Department. Miriam Ben-Shalom Papers 1971–1999. http:/digital.library .wisc.edu/1711.dl/wiarchives.uw-mil-uwmmss0237.

This collection includes the papers of the first gay or lesbian member of the military service to be reinstated after being discharged for her sexual orientation. The collection cannot be entirely retrieved onsite, and has links to retrieve other relevant material.

Vietnam's Women's Memorial Foundation. "Web-Based Bibliographies." www.vietnamwomensmemorial.org/bibliog.php.

The site has a section, Web-based bibliographies. In addition, it lists over a dozen films that cover aspects of the Vietnam War.

Wilson, Captain Barbara A. USAF (Ret.). Military Women Veterans: Yesterday-Today-Tomorrow. http:/userpages.aug.com/capt-barb/index.html.

Military Women Veterans is a compilation by Captain Barbara A. Wilson, USAF (Ret.) that demonstrates women have been involved in every conflict since the American Revolution. It has a section that favors women serving in combat.

Women In Military Service For America Memorial Foundation, Inc. www.womensmemorial.org.

The Women's Memorial is developing a comprehensive history of our American servicewomen from the American Revolution to the present. It has information on news and events, history and collections, education, and an "In Search Of" section which is a service offered to members, their family members and friends, military personnel and veteran organizations in search of women who have served or are serving in the US military.

Women and the U.S. Coast Guard. "A Historical Bibliography." www.uscg.mil/history/uscghist/womenbib.asp.

The bibliography has articles, books, and government publications, some of which extend beyond the scope of women in the Coast Guard.

Women's Research and Education Institute (WREI). www .wrei.org.

WREI has research on the status of American women since 1977 with a strong emphasis in the critical role that American servicewomen play in national defense.

Glossary

afterburner An additional component, also known as reheat, added to some jet engines, primarily those on military supersonic aircraft. Its purpose is to provide a temporary extra thrust for supersonic flight, takeoff, and combat situations. Injecting additional fuel into the jet pipe downstream of (i.e., after) the turbine accomplishes afterburner.

al-Qaeda An international terrorist organization founded in the 1980s by Osama bin Laden and Muhammed Atef. Al-Qaeda calls for the use of violence and force in bringing about the end of non-Islamic governments. It was responsible for the attacks on the World Trade Center and the Pentagon on September 11, 2001. Al-Qaeda is responsible for the proliferation of terrorists throughout the world and for providing them with military equipment and financing.

asymmetric battlefield A place where a battle is fought, with close operations taking place throughout the entire area of military operations, rather than just at the forward area, as with a linear battlefield.

balance issues Those issues that involve successfully balancing a military career and a family.

battalion An army unit usually consisting of a headquarters and three or more companies.

brigade A unit usually smaller than a division to which are attached groups and/or battalions and smaller units tailored to meet anticipated requirements.

cohesion How well soldiers function or work together.

collocation The placement and interdependence of the positions of combat support and combat service support relative to direct ground combat.

Direct Combat Probability Coding (DCPC) A system to classify positions according to the probability of direct combat.

direct ground combat Closing with and destroying the enemy with deliberate *offensive* action under fire.

forward position   The position on the battlefield that is closest to engaging the enemy.

Global War on Terror   The common term for what the George W. Bush administration perceived or presented as the military, political, legal, and ideological conflict against Islamic terrorism, Islamic militants, and the regimes and organizations tied to them or that supported them after September 11, 2000.

J5 Strategic Arms Limitation Talks (SALT)   Two rounds of talks between the United States and the Soviet Union about corresponding international treaties on armament control. The talks are referred to as SALT I (1969–1972) and SALT II (1977–1979).

Just War Tradition   A tradition with two parts: (1) the justice of war, *jus ad bellum*, deciding whether war is moral, whereas (2) justice in war, *jus in bello*, is fighting cleanly.

linear battlefield   A place where a battle is fought, with close operations taking place just at the forward area of military operations.

Military Occupation Specialty (MOS)   The name the Army calls their enlisted jobs.

North Atlantic Treaty Association (NATO)   An intergovernmental military alliance based on the North Atlantic Treaty of 1949. Member states of NATO agree to mutual defense in response to an attack.

Physical Fitness Test (PT)   Differing exercises, standards, and distances in runs and swims for all branches of the military and other special units.

platoon   A military unit typically composed of two to four sections or squads and containing 16 to 50 soldiers.

post-traumatic stress disorder (PTSD)   A type of anxiety disorder. It can occur after seeing or experiencing a traumatic event that involved the threat of injury or death. It can include persistent, frightening thoughts and memories of an ordeal and feeling emotionally numb, especially with people the PTSD sufferer was once close to. Sleep problems, feelings of detachment or numbness, and being easily startled can also be symptoms.

readiness   The ability of units and joint forces to fight and meet the demands of the national security strategy.

Risk Rule   The result of comparing the risk of exposure to direct combat, hostile fire, or capture present in noncombat units associated with combat units.

ROTC   The Reserve Officers Training Corps.

Selective Service Act, 1973   The law that ended the draft and provided for the All-Volunteer Force.

Semper Paratus, Always Ready (SPAR)   A member of the women's reserve of the U.S. Coast Guard, disbanded as a separate unit in 1946.

SERE   Survival Evasion Resistance Escape training, which prepares soldiers that have high risk of capture to survive under any conditions and anywhere in the world.

sexism   The pattern of institutional and societal responses which determines an individual's roles and status on the basis of gender.

sexual assault   Intentional sexual contact, characterized by use of force, physical threat, or abuse of authority or when the victim does not or cannot consent. It includes a broad range of sex crimes, from rape or nonconsensual sodomy to indecent assault, as well as attempts to commit these offenses.

sexual harassment   A form of sex discrimination that involves unwelcome sexual advances.

special forces   U.S. forces organized, trained, and equipped to conduct special operations with an emphasis on unconventional warfare capabilities. An example of a special force is the Navy SEAL (sea, land, and air) teams.

starboard engine   The engine on the right side of an aircraft.

state-based military   A military that is within a country and governed by that country.

Uniform Code of Military Justice (UCMJ)   The Congressional Code of Military Criminal Law applicable to all military members worldwide.

URL, Unrestricted Line   The U.S. Navy officer designation indicating who is qualified to command units, ships, or aviation squadrons.

WAAC   The Women's Army Auxiliary Corps, formed in 1942. Its auxiliary status was dropped in 1943 when it became part of the Women's Army Corps (WAC).

WAC   Women's Army Corps, established in 1943. Women were not excluded from combatant roles and had equal status, benefits, pay, and disciplinary code, but Army regulations did exclude women. WAC was abolished when women were made a permanent part of military services in 1978.

WAFS   Women's Auxiliary Ferrying Squadron, staffed by civilian women. It was formed in World War II and became part of the Women's Airforce Service Pilots (WASPs).

WASP   Women's Airforce Service Pilots, formed in World War II.

WAVES   Women Accepted for Voluntary Emergency Service, a Navy group that served in World War II; after it was abolished women were made a permanent part of military services in 1978.

Women Marines   A group for women that was abolished when women were made a permanent part of military services in 1978.

Women In Military Service For America (WIMSA)   An organization founded by Brig. Gen. Wilma Vaught to identify women who served in the military and to establish a memorial in Arlington National Cemetery to honor military women. The acronym, WIMSA, has been replaced with the Women's Memorial, which stands for the Women In Military Service For America Memorial Foundation.

Women In Military Service For America Memorial Foundation (Women's Memorial) Located in Arlington National Cemetery, the only major national memorial honoring women who have defended the nation during all eras and in all services.

Women's Armed Services Integration Act of 1948 The law which gave women permanent status in the military.

yaw rate (or yaw velocity) The angular velocity about its yaw axis, or rate of change of heading in ships and aircraft.

Index

PROPERTY RIGHTS

SOCIAL PHILOSOPHY AND
POLICY FOUNDATION

PROPERTY RIGHTS

From Magna Carta to
the Fourteenth Amendment

Bernard H. Siegan

transaction

Transaction Publishers
New Brunswick (USA) and London (UK)

Published by the Social Philosophy and Policy Foundation and by Transaction
Publishers 2001

Library of Congress Cataloging-in-Publication Data

Siegan, Bernard H.
    Property rights: from Magna Carta to the Fourteenth Amendment /
Bernard H. Siegan.
        p. cm. — (New studies in social policy ; 3)
    Includes bibliographical references and index.
    ISBN 0-7658-0057-8 (hardcover) — ISBN 0-7658-0755-6 (pbk.)
    1. Right of property—United States—History. 2. Right of property—
Great Britain—History. 3. United States. Constitution. 14th Amendment. I.
Title. II. Series.

    KF562 .S57 2001
    346.7304′2′09—dc21

                                                            00-064939

Cover Design: Lynne M. Newbound

Cover Image Credit: © Bettmann/CORBIS

To Shelley, my wife, and Jon, my son

Contents

1

Introduction

In the debates in 1787–88 to ratify the proposed United States Constitution, opponents of ratification (known as Anti-Federalists) frequently charged that the Constitution did not protect their rights, which they often referred to as the "rights of Englishmen." They based this charge on the absence of a bill of rights and the scarcity of personal protections in the document. The Anti-Federalists insisted that they had fought a war to secure their liberties, and their deaths and hardships should not have been in vain. Proponents of the Constitution (known as Federalists) replied that these apprehensions were unwarranted, and that the proposed Constitution created a government without the power to deprive the people of the rights which belonged to them under the common law, originally as English citizens and subsequently as American citizens.

To assuage these fears, the Federalists promised that if the proposed Constitution were ratified, they would introduce legislation in the First Congress to amend the Constitution by adding a bill of rights. The Federalists kept their promise and by the end of 1791, the Constitution contained a bill of rights. When the First Congress framed and the states ratified the proposed bill, most Americans believed that it protected and extended the "rights of Englishmen."

Yet, for over three years, between the ratification of the original Constitution on June 21, 1788 and the Bill of Rights on December 15, 1791, Americans lived under a Constitution that enumerated relatively few rights against the national government. Three states initially refused to ratify the proposed Bill of Rights.[1] The Anti-Federalists' fears about the absence of a bill did not resonate with the American public. The absence of this constitutional protection was not considered a matter of serious concern. Americans seemed confident that they were

protected under the original Constitution against any excesses or oppressions that the federal government might contemplate.

What were the "rights of Englishmen" that these Americans treasured as their birthright, indelibly secured in the Constitution and, for additional measure, by the Bill of Rights? England had no written constitution but, wrote United States Supreme Court Justice Joseph Bradley in 1872, the "people of this country brought with them to its shores the rights of Englishmen; the rights which had been wrested from the English sovereigns at various periods of the nation's history."[2] These migrants, explained Justice John Harlan in 1884, "brought with them, as their inheritance, which no government could rightfully impair or destroy, certain guarantees of the rights of life, liberty, and property, which had long been deemed fundamental in Anglo-Saxon institutions."[3]

Major sources for these rights were the Magna Carta, executed by King John in 1215, and many subsequent parliamentary confirmations and judicial interpretations of it. Also essential in determining the scope of individual protections were the writings of legal commentators, particularly those of Lord Edward Coke and Judge William Blackstone. Early American courts (both federal and state) utilized these sources to resolve conflicts between the government and the people. To be sure, the Americans had severed their political bonds with England but not their reliance on the English common law. For many Americans, these sources constituted an unwritten English Constitution that secured a large measure of human freedom. As historian Gordon S. Wood has put it, "what made their Revolution seem so unusual [was that] they revolted not against the English Constitution but on behalf of it."[4]

In this book, I set forth the rights of Englishmen that protected ownership, investment, and entrepreneurship, with particular emphasis on property rights. For although these rights were not enumerated in the original U.S. Constitution, they formed an essential part of its meaning and spirit. They were secured in Article IV, Section 2, as the "Privileges and Immunities of Citizens in the several States," a provision which Alexander Hamilton referred to as "the basis of the Union."[5] As James Madison stated, the Constitution would never have been ratified if the people thought that their liberties were in danger.[6] The English sources for these rights also illuminate the meaning of these rights. The language of much of the Constitution and Bill of Rights often would be unintelligible in the absence of these sources.

The legal commentaries of Coke and Blackstone concerning protection of property greatly influenced jurisprudence and legal commentary in the United States. Both were often cited by jurists in their opinions. Even when not cited, doctrines attributable to these great English commentators were evident in legal opinions of federal and state courts. With respect to U.S. jurisprudence between the ratification of the Constitution (1788) and ratification of the Fourteenth Amendment (1868), the judiciary frequently accorded

protection for property rights commensurate with the rules expressed by these Englishmen.

In 1868, the states ratified the Fourteenth Amendment. Section 1 contains broad guarantees for liberties in the states, as secured by the privileges or immunities, due process, and equal protection clauses. The language of each of these clauses is comprehensive and embodies the meanings previously accorded these concepts by the American judiciary, the branch of government entrusted with the protection of the people's liberties. The importance of judicial precedent in construing the clauses is evident from the debates of the Thirty-Ninth Congress, which framed the amendment in 1866. Representative John Bingham of Ohio was the principal author of the protective clauses of Section 1 of the Fourteenth Amendment. When asked about the meaning of "due process of law," he replied: "The courts have settled that long ago, and the gentlemen can go and read their decisions."[7] Senator Jacob Howard introduced in the Senate the legislation creating the Fourteenth Amendment and stated that prior judicial interpretations of the meaning of privileges or immunities give "some intimation of what probably will be the opinion of the judiciary."[8]

Accordingly, federal and state courts had to consider judicial precedent to understand the rights clauses of section 1. These precedents explained what the rights of Americans were in 1866 under these clauses, just as the English sources were authoritative on the rights of Americans in the late 1780s. Inasmuch as many of these judicial opinions relied for their reasoning on the English commentators and cases, it is not surprising that the interpretation of rights to ownership of property in America was not significantly different between the late 1780s and late 1860s.

What perhaps is more surprising is that the United States Supreme Court, commencing in 1987, handed down decisions in land use cases remarkably consistent with the earlier interpretations. Previously the Court had for over fifty years applied deference instead of scrutiny to regulations restricting the ownership and use of private property. This latest turn in Supreme Court interpretation would have pleased Lord Coke and Judge Blackstone who centuries earlier addressed concerns about ownership, investment in, and use of private property that still resonate with twenty-first century Americans. Events over the centuries have not lessened the vital importance of private property. Instead, experience has underscored it. World history has shown that the protection of property rights is essential to maintain human liberty as well as political and economic viability and stability. The rules promulgated by Coke and Blackstone are in this sense as current and relevant today as when they were written.

This work contains seven chapters. Chapters 2 through 6 discuss property rights in different historical periods. Chapter 2 treats the "rights of Englishmen" as they developed from Magna Carta through the great legal commentators. The latter sections of this chapter trace the influence that these English rights had in

the American colonies. The founding period in the United States is the focus of Chapter 3, which examines property rights protections in the Articles of Confederation, the new Constitution, and the Bill of Rights. State and federal court decisions in property rights cases in the period between the adoption of the Constitution and the ratification of the Fourteenth Amendment are the focus of Chapter 4. This chapter is critical to an understanding of the role of property rights in the American legal tradition, since it examines many cases that have not been mined by earlier commentators, an oversight that has inevitably skewed our understanding of our early jurisprudence on property rights. Chapters 5 and 6 examine the framing of the Fourteenth Amendment, how its framers understood such critical phrases as "due process" (Chapter 5) and "privileges or immunities" (Chapter 6), and the fate of these concepts in subsequent judicial opinions. The seventh and last chapter offers my concluding thoughts on the centrality of property rights to the American experiment in liberty and self-government. The liberty to own property undergirds the unique American perspective on government as the necessary foundation for private initiative and enterprise to advance public welfare, not the direct provider. Protection of property rights over the centuries provided the necessary conditions for the enormous material benefits presently enjoyed by Americans.

2

The Rights of Englishmen

The protection that the United States Constitution provides for property rights is contained primarily in its two due process clauses and in the takings clause. The due process clauses of the Fifth and Fourteenth Amendments prohibit the federal or state governments from depriving any person of life, liberty, or property, without due process of law. Both secure an owner from governmental deprivation of property that is not imposed pursuant to due process procedures and requirements. The takings clause of the Fifth Amendment provides that "private property shall [not] be taken for public use without just compensation." Both the due process and takings clauses curtail the power of government to confiscate or excessively regulate private property.

These clauses can be traced to Chapter 29 of the Magna Carta, executed by King Henry III in 1225, and the interpretations of that document and related English property law by the most authoritative of English legal commentators, Edward Coke and William Blackstone. The early English migrants to this continent, their descendants, and subsequent settlers possessed property rights under the laws of England that, after the American Revolution, the original U.S. Constitution, Bill of Rights, and Fourteenth Amendment confirmed and broadened.

King Henry's Magna Carta was not the first version of this document. The original document was signed in 1215 by John, king of England and Ireland. Chapter 29 of King Henry's charter was in part an extension and in part a confirmation of Chapter 39 of King John's charter. To understand the relationship between Chapters 29 and 39 of the Magna Carta and the due process and takings

clauses requires a brief discussion of early English history, beginning with the period in which the first Magna Carta was executed.

I. The Magna Carta

Commencing in 1205, King John and Pope Innocent III engaged in a struggle that led the Pope to excommunicate the king in 1209 and later in 1212 to declare him deposed of his kingdom, thereby releasing his subjects from their allegiance to him. The king fought back, however, which created serious problems both for the English Church and clergy. However, upon Pope Innocent's agreement to withdraw his decrees of excommunication, John capitulated in 1213 and transferred his kingdom of England and Ireland to the papacy. He then received it back as a feudatory of the Church of Rome, for which he agreed to pay a tribute of 1,000 marks sterling a year (seven hundred for England, and three hundred for Ireland). This arrangement was not unusual since five other European rulers previously became vassals of the Pope. In becoming a vassal of the Pope, King John acquired papal support in his conflict with the English barons.

In late 1214, the English barons, burdened by King John's serious violations of feudal law and custom, revolted against him. They attacked his castles and seized London, the principal walled town of England, where its populace welcomed them and they occupied many of its parks and palaces. In the following year, a conference to obtain peace between the king and barons was arranged to be held on the plains of Runnymede near Windsor Castle. On June 15, 1215, to terminate the conflict, the king executed a formal document containing 63 chapters that the barons submitted to him, which was originally known as the Charter of Liberties, or the Articles of the Barons, and subsequently called the Great Charter or the Magna Carta.

The barons had revolted because John violated both the substantive and procedural rights of his constituents as established by the common law, custom, and agreement. He imposed at will new rules and penalties and punished without fair or proper process those he charged with wrongdoing. In the Magna Carta John promised, among other things, to return the properties he had seized and to remit the fines he had imposed in violation of existing rules and customs. He agreed that in the future a freeman would only be punished for violating existing rules and then only in proportion to his wrongdoing and would not otherwise be deprived of his liberties and properties.

In the words of historian Charles McIlwain, "[W]hen King John substituted his will for this law, in proceeding by force against vassals whose wrong had not been judicially proved, civil war and the Great Charter were the result."[1] The barons had many grievances against King John. They suffered from gross maladministration in his government and his courts. He had exacted the sur-

render of castles and otherwise made exorbitant financial demands upon every class. He hanged prisoners whom he seized in battle and he forced barons whom he suspected of treasonable inclinations to surrender their children to him as hostages. He also seized lands of the clergy.[2]

In the Magna Carta, King John agreed to undo the deprivations he had imposed arbitrarily and retroactively and not to impose illegitimate ones in the future. Thus, in Chapter 52, the king agreed that if anyone "has been dispossessed or removed by us, without the legal judgment of his peers, from his lands, castles, franchises, or from his right, we will immediately restore them to him." Chapter 55 provided that all "fines, made with us unjustly or against the law of the land, and all amercements imposed unjustly and against the land of the land, shall be entirely remitted." Chapter 56 mandated the same relief for lands or liberties disseised or removed from any Welshman. Chapter 20 stated that a freeman, merchant, or villein shall not be amerced for either a slight or grave offense, except in accordance with the degree of the offense; Chapter 21 provided equivalent protection for earls and barons and Chapter 22 provided the same for the clergy.[3] Chapter 12 recognized the concept of no taxation without representation: "No scutage [a fee paid in lieu of military service] or aid shall be imposed on our kingdom unless by common consent of our kingdom." King John's most important commitments for the future, though, were those contained in Chapter 39, which is usually freely translated from the Latin as follows:

> No freeman shall be arrested, or detained in prison, or deprived of his freehold, or in any way molested; and we [the King] will not set forth against him, nor send against him, unless by the lawful judgment of his peers or by the law of the land.

In this chapter, King John promises never again to commit the reprehensible acts that led the barons to revolt. He agreed that in the future he would not deprive freemen of their lives, liberties, or properties unless it was required by existing and proper laws and, then, only pursuant to fair and proper procedures. He thereby relinquished authority to execute retroactive or other arbitrary laws or rules destroying or damaging freemen as had previously been his practice. A comparable chapter was included in all subsequent issues of the Magna Carta.

Three other chapters of the Magna Carta are relevant to understanding the background of the property protections in the U.S. Constitution and its amendments. Chapter 61 authorized the barons to select twenty-five of their number to receive complaints about violations of the charter. When violations occurred, "these twenty-five barons together with the community of the whole realm, shall distress and injure us [referring to King John] in all ways possible . . . until redress has been obtained as they deem fit . . . and when redress has been ob-

tained, they shall resume their old relations toward us as before." This chapter can be considered as initiating the idea of checks and balances pursuant to which different governmental branches have authority to restrain each other for the purpose of upholding constitutional provisions. No provision similar to Chapter 61 appears in any later versions of the Magna Carta. The English judiciary and Parliament subsequently assumed this role.

Chapter 28 forbade the king's constable or bailiff to "take corn, or other provisions from anyone without immediately tendering money therefor, unless he can have postponement thereof by permission on the seller." This chapter is possibly the basis for the U.S. Constitution's takings clause. (Similar provisions that permit the king to acquire private property from nonconsenting owners by paying for it appear in later versions of the Magna Carta.) In Chapter 40, the king agreed as follows: "To no one will we sell, to no one will we refuse or delay, right or justice." This chapter is a precursor to the rule that the law will be applied equally to all, without seeking to benefit or harm selected persons.

One cannot be certain as to the exact meaning of a document that was written centuries ago and at a time of limited communications. Yet history discloses information that allows for a reasonable interpretation of the event. The barons had revolted because "the necessities of King John drove him to severities that had been unknown in the preceding century."[4] The Magna Carta was essentially an agreement between the king and the barons that terminated their conflict pursuant to certain conditions. King John acceded to the barons' demands that their rights be recognized and confirmed in writing, and agreed to send a copy of the charter to each of the counties to be read to all freemen.

Much of the charter requires the king to honor his obligations under the law of the land, which at the time was, as historian Arthur Hogue explains, "principally land law, consisting of the rules, customs, and practices of those holding free tenures in a feudal society." He continues:

> Thus the common law of the twelfth and thirteenth centuries is in large part the law of land and tenures, the law of property rights and services together with rules of procedure for the administration of justice. A glance at the chapters of Magna Carta or at any collection of common-law writs will reveal the dominant concern with rights in land: the possession, or seisin, of land, the services owed for the tenure of land, the inheritance of land, the leasing of land, the wardship of land, the profits from land, the burdens on land, and the wrongs to land.[5]

Under Chapter 39, John could no longer deprive the barons of their lives, liberties, and properties, except as a penalty for violating the existing law. "A King had been brought to order . . . by the community of the land under baronial leadership; a tyrant had been subjected to laws which hitherto it had been his private privilege to administer and modify."[6] The king's legislative powers were

necessarily limited, for "if by 'law of the land' was meant any law which the king might enact, the provision was a nullity."[7] Chapter 39, wrote McIlwain, "was merely the classical statement of a fundamental principle that the king may not take the definition of rights into his own hands, but must proceed against none by force for any alleged violation of them until a case has been made out against such a one by 'due process of law.'"[8]

King John's execution of the Magna Carta was a momentous occurrence in human history. Government in the form of a king actually relinquished its powers to deprive people who are innocent of wrongdoing of their rights to life, liberty, and property. While the document was intended to protect the nobles, the principles it set forth in Chapter 39 would in time be applied to everyone. "[C]onsciously or unconsciously, the baronage . . . secured the benefits of the rule of law, not only for themselves but for all free men."[9] Persons who abided by the law would be secure from governmental violation of their persons and properties. Those accused of a crime would be entitled to fair and proper process to prove their innocence. An important legal principle was confirmed: Government cannot at will impose laws that deprive people of their liberties and possessions. In *The History of England,* David Hume describes the execution of the Magna Carta in these terms:

> It only guarded and that merely by verbal clauses, against such tyrannical practices as are incompatible with civilized government, and, if they become very frequent, are incompatible with all government. The barbarous license of the kings, and perhaps for the nobles, was thenceforth somewhat more restrained: Men acquired some more security for their properties and their liberties: And government approached a little nearer to that end, for which it was originally instituted, the distribution of justice, and the equal protection of the citizens. Acts of violence and iniquity in the crown, which before were only deemed injurious to individuals, and were hazardous chiefly in proportion to the number, power, and dignity of the persons affected by them, were now regarded, in some degree, as public injuries, and as infringements of a charter, calculated for general security. And thus, the establishment of the Great Charter, without seeming anywise to innovate in the distribution of political power, became a kind of epoch in the [English] constitution.[10]

Though King John's version of the Magna Carta would end up being largely a parchment victory, on the map of history it was an enormous substantive achievement. The king's powers were limited, and this was the beginning of the end of despotism in the English-speaking nations.

Initially, King John appeared to comply with the many requirements of the charter, but in fact he sought to revoke the promises he had made. At the instigation of King John, Pope Innocent III issued a bull dated August 24, 1215 declaring

the entire charter void, primarily on the grounds that it was invalid and derogatory to the dignity of the apostolic see; it was a "shame for England." Pope Innocent considered King John's approval of the charter as defective because the king had no authority as a feudatory of the papacy to sign it and, furthermore, his consent was obtained "by violence and fear." The pope forbade King John to obey or the nobles to enforce its terms. In September, the king recalled all the liberties he had granted his subjects in the charter, and repudiated its restraints upon him. He died in October, 1216 and was succeeded by his son Henry III.[11]

While, for the most part, the monarchy after King John's death respected the feudal rights of the barons, there were enough violations to arouse fears that it did not in fact accept limitations on its powers. To reduce and terminate conflicts with and obtain support of the nobles, Henry's regent (Henry was nine years old at his father's death) reissued King John's charter in the name of Henry on two occasions. In 1225, after he assumed personal control of the throne, King Henry in special ceremony executed a document containing 38 chapters; he identified this document as a confirmation of the original charter. The 1225 document is considered the definitive version of the Magna Carta. Henry and his successor Edward I each confirmed it three times and Parliament did likewise many times thereafter—thirty-two in total, reported Lord Edward Coke in 1628.[12] Each subsequent issue followed the form of the 1225 version, which by statute was declared to be "the birthright of the people of England."[13] These confirmations accorded the Magna Carta status as part of the common law of England.[14] Chapter 29 of the 1225 charter broadened and replaced Chapter 39 of King John's charter and provided as follows:

> No freeman shall be taken, or imprisoned, or be disseised of his freehold, or liberties, or free customs, or be outlawed, or exiled, or any otherwise destroyed; nor will we not pass upon him, nor condemn him, but by lawful judgment of his peers, or by the law of the land. We will sell to no man, we will not deny or defer to any man either justice or right.

By its terms, Chapter 29 was a much greater limitation on royal powers than was Chapter 39, but the meaning and scope of its protections had to await interpretation by the common law judges.

Among other provisions of general concern, Chapter 30 specifically extended commercial rights to "all merchants [who shall] have their safe and sure conduct to depart out of England, to come into England, to tarry in, and go through England, as well by land or by water to buy and sell without any manner of evil tolls, by the old and rightful customs, except in time of war." This chapter is similar to Chapter 41 of the 1215 Charter; both chapters intended to prevent exclusion of foreign merchants.[15] Chapter 9 is consistent with Chapter 13 of the 1215 Charter and affirmed the liberties and free customs of London

and other cities and towns. Chapter 14 is generally comparable to Chapters 20, 21, and 22 of the 1215 document; it likewise limited the imposition of amercements to the degree of fault committed by an accused.

Similar to the 1215 charter, the 1225 charter also contained provisions that foreshadowed the takings clause in the Fifth Amendment of the U.S. Constitution. Chapter 21 required payment by government officials for the acquisition of horses or carts: "No Sheriff or Bailiff of ours, or any other, shall take the horses or carts of any man to make carriage, except he pay the old price limited, that is to say, for carriage with two horse, X.d. a day; for three horse, XIV.d. a day." Similar to Chapter 28 of the 1215 charter, Chapter 19 required payment by government officials for acquisition of corn or other chattels: "No constable, nor his Bailiff, shall take corn or other chattels of any man, if the man be not of the Town where the Constable is, but he shall forthwith pay for the same, unless that the will of the Seller was to respite the payment; and if he be of the same Town, the price shall be paid unto him within forty days."

Subsequently, on four occasions during the reign of King Edward III, Parliament adopted provisions substantially augmenting Chapter 29's guarantees against arbitrary impositions and deprivations. The following provisions are contained in a statute passed in 1331 in the fifth year of King Edward III's reign:

> That no Man from henceforth shall be attached by any Accusation, nor forejudged of Life or Limb, nor his Lands, Tenements, Goods, nor Chattels seized into the King's Hands, against the form of the Great Charter, and the Law of the Land.

Other important protections were adopted in 1352, during Edward's twenty-sixth year as king:

> Whereas it is contained in the great charter . . . that none shall be imprisoned nor put out of his Freehold, nor of his Franchises nor free custom, unless it be by Law of the Land. . . .
>
> That from henceforth none shall be taken by Petition or Suggestion made to our Lord the King, or to his Council, unless it be by Indictment or Presentment of good and lawful People of the same neighborhood where such Deeds be done, in due Manner, or by Process made by Writ original at the Common Law; nor that none be out of his Franchises, nor of his Freeholds, unless he be duly brought into answer, and forejudged of the same by the course of law; and if any thing be done against the same, it shall be redressed and holden for none.

In 1354, the twenty-eighth year of King Edward's reign, a statute was adopted containing the following language:

That no man, of what Estate or Condition that he be, shall be put out of Land or Tenement, nor taken, nor imprisoned, nor disinherited, nor put to Death, without being brought in Answer by due Process of the Law.

These additions to the Magna Carta made its protections more specific and considerably enlarged their scope. According to Coke, Parliament also passed in 1363 an important statute construing the meaning of "law of the land," a construal which will be considered in the following section. The English people regarded the Magna Carta—and subsequent statutes broadening its guarantees—as preserving and protecting their lives, liberties, and properties. Those who migrated to America, and their descendants who lived there, asserted these "rights of Englishmen" against restraints imposed by the English authorities.

II. Lord Coke and His Interpretation of the Magna Carta

Edward Coke (1552–1634) was a major figure in English law. At various times, he was attorney general for the queen, chief justice both of the Court of Common Pleas and of the King's Bench, and speaker of the House of Commons. Among other publications, he authored a four-volume commentary on English law entitled *Institutes of the Laws of England* (1600–1615); in the Second Institute he interpreted King Henry III's 1225 Magna Carta, elevating it to very high status in English law. On both sides of the Atlantic Ocean, Coke's interpretation was regarded as highly authoritative on the meaning of the charter and subsequent additions to it. The *Institutes* were required reading for most colonial lawyers.

According to law professor Edward Corwin, Coke "was first on the ground" in the colonies, leading to a widespread "presence of Coke's doctrines [in the United States] . . . during the latter two-thirds of the seventeenth century."[16] Corwin asserts that Coke's statement in *Dr. Bonham's Case* (to be discussed in the following section) became the most important single source of the notion of judicial review.[17]

Some commentators have criticized Coke's writings; however, Coke's influence, "as the embodiment of the common law, was so strong, that it is useless to contend that 'he was either misled by his sources or unconsciously misinterpreted them,' for Coke's mistakes, it is said, *are* the common law."[18] In his *Institutes,* he accepted Henry's 1225 charter as the definitive one; he discusses and interprets the various chapters in light of the additions and interpretations subsequently made to it by the Parliament, judicial decisions, and authoritative legal commentaries. English and American courts accepted and cited Coke's interpretation of Chapter 29 as authoritative on the meaning of "law of the land" and "due process of law," and numerous U.S. federal and state judicial opin-

ions have cited him in various matters. Coke has been appropriately referred to as "the great light of our legal system."[19]

This great document, wrote Coke, is called "Magna Carta, not for the length or largeness of it . . . but . . . in respect of the great weightiness and weighty greatness of the matter contained in it; in a few words, being the fountain of all the fundamental laws of the realm."[20] By the time he wrote the second volume of his *Institutes,* in which he discusses and analyzes the Magna Carta, Parliament and the courts via the common law had greatly expanded and supplemented the 1225 charter. Coke viewed the common law—with its origin and basis in the Magna Carta—as a restraint on the powers of the monarchy and various other governmental bodies, including the Parliament. He looked to the judiciary to protect the people from oppression by government. The common law is, he opined, "the best and most common birthright that the subject hath for the safeguard and defense, not only of his goods, lands and revenues, but of his wife and children, his body, fame and life also."[21]

Coke considered Chapter 29 as protecting many more persons than just the class of barons who had forced King John to sign the original charter. According to him, the protections of this chapter applied to freemen as well as to villeins, "for they [villeins] are free against all men, saving against their lord."[22] Under the feudal system, villeins included persons who held lands and tenements under a villeinage agreement with the lord who owned the property. While the villeins were effectively serfs with respect to their lord, they otherwise had the rights of freemen.

Coke writes that Chapter 29 contains what he refers to as nine separate "branches." According to his interpretation, the first five established that, unless it is by due course and process of law, (1) no man shall be taken or imprisoned; (2) no man shall be disseised or dispossessed of his freehold, livelihood, liberties, or free-customs; (3) no man shall be outlawed, or denied the benefit of the law; (4) no man shall be exiled or banished; and (5) no man shall be destroyed. The last four branches relate to the king's promise to administer his high office fairly and properly: (6) no man shall be condemned at the king's pleasure or that of any commissioner or judge, (7) the king shall sell to no man justice or right, (8) the king shall deny to no man justice or right, and (9) the king shall defer to no man justice or right.

The second branch (prohibiting disseising) is especially important for our purposes, since it concerns property rights, which Coke construed broadly to include considerable protection for ownership:

> No man shall be disseised, that is, put out of seisin, or dispossessed of his free-hold (that is) lands, or livelihood, or of his liberties, or free-customes, that is, of such franchises, and freedoms, and free-customes, as belong to him by his free birth right, unless it be by the lawful judgement,

that is, verdict of his equals (that is, of men of his own condition) or by the law of the land (that is, to speak it once for all) by the due course, and process of law.[23]

With respect to the prohibition on disseising, he explains "that lands, tenements, goods, and chattels shall not be seised into the king's hands, contrary to this great charter, and the law of the land; nor any man shall be disseised of his lands, or tenements, or dispossessed of his goods, or chattels, contrary to the law of the land."[24]

Coke finds the meaning of "law of the land" in a 1363 statute of King Edward III that states "that no man be taken, imprisoned, or put out of his freehold without process of the law; that is, by indictment or presentment of good and lawful men, where such deeds be done in due manner, or by writ original of the common law." Coke explains that this provision requires that no man shall be deprived of his liberties and possessions "without being brought in to answer but by due process of the common law."[25] He writes that the law of the land includes only a general and public law, operating equally upon every person in the community; it is not intended to favor or harm certain individuals but to extend to all. "[B]ut that the law might extend to all, it is said *per legem terra* [by the law of the land.]"[26] The last sentence of Chapter 29 emphasizes the king's commitment to rule neutrally and impartially: the monarch promised to sell, deny, or defer to no man justice or right.

Limiting the standard of the law of the land invites tyranny. Coke writes that Parliament, by an act in the eleventh year of King Henry VII's reign, authorized judges—without any finding or presentment by a jury, but only on bare information—to hear and adjudicate all offenses committed by persons against laws in effect. Not being restrained by due process requirements, two judges committed "horrible oppressions" against many persons. In the first year of King Henry VIII's reign, Parliament repealed the act on the basis that it violated the Magna Carta. "[A]nd the ill success hereof, and the fearful ends of these two oppressors, should deter others from committing the like, and should admonish parliaments, that instead of this ordinary and precious trial *per legem terrae* [law of the land], they bring not in absolute, and partial trials by discretion."[27] A governmental discretion must be limited to preclude dispensing favors to or imposing penalties on certain persons or groups. Coke advised parliaments "to leave all causes to be measured by the golden and straight metwand of the law, and not to the uncertain and crooked cord of discretion."[28] Coke thus condemned retroactive justice that enables judges to impose punishment for conduct to which it was not subject at the time it was committed. Indeed, he opposed all legislation regulating prior conduct, stating that a legislative enactment ought not be retrospective in its operation.[29]

This concern about unchecked governmental powers has influenced United States Supreme Court decisions over the years. The constitutional protection

against unlimited jury or judicial discretion, Justice Stephen Breyer wrote when concurring in a 1996 case, harkens back to the Magna Carta and "arises out of the basic unfairness of depriving citizens of life, liberty or property, through the application, not of law and legal processes, but of arbitrary coercion [citations omitted]. Requiring the application of law, rather than a decisionmaker's caprice, does more than simply provide citizens notice of what actions may subject them to punishment; it also helps assure the uniform general treatment of similarly situated persons that is the essence of law itself."[30]

Unlike King John's Magna Carta, King Henry's did not create an enforcement body to monitor and secure the promises the king made in the document. In addition to being a broad limitation on the royal powers, the earlier charter is noteworthy for establishing in Chapter 61 an official body to enforce its provisions. Nonetheless, by the time Coke wrote his *Institutes,* the English judges had long ago assumed this responsibility. The judges had applied the common law to limit the king's powers as well as those of localities and guilds. They had also imposed some restraints on Parliament. In 1628, Coke told Parliament that "Magna Carta is such a fellow that he will have no Sovereign."[31] He illustrated the judicial powers by summarizing in his *Institutes* two common law decisions that explained the meaning of the provision in Chapter 29 of King Henry's Magna Carta, which stated that no freeman shall be disseised of his freehold, livelihood, liberties, or free-customs:

1. A custome was alleged in the town of C. that if the tenant ceased [to pay rent for] two years, the lord should enter into the freehold of the tenant, and hold the same until he were satisfied of the arrerages, and it was adjudged against the law of the land, to enter into a mans freehold in that case without action or answer.[32]
2. King Henry, the sixth, granted to the corporation of diers within London, power to search, and if they found any cloth died with logwood, that the cloth should be forfeit; and it as adjudged, that this provision concerning the forfeiture, was against the law of the land, and this statute; for no forfeiture can grow by letters patent.[33] No man ought to be put from his livelihood without answer.[34]

As revealed in these two cases, protection of property rights was quite broad in Coke's day, extending to ownership of certain dyed cloths and to business enterprise using these cloths, as well as to the possession of certain leasehold interests. In each case, the law of the land required a judicial hearing to determine whether existing law authorized a termination of the owner's or lessee's interest. The lease in question was apparently sufficient in law to warrant Magna Carta protection for the lessee. The Magna Carta prohibited the king from confiscating property on his own behalf; the logwood case extended this rule to apply to a

confiscatory action by the king on behalf of a private group. (The king could still acquire property under his prerogative powers, but only when it was in furtherance of those powers. The royal prerogative powers will be discussed in relation to the *Case of the King's Prerogative in Saltpeter* in Section III below.)

The lord in the first example above had a much stronger legal case. While King Henry's grant might have been a retroactive deprivation of the right of a person to use cloth dyed with logwood, the lord's case involved a custom which presumably existed when the leasehold was executed and therefore was not retroactive with respect to it. Nevertheless, common law principles prohibited any person from being a judge in his own cause. Consequently, the lord was devoid of power to limit the lessee's possessory interest without a judicial resolution of the controversy in the lord's favor. The lessee was entitled to submit in a court defenses to the action, something which the local custom prevented. However, the failure to pay rent as agreed was likely sufficient reason to enable the lord to obtain possession.

Consequently, to reiterate the foregoing, according to the common law interpretation of Chapter 29 of the Magna Carta, no person shall be deprived of his property or his livelihood, except when it is done in accordance with the law of the land. This protection requires three things: (1) the law which is alleged to have been violated must be existing and otherwise legitimate, (2) the law must be for a public and not private interest, and (3) a judicial trial conforming to the requirements of due process must be held to determine if wrongdoing has occurred that warrants a deprivation.

Coke's discussion of the meaning of "liberties" in Chapter 29 reveals his position that the scope of Chapter 29's economic protections was considerable, extending beyond ownership or possession of land. According to him, "liberties" has three significations. First, it signifies the laws of the realm. Second, it signifies the freedoms that the subjects of England have:

> [F]or example, the company of the merchant tailors of England, having power by their [royal] charter to make ordinances, made an ordinance, that every brother of the same society should put the one half of his clothes to be dressed by some clothworker free of the same company, upon pain to forfeit, . . . and it was adjudged that this ordinance was against law, because it was against the liberty of the subject, for every subject hath freedome to put his clothes to be dressed by whom he will. . . . [This is a description of the case of *Davenant v. Hurdis,* discussed in Section III below.]

Third, "liberties" signifies the franchises and privileges that Englishmen possess, which Coke (basing his position on the *Case of Monopolies,* discussed in Section III below) illustrated as follows:

[I]f a grant be made to any man, to have the sole making of cards, or the sole dealing with any other trade, that grant is against the liberty and freedom of the subject, that before did, or lawfully might have used that trade, and consequently against this great charter.[35]

Generally all monopolies are against this great charter, because they are against the liberty and freedom of the subject, and against the law of the law of the land.[36]

Coke regarded economic laws intended to benefit particular individuals or groups as invalid under the common law, because, among other things, they were special and not general laws. For example, according monopoly powers to some means depriving others of the liberty to engage in that industry or trade. It was unlawful under the common law, he concluded, for the monarch to grant or authorize the granting of monopoly powers governing entry into businesses or occupations.[37] This rule was not applicable to Parliament, which generally had authority to override the common law.

As the foregoing discussion reveals, Coke viewed Chapter 29 as a substantive protection of the people's liberties from limitation by the royal power. The argument is often made that Chapter 29 imposed only procedural requirements, that is, its protections only went so far as to require that a deprivation of life, liberty, or property by the king or his appointees be achieved with a fair and proper judicial process.[38] This would mean that the prohibition on deprivation is satisfied when the law has been passed pursuant to the required legislative processes. Life, liberty, and property would then truly be at the discretion of the lawmaker, and the judiciary would simply be a conduit to implementing these discretionary laws. Such an interpretation would undermine the libertarian objectives of Chapter 29, and thus this interpretation cannot be attributed to Coke, who was an ardent supporter of these objectives. The reason for depriving the citizen of his rights must be found in a legitimately enacted law, and not a retroactive one passed for the purpose of curtailing an existing right.

Retroactive laws are a tool of despotic government. The barons' major grievance against King John was his imposition of retroactive measures pursuant to which he seized their persons and properties; in the Magna Carta they forced him to restore both. The original, and all subsequent confirmations of, Magna Carta declared that the king could not at his will deprive a person of his freedom. Chapter 29 was intended to limit the arbitrary exercise of power, not to secure it by the application of due process procedures.[39] The due process inquiry required by Chapter 29 necessitates a judicial determination that the law in question was not retroactive or otherwise contrary to the principles of Magna Carta.

Coke considered the courts as having a decisive role in the interpretation of English law, as is evident from the famous ruling about judicial power made in

Dr. Bonham's Case (discussed in the next section) by the Court of Common Pleas in 1610, of which Coke was chief justice. The Court ruled that the London College of Physicians was not entitled to punish Bonham for practicing medicine without its approval, despite the passage by Parliament of an act authorizing this penalty:

> And it appears in our books, that in many cases, the common law will controul Acts of Parliament, and sometimes adjudge them to be utterly void; for when an Act of Parliament is against common right and reason, or repugnant, or impossible to be performed, the common law will controul it, and adjudge such Act to be void.[40]

The above-quoted statement is inconsistent with the idea of parliamentary supremacy. It was used in the American colonies to justify resistance to the British Parliament and by jurists after the Revolution as a basis for judicial review. The American colonists often cited Coke as proclaiming the supremacy of the common law. Political leaders continually invoked Coke in opposition to regulation. Thus, a prevailing argument against the highly condemned Stamp Act of 1765 that was imposed by the English on the colonies (whose legislative bodies had not consented to it), was that it violated "Magna Carta and the natural rights of Englishmen, and therefore, according to Lord Coke, null and void."[41] George Mason, the author of the Virginia Declaration of Rights and a framer of the U.S. Constitution, cited Coke in a 1772 Virginia case as authority for the proposition that "[a]ll acts of the legislature apparently contrary to natural rights and justice are, in our laws, and must be in the nature of things, considered as void."[42]

Coke's idea of judicial finality succumbed in time to parliamentary supremacy in England, but, of course, it is alive and well in the United States and many other nations. Two other major commentators, William Blackstone and John Locke, did not subscribe to Coke's position on judicial powers. Both accepted and supported legislative supremacy. Locke's solution for legislative tyranny was to be found either at the ballot box or in the rebellion of the people "whenever the legislators endeavor to take away and destroy the property of the people, or to reduce them to slavery."[43] Blackstone believed in parliamentary sovereignty: For judges to attempt to control Parliament—even when it "positively enact[s] a thing to be done which is unreasonable"—would be "to set the judicial power above the legislature, which is subversive of all government."[44] However, he acknowledged that the judges had the power to reform statutes, a matter which is discussed in Section IV below. Blackstone accepted the people's right to revolt when their rights were violated, but only after, first, seeking judicial relief and, second, petitioning the king and Parliament.[45] Nations that accord the judiciary oversight power over their government usually do so under terms of a constitution, something which England has never adopted.

Pursuant to Coke's interpretation of Chapter 29 of the Magna Carta, one might conclude that neither the king nor Parliament has the authority to deny persons of their rights to life, liberty, and property. Only the courts possess this power and, in depriving someone of his liberties, the judge must strictly adhere to the requirements of due process. However, in his capacity as a judge, Coke accepted the position that both the king and Parliament possessed some powers to restrict the exercise of liberties. I shall discuss in the next section ten English cases, seven of which Coke served in as a jurist, and three on which he wrote commentaries.

III. Coke's Judicial Record

Coke's most discussed decision was *Dr. Bonham's Case,*[46] an action for wrongful imprisonment brought by Thomas Bonham against the president and censors of the College of Physicians in London. King Henry VIII had authorized the college by letters patent, which was confirmed by Parliament, to levy a fine of 100 shillings a month, to be divided equally between the king and the college, on anyone practicing physic (medicine) in London for a month or more without a license from the college, regardless of whether or not the person has been awarded a degree in physic from any university. Having obtained the degree of Doctor of Philosophy and Physic from the University of Cambridge, Bonham practiced medicine in London without this authority and was subsequently fined 100 shillings. Rejecting the college's power to enjoin him from pursuing his practice, Bonham continued it and was fined an additional ten pounds, arrested, and committed to prison. Coke presided at the wrongful imprisonment trial as Chief Justice of the Court of Common Pleas. The court found that the statute violated common law principles, and held for the plaintiff.

Many learned commentators have debated Coke's conclusion that the existing jurisprudence empowered the judiciary to invalidate statutes of Parliament that were found to be contrary to fundamental rules of the common law. He confined the judiciary's power to void statutes to those that are against "common right and reason, or repugnant, or impossible to be performed." Statutes having these characteristics serve little or no legitimate purpose, while denying people their liberties. However, the Magna Carta was directed at the king and not Parliament, a distinction which Coke was reluctant always to accept when it came to protecting personal liberties.

Coke cited five cases as precedents to support his ruling that statutes violating the common law are void. Law professor Theodore Plucknett, after detailed analysis of all five, concludes that only the case known as *Cessavit 42,*[47] decided in 1359, was a legitimate precedent for the ruling. Plucknett suggests that two other cases that were not referred to by Coke also offered some support for the

chief justice's ruling.[48] *Cessavit 42* involved the Statute of Westminister the Second, which provided that the right to institute an action in *cessavit* should descend from a lord to his heir. A lord could obtain a writ of *cessavit* to recover the land of any of his tenants who for two years failed to perform required services or to pay the required rent and had not upon his lands sufficient goods or chattels to be distrained.[49] Courts refused to implement the Westminister Statute in two cases, thereby depriving an heir of a right of action that the statute accorded him.[50] In *Cessavit 42,* which was the second of the two cases, when an heir brought this writ, the court refused to grant it and made no reference in its ruling to principles of the common law. This decision was generally accepted as conclusive concerning the interpretation of the statute, with Coke asserting in his *Bonham* opinion, "because it would be against common right and reason, the common law [adjudged] the said act of parliament as to that point void."

Plucknett observes that the report of *Cessavit 42* does not disclose that such a judgment was entered. The court simply ignored the statute and did not hold it void. Consequently, Coke's conclusion about the judgment was extravagant and not precise. However, the court's refusal to be bound by the statute was regarded by the judiciary as final in the matter. It is not clear to me whether the *Cessavit 42* ruling qualifies as precedent under the then-current rules of the common law for Coke's famous statement in *Bonham* about judiciary power. One might also wonder if he required precedent for the statement, since common law judges often entered new rulings against oppressive statutes that had been adopted by the monarchy. In *Bonham,* Coke sought to apply the right and reason of the common law to acts of Parliament. According to Plucknett, Coke honestly believed he had incontestable precedents for his position, for he knew that without such support he would have achieved nothing.

In the subsequent years, English judges at various times followed, cited, or rejected Coke's opinion in *Bonham* concerning the authority of the common law, until it was largely abandoned in the English Revolution of 1688 (known as the Glorious Revolution), which established parliamentary supremacy in the land. Parliament was not about to share its great victory with the judges, who were at best an uncertain ally. Nonetheless, Coke's ruling continued to be held in great esteem in the United States.

Between the time that King John signed the Magna Carta in 1215 and the occurrence of the Glorious Revolution, an intense struggle existed between the forces of autocracy (the monarchy) and the forces of democracy (the Parliament). While both the Parliament and the judges sought to reduce the power of the monarchy, each had separate agendas. Parliament sought to eliminate the monarch's political powers, while the concern of the judges was to protect the people from the arbitrary designs of government, whether such designs were imposed by hereditary or elected officials. Thus the Parliament and the courts frequently were allies, but not always, as is evident from the *Saltpeter* and *Bates*

cases (discussed later in this section). In each case, the judges supported the king's prerogatives as valid under the common law, while the Parliament wanted to destroy them. The parliamentarians regarded their victory as one of democratic ideals and aspirations, and they were not disposed to allow a dominant role for the unelected judiciary.

Bonham involved a liberty of the highest priority in a free society: the right to practice a vocation of one's own choosing. The problem with the law that prohibited the practice of medicine without the requisite license was clearly not in its objective, which was to improve the "safety and health of men," but in the faulty means used to achieve that objective. The law had serious infirmities; it was both underinclusive and overinclusive in its coverage. It was underinclusive because it allowed incompetent persons to practice medicine for at least a month, and it was overinclusive since it prevented all graduates of distinguished medical schools from practicing medicine without sanction from a competing institution, the London College of Physicians. Surely, many of these graduates were competent to practice medicine.

An additional problem with the law was that the college censors were authorized, Coke wrote, to be "judges, ministers, and parties; judges to give sentence in judgment; ministers to make summons; and parties to have the moiety of the forfeiture," thus according the college censors total monopoly powers over the practice of medicine in London. While the judiciary might overrule the censors, the time, effort, and expense involved—as well as the uncertainty of success—narrowed the benefits of judicial review.

The requirement that the college receive one-half of the fine imposed on violators, made the censors judges in their own cause. Coke rebuked the censors: "[Y]ou shall not be of counsele in any case or quarrell hanginge before you." A censor might be more interested in obtaining the fine for the college than in protecting the health interests of the city. It was an established maxim of the common law that no man can be a judge in his own cause.[51] "[E]ven an act of Parliament made against national equity," Coke opined, "as to make a man a judge in his own case, is void in itself."[52]

I have previously discussed Coke's condemnation of the two judges who had complete discretion to convict and punish alleged wrongdoers under a statute of King Henry VII. Both judges were able to act oppressively because they were not confined by due process requirements.[53] Consequently, Coke noted in his *Institutes,* it is irrational to confer power on officials who have the discretion or personal interest to apply it in an oppressive manner.[54]

Bonham concerned occupational licensing, a subject as controversial in the twentieth century as apparently it was in Coke's time. Occupational licensing is typically justified as a means of protecting the public against incompetent and dishonest practitioners of a given occupation. The problem is that, over the years, experience has disclosed that these rules often exclude able and honest

individuals from their preferred occupations. Officials who have the authority to administer occupational licensing rules—such as the censors from the London College of Physicians—are on occasion likely to be motivated by interests and concerns that are personal and not public oriented.[55] These officials have at times been charged with refusing to license people to practice a profession or trade in order to favor existing licensees and limit competition. What Coke did in his *Bonham* decision was protect Bonham, who was qualified to practice medicine, in his right to practice his profession free from capricious legal limitations.

The common law in the period when *Bonham* was decided was not indifferent to two issues the case presented. Prior English cases had (1) upheld the liberty of a person to practice the trade, occupation, or vocation of his choice and had (2) held that an economic monopoly was void. While these precedents were applicable against the monarch and his appointees and commissions, their applicability to Parliament was not clear, notwithstanding Coke's certainty in the matter. But common sense argued against this distinction: the rights of Englishmen should not be affected by the source of oppression, whether it be the king or the legislature. A discussion of legal opinions follows that presents a background for the decision in *Bonham.* Although some of these cases were decided soon after *Bonham,* they reflect judicial thinking of the same period.

The first recorded common law case on monopolies is *Davenant v. Hurdis* (1598).[56] An ordinance of a tailors' guild known as the Company of Merchant Taylors of London, adopted pursuant to its royal charter, required every member who sends cloth to be finished by additional labor to have at least half the work done by members of the guild or else forfeit ten shillings per cloth. In his capacity as an attorney, Coke represented Davenant, a cloth merchant who sent out twenty cloths to be finished and refused to give the required number to guild members. Coke attacked the ordinance as tending to create a monopoly. While members were then compelled only to hire their fellow members to make or finish half their cloth, Coke argued, a ruling upholding the ordinance might in time well include all of every member's cloth. The result would be a monopoly, the establishment of which, he said, is against common law and thus void. The judges in this case generally agreed: the ordinance "was against the common law, because it was against the liberty of the subject; for every subject by the law, has freedom and liberty to put his cloth to be dressed by what cloth-worker he pleases, and cannot be restrained to certain persons, for that in effect would be a monopoly; and therefore such ordinance, by colour of a charter or any grant by charter to such effect, would be void." They explained that "a rule of such nature as to bring all trade or traffic into the hands of one company, or one person, and to exclude all others, is illegal."[57]

Based in part on the decision in *Davenant, Darcy v. Allen* (also known as the *Case of Monopolies* [1602])[58] held that a grant by Queen Elizabeth of letters patent to Darcy, her groom, for the exclusive making, importing, and mer-

chandising of playing cards contravened common law and was void. The *Davenant* case involved an ordinance of a guild, and the *Monopolies* case concerned a royal grant. Coke did not participate as a judge in the latter decision, since he was at the time Solicitor General and responsible for defending the contested patent. That he accepted (and applauded) the ruling is evident from his including its principles in defining the meaning of "liberties" in Chapter 29 of the Magna Carta.[59] He maintained that monopoly was forbidden by the civil law and by Magna Carta, as well as by certain statutes.[60] The defendant pleaded that as a resident of London he was protected under the Magna Carta to engage freely in commerce, and this included obtaining royal grants. The *Monopolies* decision held that the grant created various monopolies, and that a monopoly was against the common law because it limited trade to the detriment of the liberty and welfare of the people in three respects: it raised the prices of playing cards, impaired the quality of the playing cards, and denied a living to various workmen.[61] Not by the Crown, but only by Parliament, could a man be restrained from exercising a trade.

The *Monopolies* case factored into United States Supreme Court jurisprudence in the famous *Slaughterhouse Cases* (1872).[62] In this case, the U.S. Supreme Court upheld a Louisiana law granting a monopoly on the slaughtering of cattle in a large area of the state. In his dissenting opinion, which was joined by three other justices, Justice Stephen Field contended that "[a]ll monopolies in any known trade or manufacture are an invasion of these [Fourteenth Amendment] privileges, for they encroach upon the liberty of citizens to acquire property and pursue happiness, and were held void at common law in the great *Case of Monopolies,* decided during the reign of Queen Elizabeth." Arguing that the common law of England is the basis of jurisprudence of the United States, he contended that every U.S. citizen should be able to assert his privileges and immunities as a protection against an invasion by a monopoly. Justice Bradley made a similar argument in his dissenting opinion, though he additionally differentiated between grants of exclusive franchises to conduct such public services as provided by ferries and railroads, and grants of monopolies for commodities and for ordinary callings and pursuits. He referred to the latter monopolies as an infringement of liberty. The Court's majority responded that Parliament could never be deprived of the power to establish monopolies, and the *Case of Monopolies* "was undoubtedly a contest of the [Parliament] against the monarch." From "time immemorial to the present day," the majority opinion contended that legislative bodies have granted monopoly privileges to persons and corporations. Coke's position was that monopolies of ordinary callings and pursuits violate the common law unless they were sanctioned by Parliament, which, of course, was the rule with respect to all of the English common law.[63]

The English judges in the early 1600s viewed restraints on labor as creating monopolies. The *Case of Tailors of Ipswich* (1614)[64] involved the validity of a

tailors' guild ordinance adopted pursuant to a royal charter that no one could practice the trade of a tailor in Ipswich unless he had served his apprenticeship with the Corporation of the Tailors of Ipswich, or had been given its approval. The defendant ignored the corporation and worked as a tailor, pleading to the court that he had served seven years as a private tailor to a freeman of the locality. Chief Justice Coke and the other justices of the King's Bench held for the tailor: "That [under] the common law, no man could be prohibited from working in any lawful trade, for the law abhors idleness, the mother of all evil . . . and especially in young men, who ought in their youth (which is their seed time) to learn lawful sciences and trades, which are profitable to the commonwealth, and whereof they might reap the fruit in their old age, for idle in youth, poor in age; and therefor the common law abhors all monopolies, which prohibit any from working in any lawful trade." Consequently, the corporation's restraints on the tailor practicing his trade tended to create a monopoly, and thus "are against the liberty and freedom of the subject."

The judges cited two cases in which restraints on workmen not to work at their trades were held to be against the common law. First, a restriction on a dyer not to practice his craft for two years, and second, a restriction on a husbandman not to sow his land were both rejected. Interestingly, the judges went on to note what has become a common complaint in the twentieth century against licensure laws: they are a means "of oppression of young tradesmen, by the old and rich of the same trade, not permitting them to work in their trade freely." Apprentice requirements, the judges stated, have been enacted not only to make workmen skillful but also to educate youth in lawful sciences and trades. Laws which accord trade organizations power to forbid experienced apprentices from practicing as tradesmen discourage apprenticeship, to the detriment of both the young and the society as a whole.

In *Tooley's Case* (1613),[65] the accused person was prosecuted for violating the Statute of Artificers (1563) because he was engaged in work as an upholsterer after he had served his apprenticeship as a wool packer. The statute required that a person must be apprenticed in the trade that he practiced, but did not specify the trades to which it applied. Coke interpreted the statute as covering only skilled trades, and claimed that upholstering is clearly not included in the statute since it was neither a "trade nor a mystery and did not require any skill." Moreover, the defendant was a resident of London, a city which permitted a freeman to practice any trade or manual occupation within its area. This custom of London had been protected in both the 1215 and 1225 Magna Cartas, as well as recognized by royal charter and confirmed by Parliament. The Statute of Artificers excluded London from its scope. According to Coke, a "general law shall not take away any part of Magna Carta [and consequently] a man is not to be [unduly] restrained that he shall not labor for his living." The court terminated the prosecution of the accused.

In *Rogers v. Parrey* (1613),[66] the plaintiff sued the defendant on the ground that he had violated an agreement between them that he would not practice the trade of a joyner for twenty-one years in a house in London demised to him. The defendant answered that this agreement was invalid as a restraint on the right to work. Coke held for the plaintiff on the ground that this was not a general restraint on exercising one's trade, but one for a limited time and certain place. This decision is not difficult to explain. Unlike a governmental restriction based on a variety of political considerations, the agreement in this case was a product of private bargaining with each side obtaining and transferring something considered valuable. Freedom of the marketplace includes the freedom to accept reasonable limitations on one's own freedom. However, the case did not validate a total restraint on the practice of a trade.

In the balance of this section, I shall discuss four other English cases decided in the early seventeenth century that further illustrate the state of the law during that period in matters of property and commerce.

The *Case of the King's Prerogative in Saltpeter* (1606)[67] concerned a claim for indemnification by a landowner because the king's employees, without payment of compensation, had dug and removed saltpeter from his land to be used for making gunpowder. The king contended that this action was taken in furtherance of his prerogative powers, the exercise of which did not require parliamentary assent or payment of compensation. The king's prerogative power was an English historical institution that Blackstone understood to reflect "that special pre-eminence, which the king has, over and above all other persons, and out of the ordinary course of the common law, by right of his royal dignity."[68] The English constitutional commentator A. V. Dicey explains that "the prerogative appears to be both historically and as a matter of actual fact nothing else than the residue of discretionary or arbitrary authority, which at any given time is legally left in the hands of the Crown."[69] The king's prerogative powers in the early 1600s were extensive. They included dominion of the sea; control over navigation, foreign affairs, and defense of the realm; enforcing acts of Parliament; dispensing justice; coining money; providing for his own household; granting offices and titles of nobility; and collecting taxes. Under these powers, the king and his ministers might use and even confiscate private property without compensation. To be sure, prerogative powers and eminent domain rules and outcomes were different.[70]

The prerogative involved in *Saltpeter* was defense of the realm. The eight specially assembled judges, including Coke, then Chief Justice of the Common Pleas, issued the opinion. They observed that gunpowder was required for the nation's defense, and unfriendly foreign powers might restrain its sale to England and thus jeopardize the nation's security. They acknowledged the legitimacy of the prerogative as applied in this case, which, the justices wrote, "ought to be taken only by the ministers of the king, and cannot be converted to any

other use than for the defense of the realm." In upholding the king's exercise of this prerogative, the judges strictly confined it as follows:

1. The saltpeter acquired by the king cannot be used for his own benefit but only for the nation's defense. This prerogative is consistent with existing laws of the land. By the common law every man may enter his neighbor's land for the defense of the realm, and make bulwarks and trenches upon it for that purpose, but which ought to be removed after the danger is over.
2. In removing the saltpeter, the king's servants cannot undermine or impair any walls or foundations, or dig in the floor of a house, or in the floor of any barn storing corn or hay. But they may dig in the floors of stables and ox-houses.
3. In digging for the saltpeter, the king's servants must not damage the property containing it. They must restore the property to the same condition as they found it. They must work between sun-rise and sun-set; they must not place any furnace in any house or building without the owner's consent; and they must not stay long in one place, nor leave work in abeyance for a long time.
4. The owner of the land cannot be restrained from digging and taking saltpeter in his own interest.

According to this decision, saltpeter was essential to the national defense, and consequently the king under his prerogative powers was entitled to take it from certain areas of privately owned property pursuant to strict rules that were intended to preserve intact the balance of the estate. The sole deprivation to the landowner would be the loss of the saltpeter when demanded by the king for defense of the nation, and nothing else. Although this case is often cited as a limitation on the right of property, this interpretation is incorrect since it concerns the king's prerogatives, governed under special rules that do not relate to the protection of private property.[71]

The *Case of the Isle of Ely* (1610) was referred by the Lords of the King's Council to the justices of the Common Pleas (of which Coke was then chief justice) concerning a decree made by the king's commissioners of sewers. This decree required that a new river be created on the Isle of Ely and repairs and replacements be made to its drainage systems, all to be paid for by 15 towns on that isle with each town to pay a specified amount.[72] The drainage systems on the isle were not functioning well and required repairs and improvements. The king appointed these commissioners to execute his prerogative powers to drain the land and repair pipes, sewers, and ditches.

Coke's court held that the commissioners could not be given power by the king (1) to procure land for new drainage works (only Parliament could authorize this), (2) to create a new river and install other improvements not essential

to adequate drainage, and (3) to impose taxes upon a town instead of solely upon the persons benefited by the improvements. The justices sought to protect the residents from being taxed for unnecessary public work or for improvements from which they obtained no gain. The judicial decree mandated certain requirements, which were limited to making repairs and improvements needed for the satisfactory and safe operation of the drainage systems.

The justices ruled that the cost of the repairs and replacements should be borne only by persons who are benefited, and then according to the quantity of their land and the portion, tenure, or profit obtained from the improvements. Imposing the taxes on the various towns would burden persons not advantaged by the drainage improvements. "[N]one could be taxed towards the reparation, but those who had prejudice, damage or disadvantage by the said nuisances or defaults, and who might have a benefit by the reformation or removing of them." While this was not a case of eminent domain, it confirms the common law principle that no person should be required to contribute more than his fair share to eliminating or reducing public burdens. Or, as contemporary courts put it, a property owner should not bear public burdens, which, in all fairness and justice, should be borne by the public as a whole. It follows that an owner should be compensated when the government appropriates his property for public use; otherwise, he will be paying for benefits received by others.

Coke's opinion in *Mouse's Case* (c. 1600)[73] inaugurated the law of necessity, which permitted certain land uses to be prohibited when such action was essential to protect lives and property. In this case, a commercial barge carrying passengers had encountered heavy seas, and in order to save lives the defendant (who was a passenger) threw out of the barge the plaintiff's casket containing his valuable possessions. In a suit for damages, Coke's court held that if the danger to life occurred by act of God, without any individual's fault, everyone ought to bear his loss without indemnification. It was proved that if the possessions had not been thrown out of the barge, the passengers would have drowned.[74]

In *Bates Case* (1606),[75] the Court of Exchequer upheld the king's power to levy duties on goods imported into England on the basis that import duties were related to the king's prerogative to conduct foreign affairs and regulate foreign trade. Bates refused to pay a duty upon the import of currants, imposed by King James I, on the ground that Parliament had not authorized this tax. Coke considered the court's decision erroneous because it violated Chapter 30 of the Magna Carta, which provided that all domestic and foreign merchants are entitled "to buy and sell without any manner of evil tolls, by the old and rightful customes, except in time of war." According to him, under the common law the king's prerogative was limited to imposing import or export duties only when they were for the advancement of such foreign trade and traffic, "which is the life of every island." He writes that the king cannot at his pleasure impose

duties upon imports: "[T]he common law hath so admeasured the prerogatives of the king, that they shall not take away, nor prejudice the inheritance of any: and the best inheritance that the subject hath, is the law of the realm."[76] Coke thus strictly interprets the king's powers with respect to taxing foreign trade, contending that his prerogative to conduct foreign affairs is limited to preserving the nation's security.

The list that follows summarizes some of the important principles that Coke advanced—either as a legal commentator or as a jurist—which have influenced jurisprudence in both England and the United States.

1. No man shall be deprived of his life, liberty, or property, including his lands, tenements, goods, or chattels, unless it is done pursuant to the requirements of due process of law (2 Coke, *Institutes* 46, 47, 50, and 51).
2. The Magna Carta forbids the king or his agents from imposing laws violating its terms and depriving people of life, liberty, or property (2 Coke, *Institutes* 45–46). A legislative enactment ought to be prospective, not retroactive, in its operation (2 Coke, *Institutes* 292).
3. Judges must adhere to and apply the requirements of due process of law in all legal proceedings (2 Coke, *Institutes* 51).
4. When an act of Parliament is against common right and reason, or repugnant, or impossible to be performed, the common law will adjudge such an act to be void (*Bonham*).
5. Laws of the land include only general and public laws, operating equally upon every person in the community and do not include laws intended to favor or harm certain individuals or groups (Magna Carta, Chapter 29; and 2 Coke, *Institutes* 41).
6. Regulatory laws must substantially advance the purpose for which the government has imposed them (*Bonham*).
7. Exactions for public repairs and improvements should only be imposed in proportion to the benefits received (*Isle of Ely Case*).
8. No person should be given the power to be a judge in his own cause (*Bonham*).
9. Every person possesses the liberty to practice the trade, occupation, or vocation of his choice (*Tailors of Ipswich, Tooley, Davenant,* and *Case of Monopolies*).
10. Monopolies violate the Magna Carta because they eliminate the freedom of people to engage in economic activity (*Case of Monopolies*).
11. The prerogative powers of the king must be narrowly construed to give effect solely to the public benefits they are intended to promote (*Saltpeter* and *Bates*).
12. Property rights may be limited when it is essential to protect lives or property *(Mouse's Case)*.

As is evident from the foregoing discussion, Coke utilized numerous theories to support property rights, often simply applying a general principle to this purpose. It should not be concluded from the prior discussion, however, that Coke was dedicated to free market economics. Historian Barbara Malament writes that he was highly selective in his support of a free market, although he can be regarded as much more enlightened in this respect than most of his intellectual contemporaries. According to her, Coke did not believe in the inherent value of economic freedom: "For Coke was interested in full employment and not efficiency; just prices and not competition. Far from searching for new economic concepts, he drew upon the Commonwealth idea, arguing consistently that 'trade and traffique cannot be maintained or increased without order and government. . . .' "[77]

The better explanation of Coke's ideology is that he believed, along with many others during his life, in the supremacy of fundamental laws protecting individuals in the rights of life, liberty, and property. These protections were outside, above, and beyond the reach of the positive law, whether imposed by the king, the Parliament, or any other governmental body. Many American leaders in the revolutionary and constitutional periods of United States history held similar views, and considered Coke's commentaries and judicial opinions as offering a desirable approach to constitutional government—particularly for judicial review. Without mandate from any written constitution, Coke supported and applied the doctrine known as the separation of powers; he sought to erect a boundary between the powers of the king and the powers of Parliament, frequently to advance individual liberty. Coke and his fellow judges also annulled laws emanating from the king—and to a far lesser extent from Parliament—that abridged liberties of the people.

Coke can also be credited for paving the way for constitutional and legislative prohibitions of class legislation that benefit select portions of the population. The scrutiny tests under which regulations on private property are currently adjudicated follow Coke's distinction between a law for the general or public welfare and a law for private welfare. Under the current rules, a law intended to benefit or disadvantage a particular group would not pass constitutional muster because it does not advance a "compelling" or "substantial state interest." (These rules will be discussed in Chapter 4.)

IV. Blackstone and the Common Law

The English legal commentator William Blackstone (1723–1780) was in general accord with Coke's interpretation of the property protections of Chapter 29 of the Magna Carta, as subsequently enlarged by statute or judicial decision. He was a justice of the Court of Common Pleas (1770–1780) and the first Vinerian professor of English law at Oxford University. The legal community in North

America looked to Blackstone as another leading interpreter of English law. Among those influenced by Blackstone was the famous Chancellor James Kent of New York, who acknowledged that "he owed his reputation to the fact that when studying law . . . he had but one book, Blackstone's *Commentaries,* but that one book he mastered."[78] A biographer of Blackstone states that most members of the Constitutional Convention of 1787 "were familiar with, and they were no doubt greatly influenced by Blackstone's analysis of the English governmental system."[79] There are many terms in the Constitution that were used in the same sense that Blackstone had employed.

According to Edmund Burke, the eminent English politician of the late-eighteenth century, nearly as many of Blackstone's *Commentaries* (1765–1769) were sold in America as in England.[80] In *Hammond's Blackstone,*[81] a compilation of the original commentaries, William G. Hammond, its author, states that in examining 2,500 volumes of American law reports covering the period from 1787 to 1890, Blackstone was referred to or quoted more than any other writer by various courts in the United States. James Carey Jones, the author of *Jones' Blackstone,*[82] another compilation, states that as of 1915 Blackstone had been cited—usually approvingly—in some 10,000 cases since 1784. As indicated in a 1999 decision, U.S. Supreme Court justices refer to Blackstone as the commentator "whose works constituted the preeminent authority of English law for the founding generation."[83]

Blackstone was an admirer of Coke ("a man of infinite learning in his profession"), noting that Coke's writings were so highly esteemed "they are generally cited [as *Institutes*] without the author's name."[84] Much of Blackstone's *Commentaries* repeated and explained the common law principles Coke had set forth a century-and-a-half earlier. In one important respect, however, many early Americans rejected Blackstone's position that the legislature should be the supreme branch of government; instead, they favored a government whose powers are separated, limited, and enumerated. However, Blackstone wrote that every Englishman possessed "absolute rights . . . founded on nature and reason" that Parliament should rightfully protect. Understandably, his assertion that the natural law was legally supreme was the position in his *Commentaries* that the American colonists quoted most often.[85]

The difference in view between Coke and Blackstone about parliamentary supremacy may be attributable to the time when each wrote his commentaries. In Blackstone's day, this issue had been settled, while it was still open for Coke; Blackstone's view on the sovereignty of Parliament "would have amazed men of the thirteenth century."[86] However, notwithstanding legislative supremacy, Blackstone supported substantial roles for the judiciary in interpreting and reforming laws, as will be explained below in the last pages of this section.

Blackstone stated that Chapter 29 alone would have merited the title that the Magna Carta bears, "of the *great* charter [because] it protected every individual of the nation in the free enjoyment of his life, his liberty and his property, unless declared to be forfeited by the judgment of his peers or the law of the land."[87] Blackstone considered the rights of life, liberty, and property to be included in the common law's protection of the "absolute rights of personal security, personal liberty, and private property." For, he wrote, "the principal aim of society is to protect individuals in the enjoyment of those absolute rights."[88]

Like Coke, Blackstone was also a staunch opponent of retroactive laws. To avoid injustice, the latter wrote, people must be aware of the laws they are expected to obey. Each law must "be a rule *prescribed* [because] a bare resolution, confined in the breast of the legislator, without manifesting itself by some external sign, can never be properly a law. It is requisite that this resolution be notified to the people who are to obey it."[89] He concluded that "[a]ll laws should therefore be made to commence *in futuro* and [those affected should] be notified before their commencement." The most unreasonable method of notifying the public is by making laws *ex post facto.* When a law is *ex post facto,* "it is impossible that the party could foresee that an action innocent when it was done, should be afterwards converted to guilt by a subsequent law; he had therefore no cause to abstain from it; and all punishment for not abstaining must of consequence be cruel and unjust."[90]

Blackstone's opposition to retroactive laws, some of which he called *ex post facto,* was integrated into the U.S. Constitution. The U.S. Constitution prohibits the Congress and states from passing *ex post facto* laws (Article I, Secs. 9 and 10), though it is uncertain whether the Framers intended to ban all retroactive laws or solely what Blackstone referred to as *ex post facto* laws.[91] In *Calder v. Bull,* the U.S. Supreme Court interpreted the constitutional prohibitions on *ex post facto* laws as applying only to criminal laws.[92] Although the *ex post facto* provisions are not applicable to noncriminal matters, the Supreme Court has at times applied the due process clauses to strike down retroactive property laws.[93]

According to Blackstone, the absolute right of property "consists of the free use, enjoyment, and disposal of all [the owner's] acquisitions without any control or diminution, save only by the laws of the land."[94] As the reader will recall, the phrase "law of the land" was interpreted by Coke to mean "by the due course and process of law," and he understood this interpretation to mean "by indictment or presentment of good and lawful men, where such deeds be done in due manner." Blackstone puts this same point as follows:

> [Pursuant to Chapter 29] and by a variety of ancient statutes [citing the three statutes of King Edward III, noted in Section I above] it is enacted

that no man's lands or goods shall be seised into the king's hands, against the great charter, and the law of the land; and that no man shall be disinherited, nor put out of his franchises or freehold, unless he be duly brought to answer, and be forejudged by course of law; and if any thing be done to the contrary, it shall be redressed, and holden for none.[95]

These safeguards were essential for maintaining the integrity of private property, which for Blackstone meant "that sole and despotic domain which one man claims and exercises over the external things in the world, in total exclusion of the right of any other individual in the universe." When Blackstone wrote his *Commentaries,* and at least to and including when the U.S. Constitution and Bill of Rights were ratified (1788 and 1791), the common law accorded landowners almost total physical control of their properties. "So great moreover," he declared, "is the regard of the law of private property that it will not authorize the least violation of it; no, not even for the general good of the whole community."[96] He then went on to consider in this regard the requirement of compensation for a government acquisition of private property, and subsequently the protection for owners offered by the laws of trespass and nuisance. I shall now turn to discussing these safeguards.

The following is Blackstone's explanation of government's obligation to indemnify an owner whose property it acquires. These words have been very widely quoted in English-speaking countries on both sides of the Atlantic Ocean:

If a new road, for instance, were to be made through the grounds of a private person, it might perhaps be extensively beneficial to the public; but the law permits no man, or set of men, to do this without consent of the owner of the land. In vain may it be urged, that the good of the individual ought to yield to that of the community; for it would be dangerous to allow any private man, or even any public tribunal, to be the judge of this common good, and to decide whether it be expedient or not. Besides, the public good is in nothing more essentially interested, than in the protection of every individual's private rights, as modeled by the municipal law. In this, and similar cases the legislature alone can, and indeed frequently does, interpose, and compel the individual to acquiesce. But how does it interpose and compel? Not by absolutely stripping the subject of his property in an arbitrary manner; but by giving him a full indemnification and equivalent for the injury thereby sustained. The public is now considered as an individual, treating with an individual for an exchange. All that the legislature does is to oblige the owner to alienate his possessions for a reasonable price; and even this is an exertion of power, which the legislature indulges with caution, and which nothing but the legislature can perform.[97]

Hence, according to Blackstone, when the legislature restricts all or a portion of land for a public good such as a public road—"even for the general good of the whole community"—without fully indemnifying the owner for the loss he has sustained, it violates his property rights. Consequently, restricting a portion of land for a public road is invalid unless (1) it is accompanied by the payment of compensation and (2) it serves a public purpose. The above quotation is frequently explained as the basis for the takings clause of the Fifth Amendment of the U.S. Constitution, which prohibits government from taking private property for public use without payment of "just compensation." However, the inclusion of this clause is not necessary for protecting the property right; the failure either to pay compensation or advance a public use is itself a violation of that right, which is protected in the Fifth Amendment's due process clause. (The U.S. Supreme Court has held that "due process of law" and "law of the land" have the same meaning.[98]) In the above quotation, Blackstone illustrates an "absolute" protection afforded an owner against the imposition of governmental restrictions on his property. Other protections will be set forth later in this section.

A just and viable government is one that secures liberties as well as provides the public with essential services that are not privately available. Securing the property right mandates severely limiting governmental powers over it. At the same time, property rights must not prevent the government from providing essential services to the public. Blackstone provides a solution that is advantageous to both sides. When the legislature deprives an owner of all or a portion of his property without indemnifying the owner for his loss, it violates the owner's property rights. The public suffers little loss when it compensates the owner because it acquires actual or constructive ownership of the owner's property rights. Blackstone's position makes credible the idea that indemnifying the owner for his loss is proper and fair, whenever the government imposes serious restrictions limiting the ordinary and benign use of property.

A property owner is also protected by the laws of trespass and nuisance. According to Blackstone, "every man's land is in the eye of the law enclosed and set apart from his neighbor's: and that either by a visible and material fence; . . . or by an ideal inviolable boundary, existing only in the contemplation of law . . . and every such entry or breach carries necessarily along with it some damage or other. . . ." An action in trespass will lie both when the entry is immediately injurious to the property owner or the injury is consequential.[99]

Private property was likewise secured by the common law concerning private nuisances. He defined this protection as follows: "[I]f one does any . . . act, in itself lawful, yet which being done in that place necessarily tends to the damage of another's property, it is a nuisance: for it is incumbent on him to find some other place to do that act, where it will be less offensive."[100] A private nuisance was "any thing done to the hurt or annoyance of the lands, tenements, or heredita-

ments of another." Depriving one of a mere pleasure that abridges nothing really convenient or necessary was not actionable as a nuisance. He included as examples of nuisances offensive odors and smoke, carrying on an offensive trade, and installing structural parts that block another owner's natural light; all of these examples have usually been considered nuisances. Blackstone also included as nuisances actions which deprive an owner of all or a portion of his property, such as (1) flooding the land of another by the erection of a structure on one's own land, and (2) stopping or diverting surface water that runs to another's land.[101] Because the objective is to secure the integrity of people's property, the harms sustained by an owner whose land is flooded by the actions of government or deprived of water by a diversion required by government may also be considered as a taking of property. As such, this would—under takings law in most states of this nation—require payment of compensation. Blackstone writes that the remedies for nuisance were damages for the harm sustained and/or abatement of the nuisance. As for damages, every continuance of a nuisance was held to be a fresh one, leading to substantial penalties for such action.[102]

Accordingly, Blackstone's *Commentaries* reveal that at the time of the ratification of the U.S. Constitution in 1788 and the Bill of Rights in 1791, the common law provided two important protections for a property owner (in addition to those mentioned by Coke, as previously detailed). First, government could not acquire land for eminent domain purposes without indemnifying the owner "for the injury thereby sustained." Second, a landowner was protected from any trespass or nuisance that would harm his property. The common law very broadly defined "trespass" and "nuisance" to comprehend, among other things, a deprivation of property, which if it was imposed by government would in later years be referred to as a "taking of property." As illustrated by various decisions reported in Section III—*Saltpeter, Isle of Ely, Case of Monopolies*—agencies of the king were not exempt from these common law rules.[103]

As the New Jersey Supreme Court explained in 1795, with respect to flooding and diverting of water: "When a man purchases a piece of land through which a natural water-course flows, he has a right to make use of it in its natural state, but not to stop or divert it to the prejudice of another."[104] Nor does one man "have a right to turn more water over the land of his neighbor than would naturally go in that direction."[105]

> The water flows in its natural channel, and ought always to be permitted to run there, so that all through whose land it pursues its natural course, may continue to enjoy the privilege of using it for their own purposes. It cannot legally be diverted without the consent of all who have an interest in it. . . . I think a jury right in giving almost any valuation which the party thus injured should think proper to fix to it.

In 1816, in the widely quoted case of *Gardner v. Village of Newburgh*,[106] Chancellor James Kent, after explaining that to divert or obstruct a watercourse is a private nuisance at common law that is subject to being remedied by injunctive relief, elevated to constitutional status an aggrieved owner's rights. Combining the common law rules of eminent domain and nuisance, Kent reasoned that the village's construction of water facilities that diverted water from flowing over the plaintiff's land, had unlawfully deprived the plaintiff of his property, because the stream of water was part of his freehold.[107]

Relying on Blackstone, eminent European legal commentators (Hugo Grotius, Samuel Pufendorf, and Cornelius Bynkershoek), and English cases, Kent asserted that the payment of compensation "is a necessary qualification accompanying the exercise of legislative power in taking private property for public uses." *Gardner* arose in New York, a state whose constitution then contained no just compensation clause. Kent held the statute at issue invalid unless it was amended or interpreted to provide for compensation to indemnify the owner for his loss. "I feel myself, therefore, not only authorized, but bound to conclude, that a provision for compensation is an indispensable attendant on the due and constitutional exercise of the power of depriving an individual of his property."[108]

English courts subsumed the protections against trespass and nuisance under the right to the peaceful enjoyment of private property. Pursuant thereto, English chancery judges issued injunctions to quiet the possession of watercourses. Kent's opinion in *Gardner* cites two such cases. In 1700, an English chancery court upheld a complaint that the defendant obstructed the plaintiff's enjoyment of a watercourse to his house and garden through the land of the defendant. The court held that after a long enjoyment of this watercourse, a right to it was presumed unless disproved by the defendant. The defendant was unable to carry this burden, and the plaintiff was quieted in his enjoyment by injunction.[109] In 1720, a plaintiff's possession of a watercourse for a long time was quieted by injunction of a court of chancery against a diversion of it, though the plaintiff had not legally proven this right, since the court stated that such complaints were usual.[110] According to Kent, the basis of the chancery court's jurisdiction in these matters is the "necessity of a preventive remedy when great and immediate mischief or material injury would arise to the comfort and useful enjoyment of property. The interference rests on the principles of a clear and certain right to the enjoyment of the subject in question, and an injurious interruption of this right, which upon just and equitable ground might be prevented."[111] Inasmuch as the English law protected the right to the enjoyment of private property, one may conclude that the state cannot legitimately deprive an owner of any substantial portion of his property.

Gardner was not an isolated decision in U.S. law. Chapter 4 below contains discussion of many early cases in the United States in which both federal and state

courts required compensation when government directly deprived an owner of an interest in his property. Many courts also applied this rule to consequential (indirect) deprivations (also to be discussed in Chapter 4). Supreme Court Justice Joseph Story presented the issue in this manner: The Fifth Amendment's just compensation clause is "an affirmance of a great doctrine established by the common law for the protection of private property."[112]

While state courts varied on subscribing to *Gardner,* at least as of 1870 the U.S. Supreme Court was clearly supportive of the decision, as disclosed in *Yates v. Milwaukee,*[113] decided in that year, and *Pumpelly v. Green Bay Co.,*[114] decided the following year. (Both cases are discussed fully in Chapter 4, Section IV.) In *Yates,* the United States Supreme Court upheld unanimously Yates's common law right as a riparian property owner to construct a wharf extending from the front of his lot on the bank of a river to the navigable part of the river, despite Milwaukee's adoption of an ordinance specifically declaring this wharf to be a nuisance because it obstructed river traffic. The Court ruled that for the city to prevail, it would have to provide compensation for Yates. In *Pumpelly,* Wisconsin authorized the construction of a dam that caused the water level of a lake to rise, inundating Pumpelly's fields. Construing Wisconsin's takings clause, which was similar to that in the U.S. Constitution, the United States Supreme Court again unanimously held that a taking had occurred that required payment of compensation. The court cited as support *Gardner* and the New Jersey case of *Sinnickson v. Johnson* (to be discussed in Chapter 4, Section II).

Both *Yates* and *Pumpelly* disclose that, as of the early 1870s, Blackstone's interpretation of the common law as according near-absolute physical protection for ownership prevailed in the U.S. Supreme Court. The justices were not disposed toward limiting property rights to advance any particular conception of the public interest. Considerable public opinion in that period supported the protection of property rights as the best means of achieving the public interest, and the justices might well be included in that group. The public interest was seen as being closely tied to economic development. The uncertainty that accompanies political determination of the public interest reduces the incentives of entrepreneurs to purchase property for investment, and thus constitutes a major impairment to economic development.

When the Fourteenth Amendment was framed (1866) and ratified (1869), the U.S. Supreme Court had not adjudicated either *Yates* or *Pumpelly.* (In Chapter 5, I will explain that the meaning of a constitutional amendment must be determined by considering the prevailing and pertinent Supreme Court jurisprudence.) The clauses of the amendment that directly concern property rights are the privileges or immunities and due process of law provisions of Section 1. (The meaning of these clauses will be discussed in Chapters 5 and 6.) Although neither *Yates* nor *Pumpelly* were relevant in construing the Fourteenth Amendment, these cases confirm that as of the early 1870s the Supreme Court had not

varied from the position that the common law was applicable in determining the constitutionality of property rights.

Blackstone's perspective on the payment of compensation is in conflict with the early position of the South Carolina courts that every landowner holds land under the condition of yielding a portion of it, without compensation, when it is needed for the installation of public roads and highways.[115] This South Carolina rule did not prevail, though, because common law judges believed that it would violate private ownership and make it insecure, and would consequently be harmful to the economy. However, Blackstone's analysis falls short of fully protecting property owners. Under his position, a legislature seeking to acquire private property must give the owner "full indemnification and equivalent for the injury thereby sustained." This language has usually been interpreted to require payment of compensation both for the value of the property the public acquires and for the reduction in value to the balance of the property retained (if any). No payment is required to compensate the owner for the loss in profits he sustains because he can no longer use or develop the property, such as building and renting or selling apartments and commercial structures on it. Yet, many owners purchase certain property solely to obtain profit from its use. For example, an owner who has purchased a tract of land for a particular commercial use has thereby rejected buying other land for this use. He will not be fully compensated for his loss if, upon condemnation, he merely recovers the market value of the land.

To be sure, it is very difficult to determine the total loss suffered when a condemnation of land precludes certain use and development. Under Blackstone's formula—as judicially interpreted—many owners will not be fully reimbursed for their loss. The answer to this problem mandates restricting the legislature's eminent domain and regulatory powers to only providing essential services that cannot be offered by private ownership. His admonitions that the use be public and not intended to benefit or harm select persons should be strictly observed. Blackstone's position that the principal aim of government is to protect "absolute rights" can be implemented when such restraints on government are observed.[116]

Blackstone's stance on compensation echoed the views of prominent European legal theorists. Hugo Grotius and Samuel Pufendorf, for example, urged indemnification for losses sustained by property owners. Grotius wrote as follows:

> The property of subjects is under the eminent domain of the state, so that the state or he who acts for it may use and even alienate and destroy such property, not only in the case of extreme necessity, in which even private persons have a right over the property of others, but for ends of *public utility,* to which ends those who founded civil society must be supposed to have intended that private ends should give way. But it is to be added that when this is done *the state is bound to make good the loss* to those who lose their property.[117]

Similarly, Pufendorf wrote:

> The third right is Eminent Domain, which consists in this, that *when public necessity demands it,* the goods of any subject which are very *urgently needed* at the time, may be seized and *used for public purposes,* although they may be more valuable than the allotted share which he is supposed to give for the welfare of the republic. On this account, the excess value should, insofar as possible, be refunded to the citizen in question, either from the public funds, or from a contribution of the other citizens. [Emphases added.][118]

> Natural equity is observed, if, when some contribution must be made to preserve a common thing by such as participate in its benefits, each of them contributes only his own share, and no one bears a greater burden than another. . . . [T]he supreme sovereignty will be able to seize that thing for the necessities of the state, on condition, however, that whatever exceeds the just share of its owners must be refunded them by other citizens.[119]

Blackstone's position on compensation obtains support from Coke's *Institutes* and judicial decisions. Coke interprets Magna Carta's Chapter 29 as securing the rights of life, liberty, and property for all those who have not violated the laws of the land. In the absence of wrongdoing, a person must not be deprived of his liberties. Coke's rulings in the *Saltpeter* and *Isle of Ely* cases (among others) uphold this perspective. While not challenging the king's defense of the realm prerogative in *Saltpeter,* he otherwise protected the owner's rights to use and sell his saltpeter, and to maintain intact his estate except when the king exercised his prerogative. *Isle of Ely* protected a property owner from paying taxes in amounts excessive to the benefits he received for the public construction of sewer facilities.

Blackstone requires indemnification when there has been the "least violation" of the owner's property rights. The "least violation" of the owner's rights would include the initial passage of a law designating a road for public use. When the legislature passes the law that describes the area comprising the proposed road, the owner loses control of this area, and he will no longer be able to develop or otherwise use it, except as a public road. If at that point compensation is not guaranteed, he is the victim of a regulatory taking.

Under Blackstone's rejection of judicial review, the owner's remedies are based on the legislature's adherence to the rule of law, its good will, or its willingness to dispense mercy. The property owner has much greater opportunity to obtain compensation under a constitution containing a takings or due process clause and providing for judicial review. Under such a constitution, the judges would be obligated to declare that restriction of the land for a road without compensation violates either clause and, consequently, the legislation authorizing it is void.

This position is in accord with rulings of the United States Supreme Court. In the 1987 case of *First English v. County of Los Angeles*,[120] the Court held that under the takings clause of the Constitution's Fifth Amendment, an owner is entitled to just compensation for the taking of his property from the date the ordinance is adopted until the date that the ordinance is either rescinded or altered so that it no longer affects a taking. The result should be the same if the Constitution's due process clause were applied, since due process cannot be achieved without payment of adequate compensation. When the negative impact on an owner is more than de minimus, the United States Supreme Court has ruled that due process infractions are actionable immediately because the constitutional harm occurs at the moment the violation takes place.[121]

In addition to requiring compensation, Blackstone opines that an owner's rights are violated by a regulatory law that is designed to further a private interest and not the public interest. He explains first that such a law deprives the owner of his rights, and second the transfer constitutes special legislation. The first reason follows from his position that "the public is nothing more essentially interested than in the protection of every individual's private rights." A transfer that is not limited by a public interest requirement enables the legislators to exercise excessive discretion.[122] Blackstone's second reason relates to his opposition to "special laws," by which he meant laws that either benefit or harm individuals or classes of people. Because government represents all the people, it violates this trust when it seeks to favor or disfavor select portions of the public.

Blackstone defined "law" as "a rule of civil conduct prescribed by the supreme power in a state, commanding what is right and prohibiting what is wrong." Therefore, a law must not be "a transient, sudden order from a superior to or concerning a particular person; but something permanent, uniform, and universal."[123] Inasmuch as all the people of England are entitled to basic rights, the legislature cannot arbitrarily deprive any person or persons of these rights or elevate the rights of some persons above those of other persons. "[T]he preservation of these [rights], inviolate, may justly be said to include civil immunities in their largest and most extensive sense."[124] A law which only affects and exhausts itself upon a particular person's rights or interests and has no relation to the community in general "is rather a sentence than a law."[125] These concerns are taken up in contemporary jurisprudence. The U.S. Supreme Court has stated: "[E]lements of legitimacy and neutrality [must] characterize the performance of the sovereign's duty to govern impartially."[126] It is not every legislative act, the Court has asserted, that is law. "Arbitrary powers enforcing its edicts to the injury of the persons and property of its subjects, is not law, whether manifested as the decree of a personal monarch or of an impersonal multitude."[127]

Consequently, a law which transfers title to property from one person to another person is a prime example of a special law since it simultaneously benefits and harms specific individuals. The payment of compensation does not cure the illegitimate character of the law. Nor would a forced transfer of property

from one person to a public entity be valid; this would be special legislation, unless the transfer is for a public use and is accompanied by the payment of compensation to the original owner.

The due process clauses of the U.S. Constitution protect a person from deprivation of his property without the required application of due process of law. Recall that in its Fifth and Fourteenth Amendments, the U.S. Constitution states that the federal or state government shall not deprive any person of life, liberty, or property without due process of law. "Deprivation," in its ordinary and popular sense, means the extinction, divesting, or withholding of a personal interest. Neither Coke nor Blackstone use the word 'deprivation' in interpretations of Chapter 29. In his writings on this chapter, Coke refers to being disseised or dispossessed of one's free-hold rather than to being deprived of it. He further explains "dispossessed" as relating to "such franchises, and freedoms, and free customs, as belong to him by his free birth right."[128] Coke's enumeration is very inclusive, and covers both entire and partial interests in real property and other material interests. Blackstone refers to "seised into the king's hands," "disinherited," "put out of his franchises or freehold," "forfeited," as all being contrary to the law of the land.[129] His enumeration is also quite inclusive, and, as discussed above, covers entire and partial interests in property, such as a restriction of land for the installation of a road.

Under the reasoning of both commentators, regulation causing a reduction in value would constitute a deprivation. That Coke considered commercial value of the land as protected is evident from this comment:

> But if a man seised of lands in fee by his deed granteth to another the profit of those lands, to have and to hold to him and his heires, and maketh livery *secundum formam chartae,* the whole land itselfe doth passe; for what is the land but the profits thereof; for thereby vesture, herbage, trees, mines, and all whatsoever parcell of that land doth passe.[130]

His enumeration of the economic protections afforded under Chapter 29 of the Magna Carta shows an extensive commitment to the protection of material interests.

Blackstone also considered compensation to be an appropriate remedy for loss attributable to a governmental deprivation of the entire parcel or a portion thereof. The government must make the owner whole "by giving him a full indemnification and equivalent for the injury thereby sustained." On this issue of monetary compensation for a governmental deprivation of a property right, Blackstone was consistent with the above-quoted positions taken by Grotius and Pufendorf, as well as with those taken by eminent commentators such as Vattel, Bynkershoek, and Montesquieu.[131] These authorities believed that an owner had a tenable claim when deprived of anything having value. The views of such a formidable cast of authorities are highly relevant to ascertain the

meaning of the term "taken" in the Fifth Amendment to the U.S. Constitution, a matter that will be considered in Chapter 3.

We may at this point summarize that the common law guaranteed very strong protections to owners for the physical integrity of their properties. The protections previously enumerated applied to individual ownerships; they did not concern general legislation or regulation which affected an area or a jurisdiction. Blackstone expounded on these general laws in his explanation of civil liberty. While his standard of protection for private property was very high, his concern for other civil liberties was of a lesser variety, namely, that the law should not be arbitrary or capricious. As I shall discuss below, Blackstone wrote that the legislature may rightfully impose limited substantive restrictions on civil liberties without a finding of forfeiture or requiring payment of compensation.

Blackstone's perspective is relevant to modern views on what constitutes a legal deprivation of rights—an issue of great importance in constitutional law— much of which is involved in determining the authority of government to limit the exercise of private rights. Although Blackstone writes that the principal aim of society is to protect individuals in the enjoyment of those absolute rights vested in them by nature, he readily acknowledges that in a civilized society no person can retain the freedom of doing whatever he pleases. Political or civil liberty is, therefore, no other than natural liberty "so far restrained by human laws (and no farther) as is necessary and expedient for the general advantage of the public."[132] Accordingly, a restraint imposed by government pursuant to this standard would not constitute a legal deprivation in violation of Chapter 29 of the Magna Carta, as Blackstone explained:

> Hence we may collect that the law, which restrains a man from doing mischief to his fellow citizens, though it diminishes the natural, increases the civil liberty of mankind: but every wanton and causeless restraint of the will of the subject, whether practised by a monarch, a nobility, or a popular assembly is a degree of tyranny. Nay, that even laws themselves, whether made with or without our consent, if they regulate and constrain our conduct in matters of mere indifference, without any good end in view, are laws destructive of liberty. . . . [T]hat constitution or frame of government, that system of laws, is alone calculated to maintain civil liberty, which leaves the subject entire master of his own conduct, except in those points wherein the public good requires some direction or restraint.[133]

Blackstone presented this example of laws "without any good end in view":

> Thus, the statute of King Edward IV, which forbad the fine gentlemen of those times (under the degree of a lord) to wear pikes upon their shoes or boots if more than two inches in length, was a law that savoured of oppression; because, however ridiculous the fashion then in use might appear,

the restraining it by pecuniary penalties could serve no purpose of common utility. But the statute of King Charles II, which prescribes a thing seemingly as indifferent; vis, a dress for the dead, who are all ordered to be buried in woolen; is a law consistent with public liberty, for it encourages a staple trade, in which in great measure depends the universal good of the nation.[134]

While Blackstone's position—that, to be valid, laws must achieve their purpose—is generally acceptable, his example of woolen dress for the dead is poorly considered, as many recent judicial decisions reveal. Under the general rules applied in most fundamental rights jurisprudence in the United States, the burden is on the government to prove that a law limiting a protected liberty will, depending on the right involved, either largely or substantially achieve its purpose. This formulation requires subjective evaluation that may result in differing conclusions; the woolen dress example is much more complicated than Blackstone suggests. In Blackstone's example, the law's objective itself appears flawed because it seeks to bestow benefits on the wool industry, thus making it a special and not a general law.

Interestingly, James Madison recognized the problem of special legislation in a 1792 essay. He asked, "What must be the spirit of legislation where a manufacturer of linen cloth is forbidden to bury his own child in a linen shroud, in order to favor his neighbor who manufactures woolen cloth; where the manufacturer and weaver of woolen cloth are again forbidden the economical use of buttons of that material, in favor of the manufacturer of other materials!"[135] Madison ridiculed such specific restrictions as infringements on the right of property.

Contrary to Madison's view, Blackstone assumes that the universal good of the nation in great measure depends on the wool trade. In deciding whether the law requiring woolen dress for the dead advances the nation's economy, we must consider the percentage of the economy that the burial law affects. If the percentage is small, then the liberty to dress the dead is being curtailed to achieve a minimal public benefit. A small fit between limiting liberty and obtaining public advantage makes it difficult to conclude that the law is a justifiable restraint on liberty. For, as Blackstone states, "every wanton and causeless restraint on the will of the subject" is a degree of tyranny. A law proscribing liberty should be neither over- nor under-inclusive in achieving its objective. Thus, under current rules of the U.S. Supreme Court, a land-use regulation cannot pass constitutional muster unless it *substantially* advances a legitimate state interest.[136]

In Blackstone's explanation of compensation, he refers to the legislature acquiring land for public roads, which is a use that benefits the entire community. His position does not apply to a private road, for such a road would only benefit a particular person or persons. Many courts in the United States have applied Blackstone's position by requiring that the government's acquisition be "for pub-

lic use." What is a public use? Clearly, a public road would be an example of public use; prohibiting pikes in excess of two inches on shoes would not, however, because the law "could serve no purpose of common utility." It can be gathered from this example that "public use" is when some law does serve the "purpose of common utility." Let us apply this understanding of public use to Blackstone's woolen dress example. In his discussion of the meaning of "without any good end in view," Blackstone accepts the restriction requiring woolen dress for the dead because it benefits the wool trade. However, a restriction to benefit the wool industry seems to be for private and not public purposes, unless the restriction advances "the universal good of the nation." Blackstone's example of woolen dress offers government great discretion in defining public use, thus enlarging its power over private enterprise—an outcome which Madison's illustrations show to be harmful, unless actually justified by a legitimate public purpose.

In his role as a judge, Coke generally followed the jurisprudential approach that Blackstone would later observe, as is evident from the cases discussed above in Section III. In *Bonham,* the king and Parliament sought to protect the public health by excluding unqualified persons from the practice of medicine. This was a legitimate and important public purpose. The problem, however, was that the statute would at best only partially achieve this objective, and thus was not enough to warrant deprivation of Bonham's liberty to practice medicine. In the *Saltpeter* case, Coke narrowly construed the king's prerogative for national defense. His court allowed the landowner to otherwise retain ownership of the saltpeter, and imposed severe conditions on the king's servants to hold the owner harmless from any damage caused by and during the extraction process. Coke rejected the decision in the *Bates* case because he construed Chapter 30 of the Magna Carta as confining the king's prerogative powers to impose duties on imports to during time of war or when this would serve vital foreign trade concerns. In the absence of such restraints on his prerogative powers, the king would be able to apply this power selectively to cause benefit or harm to different merchants. The *Isle of Ely* decision required that the cost of public improvements should be borne by people only in proportion to the gains they obtain from them; there had to be a tight connection between the burden imposed and the benefits received. As can be seen from this brief summary of Coke's approach, he believed that a required restriction on human conduct be precise and narrow to avoid imposing unnecessary restraints on people. Blackstone displayed similar concerns about limiting the powers of government.

Unlike Coke, Blackstone believed in the supremacy of the Parliament, and consequently one might conclude that Blackstone's observations on protecting human rights were merely philosophical exercises. This, however, would not be a sound judgment. Blackstone's *Commentaries* was more than a philosophical exercise; it was a record of English law, setting forth rules that society either observed or should observe. This was important information for the gen-

eral public, and for lawyers, judges, and legislators in particular. Members of English society expected that their leaders would abide by these rules, even if they were not guaranteed in a constitution. Blackstone apparently believed that, for various reasons, Parliament would never violate what he referred to as the "absolute" rights of the people. First, Parliament was under a moral obligation to secure these absolute rights. Second, the Parliament had over the years generally adhered to this moral obligation. Third, with respect to property, a parliament composed exclusively of property owners was likely to respect a system largely based on the rights of property. During Blackstone's life, the richest landowners in England dominated Parliament.[137] Fourth, there is reason to conclude that Blackstone believed that Parliament would abide by the natural law. More needs to be said concerning this fourth reason.

How can one reconcile Blackstone's belief in both the supremacy of the legislature and of the natural law? "This law of nature," he wrote, "being co-eval with mankind and dictated by God himself, is of course superior in obligation to any other. It is binding over all the globe, in all countries and at all times; no human laws are of any validity, if contrary to this."[138]

Another explanation that might reconcile Blackstone's seemingly contradictory positions on the supremacy of both Parliament and the natural law, relates to his view that acts of Parliament causing "absurd consequences, manifestly contrary to common reason are void with respect to these consequences."[139] "Common reason" would seem to include natural law; and if so, the rule would be a significant limitation on parliamentary powers.[140] While Blackstone rejected giving judges the power to annul statutes that are contrary to natural law, he would permit judges to reform statutes in order to facilitate the legislative process.[141] He wrote that "acts of parliament that are impossible to be performed are of no validity, and if there arise out of them collaterally any absurd consequences, manifestly contradictory to common reason, they are, with regard to those collateral consequences, void." The judges had no power to remove such laws, but they could reform statutes to aid the legislative process.[142] He continued: "[W]here some collateral matter arises out of the general words, and happens to be unreasonable; there the judges are in decency to conclude that the consequence was not foreseen by the parliament, and therefore they are at liberty to expound the statute by equity, and only *quoad hoc* disregard it."

Accordingly, while Blackstone supported the position that the Parliament is the supreme branch of government, he did not advocate that the judges should always be deferential in interpreting statutes. When the law is "couched in such evident and express words, as to leave no doubt" about the intention of Parliament, the judges must enforce it as written. However, when the measure is ambiguous, uncertain, or contrary to common law rules, the judges have the power to reform it to make it conform with "common right and reason." The judges had to subject statutes to a high level of scrutiny in order to determine the character of the law.

When remedial statutes were involved, it was "the business of the judges so to construe the act, as to suppress the mischief and advance the remedy."

To illustrate this principle, Blackstone writes about a statute relating to religious corporations (enacted in Queen Elizabeth's reign) that the judges reformed because it did not achieve the Parliament's objective. Under the common law, religious corporations were allowed to enter into long leases without any time limitation. On occasion, they permitted long and unreasonable leases, to the detriment of the corporation. To remedy the problem, Parliament passed a statute limiting the duration of each such lease to a period of no longer than twenty-one years. However, the judges reformed the statute to provide that leases made by a bishop or a dean for a longer term were not void during his life. They theorized that since the act was passed for the benefit of the successor to the bishop or dean who executed the lease, "the mischief is therefor sufficiently suppressed" by not voiding it until after the death of the maker.[143]

Penal statutes were a different matter, though. Blackstone wrote that these must be construed precisely according to words. Thus, judges interpreted a statute penalizing stealing of "horses" not to punish the stealing of a single horse and a statute punishing the stealing of "sheep, or other cattle" as extending only to sheep. Specific legislation was needed in each instance to achieve the legislative purpose, and thus the judges would have much less interpretive discretion in such cases.

Blackstone presented other examples of judges reforming legislation in order to achieve a closer nexus between the legislative objectives of a statute and the means adopted to achieve them. Adoption of a law that would not accomplish its purpose was little more than an act both of futility in lawmaking and oppression for the persons restricted by it.[144] Coke and Blackstone approved of a judicial role in lawmaking, with Coke accepting a judicial veto while Blackstone favored only a reform authority for the judiciary. To be sure, as compared to rules in the United States, the English judges did not possess the power of judicial review. But they did have, as Blackstone approvingly reports, an important role in framing the laws of the nation. It is apparent that the power of judicial review, as exercised in the United States, had strong roots in English law.

In America, Blackstone's *Commentaries* served as very persuasive support for the judicial protection of individual rights, even though he had discussed rights within the English context of parliamentary supremacy. This is evident from two leading treatises authored in the early years of the United States, both of which were influenced by Blackstone's writings: Joseph Story's *Commentaries on the Constitution of the United States* (1833) and James Kent's *Commentaries on American Law* (1826). Story was a justice of the United States Supreme Court, and Kent was chief judge of the New York Supreme Court and Chancellor of the court of equity. Both rejected the idea of legislative sovereignty under the U.S. Constitution, yet often cited Blackstone when discussing individual rights.

Blackstone's teachings have been highly instructive for modern society. He wrote that natural liberty may be restrained "as is necessary and expedient for the general welfare of the public. . . . But every wanton and causeless restraint of the will of the subject . . . is a degree of tyranny. . . . [L]aws . . . without any good end in view, are laws destructive of liberty." Translated into modern legal terminology, Blackstone's position takes the form of tests to determine whether the legislative means substantially achieve the legislative ends; whether the means and ends are legitimate; and whether, when restraint is necessary, the measures utilized are the least onerous to liberty. The United States Supreme Court presently applies similar tests to ascertain the constitutionality of the most protected rights, identified as fundamental and intermediate rights. The Court will not uphold measures limiting the exercise of these rights that cannot be vindicated under a rigorous application of these standards. One can see that Chapter 29 of Magna Carta, as interpreted by Coke and Blackstone, provides strong support for the judicial protection of freedom.

Property regulations in the United States are currently examined under intermediate scrutiny review.[145] The U.S. Supreme Court evaluates the constitutionality of government regulations under three different standards of review: strict scrutiny for fundamental rights, intermediate scrutiny for intermediate rights, and minimal scrutiny for other rights. Property laws or regulations which satisfy the intermediate scrutiny test are valid and, consequently, do not deprive the subject of this right.[146] Property regulations which do not satisfy the test constitute "takings," in violation of the takings clause, or are deprivations of property, under the due process clause. Intermediate scrutiny imposes a considerable burden on government to prove that its restraints substantially advance legitimate governmental concerns.

V. John Locke's Influence on American Constitutionalism

The writings of John Locke, which were published about a century earlier than those of Blackstone and more than one-half century after those of Coke, were highly influential in America during the last half of the eighteenth century. "In pamphlet after pamphlet," writes historian Bernard Bailyn, "the [early] American writers cited Locke on natural rights and on the social and governmental contract."[147] According to historian Carl Becker, most Americans absorbed Locke's works as a kind of political gospel; indeed, the Declaration of Independence, in its form and phraseology, follows closely certain sentences in Locke's second treatise on government.[148] Locke's theories on the limited role of government (set forth in his *Two Treatises of Government*, written mainly in 1679–1680 and first published in 1690) were very persuasive to a colonial populace apprehensive about governmental powers. His idea of a social compact entered into by individuals in a state of nature prepatory to the for-

mation of government became increasingly meaningful in America as economic conflicts erupted with the English authorities. As historian Forrest McDonald explains, the colonists turned to Locke rather than to the other great natural-law theorists of the time, for the reason that none of the others was so well adapted to their purposes. Only Locke furnished a clear-cut rationale for independence from England.[149]

Locke wrote that people sought the sanctuary of political society because of the uncertain conditions existing in the state of nature, in which anyone who lacked the physical power to defend himself might be victimized by unscrupulous individuals. In forming society, men enter into a social compact, defining the authority and purposes of government and relinquishing many of their individual powers to the state. The state then became responsible for protecting life, personal liberties, and possessions, all of which were included in the term "property." Locke argued that life, liberty, and possessions belong to a particular person and to no one else, and that "[t]he great and *chief end,* therefore, of Men uniting into Commonwealths, and putting themselves under Government, *is the Preservation of their Property.* To which in the state of Nature there are many things wanting."[150]

According to Locke, the legislature, as the supreme body of the organized state, must have the power to rectify the defects existing in the state of nature; but that power must necessarily be limited, at least to the extent that lawmakers could not impose conditions worse than those existing in the state of nature. "[W]henever the *Legislators,*" Locke professed, "*endeavour to take away, and destroy the Property of the People* . . . they put themselves into a state of War with the People, who are thereupon absolved from any farther Obedience. . . ."[151]

The legislature, according to Locke, may not deprive the individual of fundamental rights: first, because the social compact does not provide government with this power, and second, because government's purpose is to play a fiduciary role in safeguarding and enhancing these rights. Limitations on governmental power are central to Locke's theory:

> It cannot be supposed that they [individuals] should intend, had they a power so to do, to give to any one, or more, an *absolute Arbitrary Power* over their Persons and Estates, and put a force into the Magistrates hand to execute his unlimited Will arbitrarily upon them; This were to put themselves into a worse condition than the state of Nature, wherein they had a Liberty to defend their Right against the Injuries of others, and were upon equal terms of force to maintain it, whether invaded by a single Man or many in Combination.[152]

> The *Supreme power cannot take* from any Man any part of his *Property* without his own consent. For the preservation of Property being the end of Government, and that for which Men enter into Society, it necessarily

supposes and requires, that the People should *have Property,* without which they must be suppos'd to lose that by entering into Society, which was the end for which they entered into it, too gross an absurdity for any Man to own.[153]

'Tis true, Governments cannot be supported without great Charge, and 'tis fit everyone who enjoys his share of the Protection, should pay out of his estates, his proportion for the maintenance of it. But still it must be with his own Consent, i.e. the Consent of the Majority, giving it either by themselves or their Representatives chosen by them. For if any one shall claim a Power to lay and levy Taxes on the Republic, by his own Authority, and without such consent by the People, he thereby invades the Fundamental Law of Property, and subverts the end of Government. For what property have I in that which another may by right take, when he pleases to himself?[154]

Locke did not discuss the compensation issue; the above quotation concerning taxation comes closest to it. These comments of Locke's concerning taxation can be construed as providing support for the compensation principle, for, as William Stoebuck asserts, "it would, of course, be absurd to form a government having 'the' end of preserving property, and then to use that government to take away property."[155] However, since Locke's meaning of "consent" is not confined to express consent, but also includes tacit consent, he grants power to government that may be imposed contrary to his own standards. According to Locke, the legislature is under fiduciary obligation to make laws "to no other end but the Peace, Safety, and public good of the people,"[156] with the penalty for breach being the total loss of authority. "[E]very Man, that hath any Possession or Enjoyment, of any part of the Dominion of any Government, doth thereby give his *tacit consent,* and is as far forth obliged to Obedience to the laws of that Government during such Enjoyment, as any one under it [such as one who expressly consented to its laws]."[157] But this tacit consent cannot be construed as giving absolute authority to the governors, since they must apply their authority only for the purpose of advancing the public good.

To make a law for a private and not for the public interest is an act of tyranny. Locke explains that those who are in power "are to govern by promulgated, established laws, not to be varied in particular cases, but to have one rule for the rich and poor, for the favorite at court and the country man at plough."[158] "When the Governour, however instituted, makes not the law, but his Will, the Rule; and his commands and actions are not directed to the Preservation of the Properties of his People, but the satisfaction of his own Ambition, Revenge, Covetousness, or any other irregular Passion," his powers cease,[159] and he thereafter "may be opposed, as any other Man, who by force invades the Right of another."[160] Locke

had condemned the state of nature for enabling everyone to be judge, interpreter, and executioner of the unwritten law of nature, even on their own behalf; he thought that it was unreasonable for men to be judges in their own causes. Government must, he claimed: establish settled, known law as the common measure by which to decide controversies; provide a known and indifferent judge with the authority to determine all differences according to the established law; and grant the power to execute such decisions.[161] Thus, Locke joined Coke and Blackstone in the disapproval of special laws and unrestrained judges.

The ideas of Locke, together with those of Coke and Blackstone, planted seeds for a perspective about the sanctity of human rights that in time bore fruit in the formation of a limited constitutional government. While the passions may have subsided after the Revolutionary War was won and political leadership became more pragmatic, these libertarian ideas were prominent and influential during the drafting and ratification of the United States Constitution. It is evident from the ratification debates that the protection of the individual from government oppression was still the predominant political concern. Opponents of the proposed Constitution displayed great apprehension about and antagonism toward centralized government, while the Constitution's supporters responded that the federal government would have no more power than was necessary to defend the people from foreign and domestic perils.[162] The cherished "rights of Englishmen" would be safe and secure under the Constitution—so promised the document's proponents.

Recent historical analysis of the American revolutionary period confirms that the colonists greatly feared and distrusted government. In *The Ideological Origins of the American Revolution,* Bailyn discusses the philosophy of those who inspired the American Revolution.[163] He is convinced that fear of a comprehensive conspiracy against liberty lay at the heart of American revolutionary thought. For protection against this conspiracy, many looked for guidance to the advocates of a new liberty that espoused natural rights and sought elimination of institutions and practices that harbored despotism. The key concepts were natural rights, the contractual basis of government, the uniqueness of English liberty, and the framing of constitutions founded on dispersed authority. Government was thought to be, by its nature, hostile to human liberty and happiness, and especially susceptible to corruption and despotism. Therefore, government should be confined to serving those needs of the people that could not otherwise be satisfied.

The means for restricting governmental powers was through a constitution which would define authority and create a separation and mixture of functions that would prevent any one group from gaining ascendancy. Creating this balance of forces was essential for preserving the capacity to exercise natural rights—those God-given and inalienable rights founded on immutable maxims of reason and justice, and inherent in all people by virtue of their humanity.

Those rights were expressed—not created—in the English common law, in the statutory enactments of Parliament, and in the charters and privileges promulgated by the Crown. However, because not even these sources could exhaust the great treasury of human rights, they delineated the minimum, not the maximum, boundaries of liberty. Government had to be so constituted that it could not infringe these rights, for the legitimacy of positive law (government-made law) rests on the degree to which it preserves natural rights.

VI. The Colonies Protect Rights

English migrants arriving in the American colonies maintained that they were entitled to exercise their rights as Englishmen to certain guarantees of life, liberty, and property. In 1606, King James I granted the first colonial charter to English settlers who occupied the American territory "commonly called Virginia." This charter, known as the First Charter of Virginia, declared that the settlers and their children "shall have and enjoy all Liberties, Franchises, and Immunities . . . to all intents and purposes, as if they had been abiding and born within our Realme of England."[164] The said guarantees in the 1606 charter became standard language in the founding documents that were granted for later colonies. Similar protections of the "rights of Englishmen" appeared in the colonial charters of the Massachusetts Bay Colony, Connecticut, Rhode Island, Maryland, Carolina, Georgia, and Maine.[165] Most, if not all, of the colonial charters provided that the common law was the system of jurisprudence in the colony.

As Alexander Hamilton asserted in 1804: "Our ancestors, when they emigrated to this country, brought with them the common law as their inheritance and birthright; and one of the earliest acts of our Colonial legislature [New York] was to assert their claim to the enjoyment of the common law."[166] U.S. Supreme Court Justice Smith Thompson explained that when the American colonies were first settled, the colonists (as well as the lawyers and judges of England) held that they brought with them, as a birthright and inheritance, as much of the common law as was applicable to their local situation and change of circumstances; each colony judged for itself what parts of the common law were applicable to its new condition.[167] Fundamental rights such as (but not confined to) rights of life, liberty, and property were generally considered as secured by common law. Guarantees contained in Chapter 29 of the 1225 Magna Carta appeared early in the laws of the colonies, in statutes passed by: the Maryland General Assembly in 1639; the Massachusetts Body of Liberties in 1641; the West New Jersey Charter of Fundamental Laws in 1676; and the New York "Charter of Liberties and Privileges" in 1683.[168] The policy of the American colonies, from earliest times until the revolution, was intended to encourage immigration by bestowing upon foreigners all the rights of natural born subjects.[169]

In 1765, the colonies of North America held a congress in New York and declared that their residents were entitled to all the inherent rights and privileges of natural born subjects within the kingdom of Great Britain. U.S. Supreme Court Justice Joseph Story referred to such events in his *Commentaries:* "It was under the consciousness of the full possession of the rights, liberties and immunities of British subjects, that the colonists in almost all the early legislatures of their respective assemblies insisted upon a declaratory act, acknowledging and confirming them."[170]

On September 5, 1774, the delegates from the colonies and plantations convened the First Continental Congress and made a formal declaration that the rights of their inhabitants were secured "by the immutable laws of nature, the principles of the English Constitution, and the several charters or compacts pursuant to which the colonial governments were established." This declaration asserted that those who first settled in the colonies were "entitled to all the rights, liberties and immunities of free and natural born subjects, within the realm of England," and their descendants were likewise entitled to exercise and enjoy them. Consequently, "the respective colonies are entitled to the common law of England."[171] The colonies, and subsequently the states, had adopted the common law by the time the United States Constitution was framed, as Chancellor Kent explained:

> It was not to be doubted that the constitution and laws of the United States were made in reference to the existence of the common law . . . . In many cases, the language of the constitution and laws would be inexplicable without reference to the common law; and the existence of the common law is not only supposed by the constitution, but it is appealed to for the construction and interpretation of its powers.[172]

On July 4, 1776, the Continental Congress—consisting of representatives of the thirteen states—adopted the Declaration of Independence, which justified the separation of the American colonies from Great Britain. The Declaration condemned the English violations of natural rights, which were the roots of the common law, and proclaimed that natural liberties are not defeasible: "[A]ll Men are created equal, . . . they are endowed by their Creator with certain unalienable Rights, that among these are Life, Liberty, and the Pursuit of Happiness." Liberty, the Declaration states, is the primary objective of human beings; its exercise both fulfills the needs of the people and the purposes of the state: "That to secure these Rights, Governments are instituted among Men." According to this position, rights that are unalienable cannot be limited in the name of the public interest; instead, the public interest will be achieved by protection of these rights.

The Declaration minimized the role of political authority in the advancement of people's lives and emphasized liberty as the best means for achieving human

aspirations. Thomas Jefferson explained that, in drafting the document, he sought to echo public feelings: "Neither aiming at originality of principle or sentiment, nor yet copied from any particular or previous writing, it was intended to be an expression of the American mind, and to give to that expression the proper tone and spirit called for by the occasion."[173] Indeed, the philosophy of natural rights as explained by Locke, Coke, and Blackstone prevailed in England and America. The Continental Congress had loudly and clearly affirmed the rights of Americans as well as those of all other peoples.

The early constitutions of the original states contained provisions with language—comparable to that found in Chapter 29 of the 1225 Magna Carta and in the Declaration of Independence—protecting life, liberty, and property. Massachusetts, in its constitution of 1780, and New Hampshire, in 1784, declared in the same language that "no subject shall be arrested, imprisoned, despoiled or deprived of his property, immunities, or privileges, put out of the protection of the law, exiled, or deprived of his life, liberty, or estate, but by the judgment of his peers, or the law of the land." The Virginia Declaration of Rights of 1776 provided "that no man be deprived of his liberty except by the law of the land, or the judgment of his peers." The constitutions of Maryland and North Carolina in 1776 and South Carolina in 1778, stated that "no freeman of this State be taken or imprisoned, or disseized of his freehold, liberties, or privileges, outlawed, exiled, or in any manner destroyed or deprived of his life, liberty, or property, but by the judgment of his peers or the law of the land." Vermont and Pennsylvania, in 1786, declared that all men "have certain natural, inherent and unalienable rights," among which are life and liberty and acquiring, possessing, and protecting property. In 1777, New York adopted a constitutional amendment that "no man shall be disfranchised or deprived of any right he enjoys under the constitution but by law of the land, or judgment of his peers." Delaware, in 1792, required that no person "shall be deprived of life, liberty, or property, unless by the judgment of his peers or the law of the land." Rhode Island, in 1798, enacted a statutory bill of rights, which included a provision that no person "shall be deprived of life, liberty or property unless by the judgment of his peers, or law of the land." Connecticut's first constitution in 1818 provided that no person be "deprived of life, liberty or property, but by due course of law."[174]

The importance that the original U.S. states placed on liberty and the protection of rights was reflected when subsequent U.S. states were formed. A statute adopted by Congress in July, 1787 for the government of the Northwest Territory—the area that would later become the states of Ohio, Indiana, Illinois, Michigan, and Wisconsin—referred to as the "Northwest Ordinance," required that one of the articles of compact between the original states and the people and states to be formed out of the Northwest Territory contain a commitment by the new states that "no man shall be deprived of his life, liberty, or property, but by the judgment of his peers or the law of the land."[175]

VII. The Commercial Success of English America

The Declaration of Independence speaks about political and economic liberties, both of which were very critical to the lives of the colonists. They feared that the English would threaten their accomplishments in the New World. At the date of the Declaration, English America had achieved considerable commercial success. As historian Paul Johnson puts it, the colonies satisfied man's "overwhelming dynamic . . . the lust to own land. . . . [F]or the first time in human history, cheap, good land was available to the multitude. . . ."[176] The availability of land enabled the colonists to achieve a level of prosperity and contentment not readily available in the countries from which they migrated.

Benjamin Franklin described, in a letter he wrote to one B. Vaughan, Esq. in 1784, the opportunities that America offered settlers. In reply to queries as to the kind of persons who would find emigration to America advantageous, and what were the advantages they may reasonably expect, Franklin gave a quite detailed answer:

> Land being cheap in that country, from the vast forests still void of inhabitants, and not likely to be occupied in an age to come, insomuch that the propriety of an hundred acres of fertile soil full of wood may be obtained near the frontiers in many places for eight or ten guineas, hearty young laboring men, who understand husbandry of corn and cattle, which is nearly the same in that country as in Europe, may easily establish themselves there. A little money saved of the good wages they receive there while they work for others, enables them to buy the land and begin their plantation, in which they are assisted by the good-will of their neighbors and some credit. Multitudes of poor people from England, Scotland, and Germany, have by this means in a few years become wealthy farmers, who in their own countries, where all the lands are fully occupied, and the wages of labor low, could never have emerged from the mean condition where they were born.
>
> From the salubrity of the air, the healthiness of the climate, the plenty of good provisions, and the encouragement to early marriages, by the certainty of subsistence in cultivating the earth, the increase of inhabitants by natural generation is very rapid in America, and becomes more so by the accession of strangers; hence there is a continual demand for more artisans of all necessary and useful kinds to supply those cultivators of the earth with houses and with furniture, and utensils of the grosser sorts, which cannot so well be brought from Europe. Tolerably good workmen in any of those mechanic arts are sure to find employ, and to be well paid for their work, there being no restraints preventing strangers from exercising any art they understand, nor any permission necessary. If they are poor, they begin first as servants, or journeymen; and if they are sober,

industrious, and frugal, they soon become masters, establish themselves in business, marry, raise families, and become respectable citizens.

Lastly, persons of moderate fortunes and capitals, who having a number of children to provide for, are desirous of bringing them up to industry, and to secure estates for their posterity, have opportunities of doing it in America, which Europe does not afford. There they may be taught and practise profitably mechanic arts, without incurring disgrace on that account; but on the contrary, acquiring respect by such abilities. There small capitals laid out in lands, which daily become more valuable by the increase of people, affords a solid prospect of ample fortunes thereafter for those children. The writer of this has known several large tracts of land bought on what was then the frontier of Pennsylvania, for ten pounds per hundred acres, which, after 20 years, when the settlement had been extended far beyond them, sold readily, without any improvement made upon them, for three pounds per acre. The acre in America is the same with the English acre or the acre of Normandy.[177]

Law professor William Scott writes that by 1750, the vast majority of white adult males in the colonies owned land and most families lived on farms. The laboring classes constituted a minority of the population. In the larger seaport cities, about 30 percent of free adult males were employees. As of 1763, the unpropertied or dependent laboring force in the colonies, exclusive of slaves, was no more than 20 to 30 percent of the population.[178]

By 1750, the American colonies achieved the greatest growth rate of any part of the British Empire, with a 500 percent expansion in half a century. Britain had the most modern economy in Europe, yet it advanced by only 25 percent in the same period. In 1700, the output in the colonies was 5 percent of Britain's; by 1775, it was 40 percent. According to Johnson, this was one of the highest rates of growth the world has ever witnessed.[179]

These conditions were attributable to freedom rather than to authority. Economist Chester Whitney Wright states that the colonies had been established and developed largely on private initiative and enterprise, with little aid from the government except for defense. For more than a century, England had paid little attention to them. He writes that the economic conditions in the colonies, combining an abundance of land, a scarcity of labor, a scattered population, and a relatively high degree of economic self-sufficiency among large groups, tended to increase the colonies' economic freedom, to foster a spirit of individualism and private initiative, and to make taxation particularly obnoxious.[180] Adam Smith attributed the economic success of the American colonies to an almost total commitment to agriculture—a largely individualistic endeavor—and to the genius of the British constitution, because of its protection and encouragement of freedom.[181]

The idyllic picture of life in America that Franklin presented in his letter confronted two serious problems in the years roughly between 1783 and 1789. The first problem was an inevitable downturn of the economic cycle, aggravated by the dislocations caused by the end of the revolutionary war, and the second was the imposition of economic regulation in response to the downturn—regulation that probably prolonged the downturn. Those who borrowed when prices and wages were high—according to Wright, wages dropped from between $10 and $20 per day to 50 cents—often sought and obtained political help for difficulty in repaying their loans. Laws were passed reducing, canceling, or postponing payment of debts, and some states considerably increased the money supply.[182] While debtors and politicians may have temporarily improved their lot, creditors and others viewed these laws as destructive of economic viability and well-being, and succeeded in inserting in the U.S. Constitution provisions stripping the states of the power to pass such laws.

VIII. Rejecting Authoritarian Controls

Notwithstanding constitutional and statutory safeguards for the exercise of common law rights, commerce in the thirteen states during and after the Revolutionary War was subject to a considerable amount of regulation, some of which will be discussed in Chapter 3. There was little judicial protection for these rights. Although the separation of powers was a common feature of state constitutions, judicial review was still a very weak power. Law professor Charles Haines writes that between 1778 and 1786, in only six cases in five states did a court exercise or express a right of review over a legislative act.[183] There is even some question as to whether all these cases supported the principle of judicial review.[184] Interestingly, while the Constitutional Convention was in session in 1787, the *Philadelphia Press* carried stories about judicial decisions in New Hampshire and North Carolina declaring certain statutes unconstitutional. These stories may have provided some Framers with information on the application of judicial review.

The judicial review power was advanced as being essential for preserving the people's rights. Support for judicial review was probably also encouraged by some severe failures of regulation. Judicial review, it could be argued, would serve the public interest by eliminating arbitrary and capricious legislation. Haines writes that, by 1787, a commonly held belief was that the greatest peril to liberty comes from expanding the power of government.[185]

An early experience of regulation failure occurred in the colony of Plymouth, which was founded in 1620. Initially, the colony required that its inhabitants engage in communal farming. Everyone was supposed to work in the fields and obtain their food from the produce of those fields. However, the colony faced

starvation because the demand far exceeded the supply. This outcome is inevitable when there is no monetary or regulatory limit on demand and little personal incentive for the suppliers to engage in manuring and planting the land. As a result, communal farming was eliminated and replaced with individual farming, pursuant to which every person had to obtain food from his own efforts. Governor William Bradford concluded that the change in policy made everyone industrious "so as much more corn was planted than otherwise would have been by any [other] means. . . . The women now went willingly into the fields, and took their little ones with them to set corn; which before would have alleged weakness and inability; when to have compelled would have been thought great tyranny and oppression."[186] In time, colonial settlers discarded communal farming practices. Scott writes that by 1700, except for the Southern plantations and New York's particular leasehold system, most of the land in the colonies was occupied by small, independent, freehold farmers.[187]

Another noteworthy example of regulatory failure involved the imposition of price controls during the Revolutionary War. Believing that unpatriotic speculators were responsible for the huge rise in price of the commodities required by the American army in 1777, Pennsylvania, where the main forces were quartered, enacted price controls only on those commodities. As a result, most farmers refused to sell much of their produce to the army. Indeed, some farmers sold to the British who paid in gold. The failure to obtain food nearly caused the army to starve. The Continental Congress, on June 4, 1778, adopted the following resolution that urged the termination of price restraints:

> Whereas . . . it hath been found by experience that limitations upon the prices of commodities are not only ineffectual for the purposes proposed, but likewise productive of very evil consequences to the great detriment of the public service and grievous oppression of individuals . . . resolved, that it be recommended to the several states to repeal or suspend all laws or regulations within the said states respectively limiting, regulating or restraining the Price of any Article, Manufacture or Commodity.[188]

When the controls were removed, prices rose to eighty times their prewar level for a short period before settling down to a level just greater than the prewar average, where they remained for the next decade. By the fall of 1778, the army was fairly well provided for as a direct result of this change in policy.[189]

Economist Alan Reynolds, in a study of economic controls during the American Revolution, described this unpopular experience with price controls:

> Public jawboning, private threats, ostracism, boycotts, fines—all proved useless against the flood of paper money. The price of common labor in Boston, which was fixed at three shillings a day in 1777, had risen to 60

shillings by mid-1779. In April 1779, George Washington complained that "a wagon-load of money will scarcely purchase a wagon-load of provisions." In 1779, when the Continental Congress again endorsed price controls, the request was for state laws limiting wage and price increases "not to exceed twenty fold the levels of 1774." Not even that modest goal was attainable, however, and Congress allowed controls to expire when it met again in February 1780.[190]

Economist Pelatiah Webster, writing toward the end of the war in January 1780, evaluated the sporadic record of price and wage controls in the new United States as follows:

> As experiment is the surest proof of the natural effects of all speculations of this kind, . . . it is strange, it is marvelous to me, that any person of common discernment, who has been acquainted with all the above-mentioned trials and effects, should entertain any idea of the expediency of trying any such methods again. . . . Trade, if let alone, will ever make its own way best, and like an irresistible river, will ever run safest, do least mischief and do most good, suffered to run without obstruction in its own natural channel.[191]

In *Forty Centuries of Wage and Price Controls*, Robert F. Scheuttinger and Eamonn F. Butler describe the experience of Massachusetts and Connecticut in imposing wage or price controls between 1776 and 1778, which—like the Pennsylvania controls on army commodities—had disastrous consequences. Many of these laws were repealed within several years of their passage. Such failures may help explain the limited economic powers that the Framers accorded to the government in the U.S. Constitution.[192]

When the delegates convened at the Constitutional Convention of 1787, the historical experience of England and America had already influenced the broad outlines of the constitution they came to write. The historical record was one that provided both philosophical and pragmatic dimensions to the writing of the U.S. Constitution. The Magna Carta, Coke, Blackstone, and Locke provided the perception and inspiration that led to the Declaration of Independence and to its conclusion that the protection of liberty was essential to the preservation and advancement of the human condition. The enormous successes and failures of the American economic experience had proven that limiting governmental powers was also essential for achieving a prosperous and abundant society. The American Framers thus had sufficient evidence to support the creation of a government with limited powers.

Accordingly, the Framers provided Congress with a small number of economic powers, in addition to the regulation of commerce. These powers include

the power to tax (though this is restricted on the basis of population with respect to direct taxes) and spend for constitutional purposes, borrow money, establish uniform bankruptcy laws, coin and regulate the value of money, fix standards of weights and measures, establish post offices and post roads, and grant copyrights and patents.

Law professor William Grampp observes that the economic controls that the U.S. Constitution expressly authorizes are quite modest when compared with those that France and England exercised or tried to exercise during the period of mercantilism, from the sixteenth to the middle of the eighteenth century: the fixing of prices, wages, and interest rates; prohibition of forestalling and engrossing; regulating the quality of goods; licensing of labor; programs to increase the population; sumptuary control; monopoly grants and other exclusive rights; incorporation; state enterprise; and the control of foreign trade and finance, including the protection of domestic industries. Grampp goes on to explain that

> [n]ot even proposed [at the Philadelphia Convention] were the powers to control prices, wages, interest rates, the quality of goods, the conditions of their sale, and the allocation of labor. All of these powers were cherished by the *practitioners* (although not the theorists) of mercantilism, and could they have been asked for an opinion of the Constitution, they would have said it provided a feeble economic policy indeed. Those who today believe the Federal government has extensive economic authority to exercise, if it will, cannot support their belief by the records of the constitutional convention (nor the Constitution of course), because the delegates were not agreed upon the issue.[193]

Constitutions do not emerge from thin air. They reflect to a considerable extent the experience of a nation. The commerical success of English America and the failure of economic regulation may explain in part the pronounced tilt of the U.S. Constitution toward freedom and away from authority.

IX. Freedom versus Public Virtue

It has been contended that during the period from the promulgation of the Declaration of Independence to the framing of the Constitution, important strains of thought existed in English America that would accord government an authoritarian role. These strains of thought were allegedly based on the theory that implementing the public good through authority was superior to implementing it through liberty. Historian Gordon Wood claims that such thought prevailed at the time of the American Revolutionary War and continued for some years thereafter.[194] According to this position concerning the use of po-

litical authority in attaining the public good, a monarchy is committed to achieving the common good through restraining individual desires by means of fear or force. In a republic, by contrast, the attainment of the common good is more difficult; each man must somehow be persuaded to submerge his liberties for the sake of the greater good of the whole. Such persuasion would achieve what in the eighteenth century was termed "public virtue," which was understood as subordinating one's private interests to the interests of the state.[195] It is this emphasis on public virtue, then, that Wood contends was prevalent in the early years of the American republic.

Wood's contention is difficult to accept, though. The doctrine of public virtue is completely at variance with natural rights and the common law; the positions of Coke, Blackstone, and Locke; the terms and provisions of almost all colonial and state constitutions; and the Declaration of Independence. The common concern of all these interests was the protection of individual freedom, which could only be achieved by limiting the powers of government. Government was considered more of a necessary evil than a utopian benefactor.

While there may have been some proponents of the idea of public virtue in the years before and after the Revolution, few of the political and intellectual leaders of the period favored establishing the powerful government that would be needed to bring about public virtue. It has been said Thomas Jefferson harbored thoughts in favor of a system of public virtue for a brief period in his career with respect to the regulation of property rights. However, his emphasis on unalienable rights in the Declaration of Independence reveals his considered thought for most of his life.[196] In any event, the most important political document of the revolutionary and constitutional periods is the U.S. Constitution, which is a great testament to individual rights and limited government, and thus stands as a direct challenge to the claim that public virtue was the prevalent concern during the years of its framing and adoption.

I close this chapter with some thoughts from James Madison, whom I consider to be the most important Framer. I believe that Madison represents the prevalent way of thinking of the constitutional period. In No. 10 of the *Federalist Papers,* Madison rejected theories of those who "have erroneously supposed that by reducing mankind to a perfect equality in their political rights, they would at the same time be perfectly equalized in their possessions, their opinions and their passions." These comments are consistent with the overall tenor of *The Federalist Papers* (published in 1787 and 1788), which sought to persuade the public that the proposed Constitution would establish a national government of very limited powers. These very influential commentaries, which were written to support the ratification of the Constitution, would not have found resonance with a public that supported a strong government, and they never would have been written or published if the authors believed that the public wanted such a government. This provides further evidence that the gen-

eral consensus at the time was that liberty and protection of rights were of paramount importance.

Madison ridiculed the idea that people in a nation would uphold and embody the essential elements of public virtue, that is, that they "have all precisely the same interests and the same feelings in every respect." No state ever did nor could one obtain total consent of a large mass of citizens, he claimed. A just and viable state can only exist when government is structured to successfully reconcile and benefit from the various interests and tensions that exist among its citizens.[197] "In the extent and proper structure of the Union, therefore, we behold a republican remedy for the diseases most incident to republican government."[198] Madison thus rejected, as Scott has observed, the notion of public virtue in favor of one of balanced interests.[199] Central to the balancing of these interests was the protection of life, liberty, and property.

3

Interpreting the Constitution
and the Bill of Rights

I. The Articles of Confederation

In 1781, the thirteen original colonies entered into the Articles of Confederation, which established a confederation of states that they called the United States of America. The articles asserted that the free inhabitants of each state were entitled to all of the privileges and immunities of free citizens in the several states. It granted each state one vote in the Congress of the Confederation and provided very limited legislative and executive powers to that body, with each state retaining all powers not expressly granted to Congress. Congress had the power to conduct foreign relations, establish armed services, regulate relations with Indian tribes, and issue and borrow money. It had no power to levy taxes, regulate trade and commerce, or otherwise interfere in the internal affairs of the states. Amendments could only be adopted by unanimous consent. The Articles of Confederation reflected the colonists' distrust of centralized government; they rejected it except when it was essential to the viability of the states.

The most serious problem confronted by the confederation was the prevalence in the states of economic regulations that inhibited both trade between the states and ownership and investment within the states. The official efforts to remove these barriers began in January 1786 with the passage by the Virginia general assembly of a resolution proposing a meeting of commissioners from the states to consider and recommend "how far a uniform system in their commercial regulations may be necessary to their common interest and permanent harmony." Commissioners from New York, New Jersey, Pennsylvania, Delaware, and Virginia

subsequently met in September in Annapolis, Maryland, and they recommended that a meeting of states be held in Philadelphia in May 1787 to consider changes in the Articles of Confederation in relation to commerce and other important matters. On February 21, 1787, Congress adopted resolutions calling for a convention to be held in May at Philadelphia for the sole purpose of revising the Articles of Confederation.

Under the articles, each state had virtually unlimited power to regulate all traffic and trade to and within its borders. Each state applied this power in its own self-interest, frequently to the detriment of other states. Organizers of the Constitutional Convention of 1787 sought to suppress what Alexander Hamilton referred to as the "interfering and unneighborly regulations of some states"—regulations which, "if not restrained by a national control," would result in even more "serious sources of animosity and discord."[1] A major objective of these organizers was to prohibit state or municipal laws whose purpose was to institute local economic protectionism, that is, to prohibit laws supporting local state economic interests to the detriment of other states and a national economy.

Laws regulating economic activity within the states were also of great concern. Following the American Revolutionary War, the economies in some states deteriorated markedly, leading to "an ignoble array of legislative schemes for the defeat of creditors and invasion of contractual relations."[2] Some states passed "stay laws," which extended the due date of notes; "installments laws," which allowed debtors to pay their obligations in installments after they had fallen due; and "commodity payment laws," which permitted payments in certain enumerated commodities at a fraction of actual value. Some states were reluctant to pass legislation that would allow the British to collect debts owed by Americans, payment of which had been suspended during the war. According to Alexander Hamilton, "creditors had been ruined, or in a very extensive degree, much injured, confidence in pecuniary transactions had been destroyed, and the springs of industry had been proportionately relaxed" because of the failure of the states to safeguard commercial rights.[3]

The experience of South Carolina exemplifies the problems that creditors faced. In 1782, the state passed a stay law, and, in 1785, a law terminating suits for debts. When the latter act expired, another act was passed allowing debts to be paid in installments. The state also issued public obligations that effectively increased the money supply, thus reducing the value of its currency.[4] People were reluctant to lend money or they demanded a high rate of interest if they were uncertain as to the monetary return they would receive.

Another major economic problem was the irresponsibility of some states in the issuance of their currency. The authority to print paper money was an issue of great importance to the Framers, who had personal experience with the flood of depreciated notes issued by state governments and the confederation itself, the latter in order to finance the revolution. Although the delegates to the 1787

Constitutional Convention readily admitted that such a large influx of money might at times have popular and legislative support, almost everyone who spoke on the issue recognized that the power to issue money could be employed irresponsibly with the effect of precipitating adverse consequences for the country's economy.

As law professor Kenneth Dam writes, the Framers "had seen it [paper money], and the devastating effect of issuing too much of it, in detail and profusion."[5] In June 1775, the Continental Congress began to emit bills of credit; by 1780, $100 in paper was worth only $2.50 in specie. During the following year, this paper was practically valueless—it was, as the saying goes, "not worth a Continental." Similar problems existed in the states, with Virginia's currency valued in 1780 at 0.1 percent of that which it originally had been worth. After the demise of its paper currency, the Continental Congress was forced to depend almost entirely on bond issues that were sold in Europe.[6]

Those interested in preserving and expanding a national commercial market viewed the events that transpired in Rhode Island and Massachusetts as ominous. The Rhode Island Assembly provided that if a creditor refused to accept state paper currency—which it furnished abundantly—at par, the debtor could discharge his debts simply by depositing the scrip with the local judge. As a result, some creditors were pursued by debtors who were eager to tender depreciated paper for full value of their debts. "Rather than sell for worthless paper, merchants shut up shop, hid their stock, or loaded it on a vessel and escaped to New York or the West Indies."[7]

Rhode Island had earlier adopted a law targeting the property of loyalists to the British cause that was titled an "Act to Confiscate and Sequester Estates and Banish Persons of a Certain Description"—a title reflecting the act's ominous purpose. Also targeting loyalists, in 1777, the Continental Congress recommended to all the states that the real and personal estates of "such persons as had forfeited their right to protection" (i.e., loyalists) be seized and sold and the proceeds invested in government bonds. All the states enacted legislation pursuant thereto; each declared large numbers of designated persons to be guilty of treason or of a similar offense, and proceeded to confiscate all of their property.[8] Such phenomena indicated the need for federal supervision.

In 1786, Massachusetts was the site of a relatively bloodless and unsuccessful insurrection by debt-ridden farmers who were under the leadership of Captain Daniel Shays. They protested both their high taxes and debts. The objective of Shays's Rebellion was to prevent courts from sitting, and thereby to stop the collection of unpaid debts. Due to a poor economy, judgments for overdue taxes or other debts could in most cases be satisfied only by taking a farmer's land, cattle, and personal property. The insurrection—though it was put down by the state's armed forces without help from the Confederation—forced the Massachusetts legislature to make tax and fiscal concessions.[9] Despite the failure of

Shays's Rebellion, it was apparent that the threat of class warfare (or other large-scale violence) jeopardized majoritarian rule in the states; this was a problem which required the establishment of a central authority. Indeed, James Madison feared that Shays's group contemplated "an abolition of debts, public and private, and a new division of property"; this fear is reflected in the fact that Shays's Rebellion is referred to in six numbers of the *Federalist Papers.*[10]

II. The First American Constitution

In terminating their relationship with England, the colonies cut off all legal ties to that country under whose authority they had adopted many of their laws and regulations. To overcome this legal void, various efforts were made in the colonies to adopt constitutions or other plans of government. The first colony to adopt a constitution was Massachusetts in 1780, and this document was largely the work of John Adams (who was later elected the second president of the United States). Adams was a lawyer and, like his contemporaries elsewhere in English America, he had long pondered the question of how to devise a fundamental legal system that satisfactorily reconciles authority and liberty; that is, how to obtain a strong, viable government without giving it the power to oppress its people.

Adams's philosophy on these issues echoed throughout the colonies. "Despotism, or unlimited sovereignty, or absolute power," he asserted, "is the same in a majority of a popular assembly, an aristocratical council, an oligarchical junta, and a single emperor. Equally arbitrarily, cruel, bloody and in every respect diabolical."[11] He strongly advocated a constitution that would provide for a separation of powers (legislative, executive, and judicial), a division of the legislative powers (two separate bodies), and a declaration of the rights of the people. Adams adhered to these principles in the constitution he drafted for Massachusetts, and in time all the state constitutions followed this pattern.

The idea of separation of powers was not without its critics on both sides of the Atlantic Ocean. Robert J. Turgot, the French Minister of Finance and esteemed philosopher, favored a unicameral government with a single legislative body having final authority over the state. He was joined in holding this view by some notable Americans. Benjamin Franklin, for example, the prestigious elder statesman, spoke favorably about Pennsylvania's single-branch legislature. In his influential pamphlet, *Common Sense,* Tom Paine urged the creation of a one-assembly government that would reflect the popular will.

Adams found such a system of unitary government highly objectionable, because it would enable political majorities to control the people's lives, liberties, and properties. To answer these critics of divided government, Adams wrote a three-volume work entitled, *A Defence of the Constitutions of Government of the*

United States of America. Adams pointed out the perils of a unitary government: "Without three orders and an effectual balance between them in every American constitution, it must be destined to frequent, unavoidable revolutions; though they are delayed a few years, they must come in time"; and, "[i]f the executive power or any considerable part of it is left in the hands of either an aristocratical or democratical assembly, it will corrupt the legislature as necessarily as rust corrupts iron, or as arsenic poisons the human body; and when the legislature is corrupted, the people are undone."[12] In order to avoid these perils, he claimed that "[w]hat was essential was an executive officer, hereditary or elective, who would have sufficient power as a counterbalance to the legislative branch of the government."[13] Shays's uprising in 1788 served as a background for Adams's fears. An all-powerful legislature would not always protect the people from laws—such as those favored by many persons in the Shays group—that would abolish debts, redistribute property, and do away with the offices of senators and governors. It was necessary to have a balance of powers in order to prevent oppression by any part of government. As a strong advocate of property rights, Adams greatly feared leaving its control to popular discretion.

Adams observed that in the late eighteenth century there was no functioning democracy in Europe. Nor was any democratic element part of a European constitution, with the notable exception of England. Because England was a stable and viable nation, Adams argued, Americans should recognize and follow the principles (such as the separation and division of powers) that account for its success.

III. Framing the U.S. Constitution

In the 1780s, many people expressed alarm about whether the states—if they remained largely autonomous—could sustain economic viability and stability. Not only was social chaos and even violence feared, but political forces that favored policies destructive of private ownership and enterprise were also feared. According to Madison, laws infringing on property rights "contributed more to that uneasiness which produced the Convention . . . than those which accrued . . . from the inadequacy of the Confederation." He further claimed that

> [a] constitutional negative on the laws of the states seems equally necessary to secure individuals against encroachments on their rights. The mutability of the laws of the states is found to be a serious evil. The injustice of them has been so frequent and so flagrant as to alarm the most steadfast friends of Republicanism.[14]

To the same effect, John Marshall (who later became Chief Justice of the U.S. Supreme Court) observed during the ratification debates that the Confederation

took away "the incitements to industry by rendering property insecure and unprotected." The Constitution, on the contrary, "will promote and encourage industry."[15] Marshall explained, in an opinion he later wrote as chief justice, that the union of the states was intended to create one commercial market, and "so far as respects the intercommunication of individuals, the lines of separation between states are, in many respects, obliterated." In dramatic terms, he described creditor-debtor problems as a critical reason for creating a national government:

> The power of changing the relative situation of debtor and creditor, of interfering with contracts, a power which comes home to every man, touches the interest of all, and controls the conduct of every individual in those things which he supposes to be proper for his own exclusive management, had been used to such an excess by the state legislatures, as to break in upon the ordinary intercourse of society, and destroy all confidence between man and man. This mischief had become so great, so alarming, as not only to impair commercial intercourse, and threaten the existence of credit, but to sap the morals of the people, and destroy the sanctity of private faith. To guard against the continuance of the evil, was an object of deep interest with all the truly wise, as well as the virtuous, of this great community, and was one of the important benefits expected from a reform of the government.[16]

During the Constitutional Convention, Madison said that the union must provide "more effectually for the security of private rights, and the steady dispensation of justice." He asked: "Was it to be supposed that republican liberty could long exist under the abuses of it, practised in some of the states?"[17] The *Pennsylvania Packet* described the situation in 1786: "At the commencement of the Revolution, it was supposed that what is called the executive part of government was the only dangerous part; but we now see that quite as much mischief, if not more, may be done, and as much arbitrary conduct acted, by a legislature."[18]

Whoever was in financial distress, it seemed (whether it was the small farmer, large planter, or merchant), sought and frequently obtained political aid to overcome his problems. Some used the process to acquire greater riches. Such a political climate was destructive to ownership and investment. Understandably, as Albert Beveridge, John Marshall's biographer, concluded, the "determination of commercial and financial interests to get some plan adopted under which business could be transacted, was the most effective force that brought about [the Philadelphia Convention]."[19]

To overcome these obstructions to ownership and economic enterprise, Article I, Section 10, Subsection 1 of the U.S. Constitution contains substantial protection for owners, investors and entrepreneurs. It reads:

No State shall enter into any Treaty, Alliance, or Confederation; grant Letters of Marque and Reprisal; coin Money; emit Bills of Credit; make any Thing but gold and silver Coin a Tender in Payment of Debts; pass any Bill of Attainder, ex post facto Law, or Law impairing the Obligation of Contracts, or grant any Title of Nobility.[20]

At the time the U.S. Constitution was framed in September, 1787, the Northwest Ordinance and the constitutions of nine of the thirteen states contained Magna Carta-oriented language securing life, liberty, and property. The Northwest Ordinance, as well as Vermont's and Massachusetts's constitutions included takings clauses requiring compensation when government deprived owners of their land for public use. Inasmuch as the national government was very limited in its powers, primary governmental authority existed in the states and, consequently, the state constitutions and common law served as the principal, and sometimes inadequate, barriers to governmental oppressions. The adoption of the United States Constitution was intended to create a national government and eliminate many of the economic powers of the states. It did not have the power to deprive people of the liberties ("the rights of Englishmen") to which they were entitled by virtue of the common and statutory laws of England and the states in which they lived.

In the ratification debates, the Anti-Federalists—proponents of the Constitution were labeled "Federalists," and opponents "Anti-Federalists"—charged that the Constitution created a strong, national government that seriously jeopardized the sovereignty of the states and the liberty of the people. They contended that, in relation to the people's liberties, voting majorities were decisive except when the Constitution specifically protected freedom. Since few liberties were safeguarded, the Constitution created a frighteningly powerful national state. The Anti-Federalists were correct in their count of liberties: a small number were secured. The federal government was limited in power so that it could not deprive citizens of their privileges and immunities, suspend the writ of habeas corpus, levy capitation taxes, or pass bills of attainder or *ex post facto* laws; jury trials were required in all criminal matters, usually to be held within the state where the crime was committed; treason was defined and its punishment prescribed; and no religious test was required as a qualification for any office under the United States government. No other personal guarantees of liberty were provided.

However, the absence of personal protections is not a decisive factor in determining the authority of the proposed government. According to Madison, the Constitution would never have been ratified if the people believed that all unstated liberties were totally under the control of the federal government.[21] He initially rejected a bill of rights "because the powers are enumerated. And it followed, that all that are not granted by the Constitution are retained; that the

constitution is a bill of powers, the great residium being the rights of the people."[22] In the constitutional ratification debates of 1788, the Federalists maintained that the powers of Congress were restricted to those set forth in the Constitution, plainly implied by the Constitution, or necessary and proper for executing expressed powers. The Federalists rejected the need for a bill of rights because (1) the separation of and the limitation on federal powers made it unnecessary; (2) constitutional checks and balances would ensure adherence to the Constitution's provisions; and (3) it was not possible to enumerate all of the people's rights, and those left out would be in jeopardy. Supporters of the proposed Constitution insisted that the national government did not have the power to deprive the people of their "rights as Englishmen." The Federalists' argument explaining the absence of a bill of rights is quite tenable. Most Framers favored protecting more rights than those relatively few listed in the original constitution of 1787, and they would have provided additional protection if they thought the rights they considered important would be imperiled.

Theophilus Parsons of Massachusetts, a leading Federalist who was later to become Chief Justice of the Massachusetts Supreme Court, asserted that the Anti-Federalist fears of a powerful national government were groundless since "[n]o power . . . was given to Congress to infringe on any one of the natural rights of the people by this Constitution; and, should they attempt it without constitutional authority, the act would be a nullity and could not be enforced."[23] James Wilson, a Pennsylvania delegate, explained that it was not necessary to be more definitive on this point:

> [E]very thing which is not given, is reserved. . . . [I]t would have been superfluous and absurd, to have stipulated with a federal body of our own creation, that we should not enjoy those privileges, of which we are not divested either by the intention or the act that has brought that body into existence.[24]

In No. 84 of the *Federalist Papers,* Alexander Hamilton argued against any need for including a bill of rights in the Constitution. He asserted that the proposed document was intended to regulate not personal and private concerns, but rather, the nation's general political interests. Replying to critics who noted that England had adopted considerable legislation protecting liberties, Hamilton contended that the two governments were structurally different. He explained that, unlike the English government, the American government could only exercise powers granted to it by the Constitution. The Magna Carta and subsequent enactments protecting individual rights removed the powers of the English government to deny such rights. "Here, in strictness, the people surrender nothing, and as they retain every thing, they have no need of particular reservations." Therefore, a bill of rights was superfluous. Such a declaration might

even be dangerous, Hamilton thought, because it would contain various exceptions of powers that were not conferred, and to this extent would furnish a "colorable pretext" for claiming more than was granted—possibly by those disposed to usurpation. Hamilton pointedly queried: "For why declare that things shall not be done which there is no power to do?"[25]

Any notion that the Framers sought to establish an authoritarian government is false. The people who authored the Declaration of Independence were not about to substitute one despotism for another. Even if at an earlier period some support existed for creating an authoritarian government dedicated to enforcing "public virtue," at the time the Constitution was framed and ratified the predominant concerns were otherwise.[26] Among the Framers were staunch supporters of civil liberties such as James Madison, James Wilson, Gouverneur Morris, and William Paterson (whose libertarian views will be reported later in this chapter). Each approved the proposed constitution. It is inconceivable that these ardent proponents of liberty would support a document creating an authoritarian government.

The bulk of the Framers were lawyers, property owners, and investors, and thus were persons who would likely be concerned about property rights. A major reason for the American Revolution was the English rejection of what the colonists regarded as their property and economic rights. They understood that a basic prerequisite for maintaining a voter-oriented society is the absence of power by elected officials to arbitrarily control the people's properties and enterprises. The people who voted to ratify the Constitution did not do so under the assumption that it would make them less free. On the contrary, they thought it would enhance their freedoms. The Constitution would also terminate democratic excesses, such as the passage of bills attainder, confiscatory laws, retroactive laws, and laws impairing the obligation of contracts, and other government actions that jeopardized their economic freedom.

The Framers were familiar with the common law and the many protections it offered the English and American people. The lawyers among them were well versed in the legal doctrines of Edward Coke and William Blackstone, both of whom defined the rights of the people against their government. In England and America, the courts did or were expected to advance these rights, and there is no reason to conclude that the new constitution would seriously interfere with the judiciary.

Under Coke's and Blackstone's interpretations of English law, government was substantially limited in its power to control private property. Each asserted that laws must be general and public-oriented, that is, not intended to favor or penalize select persons in the population. The legislature was deprived of the power to penalize people; this authority rested with the judiciary, which was expected to observe due process of law. Thus, retroactive laws were suspect and likely to be struck down.

The Framers of the Constitution confronted the great task of creating a strong government without it also being powerful enough to deprive its constituents of their liberties. The result was the establishment of a government of limited and enumerated powers with less authority over its constituents than probably any other government presently has or ever has had. The Framers protected liberty by eliminating the oppressive powers of government and not by mandating the government to provide people with benefits and entitlements. As with other liberties, they secured property rights by limiting government powers over them.

Accordingly, the government was structured to prevent any person or group of persons from being able to impose its unchecked will over the people. The Constitution separates the three branches of government, confines each to the exercise of specific powers, and grants each checks and balances over the others. According to James Madison, the most important of the Constitution's Framers, "[t]he powers delegated by the proposed Constitution to the federal government are few and defined [to be] exercised principally on external objects, as war, peace, negotiation and foreign commerce."[27] The federal government's "jurisdiction extends to certain enumerated objects only, and leaves to the several states a residuary and invioable sovereignty over all other objects."[28] Each of the branches has the power to monitor the other two to make certain that they stay within their limits. Even the Congress is divided into two bodies for additional dispersal of power.

The Constitution's Framers were implementing the consensus that existed in the late 1700s that a primary objective of government is to secure for its constituents "the Blessings of liberty," words which appear in the Preamble to the Constitution. Those who supported ratification of the Constitution, as well as those who opposed it, agreed on this objective, as law professor Herbert Storing has explained:

> If the Federalists and Anti-Federalists were divided among themselves they were, at a deeper level, united with one another. Their disagreements were not based on different premises about the nature of man or the ends of political life. They were not the deep cleavages of contending regimes. They were the much less sharp and clear cut differences within a family, as it were, of men agreed that the purpose of government is the regulation and thereby the protection of individual rights and that the best instrument for this purpose is some form of limited republican government.[29]

Pursuant to this perspective, the establishment of the constitutional government did not reduce the rights of the governed unless such an outcome was expressly provided for within the Constitution itself. The Constitution did not create those rights, and, therefore, it was not a source to which courts could turn for guidance about their breadth and character, except insofar as the document re-

strained and modified them. As the interpreter of the Constitution, the judiciary would be obliged to enforce the liberties of the people by striking down laws that violated them.

United States Supreme Court Justices Samuel Chase and Joseph Story later concluded that no court of justice in the country would be warranted in assuming that the power to violate and disregard the rights of personal liberties and private property lurked under any general grant of legislative authority.[30] New York Chancellor James Kent (the famous jurist and legal commentator) emphasized that the judges were not to be confined to protecting only rights enumerated in the Constitution: "Our Constitutions do not admit the power assumed by the Roman Prince and the principle we are considering [no retroactive laws] is now to be regarded as sacred. It is not pretended that we have any express constitutional provisions on the subject; nor have we any for numerous other rights dear alike to freedom and to justice."[31]

The Constitution and laws of the United States were predicated largely on the common law, which was dedicated to the rule of right and reason. English judges and Parliament had steadily expanded common-law protections; at one time only the meager rudiments of criminal procedure were required, while by Blackstone's day "absolute rights" to life, liberty, and property were acknowledged. During the late eighteenth century, the system was highly regarded in America as a guardian of individual rights. Americans looked to the common law to define their rights. For them the English constitution, which consisted of common-law rights, provided the greatest measure of human freedom.

As described above in Chapter 2, personal guarantees of rights were accepted and applied under the common law at the time the United States Constitution was ratified. Referring to advances in the criminal law, law professor J. A. C. Grant concludes that common-law processes, with occasional help from statutes, remade, in a little over two centuries, a cruel, one-sided system into the one that was inserted into the Constitution and that provided numerous guarantees for someone accused of a crime. He notes that the same general pattern of growth continued after ratification in accordance with common-law procedures.[32]

The ratification arguments over the protection of freedom of the press provide an illustration of the function that the judiciary would exercise in securing liberties. Hamilton wrote, in No. 84 of the *Federalist Papers,* that there was no need to be concerned about securing freedom of the press, inasmuch as the Constitution does not grant the government any power to restrain it.[33] Does this mean, then, that as far as the national government is concerned, freedom of the press is absolute, and not subject to any restraint? James Wilson (a framer of the Constitution, and later a Supreme Court justice) explained during the ratification debates that freedom of the press was subject to the powers of government under the common law, which were then considerable. In other words, the national government had no power to diminish freedom of the press as the term

was defined under the common law.[34] However, the national government could still penalize criminal libel, which the common law did not protect under its authority in criminal matters. Accordingly, the rights of Americans at the time of the framing of the Constitution were largely defined by the common law.

Wilson's explanation is applicable to the other rights of Englishmen. Since there was no provision in the Constitution granting the federal government the power, for example, to acquire or regulate private property, the exercise of that right remained under the substantive and procedural protections of the common law.

In addition to limiting the powers of government, the U.S. Constitution also protected liberty by separating and dividing government. The government is divided into three branches—executive, legislative, and judicial—and each has powers to curb certain powers of the other two. While governments in other countries observe some separation of powers, the branches of no other government have as much overlapping power as the executive, legislative, and judicial branches of the United States government have over each other. Suppose, for example, that the Congress passes a law imposing severe use restrictions on certain lands. The President has the power to veto the law, an action which can only be overturned by a two-thirds vote of each house of the Congress. The federal judiciary may find the law enacted by Congress unconstitutional, an action which cannot be reversed by Congress. However, Congress has the power to limit the appellate jurisdiction of the U.S. Supreme Court, a power it might use in the event it concludes that the Supreme Court is violating its constitutional responsibility.

As can be seen from the separation and division of powers, the Framers protected the people's liberties from abridgement by the national government. In addition, they protected the people's liberties by enumerating a small number of rights, most of which directly or indirectly protected property rights. Thus, the Constitution contains two *ex post facto* clauses, both of which prohibit the federal government and the states from enacting legislation that retroactively makes an action illegal that was legal at the time it occurred. The evidence is persuasive that the clauses were also intended to secure the right of property from retroactive impositions. However, the 1798 case of *Calder v. Bull* held that the *ex post facto* clauses related only to criminal and not civil matters, a decision which has never been overruled.[35] Many constitutional scholars have disagreed with this interpretation over the years, contending that the clauses were intended to be broadly construed so as to include civil matters.[36]

Another major protection for property are the two clauses prohibiting the passage of bills of attainder by the federal and state governments. A bill of attainder is a legislative act that inflicts punishment without a judicial trial. Originally, the term was limited to capital punishment, but in time it was applied to legislative confiscation of property.[37] Protection against state abridgement of property rights is also contained in Article IV, Section 5, which states that the citizens of each state "shall be entitled to all the Privileges and Immunities of

Citizens in the Several States." This clause was intended to protect the exercise of property and other fundamental rights (as will be explained in Chapter 6, Section II *infra*).

The strongest protection for property rights against infringement by the national government was the common law that defined the "rights of Englishmen," as discussed extensively in the previous chapter. The Constitution did not provide the authority for any branch of government to limit these rights. However, the structural and enumerated restraints on constitutional power were insufficient by themselves to prevent the government from treating people unequally and not impartially. Madison expressed these apprehensions in No. 44 of the *Federalist Papers:*

> The sober people of America are weary of the fluctuating policy which has directed the public councils. They have seen with regret and indignation that sudden changes and legislative interferences, in cases affecting personal rights, become jobs in the hands of enterprising and influential speculators, and snares to the more industrious and less informed parts of the community. They have seen, too, that one legislative interference is but the first link of a long chain of repetitions, every subsequent interference being naturally produced by the effects of the preceding. They very rightly infer, therefore, that some thorough reform is wanting, which will banish speculations on public measures, inspire a general prudence and industry, and give a regular course to the business of society.[38]

To prohibit such abuses by holders of political or administrative office, the Framers inserted protections against the arbitrary dispensing of favors or preferences and imposing of penalties. A summary of such protections is as follows. Consistent with the ideas of Coke, Blackstone, and Locke, they sought to eliminate legislative power to pass special laws, as distinguished from general public laws that are applicable to the entire population. The citizens of each state were entitled to all privileges and immunities of citizens in the several states (Art. IV, Sec. 2). The federal government was limited in its power to suspend the writ of habeas corpus (Art. I, Sec. 9), to give preferences to ports (Art. I, Sec. 9), to pass bills of attainder and *ex post facto* laws (Art. I, Sec. 9), and to grant titles of nobility (Art. I, Sec. 9). Moreover, jury trials were required in all criminal matters, usually to be held in the state where the crime was committed (Art. III, Sec. 2); treason was narrowly defined (Art. III, Sec. 3); and no religious test was ever to be required as a qualification for any office or public trust (Art. VI). Congress could impose and collect taxes, duties, imposts, and excises only for the purpose of paying the debts and providing for the common defense and general welfare of the United States (Art. I, Sec. 8). In No. 41 of the *Federalist Papers,* Madison explained that the term "general welfare," contained in the first

paragraph of Article I, Section 8, was confined to the specific powers listed in the balance of that section. (The general welfare clause will be discussed in Section V of this chapter.) All duties, imposts, and excises were required to be uniform throughout the nation (Art. I, Sec. 8). Direct taxes had to be levied in proportion to the population of the state (Art. I, Sec. 9). No tax or duty could be imposed on exports from a state (Art. I, Sec. 9).

With reference to property rights, these provisions limit the power of the Congress and other officials of government to either harm or help owners and entrepreneurs. Legislatures that have the power to pass the kinds of laws forbidden under the U.S. Constitution, and presidents who have the authority to veto or approve them, have enormous discretion over the lives, liberties, and properties of their constituents. Economic markets cannot function equitably or efficiently when government has great discretionary powers over participants in those markets. As Madison observed, a just security to private property "is not afforded by that government under which unequal taxes oppress one species of property, and reward another species."[39] The Framers were essentially applying the admonitions of Coke, Blackstone, and Locke against the adoption of laws that would either benefit or harm particular persons or groups.

"[T]he Constitution," Hamilton asserted, "is itself, in every rational sense, and to every useful purpose, A BILL OF RIGHTS."[40] Thus, he thought, there was no need for framing an additional bill of rights. However, the public's demand for the insertion of explicit personal protections of liberties in the Constitution led to the framing of the Bill of Rights by the First Congress in 1789.

IV. James Madison: The Most Important and Influential Framer

Of the 55 delegates to the Constitutional Convention of 1787, the most important and influential was James Madison (1751–1836). He came to the convention as a delegate from Virginia at the young age of 36, well prepared for this role. By then he was an experienced politician who had exhibited considerable pragmatic and scholarly wisdom. His accomplishments were many. In 1776 he helped draft a constitution for his state of Virginia. He served in the Continental Congress from 1780 to 1783 and 1787 to 1788, and represented his county in the Virginia legislature from 1784 to 1786. During his service in the Virginia legislature, he played an important role in disestablishing the Anglican Church. He displayed a remarkable understanding of government in the letters and papers he wrote prior to 1787, and particularly so later in his essays during the ratification debates of 1788, which, together with those of Alexander Hamilton and John Jay, became the *Federalist Papers,* considered by many to be a political science classic.

Madison sought to achieve a monumental feat of statesmanship in causing thirteen independent republics to relinquish their sovereignty and unite into one

republic. Equally important, the new nation was to be structured in order to successfully accommodate majority and minority interests, to achieve, in short, "a republican remedy for the diseases most incident to republican government."[41] As Madison later acknowledged in No. 14 of the *Federalist Papers,* the form of government that emerged from the 1787 Convention was a "novelty in the political world"; the Framers had created a political structure which had "no model on the face of the globe."

This Convention initially was intended to be a meeting of states to reform the Articles of Confederation. The states were to consider reducing their sovereignty sufficiently to eliminate local protectionism and other serious impediments to commerce that existed among them. This meant deleting barriers to economic freedom among and within the states. Instead of proposing changes to the articles, Madison drew up the Virginia Plan—submitted to the Convention by John Randolph—proposing a national government obligated to fulfill the will of the people and not of the states. Unlike the league of states that existed under the Articles of Confederation, the new national government would represent and obey the people within its borders. The states retained considerable powers, but their status was to be subsidiary to the national power. Indeed, Madison is entitled to be identified as the father of the Constitution, because the structure and organization of the United States government is substantially his creation.

Prior to the Constitutional Convention, Madison engaged in extensive preparation for his role in establishing a new government by avidly reading authoritative works he regarded as helpful to this undertaking. His good friend Thomas Jefferson served as his book buyer when the latter was in France as American minister to that country.[42] Jefferson sent him two trunks of books, including the collected works of the Scottish philosopher and historian David Hume (1711–1776). In his college years and afterward, Madison showed great interest in a group of Scottish moral philosophers—led by Hume, Adam Smith, and Adam Ferguson—that espoused the English tradition of liberty as reflected in, among other things, the common law. This group found the essence of freedom in spontaneity and the absence of governmental coercion. They believed that institutions and morals evolve by cumulative growth without authoritarian direction. This position sharply conflicted with the French tradition, which depended on the state to control society.[43]

Historian Douglas Adair referred to Madison's intensive reading of Hume as perhaps the most productive and consequential act of scholarship in American history. Hume's detailed accounts and analysis of the political and economic history of ancient and modern nations offered Madison a vast historic understanding of civil society.[44] According to historian Drew McCoy, "Hume's influence on Madison now (1989) appears indisputable."[45] Hume rejected a prevalent idea of his time that no large area could ever be modelled into a republican state. While Hume thought that it would be more difficult to form a

republican government in a large than in a small territory, "there is more facility, when once it is formed, of preserving it steady and uniform, without tumolt and faction." Madison came to the same conclusion, as he set forth in No. 10 of the *Federalist Papers* and earlier writings, and his thinking in this respect is attributed by a number of authors to the study of Hume.[46]

In view of Madison's intense exposure to Hume, it is worth considering some of the positions Hume espoused that were then relevant to Madison's constitutional concerns. Historian Forrest McDonald states that several times during the constitutional convention, Hamilton and Madison quoted or paraphrased Hume without acknowledging they were doing so.[47] The same lack of acknowledgment of Hume is also evident in some of Madison's writings.[48] Best known for his writings in history and philosophy, Hume also contributed to a host of other intellectual disciplines. I will briefly describe his views on political and economic theory.

In his *History of England,* Hume writes that the Magna Carta of 1215 provided for the equal distribution of justice and the free enjoyment of property. Both provisions were "the great objects for which political society was at first founded by men, which the people have a perpetual and unalienable right to recall, and which no time, nor precedent, nor statute, no positive institution, ought to deter them from keeping ever uppermost in their thoughts and attention."[49] However, Hume rejected Locke's idea that the state was formed by a social compact consensually adopted in the state of nature. He insisted that governments were often created by fraud, force, or conquest and, therefore, the people should exercise restraint in their allegiance to the state.[50]

Hume's economic writings are considered to be an important influence in the transition from mercantilist (i.e., government controlled) to classical liberal doctrine (i.e., market controlled). He died in 1776, the year in which his close friend Adam Smith's *The Wealth of Nations* was published. Smith is generally regarded as the founder of the laissez-faire school of economics. Before his death, Hume wrote to Smith that *The Wealth of Nations* "has Depth and Solidity and acuteness, and is so much illustrated by curious Facts, that it must at last take the public attention." While he disputed some of Smith's conclusions, Hume wrote, "I am much pleased with your performance."[51] It is apparent that the two men viewed the origins and objectives of organized society quite similarly.

Hume supported freedom for commerce as essential to the success and progress of government, accepting the following maxim as generally true:

> The greatness of a state, and the happiness of its subjects, how independent soever they may be supposed in some respects, are commonly allowed to be inseparable with regard to commerce; and as private men receive greater security, in the possession of their trade and riches, from the power of the public, so the public becomes powerful in proportion to the opulence and extensive commerce of private men.[52]

Hume also observed that while the rules protecting property benefit society, this may at times be harmful:

> All the laws of nature, which regulate property, as well as all civil laws, are general, and regard alone some essential circumstances of the case, without taking into consideration the characters, situations, and connexions of the person concerned, or any particular consequences which may result from the determination of these laws, in any particular case. . . . Public utility requires, that property should be regulated by general inflexible rules; and though such rules are adopted as best serve the same end of public utility, it is impossible for them to prevent all particular hardships, or make beneficial consequences result from every individual case. It is sufficient, if the whole plan or scheme be necessary to the support of civil society, and if the balance of good, in the main, do thereby preponderate much above that of evil.[53]

Hume was, additionally, a vigorous opponent of measures to impose "perfect equality" in property holdings. This was because first, "man's different degrees of art, care, and industry will immediately break" it, and second, it will "reduce society to the most extreme indigence; and instead of preventing want and beggery in a few, render it unavoidable to the whole community."[54]

Hume supported freedom for both domestic and foreign commerce and, consequently, opposed tariffs, duties, and domestic economic restrictions. He condemned price ceilings as applied by Parliament to farm commodities when production was low and those imposed during the reign of King Henry VII to promote archery by keeping the prices of bows low. He concluded that both efforts were counterproductive, because such laws "aggravate the evil by cramping and restraining commerce."[55] He explained the great benefits that society obtains when entrepreneurs seek their own interest by increasing production — the process Adam Smith referred to as the "invisible hand." In *The Wealth of Nations,* Smith cites Hume at least six times. When Hume died, Smith wrote that his friend was as "perfectly wise and virtuous a man as perhaps the nature of human frailty will admit."[56]

Madison gave great thought to the problem of creating a nation that would be based on the will of its constituents and that would also protect the rights of persons in that nation. In his many letters to friends and political colleagues, he frequently expressed concern about the proclivities of majorities in the economic area. Having served in legislative bodies, he was wary of the political process; yet he was always committed to a society dominated by the vote of its people. As historian Jack Rakove puts it, "[b]y 1786, Madison had come to doubt whether most state legislators could ever be relied upon to act responsibly on either state or federal issues."[57] Madison was particularly fearful that the rights of property would be insecure in the hands of an unlimited legislature; a

free society could not exist in the absence of these rights: "I see no reason why the rights of property which chiefly bears the burden of Government and is so much an object of Legislation should not be respected as well as personal rights in the choice of Rulers."[58]

Consistent with Hume's views, Madison was much less concerned about the fate of liberty in a national than in a state government. The reason was that political or economic factions would have more difficulty in achieving their goals in larger jurisdictions where there would be more of them limiting the power of each. In a large territory, the society becomes broken into a greater variety of interests, of pursuits, of passions, which check each other, while those who may feel a common sentiment have less opportunity of communication and concern.[59] Size was not to be the only factor operating to minimize the tyranny of national government. The separation of powers and the limitation of powers would also function to prevent political factions and government officials from exercising excessive influence over the populace. The extent of Madison's and other framers' concerns about governmental power are reflected in the many limitations the Constitution contains on the exercise of powers by governmental branches. Due to his concern about state governments, Madison favored giving Congress a veto over state legislation, a proposal which was never adopted. During the Convention he rejected including a bill of rights in the Constitution as unnecessary and unenforceable, but later changed his position and, as a member of the First Congress, introduced amendments that would become the major source of the Bill of Rights.

Madison's concerns about the failings and infirmities of legislative bodies resulted from his three years as a member of the Virginia House of Delegates. Far from being dedicated to the public good, he believed that most of the legislators were pursuing their own political or financial interests. Before coming to Philadelphia to participate in the Constitutional Convention, Madison wrote two memoranda. The first he titled, "Notes of Ancient and Modern Confederacies," and the second, "Vices of the Political System of the United States." In the first, he summarized the history of six confederacies, and concluded that in the past no confederacy of large size remained stable without the absolute control of a monarch. In "Vices," he raised the question of whether the majorities who ruled in the states were actually safeguarding both the public good and private rights. He concluded that neither objective had been achieved in the states and ascribed the problem to both the representative bodies and the people themselves. The expected restraints of political office had not produced just and fair governments. Reliance on (1) "a prudent regard" for the common good, (2) "respect for character," and (3) the restraints of religious faith—all of which were then considered as leading to good government—are not sufficient to cause legislatures to protect the rights of minorities and individuals. Only a republic encompassing a large area could impose "modification of the sovereignty" of the

states, because its numerous and assorted factions would be likely to neutralize each other.

Turning his attention to political leaders, Madison wrote that men seek public office to achieve ambition, personal interest, or public good. "Unhappily, the two first are proved by experience to be most prevalent," he lamented,

> [h]ence, the candidates who feel them, particularly the second, are most industrious and most successful in pursuing their object; and forming often a majority in the legislative Councils, with interested views, contrary to the interest and views of their constituents, join in a perfidious sacrifice of the latter to the former. A succeeding election, it might be supposed, would displace the offenders, and repair the mischief. But how easily are base and selfish measures masked by pretexts of public good and apparent expediency? How frequently will a repetition of the same arts and industry which succeeded in the first instance again prevail on the unwary to misplace their confidence?
>
> How frequently, too, will the honest but unenlightened representatives be the dupe of a favorite leader, veiling his selfish views under the professions of public good, and varnishing his sophistical arguments with the glowing colors of popular eloquence?
>
> A still more fatal, if not more frequent cause, lies among the people themselves. All civilized societies are divided into different interests and factions, as they happen to be creditors or debtors, rich or poor, husbandmen, merchants, or manufacturers, members of different religious sects, followers of different political leaders, inhabitants of different districts, owners of different kinds of property, &c., &c. In republican Government, the majority, however composed, ultimately give the law. Whenever, therefore, an apparent interest or common passion unites a majority, what is to restrain them from unjust violations of the rights and interests of the minority, or of individuals? Three motives only: 1. A prudent regard to their own good, as involved in the general and permanent good of the community. This consideration, although of decisive weight in itself, is found by experience to be too often unheeded. It is too often forgotten, by nations as well as by individuals, that honesty is the best policy. 2dly. Respect for character. However strong this motive may be in individuals, it is considered as very insufficient to restrain them from injustice. . . . Is it to be imagined that an ordinary citizen or evan an Assembly-man of R. Island, in estimating the policy of paper money, ever considered or cared in what light the measure would be viewed in France or Holland; or even in Massachusetts or Connecticut? It was a sufficient temptation to both that it was for their interest; it was a sufficient sanction to the latter that it was popular in the State; to the former that it was so in the neighborhood. . . . 3dly. Will

Religion, the only remaining motive, be a sufficient restraint? It is not pretended to be such, on men individually considered. Will its effect be greater on them considered in an aggregate view? Quite the reverse. The conduct of every popular assembly acting on oath, the strongest of religious ties, proves that individuals join without remorse in acts against which their consciences would revolt if proposed to them under the like sanction, separately, in their closets. . . .[60]

Madison was understandably critical of pure democracies, because of his pessimism about the motives of people generally:

A common passion or interest will, in almost every case, be felt by a majority of the whole; a communication and concern results from the form of government itself; and there is nothing to check the inducements to sacrifice the weaker party, or an obnoxious individual. Hence it is, that such Democracies have ever been spectacles of turbulence and contention; have ever been found incompatible with personal security, or the rights of property and have in general been as short in their lives, as they have been violent in their deaths. Theoretic politicians, who have patronized this species of government, have erroneously supposed in their political rights, they would, at the same time, be perfectly equalized and assimilated in their possessions, their opinions, and their passions.[61]

He thus feared that a pure democracy would render personal and property rights precarious at best.

In a subsequent essay, Madison viewed the inherent problems of representative government as also especially perilous for property rights in times of public instability, because of

the unreasonable advantage it gives to the sagacious, the enterprising, and the moneyed few over the industrious and uniformed mass of the people. Every new regulation concerning commerce or revenue, or in any manner affecting the value of the different species of property, presents a new harvest to those who watch the change, and can trace its consequences; a harvest, reared not by themselves, but by the toils and cares of the great body of their fellow-citizens. This is a state of things in which it may be said with some truth that laws are made for the *few,* not for the *many.*[62]

Although Madison based his criticism of legislative bodies on his experience as a state legislator and wrote favorably about a large republic, his support for a government of separated and limited powers shows that his concerns applied to government officials and politicians in general. Indeed, Madison viewed leg-

islators from a perspective that modern society identifies as public choice theory. Under the reasoning of public choice theory, legislators frequently vote to benefit no one other than themselves. As the leading theorists of public choice theory, economists James Buchanan and Gordon Tullock explain that in

> the face of observable pressure-group activity, with its demonstrable results on the outcome of specific issues presented and debated in legislative assemblies, the behavioral premise that calls for the legislator to follow a selfless pursuit of the "public interest" or the "general welfare" as something independent of and apart from private economic interest is severely threatened.[63]

As can be gleaned from his views on government generally, Madison showed particular interest in the protection of property rights. In an essay in the *National Gazette* of March 29, 1792, Madison offered two meanings of "property." The first meaning, paraphrasing Blackstone, was "that domination which one man claims and exercises over the external things of the world, in exclusion of every other individual," while the second meaning was that property "embraces every thing to which a man may attach a value and have a right; and which leaves to every one else the like advantages." Thus, a man's land, merchandise, and money are called his property. A man also has property in his opinions, religious beliefs, safety, and liberty of his person: "In a word, as a man is said to have a right to his property, he may be equally said to have a property in his rights."[64]

Government is instituted, Madison wrote, to protect property of every sort— that which lies in the various rights of the individual, as well as that which refers to his material possessions. "This being the end of government, that alone is just government, which impartially secures to every man, whatever is his own." Madison was critical of excessive regulation: "When an excess of power prevails, property of no sort is duly respected. No man is safe in his opinion, his person, his faculties or his possessions." He continues with a lengthy explanation of how excessive regulation can infringe on property rights:

> That is not just government, nor is property secure under it, where arbitrary restrictions, exemptions, and monopolies deny to part of its citizens the free use of their faculties, and free choice of their occupations, which not only constitute their property in the general sense of the word; but are the means of acquiring property strictly so called. . . .
>
> A just security to property is not afforded by that government under which unequal taxes oppress one species of property and reward another species; where arbitrary taxes invade the domestic sanctuaries of the rich, and excessive taxes grind the faces of the poor. . . .

If there be a government then which prides itself on maintaining the inviolability of property; which provides that none shall be taken *directly* even for public use without indemnification to the owner, and yet *directly* violates the property which individuals have in their opinions, their religion, their persons, and their faculties; nay more, which *indirectly* violates their property, in their actual possessions, in the labor that acquires their daily subsistence, and in the hallowed remnant of time which ought to relieve their fatigues and soothe their cares, the inference will have been anticipated, that such a government is not a pattern for the United States.

If the United States mean to obtain or deserve the full praise due to wise and just governments, they will equally respect the rights of property, and the property in rights.[65]

Madison voiced apprehensions about what would occur in the absence of protections for property rights:

An increase of population will of necessity increase the proportion of those who will labour under all the hardships of life, secretly sigh for a more equal distribution of its blessings. These may in time outnumber those who are placed above the feelings of indigence. According to the equal laws of suffrage, the power will slide into the hands of the former. No agrarian attempts have yet been made in this Country, but symptoms of a leveling spirit . . . have sufficiently appeared in certain quarters to give notice of the future danger.[66]

Madison briefly summarized his libertarian position on economic freedom in a speech in the First Congress on May 9, 1789:

I own myself the friend to a very free system of commerce, and hold it as a truth, that commercial shackles are generally unjust, oppressive, and impolitic; it is also a truth, that if industry and labor are left to take their own course, they will generally be directed to those objects which are the most productive, and this in a more certain and direct manner than the wisdom of the most enlightened Legislature could point out.[67]

Madison viewed the Bill of Rights as codifying the restraints of the common law on the powers of government. The Bill of Rights confirmed and broadened the "rights of Englishmen" and thereby further confined the government's authority; it clearly did not enlarge the power of government to control the people. To be sure, my interpretation of Madison's position on property rights as being libertarian is not universally accepted. Some writers reject this interpre-

tation and view Madison as favoring government controls over property in order to assure the best use of it. In his biography of Madison, Irving Brant asserts that Madison's objective with respect to property was to make certain that it was wisely used:

> It is easy and erroneous to simplify that into a mere statement that governments are set up to protect property rights. . . . But Madison was well aware that in a competitive society, with public order and private rights maintained, property would flow ceaselessly into the hands of the most able to gain and hold it. He was practically saying, therefore, that one of the first objects of government was to protect the poor and near poor by laws restraining concentration of wealth and the power of its holders.[68]

Brant's analysis completely mistakes Madison's perspective concerning property. To achieve the objective that Brant identifies requires great controls over private property, but this is the opposite of what Madison believed. He believed that the public would be better served by liberty, which would enable the creative and productive forces of mankind to flourish, and not by government, which would impede these forces. The protections of the Bill of Rights are negative in character; they are intended to negate laws that restrict the exercise of liberties. The bill does not impose affirmative economic obligations on either the government or the private sector. In the words of Judge Richard Posner: "The men who wrote the Bill of Rights were not concerned that government might do too little for the people but that it might do too much to them."[69]

V. Madison and the Separation of Powers

A separation of powers exists in nearly every government. Some of a government's officials are engaged in making laws, others are engaged in enforcing these laws, and still others are engaged in interpreting them. Thus we have a separation of legislative, executive, and judicial functions, the kind of separation the Framers required for the U.S. government. Both Charles de Secondat, baron de Montesquieu, the famed French philosopher, and Blackstone viewed the separation of powers as essential for the preservation of liberty. Montesquieu wrote that liberty is jeopardized when "the legislative and executive powers are united in the same person" and when "a judiciary power [is] not separated from the legislative and executive. . . . [A]pprehensions may arise, lest the same monarch or senate should enact tyrannical laws, to execute them in a tyrannical manner." Similar concerns should exist if the judge "were joined with the legislative . . . or executive power." He urged that the executive be given the power to restrain the legislature and that the legislature possess some controls over the judiciary.[70] Blackstone generally agreed with Mon-

tesquieu and, in addition, viewed the separation of powers as enhancing efficiency and well-being:

> Like three distinct powers in mechanics, they jointly impelled the machine of government in a direction different from what either, acting by themselves, would have done; but at the same time in a direction partaking of each, informed out of all; a direction which constitutes the true line of the liberty and happiness of the community.[71]

The U.S. Constitution was framed at an early period in the nation's history when most (or at least a large portion) of the population owned and farmed land. The Framers believed that, in the hands of this group, the country would remain politically free and the economy stable and prosperous. Many of them subscribed to Blackstone's "stake in society" theory that the interests of property owners required stable government. They wrote a document that would ensure this result under existing as well as future conditions, when much less land would be available for farming and the bulk of the population might be employees instead of landowners. Madison feared that the problems associated with widely disparate wealth and income would create serious tensions among the population, leading even possibly to insurrections. To preclude this outcome, the American republic should be large enough to include a huge diversity of interests, coupled with a diversity of state and federal powers.

English America was very receptive to the separation of powers. Over time, state and federal constitutions adopted in varying degrees the separation system. John Adams, in drafting the Massachusetts Constitution of 1780, considered the separation of powers as essential to preventing despotism—this was a common view in the states.[72] While most nations of the world have now accepted the separation principle, to the best of my knowledge none has applied it as broadly in text and as vigorously in implementation as has the United States.

Madison was the leading theoretician among the Framers on the subject of the separation of powers. In replying to the Anti-Federalists' concerns about excessive government powers in the proposed Constitution, Madison devoted five numbers of the *Federalist Papers* to explaining the Constitution's separation of powers.[73] The separation of powers consisted of two parts: first, the division of functions; and second, the checks and balances held by each branch with respect to the others. Responding to attacks on the proposed Constitution that it created a very powerful government, Madison asserted: "Were the federal Constitution, therefore, really chargeable with this accumulation of power, or with a mixture of powers, having a dangerous tendency to such an accumulation, no further arguments would be necessary to inspire universal reprobation of the system."[74] An opponent of majority rule, Madison extolled the separation principle: "No political truth is certainly of greater intrinsic value, or is

stamped with the authority of more enlightened patrons of liberty. . . ."[75] He clearly looked down upon the non-separation of powers: "The accumulation of all powers, legislative, executive, and judiciary, in the same hands, whether of one, a few, or many, and whether hereditary, self-appointed, or elective, may justly be pronounced the very definition of tyranny."[76]

Under the proposed division of government, power was to be distributed to prevent any individual, faction, or segment of the population—no matter what its political power or its numbers were—from obtaining control of the entire government. Separation would not only be accomplished by the legal text but also by "so contriving the interior structure of the government so that its several constituent parts may, by their mutual relations, be the means of keeping each other in their proper places."[77] The latter means is the system of checks and balances:

> But the great security against a gradual concentration of the several powers in the same department consists in giving to those who administer each department the necessary constitutional means and personal motives to resist encroachments of the others. The provision for defense must in this, as in all other cases, be made commensurate to the danger of attack. Ambition must be made to counteract ambition. The interest of the man must be connected with the constitutional rights of the place. . . . In framing a government which is to be administered by men over men, the great difficulty lies in this: you must first enable the government to control the governed; and in the next place oblige it to control itself. A dependence on the people is no doubt, the primary control on the government; but experience has taught mankind the necessity of auxiliary precautions.[78]

Under the separation of powers, government power would be used to control government power. As previously noted, Madison was particularly concerned about legislative excesses: "In republican government the legislative authority necessarily predominates."[79] The experience in this regard had been very poor: "The legislative department is everywhere extending the sphere of its activity and drawing all power into its impetuous vortex."[80] The legislature "was the real source of danger to the American Constitution [necessitating] giving every defensive authority to the other departments that was consistent with republican principles."[81] Madison rejected majority rule as a matter of principle. In a letter to Jefferson, he asserted that the invasion of private rights is chiefly to be apprehended "from acts in which the Government is the mere instrument of the major number of the constituents."[82] According the legislature unlimited power, Madison wrote, violated a fundamental principle of a free society:

> No man is allowed to be a judge in his own cause, because his interest would certainly bias his judgment, and, not improbably, corrupt his integrity. With

equal, nay with greater reason, a body of men are unfit to be both judges and parties at the same time; yet what are many of the most important acts of legislation but so many judicial determinations, not indeed concerning the rights of single persons, but concerning the rights of large bodies of citizens? And what are the different classes of legislators but advocates and parties to the causes which they determine?[83]

Madison's views on separation of powers were also reflected in the writings of Thomas Jefferson and Alexander Hamilton. According to Jefferson,

173 despots would surely be as oppressive as one. . . . Little will it avail us that they are chosen by ourselves. . . . The government we fought for [is] one which should not only be founded on free principles, but in which the powers of government should be so divided and balanced among several bodies of magistracy, as that no one could transcend their legal limits, without being effectually checked and restrained by the others. For this reason that convention, which passed the ordinance of government, laid its foundation on this bases, that the legislative, executive and judiciary departments should be separate and distinct, so that no person should exercise the powers of more than one of them at the same time. . . . If . . . the legislature assumes executive and judiciary powers, no opposition is likely to be made; nor, if made, can it be effectual; because in that case they may put their proceedings into the form of an act of assembly, which will render them obligatory on the other branches. They have accordingly in many instances, decided rights which should have been left to judiciary controversy. . . .[84]

Alexander Hamilton similarly wrote:

Nothing is more common than for a free people, in times of heat and violence, to gratify momentary passions, by letting into the government principles and precedents which afterwards prove fatal to themselves. Of this kind is the doctrine of disqualification, disfranchisement, and banishment by acts of the legislature. The dangerous consequences of this power are manifest. If the legislature can disfranchise any number of citizens at pleasure by general descriptions, it may soon confine all the votes to a small number of partisans, and establish an aristocracy or an oligarchy; if it may banish at discretion all those whom particular circumstances render obnoxious, without hearing or trial, no man can be safe, nor know when he may be the innocent victim of a prevailing faction. The name of liberty applied to such a government, would be a mockery of common sense.[85]

The separation of powers in the Constitution was the Framers' primary structural solution for governmental abuses and excesses; an effectual precaution "for keeping them virtuous whilst they continue to hold their public trust."[86] If the government were separated into three branches on the basis of function, each branch would exert its best efforts to consolidate and impose its powers at the expense of the other parts of government. In advancing its own interests, a particular branch would also be likely to restrain other parts of government with the result that no one part of government would be supreme—"that the private interest of every individual may be a sentinel over the public rights."[87] While the separation of functions was an organizational principle for the new government, the more important requirement for those who feared the evil propensities of officials, legislatures, and majorities was checks and balances. After all, the objective of the separation of powers, the key element of the government's structure, is to protect and preserve liberty by limiting the powers of government.

As subsequent jurisprudence has revealed, the requirements both of division of powers as well as of checks and balances are not clearly defined. Law professor Gerhard Casper—echoing the words of William Gwyn—has observed this about the Framers' position on the separation of powers: "No consensus existed as to the precise constitutional arrangements that would satisfy the requirements of the doctrine. The only matter on which agreement existed was what it meant not to have separation of powers: it meant tyranny."[88] Given this ambiguity about structure, it is understandable that the U.S. Supreme Court has decided cases with the general objective of securing liberty notwithstanding the absence of constitutional language supporting a particular outcome.

Separation of powers and checks and balances are not always compatible concerns. Checks and balances require a commingling of powers at times. As Madison put it, separation of powers "does not mean that these [three] departments ought to have no partial agency in, or no control over the acts of each other."[89] The Constitution provides for such commingling: the presidential veto over legislation, the judiciary's power of judicial review over legislation, the Congress's power to control the appellate jurisdiction of the Supreme Court and to create courts "inferior" to it, the Senate's confirmation of executive and judicial officers, the Senate's ratification of treaties negotiated by the President, and the Congress's power to impeach and remove executive and judicial officers. Because judicial review is not defined or even mentioned in the Constitution, the judiciary's power to annul legislation may at times exceed mere interpretation and include the kind of judicial policy-making consistent with common law practices.[90] (For a full discussion of judicial review, see Section VI *infra*.)

Separation of powers makes it more difficult for government to adopt legislation, thus according people greater freedom to engage in the actions and activities of their choice. Since legislation may be either good or bad in its effect, the Framers' concern was to block the undesirable variety, even at the expense

of reducing desirable legislation. One may conclude that they were willing to accept the burden of limiting legislative power because of the evils they associated with it and their belief that the nation would not suffer from the adoption of a lesser number of laws. The separation of powers doctrine is very revealing about the Framers' attitude about government; they relied on liberty rather than authority to advance individual and societal interests.

The separation of powers requirement has often been criticized as being inefficient. The comparison is made with unitary government, such as the one in England, where the decision-making process is largely the responsibility of elected legislators. Legislation under that system does not have to undergo the controversy and delay necessitated by the involvement of the executive and judicial branches. Separation of powers, however, does provide for efficiency in two respects. First, it recognizes special executive and judicial concerns that make legislation more durable and fair. Second, it provides for stable and viable legislation that may last for long periods. The checks and balances aspect of the separation of powers is premised on the belief that liberty is best served by reducing rather than enhancing government's power. The sharing of the lawmaking power between legislators, executors, and judges makes it more difficult to pass laws that control private decisions and initiatives, upon which the society depends for welfare and progress. In particular, the separation of powers seeks to prevent each branch from imposing arbitrary and capricious laws on the people—a consideration that has more to do with protecting liberty than with ensuring efficiency. As can be seen from the above discussion, though, protecting liberty does not have to come at the expense of efficiency.

Chief Justice Warren E. Burger, in *I.N.S. v. Chadha,* replied as follows to justices who sought to terminate strict interpretation of the separation doctrine:

> The choices we discern as having been made in the Constitutional Convention impose burdens on governmental processes that often seem clumsy, inefficient, even unworkable, but those hard choices were consciously made by men who had lived under a form of government that permitted arbitrary governmental acts to go unchecked. There is no support in the Constitution or decisions of this Court for the proposition that the cumbersomeness and delays often encountered in complying with explicit Constitutional standards may be avoided, either by the Congress or by the president. . . . With all the obvious flaws of delay, untidiness, and potential for abuse, we have not yet found a better way to preserve freedom than by making the exercise of power subject to the carefully crafted restraints spelled out in the Constitution.[91]

Madison, Jefferson, and Hamilton were far from being alone in fearing majoritarian power. Framer James Wilson observed that after the destruction of

royal supremacy in England, "a more pure and unmixed tyranny sprang up in the parliament than had been exercised by the monarch."[92] Other Framers viewed state legislators unfavorably. Gouverneur Morris found in every state legislative department "excesses [against] personal liberty and private property [and] personal safety,"[93] and Edmund Randolph presented the Virginia Plan to the Convention to overcome the "turbulence and follies of democracy."[94]

Hamilton described the dangers that an unlimited legislature posed for a society:

> Are not popular assemblies frequently subject to the impulses of rage, resentment, jealousy, avarice, and of other irregular and violent propensities? Is it not well known that their determinations are often governed by a few individuals in which they place confidence and are, of course, liable to be tinctured by the passions and views of those individuals?[95]

Hamilton declared that the judiciary would never endanger the liberty of the people "so long as the judiciary remains truly distinct from both the legislature and the executive. For I agree that 'there is no liberty if the power of judging be not separated from the legislative and executive powers.' "[96] Hamilton exhibited great perception in these observations. The history of the Supreme Court has shown that its major failings occur when it seeks to exercise legislative or executive powers.[97]

In the United States, the people's liberties are protected not only by the separation of powers at the national level, but also by the separation of state and national powers and by the separation of powers within the states. "Hence," wrote Madison, "a double security arises to the rights of the people. The different governments will control each other at the same time that each will be controlled by itself."[98] Madison sought to strengthen this security by supporting in the Constitutional Convention Charles Pinkney's motion giving the Congress "authority to negative all laws [adopted by the states] which they should judge to be improper." (This motion was defeated.) Madison said that such a negative on the states was "absolutely necessary to a perfect system," and "was the mildest expedient that could be devised for preventing these mischiefs [of the states.] . . . The existence of such a check would prevent attempts to commit them."[99] Here again Madison exhibited his belief in the power of a veto as an effective structural force available in a republic to secure liberty. While the proposal for a negative on state legislation might appear as nothing more than a means of increasing the powers of the national government, it would on the whole operate to reduce government power since it would be a check on the states comparable to the veto powers that each branch of the national government has over the other branches. The net result would be a lesser amount of restraints on liberty at the state level. In a letter to Jefferson, Madison contended

that a national veto over laws in the states was essential to protect individual rights, and that a reform which does not include such a provision "must be materially defective."[100]

Fearing that legislative supremacy is hostile to freedom, the delegates to the 1787 Constitutional Convention rejected an effort to give Congress immense powers. The convention's Committee of Detail recommended that Congress be granted the sweeping power to provide "for the well managing and securing the common property and general interests and welfare of the United States," but the proposal failed to appear in any drafts of the Constitution.[101] This occurrence was not unusual. The convention refused to empower the national government to act in many areas; for example, to set up temporary governments in new states; to grant charters of incorporation; to create seminaries for the promotion of literature and the arts; to establish public institutions, rewards, and immunities for the promotion of agriculture, commerce, trades, and manufactures; to regulate stages on the post road; to establish a university; to encourage, by proper premiums and provisions, the advancement of useful knowledge and discoveries; to provide for opening and establishing canals; to emit bills of credit (which then meant printing unbacked paper for circulation as currency); and to make sumptuary laws. Each of these proposals was introduced and was then either voted down or not considered further outside of committee.[102] The Constitution lists the powers delegated to Congress. According to Alexander Hamilton, acts of the federal government "which are not pursuant to its constitutional powers . . . will be merely acts of usurpation, and deserve to be treated as such."[103]

The Framers' debate over whether Congress should have the power to print paper money that was not backed by precious metals is instructive on their meaning of enumerated authority. Because the powers to borrow money and to emit bills of credit had been granted to Congress under the Articles of Confederation, they were extended to the new government in an early draft of the Constitution prepared by the Committee of Detail. Gouverneur Morris of Pennsylvania opposed giving Congress the power to emit bills of credit, and he moved to strike the phrase authorizing it. Apparently, the delegates believed that the absence of language permitting the emission of bills of credit sufficed to deny Congress this authority. Although most delegates opposed granting this power, and the states voted nine to two in support of Morris's motion, no delegate sought to insert a specific ban.[104]

Madison exhibited adherence to a "strict interpretation" of the Constitution both as congressman and as president. In February 1791, he presented a general interpretation of the federal government's powers in a speech he delivered as a member of the First Congress where he opposed the Bill to Establish the Bank of the United States. This proposed legislation chartered the bank as a private national corporation with shares to be held jointly by the United States and private individuals. Although there was no specific authority in the Constitu-

tion authorizing Congress to charter such a bank, proponents of the legislation argued that the power was implied by powers that were specified and, in addition, authorized by the "necessary and proper" clause of the Constitution. Contained in Article I, Section 8, this clause states that Congress has the power to make all laws which shall be "necessary and proper for carrying into execution the foregoing [enumerated] powers." In rejecting these arguments, Madison stated that the Constitution did not make a general grant of power to the federal government; instead it was a grant solely of particular powers. The necessary and proper clause added no powers to those enumerated. "The clause is in fact merely declaratory of what would have resulted by unavoidable implication, as the appropriate and, as it were, technical means of executing those powers."[105] Madison took essentially this position in No. 44 of the *Federalist Papers,* explaining that if the proposed Constitution did not contain such a provision, "all the particular powers requisite as a means of executing the general powers would have resulted to the government by unavoidable implication."[106]

In 1817, during Madison's second term as president, he vetoed as unconstitutional the very popular Bonus Bill passed by Congress that called for appropriating federal funds for the construction of roads and canals throughout the country. The money was to come from a bonus already paid to the national government by the Second Bank of the United States and from all future dividends that the government would receive as an investor in the bank. The measure obtained strong support from both politically powerful persons and the general public as essential for the future development of the nation because the states were unable or unwilling to install the required roads and canals. The bill's proponents relied on two constitutional provisions as authority for it: first, the domestic commerce clause, which authorizes Congress to regulate commerce among the several states, and second, the introductory first paragraph of Article I, Section 8, which states in part that Congress has the power to lay taxes and provide for the common defense and general welfare. The latter clause is followed (after a uniform clause) by the enumeration of specific authorized powers.

Madison rejected both reasons provided by the bill's proponents. For him, the Bonus Bill accorded Congress powers that belonged to the states. Its passage threatened to transform the basic character of the nation's federalist system. The commerce clause, he asserted, cannot be regarded as authorizing such fundamental changes. As for the common defense and general welfare clause, the proposed interpretation would render "the special and careful enumeration of powers, which follow the clause, nugatory and improper." Such an interpretation, he stated, would give virtually unlimited powers to Congress, contrary to the meaning of the document, and exclude the judiciary from its participation in guarding the boundary between the powers of the federal government and those of the states.[107] Madison had previously discussed this issue in No.

41 of the *Federalist Papers,* stating there that it was absurd to contend that an enumeration of particulars which neither explain nor qualify the general meaning constitute a grant of substantive power. The interpretation proposed by the proponents of the Bonus Bill would require that the enumeration of powers be considered as virtually meaningless.

Madison was, however, amenable to allowing legal precedent to be decisive in very special circumstances, even when contrary to his strict interpretation of the Constitution. In 1815, he vetoed a bill to recharter the national bank, but unlike his position in 1791 on the original bank bill, this time he did not contend that the legislation was unconstitutional. In his veto message, he wrote that the question of constitutionality of the bank had been settled "by repeated recognitions under varied circumstances of the validity of such an institution in acts of the legislative, executive and judicial branches of the Government, accompanied by indications, in different modes, of a concurrence of the general will of the nation."[108] Thus, he believed that when a precedent was generally recognized and followed, it should be binding in constitutional interpretation even if contrary to original intention.

VI. Judicial Review

The role and function of the United States Supreme Court has long been a matter of great controversy; it was no less so for the Framers. The Constitution does not mention or define judicial review. However, in a government with divided powers, final authority over the meaning of the Constitution must rest with the judicial branch. Since a primary concern of the Constitution is the limiting of legislative sovereignty, the other branches must have authority over the lawmakers. For surely, Hamilton contended, the legislators cannot be expected to deny the constitutionality of their own laws:

> From a body which had even a partial agency in passing bad laws we could rarely expect a disposition to temper and moderate them in application. The same spirit which had operated in making them would be too apt to operate in interpreting them; still less could it be expected that men who had infringed the Constitution in the character of legislators would be disposed to repair the breach in the character of judges.[109]

As is consistent with the purpose of divided government to limit governmental powers, however, the legislature is not devoid of authority over the judiciary. It participates with the president in appointing federal judges, and has structural controls over the courts. Article III, Section 1 of the Constitution provides that

the "judicial Power of the United States, shall be vested in one supreme Court, and in such inferior Courts as the Congress may from time to time ordain and establish." Article III, Section 2 confines the original jurisdiction of the Supreme Court to cases "affecting Ambassadors, other public Ministers and Consuls, and those in which a State shall be Party." In all other cases, the "supreme Court shall have appellate Jurisdiction, both as to Law and Fact, with such Exceptions, and under such Regulations as the Congress shall make." Thus, Congress has the power to establish and ordain lower courts having original and appellate jurisdiction, and it also controls the appellate jurisdiction of the Supreme Court.

Nonetheless, the history of constitutional law in the United States reveals that the major restraint on government authority is the judiciary. The question arises as to how much discretion the Supreme Court actually possesses in interpreting the Constitution. Was it confined to the text of the Constitution or could the Court go beyond the text for this purpose? The separation of powers concept provided the judiciary with two opportunities for following the latter course. First, determining the powers of the various branches is a matter of interpretation, which is a judicial function. Second, the judiciary has a duty to check the other branches in order to preserve constitutional integrity.

Madison supported judicial review as a legitimate exercise of judicial power. In introducing in the First Congress amendments to the Constitution that would in time become the Bill of Rights, Madison asserted that the courts would be "an impenetrable bulwark against every assumption of power in the Legislative or Executive."[110] He had previously told the Virginia Ratifying Convention that "[w]ere I to select a power which might be given with confidence, it would be the judicial power."[111]

One of the differences that existed between Madison and Jefferson related to the judicial power, and it reveals Madison to be a staunch advocate of judicial review. (Interestingly, Jefferson was not a delegate to the 1787 Constitutional Convention, and he was not a member of the First Congress, which framed the Bill of Rights.) In No. 49 of the *Federalist Papers,* Madison critiques a proposal Jefferson made when he authored *Notes on the State of Virginia* in anticipation of a convention that was called to draft a constitution for that state. Jefferson proposed "that whenever any two of the three branches of government shall concur in opinion, each by the voices of two-thirds of their whole number, that a convention is necessary for altering the Constitution, or correcting breaches of it, a convention shall be called for that purpose."[112] Jefferson's objective was to give the people the power to settle constitutional controversies without recourse to the judiciary, on the basis that the people were the only legitimate source of power, from which the power of all branches of the government are derived.

Madison objected to Jefferson's proposal for several reasons. First, frequent appeals of alleged constitutional violations would threaten to reduce greatly

confidence in the stability of the government. Second, the legislators would likely win in a controversy with the other branches, because they are experienced in seeking public approval; thus, the legislature would have an advantage over the other branches. Third, frequently the passions and not the reason of the public would control the outcome. In any event, however, it was apparent that Jefferson's proposal was repugnant to the constitutional system that Madison favored. Jefferson's idea was more consistent with a parliamentary than with a separation of powers system of government. Pursuant to the separation of powers, the judiciary was an independent body, largely removed from popular control, that would preserve stability and public confidence. Participants in a commercial republic expected nothing less.

But what if a judicial interpretation violated the Constitution? This very issue arose from Chief Justice Marshall's opinion in *McCulloch v. Maryland* (1819), in which he ruled that the Constitution required that the federal judiciary accord great—almost total—deference to congressional legislation that did not violate any constitutional provision.[113] A great many people protested this decision, condemning Marshall for granting Congress excessive powers— something which was inconsistent with the purpose of separating and limiting all government powers. Madison fully agreed with the opposition to Marshall's ruling, but took the matter in stride. No form of government, he later stated, can be a perfect guard against the abuse of power:

> The recommendation of the republican form is, that the danger of abuse is less than in any other; and the superior recommendation of the federo-republican system is, that while it provides more effectively against external danger, it involves a greater security to the minority against the hasty formation of oppressive majorities.[114]

Jefferson asserted that there was a constitutional alternative available for overcoming wrongful interpretations of the United States Constitution, and that this was provided by the amendment process set forth in Article V. Under this article, a constitutional convention is required either when two-thirds of both houses of Congress or two-thirds of the state legislatures deem it necessary. Either method would be superior to giving this power to an unelected body, Jefferson insisted. Madison rejected this idea as contrary to the intent of the Framers. Moreover, to refer every new point of constitutional disagreement to a national convention would be "too tardy, too troublesome, and too expensive." But if the court's abuse of its responsibility became unbearable, a national remedy would be needed in order to secure the Constitution.[115]

In No. 78 of the *Federalist Papers,* Hamilton spelled out his position on judicial review. Not only was the judiciary the guardian of the enumerated liberties, which were very few at the time because the Bill of Rights had not yet been

adopted, but also of others not stated. Hamilton asserted that the judiciary had an obligation to preserve any liberty that was not identified in the Constitution:

> This independence of the judges is equally requisite to guard the Constitution and the rights of individuals from the effects of those ill humors which the arts of designing men, or the influence of particular conjunctures, sometimes disseminate among the people themselves, and which, though they speedily give place to better information, and more deliberate reflection, have a tendency, in the meantime, to occasion dangerous innovations in the government, and serious oppressions of the minor party in the community. . . .
>
> But it is not with a view to infractions of the Constitution only that the independence of the judges may be an essential safeguard against the effects of occasional ill humors in the society. These sometimes extend no farther than to the injury of the private rights of particular classes of citizens, by unjust and partial laws. Here also the firmness of the judicial magistracy is of vast importance in mitigating the severity and confining the operation of such laws.[116]

Under Hamilton's analysis, the Supreme Court is empowered to "mitigat[e] the severity and confin[e] the operation" of "unjust and partial laws" as well as to protect against "dangerous innovations in the government, and serious oppressions of the minor party in the community."[117] Finality over unjust and oppressive measures rests, then, with the judiciary and not the legislature. By this measure, the Court could invalidate legislation that would have been condemned as oppressive by Blackstone ("wanton and causeless" restraints and those "without any good end in view") and Coke (laws "against common right and reason or repugnant or impossible to be performed").[118] In short, the judiciary protected the rights of Englishmen against legislative and executive deprivations. Hamilton believed that

> [i]n the form of this government, and in the mode of legislation, you find all the checks which the greatest politicians and the best writers have ever conceived. . . . This organization is so complex, so skillfully contrived, that it is next to impossible that an impolitic or wicked measure should pass the scrutiny with success.[119]

There is other evidence that Hamilton viewed the judiciary as the guarantor of the rights of Englishmen. He believed in natural rights, and his strong endorsement of the proposed Constitution suggests that it was satisfactory in this respect. He wrote in 1774: "The sacred rights of mankind are not to be rummaged for, among old parchments, or musty records. They are written, as with

a sun beam, in the whole *volume* of human nature, by the hand of the divinity itself; and can never be erased or obscured by mortal power."[120] Subsequently, in 1796, Hamilton in his capacity as a private attorney wrote in a brief essay that natural law was a decisive consideration in determining whether good faith purchasers of land were protected under the Constitution from the Georgia legislature's attempt to revoke their titles:

> Without pretending to judge of the original merits or demerits of the purchasers, it may be safely said to be a contravention of the first principles of natural justice and social policy, without any judicial decision of facts, by a positive act of the legislature, to revoke a grant of property regularly made for valuable consideration, under legislative authority, to the prejudice even of third persons on every supposition innocent of the alleged fraud or corruption. . . .[121]

In No. 78 of the *Federalist Papers,* Hamilton explained that in construing the Constitution, courts must never "substitute their own pleasure to the constitutional intentions of the legislature." They must act as interpreters and not as legislators. "The courts must declare the sense of the law; and if they should be disposed to exercise WILL instead of JUDGEMENT, the consequence would equally be the substitution of their pleasure to that of the legislative body." As previously explained, judges protecting the rights of Englishmen were acting within their constitutional obligation. No other branch was suited to exercise this power which is required to preserve republican government. The people's liberty can never be endangered "so long as the judiciary remains truly distinct from both the legislature and the executive."[122]

Hamilton's explanation that the judiciary was limited to a negative role in protecting the people's liberties and other constitutional provisions, was prompted by the controversy over the judicial power that existed at the 1787 Constitutional Convention. Many Framers worried that the judges would act like legislators and not like interpreters. Opponents of the Constitution argued, among other things, that since the powers of Congress were granted in general terms, the judges "may substitute their own pleasure" to that of the lawmakers.[123]

History has revealed that these concerns about judicial power were well founded. Over the years, the Supreme Court has strayed far from its role as guardian of the terms and provisions of the Constitution. It has at times, in effect, "usurped" the legislative as well as the executive powers, and it has failed to protect some important liberties. Nevertheless, despite the criticism that began in the Constitutional Convention and continues even today, the constitutional authority of the Court has not been limited in the slightest; it functions, as always, within the original constitutional language. Since the ratification of the Constitution in 1788, the nation had added to it the Bill of Rights (Amend-

ments I–X) and the civil war amendments (Amendments XIII–XV), all of which have greatly expanded the Supreme Court's authority and jurisdiction.

Whatever remained of it, the argument that judicial review is not constitutionally authorized was demolished with the ratification, on July 9, 1868, of the Fourteenth Amendment, the first sentence of which states that "[a]ll persons born or naturalized in the United States and subject to the jurisdiction thereof, are citizens of the United States and of the State wherein they reside." This sentence was adopted specifically to overcome the U.S. Supreme Court's decision in *Dred Scott v. Sandford* (1857).[124] This highly controversial decision ruled that persons of African descent were not eligible to obtain state or federal citizenship.

While some members of the Thirty-Ninth Congress, which framed the Fourteenth Amendment, sought to curtail judicial review, no such action was taken, notwithstanding the strong feeling in the nation that the Supreme Court had seriously erred in *Dred Scott.* Members of Congress who had participated in the debates over the Fourteenth Amendment generally assumed that the amendment would be subject to judicial review of the same character that already existed. Thus, Senator Jacob Howard, who introduced the proposed amendment into the U.S. Senate, stated that a prior judicial interpretation of the meaning of privileges or immunities gives "some intimation of what probably will be the opinion of the judiciary."[125]

Section 1 of the Fourteenth Amendment contains the privileges or immunities clause, the due process clause, and the equal protection clause, all of which greatly increased the Constitution's guarantee of liberties, effectively according the Supreme Court much greater power than it previously possessed to monitor and invalidate state legislation. The fact that the Thirty-Ninth Congress considered the power of judicial review and did nothing to limit it, but actually enlarged it by adopting the proposed Fourteenth Amendment, is persuasive evidence that the power was constructively approved of by the Congress sitting as a constitution-making body; that is, it refused to propose limitations on judicial review in its consideration of the amendment. Likewise, the ratification conventions in the states might have rejected the amendment for this reason, but none did. The Framers of the original Constitution and the members of the state conventions that ratified it may not have fully comprehended the potential power of the Supreme Court, but the Framers and ratifiers of the Fourteenth Amendment clearly did.

While serious controversy may rage over Supreme Court rulings, no substantial effort has existed in recent years for limiting the judicial review power. When Judge Robert Bork expressed support in his recent book, *Slouching Towards Gomorrah,* for a constitutional amendment that would enable Congress by majority vote to rescind Supreme Court decisions, the response was generally not favorable.[126] Even in the conservative community, which has often been highly critical of the Court, support for the proposal was feeble.

Congress actually has the power under the exceptions clause of Article III, Section 2 to confine the review powers of the Supreme Court. The clause states that the "supreme Court shall have appellate Jurisdiction . . . with such Exceptions, and under such Regulations as the Congress shall make." It has applied the exceptions clause only in *Ex parte McCardle,* an 1868 case dealing with federal reconstruction powers after the American Civil War.[127] In that case, Congress removed certain habeas corpus jurisdiction from the U.S. Supreme Court, which, in accepting the limitation, stated that "the power to make exceptions to the appellate jurisdiction of this court is given by express words." The fact that Congress has only once exercised its exceptions power further suggests a lack of support for such action on the part of both the politicians and the public.

Historical experience supports Madison's thesis that a major solution to the problem of excessive or oppressive government is to separate it by functions into three branches and then give each veto powers over the other branches. The objective of the separation of powers is to preserve and protect liberty by limiting government authority. To a large degree, this objective has been achieved; in each term of the court, it has struck down measures passed by Congress and/or state legislatures. Its rulings have also limited the president's powers. Despite its many failings, the Supreme Court has considerably confined the powers of government, and in this respect it has confirmed the faith of its creators. It is probably more difficult to impose legal restraints in this country than in any other; this is primarily attributable to the federal judiciary, and secondarily to the executive veto.

Consistent with the expectations of many of its creators, the U.S. Supreme Court has engaged in two kinds of inquiry in its decisions protecting liberties. First, it has inquired as to whether the law in question violates the language or meaning of a specific term or provision of the Constitution, and second, as to whether the law is oppressive. Chief Justice Marshall applied the first inquiry to determine constitutionality in *Marbury v. Madison* (1803), and Justice Chase supported the second in *Calder v. Bull* (1798). "It is emphatically the province and duty of the judicial department to say what the law is," asserted Marshall, which in *Marbury* meant interpreting constitutional text and meaning.[128] By contrast, Justice Chase did not feel bound by the language of the Constitution. He believed that the purposes for which men enter into society will determine the limits of the legislative power. In the absence of constitutional authority, the legislature may not exercise power. The theory that the legislature has the power to oppress the people if not expressly restrained, is both contrary to reason and "a political heresy, altogether inadmissible in our free republican governments."[129]

Edward Corwin, a distinguished constitutional scholar of the early twentieth century, writes that Chase's position was not unique to him. "Justices Wilson, Paterson, Story and Johnson, Chancellors Kent and Walworth, Chief-justices

Grimke, Parsons, Parker, Hosmer, Ruffin and Buchanan all appealed to natural rights and the social compact as limiting legislative powers. They and other judges based decisions on this ground. The same doctrine was urged by the greatest lawyers of the period, without reproach." He goes on to quote a view that Daniel Webster, one of the most influential lawyers in the early part of the nineteenth century, presented to the U.S. Supreme Court: "If at this period, there is not a general restraint on legislatures in favor of private rights, there is an end to private property. Though there may be no prohibition in the constitution, the legislature is restrained from acts subverting the great principles of republican liberty and of the social compact."[130] Indeed, as many jurists have asserted over the years, the object of the Constitution is not to grant legislative power but to confine and restrain it. Pursuant to the separation of powers, each branch should prove that it has constitutional authority when it seeks to exercise power. Hence, Congress should be required to show a constitutional source for the power it seeks to exercise.

These early views of the power of judicial review have existed throughout the Supreme Court's existence. In the twentieth century, natural rights may no longer be a judicially correct doctrine, but the separation of powers remains largely intact. According to Corwin, "natural rights, expelled from the front door of the Constitution, are readmitted through the doctrine of separation of powers."[131] By its rulings, dicta, and practice, the U.S. Supreme Court has acknowledged that its obligation to preserve liberty requires that it strike down laws that are oppressive, regardless of whether the Constitution's text requires such action. Accordingly, the Court presently guarantees liberties that are not enumerated, and it expands the meaning of enumerated liberties far beyond their original understanding.

VII. Constitutional Protection of Property Rights

As the architects of a free society, the Framers understood that it could not exist unless government is prohibited from confiscating private property. If government has the authority to seize something owned by a private citizen, it can exert enormous power over people. Madison put it this way: "Where an excess of power prevails, property of no sort is duly respected. No man is safe in his opinions, his person, his faculties or his possessions."[132] As Hamilton explained, "a power over a man's subsistence amounts to a power over his will."[133] "Indeed, in a free government," Justice Story opined, "almost all other rights would become worthless if the government possessed an uncontrollable power over the private fortune of every citizen."[134] Likewise, ownership and investment, upon which the economy depends, would be in jeopardy if the legislature were not deprived of confiscatory powers.[135] Hence, the viability of the

national government that the Framers contemplated required that the legislature's powers over property be substantially limited.

This view obviously was not confined to the property right, though. According to Charles Grove Haines, in his authoritative work on judicial review, a commonly held belief in 1787 was that the greatest peril to liberty comes from the expanding powers of legislative bodies:

> [T]here was more concern as to the restrictions under which governments should operate than as to the functions to be performed. Governments were to be prohibited from interfering with freedom of person, security of property, freedom of speech and of religion. The guaranty of liberty was, therefore, to give the rulers as little power as possible and then to surround them with numerous restrictions—to balance power against power.[136]

Madison's support of property rights was widely held by the other delegates. Gouverneur Morris of Pennsylvania, another prominent and influential Framer, expressed similar views about ownership at the 1787 Convention:

> Life and liberty are generally said to be of more value, than property. An accurate view of the matter would nevertheless prove that property was the main object of society. The savage state was more favorable to liberty than the civilized; and sufficiently so to life. It was preferred by men who had not acquired a taste for property; it was only renounced for the sake of property which could be secured by the restraints of regular government.[137]

William Paterson was a New Jersey delegate to the Constitutional Convention, and he subsequently became a justice of the U.S. Supreme Court. In *Vanhorne's Lessee v. Dorrance* (1795)—a United States Circuit Court of Appeals decision interpreting the Pennsylvania Constitution, which had no just compensation clause to protect owners from government seizure of their property—Paterson declared:

> [From certain provisions of the Pennsylvania Declaration of Rights and Constitution] it is evident: that the right of acquiring and possessing property and having it protected, is one of the natural, inherent, and unalienable rights of man. . . . Men have a sense of property: Property is necessary to their subsistence, and correspondent to their natural wants and desires; its security was one of the objects, that induced them to unite in society. . . . The preservation of property then is the primary object of the social compact. . . . The legislature, therefore, had no authority to make an act divesting one citizen of his freehold and vesting it in another, without a just compensation. It is inconsistent with the principles of reason,

justice and moral rectitude; it is incompatible with the comfort, peace and happiness of mankind; it is contrary to the principles of social alliance in every free government. . . .[138]

Paterson wrote that while eminent domain permitted the acquisition of property by government upon payment of compensation, it could not be applied to transfer property from one person to another. The property had to be used for the "public good."

Framer James Wilson of Pennsylvania was a prominent lawyer, a professor of law, and a justice of the U.S. Supreme Court from 1789 to 1798. He exercised an important role in framing the Constitution and obtaining its ratification. In his *Lectures on Law,* he pointed out the benefits of property ownership: "By exclusive property, the productions of the earth and the means of subsistence are secured and preserved, as well as multiplied. What belongs to no one is wasted by everyone. What belongs to one man in particular is the object of his economy and care."[139] Wilson explained the great misfortune to which the early American colony of Plymouth was subjected as a result of the regulatory programs restricting property rights.

> During seven years, all commerce was carried on in one joint stock. All things were common to all; and the necessities of life were daily distributed from the public store. . . . The colonists were sometimes in danger of starving; and severe whipping, which was often administered to promote labor, was only productive of constant and general discontent. . . . [T]he introduction of exclusive property immediately produced the most comfortable change in the colony, by engaging the affections and invigorating the pursuits of its inhabitants.[140]

Wilson rejected Blackstone's position that the legislature was the sovereign body of a nation. He agreed with Locke that individuals entered organized society in order to protect their rights to life, liberty, and property, and that, therefore, no legitimate government had authority to deprive people of these rights. He supported the judiciary's power to invalidate legislative acts that abridged natural rights.[141]

Other delegates to the Constitutional Convention emphasized property rights as well. Rufus King of Massachusetts and John Rutledge of South Carolina agreed that the protection of property was the primary object of society. Pierce Butler of South Carolina contended that "property was the only just measure of representation. This was the great object of government: the great cause of war, the great means of carrying it on." William R. Davie of North Carolina, Abraham Baldwin of Georgia, and Charles Pinkney of South Carolina thought that the Senate should represent property or wealth. George Mason of Virginia

stated that an important objective in constituting a senate was to secure the right of property. John Dickinson of Delaware considered freeholders to be the best guarantors of society.[142] Inequality of property ownership should not cause the society to abridge liberty, said Alexander Hamilton: "The differences in wealth are already great among us, nothing like equality of property exists. Inequality will exist as long as liberty exists, and it unavoidably results from that very liberty itself."[143] The records of the Convention reveal that only James Wilson disputed the primacy of property rights. For him "the cultivation and enforcement of the human mind was the most noble object" of government and society.[144] However, as previously reported, he strongly supported the right to property, believing it to be a natural right that must be protected against legislative encroachment.

It is apparent that the Framers supported property rights for both philosophical and pragmatic reasons. They regarded it as an inherent right of human beings and as essential to the well-being of society. Since of fifty-five delegates thirty-one were lawyers and several were judges, it is likely that the views of Coke, Blackstone, and Locke on property rights were known and understood by most of the fifty-five delegates. The expressions of the Framers that were favorable to private ownership were not unusual, since the right to property was an unquestioned assumption of that period. As expressed by the English scholar J. W. Gough, "[t]he sanctity of property was . . . one of the cardinal principles of English common law. Whatever rights were fundamental, we may be sure they included the right of property."[145]

VIII. The Bill of Rights

On June 8, 1789, Congressman James Madison introduced in the first House of Representatives a series of amendments to the Constitution that would protect the exercise of named and unnamed rights. Over the ensuing months, Congress debated and considered the matter, and, on October 2, 1789, transmitted to the states for ratification[146] amendments embodying most of Madison's proposals. The framing of these amendments was prompted by a number of considerations. First, to assure the ratification of the Constitution, the Federalists promised that they would seek to amend it after ratification to include a bill of rights. Second, the Federalists were concerned that failure to do so might result in the calling of another Constitutional Convention, which they strongly opposed. In May 1789, both Virginia and New York had requested Congress to convene a second Constitutional Convention. Third, North Carolina and Rhode Island had still not ratified the Constitution, presumably in part because of the absence of a bill of rights. Fourth, Massachusetts, South Carolina, New Hamp-

shire, Virginia, and New York submitted, along with their ratifications, recommendations that certain amendments be adopted. Virginia went so far as to recommend the inclusion of twenty provisions in a proposed bill of rights.[147]

Congress's task was to select rights that would accomplish the normative purpose of protecting liberty, as well as the pragmatic objective of satisfying the public's concerns. The solution rested in protecting both enumerated and unenumerated rights. This problem of enumeration had been discussed during the ratification debates, and Hamilton's objection to guaranteeing specific liberties has been noted.[148]

In this regard, the remarks of two future Supreme Court Justices, James Wilson (a framer of the Constitution) and James Iredell (former Attorney General of North Carolina), during the ratification debates on the original Constitution are instructive, since these remarks likewise presage the framing of amendments to secure both named and unnamed liberties. Wilson asserted that an effort by the Convention to protect everyone's liberties would have been futile: "[I]n no one of those books [by the great political writers], nor in the aggregate of them all, can you find a complete enumeration of rights appertaining to the people as men and as citizens. . . . Enumerate all the rights of men! I am sure, sirs, that no gentlemen in the late Convention would have attempted such a thing."[149] Moreover, as a legal matter, "every thing that is not enumerated is presumed to be given." Therefore, the consequence of an imperfect enumeration "would throw all implied power into the scale of the government, and the rights of the people would be rendered incomplete."[150] Iredell fully agreed with Wilson in an address to the North Carolina ratifying convention:

> [I]t would be not only useless, but dangerous, to enumerate a number of rights which are not intended to be given up; because it would be implying, in the strongest manner, that every right not included in the exception might be impaired by the government without usurpation; and it would be impossible to enumerate every one. Let anyone make what collection or enumeration of rights he pleases, I will immediately mention twenty or thirty more rights not contained in it.[151]

In his speech to the First Congress introducing the proposed amendments, Madison similarly expressed concern that a bill of rights might not encompass protections for all the people's liberties:

> It has been objected also against a bill of rights, that, by enumerating particular exceptions to the grant of power, it would disparage those rights which were not placed in that enumeration; and it might follow by implication, that those rights which were not singled out, were intended to

be assigned into the hands of the General Government, and were consequently insecure. This is one of the most plausible arguments I have ever
heard against the admission of a bill of rights into this system; but, I con-
ceive, that it may be guarded against. I have attempted it, as gentlemen
may see by turning to the last clause of the fourth resolution.[152]

The clause mentioned above became, in time, the Ninth Amendment, and read
initially in Madison's draft as follows:

The exceptions here or elsewhere in the Constitution, made in favor of
particular rights, shall not be so construed as to diminish the just importance of other rights retained by the people, or as to enlarge the powers
delegated by the Constitution; but either as actual limitations of such
powers, or as inserted merely for greater caution.[153]

The final form of the Ninth Amendment is essentially a shorter version of this
provision: "The enumeration in the Constitution of certain rights shall not be
construed to deny or disparage others retained by the people."[154]

Arguments such as those delivered by Madison, Hamilton, Wilson, and
Iredell made inevitable the inclusion of the Ninth Amendment in the Bill of
Rights. After continually asserting the problem of securing all rights, the Federalists, faced with fulfilling their commitment to frame a bill of rights, could
scarcely have omitted protection for those not mentioned. Madison's original
list of enumerated rights and the list Congress adopted contained a far lesser
number than seven states had recommended in their ratifications. The Ninth
Amendment provides an explicit basis for enforcing these other rights.

Perhaps more than any other provision, the Ninth Amendment discloses the
intended constitutional relationship between governor and governed. As the
Federalists explained during the ratification period, the federal government was
not granted authority to abridge the people's liberties, whether identified or not,
except when so provided in the Constitution. The limited number of rights
specifically protected in the original Constitution must have been those of greatest concern to the Framers. They expected that the judiciary would secure the
specified rights as well as the greater number they did not specify. The First Congress, which framed the Bill of Rights, followed the same approach. Under the
political pressures generated during and after the ratification proceedings, it
specified the rights considered of greatest concern. Similarly, the Congress anticipated that the judiciary would safeguard these, as well as those that were not
named. The Ninth Amendment was the vehicle they used for the latter purpose.
Without this amendment, unenumerated rights might not be protected, and freedom would have been less secure than under the original Constitution, which

safeguarded all liberties whether or not they were specified. The amendment did not accord the federal judiciary more authority than it already possessed.

IX. The Due Process Clause

The amendments that Congressman James Madison introduced in the First Congress on June 8, 1789, that would later, with changes, become the Bill of Rights, contained a due process clause identical to the one that is now in the Fifth Amendment of the Constitution. The history of this clause, therefore, begins with Madison's preparation of his amendments.

In ratifying the federal Constitution, seven states (Massachusetts, South Carolina, New Hampshire, Virginia, New York, North Carolina, and Rhode Island) recommended a series of amendments to the Constitution. Virginia and three other states (New York, North Carolina, and Rhode Island) urged the Congress to include provisions specifically guaranteeing life, liberty, and property. Virginia's recommendations contained two such provisions:

> First, that there are certain natural rights of which men when they form a social compact cannot deprive or divest their posterity, among which are the enjoyment of life and liberty, with the means of acquiring, possessing and protecting property, and pursuing and obtaining happiness and safety. . . . Ninth, that no freeman ought to be taken, imprisoned, or disseised of his freehold, liberties, privileges, or franchises, or outlawed or exiled, or in any manner destroyed or deprived of his life, liberty or property but by the law of the land.[155]

The first recommendation is declaratory in nature while the other is substantive, and together they correspond to the words and meaning of the Magna Carta's Chapter 29 (1225) as subsequently broadened by Parliament. North Carolina's ratification of the Constitution contained identical language. Rhode Island's ratification, which occurred after the Bill of Rights had been framed, differed only in the addition of the words "by the trial by jury or" preceding "the law of the land" at the end of Virginia's ninth proposal. The wording of New York's recommendation was as follows: "That no person ought to be taken imprisoned or disseised of his freehold, or be exiled or deprived of his Privileges, Franchises, Life, Liberty or Property but by due process of law."[156]

Virginia, North Carolina, and Rhode Island offered language categorically securing life, liberty, and property. Such a strong affirmation of these rights might well be responsible for the unqualified character of the due process clause. New York's use of the words "due process" in its recommendation does not

change the character of its proposed protection, which was similarly broad and unqualified, and in language otherwise generally in accord with that contained in Chapter 29 of the Magna Carta as subsequently broadened.

Hamilton explained the meaning of due process of law in a speech he made to the New York legislature on February 6, 1787. The New York Constitution, Hamilton asserted, declares that

> no man shall be disfranchised or deprived of any right, but by *due process of law,* or the judgment of his peers. The words "*due process*" have a precise technical import, and are only applicable to the process and proceedings of the courts of justice; they can never be referred to an act of legislature.[157]

Hamilton was arguing against the passage of a bill by the legislature that would disqualify former privateers from holding public office.[158] He insisted that the due process clause prohibited the legislature from depriving persons who had been privateers of their right to hold office and that only the judiciary had this power. He noted that an article of the state's constitution stated that

> no man shall be disfranchised or deprived of any right he enjoys under the constitution, but by the *law of the land,* or the judgment of his peers. Some gentlemen hold that the law of the land will include an act of the legislature. But Lord Coke, that great luminary of the law, in his comment upon a similar clause, in Magna Charta, interprets the law of the land to mean presentment and indictment, and process of outlawry, as contradistinguished from trial by jury. But if there were any doubt upon the constitution, the bill of rights enacted in this very session removes it. It is there declared that, no man shall be disfranchised or deprived of any right, but by *due process of law,* or the judgment of his peers.[159]

According to Hamilton, "due process" means the same as "law of the land," and New York's due process clause consequently confirmed the removal of the legislature's power to deprive a person of his rights. "Are we willing to endure the inconsistency of passing a bill of rights, and committing a direct violation of it [by depriving privateers of their rights] in the same session?" Hamilton asked. Understandably, he is reported to have stated in 1787 that "I hold it to be a maxim which ought to be sacred in our form of government, that no man ought to be deprived of any right or privilege which he enjoys under the Constitution, but for some offense provided in due course of law."[160] Hence, Hamilton's interpretation of New York's due process clause supports the position that, pursuant to this clause, only the judiciary and not the legislature has the power to deprive persons of their rights, and then only for wrongdoing which

has been fairly and properly determined. A legislative body does not have the powers of adjudication or punishment.

In drafting his due process clause, Madison chose language—which, to repeat, the First Congress never changed—essentially similar to that contained in the due process clause recommended by New York as an amendment to the Constitution. New York's constitution contained a due process clause that Hamilton interpreted as protective of individual rights. Since Madison and Hamilton were friends and constitutional collaborators at the time, it may be more than a coincidence that Madison chose the New York language. The use of the words "due process" instead of "law of the land" may also be attributable to Madison's desire for more clarity in meaning. The words "law of the land" may misleadingly suggest the inclusion of a greater number of laws than do the words "due process," although English law regarded the meaning of the two phrases as the same.

Furthermore, it is not surprising that Madison would draft a provision strongly securing property rights. Let me again briefly review his background. Throughout his career, he evidenced the belief that private ownership was essential to the advancement of society. This position was consistent with his conviction that the public interest was better served by freedom than authority. He was the leading proponent of the separation and limitation of powers, rejecting majority rule as a matter of principle. During his service in the Virginia legislature, he worked for the repeal of laws that excluded British creditors from the state's courts, sought to restore and opposed further confiscation of British-owned properties, opposed the issuance of paper money not backed by specie, fought measures to forestall payment of debts, and urged the elimination of state barriers to free trade.

Madison referred to protecting life, liberty, and property in another of his proposed constitutional amendments that was not accepted by the First Congress. He urged that the following language be prefixed to the Constitution, a recommendation that the First Congress, which refused to change the original preamble, consequently did not accept: "That government is instituted and ought to be exercised for the benefit of the people; which consists in the enjoyment of life and liberty, with the right of acquiring and using property, and generally of pursuing and obtaining happiness and safety."[161]

The only clause of Madison's proposed amendments that guarantees the right of acquiring and using property is the due process clause ("No person . . . shall be deprived of life, liberty or property, without due process of law"), thus suggesting that the clause was intended to implement the proposed prefix. (As will be explained in the next section, his takings clause related only to eminent domain.) If it were not implemented by language elsewhere in the Constitution, the security of the property rights referred to in the proposed prefix would have been only an aspiration in the Constitution, and it is not likely that Madison, as a

strong supporter of property rights, would have been satisfied with this kind of outcome. Substantive language is supposed to make declaratory language enforceable, a purpose which only Madison's due process provision served with respect to the right of acquiring and using property.

Another explanation for Madison's proposed due process clause is that it strongly protected the physical integrity of an owner's property. It is reasonable to assume that the Framers of the original Constitution and Bill of Rights looked to the common law and, in particular, to Blackstone's interpretation of it to understand the rights of property. At a minimum, property owners were entitled to be secure against societal wrongs. As explained in Chapter 2, Section IV, Blackstone identified what he regarded as wrongs; that is, certain acts that deprived owners of their property and were subject to penalty and legal restraint: first, a nonconsenting acquisition by government of all or a part of land for public use without payment of compensation; second, a trespass against property; and third, maintaining a nuisance that harms or destroys property. As wrongs, all three were not entitled to protection, whether they are engaged in by a public or by a private entity. The common law was concerned about the well-being of the recipient of the harm and much less about its instigator. Under the U.S. Constitution, when government agencies commit such wrongs, they may constitute deprivations of property without due process of law. Protection against the government committing or authorizing such wrongs would greatly secure the physical integrity of an owner's property, which, after all, was a prime concern of the common law.

X. The Takings Clause

The takings clause of the Fifth Amendment permits government to acquire property from nonconsenting owners for public use upon payment of just compensation. Framed together by the First Congress, the takings and due process clauses adjoin each other in the Fifth Amendment, and must be considered to be consistent with each other. Together, the two provisions are as follows: "No person shall . . . be deprived of life, liberty, or property, without due process of law; nor shall private property be taken for public use without just compensation."

There are two explanations for the insertion of the takings clause in the U.S. Constitution. First, it was intended to fortify the protection of private property by codifying the common law rule that government can acquire property for public use from a nonconsenting owner only by paying for it. Second, because of the protection against deprivation of property contained in the due process guarantee, the takings clause was necessary to preserve two unenumerated but inherent powers of government—the police power and the power of eminent domain.

I will first turn to the explanation that views the takings clause as codifying the common law protection. Blackstone interpreted England's law of the land as requiring indemnification of an owner whose land has been restricted for a public use; otherwise, the owner's property rights have been violated. Because the due process clause is considered as having the same meaning as the law of the land provision, Blackstone's interpretation of law of the land also applies to due process. The protection of the due process clause is in the form of the invalidation of the offending law. The takings clause protects ownership by way of just compensation. However, the difference in remedy between the two clauses is not as great as might appear. Under due process, government can remedy a property deprivation that arises because of failure to pay just compensation by paying just compensation. As Blackstone asserted, a legislature violates an owner's property rights when it takes land for public use without indemnifying the owner. Payment of compensation remedies the violation.[162]

Blackstone's explanation reveals in part why, as of 1800, only the constitutions of Vermont and Massachusetts and the Northwest Ordinance (of 1787) contained takings clauses and why no state urged inclusion of such a clause when submitting proposed amendments to the original U.S. Constitution. These constitutions and the constitutions of the other original states included law of the land, due process, or other such provisions protecting property. Pursuant to Blackstone, it was assumed that these provisions required payment of just compensation when government sought to acquire property for public use. There was no need, therefore, for a takings clause. In Chapter 4, I will explain that in the early years of the nation, jurists in states without takings clauses cited Magna Carta, Blackstone, and New York's Chancellor Kent, among other authorities, in ruling that the common law or natural law mandated the payment of compensation for an owner whose land is taken for public use. In effect, these judges read takings clauses into state constitutions, sometimes as ancillary to a general protection of property and sometimes solely on the basis of the common or natural law. Thus, in an 1897 case, the U.S. Supreme Court sustained this position with respect to the due process clause of the Fourteenth Amendment, holding that the "legislature may prescribe procedure to be observed in the taking of private property for public use, but it is not due process of law if provision is not made for compensation."[163]

I now turn to the second explanation, which views the takings clause as securing the eminent domain and regulatory powers. In the absence of the takings clause, the due process clause might have been interpreted as denying government the power of eminent domain, as U.S. Supreme Court Justice James Iredell (in *Calder v. Bull* [1798]) wrote might occur if the *ex post facto* provisions were interpreted as applying to retroactive laws affecting the ownership of property.[164] A retroactive property law is one that eliminates a property right that an owner had previously acquired. Iredell feared that if the *ex post facto*

clause applied to property laws, government would not be able to invoke eminent domain powers. An owner could resist eminent domain by claiming that the *ex post facto* clause was the only specified exception to the due process clause. Partly on this basis, Iredell justified his construction of the Constitution's *ex post facto* ban as not relating to property ownership and other civil matters. Similarly, the First Congress, which framed the Bill of Rights, might also have feared that the due process clause eliminated the power of Congress to impose any regulations on property rights. As the often-quoted Pennsylvania Chief Justice Gibson observed, the protection of property rights was so strong that "[i]t was deemed necessary to insert a special provision in the Constitution [the takings clause] to enable them to take private property even for public use and on compensations made."[165]

This was essentially the position of New York's highest court in the mid-nineteenth century. The state's constitution then contained the same language and same order of placement for the due process and takings clauses as did the U.S. Constitution. New York high court opinions in that period viewed the state's takings clause as implying that private property could not be taken for any other than public use. The justices acknowledged that private property can be taken for public use upon payment of just compensation, but contended that for uses not public, private property could not be taken at all, neither by an act of legislation, nor in any other manner, "for there is no provision in the Constitution, that just compensation shall be made to the owner, when his property shall be taken for private use."[166] (Chapter 4, Section II will report that some other states followed New York's position in this issue.) In the absence of a takings clause, some "strict interpretation" judges might at times have denied government the eminent domain or police (regulatory) powers.

Support for the foregoing interpretations of the due process and takings clauses comes from the language contained in one of Madison's proposed constitutional amendments, which, with several changes, became the Fifth Amendment:

> No person shall be subject, except in cases of impeachment, to more than one punishment or one trial for the same offense; nor shall be compelled to be a witness against himself; nor be deprived of life, liberty, or property without due process of law; nor be obliged to relinquish his property, where it may be necessary for public use, without a just compensation.[167]

The last clause is an exception to the categorical language of the due process clause preceding it. Both Madison's above-quoted paragraph and the final version of the Fifth Amendment provide protection from governmental oppression, and that protection would include payment for property acquired by the government for public use. The records of the First Congress do not reveal the reason that the Congress changed the language of Madison's just compensation clause.

The just compensation provision is the only clause in Madison's paragraph that relates exclusively to civil matters. The same pattern is evident in the final version of the Constitution. The Fifth and Sixth Amendments consist of criminal-law protections intended to safeguard the rights of persons who were accused or convicted of wrongdoing. The only provision in either of the amendments that concerns solely civil matters is the takings clause, and it follows the due process clause because it is applicable to it.

Additional evidence for the suggested relationship between the due process and takings clauses is provided by the text of the important Northwest Ordinance adopted by the United States Congress on July 13, 1787, while the Constitution was being framed and the Articles of Confederation were in force. This was an ordinance relating to the future government of the territory northwest of the Ohio River. Article II guarantees private property rights as follows:

> No man shall be deprived of his liberty or property, but by judgment of his peers, or the law of the land, and should the public exigencies make it necessary, for the common preservation, to take any person's property, or to demand his particular services, full compensation shall be made for the same.[168]

Again, the protection accorded to law-abiding persons was unqualified, except when the acquisition of property or services was necessary for "the common preservation," and then the payment of compensation was mandated.

This pattern is also evident in the Vermont Constitution of 1777 and the Massachusetts Constitution of 1780 (the only two constitutions adopted prior to 1787 that contain takings-type clauses). In both states the primary reason for inserting the takings clause was to strengthen the protection accorded private ownership.[169] Nonetheless, each reads as a limitation on the absolute right of property. Article I of Chapter I of the 1777 Vermont Constitution provides as follows:

> That all men are born equally free and independent, and have certain natural, inherent and unalienable rights, amongst which are the enjoying and defending life and liberty; acquiring, possessing, and protecting property, and pursuing and obtaining happiness and safety. . . .

Article II of Chapter I states the following:

> That private property ought to be subservient to public uses, when necessity requires it; nevertheless, whenever any particular man's property is taken for the use of the public, the owner ought to receive an equivalent in money.

Article X of the 1780 Massachusetts Constitution states as follows:

> Each individual of the society has a right to be protected by it in the en-
> joyment of his life, liberty, and property, according to standing laws. . . .
> And whenever the public exigencies require that the property of any in-
> dividual should be appropriated to public uses, he shall receive a reason-
> able compensation therefor.[170]

The First Congress, which accepted Madison's language for the due process
clause and most other provisions, changed the wording of his proposed just
compensation clause. Madison's language confined the clause *only* to property
obliged to be relinquished "where it may be necessary for public use," thus essentially protecting the eminent domain power, and the First Congress broadened the language to include *all* private property "taken for public use," terminology which covers not only the eminent domain power, but the police
(regulatory) power as well. Under the First Congress's language, the word
"taken" is not confined and applies to all property (that is taken for public use).

The word "taken" has a broad meaning, and there are many synonyms for
the word. Its dictionary definition includes numerous meanings, such as seized,
deprived, obtained, removed, acquired, attained, procured, and received into
possession or control. The word is used in relation to property in the following
manner: one is said to "take by purchase"; "take by descent"; "take a life interest under the devise"; and "take whichever you wish." There are therefore
various ways to take property; clearly, the word "take" is not confined to seiz-
ing property (as some have suggested).[171]

As used in the Fifth Amendment, the takings language echoes the concerns
of Coke, Blackstone, and Locke that the government should at least compensate
law-abiding persons who are deprived of their property. One objective of the
government paying compensation was to alleviate ownership from the consequences of seizure, restraint, or penalty. Since the Bill of Rights is intended to
guarantee the exercise of liberties, its protections should be read broadly to protect ownership. Under Madison's language, government had to pay compensation when it was necessary to relinquish property for a particular public use. By
contrast, the clause as fashioned by the First Congress was applicable whenever
government takes private property for public use without just compensation.

The difference between Madison's version and the final version of the takings clause is considerable. Consider, for example, the law of inverse condemnation, pursuant to which government actions that cause a reduction in the
value of private property are regarded as takings. This was the interpretation
applied by Chancellor James Kent in 1816 in *Gardner v. Trustees of the Village of Newburgh* (discussed in Chapter 4, Section II). In that case, Newburgh,
in order to provide its residents "with pure and wholesome water," diverted a

stream that had long supplied water to the plaintiff's property and as a consequence reduced the value of the plaintiff's property. Kent held that such an action required payment of compensation, even though the landowner only suffered indirect or consequential damages.

Hooker v. New Haven and Northampton Company (1841) involved the
flooding of lands caused by a government-sponsored canal construction. There
was no negligence and the flooding deprived the plaintiff of the quiet and
peaceful enjoyment of his land. Thus, the plaintiff sustained only consequential damages. Yet, he was awarded compensation by the Connecticut Supreme
Court. (This case will also be discussed in Chapter 4, Section II, which reports
other consequential damages cases.)

Both rulings would not be likely under Madison's language, which is confined to situations when the owner is "obliged to relinquish his property, where
it may be necessary for a public use." Often cited in subsequent years, *Village
of Newburgh* and *Hooker* reveal the existence of judicial opinion at an early period in United States history that protection against a takings violation is not
confined solely to damages directly caused by government in obtaining property for a public use. Compensation is also required as a result of legitimate
government actions that cause consequential property damage. In both of the
above cases, damages were suffered by owners who were never, to use Madison's language, "obliged to relinquish" their properties. These words do not or-
dinarily apply to a forced deprivation or occupation. The Fifth Amendment's
takings clause affects private property "taken for public use," which is unrestricted language that may cover many governmental restraints or actions for a
public purpose that eliminate the value of property not involved in the
achievement of that purpose. To be sure, the words "when obliged to relinquish
his property" might be judicially stretched to protect owners who are forced to
suffer consequential damages. However, the word "taken" provides greater
protection for ownership and would be more in keeping with the libertarian objectives of the Bill of Rights.

There were other reasons why members of the First Congress should have
been aware that consequential damages was an appropriate remedy when government acquires property or constructs public facilities. Law professor
William Stoebuck writes that the English Parliament had previously sought to
compensate owners who sustained consequential damages. In 1512, it passed a
statute authorizing the city of Canterbury to improve a river channel and requiring compensation for the destruction of mills and dams resulting from this
construction. English statutes adopted in 1539 and 1585 required cities or counties to pay compensation for damages to land resulting from improvements that
Parliament authorized.[172]

Stoebuck also refers to compensation requirements in the American colonies
for consequential injuries to land. In York, Maine, in 1669, a court awarded

compensation to "those whose grounds are trespassed upon" during the layout of an adjoining road. Another Maine court order in 1671 that appointed a committee to lay out a road directed that "where any person suffers Inconvenience relateing to his propriety by the Convenience of the Road, It is to bee valewd & fully made good by the Townes within whose limitts it falls, to all reasonable satisfaction." A 1693 Massachusetts statute provided compensation for the installation of new roads, as follows: "*Provided,* that if any Person be thereby damaged in his Propriety or Improved Grounds, the Town shall make him reasonable Satisfaction, by the Estimation of those that laid out the same. . . ." Similar provisions were enacted in Connecticut, New Hampshire, North Carolina, and partially in Pennsylvania.[173]

In England and America, then, there were many instances when compensation was required for deprivations of property rights that did not occur directly from eminent domain acquisitions. Owners sustaining such losses were no less entitled to indemnification from government than were owners of properties condemned for eminent domain purposes. Surely this history of the compensation principle was known to many in the First Congress—their relatives may have been involved in such enactments—and it could well have influenced their broadening of Madison's takings provision.

Another example of the right to payment of consequential damages is provided by the *Saltpeter* case (discussed in Chapter 2, Section III). While Coke's court in that case held that the king's mining of private property to obtain saltpeter was a valid exercise of his prerogative powers, it also ruled that the monarchy must indemnify the property owners for any damages they sustain that were not justified by a strict performance of the mining operation. This made the monarchy liable for all consequential damages. The *Saltpeter* case reveals the importance and fairness of requiring payment of consequential damages in condemnation cases. As the U.S. Supreme Court has asserted, no person should be forced to "bear public burdens, which in all fairness and justice, should be borne by the public as a whole."[174]

There is no difference between the burden imposed on an owner directly or consequently by construction or other development—at least not with respect to meriting compensation. For Blackstone, this distinction between the two kinds of damages did not exist in trespass law or private nuisance law. With respect to both laws, juries determined the amount of recovery to which an owner was entitled based largely on the damage that was inflicted. Even in the absence of fault or force, every entry on another's land without the owner's permission was an injury for which an action in trespass would lie. A private nuisance was anything done that caused hurt or annoyance to the lands, tenements, or hereditaments of another (see discussion in Chapter 2, Section IV). In his discussion of the crime of larceny, Blackstone provided this broad definition of the word "taking": it "implies the consent of the owner to be wanting."[175] As I have ex-

plained in Chapter 2, Section IV, under the common law almost any physical deprivation of property was in violation of the owner's right of quiet enjoyment and likely constituted either a trespass or a nuisance, for which the perpetrator thereof was subject to liability. Some courts have reasoned that when government inflicts either,[176] a taking has occurred, and this is a reasonable conclusion. It is not unreasonable to conclude that a forced governmental acquisition or deprivation of private property required payment for the compensation of both direct and consequential damages to those damaged by such action.

What then does the word "property" mean? There are various definitions of private property. According to Locke, the term included life, personal liberties, and possessions. In addition to having property in land, merchandise, or money, Madison wrote that a man has property in his opinions, religious beliefs, safety, and liberty of his person, which means that he has property in his rights. Blackstone confined his definition to material things. The right of property, he wrote, is "that sole and despotic dominion which one man claims and exercises over the external things in the world, in total exclusion of the right of any other individual in the universe."[177] He was more precise in referring to the right of property as the third absolute right "inherent in every Englishman . . . which consists in the free use, enjoyment, and disposal of all his acquisitions, without any control or diminution, save only by the laws of the land."[178] Blackstone's understanding of property is perhaps the easiest to keep track of and to compensate one for if one is deprived of it.

The right of property, Blackstone writes, is originally acquired by occupancy and is preserved and legitimately transferred only by grants, deeds, and wills, which are a continuance of that occupancy:

> [W]hen I once have gained a rightful possession of any goods or chattels, either by a just occupancy, or a legal transfer, . . . whoever either by fraud or force dispossesses me of them is guilty of a transgression against the law of society, which is a kind of secondary law of nature. For there must be an end of all social commerce between man and man, unless private possessions be secured from unjust invasions; and, if an acquisition of goods by either force or fraud were allowed to be a sufficient title, all property would soon be confined to the most strong, or the most cunning; and the weak and simple-minded (which is by far the most numerous division) would never be secure in their possessions.[179]

Blackstone's comments on indemnifying owners who are deprived of their property do not immediately reveal whether a deprivation of property occurs upon passage of a law by the legislature designating the described property as a road or whether there is no deprivation until the public occupies the property for road purposes pursuant to such legislation. His concern that not the "least

violation" of the owner's property right occurs seems to imply that the indemnification applies at the date of the adoption of the law, inasmuch as upon passage the law constitutes an encumbrance on the owner's title.

The United States Supreme Court has long recognized that regulation of property is no less detrimental to an owner than is physical occupation of it. In the famous 1922 *Pennsylvania Coal Co. v. Mahon* case, the United States Supreme Court ruled that a state's prohibition on mining coal constituted a taking of property.[180] Subsequently, it held in the 1992 *Lucas v. South Carolina Coastal Council* case that the distinction between physical and regulatory limitation on use was not legally significant when there is a deprivation of all economically viable economic use of the property.[181] Both constituted a taking of property. From the perspective of the owner, whose protection is a constitutional imperative, it makes little difference whether the limitation on use occurs because of a physical or legal impediment imposed by government. In each instance, the owner suffers a loss.

Coke's examples of illegal governmental impositions do not suggest that he observed any distinction between physical and regulatory deprivations either. The mere act of legislating a limitation on an existing interest may be sufficient to constitute an illegal imposition. Thus, the king granting a monopoly to a subject violates the Great Charter by depriving other people of their economic rights, though this deprivation has no relationship to the occupation of property.

I have previously noted Coke's explanation that if an owner of property grants to another the profits of the land, the entire parcel passes to the grantee, including both the land and all minerals and improvements that are part of it: "[F]or what is the land but the profits thereof[?]"[182] Consequently, one may conclude that a total deprivation of use is the equivalent of a physical appropriation.[183] Applying Coke's views here to Blackstone's public road example, one can conclude that once the legislature officially designates a privately owned area for future use as a public road, the owner has lost beneficial use of it, and consequently a deprivation has occurred with respect to it.

Because no record exists on the deliberations in the First Congress in framing the takings clause, it is necessary to consider history and background to make this determination. Fortunately, considerable other information exists that helps to explain the First Congress's decision on the wording of the clause.

1. As the next chapter will confirm, Blackstone was frequently cited by early American courts in relation to the requirement of just compensation for a deprivation of property both by reason of occupation and regulation. He was the most important interpreter of the common law when the Bill of Rights was framed. It is not unlikely that the First Congress applied a common law interpretation to the meaning of "deprivation" and "taken," and if so, this would require a very broad definition of these words. As a

general matter, the common law protected an owner's use of his property except when he created a nuisance on it.

2. The takings clause is part of the Bill of Rights, which was intended to guarantee individual liberties from abridgement by the national government.

3. The Bill of Rights set forth and extended the "rights of Englishmen," and therefore must be interpreted as advancing liberty and not authority. Its provisions were intended to protect the liberties of the people and not the powers of government.

4. Based on the common law, the word "taking" comprehends both a direct as well as a consequential or an indirect deprivation of property by government.

5. The Bill of Rights reveals the First Congress's general commitment to freedom and, in particular, to property rights. In addition to the due process and takings clauses, the Bill of Rights contains five provisions specifically protecting property rights (as will be explained in Section XII of this chapter). Its original author, James Madison, was a staunch proponent of property rights, believing that the nation he envisioned could not exist in their absence. He regarded these rights as essential to the nation's viability and stability.

6. So concerned were Madison and the First Congress about excessive national powers that they inserted the Ninth and Tenth Amendments to secure any rights not enumerated and powers not delegated to the national government.

7. Madison wrote his "takings" provision to secure the power of eminent domain. The First Congress changed his language to protect eminent domain and some regulatory powers. As many early justices explained, just compensation for a deprivation of property was a requirement of the natural or common law even when not mandated by a constitutional provision. They often cited Blackstone in support of this position (see Chapter 4).

XI. Correctly Interpreting the Constitution's Private Property Guarantees

A major purpose of the Constitution and Bill of Rights was to overcome impediments to ownership, investment, and enterprise. As reported above, prior to the Constitution the states frequently violated property and other economic rights. To protect these economic liberties, specific restraints on federal and state powers were set forth in the body of the Constitution and in the Bill of Rights. In interpreting these constitutional restraints, it is important to give deference to the individual liberty that they were designed to further. Surely, the scope of the broadly stated rights should not be confined in light of the practices they were

intended to prohibit. In many states at an early period in our history, the laws authorizing the building of roads made no provisions for compensating the owner when unenclosed or wild lands were involved. In some states, the timber that stood on the road could be used for road building without compensation to the owner. Compensation had only been required for the taking of properties that were enclosed or improved.

One explanation for this practice was the belief that installing a road on unenclosed or wild lands substantially elevated the property's value, and consequently no compensation was warranted. This practice was not regarded as a denial of the compensation principle, which was intended to indemnify an owner for his loss.[184] When in some areas unopened lands became more valuable than cultivated lands because of the timber on them, courts responded by broadening compensation requirements to include unenclosed or wild lands.[185]

Considerable regulation of property use also existed in the colonial period, much of which seemed to be contrary to the rules of the common law.[186] The rarity of judicial review in that period explains the considerable volume of such regulation (see Chapter 2, Section VIII). Had there been significant judicial review in the colonial period, the number of property regulations would have been much less. (The next chapter of this book sets forth decisions between 1790 and 1870 in all the states that were part of the union in 1860 and that were striking down regulatory laws largely on the basis of common-law principles.)

The scope of the takings clause should not be judicially limited because of the very questionable theory that the just compensation principle had not received general acceptance in colonial America. If this theory were adopted, the constitutional prohibition on bills of attainder and impairment of contracts would be severely compromised. During the American Revolution, the legislatures of all thirteen states passed confiscatory laws directed against persons who were loyal to the English government; among these statutes were a large number of bills of attainder. Most legislatures subsequently adopted laws impairing the obligation of contract in favor of debtors. The states also engaged in considerable currency inflation. The Constitution was ratified with provisions outlawing these practices, and it is the intent of the Framers and ratifiers that is of primary concern in determining how best to understand the Constitution and its amendments. Clearly, the due process and takings clauses were general and broad limitations on government powers. The United States Constitution is a legal document greatly premised on the principles and definitions of the common law.

XII. The Bill of Rights and Property Rights

The Bill of Rights, ratified in 1791, is very much a property-oriented document. In addition to the due process and takings provisions of the Fifth Amend-

ment, the Bill of Rights contains five other guarantees protecting private property: the prohibition on infringing the people's right to keep and bear arms (Amendment II), the prohibition on quartering soldiers on private property (Amendment III), the prohibition on unreasonable searches and seizures of property (Amendment IV), the right to trial by jury for controversies exceeding twenty dollars (Amendment VII), and the prohibition of excessive bails and fines (Amendment VIII). These guarantees shielded from federal intrusion those property interests of most concern in that period: one's home, land, office, firearms, and financial resources, highlighting, as law professor Gary Lawson puts it, "the rights that were seen in 1791 as the most likely targets of national attack."[187] For Madison, the people's rights included many protections for property in addition to those involving tangible objects since he believed that a person possesses property in his opinions, religious beliefs, safety, and liberty of his person.[188] Property rights of this character are protected in the expression and religion clauses of the First Amendment, as well as in the various other specific guarantees securing life and liberty.

The Bill of Rights originally applied to the federal government and not to the states. As explained above, the Constitution contains provisions severely limiting the economic powers of the states. However, despite the great concern of the Framers about violations of property rights in the states, the original Constitution does not contain a due process or takings clause applicable to the states. It might be asserted that the common law as well as the bill of attainder and *ex post facto* provisions in Article I, Section 10 provided protection against the deprivation of property rights by the states. However, the attainder and *ex post facto* provisions in Article I, Section 9, as well as the common law, apply to the national government, and yet the Bill of Rights contains due process and takings clauses restricting this government.

The problem with imposing these clauses against the state governments at the time of the founding was that they might have been employed to support slavery. The *Dred Scott* decision in 1857 showed that such concerns were not the products of idle speculation. In this case, Chief Justice Roger B. Taney, writing for himself and two other justices, opined that an act of Congress depriving an owner of his slaves violates the due process clause. Most delegates to the Constitutional Convention of 1787 and members of the First Congress (the Framers of the Bill of Rights) opposed slavery.[189] However, it is reported that late in his life, Madison remarked about slavery that "whatever may be the intrinsic character of that description of property [slavery], it is one known to the constitution, and as such could not be constitutionally taken away without just compensation."[190] Since most members of both bodies opposed slavery, there was probably little support for explicit property protection against the states that might in time also protect slavery.

The protection of property rights in the United States rests on the interpreta-

tion of federal and state constitutions by the high courts to which society assigns this responsibility. I have thus far provided the history and background relevant for a correct and proper interpretation of constitutional provisions on property rights. In Chapter 4 I shall discuss the early period of United States judicial history, the eighty-year period from 1790 to 1870, from the perspective of this history and background. Chapter 4 considers a large and, I believe, representative selection of federal and state decisions concerning the prevalent view of the importance of property. Notwithstanding the inherent limitations of judges who are often selected in a political process and with the many variations in their talents and concerns, the judiciary of the period generally abided by and honored their professional responsibilities to secure property rights.

4

Judicial Interpretations of Property Rights Prior to the Fourteenth Amendment

I. Introduction

In Chapters 2 and 3 of this book, I discussed legal principles that were established in England and English America protecting the ownership, use, and development of private property. In this chapter I will consider the extent to which the judiciary in the United States applied these principles in the period between the ratification of the U.S. Constitution and the ratification of the Fourteenth Amendment, specifically the eighty-year period from about 1790 to about 1870. Section II contains brief summaries of property rights decisions in thirty-three states by both the highest courts and some federal courts in those states. These were all the states in the United States as of 1860. Section III is a critique of U.S. Supreme Court Justice Harry Blackmun's dissenting opinion in *Lucas v. South Carolina Coastal Council*, in which he maintains that the American judiciary of the period provided little protection for property rights. Section IV consists of brief summaries of major U.S. Supreme Court decisions on property rights for the period. The last two sections discuss the important legal concept of due process. Section V concerns the relationship between due process and the police power, while Section VI is about the relationship between due process and class legislation.

In addition to the rules and analysis they contain, the decisions included in Sections II, III, and IV also reveal the level of property protection prevalent in

121

the latter half of the 1860s when the Fourteenth Amendment was framed and ratified. Chapters 5 and 6 of this book concern the framing and interpretation of the due process and privileges or immunities clauses of Section 1 of that amendment.

The eighty-year period that I shall discuss was a critical one for the nation. At the beginning of the period, the judiciary had not yet confirmed the written protections for private property contained in the federal and state constitutions. These rights were not self-executing and they often required judicial interpretations before they became enforceable. Pursuant to the separation of powers, jurists at both federal and state levels bore the responsibility of defining the meaning of these protections. Until these determinations were made, many constitutional provisions remained essentially aspirations without binding effect. The required adjudications took place during the eighty-year period, with the judges at federal and state levels (except for South Carolina) confirming the intentions of framers of the federal and state constitutions to secure property rights generally (but not totally) consistent with the protections provided by the common law. Hundreds of jurists at both federal and state levels were involved in adjudicating hundreds of cases. Except for South Carolina's rejection of compensation for the taking of roads, there was remarkable unity among all these courts on protecting property rights. This judicial unity is astonishing when one understands that the country was far less decisive with respect to whether the power of government in American society generally should be strong or weak. By securing property rights, the judiciary opted for a restrained government power consistent with the views of Madison, Blackstone, and Coke.

This chapter surveys state and federal decisions to determine the protection accorded property rights during the eighty-year period under consideration. Sections II and IV contain summaries of judicial opinions issued in this period adjudicating controversies concerning the protection of private property and some related rights. The issue in the property cases was whether the government had imposed excessive controls over private property, a circumstance which would require the government to pay compensation to indemnify the owner for the harm he has sustained as a result of the restriction. In the absence of such payment, the restriction would be invalid.

If a court rules that the government must compensate the owner, one may reasonably assume that thereafter it will protect property rights at least at the level involved in the adjudicated case. Such decisions should apply to equivalent or less onerous regulations. Filing lawsuits that require an appeal to a high court is expensive in money and time. Property owners will not usually file such lawsuits unless they confront highly restrictive regulations that they believe the judiciary will invalidate. Inasmuch as the restrictions judicially invalidated were generally substantial in impact, the overall effect of the various judicial opinions was to reduce substantially the power of government over property rights.

The requirement of just compensation usually guarantees owners, investors, and developers that they have the liberty to own, invest, or develop property at least without fear of confiscation, occupation, or seizure. The law of just compensation is also a standard for determining whether a government is committed to the protection of property rights. It is not the only means available for this purpose, but it has the advantage of uniformity: it is an identifiable measure applicable to every government.

II. State Decisions

In the period between 1790 and 1870, the United States Supreme Court, two federal circuit courts, a federal district court, and high and appellate courts in at least thirty-three states construed various national and state constitutional provisions securing ownership of private property and related rights. In 1860, the United States contained thirty-three states, and for purposes of the analysis presented in this section, I selected this year as representative of this period. It preceded the American Civil War (1861–1865) and the legal effects of that conflict. I believe that a survey that included other states that entered the union between 1860 and 1870 would not yield different conclusions on the subject matter. There does not appear to be sentiment that would persuade these other states to break the near-unanimity on the protection of property rights that existed among the states that were in the union in 1860.

The thirty-three states included in this section are Alabama, Arkansas, California, Connecticut, Delaware, Florida, Georgia, Illinois, Indiana, Iowa, Kentucky, Louisiana, Maine, Maryland, Massachusetts, Michigan, Minnesota, Mississippi, Missouri, New Hampshire, New Jersey, New York, North Carolina, Ohio, Oregon, Pennsylvania, Rhode Island, South Carolina, Tennessee, Texas, Vermont, Virginia, and Wisconsin. My purpose is not to present a statistical study, but instead to make a reasonable interpretation of the then prevailing position in the state courts in 1860 on the protection of private property rights. The decisions reported in Sections II through IV of this chapter confirm that a large and thoughtful body of constitutional law existed at the time of the ratification of the Fourteenth Amendment in 1868 protecting property owners from the imposition of laws that the courts viewed as confiscatory or arbitrary.

These three sections should provide the reader with an understanding of prevailing takings law for the roughly seventy-eight years preceding and two years after the adoption of the Fourteenth Amendment. I selected the decisions discussed in Sections II and IV, and the cases discussed in Section III are ones to which Justice Blackmun refers. The decisions discussed in Sections II and IV are the result of searches conducted mostly via Lexis and Westlaw of cases during the designated time period having to do with "takings," "just compensation," and "public use." The finality of each case herein reported was verified by using the

Shepard's citation service on Lexis, which is a procedure that revealed that none of the cases reported in these sections was reversed as of 1870. As will be seen, Blackmun and I part company in how we understand the cases discussed in Sections II and III with respect to the protection of property rights. Sufficient information is contained in both sections, though, to enable the reader to make an informed judgment about prevailing legal opinions of the period. Section IV discusses a number of U.S. Supreme Court opinions that reveal that the Court was also highly supportive of property rights and much in keeping with the rulings of the state courts.

Because Section II does not report all property rights cases in the states for the period in question, there might be concern that its enumeration of decisions exaggerates the extent of judicial protection given to property rights. It might be said that the survey of cases in Section II omits decisions that uphold government property regulations when no compensation was provided. The contents of Section III should eliminate this concern; this section discusses Justice Blackmun's dissenting opinion in which he refers to decisions he believes show that the state courts were far more favorable to government regulations than to property rights.

Blackmun's opinion on these matters is important not only because of the author's high judicial position, but also because it is based on well-known writings authored by persons who were not disposed to the protection of property rights and were inclined to favor government controls over them. Blackmun relies on, among others, *The Taking Issue* (1973), a 1985 *Yale Law Review* article, "The Origins and Original Significance of the Just Compensation Clause of the Fifth Amendment," a 1964 *Yale Law Review* article, "Takings and the Police Power," and *The Transformation of American Law, 1780–1860* (1977).[1] According to its authors, *The Taking Issue* was "designed to assist government officials and attorneys who seek to fashion solutions to environmental problems" by enabling them to overcome "the challenge posed by" existing interpretations of the takings issue.[2] Blackmun could not have obtained stronger support for his position than from these mentioned works.

Sections II and IV reveal a remarkable consistency between the rulings of the state and federal judges. Virtually all supported the requirement of just compensation to validate a nonconsensual government acquisition or occupation of private property. The United States has always been a land of considerable intellectual diversity. Yet for the judiciary, these differences largely evaporated with respect to property rights. There are several explanations for this consistency. First, is the influence of natural law ideas on the judiciary. Protection of property was among the highest priorities of the natural law. While this law's importance receded over time, it remained a public concern throughout the period. Second, the commentaries of Coke and Blackstone were held in high esteem in United States jurisprudence. These commentaries were often cited,

quoted, or referred to. This should not be surprising since many jurists and lawyers obtained their legal education from the commentaries themselves or from books that relied on them. In time, James Kent's judicial opinions and commentaries also became highly influential for the American judiciary, and his interpretations of property rights were often quite similar to Blackstone's. Third, there has always been considerable commonality between the constitutions and legal opinions of all the states of the union. Interestingly, Alexis de Tocqueville, the eminent French political commentator who toured this country in 1831–1832, believed that in securing property the judiciary was responding to the wishes of the people: "In no country in the world is the love of property more active and more anxious than in the United States; nowhere does the majority display less inclination for those principles which threaten to alter, in whatever manner, the laws of property."[3]

In this section, I report on over 100 decisions issued by the high and appellate courts of the thirty-three states identified above and by several federal courts relative to the protection provided for the ownership of private property. These cases separate into three categories:

1. The first category contains decisions in states whose constitutions did not contain a takings clause at the time the deprivation at issue occurred, but instead applied due process, law of the land, or something equivalent in order to vindicate the principle that a taking of property for public use is valid only if accompanied by payment of compensation. For the years applicable, there were eleven states in this category: Arkansas (1853), Connecticut (1828, 1841), Georgia (1847, 1851), Louisiana (1837), Maryland (1838, 1848), Michigan (1863), New Hampshire (1826, 1834, 1857, 1867), New Jersey (1830, 1839), New York (1816, 1819, 1823), North Carolina (1805, 1823, 1859), and Virginia (1828).

2. The second category contains high court decisions of all the surveyed states relating to takings of private property. As of 1870, the highest courts of all thirty-three states that were in the union in 1860 (with the exception of South Carolina's rejection of compensation for the taking of land for highways) were in accord that a government deprivation of a property right by law, regulation, or action from a nonconsenting private owner required payment of compensation. These deprivations usually were partial, as distinguished from total, deprivations. A "total deprivation" means that the owner is denied the rights to occupy, use, exclude, and transfer his property; these restraints can only occur when the property is permanently occupied by or at the behest of government. This accord with respect to the requirement of compensation did not exist, though, with respect to three related matters:

   (a) These courts differed on whether consequential damages sustained by an owner—that is, indirect damages inflicted as a result of a law, regu-

lation, or action—constitute a constitutional taking and thus require payment of compensation. In this survey, most of the states considering the issue held that payment for some or all consequential damages was required. These states were Arkansas, Connecticut, Illinois, Indiana, Louisiana, Maine, Massachusetts, Minnesota, New Hampshire, New Jersey, New York, Ohio, Texas, Vermont, and Wisconsin.

(b) There was disagreement among a number of states as to what damages are covered by the compensation that must be paid when a taking has occurred. Some state courts held that compensation includes payment for the total injury sustained by the property owner, while other state courts held that the benefits accruing to the owner by reason of the taking should be deducted from the amount to which the owner is entitled.

(c) Some state courts also had different positions on whether takings of land for private roads or privately owned mills constituted a public use, which the common law required for an eminent domain proceeding.

3. The third category contains high court decisions protecting general rights that indirectly support private ownership. Thirteen decisions in six states struck down laws or regulations for one of the following reasons: it gave preferential treatment to or sought to harm certain people, groups, or corporations, or it violated a specific requirement of due process of law. These six states were Alabama, Maine, Massachusetts, New York, South Carolina, and Tennessee.

The cases in this section are listed alphabetically. The reader, however, will find it convenient to read initially the New York cases and then go on to the rest, because the New York cases are often referred to in the other state cases. New York's courts of appeal were the most persuasive in influencing judicial precedent in property rights cases in the rest of the nation. As of 1860, New York had a larger population than any other state and also the most prestigious judiciary. Another reason was that James Kent occupied high judicial positions in New York as both Chancellor of the Court of Equity and Chief Justice of the Supreme Court. Kent was not only a prominent jurist, but also a legal scholar best known for his treatise, *Commentaries on the United States Constitution*. As mentioned above, his opinions and commentaries were often cited and quoted.

Alabama

In *Ex parte Dorsey* (1838), the Alabama Supreme Court addressed an act that required a person seeking to practice law in the state courts to take an oath asserting not only that he would not participate in a duel in the future, but that he had

not done so in the past.[4] A majority of the court held this provision to be unconstitutional. It found that the measure was (1) a retroactive law depriving some would-be attorneys of the fundamental right to pursue a lawful avocation, and (2) a special ("exceptional") law and not a general law because it penalized the rights of a particular class in the community. The majority opinion held that the right to practice law is "as deserving of protection as property" and an element of the unalienable right to pursue happiness secured under the state constitution's "due course of law" clause. The court interpreted this clause as originating in Magna Carta's Chapter 29—"[t]he corner stone of English liberty"—which was "intended to limit the power of the crown, and check encroachments on the liberty of the subject."

In *Sadler v. Langham* and *Moore v. Wright and Rice* (1859),[5] there were two separate actions that the Alabama Supreme Court combined for adjudication since both involved the issue of state authority to condemn land for private use. The court held that statutes of the state authorizing the condemnation of land for the establishment of private roads and the condemnation of land for the erection of private mill-dams were unconstitutional because even though they provide compensation for the landowner, they authorize the taking of private property for other than public uses. The takings clause of the state's bill of rights allowed a taking for public use upon payment of compensation, but its language did not permit it for private use even with compensation.

The court rejected the theory that the legislature is the sole judge of what is a public use. This theory, said the court, subordinates the Constitution to the legislature: "It would clothe the legislature with that absolute power of construing, as well as enacting a statute, contrary to the letter and spirit of our constitution." Moreover, if the legislature is the sole judge of what constitutes public use, its exercise of that power would be the assertion that the use was public; otherwise, they would not have the constitutional authority to so act.

Arkansas

In *Ex parte Martin* (1853),[6] an Arkansas statute for the reclaiming of swamp lands directed the swamp land commission to construct levees and drains adjoining the Mississippi River. The complainants contended that construction of certain levees would overflow a large portion of their lands and back the water up into one of their fields in cultivation. The Arkansas Constitution contained no takings provision, nor did the legislature provide for compensation for property damaged by the operations of the swamp land commission. Relying on natural-law principles and several provisions of the state constitution and declaration of rights, including a law of the land clause, the Arkansas high court held that the legislature, and, in this case, the swamp land commission, is prohibited

from taking private property for public use without just compensation: "To suppose that the legislature, under our Constitution, possessed the powers of divesting the citizen of his right to his property without . . . (equitable) compensation for it . . . would be subversive of the government and equivalent to revolution and anarchy, since it would defeat one of the primary objects for which the government was established." The court cited Chief Justice Marshall's decision in *Fletcher v. Peck* and Chancellor Kent's opinion in *Gardner v. Village of Newburgh* (both cases will be discussed later in this chapter) in support of its decision. The court stated that until a just indemnity has been afforded the landowner, the power of eminent domain cannot be legally exercised.

California

The issue in *The San Francisco, Alameda and Stockton Railroad Company v. Caldwell* (1866)[7] is whether or not the landowner whose land was subject to condemnation was entitled to the full value of the land taken, irrespective of any benefits obtained as a result of the condemnation. According to this California Supreme Court opinion, the weight of authority at the time of this decision favored allowing the value of the benefits to be deducted in ascertaining just compensation to be awarded in takings cases. However, some courts held that compensation for the value of the land taken is required in all cases, without any deduction for benefits obtained by the owner for other land he owns, by reason of the public improvement for which the property is taken. These courts held that the enhancement of the value of the property not taken is merely the owner's share of the general benefits produced by the public improvements. Why, then, these courts asked, would not the owner in such cases be entitled to the increase in the value of his property? He alone would be made to pay for the improvement by a reduction in the compensation he receives, although others whose property adjoins the improvements are equally benefited and not charged for them.

The California Supreme Court rejected the latter position:

> Just compensation requires a full indemnity and nothing more. When the value of the benefit is ascertained there can be no valid reason assigned against estimating it as a part of the compensation rendered for all the particular property taken, as all the constitution requires in such cases is a just compensation, which is all that the owners of property taken for public use can justly demand. The Constitution does not require the compensation in such cases to be rendered in money, though in the estimation of benefits the value must be measured by the money standard.

This decision was quite favorable to railroad companies and other entrepreneurs who required the acquisition of land for their business purposes. Com-

pensation indemnifying landowners was reduced by including benefits accruing to them as a result of the development of the land that was taken. In addition to the entrepreneurs who acquired the land, the general public was greatly advantaged by the development of land—an explanation which probably accounts for the ruling in this case.

In *Samuel J. Sherman v. D.S.K. Buick and John Carrick* (1867),[8] the California Supreme Court held that the legislature has no power to lay out and establish private roads, that is, roads that are the private property of particular individuals, even when just compensation is paid for damages resulting to the owner of the land on which the road is located. If, however, a private road is laid out and established pursuant to legislative authority, regardless of whether it is for public or private convenience it becomes a way over which "all may pass who have occasion." "Whenever the necessities or the convenience of the public, which includes everybody, requires a road for the purpose of trade or travel, it is the duty of government to provide one, and, if necessary, to take private property for that purpose, upon making just compensation." The court asserted that the ultimate determination of whether a given road will subserve the public need or convenience, must rest with the legislature. The fact that compensation is required to offset the damages that a landowner sustains serves as a check on the legislative excess in this area. Lawmakers may deem it just to open and maintain them at the cost of those most immediately concerned instead of at the cost of the public. The court stated that the taking of private property even for roads serving residences and farms is not a taking for private use, since they are open to everyone and under the control of the government.

The defendant railroad in *Bernard S. Fox v. The Western Pacific Railroad Company* (1867)[9] filed a petition for condemnation, gave a bond, and obtained an order authorizing it to proceed with the construction of its railroad over the plaintiff's property and to take or continue in possession of the land for that purpose. Pursuant to the authority of the Railroad Act, the defendant entered upon the land before it paid any compensation. The California State Supreme Court held that the entry of a railroad corporation on land pursuant to a condemnation order for the purposes of surveying and grading a bed for the road is not a trespass until the time for payment of compensation is past. The land is not considered "taken" so as to divest the owner of the title, until compensation is paid. When compensation is due and not paid, the owner thereafter may maintain an action and seek recovery for damages.

Connecticut

The plaintiffs in *Enfield Toll Bridge Co. v. Connecticut River Co.* (1828)[10] were authorized by state statutes in 1798 to build a toll bridge across the Connecticut River, with the proviso that they construct two locks on one side of the

river in order to allow unimpeded boat navigation. However, an 1809 statute gave the plaintiffs relief from the requirement to erect the locks. In 1824, the legislature gave the defendants the authority to construct locks and engage in work included in the original grant to the plaintiffs and to construct a shore channel instead, subject to further legislative action if the channel proved ineffective. The case raised the issue of whether a subsequent legislature has authority to deprive the plaintiffs of the rights that a prior legislature had granted them.

The Connecticut Supreme Court held that the plaintiffs were in possession of contract and property rights of which they could not be divested, except as allowed by the U.S. Constitution. The 1798 statutory grant to the plaintiffs constituted a contract that a state by its law or charter cannot constitutionally impair. The plaintiffs could not be divested of their franchise on the ground of its inutility or by nonuse. A legislative grant "vests an indefeasible and an irrevocable title," the arbitrary cancellation of which violates the U.S. Constitution and the "fundamental principles of natural justice and of the social compact." Citing Chancellor Kent's decision in *Gardner* and his *Commentaries,* they stated that compensation "is a necessary attendant on the due and constitutional exercise of the power of the lawgiver to deprive an individual of his property without his consent." The court did not identify any state compensation clause. The concurring opinion expressed doubt that, even upon payment of compensation, the vested rights of a corporation in a franchise that serves a general public interest could be abrogated by government.

Hooker v. New Haven and Northampton Company (1841)[11] was a suit brought by a landowner for damages to his land caused by the discharge of water from a canal constructed and maintained by the defendant corporation for public use, pursuant to legislative direction. The water that was discharged from the canal, after running through the lands of other persons, flowed upon the plaintiff's land, thus greatly injuring his quiet and peaceful enjoyment of it. A jury found that the discharge of water occurred without fault on the part of the corporation. The Connecticut Supreme Court of Errors held by a 3 to 2 vote that "the injury, though consequential, cannot be considered as remote," and entitled the plaintiff to compensation. The majority asserted that (1) the obligation to make compensation is commensurate with the right to take property; (2) even in the absence of negligence, an injury to land which deprives the owner of the ordinary use of it is equivalent to a taking of it; (3) it is a principle of natural equity that when private property is taken for public use, the individual whose property is sacrificed must be indemnified; and (4) when the legislature authorizes an improvement, the lawful execution of which causes the diminution of private property, without affording the owner a means of indemnification, he has an action at common law against the perpetrator. The majority opinion cited Kent, Blackstone, and numerous federal and state opinions in support of its ruling.

Woodruff v. Neal (1859)[12] raised the issue of whether an ordinance of the

town of Southington that enabled its residents to purchase licenses permitting them to pasture cows along the city's highways constituted a taking of the right of an owner to depasture the herbage on his land. The Connecticut Supreme Court held that since the state had only taken a right of passage over the land when the road was originally installed, the landowner retained rights to the property not incompatible with the public enjoyment of the right of way:

> [The landowner] retains the fee, and all rights of property in the land not incompatible with the public enjoyment of the right of way. . . . Subject to this right of the public, he may take trees growing upon the land, occupy mines, sink water courses under it, and, generally, has a right to every use and profit which can be derived from it consistent with the easement. . . . Among the rights thus retained by the owner is that of the herbage of the land, which belongs exclusively to him, and having himself thus the right to depasture it, he may maintain trespass against any one who puts his cattle upon it to graze.[13]

Delaware

In *John Whiteman's Ex'x v. The Wilmington and Susquehanna Rail Road Company* (1839),[14] which was a challenge to a statute that authorized a private railroad company to acquire property for its use as a railroad, the Supreme Court of Delaware set forth the following principles. The state, having the power of eminent domain over all the lands of its citizens, may divest private property for public use by paying just compensation. The state may exercise this power through private corporations or individuals. The legislature is to be the judge of the propriety and necessity of divesting private property for public purposes, and it may provide the mode of assessing the compensation. The taking of private property for making a public railroad is lawful. In assessing compensation, both the advantages and harms resulting to the owner of the lands from the construction of the railroad may be considered.

In the matter of a return of a private road on the petition of George Hickman (1847)[15] is a reply to an objection to a court order holding that the laying out of a private road is constitutional. In this ruling, the Court of Oyer and Terminer stated that the authority to lay out private as well as public roads has long been exercised and both are within the legislative control in the exercise of eminent domain. Private roads are part of the system of public roads, since they are essential to the enjoyment of those which are strictly public. Many people would be deprived of the benefit of the public highway, but for outlets laid out on private petition, and at private cost, and which are private roads in that

sense, but branches of the public roads and open to the public for the purposes for which they were laid out. In all instances, just compensation is made to the owner of the land to indemnify the owner for the damage he has sustained.

Florida

Pursuant to a state statute, a practicing physician filed a petition to establish a private road chiefly for personal convenience, and this petition was approved by the county commissioners. In *Bradford v. Cole* (1859),[16] the Supreme Court of Florida found the petition inadequate. Under the state statute, the petition should have been signed by twelve or more householders, setting forth a neighborhood necessity and calling for a neighborhood—not a private—road. The proceeding should be instituted by those petitioners, and not by an individual representing his own interests. Quoting Blackstone and other jurists and commentators, the court presented various opinions that the application of eminent domain to install roads must be shown to be for a public purpose; otherwise, it constitutes an invasion of the right of property.

The court refused to declare the statute unconstitutional, because the matter had not been argued as such. However, it expressed concern about protecting owners from arbitrary or capricious impositions compromising the integrity of their property rights. It referred to commentators who stated that the right of eminent domain was not applicable to a public use when merely convenient and not necessary.

Georgia

In *Young v. McKenzie, Harrison and others* (1847),[17] the Supreme Court of Georgia held that the state was bound to enforce the "great common law principle" that private property shall not be taken for public use without just compensation, even though the state's constitution did not contain such a provision. The case involved a legislative act that incorporated a private company for the purpose of erecting a bridge, and that authorized the company to take private property for building it upon payment of just compensation. The court cited Magna Carta's Chapter 29, Blackstone, and Kent (among others) in support of its ruling, stating that the eminent domain clause of the national constitution did not create any new principle of restriction, but was declaratory of a great common law principle, founded in natural justice, applicable to all republican governments, and equally applicable to the state government which existed anterior to the U.S. Constitution. The clause derived no additional force from being incorporated into the Constitution.

Parkam v. The Justices (1851)[18] concerned the constitutionality of an 1818 act of Georgia that did not require compensation for an owner when a public road is laid out on his unenclosed or wild lands. Compensation was required only when the lands were enclosed. The Georgia Supreme Court held that the state legislature had no authority to acquire property, except in situations of extreme necessity (such as foreign invasion), without payment of compensation. The court referred to no state constitutional provision; it based its decision on the common law. The requirement of compensation "came to us with the common law—it is part and parcel of our social polity—it is inherent in ours, as well as every other free government . . . [and] is admitted by able writers, as being provided in natural equity and of universal application." Henceforth, compensation would also be required for unenclosed land.

In arriving at its ruling, the court conducted an extensive analysis of English and American law beginning with the law of England prior to the Magna Carta and closing with contemporary legal rulings (from New York, South Carolina, Tennessee, and Massachusetts), and citing the commentaries or legal opinions of Blackstone, Kent, Story, Grotius, Pufendorf, Bynkershoek, and Vattel. How much and how often private property may be taken for public use, the court asserted, "are inquiries which open to the legislature a field of discretionary power, almost without bounds—a discretion which places the sacred right of property very much within their control—a discretion which no wise people will tolerate." But in cases of gross abuse of eminent domain, as when, under the pretext of public utility, the property of A is taken and given to B, the courts will interfere and set aside the law. The legislators are also subject to the corrective judgment of the courts when they grossly abuse their authority by imposing restraints on property not based on public necessity and utility.

Illinois

Peoria & Rock Island R.R. Co. v. Bryant (1870)[19] held that the loss of the enjoyment of a spring was a proper element of damage in a condemnation suit. If the owner could enjoy it only by a conveyance of the water across the railroad track, there would then be a total deprivation unless the company would give him a perpetual license to flow the water across its right of way.

St. Louis, Vandalia & Terre Haute R. Co. v. Mollet (1871)[20] discussed what constitute the proper subjects for the assessment of damages for the right of way for a railroad. The Illinois Supreme Court held that all injuries which are appreciable and result from the construction of the road, are legitimate subjects in the estimation of the damages. If, by the erection of embankments, land is submerged and rendered unfit for use and cultivation, it is also includable in the estimation of damages.

The issues before the Illinois Supreme Court in *Cook v. South Park Commissioners* (1871)[21] were (1) the date when the value of land taken for public use should be determined and (2) the date when the government was entitled to occupancy in a condemnation proceeding. An 1869 statute had authorized the Board of South Park Commissioners to select lands as sites for public parks, subject to confirmation by a popular election in certain designated towns. The trial court assumed that the proper time for valuing the land involved in the case was when the condemnation was ratified by the voters. Reversing the lower court, the supreme court construed the law of the land and takings clauses of the state's constitution as requiring the land to be valued at the date when proceedings to condemn are commenced, which might be much later than the confirmation vote and during which time the value of the land might increase greatly. Mere legislation cannot deprive an owner of his title, asserted the court; such "doctrine is monstrous, and cannot be sustained." Transfer of title and right to occupancy must await actual payment of compensation.

Indiana

Rubottom v. M'Clure (1838)[22] was a suit for trespass committed by employees of the commissioners of the Wabash and Erie Canal that was filed by a landowner. A state statute had authorized the commissioners or their agents to enter upon and use any land and take any materials necessary for the construction and maintenance of the canal. It did not require for entry the consent of the owner or prior payment of compensation. The Indiana Supreme Court held that a state statute that authorizes the appropriation of private property for public benefit, and provides for a subsequent compensation for property so applied, is valid under the Indiana Constitution. Actual payment to the owner is a condition precedent to the transfer of title to the state, but not to the appropriation of it to public use.

McIntire v. The State (1840)[23] was a claim for damages for land and material taken from the landowner for the purpose of constructing a railroad. The Indiana Supreme Court interpreted the state's takings clause as requiring that the property taken be valued and the compensation paid in money. However, if the remaining property is enhanced in value by the construction of a public improvement equal in amount to the value of the deprivation sustained, then the owner has obtained a just and constitutional compensation for the deprivation to which he has been subjected. The court went on to state that the proper rule for assessing compensation requires that the benefits resulting from the public improvement should be set off against the damages sustained by an individual on taking his property to construct that improvement. The latter rule was con-

firmed as the law of the state in *Indiana Central Railroad Company v. Hunter,* decided in 1856.[24]

The Trustees of the Wabash and Erie Canal v. Spears (1861)[25] was a suit by Spears and Case to recover damages caused by the flooding of their land, which was produced by the action of the Trustees of the Wabash and Erie Canal in raising a dam across the Wabash River and by cutting waste ways through embankments during the period between 1848 and 1854. The trial court entered judgment for the plaintiff. In affirming the judgment, the Indiana Supreme Court set forth a number of propositions relating to controversies of the kind adjudicated in the case. According to this opinion, there are many consequential damages that may harm others from the legitimate use of one's own property, for which they have no redress. Included in this class are damages resulting from the grading of streets and highways that make more inconvenient and expensive the passage to and from adjoining property.

However, there are consequential damages arising from the use of one's own or of another's property that will render the person causing them liable to pay damages, such as an unauthorized obstruction on a street or highway or a nuisance on one's land. Diversion of surface water from the land of another, by excavation on one's own land, and the backing of water, by means of dams, upon the land of another, were injuries for which an action could be brought at common law. Injuries by backing water seem, then, to be embraced within the constitutional inhibitions against injuring property by legislative authority without making compensation.

When the agent of a turnpike company commenced the excavation and grading of a prospective turnpike road, thereby causing damage to the balance of the land—which the owners alleged was much more serious than the amount determined by a jury—the owners sought and obtained an injunction against the company and its agent enjoining them from continuing with their construction of the road. On appeal, in *The Norristown Turnpike Company v. Burket* (1866),[26] the defendants insisted that even if the assessment of damages was void, the plaintiffs have an ample remedy by a suit for the trespass, and therefore there was no need for a court to forbid construction of the road. The Indiana Supreme Court upheld issuance of the injunction for three reasons: (1) The Indiana Constitution's takings clause prohibited taking of property unless just compensation is "first assessed and tendered"; (2) an injunction is more protective of the owner's interest than a suit in trespass; and (3) the plaintiffs alleged that the company was wholly insolvent. However, the court found that the assessment of damages was made by "disinterested men, acting under obligation of an oath, after hearing the evidence and viewing the premises," thereby satisfying the constitutional requirement. Finding the mode of assessment valid, it reversed the lower court's decision and dissolved the injunction.

Iowa

In 1846, the city of Davenport consented to and acquiesced in the erection of a private wharf and permitted those erecting it to continue in the undisturbed use and enjoyment of it for about fifteen years. The property became increasingly valuable during those fifteen years. The city sought to appropriate to its own use the benefits of this wharf by demanding and receiving wharfage from the steamboats landing there. The Iowa Supreme Court, in *Grant v. City of Davenport* (1865),[27] held that the city had no power to deprive the owners of the benefits of the wharf without compensation. The court explained that the city's actions over a long period of time in aiding the construction and operation of the wharf amounted to constructive approval of these activities.

In 1856, the Iowa legislature enacted a measure to extend the limits of the city of Muscatine to include, without his consent, the plaintiff's land, which was used exclusively for farming purposes. The city subsequently taxed the land at the sum of one dollar per acre. The plaintiff objected that he received no benefits from these tax payments and, consequently, his property was being taken without just compensation. He stated that his land was one mile distant from the former boundary of the city, and the same distance from any lands laid out into city lots, or used or needed for city purposes. The Iowa Supreme Court, in *Morford v. Unger* (1859),[28] asserted that if the owner of land adjoining a city or town should subdivide the property into lots and sell them to prospective homebuilders, he could not object to a law extending the authority of local government over his land so laid out for future occupation. However, if the land involved is a cultivated farm that obtains no benefits from the city's enlargement, this "is in reality nothing more than authority of the city to tax the land to a certain distance outside its limits" and, in effect, an unconstitutional taking of private property without compensation.

The Iowa Supreme Court held that legitimate taxation, whether by state or municipal authority, was not a taking of private property for public use, due to the protection afforded to the citizen by the government. However, " where an undue proportion of the burden of taxation is laid upon him, or when the power of local taxation is made to operate upon those . . . out of the reach of local benefits . . . [there is] plausible ground for alleging that property, taken for taxes authorized by law, is taken without just compensation." The court stated that if there is such a flagrant and palpable departure from the equality in the burden imposed, where many are benefited at the expense of one who is not, "it must be regarded as coming within the prohibition of the constitution designed to protect private rights against aggression, however made, and whether under the color of recognized power or not."

In *Henry v. Dubuque & Pacific Railroad Company* (1860),[29] the landowner sued the railroad company for trespass for breaking and grading his land in or-

der to install railroad tracks. The railroad had entered the property pursuant to a condemnation decree and judgment for compensation which had not been paid and had become a first lien on the railroad's real estate elsewhere in the county. The Iowa Supreme Court held for the plaintiff, stating that the condemnation judgment gave the railroad no right to enter the plaintiff's land. Until it paid the required compensation, the railroad had no possessory interest in the property. The Iowa court stated that while the Iowa Constitution contained a takings clause, the "plaintiff needed no constitutional declaration to protect him in the use and enjoyment of his property. . . . To be thus protected and thus secure . . . is a right inalienable, a right which a written constitution may recognize or declare, but which existed independently of and before such recognition, and which no government can destroy."

Kentucky

Gaines v. Buford (1833)[30] involved sections of an 1824 Kentucky statute that subjected to forfeiture to the state all lands on which there was a conflict of ownership whose owners did not make certain improvements to them. Under these provisions, every such tract 100 or more acres in size is forfeited to the state unless the owner clears, fences, and cultivates at least five acres, and in addition belts or chops trees on at least ten acres per thousand, all prior to August 1, 1825. States passed forfeiture laws to encourage development of land and industry. The particular law in question was prompted by problems relating to conflicting land claims. Two judges of the Kentucky Court of Appeals wrote opinions in the case, each applying different judicial reasoning and finding it unconstitutional as applied to a landowner who refused to comply with the said provisions of the 1824 statute.

Judge Underwood ruled that the provisions violated the federal and Kentucky constitutional provisions prohibiting the impairment of the obligation of contracts:

> The contract in the present case, as intended by the parties, was this, that Harvie [the original owner] and his heirs or assigns should enjoy the land granted, forever, in consideration of so much paid to the State for land warrants. The mode and manner of enjoyment was not prescribed: they were therefore left to the volition of the grantee. His dominion was not limited at the time of his purchase. The use to which he should apply the property, to administer to his happiness, was not then designated. In these matters he was left, by the contract, free. He had as a free man, all those rights and privileges which constitute the birthright of an American citizen. The effect of the act in question is to change the tenure and the contract.

The act subjected the owner to conditions—clearing, tending, and belting land by a given day—which were never reserved by the state in its original grant of the property:

> If an individual after selling land, was to claim the right of resuming the title, unless his vendee would submit to new conditions, one universal exclamation would denounce his claim as presumptuous, arbitrary and groundless. In matters of contract, I can not find two rules, one for states, the other for individuals. They must both share the same fate.

Underwood also ruled that the act was unconstitutional because the legislature has no power to take the property of one citizen and transfer it to another or apply it to public use without payment of just compensation:

> I am unwilling, however, to concede, that the legislature can, under the pretext of promoting the interest of the state, control and direct the citizen in the use he shall make of his private property. I subscribe to the maxim *sic utere tuo, ut alienum non laedas;* and I admit the power to punish for an injury done to individuals or the public. But I deny that the legislature can constitutionally prescribe, under color of preventing public or private mischief, the quantity of labor the citizen shall perform on his farm, the kind of improvements he shall make, and the time within which they must be constructed. The toleration of such power on the part of the government, would be conceding to it the right of controlling every man, and directing what road he shall travel in the "pursuit of happiness." Thus the freedom of the citizen would be lost in the despotic will of the government, and under the semblance of liberty, we should have the essence of tyranny.

Judge Nicholas delivered the other opinion, basing it on the separation of powers theory that the application of the forfeiture law was a matter for judicial and not legislative action: "To ascertain that Gaines had not made the required improvement, and thereupon condemn his title as forfeited to the State, belong not properly to legislation, but to adjudication." The landowner accused of violating the law was entitled to due process of law, a judicial hearing, and some mode of trial by jury before his property would be taken from him. Nicholas also viewed the forfeiture legislation as *ex post facto* and as a bill of attainder.

In the case of *Transylvania University v. Lexington* (1842),[31] the legislature enacted a law vacating a street that divided the university campus. Vacating a street requires the legislature to remove all restrictions that reserve the area primarily for movement of pedestrians and public transportation. The city of Lex-

ington opposed this vacating, contending that the legislature was devoid of power to enact it since the state had not provided compensation to all property owners who were affected. Stating that every owner has certain rights to the common and unobstructed use of a contiguous highway, the Kentucky Supreme Court ruled that the state must compensate each owner possessed of such right before the street could be vacated (or obtain his consent to it).

In *Cheany v. Hooser* (1848),[32] the Kentucky Supreme Court decided whether the plaintiff's property outside of the former limits of the city of Hopkinsville was subject to the taxing power of the city. The plaintiff owned a house within thirty feet of the former boundary from which it was separated by a street that was maintained by the town. The court held that the extension of the limits of a town whereby the property of an individual has been brought within the corporate limits without his consent, and subjected to taxation for town purposes, does not violate the state constitution's takings clause. However, the provision would be violated by a statute extending the boundary to comprehend vacant land or improved farm land occupied by the owner and his family for agricultural purposes, without being required for streets, houses, or any other purpose of the town but that of increasing its revenue. "Such an act," stated the court, "would in reality be nothing more or less than authority of the town to tax the land to a certain distance outside of its limits, and in effect take the money of the proprietor for its own use without compensation to him." Chief Justice Marshall of the Kentucky Supreme Court noted:

> There being no express constitutional declaration or prohibition directly applicable to the power or subject of taxation, and none which in terms secures equality or uniformity in the distribution of public burdens, either general or local, there is no clause to which the citizen can, with certainty, appeal for protection against an oppressive and ruinous discrimination under color of the taxing power, unless it be that which prohibits the taking of private property for public use, without compensation.

Subsequently, in *City of Covington v. Southgate* (1854),[33] the Kentucky Supreme Court adjudicated the constitutionality of a legislative statute that included, without the owner's consent, Southgate's 167 acres within the boundaries of the City of Covington. Southgate's property, which adjoined the former boundary, was utilized for farm fields, pasture, and woodland. The Kentucky high court concurred with the trial court's opinion that there was no legitimate necessity of the city that required that Southgate's land should be included within its boundary. The only apparent purpose was to subject the property to taxation for the benefit of the city. The Supreme Court held that the city may regard the land as within its boundary and subject to no other burdens than other lands outside the city. It may not be taxed until some portion of it is developed for lots or buildings, which

would indicate that it is used as part of the city. "[T]axation exercised under color of an unnecessary and unreasonable extension procured by the party to be bene-fited, and against or without the consent of those who are to be taxed, is an op-pression against which the constitution affords a protection to the individual, which the courts are bound to enforce."

Louisiana

Mabire v. Canal Bank (1837)[34] was a suit for damages which the plaintiff sustained as a result of the overflow of water caused by the defendant's con-struction of a canal on adjoining property. The defendant contended that the legislation authorizing the construction provided it with immunity against pay-ment of such damages. The Louisiana constitution did not contain a compen-sation provision until 1845. However, the trial court's charge to the jury stated that the legislature had no constitutional power to grant such immunity. The Louisiana Supreme Court upheld the verdict against the defendant, stating we "cannot entertain the idea that the legislature will ever sanction the expropria-tion of, or injury to private property, without a just indemnity."

Maine

In *Lee v. Pembroke Iron Company* (1867),[35] the plaintiff filed suit to recover damages to his grist mill, which he had owned since 1832, that were due to flooding caused by the defendant's dam that was built in 1853. The dam was erected under a statute that made no provision for compensation for damages caused by its installation and operation. The Supreme Judicial Court of Maine held that the plaintiff's property had been taken:

> It cannot be necessary to waste time or words to establish the proposition that he who assumes, under color of legislative authority, to overflow an ancient mill, "takes" that mill and privilege from the owner as directly and effectually as though he entered upon the premises and demolished the building. The truth of it is self-evident. . . . That a legislative grant of au-thority to do an act which is the immediate and sole cause of such a de-struction of his neighbor's property, shall not be so construed as to protect the party doing it from being required in some form to make just compen-sation, or to preclude the injured party from a remedy by due course of law, is a necessary sequence from the constitutional provisions referred to.

As agent of the state, the defendant in *Comins v. Bradbury* (1833)[36] located a road through the plaintiff's land without paying compensation, justifying this

on the basis that the legislature made no provision for just compensation when it authorized the road. The state attorney general contended that there was no necessity for directing a remuneration to the plaintiff since it was already secured to him in the state's constitution; a statute would have given the defendant no greater right than he already enjoyed. The Maine Supreme Judicial Court rejected this argument, though, stating that compensation must be made or provided for, when the property is taken: "It is upon that condition alone that such taking is authorized."

Lewis v. Webb (1825)[37] struck down a statute granting an appeal from a probate court's decree in a particular case. The statute allowed the probate court to adjudicate a claim on which the statutory time limit had passed. It had been enacted at the request of a bondsman who said that he was not aware of the probate proceeding until long after the time allowed by law for an appeal had elapsed. In support of its ruling, the court cited Blackstone's statement that law is defined as "a rule of civil conduct," that, hence, it must be general and prospective; a rule for all, binding on all. The court stated:

> On principle then, it can never be within the bounds of legitimate legislation, to enact a special law, or pass a resolve dispensing with the general law, in a particular case, and granting a privilege and indulgence to one man, by way of exemption from the operation and effect of such general law, leaving all other persons under its operation. Such a law is neither just nor reasonable in its consequences. It is our boast that we live under a government of laws and not of men. But this can hardly be deemed a blessing unless those laws have for their immovable basis the great principle of constitutional equality. Can it be supposed for a moment, that if the legislature should pass a general law, and add a section by way of proviso, that it never should be construed to have any operation or effect upon the persons, rights or property of [plaintiff Lewis, et al.] such a proviso would receive the sanction or even the countenance of a court of law? And how does the supposed case differ in principle from the present? A resolve passed after the general law, can produce only the same effect as such proviso. In fact, neither can have any legal operation.

This decision was cited and upheld in *Durham v. Lewiston* (1825).[38] In the latter case, Maine's high court struck down a statute granting special judicial review to the defeated party after entry of a judgment in a suit between private parties.

The Maine Supreme Court, in *Saco v. Wentworth* (1853),[39] considered the constitutionality of an act that limited a person's right to a trial by jury. The statute provided that upon an indictment of a grand jury for an alleged criminal act, the trial should be by the court, unless the accused should demand a trial by jury. However, as a prerequisite for obtaining a jury trial, the accused must post a bond, in a large penal sum, guaranteeing that he will abstain from the

commission of all criminal offenses for a given period. Citing Chapter 29 of the Magna Carta, Coke, Blackstone, Kent, and Justice Joseph Story, the court held the statute void as being in violation of the state constitution's law of the land clause. The court stated that "law of the land," as used in the state constitution,

> does not mean any act of the legislature; if such was the true construction, this branch of the government could at any time take away life, liberty, property and privilege, without a trial by jury. . . . An Act of the Legislature, which takes away this privilege of trial by jury directly, is tyrannical and a palpable violation of the constitution; one which renders it difficult to obtain, beyond what public necessity requires, impairs individual rights and is inconsistent with this provision for their protection.[40]

Maryland

The Supreme Court of Maryland, in *Regents of the University of Maryland v. Williams* (1838),[41] upheld the property (and other) rights of the university regents under a charter of incorporation issued in 1812 against changes depriving them of certain of these rights enacted by the legislature in 1825. The court held that the 1825 act violated the obligation of contracts provision in Article I, Section 10 of the U.S. Constitution. The act was also held to be a violation of the law of the land provision of the Maryland Constitution:

> By "the law of the land" is meant, by the due course and process of the law. . . . The general law, prescribed and existing as a rule of civil conduct, relating to the community in general, judicially to be administered by the Courts of justice. An Act which only affects and exhausts itself upon a particular person, or his rights and privileges, and has no relation to the community in general, "is rather a sentence than a law." 1 *Blackstone Com.* 44. A sentence that condemns without a hearing, and the very passing of which implies the absence of any general law or rule of civil conduct, by which the same purpose could be judicially effected in a Court of law.
>
> If the transferring one person's property to another, by a special and particular Act of the Legislature, is a depriving him of his property, by or according to the law of the land, then any legislative judgment or decree, in any possible form, would be according to the law of the land, although there existed at the time no law of the land upon the subject, and that too by a tribunal possessing no judicial power, and to which all power is denied by the Constitution. Such a construction would tend to the union of all the powers of the government in the Legislature, and to impart the at-

tribute of omnipotency to that department, contrary to the genius and spirit of all our institutions; and the office of Courts would be not to declare the law or to administer the justice of the country, but to execute legislative judgements and decrees, not authorized by the Constitution.

Harness v. The Chesapeake and Ohio Canal Company (1848)[42] involved the question of whether a company for whom the county had condemned the plaintiff's land could commence operations on the land prior to the payment of the condemnation award. Maryland's constitution contained no takings clause, a fact which also raised the question of whether in the absence of such a clause, the legislature was required to compensate the defendants for their land. The court held that the constitution's law of the land and separation of powers clauses required payment of compensation, citing Kent's opinion in *Gardner* and his *Commentaries*. The court asserted that the principle of just compensation for the taking of private property for public use was founded in "universal law" and "natural justice," and even in the charters which were not explicit: "[Y]et to it exists with stringent force, independent of any positive provision." The court also cited approvingly Kent's statement in his *Commentaries* that, with respect to when payment must be made, "the better opinion is that the compensation, or offer of it, must precede, or be concurrent with the seizure and entry upon private property under the authority of the state."

Massachusetts

The selectmen of Charlestown adopted a by-law prohibiting any dead body from being brought into the town for interment. The by-law allowed the selectmen to waive this prohibition. The Massachusetts Supreme Court found that the selectmen never intended to apply this waiver to the interment of Catholics. The court invalidated the law, in *Austin v. Murray* (1834),[43] holding that it was made for exclusionary purposes and not to preserve the health of the town's inhabitants:

> The illegality of a by-law is the same whether it may deprive an individual of the use of a part or of the whole of his property; no one can be so deprived, unless the public good requires it. And the law will not allow the right of property to be invaded, under the guise of a police regulation for the preservation of health, when it is manifest that such is not the object and purpose of the regulation. . . .
> The by-law "is a clear and direct infringement of the right of property, without any compensating advantages, and not a police regulation, made in good faith for the preservation of health."

Patterson v. City of Boston (1838)[44] involved a Boston ordinance widening Doane Street. It was understood that the city would pay compensation to the owners of the properties affected, but the city refused to include compensation for the front part of a store that was destroyed during the construction process. The plaintiff contended that the construction prevented him from using the store for twenty-five months, and demanded compensation for damages he sustained as a consequence of the construction. Interpreting the state's takings clause, the Massachusetts Supreme Court, per the famed Chief Justice Lemuel Shaw, held that the plaintiff was entitled to compensation for "the loss of the use of his tenement during the time he was necessarily deprived of it." Shaw also included in computing compensation the cost of building a new store front, the financial obligations under the lease, and the expense occasioned in moving the goods from the store. The plaintiff also sought compensation for the loss of profits he sustained because he had to move to a less advantageous place of business, but the court referred this issue back to the trial court for resolution.

In *Parker v. Boston and Maine Railroad* (1849),[45] the Massachusetts high court (in an opinion also written by Chief Justice Shaw) again held that a plaintiff who sustains damage as a consequence of government action is entitled to payment of compensation. The defendant railroad acting under the authority of the state had deeply excavated land adjacent to the plaintiff's property in order to enable its trains to pass under a bridge. This excavation completely drained a well on the plaintiff's property. The court interpreted the takings clause of the state constitution as requiring payment of compensation for the loss of usage of a well.

This case also concerned other construction work by the railroad that was preventing the plaintiff's free access to his property: huge embankments it had constructed along one street and deep excavations it had made along another street. The court held that each of these two acts were takings of property rights, thus requiring payment of compensation.

Frequently, when the government acquires and pays for privately owned land on which to install a road, the owner may sustain more damage than merely being deprived of this land. The new road may deny him ready access to water or make cultivation of his farm inconvenient and laborious. It may also necessitate installing fences to prevent cattle from straying on the new road. (Of course, on occasion, the owner may sustain little or no injury.) In a number of cases, the Massachussetts Supreme Court confronted the issue of whether owners should be compensated for these additional expenses.

In *Commonwealth v. Coombs* (1807),[46] the Massachusetts court recognized expenditures for the new fencing required in such situations as damages for which the owner must be indemnified in the payment of compensation. In *Commonwealth v. Justices of Middlesex* (1812),[47] it was held that no compensation is owed when the benefits to the owner are equal to or in excess of the damage sustained. In *Perley v. Chandler* (1810),[48] the court allowed inclusion of the expenses involved in construction of a culvert for the passage of water beneath a

new road as a proper item of compensation. Subsequently, the court, in *Brown v. Worcester* (1859)[49] and *Old Colony & Fall River Railroad Co. v. County of Plymouth* (1859),[50] recognized as compensable in takings cases expenses related to the property owner's moving his house away from the location of a planned highway, and the expenses for constructing cattle guards and railroad signs when the county installed a public highway across the path of a railroad. (Three other Massachusetts takings cases, *Callender v. Marsh* [1823], *Commonwealth v. Tewksbury* [1846], and *Commonwealth v. Alger* [1851], are discussed in Section III *infra*.)

Hazen v. The Essex Co. (1853)[51] concerned an incorporation statute that chartered the defendant company for the purpose of constructing a dam across a river and one or more locks and canals in connection with it to create a water power to be used for manufacturing purposes. The plaintiff owned a mill on a small stream flowing into a river above the dam, and complained that the dam caused the overflowing of his mill to its destruction and that it should not be protected as an eminent domain taking because it was constructed for a private and not a public purpose. The statute limited the compensation to those who were flooded by the dam to damages ascertained by the method provided for assessing damages for property taken by railroad corporations.

The Massachusetts high court upheld the constitutionality of the statute, rejecting the plaintiff's contention that the statute was unconstitutional because (1) the dam served a private and not a public use and (2) the provision for obtaining compensation was inadequate. Chief Justice Shaw asserted that the legislature had the power to authorize the plaintiff's land to be flowed because it effected a public use: "The establishment of a great mill-power for manufacturing purposes, as an object of great public interest, especially since manufacturing has come to be one of the great public industrial pursuits of the commonwealth, seems to have been regarded by the legislature, and sanctioned by the jurisprudence of the commonwealth, and in our judgment rightly so, in determining what is a public use, justifying the exercise of the right of eminent domain." The plaintiff's right to compensation was protected procedurally and by having access to both a special commission and a jury for determination of its amount. "It is said that compensation for property appropriated, is a common law right, independent of the (state) declaration of rights. If, by this, it is intended to state that compensation in such cases is required by a plain dictate of natural justice, it must be conceded. But this right may be regulated and remedy be made certain and definite by law."

Holden v. James (1814)[52] involved a Massachusetts statute that suspended the operation of an existing four-year statute of limitations with respect to claims that Holden had against the estate of Hannah Ranger. The Massachusetts high court found the statute unconstitutional on the ground that it was special legislation. It considered the English background of this kind of problem, that under the Magna Carta and the bill of rights passed during the reign of

William and Mary, the king was denied the power to suspend laws without the consent of Parliament. This power of suspending laws was later accorded solely to Parliament, as the supreme political body of the nation. The court reasoned:

> [In the United States] the sovereign and absolute power resides in the people; and the legislature can only exercise what is delegated to them according to the constitution. It is obvious that the exercise of the power in question would be equally oppressive to the subject, and subversive of his right to protection, "according to standing laws," whether exercised by one man or by a number of men. It cannot be supposed that the people, when adopting this general principle from the English bill of rights, and inserting it in our constitution, intended to bestow, by implication, on the General Court one of the most odious and oppressive prerogatives of the ancient kings of *England*. It is manifestly contrary to the first principles of civil liberty and natural justice, and to the spirit of our constitution and laws, that any one citizen should enjoy privileges and advantages which are denied to all others under like circumstances; or that any one should be subjected to losses, damages, suits, or actions, from which all others, under like circumstances, are exempted.

In *Piquet, Appellant* (1827),[53] Picquet sought official authority to administer the estate of her deceased father but was unable to post the $50,000 penal bond required by the probate judge to assure the faithful administration and accounting of property contained in the estate. Picquet obtained from the legislature the passage of a statute empowering the probate judge to accept a bond permitting less legal and monetary protection for the estate. The Massachusetts high court concluded that if the statute required that the probate judge accept a bond from Picquet different from that required of others, the law would be unconstitutional, citing, among other things, the decision in *Holden v. James* (discussed above) as authoritative on the issue. The court, however, concluded that the statute was not a directive to the probate judge, but only the authority to accept a bond lesser in amount that left standing the original requirements of the statute: "[W]e think it very clear that [legislators] have no authority by the constitution to suspend any of the general laws, limiting the suspension to an actual person, and leaving the law still in force in regard to every one else."

Michigan

Avery v. Fox (1868)[54] was a Michigan U.S. Circuit Court decision that upheld an owner's riparian rights to use an adjoining natural water source. (A riparian right is one enjoyed by the owner of land on the bank of a body of wa-

ter.) Congress ordered the construction of a small canal linking Lake Michigan with White Lake, which was 275 yards away. The problem was that the canal would drain water out of the White River to the detriment of persons who had been using its water to convey logs to a sawmill that they owned. The court did not find sufficient evidence to substantiate this claim. However, it did make clear what a riparian owner's rights are in such a situation:

> It is . . . well settled law, that a riparian proprietor has a property in the use of water flowing by his premises; that is, a right to it in its flow, in any manner not inconsistent with the rights of others to its use. . . . [When] a riparian owner is wholly or injuriously deprived of the use of its water which he is employing advantageously as an incident to his land, it is a taking of private property [under the common law and U.S. Constitution] of such owner in and to the use of that water for public use . . . unless just compensation is made. . . .

To alleviate the problem of obstructions and, in particular, of logs freely floating in public streams or waters, the Michigan legislature enacted a statute enabling private persons to incorporate rafting companies for the purposes of controlling such problems. The law permitted these companies, whenever a stream is obstructed by logs, to assume possession and control of them and collect their charges and expenses from the sale of the logs. In *Ames v. The Port Huron Log Driving and Booming Co.* (1863),[55] the Michigan Supreme Court held the law unconstitutional on two grounds: (1) It allowed persons to assume control over waterways, and thus to exercise a public office without an election or appointment. (2) It allowed a rafting company to assume control at will of logs that it does not own that are floating in waterways and to sell the logs to pay its charges and expenses, in violation of the state constitution's due process of law guarantees. It is "an inflexible principle of constitutional right that no person can legally be divested of his property without remuneration, or against his will, unless he be allowed a hearing before an impartial tribunal, where he may contest the claim set up against him, and be allowed to meet it in the law and the facts." The statute made the company judge in its own cause, stated the court, and empowered it to impose and execute its own monetary judgments.

In 1863, the Supreme Court of Michigan considered the constitutionality of the state's boat and vessel law in *Parsons v. Russell*.[56] Under that law, a vessel could be seized and sold upon assertion of a debt, without submission of any proof to a court to support the claim, and without any judgment of a court allowing the sale. The owner of the vessel argued that the law violated the due process clause of the state's constitution. In holding the law unconstitutional, the court majority stated that the due process clause was intended to secure the right of a proper trial before one's person or property is condemned: "[W]e recognize

and adopt the fundamental principle that no man shall be party and judge in his own case; that if tried, it shall be by his peers, and if deprived of liberty or property, it shall be by impartial judicial authority, after a trial and judgment under general laws." Due process protection "implies and includes *actor, reus, judex*—regular allegations, opportunity to answer, and trial according to some settled course of judicial proceedings."

Minnesota

The Minnesota Supreme Court held, in *Gray v. First Division, St. Paul and Pacific R. Co.* (1860),[57] that the public easement of a common street or highway does not include the right to construct and operate a railroad on it, even when the railroad company's legislative charter clearly authorizes it to construct its road upon, along, across, under, or over any public or private highway, road, or street if such construction is deemed necessary. Constructing and operating a railroad upon a public street or highway is, with respect to the owner of the fee of the street, a taking of private property for public use that requires payment of compensation in order for it to be valid. The owner had only granted the public a limited easement for street purposes. The legislature had no authority to require the owner of the fee to confer upon the public a larger interest than he is willing to grant.

The Minnesota Supreme Court ruled, in *Winona & St. Peter Railroad Company v. Denmon* (1865),[58] that in ascertaining the compensation to be paid for taking a strip of land through a tract used as a farm for public use by a railroad, it is proper to consider not only the value of this strip, but also the injury to the entire tract. In addition, the expense to the owner of fencing made necessary by this taking has to be considered in ascertaining damages. The court asserted that the primary meaning of compensation is "equivalence," and the secondary and more common meaning is "something given or obtained as an equivalent." Compensation that included only the value of a strip that divides a farm, and creates great inconvenience to the owner, does not provide an equivalent payment for the injury sustained by the owner.

An 1870 Minnesota statute for the acquisition of private property for public use from nonconsenting owners, provided for the appointment of three private persons as commissioners to determine the amount of compensation to be awarded the owners. It did not require any notice of the proceedings, nor provide that the owners may at any stage of the proceedings appear before the commissioners for any purpose. Citing Blackstone and Kent, among others, the Minnesota Supreme Court, in *Landford v. County of Ramsey* (1871),[59] held that the statute violated the state constitution's takings clause. This provision, the court asserted, requires a judicial proceeding, which would afford the landowner an

opportunity to participate in the determination of the condemnation award. "While the legislature is the judge of the necessity or expediency of the exercise of the power of eminent domain, it is not the judge of the amount or justness of compensation to be made when the power is exercised. . . ."

Mississippi

Mississippi state law provided for a forfeiture of land to the state on the failure of the owner to pay the taxes due thereon. In *Griffin v. Mixon* (1860),[60] the High Court of Errors and Appeals of Mississippi found that the act was an assumption of executive and judicial power by the legislature that divested the owner of his property, without "due course of law," without "just compensation first made" by a simple act of legislation, without hearing, without inquiry, and without notice. The court held that the summary process that was established by the act for divesting its owner of his property violated both the takings and due course of the law provisions of the state constitution. In every case where the state seeks to divest an owner of his property, judicial proceedings must intervene to decide the charge of delinquency. It cited the Magna Carta, Coke, Blackstone, Kent, Story, and similar authorities in support of its opinion.

The takings clause of the Mississippi Constitution declares that "no person's property shall be taken or applied to public use without the consent of the legislature, and without a just compensation first made therefor." The state charter of the Grand Gulf Railroad and Banking Company authorizes the company—whenever there is disagreement with landowners about the amount of compensation due—to petition a circuit court to empanel a jury to determine this amount. Then, upon valuation, the circuit court is to convey the land to the company, and give judgment and execution against the company, in favor of the landowner, for the amount of the valuation. The power in a state to appropriate by virtue of the power of eminent domain, the Mississippi high court asserted, in *Thompson v. The Grand Gulf Railroad and Banking Company* (1839),[61] should be exercised only in keeping with the strictest justice toward the owner. Citing Chancellor Kent and European commentators, the court held that the legislature acted unconstitutionally in authorizing the railroad company to take property and give the owner no other compensation than a judgment and execution. Favorably citing Kent for this position, the court concluded that compensation should proceed or be concurrent with the appropriation of private property.

Upon the application of the Mississippi Central Railroad Company, a jury was summoned under the provisions of the railroad's charter to "value the damages" that the landowner will sustain by the use or occupation of his land by the railroad. The charter required the jury, in estimating the damages, to take

into account the benefits resulting to the owner, by reason of the road running through the land, "toward the extinguishment of his claim for damages." In *Isom v. The Mississippi Central Railroad Co.* (1858),[62] the court asserted that before any person's property shall be applied to public use, just compensation shall first be made. The phrase "just compensation first . . . made" means that an equivalent in money for the injury or deprivation of rights inflicted must be provided. Moreover, said the court, compensation includes only payment for the present injury sustained by such deprivation of right, without regard to future or prospective benefits or to the "unreal advantages" likely to accrue on account of the contemplated construction of the road in the future. "Whatever is then incapable of definite ascertainment, but rests merely on conjecture, possibility, or probability, dependent on the future, cannot be taken into estimate by any rule of 'just compensation.'" The entire clause relating to the "extinguishment of his claim for damages" is consequently void.

Interpreting the separation of powers that is required under the state's Declaration of Rights, the court held that determining just compensation is a judicial and not a legislative responsibility:

> The right of the legislature or the State, by law, to apply the property of the citizen to the public use, and then to constitute itself the judge in its own case, to determine what is the "just compensation" it ought to pay therefor; or how much benefit it has conferred upon the citizen by thus taking his property without his consent; or to extinguish any part of such "compensation," by prospective conjectural advantage; or, in any manner, to interfere with the just powers and province of courts and juries in administering right and justice, cannot for a moment be admitted or tolerated under our constitution. If anything can be clear and undeniable, upon principles of natural justice, or constitutional law, it seems that this must be so.

Missouri

Wells v. City of Weston (1856)[63] involved the issue of whether the state constitution empowers the legislature to confer upon the city of Weston the authority to pass an act levying a tax, for local purposes, on land lying within one-half mile of the city boundaries. Quoting extensively from the Kentucky case of *Cheany v. Hooser,* the Missouri Supreme Court held that the act violated the state's takings clause. The court stated that under the state statute,

> those who live in the town are authorized to exact annually from those who live adjacent to it, a certain portion of their property, to be applied,

under their own direction, to their own local purposes. And this we think cannot be done under our government, which was instituted exclusively for the protection of individual rights, and where private property is expressly protected from any appropriation of it, even for public use, without full compensation to the owner.

New Hampshire

The Proprietors of the Piscataqua Bridge v. The New Hampshire Bridge (1834)[64] involved the grant to the plaintiffs by the New Hampshire legislature the exclusive right of building and maintaining a bridge over a certain stretch of river and, subsequently, the grant of a right to the defendants to build a bridge over the same area. The plaintiffs charged that the second grant violated the right of property they had previously obtained. The New Hampshire Supreme Court agreed that the plaintiffs' grant constituted property that was protected in the state's bill of rights, which provided as follows: "No part of a man's property shall be taken from him or applied to public uses, without his own consent, of that of the representative body of the people." The Court held that this article included "as a matter of right, and as one of the first principles of justice, the further limitation, that in case his property is taken without his consent, due compensation must be provided," citing (among others) Kent in *Gardner* and Blackstone. Since the statute had not provided for compensation, the court issued an injunction prohibiting the defendants from building a bridge at any place within the limits of the grant to the plaintiffs without the latter's consent.

Citing *Piscataqua Bridge,* the New Hampshire Supreme Court, in *Petition of the Mount Washington Road Co.* (1857),[65] held that, notwithstanding the absence of a takings clause in the state's constitution, the constitution's protections of property mandated application of the "well established maxim of universal law" that private property can only be taken for public use upon payment of just compensation. This was a petition for the assessment of damages to landowners caused by the laying out of a road by a private corporation under authority granted by statute. Pursuant to its interpretation of "universal law," the court held that damages must be paid for all injury done by laying out the road to the tract of land through which it passes, including not only the value of the land actually taken, but all damage from inconvenient division of the tract and the need for additional fencing. Damages need not be paid for the probable injury that the business of a landowner may suffer from competition introduced by the building of the new road.

The issue in *Company v. Fernald* (1867)[66] was whether the legislature had power under the state's constitution to authorize a corporation established for

manufacturing purposes to install a dam that would cause flooding of adjoining land without that owner's consent. The state constitution did not then contain a guarantee of just compensation. However, the New Hampshire Supreme Court acknowledged that the constitution implied this guarantee when property was taken for public use. It held that the purpose for which the dam in question was constructed was to improve water power in the state, and this purpose made the use a public one. The population of the state would benefit from the construction of such dams since they were vital for ensuring the success of the manufacturing industry. The court denied that the dam advantaged only the private corporation. According to this court, the meaning of public use reaches to all cases of general public utility, citing as further support high court decisions of California, Connecticut, Massachusetts, Wisconsin, and Indiana.

In a later case, a defendant railroad, acting under public authorization, installed its tracks on the plaintiff's farm. In so doing, it impaired a nearby ridge, thus enabling water from a river to flood the farm intermittently and to cover it with earth and rocks—an occurrence which made the land unfit for cultivation. The railroad argued that no taking had occurred, because the damages consisted only of a denial of beneficial use and the ownership was not otherwise disturbed. Rejecting this claim, the New Hampshire Supreme Court held, in *Eaton v. Boston C. & M. Railroad* (1872),[67] that a deprivation of beneficial use constituted a taking:

> Property is the right of any person to possess, use, enjoy, and dispose of a thing. [citation]. If property in land consists in certain essential rights, and a physical interference with the land substantially subverts one of these rights, such interference "takes", *pro tanto,* the owner's "property. . . ."

New Jersey

Bonaparte v. Camden & A.R. Co. (1830)[68] is a federal circuit court case that arose when the defendant (a railroad company) entered the plaintiff's land and staked out a road there without his permission. The New Jersey legislature incorporated the company for the primary purpose of installing a railroad between two cities in the state, and the company acted under color of the legislative act. The statute appointed a commission to ascertain compensatory damages, but it had made no award prior to the company's entry onto the land. At the time of entry, the New Jersey constitution did not contain a takings clause. Nevertheless, the court held that "it is an incident to the sovereignty of every government, that it may take private property for public use;

of the necessity or expediency of which, the government must judge; but the obligation to make just compensation is concomitant with the right."

According to this court, compensatory damages need not be ascertained by a jury; an appointed commission is in harmony with common law requirements. Compensation must be made prior to the divestiture of the owner's rights. An entry on private property for the mere purpose of exploration is not a taking requiring compensation (unless permanent injury is inflicted in the process); however, a permanent application of private property for public use demands compensation.

In *Sinnickson v. Johnson* (1839),[69] the New Jersey Supreme Court held that the flooding of lands caused by damming a creek during the construction of a canal was a taking of a riparian owner's property. The work was authorized by a statute of the state and performed by a private contractor, but the court held that the contractor must compensate the owner for the devaluation of his land. The New Jersey Constitution did not contain a takings clause, the absence of which, the court stated, did not eliminate the right to compensation: "This power to take private property reaches back of all constitutional provisions; and it seems to have been considered a settled principle of universal law, that the right to compensation, is an incident to the exercise of that power: that the one is so inseparably connected with the other, that they may be said to exist not as separate and distinct principles, but as parts of one and the same principle." The court cited as authority (among others) for this conclusion, Blackstone, Kent, Pufendorf, Montesquieu, and Vattel, stating further that "the legislature of this state, can no more take private property for public use, without just compensation, than if the restraining principle were incorporated into, and made part of its state constitution."

Glover v. Powell (1854)[70] concerned a dam on a small creek that had been erected and maintained pursuant to an act passed by the legislature of the then colony of New Jersey in 1760, and which the New Jersey legislature in 1854 required to be removed, declaring the creek to be a public highway. The complainants were the joint owners of land on both sides of the creek who had erected the dam and waterworks connected with it, and subsequently maintained it and alleged ownership of it. The complainants sought an injunction against demolition of the dam and waterworks. The New Jersey Chancellor held that the 1854 act violated the U.S. Constitution's prohibitions on a state passing a bill of attainder, *ex post facto* law, or law impairing the obligation of contracts. He also ruled that the statute violated the state constitution, which by then had two takings clauses:

> The value of the meadow is destroyed by the execution of the law in question, and thus may be said, with propriety, to be taken from their owners. A partial destruction, a diminution of their value, is the tak-

ing of private property. The act cannot be carried into effect without a violation of the constitution of the state.

New York

New York state decisions prior to the ratification of the Fourteenth Amendment on July 9, 1868, viewed law of the land and due process clauses as strongly protective of property ownership. According to James Kent, the celebrated New York jurist and legal commentator, writing in his *Commentaries* (1826), the words "law of the land"

> as used originally in Magna Charta [Chapter 29] are understood to mean, due process of law, that is by indictment or presentment of good and lawful men: and this, says Lord Coke, "is the true sense and exposition of those words." The better and larger definition of due process of law is, that it means law in its regular course of administration through courts of justice.[71]

> The [due process] clause means, that statutes which would deprive a citizen of the rights of person or property without a regular trial, according to the course and usage of the common law, would not be law of the land in the sense of the Constitution.[72]

With respect to compensation, Kent wrote as follows:

> A provision for compensation is a necessary attendant on the due and constitutional exercise of the power of the lawgiver to deprive an individual of his property, without his consent; and this principle in American constitutional jurisprudence is founded in natural equity; and is laid down by jurists, as an acknowledged principle of universal law.[73]

Consistent with Blackstone, Kent referred to certain personal rights as absolute: "The absolute rights of individuals may be resolved into their right of personal security, the right of personal liberty, and the right to acquire and enjoy property. These rights have been justly considered, and frequently declared, by the people of this country, to be natural, inherent, and inalienable."[74]

Kent is also noted for some of his opinions as a jurist. In *Dash v. Van Kleeck* (1811),[75] the issue before the court was whether the civil statute adopted in 1809 that eliminated certain rights contained in the civil statute passed in 1801 controls the outcome of the litigation in question. He wrote that an act of the

legislature is not to be construed to operate retrospectively so as to eliminate a vested right, that "the very essence of a new law is a rule for future cases." He held in the case that it is a principle of universal jurisprudence that laws, civil or criminal, must be prospective and cannot have a retroactive effect:

> Our case is happily very different from that of the subjects of Justinian. With us, the power of the lawgiver is limited and defined; the judicial is regarded as a distinct independent power; private rights have been better understood and more exalted in public estimation as well as secured by provisions dictated by the spirit of freedom, and unknown to the civil law. Our institutions do not admit the power assumed by the Roman prince; and the principle we are considering is now to be regarded as sacred. It is not pretended that we have any express constitutional provision on the subject; nor have we any for numerous other rights dear alike to freedom and to justice. An *ex post facto* law, in the strict technical sense of the term, is usually understood to apply to criminal cases, and this is its meaning, when used in the Constitution of the United States; yet laws impairing previously acquired civil rights are equally within the reach of that prohibition and equally to be condemned. We have seen that the cases in the English and in the civil law apply to such rights; and we shall find, upon further examination, that there is no distinction in principle, nor any recognized in practice between a law punishing a person criminally, for a past innocent act, or punishing him civilly by divesting him of a lawfully acquired right. The distinction consists only in the degree of the oppression, and history teaches us that the government which can deliberately violate the one right, soon ceases to regard the other.

In *Gardner v. Trustees of the Village of Newburgh* (1816),[76] Kent relied on due process in a case involving a partial deprivation of an owner's property that resulted from the village's improvement of its water supply that diverted water that had long flowed over the owner's land. He held that the village could not deprive an owner who was innocent of wrongdoing of a portion of his property without payment of compensation. Chancellor Kent found that a right to a stream of water "is as sacred as a right to the soil over which it flows." It was, therefore, "part of the freehold of which no man can be disseised 'but by lawful judgment of his peers, or by due process of law.' This is an ancient and fundamental maxim of common right to be found in Magna Charta, and which the legislature has incorporated into an Act declaratory of the rights of the citizens of this state." The New York Constitution contained no takings clause until 1821. Kent held that the state's due process guarantee would be violated if the owner of the land through which the stream flowed was not compensated for the loss he suffered in the event that the flow over his land was diverted by the

city. "I feel myself, therefore, not only authorized, but bound to conclude that a provision for compensation is an indispensable attendant on the due and constitutional exercise of the power of depriving an individual of his property. . . . "

People v. Platt (1819)[77] involved two statutes requiring riparian owners of dams that obstructed the usual course of salmon in going up any river or creek flowing into the great lakes to alter their dams in order to enable the salmon to pass. Platt owned land on both sides of the Saranac River, which was a nonnavigable waterway, and had previously erected a dam across it that blocked the passage of salmon. Compliance with the statute required him either to destroy or substantially to modify the dam. Because the river was nonnavigable, New York's Supreme Court of Judicature found that Platt's land was "wholly and absolutely" his and ruled that the statutes violated his property rights. Inasmuch as no equivalent was offered "for the loss which must inevitably ensue, upon compliance," and since "such appropriations are constitutional, legal, and justifiable only when a fair and just equivalent is awarded," the statute could not be sustained under the power of eminent domain. Nonnavigable rivers are capable of serving only local commerce and travel. The court noted that the legislature was empowered to regulate navigable rivers to improve navigation. The latter are part of water highways accommodating extensive commerce and travel.

The extent of such power was decided in *Canal Fund v. Kempshall* (1841)[78] by New York's Court for the Correction of Errors. This case involved a temporary obstruction to water conduits providing water from the Genesee River, which was a navigable waterway, to Kempshall's mill. The state's construction of a new aqueduct blocked for a short period water service to the mill. The court held that a taking had occurred, since the common law authority of the state over such rivers related only to navigation and did not comprehend the power to divert the waters for other purposes, such as construction of the aqueduct. The state may divert navigable waters for these other purposes, but only under eminent domain authority and payment of compensation.

Decided prior to inclusion of a takings clause in the New York Constitution, *Rogers v. Bradshaw* (1823)[79] involved a statute that authorized the canal commissioners to acquire land for extending a canal across a part of a turnpike road, but it contained no provision for compensation. The trial court stated that a just compensation provision was merely declaratory of a great and fundamental principle, and that any law violating that principle would be deemed a nullity, as being against natural rights and justice. It accordingly held the statute to be invalid. On appeal, the Court of Errors agreed: "This equitable and constitutional right to compensation, undoubtedly imposes it as an absolute duty on the legislature to make provision for compensation, whenever they authorize an interference with private right."

Taylor v. Porter (1843)[80] concerned a New York statute that authorized the commissioners of highways to lay out a private road for the benefit of persons

who did not own the land on which the road was to be situated. When every such private road was so laid out, it was for the use solely of the applicant, his heirs and assigns, and persons doing business with him, and was not to be considered a public highway, nor converted to any other use than that of a private road. The owner of the land through which such a road was laid out was permitted to use the road only if he signified his intention to do so prior to the determination of the amount of compensation due him. Compensation was assessed by a jury of six freeholders of another town and paid by the applicant for the road. This was an action of trespass for making and laying out a private road through and over the plaintiff's land.

The New York Court of Appeals, per Justice Bronson, held that a private road cannot be laid out without the consent of the owner of the land over which it passes. It interpreted the statute as requiring a transfer of land from one person to another and not as a matter of eminent domain, which involves a transfer to the public. "In short," said the court, "the road is the private property of the applicant." The court ruled that the statute violated the law of the land and due process clauses of the state constitution. The law of the land, wrote Justice Bronson, requires that before a person can be deprived of his property for private and not public purposes, "it must be ascertained judicially that he has forfeited his privileges, or that someone else has a superior title to the property he possesses. It cannot be done by mere legislation." Payment of compensation does not make legitimate the taking of private property for private purposes:

> The words "by the law of the land," as here used, do not mean a statute passed for the purpose of working the wrong. That construction would render the restriction absolutely nugatory, and turn this part of the Constitution into mere nonsense. The people would be made to say to the two [legislative] houses: "You shall be vested with 'the legislative power of the state;' but no one 'shall be disenfranchised, or deprived of any of the rights or privileges of a citizen, unless you pass a statute for that purpose;' in other words 'You shall not do the wrong, unless you choose to do it.'" The section was taken with some modifications from a part of the twenty-ninth chapter of the Magna Charta, which provided, that no freeman should be taken, or imprisoned, or be disseised of his freehold, etc., but by lawful judgment of his peers, or by the law of the land. Lord Coke in his commentary upon this statute, says, that these words, "by the law of the land," mean "by the due course and process of law;" which he afterwards explains to be, "by indictment or presentment of good and lawful men, where such deeds be done in due manner, or by writ original of the common law."

The Court held that the statute also violated the due process clause of the state's constitution:

> The words due process of law . . . cannot mean less than a prosecution or
> suit instituted and conducted according to the prescribed forms and
> solemnities for ascertaining guilt, or determining the title of property. It
> will be seen that the same measure of protection against legislative en-
> croachment is extended to life, liberty and property; and if the latter can
> be taken without a forensic trial and judgment, there is no security for the
> others. If the legislature can take the property of A and transfer it to B,
> they can take A himself, and either shut him up in prison, or put him to
> death. But none of these things can be done by mere legislation. There
> must be "due process of law."[81]

The New York court thus struck down a colonial statute which, according to
legal scholar Morton Hurwitz, "had been employed hundreds of times before
to enable landowners to build private roads through another's property. . . .
[T]he court refused to accept what before had been a standard and virtually unchallenged utilitarian justification of these acts."[82] However, the court viewed
the issue differently and applied a strict interpretation of property rights, a move
which also qualifies generally as a utilitarian approach. As U.S. Supreme Court
Justice Anthony Kennedy put it in a 1992 case: "The takings clause . . . protects
private expectations to ensure private investment."[83] The requirement of public use is an important protection against the legislature transferring property at
will. When the judiciary protects private ownership from government regulation, it removes the high cost of political unpredictability from the investor's
balance sheet. Investors purchase property on the basis of the risks they expect
to encounter as owners. The higher the risk, the fewer the number of investors.
The result of such increased risk is not only higher prices but also reduced production, creativity, and competition, which are all factors essential to societal
advancement, well-being, and prosperity.[84]

In *Embury v. Conner* (1850),[85] the New York high court concluded that *Taylor v. Porter* and earlier rulings of that court settled the point that "a statute is
unconstitutional and void which authorizes the transfer of one man's property
to another without consent of the owner, although compensation is paid." While
consent of the owner was not required to take private property in an eminent
domain suit for the use of the public, it was essential when the transfer was
made to a private person. In *Embury,* the New York statute under review had
authorized the city, upon payment of the compensation, to obtain title to the
whole of a lot when only part was required for the use of a street. The act, said
the court, would only be constitutional if it required the consent of the owner
for the acquisition of the part not required for public use. In further support of
its position, the court cited Chancellor Kent's comment on the *Taylor* case that
the "taking (of) private property for *private* uses without the consent of the
owner, is an abuse of the right to eminent domain, and contrary to fundamen-

tal and constitutional doctrine in English and American law." The *Embury* court noted that the *Taylor* decision relied mainly on the due process clause of the state constitution.

The New York Court of Appeals, in the 1852 case of *Powers v. Bergen*,[86] considered the constitutionality of a special act of the legislature authorizing a sale of lands by the trustees named in a will that was not authorized by the provisions of that will. The will gave a life estate to Eliza and upon her death to her lawful issue in fee simple, and in the absence of such issue to the testator's grandchildren then living or their heirs and assigns forever. The trustees under the will had no authority to sell the property. However, the legislature adopted legislation giving them this authority and requiring that the proceeds of the sale be paid to the devisees under the will. According to the high court, the effect of the statute is to divest the owners in remainder of these lands of their estate in them, disqualifying them from disposing of their estate in the property, if they desired to do so. Conceding that the legislature had power to control land dispositions when a party was incapacitated, the court ruled that the power is not granted when no incapacity exists.

The court also held that this special act was for private and not public benefit, and constituted a taking from one individual to give to another. Not only was there no constitutional authority for what the legislature had done, it was actually prohibited by the New York Constitution's takings clause:

> It follows, that if the legislature should pass an act to take private property, for a purpose not of a public nature; as if it should provide, through certain forms to be observed, to take the property of one and give it (or sell it, which is the same thing in principle) to another, or if it should vacate a grant of property, under the pretext of some public use, such cases would be gross abuses of the discretion of the legislature, and fraudulent attacks on private rights, and the law would clearly be unconstitutional and void. (2 Kent's Com. 340.) If the power exists, to take the property of one without his consent, and transfer it to another, it may as well be exercised, without making compensation, as with it; for there is no provision in the constitution, that just compensation shall be made to the owner, when his property shall be taken for *private* use. The power of making contracts for the sale and disposition of private property for individual owners, has not been delegated to the legislature, nor to others, through or by any agency conferred on them for such purpose, by the legislature; and if the title of A. to property can, without his fault or consent, be transmitted to B., it may as well be effected without, as with, a consideration.[87]

In *Westervelt v. Gregg* (1854),[88] New York's high court struck down provisions of the Woman's Protection Act of 1848, which extinguished a husband's

claim to a legacy bequeathed to his wife prior to the passage of the act. Under the common law, a husband acquired upon marriage certain rights in the real and personal property which the wife then possessed. The 1848 act declared that the property of the wife shall remain her sole and separate property, as if she were a single female, except so far as the same may be liable for the debts of her husband theretofore contracted. The court held that the act violated the state constitution's due process clause with respect to his wife's property, to which the husband was entitled under the common law. These rights immediately vested and could not be divested by any subsequent change in the law. "Such an act as the legislature may, in its uncontrolled exercise of its power, think fit to pass, is, in no sense, the process of law designated by the constitution."

The New York decisions protecting property culminated in the famous case of *Wynehamer v. People,* an 1856 case[89] involving a New York State penal statute that forbade the sale of intoxicating liquor owned at the time of enactment (except those for medicinal and religious purposes) and those acquired afterward. The court held that applying the law retroactively to liquor already owned violated the state constitution's due process clause. Had the act been applicable only to liquor acquired or manufactured after it took effect, it would not conflict with the clause. Since the act makes no distinction between liquor acquired before or after its adoption and is made operative to both, it violates the clause and is unconstitutional.

Justices Comstock, Johnson, and Selden wrote separate and extensive opinions finding the law unconstitutional. Each relied in part on Magna Carta's Chapter 29, Coke, Blackstone, and Kent. Noting that the Magna Carta was intended to prevent the imposition of retroactive restraints on life, liberty, and property, Justice Comstock stated:

> To say, as has been suggested, that "the law of the land," or "due process of law," may mean the very act of legislation which deprives the citizen of his rights, privileges or property, leads to a simple absurdity. The constitution would then mean, that no person shall be deprived of his property or rights, unless the legislature shall pass a law to effectuate the wrong, and this would be throwing the restraint entirely away. The true interpretation of these constitutional phrases is, that where rights are acquired by the citizen under the existing law, there is no power in any branch of the government to take them away; but where they are held contrary to the existing law, or are forfeited by its violation, then they may be taken from him—not by an act of the legislature, but in the due administration of the law itself, before the judicial tribunals of the state. The cause or occasion for depriving the citizen of his supposed rights must be found in the law as it is, or, at least it cannot be *created* by a legislative act which aims at their destruction. Where rights of property are admitted to exist, the legislature cannot say they shall exist no longer; nor

will it make any difference, although a process and a tribunal are appointed to execute the sentence. If this is the "law of the land," and "due process of law," within the meaning of the constitution, then the legislature is omnipotent. It may, under the same interpretation, pass a law to take away liberty or life without a preexisting cause, appointing judicial and executive agencies to execute its will. Property is placed by the constitution in the same category with liberty and life.[90]

Justice A. S. Johnson stated the following:

The clauses of the bill of rights, before cited, together with the provisions in respect to jury trials, contain the substance of the provisions of chap. 29 of Magna Charta. These clauses have always received a large and liberal interpretation in favor of private rights and against power.

The expression, "by the law of the land," is interpreted by Lord Coke to mean "by the due course and process of law" (2 Ins., 46); and this last expression is afterwards expounded to mean by indictment or presentment of good and lawful men, where such deeds be done in due manner, or by writ original at the common law. (2 Ins., 50.) . . . Without judicial investigation, without a "due process of law," no act of legislators can deprive a man of his property, and that in civil cases an act of the legislature alone is wholly inoperative to take from a man his property.[91]

Justice Selden wrote as follows:

The first of these clauses [law of the land] which had its origin in Magna Charta, brief as it is, embodies the most essential guarantees against the exercise of arbitrary power which the instrument contained. Its meaning, as there used, is plain, when we consider that it was the result of a struggle which had lasted for more than a century between the English people and the Norman kings, who had supplanted the laws and customs of the Anglo Saxons, and established in their place the prerogatives of royalty. The English yeomanry, at whose instance this clause was inserted, meant by the terms, "law of the land," the ancient Saxon or common law. To put any other construction upon it, would render the clause utterly unmeaning. At that period in English history, the king exercised legislative power; and if by "law of the land" was meant any law which the king might enact, the provision was a nullity. But the meaning was rendered more clear by the paraphrase of this article of Magna Charta, which was inserted in a subsequent statute securing privileges to the people, passed in the reign of Edward III., in which the clause, "but by the land of the land or the judgment of his peers," was changed to the words, "without being brought to answer by due process of

law." This change shows that the object of the provision was, in part at least, to interpose the judicial department of the government as a barrier against aggressions by the other departments. Hence, both courts and commentators in this country have held that these clauses, in either form, secure to every citizen a judicial trial, before he can be deprived of life, liberty or property.[92]

Coming from the highly respected New York high court, these legal interpretations proved to be influential in forming the nation's jurisprudence. The basic principle of the decision was merely an affirmation that a person who abides by the law and commits no wrong shall not be penalized. The statute was penal and the court found no procedural defects. As Edward Corwin, a leading legal commentator on that period, puts it, for the *Wynehamer* court, process was not the issue; the due process clause "was thereby plainly made to prohibit, regardless of the matter of procedure, a certain kind and degree of exertion of legislative power altogether." Corwin continues:

> The main proposition of the decision in the *Wynehamer* case is that the legislature cannot destroy by any method whatever what by previous law was property. But why not? To all intents and purposes the answer of the court is simply that "no person shall be deprived of life, liberty or property."[93]

Corwin subsequently notes, however, that because the *Wynehamer* judges acknowledge the validity of reasonable regulation, the word "deprived" remains as an important part of the clause.

Insofar as it restricted legislative power in the control of liquor traffic, the *Wynehamer* precedent was generally not followed in the other states. The alcohol control statutes were generally upheld under the police power of a state on the theory that alcohol consumption was tantamount to a nuisance. However, as is evident from the prior discussion in this chapter, at the time *Wynehamer* was decided there was a considerable body of law that supported its interpretation of the due process guarantee. According to Corwin, in less "than twenty years from the time of its rendition, the crucial ruling in *Wynehamer v. People* was far on the way to being assimilated into the accepted constitutional law of the country."[94]

North Carolina

The North Carolina Supreme Court, in *University of North Carolina v. Foy and Bishop* (1805), held that the state constitution's law of the land clause pro-

hibited the legislature from repealing a prior grant of lands to a university.[95] In 1789, North Carolina's legislature granted to the trustees of the University of North Carolina all the property that had escheated or will escheat to the state, and, in 1794, it also granted to the trustees property that the state had "confiscated" and was then unsold. However, in 1800 it repealed these laws and provided that all escheated and confiscated property that the trustees still owned should revert to the state. (Escheated property is property that is transferred to the state when a person who is legally qualified to own it fails to claim it.)

The trustees of the University brought suit to obtain possession of a tract of land escheated to the state prior to the passing of the Repealing Act of 1800. The state argued that the term "law of the land," does not impose any restrictions on the legislature, and was only intended to prevent abuses in the other branches of government. The state also contended that the protections of the law of the land clause did not apply to public corporations. The North Carolina Supreme Court held in favor of the trustees and stated as follows:

> It seems to us to warrant a belief that members of a corporation as well as individuals shall not be so deprived of their liberties or properties, unless by a trial by Jury in a Court of Justice, according to the known and established rules of decision, derived from the common law, and such acts of the Legislature as are consistent with the Constitution—although the Trustees are a corporation established for public purposes, yet their property is as completely beyond the control of the Legislature, as the property of individuals or that of any other corporation. . . . The property vested in the Trustees must remain for the uses intended for the University, until the Judiciary of the country in the usual and common form, pronounce them guilty of such acts, as will, in law, amount to a forfeiture of their rights or a dissolution of their body.[96]

In the North Carolina decision of *Hoke v. Henderson* (1833),[97] a much-cited case, Chief Justice Ruffin of North Carolina's Supreme Court asserted in his opinion that once there had been a legitimate vesting of property rights, only the owner's wrongdoing could be cause for forfeiture. According to him, the "law of the land" provision of the state's constitution requires that before anyone shall be deprived of property, he is entitled to a judicial trial and process according to the common law.

In this case, Hoke claimed the office of the Clerk of the Superior Court of Law by virtue of his election thereto under the act of 1832; and his claim was opposed by Henderson, who held the office under a previous appointment pursuant to the act of 1806. The state argued that the statute was general in its terms, not intended to harm specifically any incumbent officeholders. In holding for Henderson, Ruffin reasoned as follows:

Those terms "law of the land" do not mean merely an act of the General Assembly. If they did, every restriction upon the legislative authority would be at once abrogated. For what more can a citizen suffer, than to be "taken, imprisoned, disseized of his freehold, liberties and privileges; be outlawed, exiled and destroyed; and be deprived of his property, his liberty and his life," without crime? . . . In reference to the infliction of punishment and divesting of the rights of property, it has been repeatedly held in this State and it is believed, in every other of the Union, that there are limitations upon the legislative power, notwithstanding those words; and that the clause itself means that such legislative acts, as profess in themselves directly to punish persons or deprive the citizen of his property, without trial before the judicial tribunals, and a decision upon the matter of right, as determined by the laws under which it vested, according to the course, mode and usages of the common law as derived from our forefathers, are not effectually "laws of the land," for those purposes. . . .

The sole inquiry that remains, is whether the office of which the Act deprives Mr. Henderson is property. It is scarcely possible to make the proposition clearer to a plain mind, accustomed to regard things according to practical results and realities, than by barely stating it. For what is *property*; that is, what do we understand by the term? It means, in reference to the thing, whatever a person can possess and enjoy by right; and in reference to the person, he who has the right to the exclusion of others, is said to have the property.[98]

State v. Glen is an 1859 North Carolina case involving a dam that the defendant built across the Yodkin River to supply his grist and saw mills with water.[99] The river was considered nonnavigable, never having been navigated with steamboats or any other sailing vessel, and, therefore, the soil under it could be privately owned under state law. The defendant was the owner of land on both sides of the river and the river bed. His dam blocked the passage of fish beyond it, and he was indicted under a state statute for failing to remove obstructions to the passage of fish. The case presented the question of whether the legislature had the power to compel the defendant to take away, at his own expense, a part of the dam so as to make an opening for the passage of fish, without providing compensation for the defendant to indemnify his loss. The North Carolina Supreme Court held that while the state's constitution did not contain a takings clause, its existence is implied from the law of the land clause. The owner's rights to the dam could not be taken except in the exercise of the power of eminant domain, and then only for public use, with just compensation. The state's high court thus reversed *Railroad Co. v. Davis* (1837), which was a case that rejected the concept of a "higher law" requiring payment of just compensation.[100]

Ohio

The question presented in *Gavit v. Chambers and Coats* (1828)[101] was whether the owner of lands on a navigable stream also owned property interest in and to the bed of the river. The court's answer was this: He who owns the lands upon both banks, owns the entire river, subject only to the easement of navigation, and he who owns the land upon one bank only, owns to the middle of the river, subject to the same easement.

In *Cooper v. Williams* (1832),[102] the Ohio Supreme Court considered a claim that the state had caused a diversion of water from the Mad River in order to benefit a public canal causing harm to the plaintiff, who was a riparian owner. The court found that no surplus water had been withdrawn from the river. It did acknowledge that such a diversion would be compensable as a taking of property:

> A riparian proprietor possesses the same right to the use of the water flowing through his land that he does to the land itself. The water itself is not his. It is the use . . . of this right he may be deprived, if the "public welfare" require it, so far as that public welfare does require, he first having been compensated for the injury.

Subsequently, in *Walker v. Board of Public Works* (1847),[103] the court reiterated that for the state's acquisition of riparian usage rights to be constitutionally valid, payment of compensation to an aggrieved owner is required. At issue was state legislation declaring that a certain portion of a river was navigable, making it a public highway, and that consequently the plaintiff's dam was an unlawful obstruction to the navigation of the river, constituting a nuisance.

The court found that, in fact, the river was not navigable at the location in question, and held that effectuation of the state's declaration would constitute a taking, which required compensation:

> [Before these acts were passed], the owners of the lands on both banks of such streams owned the streams and the right to use the water flowing in them, in any manner consistent with the rights of persons above and below them, without let or hindrance. They might erect dams or other obstructions to direct the water from the bed of the stream to any point of their premises, returning it to its natural channel after using it at their pleasure or convenience. A right of this description is a right of property within the protection of the constitution, and

that can not be impaired by a legislative enactment which provides no compensation to the proprietor for the injury.

The court went on to explain that even if a river is navigable, the owner of lands on its banks is entitled to use its water in any way not inconsistent with the public's navigation easement. "Hence the state in the exercise of the right of eminent domain, can subject the waters of such stream to other public uses the same as any other private property, by making a just compensation for the injury, and not otherwise."

Oregon

In *The Oregon Central R. R. Co. v. Wait* (1869),[104] which concerned an action to condemn land for a railroad, the Oregon Supreme Court interpreted the compensation requirements of the state's takings clause. First, compensation must be paid for the true value of the land appropriated. Second, this compensation is to be estimated irrespective of any additional value which may be given to the balance of the owner's land by any buildings or other improvement which may in time be erected there by the railroad company. Third, if the condemnation injures other land of the owner, over and above the benefits or additional value of that land created by the company's improvements, an additional amount is to be awarded to cover such excess of injury over benefit. The rulings of this decision were approved in *Willamet Falls Canal and Lock Co. v. James K. Kelly* (1869).[105]

Pennsylvania

McMasters v. Commonwealth of Pennsylvania (1834) involved an 1833 statute on the acquisition of private property for the installation of public streets.[106] While acknowledging that the state's power of eminent domain required just compensation, the state's supreme court allowed the legislature to determine the nature and kind of compensation. In this case, no compensation was paid, under the state's reasoning that the building of public roads increased the value of the land "fourfold"; therefore, monetary compensation was deemed unnecessary.

Norman v. Heist (1843) involved a Pennsylvania statute passed in 1841 declaring that the children of Christopher, who was an illegitimate son of Ann, shall have the same rights as if their father had been born in wedlock.[107] The statute's purpose was to reverse the common law rule that a bastard cannot in-

herit property. Ann died in 1840, and her brothers as her only heirs at law claimed title to the property in question, which Christopher's children also claimed under the statute. Pennsylvania Chief Justice Gibson held that the statute violated the state constitution's law of the land provision. This provision's protection applied to "a pre-existent rule of conduct, declarative of a penalty for a prohibited act; not an *ex post facto* rescript or decree made for the occasion." The brothers acquired title to the property immediately upon the decease of their sister, and before the passage of the act. Gibson explained his decision, as follows:

> The design of the [constitutional] convention was to exclude arbitrary power from every branch of the government; and there would be no exclusion of it, if such rescripts or decrees were allowed to take effect in the form of a statute. The right of property has no foundation or security but the law; and when the Legislature shall successfully attempt to overturn it, even in a single instance, the liberty of the citizen will be no more. This estate was lawfully vested in the plaintiffs, who were the next heirs to their intestate sister, at her death; it was theirs in full property; it was guaranteed to them by the Constitution and the laws; and to have despoiled them of it in favour of the supposed natural right of the grandchildren, would have been as much an act of despotic power, as it would had the grandchildren been strangers to the intestate's blood. Take it that they had the same claim, on the score of birthright, which their father might be supposed to have had; yet still, as title is the creature of civil regulation, even a legitimate child has no natural right of succession to the property of its parent. The right of a proprietor, living or dying, to pass by those who are nearest in blood to him, and bestow his bounty on strangers, is one of the most sacred incidents of ownership; and it is very often exercised. This intestate had a right to give her estate at her pleasure; and she did no less by leaving it to pass to her legitimate brothers by the intestate laws, instead of giving it to the children of her illegitimate son by will.[108]

Interestingly, the opinion was authored by a chief justice known for his belief in legislative sovereignty and as a critic of judicial review.

Rhode Island

Clark v. Peckham (1871)[109] was a suit for damages by the owner or occupant of a certain dock against the city of Providence for constructing and maintaining a sewer at the head of the dock that discharged a great quantity of mud

into and partially filling it. The court stated that a riparian owner bounded by navigable water has a right of access to navigate it, a right which can only be taken by payment of compensation. It held that the city had no right to fill up the dock, and that the plaintiff was entitled to damages.

South Carolina

I begin with the 1789 South Carolina case of *Ham v. McClaws,*[110] which did not involve a law of the land or due process clause, but discloses a judicial perspective consistent with the position espoused by both Coke and Blackstone that laws should conform to the common law requirements of common right and reason. In this case, the court protected liberty and property by interpreting a law consistent with justice and natural reason, though it was contrary to the strict letter of the law as applicable to the facts.

Seven slaves had traveled with their master from the Bay of Honduras to South Carolina unaware that, subsequent to their departure, the state legislature passed a law prohibiting importation of slaves under penalty of forfeiture and fine. At the time of their departure, South Carolina law allowed foreign masters to import their slaves into the state. The defense argued that statutes made against common right and reason, common equity, and the Magna Carta are void, for these principles are "paramount to all statutes." The court held that "statutes passed against the plain and obvious principles of common right, and common reason, are absolutely null and void, as far as they are calculated to operate against these principles." The court construed the law in a manner that would make it consistent with justice and natural reason, ruling that the legislature never contemplated applying it to these slaves, since it was passed while they were traveling to South Carolina in reliance on the provisions of the earlier statute. The slave owner could, therefore, import his slaves despite the new law.

In 1792, the South Carolina Supreme Court, in *Bowman v. Middleton,* considered a challenge to a state law passed in 1712 that transferred a freehold from the heir at law to another person, and also from the oldest son to a second son, without provision for a trial by jury or other judicial process.[111] Declaring the statute invalid, the court held that "it was against common right, as well as against *Magna Charta,* to take away the freehold of one man and vest it in another, and that, too, to the prejudice of third persons, without any compensation, or even a trial by the jury of the county, to determine the right in question."

In 1794, in *Zylstra v. Corporation of Charleston,* the Supreme Court of South Carolina unanimously invalidated Charleston's ordinance enabling the Court of Wardens to impose fines without a jury trial on any person making soap or candles within the city limits.[112] The city contended that the law was intended to prohibit nuisances. Writing for two of the four members of the court, Justice

Waites stated the following, citing the Magna Carta, Coke, and Blackstone (among others):

> How then can a law be valid, which constrains a citizen to submit his person and his property, to a tribunal, that proceeds to give judgment on both, without the intervention of a jury? Do these words of the constitution, "or by law of the land," authorize it? Do they mean any law which may be passed, directing a different mode of trial? Such a construction would be incompatible with the declaration of this privilege; it would be taking away all the security which that intended to give it; it would do more, it would by making the constitution itself authorize the means of destroying a right which it afterwards declares shall be inviolably preserved. For if the law may abridge the trial by jury, it may also abolish it; and then this great privilege would be held only at the will of the legislature. . . .[113]

> [B]y virtue of the charter, the city council makes by-laws; they appoint, as is frequently the case, some of their own members the commissioners to carry them into effect; and the same members afterwards may take their seats as judges, to determine on any breaches of them which may have been committed. It may sometimes happen, too, that, in the course of their duty as commissioners, they are witnesses to the violation of some by-law; they may then add one more character to this multiform political monster, and exhibit legislators, executors, prosecutors, witnesses, and judges, all in the same persons.
>
> There surely could not be contrived, by the most ingenious tyrant, a more complete instrument for all the purposes of oppression.[114]

In the 1796 case of *Lindsay v. East Bay Street Commissioners,* the South Carolina Court was equally divided on the constitutionality of a Charleston ordinance laying out a new street without providing for compensation.[115] The city contended that the land over which the street in question was to be installed was valueless since the tide flowed over it twice a day, and would never be of value until the street was established. According to two justices, every landowner holds land upon condition of yielding a portion of it when wanted for public roads and highways. The state has this power as an original right of sovereignty—like the power of collecting taxes—to appropriate the lands for this purpose without being liable for compensation. Justice Waites acknowledged the power of the state to take the property of an individual, for purposes of public necessity or even for public utility, but it can only be exercised on condition that the owner receive compensation "for every injury the individual might suffer." He cited the Magna Carta, Coke, and Blackstone as authorities in support of this position.

In *State v. Dawson* (1836),[116] the South Carolina Supreme Court upheld a constitutional position which the majority opinion stated it had maintained for forty-five years with respect to the public acquisition of private land for public roads.

According to this position, the state's constitution authorizes the legislature to acquire private property for public roads, and to use so much timber, earth, or rock near the road as was necessary to keep the road in repair, and this could be done without the consent of the owner of the land and without making compensation. The court held that the right of eminent domain is a tacit condition of every land in the state and does not require payment of compensation. The state's constitution contained a law of the land provision protecting property. To the best of my knowledge, South Carolina is the only state that, prior to the framing of the Fourteenth Amendment, did not require compensation to be paid for the taking of property for public roads. (See Section III *infra* for further discussion of the *Lindsay* and *Dawson* cases.)

Tennessee

In *Woodfolk v. Nashville & Chattanooga Railroad Company* (1852),[117] the issue before the Tennessee Supreme Court was the meaning of "the just" compensation requirement of the state constitution's takings clause. The court asserted that when the legislature, in furtherance of its takings powers, seeks to appropriate private property for public use in the construction of a railroad, it cannot prescribe how much and in what way the owner shall be compensated for the loss he has suffered. The value of the property taken, said the court, must be assessed by an appropriate tribunal and the amount paid in money. The "benefits and advantages" the owner will allegedly receive as a result of the taking cannot be applied to reduce this amount. The measure of compensation must be limited to determining the fair cash value of the property appropriated; to do otherwise is grossly unfair to the property owner:

> The increase of price, without any improvement of its fertility or beauty, is no advantage to him if he does not wish to sell; it only increases his public burdens in the way of taxation. What others might regard as a great "advantage and benefit," he might consider a decided injury. If his lands are appreciated, and his facilities of travel and trade increased, by this improvement, these are benefits to which he is entitled with the community in general, and for which he has to pay, in common with others, in taxes and other burdens. But there can be no good reason, why any more should be taken from him than others, for these common benefits.

In *Red River Bridge Company v. Mayor and Alderman of Clarksville* (1853),[118] the Supreme Court of Tennessee held that an exclusive franchise to maintain a toll bridge is subject to the power of eminent domain and may be destroyed only on payment of compensation to its owner. In 1829, the legisla-

ture granted to the Red River Bridge Company a charter authorizing it to erect a bridge across Red River with the power to collect tolls from persons crossing the bridge. The charter provided that no other toll bridge should be at any time erected within one-half mile of this bridge. The company erected its bridge at the place designated in the charter and received tolls as authorized. In 1847, the legislature authorized the municipal authorities of Clarksville to purchase the company's bridge, or to erect a free bridge near it. Pursuant to this authority, Clarksville authorized the building of a new bridge within a few feet of the existing bridge. The court held that the city authorities could only support the building of the new bridge upon the condition of paying just compensation for the franchise that was thus destroyed.

Between 1829 and 1842, the Tennessee Supreme Court declared a number of laws it construed as special and not general laws to be invalid under the law of the land provision of the state's constitution. One of the first of these decisions was in *Vanzant v. Waddel* (1829),[119] which concerned an 1821 Tennessee statute prescribing the mode by which the holders of the promissory notes of the Farmers' and Mechanics' Bank and the Fayetteville Tennessee Bank could, on the bank's refusal to pay the same, recover judgment from persons owing money to the bank. Under this act, a summons could be issued and served upon those persons before the final judgment against the bank.

The court sustained the statute in this case. It found that, in passing this law, the legislature had not deprived particular individuals of the benefit of the general laws, and was accordingly not a partial law in its operation. Of particular interest is the concurring opinion of Judge John Catron, who later from 1837 to 1865 served as a justice of the United States Supreme Court. In agreeing with his colleagues, Catron stated that the law of the land clause of the Tennessee Constitution refers to "a general and public law, equally binding upon every member of the community." Catron continued:

> The right to life, liberty and property, of every individual must stand or fall by the same rule or law that governs every other member of the body politic, or "LAND," under similar circumstances; and every partial or private law, which directly proposes to destroy or affect individual rights, or does the same thing by affording remedies leading to similar consequences, is unconstitutional and void. Were this otherwise, odious individuals and corporate bodies would be governed by one rule, and the mass of the community who made the law, by another. The idea of a people through their representatives making laws whereby are swept away the life, liberty and property of *one* or a *few* citizens, by which neither the representatives nor their other constituents are willing to be bound, is too odious to be tolerated in any government where freedom has a name. Such abuses resulted in the adoption of Magna Charta in England, securing the

subject against odious exceptions, which is, and for centuries has been, the foundation of English liberty. Its infraction was a leading cause why we separated from that country, and its value as a fundamental rule for the protection of the citizen against legislative usurpation was the reason of its adoption as part of our constitution. [Citing 2 Coke, Institutes 46, and the American Declaration of Independence.][120]

In 1829, the Tennessee legislature created a special tribunal, composed of existing judges, for the disposition of suits commenced by the Bank of the State of Tennessee against its officers, their sureties, and customers of the bank who had written bad checks and from whose decision there was no appeal. The state's supreme court, in *Bank of the State v. Cooper* (1831),[121] held the law to be unconstitutional because, among other things, it was a law partial in its operation, which was in violation of the law of the land provision of the state's constitution. Citing Coke's *Institutes,* the judges in different opinions agreed that the law of the land required that a law extend to all, not just to benefit or punish a special group. The judges concluded that the law in question was intended to affect only the few of those indebted to the Bank of the State of Tennessee. Judge Green stated that if "the construction here contended for be not the true one, it seems to me, that an edict in the form of a legislative enactment, taking the property of A, and giving it to B, might be regarded as the 'law of the land,' and not forbidden by the constitution; but such a proposition is too absurd to find a single advocate." Green elaborated further:

> This provision was introduced to secure the citizens against the abuse of power by the government. Of what benefit is it if it impose no restraint upon legislation? Was there not as just ground to apprehend danger from the legislature as from any other quarter? Legislation is always exercised by the majority. Majorities have nothing to fear, for the power is in their hands. *They* need no written constitution, defining and circumscribing the powers of the government. Constitutions are only intended to secure the rights of the minority. They are in danger. The power is against them; and the selfish passions often lead us to forget the right. Does it not seem conclusive then, that this provision was intended to restrain the legislature from enacting any law affecting injuriously the rights of any citizen, unless at the same time the rights of all others in similar circumstances were equally affected by it? If the law be general in its operation, affecting all alike, the minority are safe, because the majority, who make the law, are operated on by it equally with the others.[122]

In 1825, Tennessee passed a private law pursuant to the application of a guardian of infants authorizing the guardian to sell land inherited from the par-

ent to pay the debts of the parent. In *Jones' Heirs v. Perry* (1836),[123] the Tennessee Supreme Court declared the act invalid, since it violated the state constitution's law of the land provision. Citing Coke (2 Inst. 51), the court defined the phrase as requiring "a general and public law, operating equally upon every member of the community." The court explained further:

> It is, however, contended that this provision of the constitution was not intended to apply to a case like the present, but was intended to prevent majorities in times of high political excitement from passing partial laws, whereby to create forfeitures of estates and otherwise to destroy obnoxious individuals. It is true, no doubt, but that the primary object of the framers of the constitution was to protect individuals in cases like those suggested in the argument. But the language used is of general application, and forbids the enactment of a partial law by which the rights of any individual shall be abridged or taken away.[124]

An 1827 Tennessee act directed the dismissal of a certain class of lawsuits then brought, or which might thereafter be brought, in the name of any Indian reservee, to recover lands under the provisions of the treaties of 1817 and 1819 between the United States and the Cherokee Nation of Indians. In an opinion by Judge Catron, the state supreme court declared the act unconstitutional, in *Wally's Heirs v. Nancy Kennedy* (1831).[125] Citing the law of the land provision, the court held that the act "is peculiarly partial. It is limited in its operation to a comparatively small section of the state, and to a very few individuals claiming a very small portion of the section of the country referred to." Catron also viewed the 1827 law as contrary to the clause of the state constitution prohibiting adoption of retrospective laws and laws impairing the obligation of contracts:

> The act of 1827 proposed to legislate out of court actions of ejectment lawfully brought before its passage, by letting in parol proof of an outstanding trust created by contract long before the act was passed; which contract, for anything appearing to the contrary on this record, was lawful when made, and for the first time declared otherwise by this act. The letting in new, and in the grade of evidence, unheard-of, proof in the pending action of ejectment, and declaring the effect of that proof, is to my mind very dangerous legislation. . . .

Budd v. The State (1842)[126] was concerned with a prosecution against a clerk of the Union Bank for making a false entry in order to defraud the bank. The indictment was founded upon a provision of the statute that chartered the bank creating a new felony applicable only to certain clerical frauds committed by

officers, agents, and servants of the bank. The court held that this statute was not a law of the land, because it affected only particular bank employees and did not equally embrace similar employees of other banks:

> At the time of the enactment of this statute, there were other banks having actual corporate existence, as we can see from our statute book, with like faculties and functions. They were not embraced; other banks had a potential existence; that is, the Legislature had power to make others. The act, however, embraces the Union Bank alone and its servants, etc., and not all who are or may be, in the like state and circumstances. If, as in Alabama and Arkansas, the Legislative power being constitutionally expended by the creation of one bank, a felony had been created, limiting itself in its terms to the bank established, we do not doubt that under such a bill of rights as ours such law would be constitutional. We do not think the law in question partial, because merchants, clerks, or the public officers, called clerks, were not embraced; but because the officers, agents, and servants of banks in general, persons in like situations and circumstances, were not embraced. It matters not how few the persons are; if all who are or may come into the like circumstances and situations, be embraced, the law is general, and not a partial law.

Texas

The overseer of roads, an agent of Walker county, cut and carried away from the plaintiff's land a large amount of trees growing on it for the purpose of repairing a public road. The overseer acted under the authority of a statute providing that "when to the overseer of the roads, it may appear expedient to make causeways and build bridges, the timber most convenient may be used." In a suit for payment of compensation— *Watkins v. Walker County* (1857)[127]—the Supreme Court of Texas ruled in favor of the plaintiff on the basis that the action of the overseer constituted a taking:

> There may be cases where the right of the public rests upon a principle of necessity which will justify the appropriation or destruction of private property, without rendering the public liable to make reparation. If a public highway be out of repair, the passengers may lawfully go through an adjoining private enclosure. It is lawful to raze houses to the ground to prevent the spreading of a conflagration. These, it is said, are cases of urgent necessity, in which no action lay at common law by the individual

who sustained the injury. And it is true, too, that the right of public domain, or inherent sovereign power, gives to the legislature the control of private property for public uses. Roads may be cut through the lands of individuals without their consent; and timber may be taken from the adjacent lands to make the necessary causeways and repairs without the consent of the proprietor. But to this right there is, in this state, a qualification annexed by the declaration in the bill of rights, that "no person's property shall be taken or applied to public use without adequate compensation being made, unless by the consent of such person."

Miller and his wife owned buildings that had formerly been used as a livery stable, which, when left unoccupied, became dilapidated. The town council declared the buildings a nuisance, and ordered them to be sold at a public sale and demolished. The Texas Supreme Court held, in *Miller v. Burch* (1869),[128] that the town had exceeded its authority in having the houses sold and demolished. While the town had the authority to suppress a nuisance, this authority did not extend to selling the houses containing the nuisance. The nuisance was not caused by the building, but by the abuse of it, and the municipal authorities have sufficient power to terminate the nuisance without resorting to the demolition of the building. The property in these buildings is protected by the constitution and can only be taken upon payment of compensation.

In *Janes v. Reynolds' Adm'rs* (1847), the Texas Supreme Court considered the constitutionality of a statute authorizing the entry of summary judgments on forfeited bonds without notice or a trial by jury.[129] It was contended that the law violated the "due course of the law of the land" provision of the Texas Constitution. According to the court, this provision requires passage of "general public laws, binding all members of the community under similar circumstances, and not partial or private laws; affecting the rights of private individuals, or classes of individuals [citing the Tennessee cases of *Bank of the State v. Cooper* and *Vanzant v. Waddel*]." While the right of notice and a fair and proper jury trial are cardinal principles of the common law, there are exceptions to the rule. These include the entry of summary judgments against the sureties on certain bonds when their conditions are forfeited.

In this case, the court observed that the sureties knew about the summary judgment statute as well as the relief available to holders of the bonds. Texas law gave obligors in such bonds one year after forfeiture within which they could move to quash the bond, and have issues relating to their liability tried by a jury. However, the court held that the bond in this case did not conform essentially to requisites prescribed by statute, and therefore summary judgment could not be entered against the sureties.

Vermont

In determining the compensation due landowners for a taking of their property for a portion of a highway, the commissioners who were appointed for this purpose disallowed the landowners' claim for damages on the ground that the benefits the owners would receive would be quite equal to any damage they would sustain. The landowners claimed that they were entitled to the value of the land that was taken, independent of any advantages they may obtain from installation of the road. In *Livermore v. Town of Jamaica* (1851),[130] the Supreme Court of Vermont rejected this claim. The court stated that acquiring land for a highway does not divest an owner of his full title. The public only acquires an easement for road purposes. Upon a discontinuance of the highway, the possession of the land reverts to the owner. The court held that this was not such a taking of property for public use under the state constitution that would require payment of compensation to be made in money. To qualify as a taking under the constitution, a divesting of all of the owner's title or control for the benefit of the public is required.

In *Joseph Hatch, et al. v. Vermont Central Railroad Company* (1852),[131] the Vermont Supreme Court combined and adjudicated two separate lawsuits against a company chartered by the state to construct and operate a railroad. Plaintiff Hatch alleged (among other things) that in installing its tracks the company constructed a three-and-one-half foot high embankment and excavated deeply near his home and business, which together caused water to flood his basement and seriously impede traffic to and from his business. Plaintiff Whitcomb alleged that the defendant company, in constructing its road over a stream on his land, had not built a culvert to maintain the channel of the stream and had instead diverted the stream from its course, an action which was to his injury. The case presented the issue of whether the railroad company was liable for consequential damage to lands near their track, no part of which was taken for the railroad. The plaintiffs argued that their damages constituted a taking under the Vermont Constitution, which required payment of compensation for the taking of property. However, the Vermont Supreme Court disagreed:

> [T]he general rule may now be regarded as settled in this country, that any advantages accruing to the proprietor of the land taken by the contemplated public work, may be taken into account in appraising the damage. So, too, where any portion of the land is taken, the commissioners may doubtless estimate consequential damages, to the remaining portion of the land . . . [b]ut [not for] merely consequential damages to lands not taken. . . .[132]

According to the court, since the legislature made an unqualified grant to the railroad company, thereby legalizing its building and operating the road, it is

subject to no further liability for damages to property outside of the property affected by the taking. The plaintiffs therefore must look for relief, if any, to the statutes and common law of the state. The court observed that in the absence of a statutory provision to that effect, "no case, and certainly no principle seems to justify the subjecting of a person, natural or artificial, in the prudent pursuit of his own lawful business, to the payment of consequential damage, to other persons, in their property or business." Once a railroad is installed, some people will suffer or perceive harm that previously did not exist. But, after the legislature had made an unqualified grant to the railroad company, "it is impossible for the court to impose any further restrictions upon them, than upon other legal business, which one carries on upon his own land."

But all was not lost for Whitcomb. Citing *Hooker v. New Haven and Northampton Company* (a Connecticut case) and *Gardner v. Newburgh* (a New York case) (both previously discussed in this section), the court noted that some existing judicial opinions justified some limitations upon the right of railroad companies to divert water courses, rivers, and other streams. These and some other cases of a similar character "seem to be founded in reason and justice," and not at all in conflict with a constitutional rule that a defendant railroad was not liable for merely consequential damages:

> [U]pon general principles, every one is liable for diverting a stream of water. . . . The state cannot do this, more than an individual, unless it become necessary, to the accomplishment of some public work, and in that case, is bound to make compensation. Here the land is not taken, but the water, which makes the land valuable, is taken, and that is the same in law, as if the land were taken.

As for the plaintiff Hatch, the court gave him the option of having a jury decide whether the railroad "was built in a manner to do him unnecessary damage." Vermont thus protected property rights under both its constitution and common law. Consequential damages was a matter for common law adjudication in this state, just as the entire issue of takings was protected under the common law in states that had no takings clause in their constitutions.

Virginia

In *Crenshaw v. State River Company* (1828),[133] the owners of a water-grist mill and nearby dam sought an injunction to prevent enforcement of a Virginia statute requiring them to erect locks through the dam, to keep the locks in repair, and to attend to them, all upon pain of otherwise having the dam declared a nuisance. These requirements were part of a state program to make the river,

which was not previously navigable, a navigable public highway. The statute did not provide for indemnifying the mill and dam owners for any costs they incurred in carrying out the said provisions. The four judges of the Virginia Supreme Court who wrote opinions agreed that the statute was invalid under the state constitution because it did not provide compensation to indemnify the owners. The Virginia Constitution contained a Magna Carta-type provision protecting life, liberty, and property, but it had no takings clause. The court declared the statute unconstitutional and void. The judges referred to Blackstone, Magna Carta, common and natural laws, the U.S. Constitution, and "the law of every civilized country" to support their holding that the statute's mandates could not be imposed without payment of fair compensation, based upon the equitable assessment of the taking.

Wisconsin

Pursuant to a law enacted by the territory of Wisconsin, Thien constructed and maintained a dam across the Milwaukee River, which caused Voegtlander's land to be overflowed. In *Thien v. Voegtlander* (1854),[134] the Supreme Court of Wisconsin construed the state's constitution as prohibiting the taking of private property for use of the public unless compensation was made to the owner, and further forbidding the property of one person to be given without his consent to another, even if compensation is paid. In this case, the court held that a plea of justification for the overflowing of the land was bad because it did not aver compensation or an offer of compensation for the lands so overflowed.

Newell v. Smith (1862)[135] concerned the constitutionality of an act of the legislature authorizing proprietors of a mill dam to flow lands of other persons, without any provision for compensation, except that they should pay the landowners the value of the land damaged. This value was to be ascertained by the verdict in an action of trespass. The response of the Wisconsin Supreme Court was unequivocal:

> We do not know upon what principle of law, reason or justice, such an enactment of the legislature, under the constitution of this state, can be sustained. Within repeated decisions of this court, it is clearly unconstitutional and void. It professes to authorize the respondents to overflow, use, enjoy and practically destroy the value of lands of an individual, without first making compensation therefor. The only compensation in fact given by the law, is an action of trespass against the respondents for the value of the lands overflowed. It is not readily perceived how an action of trespass for the permanent use and enjoyment of land places the owner in any better condition for the redress of his injury than he would

have been at common law. At all events, an action of trespass, for the permanent use and enjoyment of private property is not just compensation therefor, either in a constitutional sense or any other.

The court also ruled on the rights of a purchaser of land already flowed and for which no compensation relating to the flow had ever been paid to the prior owner. The court held that the injury to land caused by overflow is in the nature of a continuing trespass, for which he should receive such compensation for the injury to the land as he may have sustained.

In *Norton v. Peck* (1854),[136] the Wisconsin Supreme Court held that under the Wisconsin Constitution all taxable property of a town was liable for payment of compensation when a taking has occurred and constituted a fund to which the owners of land might resort for payment as soon as the amount of damages was ascertained. While this fund might supercede the necessity of actual payment, the town could not take the land without at least making provision for ascertaining the value of the land taken. If the state statutes make no provision for ascertaining and paying the damages sustained by the owners, the legislature should remedy the defect. Moreover, opined the court, unless some mode exists, the property cannot lawfully be taken. These principles were affirmed in *Shepardson v. The Milwaukee and Beloit Railroad Company* (1857),[137] which also held that the defendant railroad company would not enter the plaintiff's land and commence construction of the road without first ascertaining the landowners' damages and paying them compensation.

In *Ford v. The Chicago and Northwestern Railroad Company* (1861),[138] the plaintiff was the owner of certain lots that were located on each side of a public street. He sued the railroad company to recover damages caused by the construction of its road bed in the street in front of his lots, and also for a perpetual injunction to restrain the company from laying its track or otherwise encumbering the street. Because the owner of adjacent lots owns to the center of the street, subject only to the public use of the land as a public highway, the Wisconsin Supreme Court stated that a railroad company cannot appropriate and occupy it with its track without the consent of the owner or without compensation, and neither the legislature nor any other government authority had the power to dispense with such compensation.

A state statute provided for laying out and compensating the landowner for the creation of a private road on his property. Such a road would be for the use of the applicant, his heirs, and assigns, and the owner of the land through which it is laid would not be permitted to use it as a road unless he should have signified his intention of doing so before the damages were determined. In *Osborn v. Hart* (1869),[139] the Wisconsin Supreme Court ruled that a state legislature cannot authorize the taking of private property for a merely private use, even upon payment of compensation. The public has no right to use a private road,

which is created solely for the benefit and convenience of the applicant. According to this court, citing *Taylor v. Porter* (a New York case previously discussed), the "assertion of a right on the part of the legislature to take the property of one citizen and transfer it to another, even for a full compensation, where the public interest is not promoted thereby, is claiming a despotic power, and one inconsistent with every just principle and fundamental maxim of a free government."

If there was any doubt that the United States was a country committed to economic freedom, it was clearly dispelled by the practices of the judiciary in the eighty-year period following the ratification of the Constitution. With the exception of South Carolina, high courts in the other thirty-two states that were surveyed observed the position that an owner who has been deprived of his property by the state—whether for public or private purpose—is entitled to be indemnified for damages he has sustained. This rule did not apply to the creation or maintenance of a nuisance because such harmful conduct was not entitled to legal protection. In implementing the compensation rule, the courts differed over whether an owner who suffers indirect or consequential damage is entitled to indemnification, whether the benefits that an owner obtains by reason of a government condemnation should be deducted from his award, and whether the state had the authority to acquire property from a nonconsenting owner for private purposes upon payment of compensation.

The reader should not conclude that judges who adopt one or more of these exceptions were necessarily antagonistic to property rights. They were often motivated by a desire to encourage the nation's growth and development, which they believed was impeded by these rules. Fully compensating owners whose property was condemned and not allowing eminent domain for private roads and mills added to an investor's costs and lessened the desirability of a proposed venture. The strict interpreters of property rights reply that private investment is adversely affected when these rights are not guaranteed. Who would want to purchase property in a developing area if the government could control the amount of compensation that could be awarded in a condemnation proceeding? Although the impact would likely not be as severe as the previous questions suggest, property value would suffer if an owner's land was subject to eminent domain for the installation of a private road at the will of another person. In short, a system of property rights cannot exist if its protections are substantially compromised.

III. Justice Blackmun's Dissent in the *Lucas* Case

In *Lucas v. South Carolina Coastal Council* (1992), the United States Supreme Court held that a regulation that deprives an owner of all economically viable use of his property violates the takings clause of the U.S. Consti-

tution. Justice Harry Blackmun filed an extensive dissent, part of which related to the history and background of this clause.[140] I discuss this portion of his dissent in this section, including all of the pre-1892 cases he refers to,[141] and explain why I do not find his position persuasive.

In his dissenting opinion, Blackmun took particular exception to what he saw as the majority justices in the *Lucas* case creating a "new rule that the legislature may not deprive a property owner of the only economically valuable use of his land, even if the legislature finds it to be a harmful use, because such action is not part of the 'long recognized' 'understandings of our citizens.'" According to Blackmun, "It is not clear from the Court's opinion where our 'historical compact' or 'citizens understanding' comes from, but it does not appear to be history." Regrettably, Justice Scalia, author of the majority opinion, did not refute Blackmun's assertions regarding the history of takings jurisprudence. Instead, Scalia merely asserted that the majority's approach was consistent with "the historical compact recorded in the takings clause that has become part of our constitutional culture." In this section, I will show that Justice Blackmun's dissent lacked historical understanding of takings law in early America.

The *Lucas* case involved two ocean front lots purchased by Lucas in 1986 for the construction of a house on each lot. In 1988, the South Carolina legislature enacted legislation forbidding Lucas and other owners of land similarly situated from erecting any permanent habitable structures on the land. The state legislature asserted that the regulation was required (among other things) to prevent erosion and destruction of the state's beach/dune system, which had been created to safeguard lives and property from destructive weather conditions. In a suit filed by Lucas, the trial court found that a taking had occurred and awarded him substantial damages. The South Carolina Supreme Court reversed this decision, declaring that when a land-use regulation is designed "to prevent serious public harm," as determined by the legislature, a taking has not occurred regardless of the impact on the property's value. On appeal, the U.S. Supreme Court reversed and held that South Carolina's law denying Lucas all economically viable use of his property is an unconstitutional taking, unless his proposed use constituted, under state law when he purchased the property, a nuisance or other grave threat to lives and property. (On remand, the South Carolina Supreme Court found that there was no nuisance basis for denying Lucas's proposed use of the land.) Nothing in Blackmun's dissenting opinion reveals information that most courts in early America would have to come to a different conclusion. Blackmun's position was that, under takings law, a state has the power to prevent without payment of compensation the use of property it finds to be harmful to its citizens. He considered such legislation to be entitled to a presumption of constitutionality.

Justice Blackmun's flat assertion in his dissent was: "The principle that the State should compensate individuals for property taken for public use was not

widely established in America at the time of the Revolution." He cited as the sole authority for this proposition a discussion of the 1606 *Case of the King's Prerogative in Saltpeter,*[142] and concluded: "The colonists [inherited] a concept of property which permitted extensive regulation of the use of property for the public benefit—regulation that could even go so far as to deny all productive use of the property to the owner if, as Coke himself stated, the regulation 'extends to the public benefit.'"[143] As discussed in Chapter 2, the *Saltpeter* case involved the king's prerogative to defend the realm, which was a special historical exception to the common law protection of private property. Coke's comment concerning *Saltpeter* related to the prerogative and not to the general common law. This case did *not* allow the king to deprive a landowner of all productive use of his property. Coke and his fellow judges strictly confined the king's servants to removing only the saltpeter that was needed for national defense. The owner of the land could not be restrained from digging and removing saltpeter in his own self-interest. When obtaining saltpeter, the king's agents were required to restore the property to the same condition as they found it. They were prohibited from otherwise damaging the property; from working at night; from erecting furnaces on the property without the owner's consent; and from staying for long in any one place, or returning before a long while had passed.

Blackmun then asserted: "Even into the 19th century, state governments often felt free to take property for roads and other public projects without paying compensation to the owners."[144] He cited as authority an 1802 Pennsylvania case, *M'Clenachan v. Curwin,* quoting from it that citizens "were bound to contribute as much of [land], as by the laws of the country, were deemed necessary for the public convenience."[145] This case involved an action of trespass brought against the superintendent of a turnpike company, for entering the cleared, tilled, and enclosed land of the plaintiff in order to lay out and install a public road without having made *prior* compensation for the land or for injury to improvements on the land. The *M'Clenachan* court noted a unique aspect of Pennsylvania land titles; it found that an extra amount of 6 percent was added to the land purchased by the original buyers from the first proprietor, William Penn, to be used for the installation of roads: "[F]rom that early period to the present time, no grant has been made either by the proprietaries or the commonwealth, without this addition of 6 percent, expressly for the purpose of contributing to the establishing of the roads and highways." The court held that this original grant satisfied the mandate of the Pennsylvania Constitution "that no man's property shall be taken for public use without his own consent, or that of his legal representatives, nor without compensation."[146] Contrary to Blackmun's claim, just compensation was not unnecessary; it was merely paid in advance.

The *M'Clenachan* court also distinguished improved from unimproved land, and stated that just compensation would be required for government damage to certain improvements on the land: "[I]f it has in any case been necessary to pull

down houses, destroy orchards, or spoil grain in the track or route of the road, the company are undoubtedly bound to make compensation to the owners, as well as the adjacent grounds from whence they are to collect the material."[147] This case thus does not support Blackmun's conclusion about it.

Blackmun then cited another Pennsylvania case, *Commonwealth v. Fisher* (1830), to show that "[t]here was an obvious movement toward establishing the compensation principle during the 19th century, but there continued to be a strong current in American legal thought that regarded compensation simply as a 'bounty given . . . by the State' out of 'kindness' and not out of justice."[148] The *Fisher* case involved compensation claims by landowners against the state for land taken for the Pennsylvania Canal. As in *M'Clenachan*, the *Fisher* court held that "[t]he right of the state to take six acres out of every hundred acres sold, is not an implied right but an express reservation. It infringes no private right nor does it injure any man by using this right."

However, *Fisher* involved the state legislature authorizing a private enterprise to build the canal:

> When the state authorized private corporations to make turnpike roads or canals, it compelled them to pay for the land occupied by such road or canal, for such corporation was very different from the state; its rights were very different; no reservations had been made for its use, no contract for its benefit. But when the state itself undertook to make public canals, its right was unquestionable. These petitioners, then, ought to be grateful for a bounty given them by the state; to be thankful rather than presumptuous; to acknowledge kindness rather than to assume the attitude of injured persons.[149]

In other words, landowners should be grateful for a windfall (the right to compensation from a private entity, a right which they would not be entitled to from the state) and they should be willing to wait until after completion of the canal (when its effect on their property values could be determined), prior to filing claims for payments which they would not have had a right to under eminent domain. The court did not state that all government compensation stemmed from kindness (and it affirmed in dicta that compensation was constitutionally required for the disruption of improvements).

Blackmun also cited cases in South Carolina to demonstrate the proposition that compensation was not historically required in early American takings cases. In the case of *Lindsay v. Commissioners* (1796), the court split 2–2, allowing to stand the City of Charleston's action of taking land from lot owners to build a street without compensation. Two judges took the position that "[t]he authority of the state . . . to appropriate a portion of the soil of every county for public roads and highways was one of the original rights of sovereignty, re-

tained by the supreme power of every community at its formation, and like the power of laying on, and collecting taxes, paramount to all private rights. . . ."[150] The state attorney general is quoted by Blackmun as stating that "there is not one instance on record, and certainly not within the memory of the oldest man now living, of any demand being made for compensation for the soil or freehold of the lands. . . ."[151]

Not mentioned by Justice Blackmun is the fact that the other two judges in *Lindsay* believed just as strongly that compensation was required for eminent domain acquisitions under the South Carolina state constitution. Judge Burke "was of opinion that there should be a fair compensation made to the private individual for the loss he might sustain by it, to be ascertained by a jury of the county." Citing Blackstone and the rights of property owners, Judge Waites asserted that "in exercising this power, it was essential to its validity, that a full compensation should be provided at the time, for every injury that the individual might suffer."

Blackmun also cited on behalf of his claims the South Carolina case of *State v. Dawson,* decided in 1836, where the defendant had been indicted for obstructing the road commissioner. A statute authorizing the commissioner to cut timber on private land for the repair of highways, without compensation, was held not to violate the state constitution of 1790 (with its "law of the land" provision). The court relied on *Lindsay,* a case which dissenting Justice Richardson said "decided no doctrine whatever, yet left a false gloss, which has unduly beset our successive cases. . . ."[152] According to Richardson, South Carolina's policy of non-compensation for the taking of private property for public use was out of step with both English legal theory and the "great American commentators," including Chancellor Kent and Justice Story.

South Carolina appears to be the only state that was part of the Union in 1860 that failed to provide compensation for takings by the state in eminent domain actions for public highways. This unusual aberration on the part of South Carolina hardly provides grounding for the position that Blackmun espoused. In addition, the South Carolina Supreme Court noted in a 1956 case that this policy of non-compensation ended with the ratification of the state's constitution of 1868, which contains two compensation provisions.[153] The court also observed that, prior to the adoption of the 1868 constitution, it was customary in the incorporation of railroad companies to provide for an assessment of compensation to landowners for property taken for the rights of way.

Blackmun asserted that "[a]lthough prior to the adoption of the Bill of Rights, America was replete with land-use regulations describing which activities were considered noxious and forbidden, . . . the Fifth Amendment's Takings Clause originally did not extend to regulations of property, whatever the effect." To support this assertion, he erroneously cited the takings clause that Madison originally drafted but which was rewritten by the First Congress (as explained in Chapter 3, Section V). He was also wrong in stating that

"[n]othing in the discussion in [the First] Congress concerning the takings clause indicates the Clause was limited by the common law nuisance doctrine."[154] I am not aware of any meaningful discussion of the takings clause in the First Congress. However, its members were most likely knowledgeable about two rules of the common law. First, the common law strongly protected an owner's use of his property. Second, it provided no protection—and even penalized an owner—for maintaining a nuisance on it (see Chapter 2, Section IV). These two rules provide general support for the nuisance doctrine.

Blackmun cited the 1823 Massachusetts case of *Callender v. Marsh* to support the proposition that "[u]ntil the end of the nineteenth century . . . jurists held that the constitution protected possession only, and not value. . . . Even indirect and consequential injuries to property resulting from regulations were excluded from the definition of a taking."[155] However, *Callender v. Marsh* did *not* involve a regulation of the plaintiff's property. It was an action of trespass by the owner of a dwelling house in Boston against a surveyor of highways who dug down an existing street that ran alongside the plaintiff's home, causing its foundation to be laid bare and requiring expensive refortification by the owner.

The appellate court reversed the trial court's judgment for the plaintiff, stating that even though the Massachusetts Declaration of Rights provided "that whenever the public exigencies require the property of any individual should be appropriated to public uses, he shall receive a reasonable compensation therefore," this provision did not apply to "indirect or consequential damage or expense, by means of the right use of property already belonging to the public."[156] The court did not view the state as regulating the plaintiff's property. Rather, the court defended the right of the public to make necessary improvements to preexisting streets: "Those who purchase housing lots bordering upon streets are supposed to calculate the chance of such elevations and reductions as the increasing population of a city may require, in order to render the passage to and from the several parts . . . and as their purchase is always voluntary, they may indemnify themselves in the price of the lot which they buy, or take the chance of future improvements as they see fit."[157] Just compensation is required, however, "[w]henever a new road or way is to be laid out, or an existing one enlarged or widened. . . ."[158] The court was defending the right of the public to improve its own property (the roads) even if the adjacent owner suffered a loss, since it was foreseeable at the time of purchase that streets might have to be altered in the future. Moreover, explained the court, the original condemnation award included payment for the diminution of the value of the adjoining lots, "calculating upon the future probable reduction or elevation of a street or road." When the street was legally established, "the public acquired the right, not only to pass over the surface in the state it was in when first made a street, but the right to repair and amend the street, and, for this purpose, to dig down and remove soil sufficiently to make the passage safe and convenient."

Blackmun's opinion concerning takings continued: "Even when courts began to consider that regulation in some situations could constitute a taking, they continued to uphold bans on particular uses without paying compensation, notwithstanding the economic impact, under the rationale that no one can obtain a vested right to injure or endanger the public."[159] Blackmun criticized the *Lucas* majority's view of history, challenging their view that only common law nuisance justified regulatory takings without compensation. He cited *Coates v. City of New York* (1827), in which the Supreme Court of New York found no taking in New York's ban on the interment of the dead within the city, although "no other use can be made of these lands."[160] In *Coates,* the court held that the act prohibiting further interment of the dead in the city was "not unconstitutional, either as impairing the obligation of contracts, or taking private property for public use, without compensation; but stands on the ground of being an authority to make police regulations in respect to nuisances."[161] Thus, according to this court, *Coates* involved a legal nuisance, which is by definition such a harmful use that it is not entitled to constitutional protection. Blackmun, of course, contended that *any* use the legislature found to be harmful, whether or not it is a legal nuisance, is not constitutionally secured. He also believed that such a legislative determination was presumed to be constitutional.

Nuisances and the virtually equally harmful grave threats to life and property are precisely what the *Lucas* majority recognized as justifying uncompensated economic loss. Since nuisances and such grave threats are not constitutionally protected, the owners are not entitled to compensation when such uses are prohibited or abated.

Blackmun also relied upon the *Coates* decision to support his view that "the retroactive application of the regulation to formerly lawful uses was not a controlling distinction in the past."[162] He then quoted the following from *Coates:*

> Nor can it make any difference that the right is purchased previous to the passage of the by-law . . . for [e]very right, from an absolute ownership in property, down to a mere easement, is purchased and holden subject to the restriction, that it shall be so exercised as not to injure others. Though, at the time, it be remote and inoffensive, the purchaser is bound to know, at his peril, that it may become otherwise.[163]

The *Coates* court, however, was not talking about all retroactive applications of all regulations, but only those suppressing nuisances. Blackmun omitted the court's language after the word 'otherwise', which is as follows: "by the residence of many people in its vicinity; and that it must yield to by-laws, or other regular remedies, for the suppression of nuisances." The *Coates* court actually upheld the principle that the *Lucas* court considered to be the nuisance exception to the takings doctrine:

We are of opinion that this by-law is not void, either as being unconstitutional, or as conflicting with what we acknowledge as a fundamental principle of civilized society, that private property shall not be taken, even for public use, without just compensation. No property has, in this instance, been entered upon or taken. None are benefited by the destruction, or rather the suspension of the rights in question, in any other way than citizens always are, when one of their number is forbidden to continue a nuisance.[164]

Blackmun cited other cases to support his view that "retroactive application of regulation was not a controlling distinction in the past," including *Brick Presbyterian Church v. City of New York* (1826). In this case, New York's Supreme Court voided the city's covenant with a church for the quiet enjoyment of its property as a cemetery. The court held:

Sixty years ago, when the lease was made, the premises were beyond the inhabited part of the city. They were a common, and bounded on one side by a vineyard. Now they are in the very heart of the city. When the [city] covenanted that the lessees [the church] might enjoy the premises for the purposes of burying the dead, it never entered into the contemplation of either party that the health of the city might require the suspension or abolition of that right. It would be unreasonable, in the extreme, to hold that the plaintiffs should be at liberty to endanger not only the lives of such as belong to the corporation of the church, but also those of the citizens generally, because their lease contains a covenant for quiet enjoyment.[165]

This holding is not a blanket approval of retroactive regulation that destroys economic value without compensation; the court merely affirmed the city's right to curb a health hazard. The discussion above of the New York property rights decisions in Section II *supra* reveals that its courts strongly protected private ownership and generally rejected Blackmun's position of great deference to the legislature in this area of the law.

Blackmun also cited in support of his dissenting opinion the 1846 Massachusetts case of *Commonwealth v. Tewksbury*. The defendant was indicted for removing a quantity of sand and gravel from the beach in the town of Chelsea, an action that was contrary to local ordinance. The ordinance was adopted to protect Boston Harbor by conserving the natural embankment of its beaches. Tewksbury did not deny the charge. He countered that he was the owner of the land in fee, and that an ordinance prohibiting him from removing gravel from his own land was a taking of the private property for public use, requiring reasonable compensation. The court disagreed, holding that "a law prohibiting an owner from removing the soil composing a natural embankment to a valuable,

navigable stream, port or harbor, is not such a taking, such an interference with the right and title of the owner, as to give him a constitutional right to compensation, and to render an act unconstitutional which makes no such provision, but is a just restraint of an injurious use of the property, which the legislature have authority to make."[166] According to this court, the legislative power to limit property rights "is undoubtedly a high power; and is to be exercised with the strictest circumspection, and with the most sacred regard to the right of private property, and only in cases amounting to an obvious public exigency."

Blackmun argued that common law courts rejected "any common-law limit on the State's power to regulate harmful uses even to the point of destroying all economic value."[167] He quoted the *Tewksbury* decision as recognizing that it is "for the legislature to interpose, and by positive enactment to prohibit a use of property which would be injurious to the public."[168] However, the *Tewksbury* court was careful to note that "[i]t is extremely difficult to lay down any general rule, or draw a precise line between the cases where the restraint of the right of the owner is such that compensation ought to be provided, and where the regulation is such only as to prevent a particular use of the property from being a public nuisance."[169] The court's decision was narrow, merely holding that removing soil from the natural embankments of navigable waterways was a threat to life and property, which was the kind of harm that the legislature was constitutionally permitted to prohibit without compensation. The court did not express or imply that the legislature's powers to create new "harms" to regulate were without limit; on the contrary, the court refused to issue an opinion as to what the precise nuisance rule should be, leaving open the question of whether each future statutory restraint on property rights would require just compensation under the Massachusetts Constitution.[170]

Blackmun also cited *Commonwealth v. Alger* (1851), another Massachusetts case, to support his contention that early cases did not indicate any limit on the state's power to regulate harmful uses, even if that meant destroying all economic value. "Chief Justice Shaw explained in upholding a regulation prohibiting construction of wharves, the existence of a taking did not depend on 'whether a certain erection in tide water is a nuisance at common law or not.'"[171] The case involved an 1841 Boston statute that established a line in Boston Harbor beyond which no wharf could be extended or maintained, declaring any structure beyond that boundary to be a public nuisance. The statute did not affect the right to maintain wharves erected before its passage. Alger was indicted for building a pier, part of which extended beyond that line, on submerged land that he owned. Alger contended that he was entitled to build on this land, and if prohibited, that he was due just compensation under the Massachusetts Declaration of Rights' takings clause.

The Massachusetts high court held that the regulation in question did not effect a taking, because of the "subject matter to which such a restraint applies." The court explained:

The value of this species of estate, that of shore and flats, consists mainly in the means it affords of building wharves from upland towards deep water, to place merchandise and build wharves upon, and principally to afford access, to vessels requiring considerable depth of water. . . . Now if along a shore where there are flats of considerable extent, one were restrained to a certain length, while others were allowed to extend further, the damage might be great. . . . The one extended would stop or check the current along the others, cause mud to accumulate near them, and thus render the water shoal at those wharves.[172]

Thus, the court concluded, the legislature acted properly in drawing a line "adapted to the course of the current," to prevent shoaling at neighboring docks—the occurrence of which would constitute a harm. The court noted the

difficulty, not to say impracticability, of inquiring and deciding as a fact, in each particular case, whether a certain erection in tide water was a nuisance at common law or not. It is this consideration (the expediency and necessity of defining and securing the rights of the public) which creates the exigency, and furnishes the legislature with the authority to make a general and precise law. . . . If such a wharf or other erection were such as to interfere essentially with the common right of navigation, it would be held by the common law to be a common nuisance. . . .[173]

Ships benefit when they have access to their wharves with the same depth of water and the same strength of current at their heads. The Boston ordinance did not destroy all economic value, because property owners were free to build wharves and piers that did not cross the statutory boundary. The judicial problem, Chief Justice Shaw asserted, was to determine when the "regulation is such only as to prevent a particular use of the property from being a public nuisance." In contrast to the earlier cases, the court in *Alger* was persuaded that the legislation in question was dealing with a nuisance rather than a taking. Justice Blackmun did not refer to the Massachusetts cases of *Patterson* and *Parker* (discussed in Section II *supra*), authored also by Chief Justice Shaw, that revealed the court's strong commitment to the protection of property rights, including payment for consequential damages when a taking occurs.

Justice Blackmun also cited the 1858 Rhode Island case of *State v. Paul*, which was another nuisance case. The defendant was indicted for "keeping and maintaining a grogshop, and place of resort for noisy and disorderly persons, in the City of Providence," contrary to recently enacted statutes that declared such places to be "common nuisances."[174] The court upheld the conviction and its retroactive effect on Paul's property. The court reasoned that "rights of property . . . (are) restricted, as they necessarily must be, by the greater right of the community to have them so exercised within it as to be compatible with its

well-being. . . . [N]o one dreams that he can use his pick for burglary, or his sword for murder, merely because they are his. . . . The vile and poisonous compounds so generally sold at such places to the ignorant or degraded in taste, destructive alike to the body and the soul, have called aloud for regulation of some sort, in this dangerous trade."[175] Although the manufacture and sale of intoxicating liquors did not meet the definition of a common law nuisance for much judicial opinion of the period, the impact was no less destructive (see Section V *infra*).

In *Coates, Brick Presbyterian Church, Tewksbury,* and *Paul,* state courts determined that each use constituted a nuisance. As such, it was not entitled to constitutional protection. Nothing in the *Lucas* majority opinion holds otherwise. The U.S. Supreme Court remanded the *Lucas* case to the South Carolina courts to ascertain whether a nuisance law existed at the time Lucas purchased the property that could be construed to prohibit his proposed construction. The court's action appears to be consistent with the common law rules against retroactive legislation as reported by Coke and Blackstone.

Blackmun contended that prior to and during much of the eighteenth century, "the common agrarian conception of property limited owners to 'natural uses' of their land. . . . Thus, for example, the owner could build nothing on his land that would alter the natural flow of water."[176] He cited as authority the 1795 case of *Meritt v. Parker,* in which the New Jersey Supreme Court ruled on questions of riparian rights between owners of property on a stream (discussed in Chapter 2, Section IV). The common law protected an owner's right to enjoyment of his property, which included protection against the flooding of one's property and the stopping or diverting of an existing waterway. The case was not about natural uses of land, though; it was about uses of public waterways that affect the property rights of others. According to Chief Justice Kinsey, "[i]n general, it may be observed, when a man purchases a piece of land, through which a natural watercourse flows, he has a right to make use of it in its natural state, but not to stop or divert it to the prejudice of another." If one man

> by any contrivance causes to flow over the land of another a greater quantity of water that it is naturally subjected to, against his will, or without his consent, such other has a legal right to resort to any device, or may erect any banks or, dams, etc., on his own land, to prevent this additional current of water; and if any consequences injurious to the first wrongdoer result from this course, he must submit to them, and cannot recover in damages.[177]

Clearly, the court sought to protect property rights and not to further some late-twentieth century ecological, anti-development standard concerning property. As Chancellor Kent in 1816 put it in a comparable situation: "A right to a

stream of water is as sacred as a right to the soil over which it flows. It is part of the freehold of which no man can be disseized 'but by lawful judgment of his peers, or by due process of law.' "[178] Applying the rules expressed in *Meritt,* in 1839, the New Jersey Supreme Court, in *Sinnickson v. Johnson* (discussed in Section II *infra*), held that the flooding of lands caused by the damming of a creek was a consequential taking of a riparian owner's property. These important property rights decisions were not taken into account by Blackmun.

Blackmun sought to show that the legislature was entitled to maximum deference in determining the existence of a nuisance or any other harmful use. Departing from his discussion of early cases, Blackmun quoted Justice Oliver Wendell Holmes in the 1892 Massachusetts case of *Commonwealth v. Parks* on nuisance: "[T]he legislature may change the common law as to nuisances, and may move the line either way, so as to make things nuisances which were not so, or to make things lawful which were nuisances."[179] In *Parks,* the court upheld the conviction of the defendants for violating a statute prohibiting blasting rock with explosives without written permission from the city. Blackmun, however, omitted Holmes's next sentence: "It is still plainer that it may prohibit a use of land which the common law would regard as a nuisance if it endangered adjoining houses or the highway, and the legislature may authorize cities and towns by ordinances and by-laws to make similar prohibitions."[180] This is a very clear statement of the common law principle upon which nuisance law was based: the authority of the state to prevent serious public or private harm.

Noting that "blasting might be a private or a public nuisance" under Massachusetts's common law, Holmes wrote: "Forbidding it does not trench upon the rights of ownership to such an extent as necessary to require compensation."[181] However, he noted, even the regulation of an ultrahazardous activity such as blasting has its constitutional limits. Far from granting the legislature unlimited power, "[i]t may be that a by-law absolutely prohibiting blasting would be invalid in some towns of this commonwealth. It may be that, in order to determine the question, we should have to take into account facts touching the mode in which the particular town was occupied, and the nature of its industries, whether we listen to evidence of such facts or notice them judicially."[182] In other words, the regulation would only be constitutionally valid if the judiciary found that it actually prevented a nuisance or grave public harm.

Holmes was hardly a champion of the legislature having the final word when the regulation of private property was involved. In his famous 1922 U.S. Supreme Court opinion in *Pennsylvania Coal v. Mahon,* he wrote: "As long recognized some values are enjoyed under an implied limitation and must yield to the police power. But obviously the implied limitation must have its limits or the contract and due process clauses are gone. One fact for consideration in determining such limits is the extent of diminution. When it reaches a certain

magnitude, in most if not all cases there must be an exercise of eminent domain and compensation to sustain the act."[183] He warned that "[w]e are in danger of forgetting that a strong public desire to improve the public condition is not enough to warrant achieving the desire by a shorter cut than the constitutional way of paying for the charge."[184] This opinion is consistent with Holmes's view in *Parks* that the legislature does *not* have unlimited authority under the police power to redefine nuisance law. Even public safety regulation has limits, beyond which government regulation becomes a taking requiring compensation. Thus, in *Mahon,* Holmes rejected claims by the state (and Justice Brandeis) that the law at issue was necessary to abate nuisances, and instead held that it was constitutionally invalid.

Justice Blackmun concluded in his dissenting opinion: "In short, I find no clear and accepted 'historical compact' or 'understanding of our citizens' justifying the court's new takings doctrine."[185] However, the sources he cited on behalf of his opinion, when examined, provide support for an opposite conclusion: The principle that the state should compensate individuals for property taken for public use (except in cases of nuisance and grave threats to life and property) *was* widely established in America at the time of the Revolution and beyond. This principle is confirmed by numerous cases discussed in Section II (and that will be discussed in Section IV) of this chapter. Blackmun's opinion contained no references to U.S. Supreme Court or other federal court cases decided prior to the early 1870s, which, as the next section will reveal, were cases highly protective of property rights.

IV. Federal Cases

This section concerns the jurisprudence of the U.S. Supreme Court and other federal courts during the period from the late 1780s to the early 1870s that relates directly or indirectly to the protection of private property. Judicial review arrived at the federal level with Chief Justice John Marshall's unanimous opinion in *Marbury v. Madison* (1803),[186] in which he ruled that the Supreme Court had the power to invalidate a congressional statute that violated the terms of the Constitution.

In *Marbury*, Marshall applied customary rules of statutory construction in interpreting a provision of the Constitution, similar to what he would have done if only a statute were involved. Congress authorized the filing of a mandamus suit directly in the U.S. Supreme Court as a matter of original jurisdiction, but the Chief Justice held that the Supreme Court had no authority under the Constitution to adjudicate such suits as original matters. (The purpose of a mandamus suit is to require a government official to execute a rule or carry out a duty that he is required to do by existing law.) Article III, Section 2 enumer-

ated the actions that could be filed in the Supreme Court under its original jurisdiction, and these actions did not include a mandamus proceeding. This section of the Constitution allowed only cases affecting ambassadors, other public ministers and consuls, and those in which the state is a party to be filed as original matters. In all other matters, the Supreme Court had appellate jurisdiction. Once Marshall resolved the issue of the judicial review power, there was nothing extraordinary about the analysis that he employed in interpreting the constitutional provision as not authorizing a mandamus action.

The 1798 U.S. Supreme Court case of *Calder v. Bull*[187] involved the interpretation of the provision of the Constitution that prohibits state governments from passing *ex post facto* laws. The case relates to property rights in two important respects. First, the Supreme Court construed the *ex post facto* clauses as a protection solely against retroactive criminal laws and not civil laws. Since laws regulating property are frequently retroactive in character—that is, they eliminate rights an owner acquired at the time of his original acquisition—this decision denied owners an important protection against confiscation and regulation.

Second, the case is also noted for Justice Chase's observations on the inherent limitations of legislative bodies under the U.S. Constitution. Chase reasoned that the noble purposes for which people enter into society determine the nature and terms of the social compact. The legislature does not possess the power to pass measures in violation of these purposes. Chase wrote:

> I cannot subscribe to the omnipotence of a state legislature; or that it is absolute and without control; although its authority should not be expressly restrained by the constitution, or fundamental law, of the state . . . There are certain vital principles of our free Republican governments, which will determine and over-rule an apparent and flagrant abuse of legislative power. . . . An ACT of the Legislature (for I cannot call it a law) contrary to the great first principles of the social compact, cannot be considered a rightful exercise of legislative authority. The obligation of a law in governments established on express compact, and on republican principles, must be determined by the nature of the power on which it was founded.[188]

Chase proceeded to provide illustrations explaining his position:

> A law that punished a citizen for an innocent action, or in other words, for an act, which, when done, was in violation of no existing law; a law that destroys, or impairs, the lawful private contracts of citizens; a law that makes a man a Judge in his own cause; or a law that takes property from A and gives it to B: It is against all reason and justice, for a people

to entrust a legislature with SUCH powers; and, therefore, it cannot be presumed they have done it. The genius, the nature, and the spirit, of our State Governments, amount to a prohibition of such acts of legislation; and the general principles of law and reason forbid them.[189]

These observations by Chase are a distillation of the principles espoused by Coke and Blackstone. Both Coke and Blackstone viewed government as limited by the people's rights and liberties, for the protection of which the political society was created. This principle is also consistent with those of Locke, who wrote that, in forming political society, men entered into a social compact where the authority of government was limited.

The Supreme Court's language and terminology has changed over the years, but the justices have followed a course of dispensing justice quite consonant with Chase's position. The inclusion in his opinion of property confiscation as a flagrant abuse of power reveals the high priority accorded ownership in the early years of this nation. Another early American jurist who subscribed to Chase's position on constitutional interpretation was Joseph Story, a justice of the United States Supreme Court between 1811 and 1845 and the author of the highly authoritative *Commentaries on the Constitution.* In providing meaning for the Fifth Amendment's due process clause, in his *Commentaries,* Story quoted Lord Coke:

> The [due process] clause is but an enlargement of the language of magna charta, *nec super eum ibimus, nec super eum mittimus, nisi per legale judicium parium suorum, vel per legem terrae,* neither will we pass upon him, or condemn him, but by the lawful judgment of his peers, or by the law of the land. Lord Coke says, that these latter words, *per legem terrae* (by the law of the land), mean due process of law, that is, without due presentment or indictment, and being brought in to answer thereto by due process of the common law. So that this clause in effect affirms the right of trial [among other things] according to the process and proceedings of the common law.[190]

Story wrote two opinions concerning the property laws of the states, which at that time were not subject to the Bill of Rights since it then applied only to the national government. (The Fourteenth Amendment, which was ratified in 1868, applied most guarantees of the Bill of Rights to the states.) For a unanimous court in both cases, Story wrote that a legislature was limited in its powers over life, liberty, and property. While he did not expressly cite the Magna Carta or Lord Coke, the language he used was in accord with Coke's interpretations of Chapter 29 of the great charter.

In *Terrett v. Taylor* (1815),[191] Justice Story invoked the principles of natural justice, the fundamental laws of every free government, the spirit and letter of

the Constitution, and "the decisions of the most respectable judicial tribunals" to strike down a Virginia statute divesting the Protestant Episcopal Church of its property. The state had previously incorporated the church, and given it authority to demise, improve, and lease the lands belonging to it. The church had acquired the property before the American Revolution when it was the established church of Virginia and received financial and other assistance from the government. Virginia argued that the grant of lands was revocable because it was owned by a corporation and its continued existence was contrary to the Virginia Declaration of Rights and statutory law. Story did not base his opinion on any specific provision of the Constitution. Any doctrine that a legislative grant of property is revocable, he concluded, would be "utterly inconsistent with a great and fundamental principle of republican government, the right of the citizens to the free enjoyment of their property legally acquired." The property rights of the owners of corporate stock were no different than the property rights of natural persons.

Subsequently, in *Wilkinson v. Leland* (1829),[192] the Supreme Court (again, per Justice Story) upheld the validity of a 1792 Rhode Island statute confirming the sale of lands in that state by the executrix of an estate to pay debts of the testator, who was a citizen of New Hampshire. At the time of the sale, the will had not been probated in Rhode Island, and the executrix did not have the authority to make the sale. The Rhode Island statute sought to eliminate this defect, and second-generation heirs of the estate contested the power of the state to adopt the statute.

Justice Story reasoned that under law the devise in question was transferred immediately to the devisees upon the death of the testator, and that Rhode Island had no authority to divest it. In passing the 1792 statute, the legislature had merely ratified a conveyance of the right and interest of the testator. Echoing the position of Justice Chase in *Calder v. Bull,* Story asserted that in the absence of specific authority, Rhode Island did not possess the power to disregard the "great principles of Magna Carta" by taking away the purchaser's property "without trial, without notice, and without offense." Even if the general assembly had such power prior to the American Revolution,

> it can scarcely be imagined that that great event could have left the people of that state subjected to its uncontrolled and arbitrary exercise. That government can scarcely be deemed free, where the rights of property are left solely dependent upon the will of the legislative body, without any restraint. The fundamental maxims of a free government seem to require, that the rights of personal liberty and private property should be held sacred. At least no court of justice in this country would be warranted in assuming, that the power to violate and disregard them; a power so repugnant to the common principles of justice and civil liberty; lurked under any general

grant of legislative authority, or ought to be implied from any general expressions of the will of the people. The people ought not to be presumed to part with rights so vital to their security and well being, without very strong and direct expressions of such an intention.[193]

Story affirmed that under existing precedents the legislature was limited in its power to restrict the rights of ownership: "We know of no case in which a legislative act to transfer the property of A to B without his consent has ever been held a constitutional exercise of legislative power in any State of the Union. On the contrary, it has been consistently resisted as inconsistent with just principles by every judicial tribunal in which it has been attempted to be enforced." The Supreme Court expressed strong support for the right of property in language echoing Chase's position in *Calder v. Bull.*

The positions of Justices Chase and Story on the fundamental status of property rights were applied over one hundred years later to protect purchasers of municipal bonds. In *Gelpcke v. Dubuque* (1864), the Supreme Court upheld the validity of Dubuque, Iowa municipal bonds that were issued in aid of railroads, notwithstanding a state supreme court decision which held the bonds invalid under the state's constitution.[194] The bonds were issued on the authority of state legislation, Iowa Supreme Court decisions sustaining the constitutionality of such bonds, and similar decisions in sixteen states. The U.S. high court thus rejected the generally accepted doctrine that a state supreme court's interpretation of its own constitution is final and conclusive. While acknowledging the existence of this doctrine and the court's adherence to it in the past, the high court insisted that "truth, justice and the law" as well as the "plainest principles of justice" required it to uphold a contract which, when made, was valid by the law of the state as then expounded by all branches of its government.

In *Fletcher v. Peck* (1810),[195] the Supreme Court applied both constitutional provisions and unenumerated principles of natural law to annul a Georgia law that canceled the purchasers' title to millions of acres of land in what is now most of Alabama and Mississippi. This land had been bought in good faith from grantors who had acquired it through legislative corruption. Chief Justice Marshall combined grounds for decision making by holding that the law in question was contrary to general principles of law as well as a violation of the obligation of contracts provision (Article I, Section 10, which bars states from passing any "Law impairing the Obligation of Contracts"). He observed that if the legislature

> feel(s) itself absolved from those rules of property, which are common to all the citizens of the United states, and from those principles of equity which are acknowledged in all our courts, its act is to be supported by its power alone, and the same power may divest any other individual of his lands, if it shall be the will of the legislature to exert it.

It may well be doubted whether the nature of society and of government does not prescribe some limits to the legislative power; and, if any be prescribed, where are they to be found, if the property of an individual, fairly and honestly acquired, may be seized without compensation.

To the legislature all legislative power is granted; but the question whether the act of transferring the property of an individual to the public, be in the nature of a legislative power is well worthy of serious reflection. . . .[196]

[T]he estate having passed into the hands of a purchaser for a valuable consideration, without notice, the State of Georgia was restrained, either by general principles which are common to our free institutions, or by the particular provisions of the Constitution of the United States, from passing a law whereby the estate of the plaintiff in the premises so purchased could be constitutionally and legally impaired and rendered null and void.[197]

In ruling on the contracts issue, Marshall interpreted the obligation of contracts clause by examining its language and meaning, concluding that it prohibited the passage of the challenged statute. Justice Johnson wrote a separate opinion maintaining that a state has no power to deprive people of property it has given them: "I do not hesitate to declare that a state does not possess the power of revoking its own grants. But I do it on a general principle, on the reason and nature of things: a principle which will impose laws even on the Deity."

I have previously quoted United States Supreme Court Justice William Patterson's views in *Vanhorne's Lessee v. Dorrance,* a case he decided while on circuit in Pennsylvania in 1795, where he applied principles of natural law to declare unconstitutional restraints imposed on property ownership by a Pennsylvania statute.[198] The state constitution contained no takings clause and Patterson held that common law principles mandated payment of just compensation to indemnify an owner:

When the legislature undertake to give away what is not their own . . . even upon complete indemnification, it will naturally be considered as an extraordinary act of legislation, which ought to be viewed with jealous eyes, examined with critical exactness, and scrutinized with all the severity of legal exposition. An act of the sort deserves no favor; to construe it liberally would be sinning against the rights of private property.

In *Bank of Columbia v. Okely* (1819),[199] Supreme Court Justice Johnson interpreted the twenty-first article of Maryland's Declaration of Rights, which, following the words of the Magna Carta, stated that "no freeman ought to be

taken or imprisoned, or deprived of his life, liberty and property, but by the judgment of his peers, or by the law of the land." Johnson wrote that these words "were intended to secure the individual from the arbitrary exercise of the powers of government, unrestrained by the established principles of private rights and distributive justice."[200] The case involved a Maryland statute allowing a bank to obtain summary judgments against its debtors who have consented in writing to this process. The Supreme Court held that because this law was in derogation of the ordinary protection of private rights (such as a trial by jury), it must be subjected to a strict construction. However, it concluded that a person may renounce this constitutional right, and this had voluntarily occurred in this case.

In *Corfield v. Coryell* (1823), United States Supreme Court Justice Bushrod Washington, in his capacity as a circuit court judge for the district of Pennsylvania, interpreted the privileges and immunities clause of Article IV, Section 2 of the Constitution as protecting "those privileges and immunities which are in their nature fundamental; which belong of right, to the citizens of all free governments; and which have, at all times, been enjoyed by the citizens of the several states which compose this union."[201] These protections included "the enjoyment of life and liberty, with the right to acquire and possess property of every kind, and pursue and obtain happiness and safety," subject to reasonable regulations. Washington wrote that these fundamental liberties also comprehended the "right of a citizen of one state to pass through, or to reside in any other state, for purposes of trade, agriculture, professional pursuits or otherwise: to claim the benefit of habeas corpus; to institute and maintain actions of any kind in the courts of the state; to take, hold and dispose of property, either real or personal." The enjoyment of these liberties "by the citizens of each state, in every other state was manifestly calculated" to achieve friendship and interaction among the states.

Proponents of the Fourteenth Amendment in the Thirty-Ninth Congress (which framed the amendment) considered Washington's interpretation as constitutionally guaranteeing fundamental rights to be secure from violation by the state or federal governments. They reasoned that if nonresidents of states were guaranteed these fundamental rights, then surely residents would be entitled to no less protection. While for a long time (1823–1869) the Supreme Court embraced this position, it subsequently ruled otherwise. In *Paul v. Virginia* (1868), it held that the clause was intended to relieve "state citizens of the disabilities of alienage in other states and of inhibiting discriminatory legislation against them by other states."[202] A state only had to provide nonresidents living in the state the same protection of fundamental rights as it accorded its own residents.

The Fifth Amendment's due process clause was first interpreted by the Supreme Court in *Murray's Lessee v. Hoboken Land and Improvement Com-*

pany (1855).[203] The Court was asked to declare unconstitutional a federal statute that provided for the imposition of a summary judgment at the direction of the Secretary of the Treasury without the exercise of judicial power against a collector of customs for a balance due on his account. The Court stated that the words "due process of law were undoubtedly intended to convey the same meaning of the words 'by the law of the land' contained in the Magna Charta." Rejecting the position that the Fifth Amendment's due process clause placed no restrictions on the legislative power, the Court interpreted it as a restraint on every branch of government:

> It is manifest that it was not left to the legislative power to enact any process which might be devised. The article is a restraint on the legislative as well as on the executive and judicial powers of the government and cannot be so construed as to leave congress free to make any process "due process of law," by its mere will.[204]

The Court went on to ascertain whether, since the statute did not require the judiciary to enter a summary judgment, the process at issue was due process:

> To what principles, then, are we to resort to ascertain whether this process, enacted by Congress, is due process? To this the answer must be twofold. We must examine the Constitution itself to see whether this process be in conflict with any of its provisions. If not found to be so, we must look to those settled usages and modes of proceeding existing in the common and statute law of England, before the emigration of our ancestors, and which are shown not to have been unsuited to their civil and political conditions by having been acted on by them after the settlement of this country.[205]

The Supreme Court concluded that the sort of summary proceeding provided for by the federal statute was in accordance with such "settled usages and modes of proceeding" and was exercised subsequent to settlement. By the common law of England, the laws of many of the colonies before the American Revolution, and the laws of states before the framing of the federal constitution, a summary process (devoid of judicial participation) existed for the recovery of debts due to the government:

> For, though "due process of law" generally implies and includes *actor, reus, judex,* regular allegations, opportunity to answer, and a trial according to some settled course of judicial proceedings, [citations discussed below] yet, this is not universally true: There may be, and we have seen that

there are cases, under the law of England after *Magna Charta,* and as it was brought to this country and acted on here, in which process, in its nature final, issues against the body, lands, and goods of certain public debtors without any such trial. . . .[206]

The Supreme Court's citations in support of its view on the general meaning of due process consisted of Lord Coke's *Institutes* (citing 2 Inst. 47, 50), *Greene v. Briggs* (a U.S. Circuit Court decision in Rhode Island that will be discussed later in this section), and five state court decisions that were discussed earlier in this chapter (*Hoke v. Henderson,* a North Carolina case, *Taylor v. Porter,* a New York case, and three Tennessee cases, *Vanzant v. Waddel, State Bank v. Cooper,* and *Jones' Heirs v. Perry*). These decisions accord "law of the land" and "due process of law" the same meaning that Alexander Hamilton gave them in his speech to the New York legislature on February 6, 1787 (previously discussed above in Chapter 3). Also citing Lord Coke in support of his position, Hamilton stated that by reason of either due process or law of the land provisions, legislators have no authority to deprive people of their rights. Only the judiciary has this authority, and then solely when it adheres to principles of due process or law of the land. In this opinion, the Supreme Court agreed with Hamilton with respect to the usual and ordinary legislative actions. However, as previously noted, the Court stated that "there are cases . . . in which process . . . issues against . . . certain public debtors without any such trial," but these exceptions were based upon particular historical practices and they still left Hamilton's basic reasoning intact.

Justice Benjamin Curtis, who authored the Supreme Court's opinion in *Murray's Lessee,* had previously written (in his capacity as a circuit justice) the opinion in the circuit court case he cited, *Greene v. Briggs* (1852).[207] *Greene* involved a Rhode Island law that precluded an accused person from answering and contesting the charge against him, unless he first gave a security, in the sum of $200 with two sufficient sureties, to pay all fines and costs. If the accused failed to comply with these requirements, courts were empowered to impose a fine and/or forfeiture pursuant to statute. Writing for the circuit court, Curtis held that such a law would deprive an accused of his liberty or property, not by the law of the land, but by arbitrary exertion of the legislative power. The Constitution of Rhode Island provided that no person "shall be deprived of life, liberty or property, unless by the judgment of his peers, or the law of the land." In his opinion, Curtis stated the following:

[Law of the land] does not mean any act which the assembly may choose to pass. If it did, the legislative will could inflict a forfeiture of life, liberty, or property, without a trial. The exposition of these words, as they

stand in Magna Charta, as well as the American Constitutions, has been that they require "due process of law;" and in this is necessarily implied and included the right to answer to and contest the charge, and the consequent right to be discharged from it, unless it is proved. Lord Coke, giving the interpretation of these words in Magna Carta (2 Institute, 50, 51), says they mean due process of law, in which is included presentment or indictment and being brought in to answer thereto. And the jurists of our country have not relaxed this interpretation.[208]

The Court also cited *Hoke v. Henderson, Taylor v. Porter,* and commentaries of Justice Story and Chancellor Kent. In later years, the meaning of due process protection with respect to slavery became an issue. People who viewed slavery favorably argued that the due process clause supported their position. They found support in Chief Justice Roger Taney's decision in the highly controversial *Dred Scott* case, decided in 1856.[209] Dred Scott was a slave who traveled to and lived with his master for five years in free territory (the state of Illinois and the Minnesota territory) and subsequently moved to Missouri, which was then a slave state. Alleging that he was a citizen of Missouri, Scott filed suit in a federal court in St. Louis against John Sandford of New York, his master, for assault and sought damages in the amount of $9,000. Pursuant to Article III, Section 2 of the U.S. Constitution, Congress had authorized the federal courts to adjudicate cases between citizens of different states. The case reached the United States Supreme Court on the question of whether the federal court had jurisdiction to decide the case, and the decision rested on Scott's citizenship status. He claimed freedom because he had traveled to and lived in territory declared free by the United States Congress.

Taney wrote that blacks could not be considered citizens because they were not "people of the United States." As part of his opinion, he held that Congress had no power to prohibit slavery in specified areas because the "powers over person and property . . . are not granted to Congress, but are in express terms denied, and they are forbidden to exercise them." Taney explained this "express" limitation as follows:

[A]n act of Congress which deprives a citizen of the United States of his liberty or property, merely because he came himself or brought his property into a particular Territory of the United States, and who has committed no offense against the laws, could hardly be dignified with the name of due process of law.

Although a majority concurred with Taney's general decision, only two justices went along specifically with this reasoning.

Justice Curtis disagreed with Taney. He asserted that the due process clause was not violated because no deprivation had occurred. According to Curtis, a property right in a slave existed only pursuant to the laws of the state in which the slave was held, and that condition terminated when the owner voluntarily placed his slave permanently within another jurisdiction where no municipal law on the subject of slavery existed.

For many if not most people in the nation, and clearly the bulk of the population today, both Taney's and Curtis's view of due process with respect to racial restrictions was perverted. In Taney's day, abolitionists interpreted the due process clause as meaning that "no person shall be deprived of his self ownership and earning power." They contended that the due process principle is intended to protect the life, liberty, and property of every person, and must not be applied by government to destroy them. As a matter of legal precedent, however, Taney's interpretation of the meaning of the due process clause was frequently cited.

Taney had previously interpreted the Fifth Amendment's due process clause as banning Congress from depriving an owner of property rights. In writing for the Court in *Bloomer v. McQuewan* (1853),[210] he had observed that a special act depriving licensees of their right to use property protected by patent "certainly could not be regarded as due process of law"; however, the case was resolved on other grounds.

Yates v. Milwaukee (1870)[211] involved a Wisconsin law of 1854 that authorized Milwaukee "by ordinance, to establish dock and wharf lines on the banks of the Milwaukee and Menomonee rivers, [and to] restrain and prevent encroachments upon said rivers and obstructions thereto." Subsequently, Yates built a wharf over property he owned on the Milwaukee River, extending 150 feet in order to reach the navigable part of the river. Thereafter, the city—without evidence that the wharf actually constituted an obstruction to navigation—adopted an ordinance declaring Yates's wharf an obstruction to navigation and consequently a nuisance, and ordered it to be abated. Yates filed suit to restrain the city and its contractor from demolishing the wharf. The Wisconsin Supreme Court upheld the city.

On appeal, the United States Supreme Court, per Justice Samuel Miller, reversed and enjoined the defendants from interfering with the wharf, reserving the right of the city to make changes for the actual improvement of the navigability of the river upon payment of compensation. The Court decided the case on the basis of the common law without reference to any state or national takings clause. It held that the owner of land bounded by a navigable river has certain riparian rights, including free access to the navigable part of the stream by constructing a landing, wharf, or pier for his own or the public's use:

> The mere declaration by the city council of Milwaukee that a certain structure was an encroachment or obstruction did not make it so, nor

could such a declaration make it a nuisance unless it in fact had that character. It is a doctrine not to be tolerated in this country, that a municipal corporation, without any general laws either of the city or of the State within which a given structure can be shown to be a nuisance, can by its mere declaration that it is one, subject it to removal by any person supposed to be aggrieved, or even by the city itself. This would place every house, every business, and all of the property of the city, at the uncontrolled will of the temporary local authorities.

Although decided in 1870, four years after the framing of the Fourteenth Amendment, *Hepburn v. Griswold*[212] reflects considerable judicial opinion existing at the time of its framing and ratification. In 1862, in the midst of the Civil War, Congress passed an act authorizing the issuance of $150 million of notes redeemable only in six-percent, twenty-year bonds and not in gold or silver coin, and providing that these notes should "be lawful money and a legal tender in payment of all debts, public and private, within the United States," except for duties on imports and interest on the public debt, which were still payable in specie. These notes—and others of similar character issued subsequently—became known as "greenbacks" because of their distinctive color.

Hepburn raised due process and takings issues relevant to the analyses presented in this chapter. The legal issue arose as a result of a promissory note executed by Mrs. Hepburn on June 20, 1860, agreeing to pay Mr. Griswold $11,250 on February 20, 1862. At the time that she made the note, and on the date of its maturity, the only form of money that could be lawfully tendered in payment of private debts was gold or silver coin. The holder of the promissory note subsequently filed suit to collect on it. In March of 1864, Hepburn tendered the holder greenbacks issued under the act in the amount of $12,720, which included principal, accrued interest, and some court costs, in full satisfaction of her note. The payment was refused. The greenbacks were then tendered to the trial court, which found the tender good and the debt fully discharged.

Throughout this litigation, the value of a dollar in gold was more than the value of a dollar in U.S. notes. At that time, a dollar in gold meant the physical amount of gold that was designated a dollar before the Civil War. From mid-1864 to early 1865, this amount of gold was worth more than $2 in notes and was close to that figure at the time of Hepburn's tender. The holder denied that Congress had the power to make the greenbacks a legal tender in payment of debts, which, when contracted, were payable only in gold or silver coins.

The U.S. Supreme Court decided 4–3 that the 1862 act was unconstitutional with respect to existing contracts. In addition, the Court found other defects. It held that the law violated the Fifth Amendment's takings clause, because it appropriated property from one group for the benefit of another. The Court proceeded to consider the application of the Fifth Amendment's due process

clause—"whether an act which compels all those who hold contracts for the payment of gold and silver money to accept in payment a currency of inferior value deprives such persons of property without due process of law." It concluded:

> It is quite clear, that whatever may be the operation of such an act, due process of law makes no part of it. Does it deprive any person of property? A very large proportion of the property of civilized men exists in the form of contracts. These contracts almost invariably stipulate for the payment of money. And we have already seen that contracts in the United States, prior to the act under consideration, for the payment of money, were contracts to pay the sums specified in gold and silver coin. And it is beyond doubt that the holders of these contracts were and are as fully entitled to the protection of this constitutional provision as the holders of any other description of property.

President Grant subsequently appointed two justices who, on May 1, 1871 in *Knox v. Lee,*[213] joined with the three dissenters in *Hepburn* to reverse the latter case. Justice Noah H. Swayne dissented in *Hepburn,* and he and newly appointed Justice Bradley voted with the majority in *Knox.* Neither, however, should be considered antagonistic to the protection of property rights. On the contrary, both contended in their dissents in the *Slaughterhouse Cases,* decided the following year (and will be discussed in Chapter 6), that the Fourteenth Amendment's privileges or immunities and due process clauses secured property and economic interests.

Decided unanimously the following year, *Pumpelly v. Green Bay Co.* (1871)[214] upheld the position that a partial conversion to public use was sufficient to constitute a taking and thus requiring payment of compensation. The case involved a physical invasion by government of private property that did not affect the title but "almost complete[ly]" destroyed the property's value by denying the owner beneficial use of it. Under authority of the state of Wisconsin, Green Bay Company had built a dam across Fox River, raising the level of Lake Winnebago and flooding the property of Pumpelly, who thereafter claimed compensation under the takings clause of the Wisconsin Constitution that was similar in language to the federal version.[215]

The company conceded that Pumpelly's property had been flooded, but claimed that (1) the dam was authorized by statute and built in conformity with the requirements of existing law, (2) a takings claim was precluded by another law which provided the sole remedy for property flooded by dams, and (3) the damage was not compensable as a taking because it was the remote and consequential result of the government exercising its power to im-

prove a navigable stream. It had not intentionally harmed Pumpelly or acted negligently.

The United States Supreme Court was not convinced by the Green Bay Company's reasoning. Writing for the Court, Justice Samuel Miller asserted that the defendant raised no valid defense to the claim for compensation under Wisconsin's takings clause:

> It would be a very curious and unsatisfactory result, if in construing a provision of constitutional law, always understood to have been adopted for protection and security to the rights of the individual as against the government, and which has received the commendation of jurists, statesmen and commentators as placing the just principles of the common law on that subject beyond the power of ordinary legislation to change or control them, it shall be held that if the government refrains from the absolute conversion of real property to the uses of the public it can destroy its value entirely, can inflict irreparable and permanent injury to any extent, can, in effect, subject it to total destruction without making any compensation, because, in the narrowest sense of that word, it is not *taken* for the public use. Such a construction would pervert the constitutional provision into a restriction upon the rights of the citizen, as those rights stood at the common law, instead of the government, and make it an authority for invasion of private right under the pretext of the public good, which had no warrant in the laws or practices of our ancestors.[216]

The Court cited *Sinnickson v. Johnson,* an 1839 New Jersey case, and Chancellor James Kent's famous decision in *Gardner v. Trustees of the Village of Newburgh* (1816) (both of which were discussed earlier in this chapter). Conceding that cases in some states supported the Green Bay Company's position, and that the principle of no redress for "consequential injury to property of the individual arising from the prosecution of improvements of roads, streets, rivers, and other highways, for the public good" is a "sound one in its proper application," the *Pumpelly* opinion criticized those decisions as having "gone to the uttermost limit of sound judicial construction in favor of this principle, and in some cases beyond it."[217] The opinion continued:

> But there are numerous authorities to sustain the doctrine that a serious interruption of the common and necessary use of property may be, in the language of Mr. Angell, in his work on water-courses, equivalent to the taking of it, and that under the constitutional provisions, it is not necessary that the land should be absolutely taken.

The U.S. Supreme Court went on to note that the Wisconsin Supreme Court, among others, has consistently upheld overflow as a taking. It concluded the opinion with this statement: "[W]here real estate is actually invaded by super-induced additions of water, earth, sand, or other material, or by having any artificial structure placed on it, so as to effectually destroy or impair its usefulness, it is a taking, within the meaning of the Constitution."[218] The U.S. Supreme Court thus defined takings to include a physical invasion, a concept which is now firmly entrenched in takings law.[219]

During the eighty-year period surveyed in this book, little change occurred in the position of the U.S. Supreme Court on the protection of property rights. For a unanimous U.S. Supreme Court, Justice Miller in support of his opinions in *Yates* (1870) and *Pumpelly* (1871) applied Blackstone's interpretations of the common law. To uphold his ruling in *Pumpelly,* he cited *Gardner* and *Sinnickson,* both of which also were consistent with Blackstone's commentaries. Miller's opinions were no less supportive of property rights than those expressed for a unanimous court by Justice Story in *Terrett* (1815) and *Wilkinson* (1829). I believe that in these opinions, the Supreme Court was implementing the intentions of both the framers of the original constitution and of the Bill of Rights.

One of the major reasons that persuaded James Madison and his colleagues at the 1787 Constitutional Convention to support the separation of powers was that it would protect property rights. Without this protection, the commercial society they envisioned could not exist. A similar perspective likely prevailed among framers of state constitutions who were also concerned about the egalitarian proclivities of the public that operate to limit the rights of property. There are always factions that seek to occupy, seize, or control other people's property. Many times, these efforts succeed in the legislature. In the absence of the judicial check on the legislative and executive branches of government, the history of the United States would have been much different.

The judges enabled the productive and innovative talents of the American people to flourish to the general benefit of all. The judiciary is also responsible for setting the moral tone of the U.S. government. Government must not confiscate the people's assets. It must not deprive the people of their rights to life, liberty, and property, except when they violate existing laws. All laws must be prospective and not retroactive so that persons will be aware of them when they act, and the government must not have the power to specially harm or benefit any person or group.

V. Due Process and the Police Power

A great many judicial decisions in the years prior to the framing of the Fourteenth Amendment are consistent with the rules set forth by Coke and Black-

stone. The decisions briefed in the foregoing sections of this chapter indicate that most state high courts, at least two federal circuit courts, and the United States Supreme Court followed Coke's and/or Blackstone's interpretations of the Magna Carta's Chapter 29, which was the source for due process of law and law of the land provisions. It is important to note that in *Murray's Lessee* the U.S. Supreme Court premised its interpretation of the Fifth Amendment's due process clause on Coke's *Institutes,* and a federal circuit and five state court decisions, all of which were also based on the *Institutes.* For the Supreme Court, these decisions were sufficient to support its interpretation of due process of law. Courts interpreting just compensation issues frequently cited Blackstone's requirements for compensation. They often referred to Coke and Blackstone in support of their rulings that laws must have a public and not a private purpose. Clearly, Coke and Blackstone were widely accepted with respect to their interpretation of the common law's protection of private property.

Some commentators state that prior to the adoption of the Fourteenth Amendment, the prevailing view of American courts was that, except for perhaps a dozen major cases, the phrases "due process of law" and "law of the land" related largely to procedural rights.[220] These protections, it was said, were of little significance as a standard to test the validity of legislative acts.[221] The case summaries presented in the prior sections of this chapter reveal the inaccuracy of these comments. This was surely not the position of the U.S. Supreme Court in 1856 when it decided *Murray's Lessee* and interpreted the Fifth Amendment's due process clause as a substantive restraint on all branches of government. The Court in that case cited decisions based on substantive due process; it obviously did not support this interpretation with cases confining due process or law of the land clauses to procedural protection or with cases subordinating due process concerns to those of the police powers. Nor did Congressman John Bingham, the principal author of the due process clause of the Fourteenth Amendment, harbor any doubt that due process was a substantive limitation on government. References to due process by Bingham and other members of the Thirty-Ninth Congress who supported the proposed Fourteenth Amendment indicate that they viewed due process as a substantive and procedural restraint on legislative and executive power.[222]

Moreover, the line between substantive and procedural due process is nebulous. As defined by Coke, due process of law imposes various procedural requirements on the judiciary, such as jury trial and the right to answer, each of which is also a substantive restraint on the power of the legislature to restrict liberties and to penalize people. As the Supreme Court has asserted, the due process clause forbids Congress from making "any process 'due process of law,' by its mere will."[223]

Law professor Kris Kobach has identified another common misunderstanding about takings law. It has often been professed that requiring compensation

for excessive regulation of property was utterly alien to nineteenth century jurisprudence. Kobach notes that many commentators trace the requirement of compensation for a regulatory taking to Justice Holmes's opinion in *Pennsylvania Coal Co. v. Mahon* (1922).[224] Holmes held that a Pennsylvania state regulation limiting the mining of anthracite coal in the state violated the property protections of the Fourteenth Amendment. The commentators to whom Kobach is referring contend that compensation for takings was a recent judicial invention without a fundamental basis in constitutional law. As the preceding summary of cases reveals, this contention is not correct. Excessive government regulation of property was considered a taking from the earliest days of constitutional jurisprudence. Kobach discusses a multitude of decisions supporting this conclusion, most of which I have also reported in the preceding pages.[225]

Prior to the U.S. Civil War, the principal area of the law upholding governmental restraints on property rights involved the validity of liquor prohibition legislation.[226] Insofar as it denied legislatures the power to restrict the manufacture and sale of liquor, the *Wynehamer* precedent was generally not followed. With the exception of Indiana, all other state courts where the issue was raised—eleven, according to Corwin[227]—ruled that inherent legislative powers, or more specifically the police powers, enabled the legislature to adopt laws for this purpose. In 1855, the Indiana Supreme Court held that the state prohibition laws were void because prohibiting the manufacture, sale, and consumption of spiritous liquors unlawfully interfered with individual rights and the pursuit of happiness.[228] However, this decision was overturned seven years later on the premise that the legislature was authorized under the police powers to enact such legislation.[229]

The most famous liquor prohibition case is *Mugler v. Kansas,*[230] decided by the U.S. Supreme Court in 1887. The decision in this case reveals the reasoning of courts in upholding liquor prohibitions under the police power. The Court considered whether a state law prohibiting the manufacture of alcoholic beverages violated the due process clause of the Fourteenth Amendment. The law had been enforced against Mugler, to forbid him without payment of any compensation, from operating his brewery contrary to the legislatively forbidden purpose. Although the law destroyed the value of the brewery and greatly reduced the value of the entire property on which the brewery was located, the Court held that no compensation was owed, because the state was exercising its police power to protect the public's health, safety, and morals. According to the Court, the legislature, not the judiciary, should decide when the use of property adversely affects the public: "It belongs to that department to exert what are known as the police powers of the state, and to determine, primarily, what measures are appropriate or needful for the protection of the public morals, the public health, or the public safety." The Court would uphold a regulation as long as there was a "real" or "substantial relation" between it and the public

harm, and no "palpable invasion of rights secured by the fundamental law." The entire scheme of prohibition might fail "if the rights of each citizen to manufacture intoxicating liquors for his own use as a beverage were recognized."

It is difficult to envision a prohibition measure that might fail such a weak constitutional test, since most tend to be part of "the entire scheme of prohibition." However, this rule has no relevance to the actual deprivation Mugler sustained. The Court did not consider the linkage between destroying Mugler's brewery and the problems caused by alcohol consumption, or whether these problems could be reduced with less restrictive measures than depriving an owner of the use of his property. In later years, such concerns would be considered as factors in determining whether government had sufficient justification for depriving individual owners of their property.

The liquor prohibition cases were decided during a period when much American public and professional opinion viewed the consumption of intoxicating liquors as a serious threat to the health, safety, morals, and welfare of the nation. Although the manufacture or sale of intoxicating liquors did not meet the legal definition of a common law nuisance, considerable opinion of that period considered the impact as no less destructive. Indeed, some states barred the manufacture and sale of liquor under statutes passed for the suppression of nuisances.[231] The usual common law nuisances were highly offensive activities—loud noises, bad smells, glaring lights, particle emissions—or were otherwise noxious and dangerous to health and safety.[232] Even though prohibition laws did not meet nuisance criteria, most judges in that period were reluctant to overturn legislation intended to reduce the consumption of liquor. Prohibition zealotry existed in this period of the nation's history. However, by choosing to attack the manufacture and distribution of alcohol as a nuisance, prohibitionists did not reject the principle of substantive due process, because it does not protect a nuisance. A constitution intended to advance the public welfare could hardly be interpreted to protect the harmful use of property.

The concept of state police power appears nowhere in the United States Constitution, but was developed over the years from the theory of popular sovereignty. The idea is that when democratic government (state or federal) is exercising police power, it is securing vital public concerns and, consequently, is not subject to constitutional protections for personal liberty and property. Thus, in *Mugler,* the Supreme Court stated that the Fourteenth Amendment's due process clause was not

> designed to interfere with the power of the States, sometimes termed police power, to prescribe regulations to promote the health, peace, morals, education, and good order of the people, and to legislate so as to increase the industries of the State, develop its resources, and add to its wealth and property.[233]

Initially, the United States Supreme Court was hostile to this idea of unlimited popular sovereignty, as revealed in the statement by Justice Joseph Story, in *Wilkinson v. Leland* (1829), that the rights of personal liberty and property "should be held sacred. At least no court of justice in this country would be warranted in assuming, that the power to violate and disregard them . . . lurked under any general grant of legislative authority, or ought to be implied from any general expressions of the will of the people."[234]

But this concern for liberty faded with the advent of the Supreme Court presided over by Chief Justice Roger Taney (1836–1864), which succeeded the Marshall Court (1801–1835). Taney's Court supported the idea of popular sovereignty as embodied in state legislation and upheld legislation on the basis of this theory that the Marshall Court would have struck down.[235] This theory of legislative supremacy also found support in state courts.[236]

The theory runs counter to Coke's and Blackstone's view that the purpose of government is not to protect legislative power, but to confine and restrain it. After all, the Magna Carta is eulogized not because it expands government powers, but because it limits them. As evident from the earlier discussion in this chapter, the positions of Coke and Blackstone were held by many if not most jurists in the nation prior to the ratification of the Fourteenth Amendment.

Chancellor Kent urged great caution in applying the police power:

> But the acts which can only be justified on the ground that they are police regulations, must be so clearly necessary to the safety, comfort or well being of society, or so imperatively required by the public necessity, that they must be taken to be impliedly excepted from the words of the constitutional prohibition.[237]

According to Thomas Cooley, probably the most important legal commentator prior to the framing of the Fourteenth Amendment, in the exercise of the police power, "regard must be paid to the fundamental principles of civil liberty, and to processes that are adopted to preserve and secure civil rights; persons cannot arbitrarily be deprived of equal protection of the laws, or of life, liberty and property, because the State purports to be exercising the police power."[238]

In the *Wynehamer* case, Justice Selden viewed the police power as limited to protecting those interests which "exist in every individual to protect his life and property from immediate destruction." Thus, for example, the blowing up of buildings during fires, the destroying of infected articles, and the enacting of quarantine laws in times of pestilence are rights "which individuals do not surrender when they enter into the social state, and which cannot be taken from them. The acts of the legislature in such cases do not confer any right of destruction which would not exist independent of them, but they aim to introduce some method into the exercise of them. . . . [I]t may well be doubted whether

the legislature can add to the extent or force of [this] natural right." According to Selden, the justification for such laws rests upon the immediate and imminent danger to life and health which they are enacted to avert.[239]

The many cases over the years applying the police power can be viewed as falling into two categories. First, there are opinions that consider the police power as confined to the inherent power of government to protect itself from destruction and the people from severe injury. Kent and Selden support this perspective. Second, there are opinions that identify the police power with the power of government to advance the public interest, except when it does so in a very arbitrary and capricious manner. *Mugler* supports that position. Under the first category the police power is very limited, while under the second it is very broad. The role of judicial review plays a major role in the first category and a minor one in the second. The first is consistent with the separation of powers concept, because it limits the legislature to a role that it must exercise for society to function, that is, adopting laws protecting the society from severe injury. The second violates the separation of powers, because it accords the legislature largely unrestricted power, which is proper in a parliamentary system but improper in a government requiring the separation and limitation of powers.

The second category also governed the application of the police power to expression cases for a long period. Thus, in the very important 1925 *Gitlow* decision, the Supreme Court held that the due process clause of the Fourteenth Amendment incorporated the expression guarantees of the First Amendment and secured them from impairment by the states.[240] Nonetheless, citing *Mugler*, the Court ruled that under the police power a state may penalize utterances advocating the overthrow of government by force, violence, or other unlawful means. The state's determination that such utterances "are inimical to the general welfare and involve danger of substantive evil," the Court held, "must be given great weight. Every presumption is to be indulged in favor of the validity of the statute." In reply to the defendant's plea that his statements were not dangerous, the Court explained that "a single revolutionary spark may kindle a fire that, smoldering for a time, may burst into a sweeping and destructive conflagration."[241] *Gitlow* seemed to accept legislative omnipotence.

The Supreme Court in time adopted the "clear and present danger" test, which reversed the *Gitlow* holding on the police power. The current standard for expression which might provoke violence is set forth in *Brandenberg v. Ohio* (1969),[242] the most recent version of the "clear and present danger" test. This test requires the government to prove the existence of a likelihood that serious harm will occur as a result of the particular utterance under consideration.

A similar approach to the police power in liberty of contract cases existed at the beginning of the nineteenth century, as indicated in this quotation from *Lochner v. New York* (1905):

It is a question of which of two powers or rights shall prevail—the power of the state to legislate or the right of the individual to liberty of person and freedom of contract. The mere assertion that the subject relates, though but in a remote degree, to the public health, does not necessarily render the enactment valid. The act must have a more direct relation, as a means to an end, and the end itself must be appropriate and legitimate, before an act can be held to be valid which interferes with the general right of an individual to be free in his person and in his power to contract in relation to his own labor.[243]

This limitation on the police power adopted in the expression cases and the *Lochner*-era liberty-of-contract cases should apply generally. The authority of the legislative branch under the separation-of-powers doctrine should not be dependent on the liberty at issue, whether it involves speech, contract, or property. In order to control this legislative authority so that it does not overstep its legitimate bounds and encroach upon liberty, the Constitution requires that the judiciary monitor the legislature. Free-speech advocates have noted how bizarre the *Gitlow* decision was, "for it effectively permitted legislatures to legislate themselves out from under the restrictions of the First Amendment. . . . [T]his placed the fox in charge of the chicken coop, and turned the First Amendment on its head."[244] The same reasoning applies when the endangered liberty is the right to property.

VI. Observations about Due Process and Class Legislation

A major restraint on the police power is the common-law principle that laws must be neutral and not partisan in purpose. The legislators must seek to further the general public interest and not intentionally favor or disfavor particular persons or groups. This principle has strong support in both English and American law. Coke, Blackstone, and Locke advanced it, as have many courts and commentators over the years. This position is essential to the maintenance of a free society. If the legislature passes a law restraining individual freedom solely to benefit particular individuals or classes, the lawmakers are taking rights or interests from one group and giving them to another; this is a heresy in a government dedicated to the common good. Jurists and legal commentators over the years often rebuked legislators' removing property from A and transferring it to B in order to benefit the latter. It is no different when other rights or interests are involved. A legislature elected by all the people must govern neutrally and impartially; it should not intentionally advantage or disadvantage some of the people.

Theodore Sedgwick, the noted nineteenth century legal and social commentator, classified such objectionable special laws into three groupings: first, where the legislature, by a special act, has sought to dispense with a general law to help or hurt an individual; second, where the act is one of legislation for a particular case; third, where the act is, in its nature, judicial, that is, it seeks to influence, directly or indirectly, the determination of private controversies.[245]

Many early American judges ruled against special interest legislation on the basis of the common or natural law. Supreme Court Justices Chase and Story, among many others, maintained that the Constitution never empowered the legislature to deprive one group of people of their property rights for the sake of enriching another group. Property rights and liberty were not absolute, but they could only be limited when the public interest justified it.[246] Blackstone asserted that for government to deprive a person of his liberties when no public purpose is involved "is rather a sentence than a law."

Like many other legal concepts, it is difficult at times to distinguish between laws intended to serve public interests and laws intended to serve private interests. Some commentators contend that the distinction cannot be judicially defined or applied and, therefore, the courts should defer the application of the distinction to the legislature.[247] Such practices would of course negate the judicial protection to which all members of the society are entitled. Moreover, if difficulty of legal interpretation is a critical factor, not many legal concepts would survive. At the edges, legal concepts are quite often uncertain. Consider, as an example, the clear and present danger rule, which is one of the most accepted standards in American jurisprudence. While most of the time judges can readily determine the meaning of clear and present danger, this does not always occur. Under this rule, government may not forbid the advocacy of force and violence unless such advocacy is likely to produce a clear and present danger. The best that can be said is that the concept will be correctly applied on most occasions, and judges will attempt to make the "close calls" as fairly and judiciously as possible.

Courts have often cited Blackstone for the proposition that private property can only be restricted or acquired by government when the purpose is a public and not a private one and compensation is paid to the owner. This is an accurate but not complete description of his position in two respects. First, he rejected laws that inflicted "wanton and causeless" restraints (see Chapter 2, Section IV), even when the restriction was for a public purpose. Second, he approved of laws abating nuisances or other conditions that endangered life and property, even when these restrictions served a private and not a public purpose. Contemporary jurisprudence has responded favorably to these concerns.

Under contemporary U.S. Supreme Court jurisprudence, regulatory legislation that serves the general public interest and limits speech, press, race, property, gender, and some other rights must also be "compelling," "legitimate," or "important" in order to be upheld, depending on the right or interest involved. These rules reduce the scope of legislative discretion and thereby curtail the power of the legislature to pass measures benefiting or harming particular persons or groups. Proving that the legislation seeks to advance the general public good is not enough. Thus, expression and racial restrictions must be justified by a *compelling* governmental interest,[248] requiring a strict scrutiny analysis, which is the highest level of judicial scrutiny. A land-use regulation must substantially advance a *legitimate* state interest, and a gender restriction must serve *important* governmental interests—both categories invoke intermediate scrutiny, which is also a high level of scrutiny. In the expression area, a public purpose short of preventing expression that is likely to cause imminent lawless actions would not suffice as a compelling governmental interest. With respect to gender, the legislative objective must not reflect "archaic and stereotypic notions." Thus, if the statutory objective is to save the public interest by protecting members of one gender because they are presumed to suffer from an inherent handicap or to be innately inferior, the objective itself is illegitimate.[249]

In creating these rules, the Supreme Court reasons that even when a public purpose exists the legislature must still have a much more persuasive justification to limit the exercise of constitutionally protected liberties. These rules retain the requirement of public purpose and add a means-end inquiry that the regulation will substantially achieve its objective. The court may also seek to determine whether the same objective can be achieved by a law less harmful to liberty, again limiting legislative discretion.

Let me briefly examine these rules. Under current Supreme Court review standards requiring strict or intermediate scrutiny in rights litigation, the U.S. Supreme Court applies two rules to determine whether the regulation is advancing the required governmental interest. The first is the intention of the legislature: What was the purpose of the lawmakers? A law that the court finds was intended largely to further private interests will be declared invalid. The second rule requires a means-end inquiry: Will the law substantially advance the public benefit that the legislature contends was the purpose of the law? A law that excessively advantages or disadvantages particular persons or groups or remotely advantages or disadvantages the general public does not substantially benefit the public. This outcome will fail the second rule because it is either too broad or too narrow. The impact of the law is either overinclusive, that is, it affects more people disproportionately than necessary to achieve the law's purpose, or it is underinclusive, affecting fewer people than required to achieve the law's purpose. If the law fails means-end inquiries, we may reasonably conclude that the law does not serve the public interest, and consequently is futile or special interest legislation.

In determining whether the legislature has advanced the public interest, the means-end test operates as a check on the public interest test, since matters that erroneously get by the first test will again be examined under the second test. "By requiring that the classification bear a rational relationship to an independent and legitimate legislative end," the U.S. Supreme Court has asserted, "we ensure that classifications are not drawn for the purpose of disadvantaging the group burdened by the law."[250] In *City of Richmond v. Croson,*[251] the Court noted how an inquiry as to the means chosen by the legislature to effectuate its purpose is revealing of the true purpose of the legislation:

> Indeed, the purpose of strict scrutiny is to "smoke out" illegitimate uses of race by assuring that the legislative body is pursuing a goal important enough to warrant use of a highly suspect tool [racial classification]. The test also ensures that the means chosen "fit" this compelling goal so closely that there is little or no possibility that motive for the classification was illegitimate racial prejudice or stereotype.

Jurisprudence that buttresses the public interest requirement with a means-end test makes more certain that the legislation serves the general public interest than does merely relying on a public interest inquiry.

Let us now turn to offensive and obnoxious uses of property that are not entitled to legal protection. The scrutiny rules protect property owners who pursue the normal and benign prerogatives of ownership. They do not secure owners who are engaged in clearly harmful uses such as nuisances and those gravely endangering lives and property, since the Constitution cannot be construed as protecting evil. When government abates a nuisance, there is no taking or deprivation of any property right recognized in the due process or takings clauses.

This issue came up in *Lucas v. South Carolina Coastal Council*[252] (discussed above in Section III *supra*), in which the South Carolina Supreme Court upheld a ban on land development "to prevent serious public harm," on the basis of a laundry list of alleged harm that the construction of two separate houses would create. On appeal, the U.S. Supreme Court returned the case to the South Carolina courts to determine whether, at the time the owner bought his lots, the land was subject to nuisance laws or other laws prohibiting uses that gravely threatened lives and property. The law would be upheld only if the development were to create a nuisance or such other extraordinarily harmful use. The state had passed the law to, among other things, increase public beach access and promote tourism. The difference between legislation seeking to prevent nuisances and legislation to provide more beach access and increase tourism is that in the former the state prevents harm while in the latter it provides benefits. When an owner's land is restricted to provide benefits for others, property rights are be-

ing taken from A and given to these others. On the other hand, a nuisance is clearly a harmful use, which is not entitled to constitutional protection. According to Chief Justice William Rehnquist, the nuisance exception to the protection of the takings guarantee is a narrow one that is intended only to prevent a "nuisance or illegal use" and is not concerned with "the prevention of legal and essential use."[253]

Policy considerations have often complicated the distinction between public and private interests. Welfare legislation that is intended to help mortgage debtors, tenants, tobacco growers, low income workers, and taxicab owners, and that is often viewed as advancing the public interest, can be interpreted as class legislation that takes property from one group and gives it to another. These redistributions of income are seen as measures that help the poor and reduce inequality in the society, and thus seen as benefiting the general public. Consider in this regard the famous 1905 *Lochner* case, which invalidated a New York statute as violating the due process clause of the Fourteenth Amendment because it restricted the working hours of bakery workers to ten per day and sixty per week. For purposes of its analysis, the majority of the U.S. Supreme Court assumed that the purpose of the work-hours limitation law was to protect the health of bakery workers. The Court concluded that the law did not achieve this objective and, therefore, was an unconstitutional restraint on the employer.[254] Some commentators have contended that the law served the public interest in a different respect, and that the outcome of the case would have been different had this purpose been invoked. Law professors Gerald Gunther and Kathleen Sullivan write that the bakery workers had unequal bargaining power and the state may, under its police powers, redress perceived economic inequalities.[255] Let us examine this position in some detail, since the analysis will often also apply to other welfare laws.

Simply put, the legislature attempted to reduce the alleged unequal bargaining powers of the bakery workers by limiting their work hours at the expense of the employer, something which the workers could not achieve on their own because of their "inequality." It took from A and gave to B. Since the parties originally freely entered into their bargains, the conclusion that unequal bargaining power existed would be rejected by many economists. But, the reader might insist that the legislature's action was not arbitrary; it was done to preserve the workers' health. This, of course, is the purpose that the Court ascribed to the legislature. If removing inequality of wealth or power is considered a legitimate public purpose, legislative discretion is enormous and may often be applied in a partisan manner. Liberty inevitably results in many inequalities. The U.S. Supreme Court held early in the twentieth century that the police power was not applicable to curing inequalities "that are the necessary result of the exercise of [contract and property] rights."[256]

Law professor Alan J. Meese points out that U.S. courts have accepted as legitimate and not an abridgement of constitutional freedom antitrust laws that

enable parties to a contract to bargain more equally. However, such laws are not applicable to the *Lochner* situation. In New York in 1905 there were over 3,000 bakeries and over sixty percent of these bakeries employed an average of 3.76 workers per firm. "Far from evincing any unequal bargaining power," he writes, "these circumstances suggest a textbook example of perfect competition." No firm had any power over the terms of employment.[257]

The New York law cut appreciably the working hours of the bakers. There are various benefits that a worker obtains from a shorter work day, but one of these is not more wages. Workers who worked fewer hours received less wages. If we assume that the general purpose of New York's law was to improve the well-being of the bakery workers (the *Lochner* court ruled out the health issue), for many workers this would not be achieved by a law that operated to reduce wages. One may speculate that some or even many workers would seek other employment to compensate for the loss in wages, but then the law for these persons has served no other purpose than to require the employee to work for two employers instead of one in order to obtain the same wages. Adding to a worker's woes, the economic restrictions of the *Lochner* law also operated to increase production costs and thereby to eliminate some of the small bakeries, thus reducing employment for that section of the bakery market. The lesson of *Lochner* is one prominently advanced in this book: regulations often exacerbate rather than alleviate the problems of the marketplace.*

---

* Michael Giorgino aided me in researching the cases reported in this chapter.

5

The Due Process Clause of the Fourteenth Amendment

I. Introduction

Section 1 of the Fourteenth Amendment to the U.S. Constitution reads as follows:

> All persons born or naturalized in the United States and subject to the jurisdiction thereof, are citizens of the United States and of the State wherein they reside. No State shall make or enforce any law which shall abridge the privileges or immunities of citizens of the United States; nor shall any State deprive any person of life, liberty, or property, without due process of law; nor deny to any person within its jurisdiction the equal protection of the laws.

In this and the next chapter, I shall discuss the due process and privileges or immunities clauses of Section 1 of this amendment. Both clauses were drafted in large part to secure property rights. This chapter will chiefly be devoted to the meaning of the due process clause, and the next chapter will largely concern the privileges or immunities clause.

In 1897, the Fourteenth Amendment's due process clause was interpreted to incorporate the takings clause of the Fifth Amendment, and thereby make it applicable to the states.[1] In recent years, the U.S. Supreme Court has, in my opinion, generally adjudicated the takings clause consistent with the meaning of this provision.[2] However, the privileges or immunities clause of the Fourteenth Amendment has never been construed to secure property rights, even though the argument for doing so is very strong. In 1999, the Supreme Court decided

z v. Roe, which concerned the privileges or immunities clause of the Fourteenth Amendment. The Court accorded the clause a substantive character, which may in time be interpreted as applicable to the ownership of private property.[3] (This case will be reported and analyzed in Chapter 6.)

Before considering the meaning of Section 1 with respect to the protection of private property, let us consider the role of the Supreme Court in interpreting amendments to the Constitution. The Thirty-Ninth Congress framed the Fourteenth Amendment in 1866 and by 1868 it was ratified by three quarters of the states, thus making it part of the Constitution. The protection of individual rights is contained in the second sentence of Section 1. Section 5 of the Fourteenth Amendment relates to its enforcement and it states the following: "The Congress shall have power to enforce, by appropriate legislation, the provisions of this article."

Ever since the Thirty-Ninth Congress approved the proposed Fourteenth Amendment (by the required two-thirds vote of each house), controversy has existed as to the meaning of various words and phrases of Section 1. Much of the language is not unique to this amendment. The words "privileges and immunities of citizens in the several States" are in Article IV, Section 2 of the Constitution, and a clause virtually identical in language to Section 1's due process clause is in the Fifth Amendment (except that it applies only to the national government). Since the same words cannot be defined differently in separate parts of the Constitution, the meaning of language that is added to the Constitution should be the same as that for existing language.

The terms and provisions of the U.S. Constitution are defined by the judiciary, principally the United States Supreme Court. The high court is often influenced by the constitutional interpretations applied by lower federal courts and by state courts, the latter being responsible for construing state constitutions that may contain language similar to that in the federal constitution. It can be assumed that the judiciary will continue—after the ratification of an amendment—to apply the same definition to words and concepts that it did before ratification. The acts of framing and ratification have no bearing on the meaning of "privileges or immunities" or of "due process of law."

The members of Congress accept this understanding of the role of the judiciary in construing the U.S. Constitution. Representative John Bingham of Ohio was the principal draftsman of the second sentence of Section 1 of the Fourteenth Amendment. During the debates on the amendment, he was asked by one of his colleagues to explain the meaning of "due process of law." Bingham replied that "[t]he courts have settled that long ago, and the gentleman can go and read their decisions."[4] Bingham was stating the obvious: the judiciary had defined the legal meaning of the term, and the framers of the amendment were obliged to accept this meaning. Similarly, Senator Jacob Howard, in introducing the proposed Fourteenth Amendment in the U.S. Senate, explained

that existing judicial opinion as to the meaning of privileges or immunities gives "some intimation of what probably will be the opinion of the judiciary" in deciding its meaning in the future.[5]

After Congress framed the amendment, it was submitted for ratification to the people of the various states who likewise had to consider existing jurisprudence to determine the meaning of the proposed amendment's language. We are told that many people and newspapers considered the protections of Section 1 as being very modest in scope.[6] I have no doubt that some were of this view, but millions of people in many states voted on the amendment and ascertaining prevailing opinions of the public as to the meaning of its various parts is quite difficult at best. When Congress or state legislatures pass laws, the persons affected cannot on their own decide what these laws mean. Whether they are acting as constitutional framers or in their usual law-making roles, legislatures pass measures pursuant to existing judicial interpretations, in both instances expecting that these meanings will bind public conduct. It does not matter that some segments of the public attach other meanings to the words that the legislature uses. During the ratification process, the public usually seeks to obtain definitions from constitutional authorities who will likely explain their meanings pursuant to the prevailing jurisprudence.

Bingham believed that the existing law supported his interpretation of the due process clause of the Fifth Amendment: that it was a guarantee against being deprived by government of life, liberty, or property without adequate cause and a fair and proper judicial proceeding. The most important decision on the due process clause prior to the framing of the Fourteenth Amendment in 1866 was the United States Supreme Court's unanimous opinion in *Murray's Lessee* (1855) (previously discussed in Chapter 4, Section IV). In this case, the Court interpreted the Fifth Amendment's due process clause in a way essentially similar to Bingham's view, except in terms of its impact for a relatively minor historical precedent, which was the acceptance of summary and not judicial process for the recovery of certain debts owed to the national government.[7]

What relation does the framers' intent in writing an amendment have to the judicial meaning of the words they use? Suppose that the framers seek to accomplish a purpose with language that is not consistent with the judicial meaning of that language. Say, for example, that the framers of the Fourteenth Amendment sought only to protect fair and proper process and not matters of substance by way of the due process clause. They could not achieve this purpose with the language they actually used, inasmuch as the judiciary had already interpreted the due process clause of the Fifth Amendment as securing both procedural and substantive due process. This example is also relevant to ratification. Let us assume that the ratifying conventions in the states approved the due process clause because they believed that it related only to procedure. Nonetheless, the judiciary would interpret the clause in a way that is consistent

with existing judicial precedent, although it differed from the intent of the framers. The meaning of what has been framed or ratified must be based on existing judicial interpretations with respect to that language.

The foregoing comments relate only to the use of language in an amendment to the Constitution that is the same or virtually the same as existing language elsewhere in the Constitution. The Supreme Court will interpret the language of the amendment exactly the same as it does for existing language. However, where an amendment contains terms and provisions not present in other parts of the Constitution, the Court is not limited in its interpretation, except, of course, by the usual rules appropriate to this responsibility. The question then arises whether the Court is bound by the intentions of the framers of the amendment or by the intentions of the voters who ratify it. As I have previously suggested, to determine the intentions of the millions of people who vote favorably on a constitutional amendment would be extremely difficult if not impossible. Instead, the ratification process should be considered as a general endorsement or rejection of a proposed amendment. If the voters accept the amendment, the Court in construing it must determine the intentions of the body that framed it. A voter who is uncertain about the amendment's meaning or objects to some of its language has the option to vote against it.

As it happens, the framers of the due process clause of the Fourteenth Amendment defined its language consistent with existing judicial meaning. I shall, in the discussion below, show what those framers believed due process of law meant. Actually, it makes little difference as to how the framers and ratifiers define language, since no matter what they state they lose control of its meaning to existing jurisprudence. Let us now briefly consider the debates and deliberations that culminated in the due process language of Section 1 of the Fourteenth Amendment.

When the Fourteenth Amendment was framed, the Constitution of the United States and the constitutions of most states contained a due process or law of the land clause. While the cases briefed in Chapter 4 suggest a judicial consensus on the meaning of these clauses this information is not necessary for determining the meaning of the due process clause in the Fifth Amendment. Under the rule of *stare decisis,* only the decisions in which the U.S. Supreme Court construed the Fifth Amendment's due process clause are relevant to ascertaining the meaning of the Fourteenth Amendment's due process clause. In 1866, any judge, lawyer, or private individual who wanted to know the meaning of the due process clause of the Fifth Amendment would have to read and be guided by the *Murray's Lessee* case, which was the most important U.S. Supreme Court decision on the issue as of that time.[8] *Murray's Lessee* was not an isolated decision on the meaning of due process; it likely conformed with most jurisprudence in the state courts since it was based on Coke's *Institutes.* As of 1866, when the Fourteenth Amendment was framed, or 1868, when it was

ratified, no U.S. Supreme Court decision had reversed or limited the opinion in this case. In *Murray's Lessee,* the Court's interpretation of the due process guarantee was premised on an impressive list of authorities: Coke's *Institutes of the Laws of England,* a Federal Circuit Court of Appeals decision, and five state high court decisions from North Carolina, New York, and Tennessee. (The circuit court and the five state cases also relied on Coke.)

According to the five state cases and the federal appeals court case (all discussed in Chapter 4, Sections II and IV), the due process of law (or its equivalent, the law of the land guarantee) stands for the following propositions:

1. An owner cannot be deprived of his life, liberty, or property, except as a penalty for wrongdoing determined in a fair and proper judicial trial. For purposes of this rule, wrongdoing means a violation of a law existing at the time of the offense and not a retroactive law passed to deprive a person of his rights (*Hoke v. Henderson* and *Taylor v. Porter*).
2. A law transferring property from A without his consent to B in order to achieve a private purpose is invalid even when just compensation is paid to the owner (*Taylor v. Porter*).
3. A law transferring property from a nonconsenting owner to the public for public use is valid only when just compensation is paid (*Taylor v. Porter*).
4. Due process requires the state to provide an accused person a fair and proper trial that includes a jury and other procedural protections (*Greene v. Briggs*).
5. Laws must have an impact on the public neutrally and impartially and not specially benefit or harm particular persons or groups (*Vanzant v. Waddel, State Bank v. Cooper, Jones' Heirs v. Perry*).[9]

As explained in Chapter 4, the bulk of the state cases briefed in Section II of that chapter support one or more of the above propositions. The federal cases briefed in Section IV of Chapter 4 are also generally supportive of these propositions. Thus, as of the framing of the Fourteenth Amendment in 1866, a due process of law clause was generally considered by the judiciary to be a powerful substantive protection for the preservation of life, liberty, and property.[10]

Justice Curtis's opinion in *Murray's Lessee* reveals what was meant at the time of the nation's founding by the words "rights of Englishmen." He confirms that these rights included those accorded persons by the common and statute law in England "before the Emigration of our ancestors." The sources of these rights were the "settled usages and modes of proceeding" that were then extant in England. He conditions the acceptance of these English rights in America to those "shown not to have been unsuited to their civil and public condition by having been acted on by [our ancestors] after the settlement of this country," a qualification which seems

to meet the common law requirement that laws be of "common right and reason." If prior to the framing of the Constitution these English rights had been rejected in America, they surely should not have been secured in the Constitution.

The opinions in all six cases that Curtis cited are based on interpretations of English common law. Each sets forth substantive rights of property consistent with views expressed by Coke and Blackstone. When considered in light of both Curtis's reasoning in the case and his reference to the six opinions, the conclusion is reasonable that the U.S. Supreme Court, as of 1855, generally accepted Coke and Blackstone as leading expositors of the rights of Englishmen at the time of the framing of the Constitution in 1787. The Supreme Court's interpretation of due process in *Murray's Lessee* is generally consistent also with the highly regarded constitutional commentaries of Justice Joseph Story and Chancellor James Kent, and with Alexander Hamilton's interpretation of New York's due process clause (see Chapters 3 and 4). Chief Justice Taney's opinions in *Dred Scott* and *Bloomer* (both discussed in Chapter 4) likewise support the *Murray's Lessee* interpretation of due process.

In a speech he delivered several years before he drafted the second sentence of Section 1 of the Fourteenth Amendment, Bingham stated that the due process guarantee of the Fifth Amendment secures natural rights for all persons, requires equal treatment by the law, and comprehends the highest priority for ownership. He believed that the acquisition of private property by government required the owner's consent; this is a stronger affirmation of property rights than that set forth in the Fifth Amendment's takings clause, which contains no such qualification.[11]

Justice Hugo Black, in a 1947 dissent, dubbed Bingham "the Madison of the first section of the Fourteenth Amendment."[12] Regarded as an expert on constitutional law by his colleagues, Bingham served for sixteen years in the House of Representatives and spoke a great deal there about the Constitution and its protection of liberty. He was a moderate in his party, and unlike most of his Republican colleagues—the architects of Reconstruction—he opposed the Civil Rights Act of 1866 (discussed in the next section) because he could find no authorization for it in the Constitution. He viewed the adoption of Section 1 of the proposed Fourteenth Amendment as a remedy for this constitutional problem. Though Bingham was not known for the orderliness of his thinking, his interpretations of such key guarantees as provided by the privileges or immunities and due process of law clauses were generally consistent with those of most Republicans in Congress. It was these Republicans who comprised the political wing of the abolitionist cause. They included many passionate believers in freedom, human dignity, and the equality of all men, irrespective of race. Abolitionist philosophy was generally libertarian, particularly in its antagonism toward state economic powers. Consider in this respect Bingham's remarks that he made at various times concerning the meaning of due process of law:

Natural or inherent rights, which belong to all men irrespective of all conventional regulations, are by this constitution guarantied [sic] by the broad and comprehensive word "person," as contradistinguished from the limited term citizen—as in the fifth article of amendments, guarding those sacred rights which are as universal and indestructible as the human race, that "no person shall be deprived of life, liberty, or property but by due process of law, nor shall private property be taken without just compensation."[13]

Who . . . will be bold enough to deny that all persons are equally entitled to the enjoyment of the rights of life and liberty and property; and that no one should be deprived of life or liberty, but as punishment for crime; nor of his property, against his consent and without due compensation?[14]

It must be apparent that the absolute equality of all, and the equal protection of each, are principles of our Constitution, which ought to be observed and enforced in the organization and admission of new States. The Constitution provides, as we have seen, that *no person* shall be deprived of life, liberty, or property, without due process of law. It makes no distinction either on account of complexion or birth—it secures these rights to all persons within its exclusive jurisdiction. This is equality. It protects not only life and liberty, but also property, the product of labor. It contemplates that no man shall be wrongfully deprived of the fruit of his toil any more than of his life.[15]

Representatives, to you I appeal, that hereafter, by your act and the approval of the loyal people of this country, every man in every State of the Union, in accordance with the written words of your Constitution, may, by the national law, be secured in the equal protection of his personal rights. Your Constitution provides that no man, no matter what his color, no matter beneath what sky he may have been born, no matter in what disastrous conflict or by what tyrannical hand his liberty may have been cloven down, no matter how poor, no matter how friendless, no matter how ignorant, shall be deprived of life, or liberty or property without due process of law—law in its highest sense, that law which is the perfection of human reason, and which is impartial, equal, exact justice; that justice which requires that every man shall have his right; that justice which is the highest duty of nations as it is the imperishable attribute of the God of nations.[16]

Thus, asserts Bingham, no one can be deprived of life, liberty, or property without a fair, just, and proper judicial proceeding to determine whether an accused person has violated the law and is deserving of a penalty. This is a view on the

meaning of due process that is essentially in accord with the position of the U.S. Supreme Court in *Murray's Lessee.*

The legislative history of the Fourteenth Amendment reveals that Section 1 was drafted to embody rights that the judiciary already protected against the national government but did not necessarily have authority to enforce against the states. I shall discuss this legislative history in the balance of this chapter and in the next chapter.[17] There were three important events related to the framing process: the adoption of the Civil Rights Act of 1866, the drafting of the initial version of Section 1 of the proposed amendment, and the adoption of the final version of Section 1. Each event is discussed, respectively, in the three sections that follow.

II. The Civil Rights Act of 1866

While opinion was divergent as to the full meaning of Section 1 of the proposed Fourteenth Amendment, commentators generally agreed that it was intended to authorize passage of and constitutionalize the principles of the Civil Rights Act of 1866—that is, to assure that the latter's provisions were permitted by the Constitution and to place its safeguards on a constitutional level beyond the power of any subsequent Congress to repeal by majority votes. The act's immediate purpose was to provide federal protection for the slaves who were emancipated by the Thirteenth Amendment (ratified July 6, 1865) to exercise certain enumerated liberties. However, the act applied to all the states and benefited most other people as well. Section 1 of the Civil Rights Act stated:

> *Section 1.* That all persons born in the United States, and not subject to any foreign Power, excluding Indians not taxed, are hereby declared to be citizens, of the United States; and such citizens, of every race and color, without regard to any previous condition of slavery or involuntary servitude, except as a punishment for crime whereof the party shall have been duly convicted, shall have the same right, in every State and Territory in the United States, to make and enforce contracts, to sue, be parties, and give evidence, to inherit, purchase, lease, sell, hold, and convey real and personal property, and to full and equal benefit of all laws and proceedings for the security of person and property, as is enjoyed by white citizens, and shall be subject to like punishment, pains and penalties, and to none other, any law, statute, ordinance, regulation or custom, to the contrary notwithstanding.

Section 2 of the act provided "[t]hat any person who under color of any law, statute, ordinance, regulation, or custom, shall subject" a person so protected to the deprivation of any right secured by the act would be liable to trial and punishment in a federal court.

The Civil Rights Bill was introduced in the Senate on January 29, 1866 by its author, Senator Lyman Trumbull of Illinois, who was chairman of the Judiciary Committee, and in the House of Representatives on March 1, 1866 by James F. Wilson of Iowa, who was chairman of its Judiciary Committee. Both were members of the Republican party, which held substantial majorities in the two bodies. Forty-two Republicans and ten Democrats occupied the Senate, and 145 Republicans and forty-six Democrats were in the House. At that time, the eleven states that had participated in the Civil War were not represented. The Republicans overwhelmingly supported the Civil Rights Act both before and after President Andrew Johnson's veto, while the Democrats opposed it.

Trumbull and Wilson found authority for Congress to pass the Civil Rights Act in two parts of the Constitution: Section 2 of the Thirteenth Amendment and Section 2 of Article IV. Section 2 of the Thirteenth Amendment gave Congress the power to enforce "by appropriate legislation" Section 1, which abolished slavery. They read Section 2 of Article IV—"The citizens of each state shall be entitled to all the Privileges and Immunities of Citizens in the Several States"—as protecting citizens from state interference in the free exercise of their privileges and immunities.

Both men argued that the bill would make the Thirteenth Amendment meaningful by securing practical freedom for the former slaves: "Of what avail will it now be that the Constitution of the United States has declared that slavery shall not exist, if in the late slaveholding States laws are to be enacted and enforced depriving persons of African descent of privileges which are essential to freemen?"[18] A statute depriving a citizen of civil rights that are secured to other citizens constitutes "a badge of servitude which, by the Constitution, is prohibited."[19]

By conferring citizenship, the bill entitled former slaves to exercise those rights guaranteed to citizens by the Constitution. To determine what those rights were, Trumbull referred to judicial decisions that interpreted Article IV, Section 2. He concluded that the decision that most elaborated upon this clause and contained the settled judicial opinion was that delivered by Supreme Court Justice Bushrod Washington in 1823, while serving on a federal circuit court of appeals, in *Corfield v. Coryell*.[20] Cited at various times in the debates over the Civil Rights Act and the Fourteenth Amendment, Justice Washington's famous pronouncement on the meaning of the privileges and immunities clause of Article IV (previously discussed in Chapter 4) is, in part, as follows:

> We feel no hesitation in confining these expressions to those privileges and immunities which are, in their nature, fundamental; which belong, of right, to the citizens of all free governments; and which have, at all times, been enjoyed by the citizens of the several states which compose this Union, from the time of their becoming free, independent, and sovereign. What these fundamental principles are, it would perhaps be more tedious than difficult to enumerate. They may, however, be all comprehended under the

following general heads: Protection by the government; the enjoyment of life and liberty, with the right to acquire and possess property of every kind, and to pursue and obtain happiness and safety; subject nevertheless to such restraints as the government may justly prescribe for the general good of the whole. The right of a citizen of one state to pass through, or to reside in any other state, for purposes of trade, agriculture, professional pursuits, or otherwise; to claim the benefit of the writ of habeas corpus; to institute and maintain actions of any kind in the courts of the state; to take, hold and dispose of property, either real or personal; and an exemption from higher taxes or impositions than are paid by the other citizens of the state; may be mentioned as some of the particular privileges and immunities of citizens, which are clearly embraced by the general description of privileges deemed to be fundamental; to which may be added; the elective franchise, as regulated and established by the laws or constitution of the state in which it is to be exercised. These, and many others which might be mentioned, are, strictly speaking, privileges and immunities, and the enjoyment of them by the citizens of each state, in every other state, was manifestly calculated (to use the expressions of the preamble of the corresponding provision in the old articles of confederation) "the better to secure and perpetuate mutual friendship and intercourse among the people of the different states of the Union."[21]

Senator Trumbull observed that Justice Washington's understanding of the privileges and immunities clause included all the rights contained in the proposed legislation. Thus, the bill did not do more than protect the "fundamental rights belonging to every man as a free man, and which under the Constitution as it now exists we have a right to protect every man in."[22]

Representative Wilson offered a similar interpretation.[23] He likewise asserted that the law, instead of creating rights, merely enforced the fundamental rights to which citizens already were entitled under the Constitution, and he also quoted from Justice Washington's construction of Article IV's privileges and immunities clause.[24] Wilson emphasized the basic character of the bill's protections and identified them as natural rights.[25]

In addition to arguing, as Trumbull did, that the Civil Rights Act was authorized under the Thirteenth Amendment and Article IV, Wilson contended that Congress had implied powers under the Constitution to protect fundamental liberties of United States citizens from abridgement by the states. According to Wilson, the "great fundamental civil rights which it is the true office of Government to protect" were named in the celebrated commentaries of England's Sir William Blackstone and New York's Chancellor James Kent. Both Blackstone and Kent had declared that the three absolute rights of individuals were personal security, personal liberty, and personal property. All the liberties set

forth specifically or generally in the proposed Civil Rights Act, Wilson concluded, were either embodied in these rights or necessary for their enjoyment. He believed that, in particular, the due process clause of the Fifth Amendment authorized Congress to set aside state laws abridging the rights of life, liberty, and property[26] (a position not generally shared at that time, since the Fifth Amendment then applied only to the national government).

Not only would the bill protect the fundamental rights of the former slaves, Trumbull and Wilson asserted, it would also secure an equality of rights for blacks as well as for other citizens. Senator Trumbull viewed the bill as affecting state legislation generally, quoting in his introductory statements to the proposed Civil Rights Bill from a note to Blackstone's *Commentaries*: "In this definition of civil liberty it ought to be understood, or rather expressed, that the restraints introduced by the law should be equal to all, or as much so as the nature of things will admit."[27]

Wilson asserted that "the entire structure of this bill rests on the discrimination relative to civil rights and immunities made by the States on 'account of race, color, or previous condition of slavery.' "[28] Many Southern states refused to allow the former slaves to exercise the rights enjoyed by white people, and Wilson thought that the Thirteenth Amendment empowered Congress to protect the former slaves in exercising such rights. However, recognizing that the measure required a broader application, he argued that Congress had the authority to enforce the rights of others in the nation as well, as explained above. Enacting the statute was also necessary "to protect our citizens, from the highest to the lowest, from the whitest to the blackest, in the enjoyment of the great fundamental rights which belong to all men."[29]

Representative John Bingham agreed; he also viewed the measure as affecting the entire nation. It was not proposed

> simply for the protection of freedmen in their rights for the time being in the late insurrectionary States. That is a great mistake. It applies to every State in the Union, to States which have never been in insurrection, and is to be enforced in every State in the Union, not only for the present, but for all future time, or until it shall be repealed by some subsequent act of Congress. It does not expire by virtue of its own limitation; it is intended to be permanent.[30]

Most congressmen accepted these interpretations, but not all. Some considered only the effect on emancipated persons and did not comment on the statute's meaning for the rest of the population. Senator Howard of Michigan (a supporter) insisted that the bill was confined to eliminating discrimination on the basis of race or color.[31] Opponents Senator Guthrie of Kentucky and Representative Eldridge of Wisconsin indicated that this was also their understanding.[32] Senator

Stewart of Nevada (a supporter) asserted that the bill did no more than strike at the renewal of any attempt to return the freedmen to slavery or peonage. Senator Henderson of Missouri (a supporter) thought that its sole object was to break down the system of oppression in the seceded states.[33]

These narrow interpretations are difficult to reconcile with abolitionist doctrine that emphasized legal equality generally and not just with respect to race. The former abolitionists, who were very influential in Republican ranks, had as a goal that "slaves and free Negroes . . . receive legal protection in their fundamental rights along with all other human beings."[34] They had long comprehended the moral and practical problems of isolating their pleas for legal equality to one area. Because the result would be to limit the powers of government, this perspective was highly acceptable in the generally laissez-faire climate of the Republican Party.

Among the rights to which the abolitionists gave prime attention were those of property and contract. They argued that these liberties be extended to all people, for they were natural rights that would enable the dependent poor to become financially secure and thus independent.[35] In the congressional debates, it was charged that specific economic rights belonging to the freedmen were being denied to them in the South. Senator Trumbull said that all men have the right to make contracts, to buy and sell, and to acquire and dispose of property.[36] Senator Howard of Michigan asserted that each freedman must be able to earn and purchase property and to benefit by the "fruits of his toil and his industry."[37] Representative Thayer of Pennsylvania contended that the freedmen must have the ability to contract for their labor and to purchase a home and to have the liberty to enjoy the ordinary pursuits of civilized life.[38] Representative Lawrence of Ohio stated that all citizens have the right to make contracts to "secure the privilege and the rewards of labor."[39] Representative Windom of Minnesota was also concerned that all citizens have the right to contract for their labor, to enforce the payment of their wages, and to have the means of holding and enjoying the "proceeds of their toil."[40]

Trumbull and Windom gave examples of statutes (known as the "Black Codes") depriving the freed blacks of their rights, that would be outlawed by the Civil Rights Act. Mississippi, for instance, had passed a statute authorizing local officials to prevent freedmen from carrying on independent business and to compel them to work only as employees. It also barred freedmen from holding, leasing, or renting real estate. In addition, Georgia and South Carolina prohibited any freedman from buying or leasing a home.[41] Representative Cook was alarmed by laws which stated "that a man not supporting himself by labor shall be deemed a vagrant, and that a vagrant shall be sold."[42]

The explanations of the bill by both Trumbull and Wilson reflected important philosophical concerns about the citizens being able to exercise fundamental rights, and these concerns appealed to the vast majority of the congressmen from

their party who shared them. (The remarks of supporters of this perspective are set forth in the discussion of privileges or immunities in Chapter 6.) However, opponents of the legislation focused on the serious constitutional problems that it raised. First, there was the questionable relationship between the goal of the Thirteenth Amendment—to eliminate slavery—and the goal of the bill—to eliminate denials of other personal rights. The second issue was how the proposed law could apply to blacks or whites who were free and thus never affected by the amendment. Third, the opposition contended that under the *Dred Scott* decision,[43] Congress did not have the authority to confer citizenship on former slaves. Fourth, opponents argued that Congress could not require the states to observe provisions in the Bill of Rights, for that document was solely a limitation on the federal government. Fifth, opponents doubted that Congress had the power to penalize persons who in good faith obeyed state laws. To survive these challenges, it was evident that the proposed legislation required a firmer constitutional foundation, which in time the Fourteenth Amendment provided.

III. Bingham's Early Version of Section 1

Prior to the House debates on the Civil Rights Bill, the select Joint Committee on Reconstruction voted to submit to Congress a resolution proposing a Fourteenth Amendment to the Constitution. Committee member Bingham, the proposed amendment's primary author, presented this resolution to the House on February 26, 1866. It was introduced concurrently in the Senate but was never considered by that body. This earlier version of what was to become in time the second sentence in Section 1, provided as follows:

> The Congress shall have power to make all laws which shall be necessary and proper to secure to the citizens of each State all privileges and immunities of citizens in the several States, and to all persons in the several States equal protection in the rights of life, liberty, and property.

The first part was worded to incorporate Article IV, Section 2, while the second used terminology not found elsewhere but which reflected the due process language in the Fifth Amendment. According to Bingham, the amendment would enable Congress to apply fundamental rights contained in the Constitution to the states: "Every word of the proposed amendment is today in the Constitution, save the words conferring the express grant of power upon the Congress of the United States." The Framers of the original Constitution had omitted inserting the authority for Congress to enforce against the states "the great canons of the supreme law." The amendment would, among other things, Bingham said, arm Congress "with the power to enforce the Bill of Rights as it

stands in the Constitution today."[44] It encompassed no more than those safe-guards granted by two provisions of the Constitution: the privileges and immunities clause of Article IV and the due process clause of the Fifth Amendment.[45] He charged that, within the previous five years, the officials of eleven states that had seceded had violated these provisions. Constitutional credibility required the adoption of an amendment to cure this problem.

An opponent of the Civil Rights Act, Bingham believed that a constitutional amendment was required before Congress could impose civil rights restraints on the states. The House, although not disposed toward the general structure of the proposed amendment, refused to table it, and on February 28, after some debate, postponed consideration of it, by a vote of 110–37, until the second week of April. Bingham voted with the majority. This measure was never taken up again and was eventually replaced by the final version.

The problem with this earlier version of the proposed amendment was that instead of prohibiting state action that infringed on liberties, the amendment placed the obligation entirely on Congress to make laws that would keep the states in check. The latter granted to Congress what was considered either excessive or ill-defined authority over the states and it enabled future congresses to change policy. The final version of the Fourteenth Amendment was drafted to meet these concerns. Consistent with the form of other constitutional protections, it prohibited certain actions by all of the states, and its purposes could be negated not by the majority will of another congress but only by another amendment.

From Bingham's perspective, an amendment giving Congress civil rights authority would have made the Civil Rights Act unnecessary. He rejected the proposed act, in part, because it removed some inherent state powers and centralized them in the federal government.[46] In contrast, his proposed amendment would greatly advance freedom and yet maintain the federal/state balance: "The care of the property, the liberty, and the life of the citizen . . . is in the States, and not in the Federal Government. I have sought to effect no change in that respect in the Constitution of the country."[47] Under the amendment, state authorities would have to answer nationally only if "they enact laws refusing equal protection to life, liberty or property."[48]

Bingham explained that the equal protection provision of the amendment also applied the due process guarantee to the states. He equated these two concepts with one another; there could be no liberty without equality and vice versa. On initial consideration, this position might appear untenable, for many commentators believe that irreconcilable tension exists between liberty and equality. Governments impose myriad laws and regulations that achieve the latter at the expense of the former. This version of equality is statist, though, and is brought about by the adoption of laws that make people alike in their condition. However, the libertarian version, which was advanced by Bingham and espoused by John Locke, Edward Coke, and William Blackstone (among

others), is based on the protection of individual rights. For Bingham and these commentators, equality before the law meant that all laws should apply equally and that no person or group should be favored or disfavored. No one is entitled to more or fewer rights than anyone else. Locke offered this perspective on equality:

> Though . . . all men by nature are equal, I cannot be supposed to understand all sorts of equality. Age or virtue may give men a just precedency. Excellency of parts and merit may place others above the common level. Birth may subject some, and alliance or benefits others, to pay an observance to those to whom Nature, gratitude or other respects, may have made it due; and yet all this consists with the equality which all men are in respect of jurisdiction or dominion one over another, which was the equality . . . being that equal right that every man hath to his natural freedom, without being subjected to the will or authority of any other man.[49]

Bingham was far from being alone among his colleagues in this thinking. For a great many years prior to the U.S. Civil War, abolitionists had maintained that the Fifth Amendment's due process clause required that the laws treat equally with respect to life, liberty, and property all persons similarly situated. Legislation treating certain people in a different or special way without adequate cause — and, therefore, unequally — was found to be violative of due process in a number of judicial decisions prior to the Civil War.[50] Subsequent to ratification of the Fourteenth Amendment, courts employed either the due process clause or the equal protection clause (or both) in order to nullify legislation that arbitrarily denied liberties to individuals or groups. To preserve a statute under either clause, a state had to show that sufficient reason existed to account for the differential treatment.

Bingham's concern for constitutionally guaranteeing property rights and other rights not related to race is evident in a change he sought to a draft of a proposed constitutional amendment that was adopted by the Reconstruction Committee and authored by Representative Thaddeus Stevens. This proposal occurred after the House postponed consideration of Bingham's early version of the Fourteenth Amendment. A section of Stevens's amendment provided: "No discrimination shall be made by any State, nor by the United States, as to the civil rights of persons because of race, color, or previous condition of servitude." Bingham moved to add the following provision to the amendment: "[N]or shall any state deny to any person within its jurisdiction the equal protection of the laws, nor take private property for public use without just compensation." This motion lost in the committee 5–7, with three absent.[51] Presumably, Bingham desired to extend the protections of the draft amendment beyond race relations to other personal freedoms.

It is doubtful that Bingham's primary purpose was to augment the section's racial protections. Stevens's proposed section was similar in language to the provision in the original Civil Rights Bill forbidding "discrimination in civil rights and immunities" that the House, and subsequently the Senate, deleted.[52] Bingham had urged this deletion because "the term civil rights includes every right that pertains to the citizens under the Constitution, laws, and government of this country."[53] A person given to such an understanding of "civil rights" would hardly have thought that more protection for such rights would be needed than was already provided by Stevens's section. Nor does it seem that Bingham would have received the support for his proposal that he did from Representative Rogers and Senator Johnson—both Democrats and opponents of the Civil Rights Act—had they believed that the proposal was so directed.

In the debates on Bingham's proposed constitutional amendment, ten congressmen, divided equally between supporters and opponents, made substantive comments. No one seriously quarreled with Bingham's definitions of privileges and immunities, due process, and equal protection. Opponents, however, feared that Congress would use these concepts excessively against the states, something which Bingham vigorously denied would occur, because the amendment would only authorize Congress to enforce the Bill of Rights.

When asked by Representative Hale of New York whether his first proposed Fourteenth Amendment was aimed solely at protecting American citizens of African descent in rebellious states, Bingham denied this intent, responding that it would apply to other states and that it would also safeguard thousands of Union supporters in the erstwhile confederacy from confiscation of property and banishment.[54] Subsequent discussion discloses the extent to which the amendment would govern the states. Bingham asserted that the amendment would confer upon Congress a general power to secure for all persons protection from the states with respect to life, liberty, and property. However, since it did not have discriminatory laws, Hale's New York did not require congressional intervention. Bingham was uncertain about the amendment's impact in Indiana.[55] As to real estate,

> every one knows that its acquisition and transmission under every interpretation ever given to the word property, as used in the Constitution of the country, are dependent exclusively upon the local law of the States, save under a direct grant of the United States. But suppose any person has acquired property not contrary to the laws of the State, but in accordance with its law, are they not to be equally protected in the enjoyment of it, or are they to be denied all protection? That is the question, and the whole question, so far as that part of the case is concerned.[56]

Two exchanges between Representative Hale and Representative Stevens, who supported Bingham's measure, further clarify the intended scope of con-

gressional authority pursuant to the amendment. Hale charged that under the equal protection provision, Congress would be able to override a state's civil and criminal legislation and establish its own laws instead. Stevens replied that the authority was far less broad than this:

> Does the gentleman mean to say that, under this provision, Congress could interfere in any case where the legislation of a State was equal, impartial to all? Or is it not simply to provide that, where any State makes a distinction in the same law between different classes of individuals, Congress shall have the power to correct such discrimination and inequality?[57]

In response to Hale's assertion that Congress would be empowered to overrule the states with respect to the property rights of women, Stevens explained: "When a distinction is made between two married people or two *femmes sole,* then it is unequal legislation; but where all of the same class are dealt with in the same way then there is no pretense of inequality." Stevens's explanation would require the application of reasonableness distinctions to Section 1 of the Fourteenth Amendment that the judiciary later utilized under substantive due process.[58] While their responses and examples may suggest wider coverage for the equal protection provision, both Bingham and Stevens maintained that state legislation that did not abridge fundamental liberties would not be affected.

IV. The Final Version of Section 1

On April 28, 1866, the select Joint Committee on Reconstruction voted 12–3 (with only Democrats opposing) to report out another proposed version of the Fourteenth Amendment, the first Section of which had been largely authored by John Bingham. Section 1 consisted solely of what is now its second sentence; a prior sentence on citizenship would be added subsequently. Representative Thaddeus Stevens presented this version to the House on May 8, and Senator Jacob Howard introduced it to the Senate on May 23. Both men were members of the joint committee. To better comprehend Section 1's meaning, it is best to discuss the Senate debate prior to that of the House; the subsequent commentary will proceed on this basis.

In a statement corresponding to Bingham's assertion made when presenting his earlier version, Howard claimed that all the restraints in the Constitution then bound the federal government but not the states:

> These immunities, privileges, rights, thus guaranteed [sic] by the Constitution or recognized by it, are secured to the citizen solely as a citizen of the United States and as a party in their courts. They do not operate in the

slightest degree as a restraint or prohibition upon State legislation. . . . [Moreover,] there is no power given in the Constitution to enforce and to carry out any of these guarantees. They are not powers granted by the Constitution to Congress, and of course do not come within the [necessary and proper] clause of the Constitution. . . . But they stand simply as a bill of Rights in the Constitution, without power on the part of Congress to give them full effect; while at the same time the States are not restrained from violating the principles embraced in them except by their own local constitutions, which may be altered from year to year. The great object of the first section of this amendment is, therefore, to restrain the power of the States and compel them at all times to respect these great fundamental guarantees.[59]

Instead of offering separate meanings for the due process and equal protection clauses, Howard lumped his understanding of them together in a short explanation:

The last two clauses of the first section of the amendment disable a State from depriving not merely a citizen of the United States, but any person whoever he may be, of life, liberty, or property without due process of law, or from denying to him the equal protection of the laws of the State. This abolishes all class legislation in the States and does away with the injustice of subjecting one caste of persons to a code not applicable to another. It prohibits the hanging of a black man for a crime for which the white man is not to be hanged. It protects the black man in his fundamental rights as a citizen with the same shield which it throws over the white man. Is it not time, Mr. President, that we extend to the black man, I had almost called it the poor privilege of the equal protection of the law? Ought not the time to be now past when one measure of justice is to be meted out to a member of one caste while another and a different measure is meted out to the member of another caste, both castes being alike citizens of the United States, both bound to obey the same laws, to sustain the burdens of the same Government, and both equally responsible to justice and to God for the deeds done in the body?[60]

Both of these clauses thus outlaw racial and other preferences and class and caste legislation in general. Here Howard spoke of protecting legal equality, both racial and otherwise, as being under the Civil Rights Act. The extent of this commitment is not defined, but because of its origins and Howard's explanation, it is substantive, general, and substantial. Not being limited by the specifics contained in the act, its impact on the states would be greater.

The three clauses of Section 1 provided sweeping protection for fundamental liberties. Except for eliminating direct congressional oversight, the final version is similar conceptually to Bingham's earlier one that had been introduced in the House in February, 1866. The privileges or immunities clause reads as Bingham interpreted his February version of it (and of Article IV, Section 2). Because he used equal protection and due process interchangeably, the addition of due process language and the alteration in equal protection wording clarified the meaning and provided added safeguards. In a speech to Congress in 1871, Bingham asserted that the final version was "more comprehensive than as it was first proposed. . . . It embraces all and more than did the February proposition."[61]

Bingham's speeches reveal that he, like many of similar persuasion, employed the three concepts (privileges or immunities, due process of law, and equal protection) interchangeably to condemn oppressive state legislation. All were catch phrases of the antislavery movements. Absent from the amendment is any reference to civil rights—an omission probably attributable to the fact that the term was thought to include political rights. As previously explained, this same concern had led to the deletion of this term in the Civil Rights Act.

At the prompting of other senators, Senator Howard subsequently offered specific changes to the amendment. One that was adopted was the addition of the definition of citizenship that became the first sentence of Section 1. In the ensuing debate, only six senators, three from each party, commented substantively on what had by that time become the second sentence of Section 1. The sparsity of the discussion may in part be attributable to the greater passions and concerns that other sections aroused among the senators.

Debate in the House on Section 1 was also not very extensive. In describing the contents of this section, Representative Stevens read *verbatim* the privileges or immunities and equal protection clauses and paraphrased the due process clause as prohibiting the states from "unlawfully depriving [citizens] of life, liberty, or property." He maintained that the provisions of what is now the second sentence of Section 1 are

> all asserted, in some form or other, in our Declaration or organic law. But the Constitution limits only the action of Congress and is not a limitation on the States. This amendment supplies that defect, and allows Congress to correct the unjust legislation of the States, so far that the law which operates upon one man shall operate *equally* upon all.[62]

Stevens explained that whatever law applied to a white man would apply to the black man precisely in the same way and to the same degree. He did not otherwise elucidate the section, except to assert that it would maintain the principles of the Civil Rights Act in the event that the latter was repealed by another

congress. After this short explanation, Stevens went on to Section 2, which he considered to be the most important section.

Bingham presented this explanation of Section 1 of the proposed constitutional amendment:

> There was a want hitherto, and there remains a want now, in the constitution of our country, which the proposed amendment will supply. What is that? It is the power in the people, the whole people of the United States, by express authority of the Constitution to do that by congressional enactment that they have not had the power to do and have never attempted to do; that is, protect by national law the privileges and immunities of all of the citizens of the Republic and the inborn rights of every person within its jurisdiction whenever the same shall be abridged or denied by the unconstitutional acts of any State.
>
> Allow me, Mr. Speaker, in passing, to say that this amendment takes from no State any right that ever pertained to it. No State ever had the right, under the forms of law or otherwise, to deny to any freeman the equal protection of the laws or to abridge the privileges or immunities of any citizen of the Republic, although many of them have assumed and exercised the power, and that without remedy.[63]

Probably the most powerful member of Congress, Stevens was more radical than Bingham on Reconstruction policy. Thus, he sought a provision to guarantee black suffrage constitutionally, but he could not obtain enough votes for passage. Bingham did not help him in this quest. However, the two took similar positions on amending the Constitution. Stevens supported Bingham's main efforts—first on the latter's earlier version of the Fourteenth Amendment, and then on his addition to Section 1 of the draft amendment that he authored. Additionally, Stevens voted to delete this Section 1 in favor of the one drafted by Bingham, which now constitutes the second sentence.

The two men had similar ideas in another area that may also be revealing of their perspective on Section 1. During the drafting of the Fourteenth Amendment, Stevens sponsored bills to support the economic interests of certain railroads against hostile state legislatures on the ground that their vested rights had been impaired. Bingham voted for these measures. Commentators have speculated about the effect of such economic issues upon the drafting of the amendment.[64] It is difficult to believe that they and other congressmen supporting the amendment were not aware that the broad language would be invoked in support of commercial interests.

In a speech near the close of the House debate on the proposed amendment, Representative Bingham explained that Section 1 protected, by national law, from abridgement or denial by a state "the privileges and immunities of all of the citizens of the Republic and the inborn rights of every person within its jurisdiction. . . ."[65] In light of Bingham's known perspective, "inborn" most likely

meant natural rights. He used the same term in his previously mentioned 1857 speech, when he condemned states that "trample upon the inborn rights of humanity" and lauded those that "defend the inborn rights of each against the combined power of all."[66]

In the sentence from his closing speech (quoted above), Bingham summed up the significance and importance of Section 1. For him, privileges and immunities encompassed natural or fundamental liberties, including those contained in the first eight amendments and that applied only to citizens. Both the due process and the equal protection clauses were open-ended protections of life, liberty, and property for all persons, regardless of citizenship: "That great want of the citizen and stranger, protection by national law from unconstitutional State enactments, is supplied by the first section of this Amendment."[67]

The balance of the House debate is not very enlightening on how the representatives construed what is now the second sentence of Section 1. Much of the debate concerned other sections, with a number of legislators making no reference to Section 1. In all, fewer than twenty representatives dealt with that section. Most of the Republicans who participated mentioned its relationship to the Civil Rights Act—that the amendment supplied the necessary congressional authority either to enact it or to constitutionalize its protections against diminution or extinction by subsequent congresses.

Some spoke about the personal rights, other than those concerning race, secured by the amendment. Representative Thayer said that it "simply brings into the Constitution what is found in the bill of rights of every State."[68] Equality guarantees were stressed by Representatives Raymond[69] and Farnsworth;[70] Representative Miller said that the due process and equal protection clauses were within the spirit of the Declaration of Independence;[71] Representative Eckley believed that the amendment afforded "security of life, liberty, and property to all the citizens of all the States."[72]

Of the Democrats, only Representative Rogers of New Jersey (a member of the reconstruction committee) spoke extensively. He warned that the privileges or immunities clause would revolutionize the entire constitutional system by eliminating the states' powers. "All the rights we have under the laws of the country are embraced under the definition of privileges and immunities." He asserted that the amendment embodies "that outrageous and miserable Civil Rights Bill."[73] (See Chapter 6 for discussion of the Thirty-Ninth Congress's debates on the proposed privileges or immunities clause.)

During the debates on the Civil Rights Bill and the two proposed constitutional amendments, the term "privileges or immunities" was frequently mentioned and defined. Less attention was directed at the term "due process of law," which has so much more influenced the course of the nation's laws. When the latter term was mentioned, it was always in the context of limiting governmental powers. As we have seen, this perspective was shared by Representative Bingham. He equated due process with equal protection of the laws and of fundamental and

natural rights. No representative disputed Bingham's explanation that the equal protection provision of his first version, which was clearly substantive in character, did no more than apply the due process clause to the states. Representative Higby specifically agreed, asserting that the language of the two guarantees "is very little different."[74]

The previous discussion of the Civil Rights Act disclosed Representative Wilson's convictions about due process. He believed that the act enforced the protections of the Fifth Amendment's due process clause against the states.[75] For Representative Baker of Illinois, the proposed due process clause was "a wholesome and needed check upon the great abuse of liberty which several of the states have practices, and which they manifest too much purpose to continue."[76] Senator Poland and Representative Miller identified the due process and equal protection clauses with the Declaration of Independence.[77] Representative Williams of New Jersey opined that if suffrage was regarded as a property right, its deprivation would violate the due process clause.[78] Thus, for these congressmen, due process of law meant a substantive guarantee of life, liberty, and property. Representative Stevens so construed the clause in introducing the amendment in the House.

It is likely that most Republican congressmen, particularly those who had been active in or associated with the antislavery movement, held similar views. Due process was a term used often before, during, and after the U.S. Civil War. Both sides of the slavery controversy employed it to further their cause. Proslavery forces contended that slaves were property and that, therefore, owners were protected against their loss without due process. In contrast, beginning in the mid-1830s, antislavery activists thought of the due process guarantee as constitutionalizing their natural rights beliefs in the sanctity of life, liberty, and property.[79] They repudiated any notion that a person could be someone else's property; people possessed human property only in and to their own selves. The Fifth Amendment's due process clause, accordingly, obligated the national government to secure life and liberty in addition to real and personal property in the areas under its authority.

The due process concept was a major verbal weapon for the abolitionists. H. J. Graham observed that due process

> was snatched up, bandied about, "corrupted and corroded," if you please, for more than thirty years prior to 1866. For every black letter usage in court, there were perhaps hundreds or thousands in the press, red schoolhouse, and on the stump. Zealots, reformers, and politicians—not jurists—blazed the paths of substantive due process.[80]

Thus, the political parties committed to eradicating slavery used the term to advance their position. In 1843, the Liberty Party platform declared that the Fifth

Amendment's due process clause legally secured the inalienable rights referred to in the Declaration of Independence.[81] The 1848 and 1852 platforms of the Free Soil Party contended that the clause served both as a restraint on the federal government and as an obligation that it enforce the inalienable rights enumerated in the Declaration.[82] More significant, according to the 1856 and 1860 platforms of the Republican Party, the clause denied Congress the power to allow slavery to exist in any territory in the Union: "It becomes our duty to maintain [the due process provision] of the Constitution against all attempts to violate it."[83] Some of those involved in the drafting or consideration of the Republican platforms may have later, as members of Congress or in other political roles, been responsible for framing or adopting the Fourteenth Amendment. In the 1856 political campaign, "due process of law" was a leading catch phrase of Republican orators.[84]

Due process advocacy was not confined to the antislavery movement. When the Fourteenth Amendment was being framed, insurance and other corporations submitted large numbers of petitions to Congress that were permeated with due process of law reasoning, urging federal relief from state legislation that deprived them of property and economic freedoms.[85] Commentators have noted the commonality of interest between corporate and antislavery groups: each thought that it would benefit from the imposition of due process, just compensation, and privileges or immunities restraints on the states. Accordingly, both groups lobbied for these positions.[86] The abolition of slavery eliminated the argument over ownership of the person, and both sides of this controversy could thereafter promote personal freedom under the same reasoning.

It is evident that in the period covering the framing and ratification of the Fourteenth Amendment, many political, commercial, and ideological leaders viewed the concept of due process of law as strongly protective of individual liberty.

To be sure, in our society it is the Supreme Court and not the public that decides the meaning of the Constitution. The people, however, determine whether or not an amendment to the Constitution should be adopted, and to this extent they control constitutional meaning. The foregoing discussion indicates that when the Fourteenth Amendment was ratified, the concept of due process of law was in considerable use and many people viewed it as a protection against government oppression; it was not seen as merely a safeguard for proper procedures. The words would hardly have been elevated to a battle-cry had the public's understanding been so confined. For John Bingham—and presumably other congressional supporters of the proposed amendment—the due process clause guaranteed the people that the states could not deprive them of the protections of the Constitution. Bingham and his allies did not seem reticent in the least to declare this to be the meaning of the due process clause. It is likely that during the ratification period, the public's understanding of the due process clause was greater than for most provisions of the proposed amendment.

6

The Privileges or Immunities Clause
of the Fourteenth Amendment

I. Introduction

The words "privileges" and "immunities" are contained in two separate clauses of the Constitution. Article IV, Section 2 states: "The Citizens of each State shall be entitled to all Privileges and Immunities of Citizens in the several States," and the second sentence of Section 1 of the Fourteenth Amendment provides: "No State shall make or enforce any law which shall abridge the privileges or immunities of citizens of the United States." Considerable controversy has existed over the years as to the meaning of each clause. In his dissenting opinion in the 1999 case of *Saenz v. Roe,* U.S. Supreme Court Justice Clarence Thomas traces the meaning of both clauses to the original understanding between the English settlers in America and the English authorities who governed these settlements.[1]

Justice Thomas writes that at the time of the founding, the terms "privileges" and "immunities" and their counterparts were understood to refer to those fundamental rights and liberties enjoyed by English citizens (and all persons)—what I have referred to in this book as the "rights of Englishmen." Thomas supports this assertion by referring to official documents that were executed prior to independence of the colonies from England.

English settlers sought and usually obtained assurance from the English authorities that their rights as Englishmen would not be affected by their move to the new territory. This is evident in the papers that were executed relating to the new settlements. For example, the Charter of Virginia of 1606 safeguarded "all

243

ies, Franchises, and Immunities [of the emigrants] as if they had been
ding and born, within our Realme of England."[2] Other colonies adopted similar resolutions, asserting their entitlements to the liberties, franchises, privileges, and immunities of Englishmen. The 1620 Charter of New England guaranteed "[l]iberties, and franchizes, and Immunities of free Denizens and
naturall subjects."[3] The 1622 Charter of Connecticut guaranteed "[l]iberties
and Immunities of free and natural subjects";[4] the 1629 Charter of the Massachusetts Bay Colony guaranteed the "liberties and Immunities of free and naturall subjects";[5] the 1632 Charter of Maine guaranteed "liberties[,] Franchises
and Immunityes of or belonging to any of the naturall borne subjects";[6] the
1632 Charter of Maryland guaranteed "Privileges, Franchises and Liberties";[7]
the 1663 Charter of Carolina referred to the colonists' "liberties, franchises and
privileges" as inviolate";[8] the 1663 Charter of the Rhode Island and Providence
Plantations guaranteed "libertyes and immunityes of free and naturall subjects";[9] and the 1732 Charter of Georgia guaranteed "liberties, franchises and
immunities of free denizens and natural born subjects."[10]

In their disputes with the English authorities, the colonists frequently insisted
that England was violating the liberties that they had been guaranteed. They
adopted resolutions reasserting their entitlement to the privileges and immunities of English citizenship. The Massachusetts Resolves stated:

> Resolved, That there are certain essential Rights of the British Constitu-
> tion of Government, which are founded in the Law of God and Nature,
> and are the Common Rights of Mankind—Therefore, . . . Resolved that
> no man can justly take the Property of another without his consent. . . .
> [T]his Inherent Right, together with all other essential Rights, Liberties,
> Privileges and Immunities of the People of Great Britain have been fully
> confirmed to them by Magna Carta.[11]

In 1765, the Resolutions of the Stamp Act Congress condemned the Stamp Act
imposed by the British as violating their "inherent rights and privileges": "That it
is inseparably essential to the freedom of a people, and the undoubted rights of
Englishmen, that no taxes should be imposed on them, but with their own consent,
given personally, or by their representatives."[12] The Virginia Resolves stated:
"[T]he Colonists aforesaid are entitled to all Liberties, Privileges and Immunities
of Denizens and natural subjects, to all Intents and Purposes, as if they had been
abiding and born within the Realm of England."[13] The 1774 Statement of Violation of Rights issued by the Continental Congress provided as follows: "[O]ur ancestors, who first settled these colonies, were at the time of emigration from the
mother country, entitled to all the rights, liberties, and immunities of free and nat-
ural-born subjects, within the realm of England . . . Resolved . . . [t]hat by such
emigration they by no means forfeited, surrendered or lost any of those rights."[14]

Privileges and immunities included the substantive and fundamental rights of Englishmen, which, in the words of Justice Bushrod Washington, "belong, of right, to the citizens of all free governments."[15] The colonists claimed these privileges and immunities as a matter of birthright, though, and not by reason of having equality with those citizens of England who did not migrate to America. As they proclaimed in the Declaration of Independence, these were the unalienable rights of life, liberty, and the pursuit of happiness that they were endowed with by their Creator. These privileges and immunities were identified or implicit in the Magna Carta, the common law, the English statutes, and the commentaries of Coke and Blackstone. The protection of these rights was inapplicable to rights and liberties that were not deemed fundamental, a distinction which continues to exist in rights jurisprudence to this day (although the definitions of "fundamental" and "nonfundamental" are disputed). The colonists' entitlement to privileges and immunities were accordingly reaffirmed in the two constitutional documents that they adopted subsequent to independence from the English: the Articles of Confederation (1781) and the Constitution of the United States (1788).

In the Articles of Confederation, which had little to say about liberties, the states did provide protection for the privileges and immunities of the people in Article IV:

> The better to secure and perpetuate mutual friendship and intercourse among the people of the different states in this union, the free inhabitants of each of these states, paupers, vagabonds and fugitives from justice excepted, shall be entitled to all privileges and immunities of free citizens in the several states; and the people of each state shall have free ingress and regress to and from any other state, and shall enjoy therein all of the privileges of trade and commerce, subject to the same duties, impositions and restrictions as the inhabitants thereof respectively, provided that such restriction shall not extend so far as to prevent the removal of property imported into any state, to any other state, of which the owner is an inhabitant; provided also that no imposition, duties or restrictions shall be laid by any state, on the property of the United States, or either of them.[16]

This article confirmed the privileges and immunities to which inhabitants of the colonies were entitled, and which had previously under English rule been guaranteed. The newly created and independent states were not about to deprive their inhabitants of their rights and liberties. The article assured inhabitants of one state that they could exercise in their own state or in any other state the rights and freedoms to which they were entitled. Moreover, a common meaning of privileges and immunities was required to facilitate and enhance intercourse, cooperation, business, and commerce between the States, reducing the disabling consequences

of excessive and unfamiliar regulation. It would also diminish jealousies and retaliatory measures that might imperil harmony among the states.

II. The Privileges and Immunities Clause of Article IV

Article IV, Section 2 of the U.S. Constitution is modeled after the first clause of Article IV of the Articles of Confederation. It states the following: "The Citizens of each State shall be entitled to all Privileges and Immunities of Citizens in the several States." This clause imposes the constitutional guarantee of unenumerated privileges and immunities on the states, limiting their powers to infringe these vital protections. As explained in Chapter 3, it was assumed at the founding of the nation in 1789 that the federal government was devoid of the power to deprive its citizens of their rights as Englishmen.

Accordingly, for Alexander Hamilton writing in No. 80 of the *Federalist Papers,* the privileges and immunities clause was not only a "fundamental" provision, but also "the basis of the Union." Citizens expected, he asserted, "the inviolable maintenance of that equality of privileges and immunities to which [they] will be entitled."[17] They never relinquished them nor were they deprived of them either as English or American citizens. Their freedom was comprised of the safeguards inherent in their privileges and immunities.

Hamilton was concerned that the judicial system fully and fairly enforce this understanding. "To secure full effect of so fundamental a provision against all evasion and subterfuge," he urged that controversies concerning the application of this clause be adjudicated by the federal judiciary because it would be more impartial than a state court in controversies involving states. To this extent, his position would provide federal protection for a citizen's privileges and immunities, which (as previously reported in Chapter 5) was an important objective of the Fourteenth Amendment's framers.

Early cases and legal commentaries supported Hamilton's interpretation that the clause was of major importance in the constitutional scheme. One of the earliest judicial explanations of the privileges and immunities clause of Article IV was given by Judge Samuel Chase in the 1797 Delaware case of *Campbell v. Morris.*[18] Chase did not give a comprehensive definition of privileges and immunities, and instead offered a particular and limited one related to the controversy before the court. According to Chase, one of the privileges and immunities was the right of "citizens of the several states to acquire and hold real property in any of the states," and another was to "secure and protect personal rights." Chase explained that the clause was taken verbatim from the Articles of Confederation, which required, among other things, each of the states to protect ownership of property. Chase stated that the clause in Article IV "means that the citizens of all the States shall have the peculiar advantage of acquiring

and holding real as well as personal property, and that such property shall be protected and secured by the laws of the State, in the same manner as the property of the citizens of the States is protected." The clause also means that the property of non-citizens "shall not be liable to any taxes or burdens which the property of the citizens is not subject to"; it does not mean the right of election or the right of holding offices.

However, Chase asserted, the Constitution does not abridge the power of the states to make local regulations, the operation of which is confined to individual states. While the states could not deprive their citizens of the fundamental right of property ownership, they could, said the judge, make creditors (who were plaintiffs in the case) be "on the same footing with a state creditor, in the payment of the debts of a deceased debtor." The privileges and immunities clause does not limit the power of the states to establish modes of proceedings for the recovery of such debts.

Douglas, Admin. v. Stephens[19] is an 1821 Delaware chancery court decision on the broad question of whether the privileges and immunities clause of Article IV places a citizen of the state of Maryland on an equal footing with a citizen of Delaware with respect to the recovery of debts. At issue was the constitutionality of a Delaware statute providing that debts due by any person to any inhabitant of the state shall receive priority of judgment and execution over a debt due a noninhabitant of the state. According to Justice Ridgely, privileges and immunities "comprehend all the rights, and all the methods of protecting those rights, which belong to a person in a state of civil society, subject to be sure, to some restrictions, but to such only as the welfare of society, and general good require." He found the statute invalid because in the "payment of debts by an executor or administrator there can be no other distinction than according to the dignity of the debt." Chief Justice Johns and a majority of the court disagreed that the priority in payment of debts required by the state violated the privileges and immunities clause. Johns asserted that the privileges and immunities secured "are not such as are given to citizens in one or more states by the state laws, but must be such as citizens in the several states, that is, in *all* the states, are entitled to." He went on to state that the great object to be attained was to secure the right to acquire and hold real property. Despite some disagreement, it was apparent from this case that all of the justices agreed that the clause at the very least protected fundamental rights from abridgment by the states.

The uncertainties of the privileges and immunities clause were settled for a long time by Justice Washington's 1823 opinion in *Corfield v. Coryell,*[20] in which he ruled that the clause secured the fundamental rights of citizens that "belong, of right, to the citizens of all free governments." However, continued Washington, this provision of the Constitution does not entitle the citizens of the several states to participate in all of the rights which belong exclusively to the citizens of

any particular state. Hence, the New Jersey statute involved in *Corfield* that limited the right of removing oysters from the beds in which they grew to the citizens or inhabitants of the state does not violate the clause. The state law did not inhibit the buying and selling of oysters once they are lawfully gathered. The oyster beds, the justice stated, are the common property of the citizens of New Jersey. It would be going too far to construe the grant of privileges and immunities as amounting to a grant of a cotenancy in the common property of a particular state to the citizens of all the other states. Washington thus distinguished between fundamental rights that were guaranteed to citizens of all the states and rights to which only citizens of a particular state were entitled. Article IV, Section 2 of the U.S. Constitution protects solely the former group of rights.

Washington's interpretation of the privileges and immunities clause was constitutional orthodoxy for the next 45 years until the *Paul v. Virginia* decision in 1868 (discussed later in this chapter).[21] This is not surprising, inasmuch as citizens from the time of the early English settlements to the framing of the Bill of Rights took it for granted that they possessed fundamental rights—that is, privileges and immunities—of which government could not deprive them. An important New York decision in 1844 went so far as to interpret the privileges and immunities clause of Article IV as stripping the states of the authority to "define, abridge, or enlarge the important privilege of citizenship in the United States. It was purely a natural right and one which must for the future be governed by rules operating alike upon every part of the Union."[22] Washington's position was subscribed to by Chief Justice Taney and Justice Curtis in the *Dred Scott* case. Thomas Sergeant, in his *Constitutional Law* (1822); William Rawles, in his *The Constitution of the United States of America* (1825); and commentators William Goodell, in 1844, James Birney, in 1847, and Joel Tiffany, in 1847, endorsed it. Chancellor James Kent, in his *Commentaries* (1832) and his opinion in *Livingston v. Van Ingen* (1812),[23] accepted it. Justice Joseph Story was somewhat unclear about the clause, but cited the decisions in *Corfield* and *Livingston* and the commentary of Sergeant in support of his interpretation, all of which maintained Justice Washington's position.[24]

III. Congress Defines Privileges and Immunities

Of considerable importance to comprehending the meaning of privileges and immunities are also the interpretations of this term in the congressional debates on the Civil Rights Act of 1866 and on Section 1 of the then-proposed Fourteenth Amendment. As explained in Chapter 5, Section I, existing jurisprudence at the time of ratification is vital to determining the meaning of language contained in Section 1 of the Fourteenth Amendment. Congressional discus-

sions and debates are helpful in ascertaining the meanings that the Supreme Court has accorded the critical words and phrases of that amendment. Since most members of the Thirty-Ninth Congress were lawyers and former judges, these debates provide a highly informed source of information about the meaning of the proposed amendment.

Recall that the chief purpose of the Civil Rights Act was to provide federal protection for the slaves who were emancipated by the Thirteenth Amendment so that they could exercise certain enumerated liberties. The act applied to all the states and benefited other people as well. It extended citizenship to most persons born in the United States and gave each the same rights to make and enforce contracts, to sue, to be parties and give evidence, and to inherit, purchase, lease, sell, hold, and convey real and personal property. As explained in Chapter 5, its sponsors found the authority for Congress to pass the law under the Thirteenth Amendment and Article IV. First, under Section 2 of the Thirteenth Amendment, they contended that Congress had the authority to enforce the amendment on southern states that maintained discriminatory practices against the emancipated slaves. Second, these discriminatory practices also deprived these blacks of the fundamental rights that are protected by the privileges and immunities clause of Article IV. Third, these states deprived the emancipated slaves of rights practiced and enjoyed by white citizens, thus denying them the equality of rights required by Article IV's privileges and immunities clause. The discussion that follows will be largely confined to the constitutional meaning of the privileges and immunities clause.

In introducing the Civil Rights Bill in their respective bodies, Senator Trumbull and Representative Wilson both contended that all of the protections accorded under the act were already secured against the states under Article IV, Section 2. They quoted approvingly Justice Washington's opinion in *Corfield*. Citing his opinion, Trumbull stated that every citizen "is entitled to the great fundamental rights of life, liberty and the pursuit of happiness, and the right to travel, to go where he pleases." By making the freed slaves citizens, the Civil Rights Bill would protect their fundamental rights: "the right to acquire property, the right to go and come at pleasure, the right to enforce rights in the courts, to make contracts and to inherit and depose of property." A law that does not allow a "colored person" to go from one county to another, "does not allow him to teach, does not allow him to preach, is certainly a law in violation of the rights of a freeman, and may so properly be declared void."[25] However, he insisted, this "bill has nothing to do with the political rights or status of parties," which are matters that the states would continue to control. Subsequently, after President Johnson vetoed the Civil Rights Bill, Trumbull, in urging an override of the veto, stated the following:

> To be a citizen of the United States carries with it some rights. . . . They are those inherent, fundamental rights which belong to free citizens or

free men in all countries, such as the rights enumerated in this bill and they belong to them in all the States of the Union.[26]

Wilson contended that "[b]efore our Constitution was formed, the great fundamental rights . . . belonged to every person who became a member of our great national family. No one surrendered a jot or tittle of these rights by consenting to the formation of the Government." The Civil Rights Bill would not be needed, Wilson argued, if all the states observed Article IV's privileges and immunities clause. "It is not the object of this bill to establish new rights," Wilson explained, "but to protect and enforce those which already belong to every citizen. . . . If the States would all observe the rights of our citizens, there would be no need of this bill."[27]

Wilson also cited *Bouvier's Law Dictionary*: "Civil rights are those which have no relation to the establishment, support, or management of government." For Wilson, this definition of civil rights did not include political rights, which remained within the powers of the states. This bill, he stated, refers to those rights which belong to men as citizens of the United States: "[T]his bill can only relate to matters within the control of Congress."[28] As to school, jury, and election laws, these are matters under the control of the states.

John Bingham construed Article IV, Section 2, as guaranteeing fundamental rights. These rights were, he contended, natural or inherent liberties of United States citizens that were intended to be secure from infringement by the states. A strong believer in natural rights, he maintained a distinction between them and political rights, and he did so by relating the former to life, liberty, and property. Natural rights were insulated from the opinion of the majority, while political rights were its product. He expressed these ideas, which related to the constitutional meaning of privileges and immunities, at various times in his career as a congressman:

> I deny that any State may exclude a law abiding citizen of the United States from coming within its Territory, or abiding therein, or acquiring and enjoying property therein, or from the enjoyment therein of the "privileges and immunities" of a citizen of the United States. . . . [Pursuant to Article IV, Section 2], citizens of each State, all the citizens of each State, being citizens of the United States, shall be entitled to "all privileges and immunities of citizens in the several States." Not to the rights and immunities of the several States; not to those constitutional rights and immunities which result exclusively from State authority or State legislation; but to "all privileges and immunities" of citizens of the United States in the several states. . . . Citizens of the United States . . . are entitled to all of the privileges and immunities . . . amongst which are the rights of life, liberty and property, and their due protection in the enjoyment thereof by law. . . .[29]

All free persons, then, born and domiciled in any State of the Union, are citizens of the United States; and, although not equal in respect of political rights, are equal in respect of natural rights. Allow me, sir, to disarm prejudice and silence the demagogue cry of "negro suffrage," and "negro political equality," by saying, that no sane man ever seriously proposed political equality to all, for the reason that it is impossible. Political rights are conventional, not natural; limited, not universal; and are, in fact, exercised only by the majority of the qualified electors of any State, and by the minority only nominally.[30]

Senator Jacob Howard introduced the resolution in the Senate to approve the proposed Fourteenth Amendment. After quoting Justice Washington's broad definition of Article IV's privileges and immunities clause, and adding that it gives "some intimation of what probably will be the opinion of the judiciary," he interpreted the privileges or immunities clause of the Fourteenth Amendment as follows:

To these privileges and immunities [as set forth by Justice Washington], whatever they may be—for they are not and cannot be fully defined in their entire extent and precise nature—to these should be added the personal rights guarantied [sic] and secured by the first eight amendments of the Constitution; such as the freedom of speech and of the press; the right of the people peaceably to assemble and petition the Government for a redress of grievances, a right appertaining to each and all the people; the right to keep and to bear arms; the right to be exempted from the quartering of soldiers in a house without the consent of the owner; the right to be exempt from unreasonable searches and seizures, and from any search or seizure except by virtue of a warrant issued upon a formal oath or affidavit; the right of an accused person to be informed of the nature of the accusation against him, and his right to be tried by an impartial jury of the vicinage; and also the right to be secure against excessive bail and against cruel and unusual punishments.

Now, sir, here is a mass of privileges, immunities, and rights, some of them secured by the second section of the fourth article of the Constitution, which I have recited, some by the first eight amendments of the Constitution. . . . The great object of the first section of this amendment is, therefore, to restrain the power of the States and compel them at all times to respect these great fundamental guarantees.[31]

Senator Poland of Vermont, a lawyer who had served for 17 years in the state's highest court, supported and amplified Howard's explanation. He maintained that the amendment's privileges or immunities clause "secures nothing

beyond what was intended" in Article IV, Section 2. Inasmuch as Poland did not challenge Howard's explanation, he apparently assumed, as did other Republicans and some Supreme Court Justices, that Article IV, Section 2 was intended to protect all fundamental liberties, including those in the first eight amendments. Poland went on to argue that many of the states had repudiated or disregarded this important clause and that investing Congress with the power to enforce it was now eminently proper and necessary.[32]

Senator Howe of Wisconsin, a lawyer formerly on the highest court of his state, supported Section 1 as a means to combat the wrongs that the rebellious states had committed and might continue to commit. They had "denied to a large portion of the population the plainest and most necessary rights of citizenship." These included, among others, the right to hold land that had been paid for, the right to sue for wages that had been withheld, and the right to give testimony. No state should be able to deny its citizens their privileges and immunities or the equal protection of the laws.[33] Senator Henderson of Missouri chose to discuss only that part of Section 1 relating to citizenship. The other clauses, he asserted, merely secured the rights that attached to citizenship in all free countries. He implied that the amendment would overcome the Black Codes that had made the black man a "degraded outcast" deprived of the "commonest rights" of property and legal processes.[34]

Senator Davis of Kentucky (a Democrat) saw no need for a new privileges and immunities clause because, he stated, Article IV "comprehends the same principle in better and broader language." However, he offered no explanation for this conclusion. Davis argued, additionally, that due process should be left to the states where it was already assured in their constitutions. Equal protection was also their concern.[35] Senators Hendricks of Indiana and Johnson of Maryland (both Democrats) spoke about the ambiguity of the privileges clause. The former complained that he had not heard any senator or other statesman accurately define the rights and immunities of citizenship.[36] The latter, a member of the Reconstruction Committee, disapproved of only this clause because he did not understand what its effect would be.[37] His motion to delete it was rejected in an unrecorded vote. Although this limited debate may not be very revealing as to meaning, it does evidence an absence of serious opposition to Howard's explanation of the privileges and immunities clause and a willingness to accept it.

Senator Johnson's position that he did not understand what the effect of the proposed privileges and immunities clause would be raises questions about the meaning of the clause—as well it should. He was a member of the Joint Committee of Congress that approved it and was a distinguished and prominent lawyer. From 1849 to 1850, he was Attorney General of the United States and for most of his career a leading practitioner before the U.S. Supreme Court. Johnson's uncertainty about the meaning of the clause is somewhat difficult to

comprehend since he found no such problem with the proposed due process clause, which at the time was hardly more fixed in meaning than was the privileges and immunities clause. The United States Constitution is not written as a civil code, and its terminology, not always being clear and precise, continually requires interpretation as to its applicability in particular situations. When the Thirty-Ninth Congress framed the Fourteenth Amendment, the courts and legal community generally recognized Justice Washington's opinion in *Corfield* as being the definitive interpretation of Article IV's privileges and immunities clause. Washington asserted that the clause protected fundamental rights, but, because it was too tedious and difficult, he did not enumerate all those rights. Senator Howard felt free to include in the definition of fundamental rights the first eight amendments to the Constitution, which Representative Stevens (and probably most of Congress) accepted on the premise that they constituted or would be judicially found to constitute fundamental rights. To be sure, in 1868, *Paul v. Virginia* (discussed in Section IV *infra*.) effectively reversed Washington's decision, but no lawyer or layman can be certain about future judicial opinions. Johnson may have rejected the clause on policy grounds, but it surely was within a constitutional standard of precision.

Because of the limited meaning currently given the term "privileges and immunities" as it appears in Article IV, it may seem surprising that only a few senators challenged Howard's extensive definition. However, the debates relating to the Fourteenth Amendment reveal (as heretofore noted) that most of the Republicans regarded privileges and immunities as encompassing all fundamental liberties secured in the Constitution, which necessarily would include those set forth in the first eight amendments. Antislavery doctrine advanced this position.[38] Were it otherwise, the clause might secure only a portion of those liberties identified in the eight amendments—a far lesser and seemingly incoherent commitment to freedom. Moreover, Washington had indicated that his list of liberties was not final and that unnamed liberties were also included. Howard's broad definition, accordingly, was consistent with such thinking.

While introducing the proposed Fourteenth Amendment to the House, Representative Thaddeus Stevens took a position similar to the one Senator Howard presented; that the amendment would enable the Congress (and, presumably, the Supreme Court) to enforce the protections of the Civil Rights Bill, which, because it was a product of the legislature, could be rescinded by a subsequent Congress. Stevens asserted that "the first time the South with its copperhead allies obtain the command of Congress it will be repealed." These rights, Stevens stated, correct the unjust legislation of the states and demand a constitutional guarantee.

In the debates both on the Civil Rights Bill and the proposed Fourteenth Amendment, most members of Congress favoring these measures agreed with Trumbull, Wilson, and Bingham on the meaning of privileges and immunities. President Johnson, in vetoing the Civil Rights Bill, acknowledged in his veto

message that privileges and immunities included only fundamental rights.[39] Supporters generally accepted—either specifically or in principle—Justice Washington's interpretation that Article IV, Section 2 protected fundamental rights, and many interpreted fundamental rights as not including political rights. Both Trumbull and Wilson asserted that the privileges and immunities clause of the proposed constitutional amendment related only to fundamental rights and did not abridge existing state laws on voting, jury service, and separate schools. Bingham also distinguished between fundamental and political rights. About thirty members of Congress, in addition to the proposed amendment's three principal advocates, spoke on the bill and the amendment. To enable the reader to comprehend the perspectives in the Congress, I will turn, in the balance of this section, to excerpts from those remarks illustrating the character of the debate over the bill and amendment.

Congressman William Lawrence of Ohio, a common pleas judge and editor of the *Western Law Monthly,* approvingly quoted Washington's opinion. He asserted that "there are some inherent and inalienable rights, pertaining to every citizen which cannot be abolished or abridged by state constitutions or laws." These rights include "the absolute right to life, the right to personal security, personal liberty, and the right to acquire and enjoy property. These are the rights of citizenship."[40] He asserted that the Civil Rights Bill would have a very broad impact; it would protect every citizen in the exercise of fundamental liberties. "It is scarcely less to the people of this country than Magna Charta was to the people of England."[41] The legislation required that "whatever of certain civil rights may be enjoyed by any shall be shared by all citizens in each State and in the Territories."[42] He maintained that the bill did not affect any political right, as that of suffrage, the right to sit on juries, and hold office.

Representative Cook of Illinois strongly supported the Civil Rights Bill.

> Now, sir, I am prepared, for myself, to say that when those rights which are enumerated in this bill are denied to any class of men on account of race or color, when they are subject to a system of vagrant laws which sells them into slavery or involuntary servitude, which operates upon them as upon no other part of the community, they are not secured in the rights of freedom. If a man can be sold, the man is a slave. If he is nominally freed by the [Thirteenth] amendment to the Constitution, he has nothing in the world he can call his own; he has simply the labor of his hands on which he can depend. Any combination of men in his neighborhood can prevent him from having any chance to support himself by his labor. They can pass a law that a man not supporting himself by labor shall be deemed a vagrant, and that a vagrant shall be sold . . . .[43]

Representative Raymond of New York (editor of the *New York Times*) construed the Civil Rights Act as "securing an equality of rights to all citizens of

the United states, and of all persons within their jurisdiction."[44] Although he favored its principles,[45] he voted against the bill because of his belief that Congress lacked authority to enact it.[46] He was therefore pleased to support the proposed Fourteenth Amendment because it secures equality of rights among all citizens of the United States.

Senator Hendricks of Indiana (an opponent) stated that the act would provide "that the civil rights of all men, without regard to color, shall be equal."[47] Congressman Kerr of Indiana (an opponent) believed that, under the measure, "Congress may, then, go into any State and break down any State constitutions or laws which discriminate in any way against any class of persons within or without the State." It would be able to "determine for each State the civil *status* of every person, of any race or color, who should elect to settle therein."[48]

Senator Davis spoke at length against the Civil Rights Bill, asserting that it violated both the Ninth Amendment and the meaning of the "privileges and immunities" clause by imposing congressional power over the states as opposed to the rights of the citizens of one state who go to another state. He contended that a constitutional amendment would be needed to assert the power that the Civil Rights Bill was intended to wield. Davis argued that "every doctrine [in *Corfield*] and every right and privilege of the citizen it establishes under the [privileges and immunities clause] appertains to a citizen residing in his own state and claiming these immunities or privileges in another State, or they attach to a citizen of one State who has removed into the other State and changed his relationship." Therefore, the proposed Civil Rights Act, which would "legislate upon the person or property of white citizens or negroes who have always lived in one State, and who have no business and no transactions and claim no rights or immunities in another state, is flagrantly unconstitutional and void."[49]

Senator Trumbull replied to Davis:

> Sir, this bill applies to white men as well as black men. It declares that all persons in the United States shall be entitled to the same civil rights, the right of the fruit of their own labor, the right to make contracts, the right to buy and sell, and enjoy liberty and happiness . . . it does not propose to regulate the political rights of individuals; it has nothing to do with the right of suffrage, or any other political right; but is simply intended to carry out a constitutional provision, and guaranty to every person of every color the same civil rights.[50]

Representative Shellabarger of Ohio noted that the Civil Rights Bill was limited to protecting citizens from deprivations on account of race or color:

> It does seem to me that Government which has the exclusive right to confer citizenship, and which is entitled to demand service and allegiance, which is supreme over that due to any State, may, nay, must, protect those

citizens in those rights which are fairly conducive and appropriate and necessary to the attainment of his "protection" as a citizen. And I think these rights to contract, sue, testify, inherit, etc., . . . are of that class which are fairly conducive and necessary as means to the constitutional end, to wit, the protection of the rights of person and property of a citizen.[51]

Representative Hill of Indiana sought unsuccessfully to amend the bill by excepting from its protection "those who have voluntarily borne arms against the Government of the United States or given aid and comfort to the enemies thereof." He concluded that the bill protected these individuals.[52]

Senator Cowan of Pennsylvania contended that the bill

confers . . . upon everybody native born in all the States, the right to make and enforce contracts, because there is no qualification in the bill, and the very object of the bill is to override the qualifications that are upon those rights in the States. . . . I . . . am quite willing . . . that all the people of this country shall enjoy the rights conferred by this bill. . . . That all men should have the right to contract, I agree. . . . I might limit the right of a great many people to purchase and hold real estate, but as a general proposition I would allow them to purchase, hold, and lease, and to be entitled to their remedies for the defense of their property. There is no doubt in my mind about that.

But, Cowan insisted, these rights should be regulated by state legislation.[53]

Senator Wilson of Massachusetts denounced a Louisiana law that required freedmen to get home in twenty days, or else be subject to prosecution under vagrancy laws, and that also denied them the right to sell or lease land:

We must annul this; we must see to it that the man made free by the Constitution of the United States, sanctioned by the voice of the American people, is a freeman indeed; that he can go where he pleases, work when and for whom he pleases; that he can sue and be sued; that he can lease and buy and sell and own property . . . that the rights and guarantees of the good old common law are his, and that he walks the earth, proud and erect in the conscious dignity of a free man, who knows that his cabin, however humble, is protected by the just and equal laws of this country.[54]

According to Senator Sherman of Ohio, there was never any doubt about the construction of the privileges and immunities clause of Article IV: "that is, a man who was recognized as a citizen of one state had a right to go anywhere within the United States and exercise the immunities of a citizen of the United States."[55] Congressman Higby of California argued that Article IV's privileges

and immunities clause had been "trampled under foot; it has been considered in certain States of this Union as nugatory and of no force whatsoever." If it had been properly enforced, "a citizen of New York would have been treated as a citizen of South Carolina. . . . The man who was a citizen of one State would have been considered and respected as a citizen in every other State in the Union." The intent of the proposed Fourteenth Amendment was "to give force and effect and vitality to that provision of the Constitution which has been regarded heretofore as nugatory and powerless."[56]

Congressman Kelley of Pennsylvania contended that the Constitution was intended to cure the defects of the Articles of Confederation, which had "failed utterly to accomplish its purpose" as a national government. He pointed to the privileges and immunities clause in Article IV of the Constitution as a dormant power that required reaffirmation: "The war against the rebellion called into energetic activity vital powers of the Government that had lain dormant since the adoption of the Constitution because they had never been called into action by the exigency against which they were ordained to provide."[57]

Speaking in favor of the bill, Congressman Thayer of Pennsylvania distinguished fundamental from political rights:

> [T]he words themselves are 'civil rights and immunities,' not political privileges; and nobody can successfully contend that a bill guarantying simply civil rights and immunities is a bill under which you could extend the right of suffrage, which is a political privilege and not a civil right. . . . The sole purpose of the bill is to secure to that class of persons (freedmen) the fundamental rights of citizenship; those rights which constitute the essence of freedom, and which are common to the citizens of all civilized States; those rights which secure life, liberty, and property, and which make all men equal before the law, as they are equal in the scales of eternal justice and in the eyes of God.[58]

Congressman Broomall of Pennsylvania asserted that the object of the Civil Rights Act is two-fold: to declare who are citizens of the United States and to secure them the protection that every government owes its citizens: "For thirty years prior to 1860 everybody knows that the rights and immunities of citizens were habitually and systematically denied in certain States to the citizens of other States: the right of speech, the right of transit, the right of domicile, the right to sue, the writ of *habeas corpus,* and the right of petition." Broomall argued that this state of affairs would not disappear simply by abolishing slavery. In addition, loyal whites were also denied their rights in the post-war South.[59]

Broomall asserted that the bill's "terms embrace the late rebels, and it gives them the rights, privileges, and immunities of citizens of the United States." The bill would help "secure protection to the loyal men of the south" who were

victims in their person and property of oppression and prosecution in Southern states only because of their loyalty to the Union. "[L]oyal men who . . . have had their property confiscated by the State courts, and are denied remedy in the courts of [the] reconstructed South" would deservedly be accorded federal protections.[60]

Congressman Kerr, speaking against the bill, stated:

> This bill rests upon the theory that Congress has the right to declare who shall be citizens of the United States, and then to provide that *such* citizens shall enjoy in the *States* all the privileges and immunities allowed therein to the most favored class of citizens of such State. . . . We may thus . . . become *Africanized, Mexicanized, or Coolyized,* and our glorious institutions and national and personal individuality give place to anarchy and weakness.

He declared that Judge Washington's description of privileges and immunities in *Corfield* was correct; however, "[t]hese views were uttered in reference alone to white citizens." Criticizing the Civil Rights Bill, he stated: "It asserts the right of Congress to regulate the laws which shall govern in acquisition and ownership of property in the States, and who may go there and purchase and hold property, and to protect such persons in the enjoyment of it. The right of the State to regulate its own internal and domestic affairs . . . is denied. . . . Congress, in short, may erect a great centralized, consolidated despotism in this capital."[61]

Representative Price of Iowa, who identified himself as a layman and not as a constitutional lawyer, said that the privileges and immunities clause of the proposed Fourteenth Amendment meant "to give the same rights, privileges and protection to the citizen of one state going into another that a citizen of that state would have who had lived there for years."[62]

Representative Woodbridge of Vermont stated that the object of the proposed amendment was to give Congress the power to enact laws to protect the natural rights pertaining to citizenship, the inalienable rights to life and liberty, the privileges and immunities already secured, and property rights. This congressman believed that the adoption of the amendment "will be no shock upon the present well arranged system, defining the powers of the General Government and the States, under which we have so happily lived."[63]

IV. *Paul v. Virginia*

Representatives John Bingham, Thaddeus Stevens, and James F. Wilson, and Senators Jacob Howard and Lyman Trumbull, the principal congressional proponents of Section 1 of the proposed Fourteenth Amendment, and at least

most of the other supporters of the proposed amendment, generally agreed with Justice Washington's interpretation of the meaning of privileges and immunities in Article IV of the Constitution. They regarded the privileges and immunities clause of Article IV as a major protection for the fundamental rights of the people and sought to secure it nationally under the proposed amendment. After all, many of their ancestors had likely migrated to the new world trusting the English government's promise to fully protect all migrants' privileges and immunities. And, as Wilson put it, no one had since then "surrendered a jot or tittle of these rights."

In accepting Washington's opinion on the meaning of the clause, the Thirty-Ninth Congress was echoing the prevailing judicial opinion. Historical background, judicial opinions, and the plain language of the clause strongly supported Washington's interpretation. Nevertheless, beginning in 1868, the United States Supreme Court entered opinions that basically reversed Washington. In that year, the Court decided *Paul v. Virginia,*[64] which rejected the fundamental liberties approach of *Corfield,* and in 1872, in the *Slaughterhouse Cases,*[65] the Court threw out of the Constitution any significant substantive meaning for the privileges or immunities clause of the Fourteenth Amendment.[66] I shall discuss these cases in this and the next section.

The *Paul* case interpreted the privileges and immunities clause of Article IV. It involved an 1866 Virginia statute that barred any insurance company not incorporated in the state from carrying on its business within the state without previously receiving a license for that purpose, which it could only obtain by depositing state or certain other bonds in an amount varying from thirty to fifty thousand dollars. No such deposit was required of a domestic insurer. The statute was assailed for, among other things, violating the privileges and immunities clause of Article IV, because Virginia discriminated between its own corporations and those of other states. The United States Supreme Court, in a unanimous opinion by Justice Field, upheld the statute for two reasons. First, corporations are not citizens within the meaning of the privileges and immunities clause of Article IV. Second, corporations are creations of local law, and have no absolute right of recognition in other states, but depend for that and for the enforcement of their contracts upon the assent of other states, which the latter may give on such terms as they please. According to Field, a grant of corporate existence is a grant of special privileges to the corporators, which, as special privileges enjoyed by citizens in their own states, are not secured by the Article IV clause. He thus excluded special state privileges, which he defined only with respect to corporations, from the protections offered by the clause.

After discussing the paucity of rights that corporations possess under the privileges and immunities clause (of Article IV)—and without any reference to *Corfield* or any other decision or commentary—Field went on to assert that it was "undoubtedly the object of the clause in question to place the citizens of

each State upon the same footing with citizens of other states, so far as the advantages resulting from citizenship in these states are concerned." He feared that states could create corporations that other states would have to recognize, giving each originating state excessive powers "utterly destructive of the independence and the harmony of the States." This position ignored the vital character of the privileges and immunities clause in the American political system, what Hamilton referred to as "the basis of the Union": the protection of fundamental rights. Instead, he pursued a vastly different position based on an idea of a limited equality between citizens in different states:

> [Article IV's privileges and immunities clause] relieves [citizens of each state] from the disabilities of alienage in other States; it inhibits discriminatory legislation against them by other States; it insures to them in other States the same freedom possessed by the citizens of those States in the acquisition and enjoyment of property and in the pursuit of happiness; and it secures to them in other States the equal protection of their laws.

Field thus rejected the idea that the clause was a substantive guarantee of fundamental rights. Instead, he decided that the clause embraced a much more limited anti-discrimination principle. Thus, if a person from New York went to Mississippi and was totally denied freedom of speech and other basic rights, there would be no constitutional difficulty so long as the citizens of Mississippi had likewise been denied the same rights.[67] Field was in time to recognize the great error in his interpretation of the clause, but a majority of the court has never reversed his opinion in the *Paul* case. Writing in 1873, for himself and three other dissenting justices in the *Slaughterhouse* cases (discussed subsequently in this chapter), Field approved Justice Washington's understanding of the clause in *Corfield* and stated as follows:

> The privileges and immunities of citizens of the United States, of every one of them, is secured against abridgment in any form by any State. The Fourteenth Amendment places them under the guardianship of the National Authority. . . .
>
> The amendment was intended to give practical effect to the declaration of 1776 of inalienable rights, rights which are the gift of the Creator, which the law does not confer, but only recognizes. . . .
>
> [The] equality of right with exemption from all disparaging and partial enactments in the lawful pursuit of life, throughout the whole country, is the distinguishing privilege of citizens of the United States. . . .

In his discussion of the privileges or immunities clause of the Fourteenth Amendment in the *Slaughterhouse Cases,* Field approved Washington's inter-

pretation of the privileges and immunities clause of Article IV, thereby reject-ing the meaning he had presented in *Paul*. In *Paul*, Field got it right with re-spect to the absence of rights for foreign corporations under the privileges and immunities clause of Article IV, since only fundamental liberties, regardless of whether or not they are in corporate form, were protected by the clause. But, as his later opinions acknowledged, he initially misunderstood the full meaning of this critical provision. The clause secured against the denial of fundamental lib-erties and not merely against discrimination. As a result of *Paul*, Article IV, Section 2 has long been interpreted to require that the rights a state grants or es-tablishes for its own citizens, neither more nor less, is the measure in that state of the rights of citizens of other states.

V. The *Slaughterhouse Cases*

The first test of the protections contained in Section 1 of the Fourteenth Amendment occurred in the famous *Slaughterhouse Cases*, decided in 1872. Also at issue in *Slaughterhouse* was the Thirteenth Amendment (1865), which prohibits slavery and involuntary servitude.

The problem presented in this first test did not directly involve the Fourteenth Amendment's central concern, which was securing fundamental rights for the recently emancipated blacks and providing them federal protection against in-fringement of such rights by the states. In 1869, Louisiana's legislature granted a twenty-five year exclusive privilege to a private corporation it had created to operate a regulated livestock and slaughterhouse business within a specified area of about 1,150 square miles, comprising New Orleans and two other parishes. The statute required that all cattle brought into this area for commercial purposes be slaughtered by the corporation or in its facilities, and it ordered the closing of other existing slaughterhouses. An association of butchers who were adversely affected brought suit on the basis that the monopoly grant violated the Thirteenth and Fourteenth Amendments—the former by creating an involuntary servitude, and the latter by depriving plaintiffs of their privileges and immunities as United States citizens, of liberty and property without due process of law, and of equal protection under the laws. However, the argument principally involved the priv-ileges or immunities clause. The Supreme Court upheld the monopoly grant by a 5–4 vote, with the dissenters contending that despite the facts' seeming re-moteness to the Fourteenth Amendment's purposes, the Louisiana statute vio-lated one or more of the last three clauses of Section 1.

As their counsel, the butchers hired John Campbell, a former member of the Supreme Court, who had resigned when his home state of Alabama seceded from the Union. He argued that the privileges or immunities clause of the Fourteenth Amendment extended to all citizens federal safeguards for a variety of civil rights,

including the protection of the plaintiffs' interests in pursuing their occupations and businesses. According to Campbell, the amendment's framers intended to convert the privileges and immunities of state citizenship into privileges and immunities of national citizenship: "The States . . . have been placed under the oversight and restraining and enforcing hand of Congress." Supporting Campbell's position was the meaning Justice Washington gave, in *Corfield v. Coryell,* to the privileges and immunities phrase contained in Article IV, Section 2.

Justice Samuel F. Miller, writing for the majority, rejected Campbell's argument that the Fourteenth Amendment provides federal protection for the rights mentioned by Justice Washington. In its opinion, the Court's majority virtually removed the privileges or immunities clause from the Fourteenth Amendment. Miller divided the rights of citizenship into two categories: federal and state. He said that the category Justice Washington defined was not intended as protection for the citizens of a state against the legislative power of their own state; instead, the rights enumerated by Washington were solely rights of state citizenship and under state protection. The constitutional amendment placed only the privileges and immunities of United States citizens under federal protection. These were those privileges and immunities that "owe their existence to the Federal government, its national character, its Constitution, or its laws," and they are quite limited. They include the right to come to the seat of government, to assert claims against it, to seek its protection from foreign governments, to transact business with it, to have free access to the nation's seaports and courts, to peacefully assemble and petition for redress of grievances, to be protected by the writ of habeas corpus, and to demand the protection of the federal government when outside the country.

Dissenting justices asserted that preservation of these rights hardly required an extensive constitutional amendment. However, Miller contended that the construction that was sought by the butchers would

> constitute this court a perpetual censor upon all legislation of the States, on the civil rights of their own citizens, with authority to nullify such as it did not approve as consistent with those rights, as they existed at the time of the adoption of this amendment. . . . But when, as in the case before us, these consequences are so great a departure from the structure and spirit of our institutions; when the effect is to fetter and degrade the State governments by subjecting them to the control of Congress, in the exercise of powers heretofore universally conceded to them of the most ordinary and fundamental character; when in fact it radically changes the whole theory of the relations of the State and Federal governments to each other and of both these governments to the people; the argument has a force that is irresistible, in the absence of language which expresses such a purpose too clearly to admit of doubt.

Miller asserted that he was "convinced that no such results were intended by the Congress which proposed these amendments, nor by the Legislatures of the States, which ratified them." It was not the purpose, he claimed, of the Fourteenth Amendment to transfer the security and protection of civil rights from the states to the federal government. The interpretation the butchers sought would transform the character of the United States government at the expense of the states, and is not persuasive "in the absence of language which expresses such a purpose too clearly to admit of doubt."

It is impossible to read the Thirty-Ninth Congress's debates on the Fourteenth Amendment and be persuaded by Justice Miller's conclusion that the Congress did not intend to secure nationally the liberties expressed in Section 1 of the amendment. As Justice Thomas explained in the *Saenz* case,

> Justice Washington's opinion in *Corfield* indisputably influenced the members of Congress who enacted the Fourteenth Amendment. When Congress gathered to debate the Fourteenth Amendment, members frequently, if not as a matter of course, appealed to *Corfield,* arguing that the Amendment was necessary to guarantee the fundamental rights that Justice Washington identified in his opinion.[68]

Thus, it appears that their concern for the maintenance of the existing federal system caused the Court's majority to reject national involvement in the protection of the fundamental rights of citizens—a legitimate purpose and one which the congressional debates show was actually intended by the amendment's framers. Bingham and the other framers correctly interpreted the privileges and immunities clause of Article IV, Section 2 as belonging, as Justice Washington asserted, "of right, to the citizens of all free governments," and did not distinguish between those belonging to citizens of states and those belonging to citizens of the federal government. As law professor Charles Fairman put it: "In recoiling from consequences they considered too subversive of the federal system, the majority felt driven to a construction that made the clause trivial."[69] In time, the Court interpreted the due process clause of the Fourteenth Amendment to secure many rights that the amendment's framers assigned to the privileges or immunities clause.[70]

Miller was even less impressed with the plaintiffs' arguments concerning due process and equal protection. He did not address their contention concerning the deprivation of liberty and he dismissed their property arguments almost in passing. He stated that inquiring into the meaning of the due process clause was unnecessary, for

> it is sufficient to say that under no construction of that provision that we have ever seen, or any that we deem admissible, can the restraint imposed

by the State of Louisiana upon the exercise of their trade by the butchers of New Orleans be held to be a deprivation of property within the meaning of that provision.

Miller did not cite any cases in support of this statement. As for the equal protection clause, he claimed that it was intended to remove discrimination against blacks and doubted very much whether any state action not directed toward such discrimination would ever be held to come within the purview of this provision.

Miller's opinion has been subject to considerable criticism in the legal community, both for his constitutional and common law interpretations. Interestingly, the opinion was written by a justice who on other occasions displayed an acute understanding of the law of private property. Notwithstanding what may be implied by the quoted portions of his *Slaughterhouse* opinion, there is reason to conclude that Miller did believe that the due process clause provided certain substantive protections for the ownership of private property. A literal reading of Miller's language suggests no more than that the commercial activities in question were not secured by due process. This conclusion, however, does not mean that vested property rights (as distinguished from economic rights) were outside the clause's scope. That Miller was inclined to include such rights is revealed by his decision in a case (*Bartemeyer v. Iowa*) that was submitted in briefs at the time that *Slaughterhouse* was argued, but that was not decided until the following year. In *Bartemeyer,* Iowa's statewide prohibition law, which had been enacted in 1851, came under attack as a violation of the due process clause of the Fourteenth Amendment. Miller wrote that a statute prohibiting the sale of property would raise "very grave questions" under the Fourteenth Amendment's due process clause and he cited *Wynehamer* (discussed in Chapter 4) as supporting such a proposition. However, according to Miller, the Iowa case did not present this issue, for it was "absurd to suppose that the plaintiff, an ordinary retailer of drinks, could have proved [in 1870] . . . that he had owned that particular glass of whisky prior to the prohibitory liquor law of 1851."[71]

In *Yates v. Milwaukee* (1870), Miller, writing for a unanimous Court, threw out Milwaukee's declaration that a certain structure was an obstruction in a river (thus making it a nuisance) without the city proving that it in fact had that character. The city sought to demolish the structure merely on the basis of this declaration. The existence of such power, Miller stated, "would place house, every business, and all of the property of the city, at the uncontrolled will of the temporary local authorities." Subsequently, in 1871, Miller—again for a unanimous court—authored the opinion in *Pumpelly v. Green Bay & Mississippi Canal Co.,* holding that a flooding of private property caused by the installation of a government-sponsored dam constituted a taking of private property and thus required the payment of compensation. The record shows that, on the

whole, Miller supported property rights. (Both *Yates* and *Pumpelly* are discussed in Chapter 4, Section IV.)

In 1869, a 6–3 majority of the Supreme Court held that the Legal Tender Act of 1862 violated, among other provisions, the Fifth Amendment's due process clause by impairing the value of property held by creditors. This act had compelled creditors to accept legal tender worth far less than any amount originally contracted for.[72] The Court viewed the act as being confiscatory. Although two years later the Court reversed its holding, it did not reconsider that portion of the decision relating to due process.[73]

Based on this context, had vested property rights been at issue in the *Slaughterhouse Cases,* the due process clause might possibly have demanded a different outcome. However, at that time the majority was not prepared to regard a person's calling, trade, occupation, or labor as property, or the right to engage in it as a protected liberty (or as property).

Each dissenting *Slaughterhouse* opinion viewed property and liberty in the more expansive terms that would later in the century become judicially acceptable. Justices Field, Bradley, and Swayne filed separate dissents, with Chief Justice Chase and the two other dissenters joining with Field. Justice Swayne concurred in Bradley's opinion. The dissenters acknowledged that the well-being of the former slaves may have been the amendment's primary concern, but they nevertheless maintained that its language was purposefully made general in order to embrace citizens and persons. They accepted Campbell's argument that the amendment provided federal safeguards for all people in the United States against deprivation of their fundamental rights by state legislatures.

The written dissents contain many memorable passages on the relationship between the government and the governed. For the most part, Field limited his remarks to privileges or immunities, but in later opinions he applied this same reasoning to due process. Bradley and Swayne argued that all three clauses had been violated. Field castigated legislative monopoly as encroaching "upon the liberty of citizens to acquire property and pursue happiness" contrary to the privileges or immunities clause; Bradley declared that "a law which prohibits a large class of citizens from adopting a lawful employment, or from following a lawful employment previously adopted, does deprive them of liberty as well as property, without due process of law." United States citizenship, he wrote, "is not an empty name—citizenship means something—it carries certain incidental rights, privileges and immunities of the greatest importance." For Justice Swayne, the language of all three clauses is unqualified in its economic scope: "[A] more flagrant and indefensible invasion of the rights of many for the benefit of a few has not occurred in the legislative history of the country." Fairly construed, he stated, "these amendments may be said to rise to the dignity of a new Magna Charta."

Field asserted that the Fourteenth Amendment was intended to give practical effect to the Declaration of Independence, and he interpreted the privileges

or immunities clause to mean that all pursuits were open to citizens, subject to some regulations imposed equally upon everyone similarly situated:

> What the clause [in Article IV] did for the protection of the citizens of one State against hostile and discriminating legislation of other States, the fourteenth amendment does for the protection of every citizen of the United States against hostile and discriminating legislation against him in the favor of others, whether they reside in the same or in different States. If under the fourth article of the Constitution equality of privileges and immunities is secured between citizens of different States, under the fourteenth amendment the same equality is secured between citizens of the United States.

The dissenting justices saw no problem in considering the butchers' loss to be one of both liberty and property. Thus, as Bradley stated, "[t]his right to choose one's calling is an essential part of that liberty which it is the object of government to protect; and a calling, when chosen, is a man's property and right. . . . Their right of choice is a portion of their liberty; their occupation is their property."

Swayne gave an extensive meaning to property and emphasized its importance in the larger society:

> Property is everything which has an exchangeable value, and the right of property includes the power to dispose of it according to the will of the owner. Labor is property, and as such merits protection. The right to make it available is next in importance to the rights of life and liberty. It lies to a large extent at the foundation of most other forms of property, and of all solid individual and national prosperity.

Consistent with Justice Washington's position, four Supreme Court justices believed that the Fourteenth Amendment safeguarded from state limitations "those privileges and immunities which are, in their nature, fundamental." For them, the amendment meant that the federal judiciary would have the power to perpetuate individual liberties by the exercise of a veto over state economic regulation. They saw the amendment as achieving a free society's goals of maintaining liberty at a maximum and of removing restraints that impede individuals from fulfilling their rightful ambitions. Under this view, the amendment applied the libertarian foundations of American constitutional government to the states.

Bradley and Field were strong opponents of slavery (Field was appointed by Lincoln, and Bradley by Grant), and the opinions they expressed in this case reflect the convictions of the antislavery movement and the principles of what has

been referred to as the "jurisprudence of antislavery." Among the rights to which the abolitionists gave prime attention were those of property and contract, both of which were demolished by the statute at issue in *Slaughterhouse*. The abolitionists wanted Section 1 of the Fourteenth Amendment to be the federal government's broad and sweeping guarantee of fundamental political, material, and intellectual rights, thus enabling the poor to elevate their economic condition. The ruling in *Slaughterhouse* that fundamental rights are not attributes of United States citizenship and therefore not constitutionally protected against state action, was a severe blow to the civil rights movement of that period.

In 1879, Louisiana adopted a new constitution that abolished monopoly grants. In 1884, the United States Supreme Court, confronted with the issue of whether Louisiana could limit the slaughterhouse monopoly under the terms of the federal Constitution's contracts clause, unanimously upheld this power.[74] Justices Field and Bradley, along with two justices who had been appointed after the *Slaughterhouse* decision, concurred in the result, contending that the grant had never been valid. Both of the former reiterated the positions they had taken twelve years earlier. Bradley's remarks provided one of the foundations for the 1897 decision in *Allgeyer v. Louisiana,* in which the U.S. Supreme Court constitutionalized liberty of contract under the Fourteenth Amendment's due process clause and thereby formally commenced the economic due process period of the federal judiciary.[75] During this period, which commenced in the late 1890s and terminated in the 1930s, the Court protected economic activity against federal and state regulation under the due process and equal protection clauses.[76] In time, Justice Field embraced the due process clause as a guarantor of economic liberty and he had far-reaching influence among the state courts in fostering acceptance of the liberty of contract doctrine. He subsequently wrote a number of opinions emphasizing the inclusiveness of substantive due process.

VI. *Saenz v. Roe*

The 5–4 decision in the *Slaughterhouse Cases* effectively removed the privileges or immunities clause of Section 1 of the Fourteenth Amendment as a protection for fundamental rights. Since that decision, the U.S. Supreme Court has held in only two cases that the amendment's privileges or immunities clause was violated. The first decision was *Colgate v. Harvey* (1935),[77] which was overruled five years later by *Madden v. Kentucky* (1940).[78] *Colgate* invalidated a Vermont statute that taxed dividends and interest earned outside the state but none on such earnings made within the state. Applying the views of the dissenting justices in the *Slaughterhouse Cases,* the majority opinion held: "The right of a citizen of the United States to engage in business, to transact any lawful business, or to make a lawful loan of money in any state other than that in

which the citizen resides is a privilege equally attributable to his national citizenship." The power asserted by Vermont enabled it to tax so heavily as to limit loans made outside the state. In response to this, the Court stated: "It reasonably is not open to doubt that the discriminatory tax here imposed abridges the privilege of a citizen of the United States to loan his money and make contracts with respect thereto in any part of the United States."

Four years later, the Court in *Madden* overruled *Colgate* by upholding a Kentucky statute that taxed money deposited in banks outside the state five times as much as on money deposited in banks within the state. The minority in *Colgate* and the majority in *Madden* each contended that the privileges or immunities clause of the Fourteenth Amendment only protected interests growing out of the relationship between the national government and its citizens, which was the position originally taken by Justice Miller. *Madden* reflected the change that occurred on the Supreme Court with respect to the protection of economic liberties. In 1938, in *United States v. Carolene Products Co.*,[79] the Court held that legislative bodies were entitled to great deference in upholding economic regulations, virtually removing constitutional protection for economic liberties. *Madden* was consistent with that position, while *Colgate* was contrary to it.

Mention might also be made of *Edwards v. California*,[80] in which the Court in 1941 unanimously secured the right of interstate travel against a California statute that prohibited indigents from freely moving into the state. Five justices held that the statute imposed an unconstitutional burden on interstate commerce. For the other four justices, the right to move and locate freely from state to state was one of national citizenship that was protected by the privileges or immunities clause of the Fourteenth Amendment against state interference.

The second case in which the Court held that the Fourteenth Amendment's privileges or immunities clause was violated is *Saenz v. Roe* (1999). This case involved a 1992 California statute limiting the maximum welfare benefits available to a family during its first year of residency in the state to the amount payable by the state of the family's prior residence. This case raised the issue of whether the 1992 enactment was consistent with both the privileges or immunities clause of the Fourteenth Amendment and the right to travel and, if not, whether an amendment to the Social Security Act enacted by Congress in 1996 supporting California's law validates it.

The plaintiffs in *Saenz* were three California residents, each of whom alleged she had recently moved to the state to live with relatives in order to escape abusive family circumstances. As a result of the statute, the former residents of Louisiana and Oklahoma would receive monthly $190 and $341, respectively, for a family of three, even though the full California grant was $641. The former resident of Colorado, who had just one child, was limited to $280 a month as compared to the full California grant of $504 for a family of two. The cost

of living for welfare recipients was much higher in California than in the three other states. The state justified its statute concerning the reduction of welfare benefits chiefly on the undisputed evidence that it would save the state some $10.9 million in annual welfare costs, which themselves totaled $2.9 billion. The federal district and circuit courts struck down the statute on the basis that it created a substantial difference in benefits awarded to newer residents and longer term residents of California.

In sustaining the opinions of the lower courts, a Supreme Court majority of 7–2, per Justice John Paul Stevens, viewed prior decisions upholding the "right to travel" as determinative of the outcome:

> The "right to travel" discussed in our cases embraces at least three different components. It protects the right of a citizen of one State to enter and to leave another State, the right to be treated as a welcome visitor rather than an unfriendly alien when temporarily present in the second State, and, for those travelers who elect to become permanent residents, the right to be treated like other citizens of that State.

Stevens stated that, for purposes of this case, the Court "need not identify the source" of the first component in the text of the Constitution. The right to travel freely across state lines was vindicated in the 1941 *Edwards* case and in subsequent decisions. The source of the second component is the privileges and immunities clause of Article IV, and the source of the third component is "plainly identified in the opening words of the Fourteenth Amendment." According to Stevens, the right to travel in this case involved the right of a recently arrived citizen to enjoy the same privileges and immunities enjoyed by other citizens of the same state. In contrast to Justice Miller's opinion in the *Slaughterhouse Cases,* Stevens declared that this right "is protected not only by the new arrival's status as a state citizen, but also by her status as a citizen of the United States." Miller had insisted that the Fourteenth Amendment's privileges or immunities clause was not intended as federal protection for the citizens of a state against the legislative power of their own state. Unlike Miller, who distinguished between the rights of state and federal citizenship, Stevens viewed the two political sources as together adding "special force" to the claim of the newly arrived citizens that they have the same rights as others who share their citizenship:

> Neither mere rationality nor some intermediate standard of review should be used to judge the constitutionality of a state rule that discriminates against some of its citizens because they have been domiciled in the State for less than a year. The appropriate standard may be more categorical than that articulated in [*Shapiro v. Thompson*], but it surely is no less strict.

Decided in 1969, *Shapiro v. Thompson*[81] involved laws of Connecticut, Pennsylvania, and the District of Columbia denying welfare assistance to residents who had resided in those jurisdictions less than one year. The Court struck down these laws as violating the right to travel, making no reference to the Fourteenth Amendment's privileges or immunities clause. The Court in *Shapiro* did not designate the source of this right to travel to a particular constitutional provision, stating that it had long "recognized that the nature of our Federal Union and our constitutional concepts of personal liberty unite to require that all citizens be free to travel throughout the length and breadth of our land uninhibited by statutes, rules or regulations which unreasonably burden or restrict this movement." The *Shapiro* Court further held (1) that it was "constitutionally impermissible" for a state to enact durational residency requirements for the purpose of inhibiting the migration of needy persons into the state, and (2) that a classification that effectively imposed a penalty on this right of travel violated this right "unless shown to be necessary to promote a compelling governmental interest." No such showing was made in the case sufficient to satisfy the high standard of scrutiny that the Court imposed. Stevens rejected any constitutional distinction between the difference in welfare payments required in *Shapiro* and *Saenz,* because, in both cases, recipients were treated differently than persons who were citizens of longer duration.

Despite varying views concerning the coverage of the Fourteenth Amendment's privileges or immunities clause, such as those expressed in the majority and dissenting opinions in the *Slaughterhouse Cases,* Stevens asserted that it has always been common ground that this clause protects the right of recently arrived persons, who elect to become permanent residents, to be treated like other citizens of that state who have resided there for longer periods. Stevens subjected to strict scrutiny California's reason for limiting payments to residents of less than a year, and he found no compelling interest justifying the statutory restriction. Neither deterring welfare applicants from migrating to California nor the state saving $10.9 million annually justified the law:

> Were we concerned solely with actual deterrence to migration, we might be persuaded that a partial withholding of benefits constitutes a lesser incursion on the right to travel than an outright denial of all benefits [citations]. But since the right to travel embraces the citizen's right to be treated equally in her new state of residence, the discriminatory classification is itself a penalty.

However, the Court had previously upheld one-year residency requirements for obtaining in-state college tuition benefits and a divorce, and sustained durational residency requirements for voting in primary elections. It distinguished these requirements on the basis that "readily portable" benefits are involved

which will be enjoyed after the recipient returns to his original domicile. By contrast, welfare benefits will be consumed "while they remain in California [so] there is no danger . . . that citizens of other states will be encouraged to establish residency for just long enough" to obtain the benefit and then depart.

With respect to the 1996 congressional legislation that amended the Social Security Act, Stevens held that this enactment which approved California's durational residency requirement did not resuscitate its limitation on the welfare payments litigated in *Saenz*. Congress, he asserted, does not possess constitutional authority to authorize the state to violate the Fourteenth Amendment.

Thus, the Supreme Court in *Saenz*—by an impressive margin—interpreted the Fourteenth Amendment's privileges or immunities clause as protecting, under a strict scrutiny analysis, certain welfare rights of residents of less than a year. It thereby reversed the *Slaughterhouse Cases* interpretation that the clause protected solely the relatively minor activities that Justice Miller identified in his opinion. The *Saenz* decision must be considered against the background of the 1969 *Shapiro* case, as well as a number of others over the years, construing the right to travel as a serious limitation on the power of the states to restrict welfare spending for newcomers. However, if one considers as its major holding the requirement that recently arrived persons in a state who elect to become permanent residents are entitled to equal treatment with longer residents of the state, the decision would protect numerous rights.

Chief Justice Rehnquist and Justice Thomas filed dissenting opinions in *Saenz*. Rehnquist viewed the case as affecting the privileges and immunities of recent citizens of California, that is, he considered whether the state could constitutionally provide welfare benefits for these citizens substantially less than for citizens who have lived in the state for at least one year. He concluded that the Supreme Court's prior decisions sustaining a one-year residency requirement (1) for obtaining an in-state level of tuition for state universities, (2) for eligibility to obtain a divorce in state courts, and (3) for the right to vote in primary elections should also be sustained for welfare payments. Rehnquist rejected any constitutional distinction between residency requirements for these three cases and those for welfare eligibility. He asserted that the distinction is judicially untenable because it requires investigation of the "essence" and "portability" of various benefits.

Justice Thomas's dissenting opinion, in which Rehnquist concurred, protested the failure of the majority to abide by the intended meaning of the privileges and immunities protections in the Constitution. He writes that at the time the Fourteenth Amendment was adopted, "[p]eople understood that 'privileges and immunities of citizens' were fundamental rights, rather than every public benefit established by positive law." Accordingly, the majority's conclusion in the case "appears contrary to the original understanding and is dubious at best." Furthermore, he states that it appears that no member of the Thirty-Ninth Congress

(which drafted the Fourteenth Amendment) rejected the notion that Justice Washington's analysis undergirded the meaning of the privileges or immunities clause.

Thomas objects that the course taken by the majority will yet be another convenient tool for inventing new rights, limited solely by the "predilections of those who happen to be Members of this Court." As explained earlier in this chapter, until the decision in *Paul v. Virginia* in 1868, the jurisprudence of the privileges and immunities clause of Article IV confined its protections to those which, as Justice Washington put it, "are, in their nature, fundamental; which belong of right, to the citizens of all free governments." Obviously, this meant that the protections of this clause were not applicable to rights not held to be fundamental. The rights not protected were those vested by the state for the benefit of the citizens of that state, as well as other political rights. Many members of the Thirty-Ninth Congress accepted this limitation upon the Fourteenth Amendment's privileges or immunities clause. In the Congressional debates on the Fourteenth Amendment, its proponents sought to assure states that the protections of Section 1 were not intended to deprive state legislators of their constitutional lawmaking powers. They contended that the states never possessed the power to abridge fundamental rights, and therefore should have no cause for complaint.

The funding required under the *Saenz* decision invades the political powers of states in respects other than the one that Justice Thomas alluded to. *Shapiro* struck down welfare statutes in various states and the District of Columbia that denied welfare assistance to those residing there for less than one year. These jurisdictions were, as a result, required to fund indigents from monies that had to be obtained from other welfare recipients or other state programs or new taxes, thereby invading the spending and taxing prerogatives of those states' legislatures.

Judges do not have the same options as legislators, who can choose among a great number of competing interests and values. Courts are supposed to decide only the matters that are submitted to them for adjudication. As the interpretive branch of government, they do not have the option of determining, for example, how much taxes should be collected and how much should be spent; they cannot determine the amount of funds that are designated for welfare or any other purpose, or how the welfare or other budgets should be allocated among competing interests. "Then," said the court in *San Antonio v. Rodriguez* (1973), a case which involved funding for public schools, "we stand on familiar grounds when we continue to acknowledge that the Justices of this Court lack the expertise and familiarity with local problems so necessary to the making of wise decisions with respect to the raising and disposition of public revenues."[82]

In *Dandridge v. Williams* (1970), the Supreme Court recognized the perils of exercising legislative powers when it sustained a Maryland regulation mandating a welfare limit of $250 monthly for each family, regardless of the family's size or need. According to the majority opinion in this case,

the intractable economic, social and even philosophical problems presented by public welfare assistance programs are not the business of this Court. . . . [T]he Constitution does not empower this Court to second-guess state officials charged with the difficult responsibility of allocating limited public welfare funds among the myriad of potential recipients.[83]

The majority opinion in *Saenz* ignores this position concerning the limited role of the courts. As is evident from the debates of the Thirty-Ninth Congress, Section 1 of the Fourteenth Amendment was intended to protect liberty and not to provide benefits and entitlements. In an opinion in another matter, U.S. Circuit Judge Richard Posner put the issue this way:

The men who wrote the Bill of Rights were not concerned that government might do too little for the people but that it might do too much to them. The Fourteenth amendment, adopted in 1868 at the height of laissez-faire thinking, sought to protect Americans from oppression by state government, not to secure them governmental services.[84]

Maher v. Roe, decided in the United States Supreme Court in 1977, presented an equal protection issue not unlike that involved in the *Saenz* case. In *Maher,* Connecticut displayed favoritism toward childbirth over abortion. It subsidized the medical expenses incident to pregnancy and childbirth, but not the expenses related to first trimester abortions except those that were medically necessary. Prior to the *Maher* case, the court in *Roe v. Wade* ruled that a woman had a constitutional right to obtain an abortion during the first trimester and up to the time when viability of the fetus occurs. Two indigent women who were unable to pay for an abortion sued Connecticut on the basis that it (1) had refused to fund the fundamental liberty of abortion and (2) had denied them equal treatment with women opting for childbirth. The Court rejected these arguments, stating that *Roe v. Wade* protected a woman seeking an abortion only from the enactment of legislation unduly burdening that right, and that nothing of this character had occurred. The reason that the woman could not obtain an abortion was her indigency and not because of any law passed by the state legislature.[85] Likewise in *Saenz,* California stated that its objective in passing the law was to conserve the state's financial resources, a claim which the Supreme Court did not reject with respect to saving money, but did reject as a justification for the legislation.

As explained above in Chapter 4, Section I, in determining the meaning of the privileges or immunities clause of the Fourteenth Amendment, the most important factor is the legal meaning at the time that it was submitted for ratification. Regardless of the meaning of this particular clause, people may have voted for the amendment because they favored some of its other provisions. Nevertheless, the political process generally assumes that a vote in favor of ratification of an amendment signifies a person's general acceptance of all its terms

and provisions. Yet, it is possible that many affirmative votes for the amendment did not constitute approval of the privileges or immunities clause. The situation is analogous to election of political candidates, since an individual candidate may support various positions that a voter rejects but who still obtains his vote because of the candidate's views on a particular matter.

Despite these limitations, the judiciary still is the final authority on the meaning of each provision of an amendment to the Constitution. It generally agrees with the view that a vote in favor of ratifying an amendment evidences the voter's approval of all its parts. However, there is no need to apply this rule to ascertain the meaning of the amendment's privileges or immunities clause. At the time the Fourteenth Amendment was approved by the Thirty-Ninth Congress in 1866, the most accepted judicial meaning for the privileges and immunities clause of Article IV was that issued by Justice Washington in the *Corfield* case. The amendment was ratified in July 1868. In December 1868, the U.S. Supreme Court decided *Paul v. Virginia,* substantially modifying the rule of *Corfield*. Accordingly, ratification by the states took place at a time when *Corfield* and not *Paul* provided the prevalent meaning for the clause. This kind of determination may seem "technical"; however, in the case of interpreting the Fourteenth Amendment's privileges or immunities clause, it is consistent with the history and background of the Article IV clause on which it was based.

In *Saenz,* Justice Stevens applied a measure of constitutional validity that is quite different than the one Justice Thomas seems to approve, which is essentially the *Corfield* standard. For Stevens, validity is determined by subjecting the state's durational classification for welfare payments to a strict scrutiny standard, regardless of whether or not a fundamental right is involved. (*Dandridge v. Williams* held that welfare was not a fundamental right.) However, *Corfield* confines privileges and immunities to fundamental rights; Washington's opinion does not protect benefits and entitlements that are enacted by a legislature, since none of these is a fundamental right.

Over the years, there have been many calls for reversal of the *Slaughterhouse Cases,* which some have referred to as the *Plessy v. Ferguson*[86]—the separate but equal decision—of economic liberties. This call has been answered, but with a very uncertain outcome. For many, the objective of reversing the *Slaughterhouse* decision was to protect economic liberties that the U.S. Supreme Court has not secured since 1938, when it issued *United States v. Carolene Products Co.*[87] In reversing the *Slaughterhouse Cases, Saenz* may be a step in that direction, but at best only a small one.

Let me briefly summarize this chapter up to this point. Section 1 of the Fourteenth Amendment is an important provision of the U.S. Constitution. Pursuant to it, the enumerated and unenumerated protections of the Constitution are applied to the states. The Thirty-Ninth Congress framed this amendment, and a majority of its members believed that both the privileges or immunities and due

process clauses of the amendment secured fundamental liberties that comprehended property and economic rights. This chapter thus far reveals that these intentions with respect to the privileges or immunities clause were applied only once in its long history, and that was in 1935 in the *Colgate* case, which struck down an effort by Vermont to protect the state's financial interests at the expense of financial interests outside of the state. The only other time that the amendment's privileges or immunities clause was used to invalidate state legislation occurred in 1999 in the *Saenz* case, an opinion with which the framers of the amendment would probably differ. In *Saenz,* the U.S. Supreme Court ruled that the privileges or immunities clause protected, under a strict standard of scrutiny, a state's payment of a prescribed amount of welfare funds to those in need. The difficulty with this decision is that the clause was not intended to relate to benefits and entitlements. Instead, it was intended to protect fundamental liberties, that is, liberties that an individual exercises largely on his own and independent of government.

VII. Section 1: Beyond Property Rights

I have, in this and the preceding chapter, considered the relation between Section 1 of the Fourteenth Amendment and property rights and concluded that both the due process and privileges or immunities clauses of that section secure property rights. This section will augment the discussion of property rights to cover other rights protected in the Constitution and explore whether these other rights are also made applicable to the states. I conclude that the reasoning supporting Section 1's protection of property rights is applicable to other rights, with the decision as to its applicability to be decided separately for each right on a case-by-case basis.

The objectives of the Thirty-Ninth Congress were much more grandiose than merely shielding property rights from excessive state regulations. The congressmen sought in Section 1 to accord persons the same guarantees against state legislation that they already possessed under the Constitution against federal legislation. The three rights clauses of Section 1 accomplished this purpose. However, as I explained in Chapter 5, Section I, the intentions of constitutional framers are subordinate to the language they have used to achieve their goals. The meaning and impact of what they have written must be determined by interpreting their language. When constitutional framers employ terminology already in the document, constitutional meaning must be derived from the existing language.

Because a majority of its members have never been convinced that Section 1 incorporated either the privileges and immunities clause of Article IV or the Bill of Rights, the U.S. Supreme Court has on a selective basis applied to the

state governments individual protections of these provisions, usually by way of the Fourteenth Amendment's due process clause. This practice seems plausible, because adding protections to the Constitution is a matter of great importance, requiring unequivocal evidence of such intention. The addition of each protective right operates negatively and enlarges individual liberties and simultaneously reduces government's powers. Thus, in 1833, in *Barron v. Baltimore,* Chief Justice John Marshall, in rejecting the position that the Bill of Rights was intended to be applicable to the states, stated the following:

> Had the framers of these amendments intended them to be limitations on the powers of the state governments, they would have imitated the framers of the original constitution, and have expressed that intention. Had Congress engaged in the extraordinary occupations of improving the constitutions of the several states by affording the people the additional protection from the exercise of power by their own governments, in matters which concern themselves alone, they would have declared this purpose in plain and intelligible language.[88]

As explained above in Chapter 5 and earlier sections of Chapter 6, a substantial majority of the Thirty-Ninth Congress sought to eliminate the powers of the states to impair individual rights, and its leaders continually expressed this objective in the debates on the proposed Fourteenth Amendment. This goal was never achieved, but it came very close to realization. In 1946, the U.S. Supreme Court came within one vote of adopting Justice Hugo Black's position that Section 1 of the Fourteenth Amendment guaranteed that "no state could deprive its citizens of the privileges and protections of the Bill of Rights."[89]

The problem with Black's position is that not every provision in the Bill of Rights can be regarded as a guarantee of liberty. The Bill of Rights' various guarantees of life, liberty, and property readily qualify as fundamental protections, but not all of its provisions are of this character. For example, the First Amendment contains—in addition to the free exercise of religion clause—the establishment clause prohibiting Congress from making a law "respecting an establishment of religion." The two religion clauses (free exercise and establishment) restrict by their terms only the U.S. Congress. (The U.S. Supreme Court has held that both clauses are incorporated into the Fourteenth Amendment's due process clause.) Nevertheless, there is little difficulty in incorporating the free exercise clause, which protects the free exercise of religion, because the word 'liberty' in the due process clause secures individual rights. The establishment clause cannot be similarly interpreted. The imposition of the forbidden establishment does not deprive anyone of the free exercise of religious or any other liberty. Since the clause is not subsumed in any provision of Sec-

tion 1 of the Fourteenth Amendment, its incorporation does not meet Chief Justice Marshall's "plain and intelligible language" standard.[90]

The problem of incorporation of other rights also arises when a provision pertinent to the original Constitution is no longer relevant in a later period. Examples of this problem are the requirement in the Fifth Amendment of a grand jury indictment for a capital crime and the prohibition in the Seventh Amendment of any reexamination by a court of a fact tried by a jury. These provisions related to the common law as of 1789, and they had little relevance to the jurisprudence of nearly a century later.[91] The Ninth and Tenth Amendments are generally considered to be part of the Bill of Rights, yet they contain no specified rights for incorporation. Moreover, they also concern the powers of the federal government in relation to the states, which is an issue of federalism. Law professor Akhil Reed Amar raises queries about the capitation clause in Article 1, Section 9, which constitutes a protection against the imposition of capitation or other direct taxes not in proportion to the census.[92] Is this a matter of individual or states rights? The point of this brief discussion is that the question of incorporation requires individual consideration for each candidate for inclusion.

As explained in Chapter 5, the meaning of particular constitutional amendments must be the same as those for identical provisions that are already part of the Constitution. The same language cannot receive different interpretations premised on when the provisions became part of the Constitution. Accordingly, the meaning of the privileges or immunities and due process clauses of Section 1 of the Fourteenth Amendment must be the same as the meaning of identical clauses in other parts of the Constitution, namely, the privileges and immunities clause of Article IV and the due process clause of the Fifth Amendment. With respect to the privileges and immunities clause of Article IV, I have explained that at the dates of the framing and ratification of the Fourteenth Amendment, Justice Bushrod Washington's interpretation of the meaning of the privileges and immunities clause of Article IV, in *Corfield v. Coryell,* prevailed in United States jurisprudence. He confined the privileges and immunities of Article IV to those "which are in their nature, fundamental, which belong of right, to citizens of all free governments." Washington's interpretation provided meaning for the phrase "privileges or immunities" at the time of the ratification of the Fourteenth Amendment. No such ruling was ever entered, however, and the burden of fulfilling the Framers' intentions therefore rested with the due process and equal protection clauses.

As explained above in Chapters 4 and 5, the most important due process case affecting the meaning of Section 1 at the time of the framing and ratification of the Fourteenth Amendment was *Murray's Lessee.* Its relevancy to Section 1 rests in two portions of its reasoning. First, "due process of law" means the same as "law of the land," both of which were interpreted by Coke

as providing protection against legislative deprivations. Second, the Court's opinion in that case cites and refers to certain jurisprudence—Coke's *Institutes* and six state cases—that explains the meaning and coverage of due process of law.

Coke construes Magna Carta's chapter 29 as providing "that no man be taken, imprisoned, or put out of his freehold without process of law [that is] without being brought in to answer but by due process of the common law." In addition, Coke states: "No man ought to be put from his livelihood without answer." These provisions meant that a person could not be deprived of life, liberty, or property in the absence of wrongdoing that is proven in a fair and proper trial pursuant to the law existing at the time that the alleged wrongdoing occurred.[93]

The six cases cited in *Murray's Lessee* include one each from North Carolina, New York, and a federal circuit court in Rhode Island, and three from Tennessee. These various courts together entered opinions that applied due process or law of the land to strike down a considerable amount of legislation. *Hoke v. Henderson* (North Carolina) threw out a law that deprived an elected office holder of his position during a prescribed term of office, because there was no judicial finding that he had violated an existing law warranting such action. *Taylor v. Porter* (New York) invalidated a law for the creation of private roads, because due process prohibited a forced transfer of property from one person to another even when payment of compensation was made. To survive judicial review, the transfer must be for a public purpose and just compensation must be paid. An owner cannot otherwise be deprived of his property unless he had engaged in wrongdoing that required a forfeiture. *Greene v. Briggs* (federal circuit court of Rhode Island) voided a law that made a trial by jury in a criminal case dependent on giving a bond with surety for the payment of penalty and court costs. The court held that a legislature could not deprive an accused person of a right essential to prove his innocence.

Coke states in his *Institutes,* after rejecting language that might be interpreted as upholding special laws, "that the law might extend to all, it is said *per legem terra* [by the law of the land]."[94] The three Tennessee courts cited in *Murray's Lessee* interpreted Coke's rule here to require that every law must be a general public law, operating equally upon all members of the community. In *Bank v. Cooper,* a Tennessee act created a special tribunal, composed of existing judges, for the disposition of lawsuits commenced by a named bank against its officers, their sureties, and customers of the bank who had overchecked, and from whose decision there was no appeal. The supreme court of the state held this provision to be unconstitutional, since it was special legislation in violation of the state constitution's law of the land clause. In *Jones' Heirs v. Perry,* the Tennessee Supreme Court held as invalid a private act passed, upon application of court-appointed guardians of infants, that authorized the guardians to sell land inherited from the parent to pay his debts. However, in *Vanzant v. Waddel,* the court

upheld a law authorizing a holder of the notes of two named banks, at their election, to summon persons as garnishees when the original writ issues against the bank, instead of waiting until the judgment is recovered as in ordinary cases. Although it was a special law, the court found that the act did not deprive the garnishees of any right and was enacted to enforce an existing right.

In every one of the six cases, a court imposed or reiterated severe limitations on the power of legislatures to deprive people of their rights. Each case was based in part on Coke's interpretation of the Magna Carta, which prohibited the termination of an existing right without due process of law or according to the law of the land. The variety of rights protected in these cases discloses the wide coverage of the due process of law concept and its general applicability for securing liberty. Although the United States Supreme Court refers to the due process clause as "process" and "proceeding" in its *Murray's Lessee* opinion, the cases here reported relate to substantive and procedural due process, as is evident from its citation of both substantive (*Taylor v. Porter, Hoke v. Henderson,* and the three Tennessee cases) and procedural (*Greene v. Briggs*) due process cases. According to the court, due process of law means the same as law of the land, which Coke interpreted as a general protection against governmental oppression.

Moreover, in the pursuit of liberty, protection of process becomes meaningless if the legislature retains the power to impose laws restricting the exercise of substantive rights. As U.S. Supreme Court Justice John Harlan explained: "Were due process merely a procedural safeguard it would fail to reach those situations where the definition of life, liberty or property was accomplished by legislation which by operating in the future could, given the fairest possible procedure in application to individuals, nevertheless destroy the enjoyment of all three."[95]

Accordingly, due process of law shields persons from laws that deprive them of their rights, which means that it necessarily applies to protections contained elsewhere in the Constitution. In five of the six cases, a state supreme court or a federal appeals court upheld the aggrieved person's complaint that he had been deprived of liberty or property without any finding of wrongdoing. In the other case, the court sustained the rule but found that it had not been violated. Each case was decided prior to the ratification of the Fourteenth Amendment or concerning a statute violating due process or law of the land. Surely, a claim that one has been deprived of the liberty of speech, press, religion, property, or any other fundamental right, is entitled to similar consideration. Pursuant to such reasoning, the U.S. Supreme Court has included most of the rights contained in the first eight amendments of the Bill of Rights as protected under the due process clause of the Fourteenth Amendment.

One may regard this approach as redundant, which to an extent is correct because it invokes protection of a right by means of two separate constitutional

provisions—due process and the one directly at issue—but this fact should not compromise meaning. Lawyers often employ or accept redundancy as a necessary tool in draftsmanship in order to overcome what Chief Justice Marshall referred to as the "imperfection in human language, which often exposes the same sentence to different constructions."[96] The general purpose of each of three clauses of Section 1 was to protect liberty. Because of the uncertainty of, say, the judicial interpretation of privileges or immunities, why not insert after it a due process or equal protection clause (or both) as a backup to ensure an equivalent or even a broader coverage of individual rights? As it happens, the redundancy of the due process and equal protection clauses saved some protections from oblivion when the Supreme Court largely nullified the privileges or immunities clause in the *Slaughterhouse Cases*. In the virtual absence of the Fourteenth Amendment's privileges or immunities clause, the only path to impose specific liberties on the states (that are contained in the original Constitution and Bill of Rights) was by way of Section 1's due process and equal protection clauses.

Coke interpreted law of the land and due process of law as protection against government oppression. Lawmakers are in a position to inflict harm by depriving a person of a substantive or procedural protection. Under the Constitution, there is no clear distinction between substantive and procedural protections. Almost every procedural protection is also a limitation on the power of the legislature, and as such is a substantive restraint on it. Except for rules issued by the judiciary concerning that branch of government, there is no such thing as an exclusively procedural right. As revealed in *Murray's Lessee,* the U.S. Supreme Court did not interpret due process solely as a separate and distinct guarantee, but as comprehending and augmenting safeguards contained elsewhere in the Constitution. Indeed, Bingham and many of his colleagues referred to due process as a mere shorthand for the Bill of Rights. In his first version of Section 1, Bingham included this equal protection provision: "Congress shall have the power [to make laws to secure] to all persons in the several states equal protection for the rights of life, liberty and property." In the final version he changed this language to "no state [shall] deny to any person within its jurisdiction equal protection of the law." Bingham's insertion of this equal protection clause was another exercise in redundancy. Both privileges and immunities and due process required that government treat everyone who is similarly situated equally and fairly. When government limits the liberties of certain individuals, it also denies them equality with those not so incapacitated.

The equal protection clause was the third barrier of Section 1 of the Fourteenth Amendment against state oppression, one that also dates back to Coke's interpretation of "law of the land." For many years prior to the U.S. Civil War, abolitionists maintained that the due process clause of the Fifth Amendment required that laws treat equally all persons similarly situated with respect to life,

liberty, and property. Chapter 4, Section II reveals that courts in Tennessee and at least three other states struck down legislation treating people in a different or special way without adequate cause—and therefore unequally—as in violation of law of the land clauses. The United States Supreme Court accepted such holdings in *Murray's Lessee.*

Considering the substance of the debates in the Thirty-Ninth Congress, I conclude that most of its members sought to remove the power of government to inflict pain and suffering on law-abiding persons. The congressmen believed that the most effective tool for this purpose was the privileges or immunities clause of the Fourteenth Amendment. They thought that both the due process and equal protection clauses of the amendment also served this purpose but to a lesser degree. As it happens, the due process clause in this respect was as or possibly even more effective than the privileges or immunities clause. In *Murray's Lessee,* the U.S. Supreme Court interpreted the due process clause of the Fifth Amendment as providing great protection for personal liberties. According to the six cases approvingly cited there, the due process clause protected a person from being deprived of life, liberty, or property in the absence of a fair and proper judicial finding that he has violated an existing law and not one imposed retroactively or punitively. Due process of law also required that all laws be general and public, equally binding on every member of the community without intention to harm or benefit any person or group.

The three leading commentators for members of the Thirty-Ninth Congress were Blackstone, Kent, and U.S. Supreme Court Justice Joseph Story. All supported Coke's interpretation of Magna Carta, as above reported. The views of Blackstone on this subject are discussed above in Chapter 2, Section IV, and those of Kent in the same section and in Chapter 4, Section II. United States Supreme Court Justice Joseph Story was similarly supportive, as he set forth in his influential *Commentaries on the Constitution*: "Lord Coke says that the [words 'by law of the land'] mean by due process of law, [that is,] due presentment or indictment, and being brought into answer thereto by due process of the common law. So that [the due process clause of the Fifth Amendment] in effect affirms the right of trial according to the process and proceedings of the common law."[97]

The philosophy and position of the judges in the cases previously discussed in this chapter are quite consistent with the constitutional interpretations of Congressman Bingham. Given his interpretations of the law, it was not unreasonable for Bingham to author a broad constitutional provision such as the second sentence of Section 1 of the Fourteenth Amendment that removed the powers of the states to deprive people of their liberties, which were separately protected in the Constitution. Consistent with the general language of the Constitution, Bingham drafted section 1 in language that enabled the judiciary to exercise the same level of discretion as with other parts of the Constitution.

7

Concluding Remarks

Our account of property rights from the execution of the Magna Carta by John, king of England and Ireland, in 1215 to the early 1870s, the years immediately following the ratification of the Fourteenth Amendment in 1868, is now concluded. We have seen how early English property law greatly influenced property law in the United States prior to the adoption of this amendment and has continued to do so into the twenty-first century. In particular, the interpretations of English property law by Lord Edward Coke (1552–1634) and Sir William Blackstone (1723–1780) set forth property rules which American jurists routinely apply today.

Thus, when adjudicating land-use regulations, judges inquire whether a regulation substantially advances a legitimate state interest, or deprives an owner of the economically viable use of his land—the current tests for adjudicating the legitimacy of land-use regulation—they are applying rules articulated by Coke and Blackstone. The long historical provenance of these rules should help still criticism that they are of recent vintage, not secured in the original U.S. Constitution or in its Bill of Rights. Understanding the history of property rights, the mission of this work should finally put such concerns to rest. Strong support for property rights was confirmed in King John's and subsequent issues of the Magna Carta and it continued in the United States with the Constitution, Bill of Rights, and the ratification of the Fourteenth Amendment in 1868.

When King John signed the Magna Carta, judges in England and Ireland were already applying and extending the common law to protect the people's liberties, a task which they have continued over the years. The laws of England consist of the common law and statute law. In the seventeenth and eighteenth centuries, in the absence of any document cataloging these laws, Coke and

Blackstone wrote widely read and very influential commentaries interpreting, explaining, and expounding the English laws of their times. These commentaries were highly important and persuasive to Englishmen on both sides of the Atlantic Ocean. When the English settlers migrated to America, the English government assured them that they were entitled to the same privileges and immunities in their new land as they had enjoyed in England. These privileges and immunities largely embodied the common law. The English and subsequently the American authorities continued to abide by and generally apply the common law as had been the practice in England.

King John revoked the Magna Carta a few months after he signed it, and it was replaced by other versions executed in the reign of his son, Henry III. Both Coke and Blackstone interpreted the Magna Carta that Henry executed in 1225. This great charter is considered the fundamental English document securing the people's liberties. With respect to the protection of property, Coke emphasized that the Magna Carta required that no freeman be deprived of his life, liberty, or property, unless it be done pursuant to the requirements of due process of law, which meant a fair and proper judicial trial. Laws should not be retroactive and must serve a public and not a private interest. Blackstone underscored, among others, two very important safeguards for property owners. First, indemnification must be awarded to a nonconsenting owner whose property is taken for a public purpose. Second, the laws of trespass and nuisance guarantee a property owner against any physical deprivation of his property.

Nor could government rightfully adopt arbitrary or capricious laws. Blackstone condemned laws "without any good end in view" and those which are "wanton and causeless" restraints of persons. In the famous *Dr. Bonham's Case*, Coke's court struck down as capricious (against the common law standard of "common right and reason") a statute of Parliament that accorded the London College of Physicians complete discretion to bar graduates of professional universities from the practice of medicine.

For most of the period from their migrations in the early seventeenth century to the years prior to the American Revolution, the residents of English America enjoyed considerable freedom and prosperity and their numbers steadily rose. Economic well-being reached historically high levels. The English efforts to impose regulations and taxes on Americans who experienced until then relatively little government control met with great resistance and, ultimately, revolution and led in time to the creation of a new nation with a central government of substantially confined powers. John Locke's principles of freedom and limited government, coupled with the commentaries of Coke and Blackstone, provided intellectual support for the freedom that the settlers had learned to cherish as the cornerstone of their occupations and professions.

Revolution brought each of the thirteen colonies their independence. The newly minted states first joined together loosely under the Articles of Confed-

eration. The Articles proved unworkable because each of the states operated as a separate nation, applying protectionist measures against its neighbors and rejecting any serious limitation on its powers, thereby creating commercial problems for all.

Many political and intellectual leaders concluded that unless the Confederation was abolished and replaced by a single union of the states, chaos and maybe even civil strife would result. Although convened to reform the Articles of Confederation, the Constitutional Convention of 1787 decided that the establishment of a single union of all the states was required to reduce or eliminate existing commercial problems. Instead of reforming the Articles, the Convention decided to frame a constitution for a new nation. The most important and influential framer was James Madison, who was well prepared for this responsibility. He had studied the works of great political and legal minds and had thought deeply about the creation of this nation. Most of his proposals were embraced by his fellow delegates.

Delegates to the 1787 Constitutional Convention recognized the tension between majority rights and personal rights and sought to achieve reasonable accommodation between the two. They created a nation of limited authority by separating the government into three branches—legislative, executive, and judicial—and greatly confining the powers of each. To prevent the accumulation of excessive powers by any one group, every branch would have some veto over each of the other two. This new nation would be a commercial republic that relied principally on the productivity and ingenuity of its citizens to sustain and advance the public welfare.

The constitutional generation strongly believed in the protection of property rights. The nation that the Framers contemplated would be viable only if the means of production and distribution of goods and services were largely unrestrained by government. The government that they established under the original Constitution ratified in 1788 had no power to deprive owners of their property rights, rights protected by the common law. This original Constitution contained few guarantees directly protecting individual freedom, but secured freedom by greatly limiting the power of government to deprive people of their liberties. The public was assured that the government had no authority to eliminate their "rights as Englishmen," which meant their rights under the common law. In the amendments to the Constitution that Madison proposed after its ratification, which became in time the Bill of Rights, he inserted two major protections for property in what later became the Fifth Amendment: the due process of law clause and the takings clause. He intended both to be consistent with the protections afforded by the common law, but the First Congress changed his takings clause to be an even more comprehensive protection of property.

In the period following ratification of the U.S. Constitution until the ratification of the Fourteenth Amendment in 1868, the U.S. Supreme Court and the

state courts strongly protected property rights under various theories. Most interpreted national and state due process (or law of the land) and takings clauses to this effect, and some applied common law interpretations advanced by Coke and Blackstone. In many states, the courts applied such protections even in the absence of any takings provision. By the early 1870s, prevailing jurisprudence in the United States invoked various constitutional provisions and common law principles to invalidate state and federal restraints on the ownership and use of private property when compensation was not forthcoming.

Article IV, Section 2 of the United States Constitution states: "The Citizens of each State shall be entitled to all Privileges and Immunities of Citizens in the several States." Section 1 of the Fourteenth Amendment mandates: "No State shall make or enforce any law which shall abridge the privileges or immunities of citizens of the United States." At the time when the Fourteenth Amendment was framed (1866) and ratified (1868), the prevailing judicial opinion in the United States was that the term "privileges or immunities" meant those fundamental rights and liberties "which belong, of right, to the citizens of all free governments." These would surely include the rights of property, as explained in the works of Coke and Blackstone.

Similarly, the due process clause, originating in the Magna Carta, protected people against deprivation by government of their life, liberty, or property without a judicial determination that they had engaged in conduct warranting such deprivation. The takings clause makes an exception to this rule when eminent domain or excessive regulation is involved, and then by requiring that compensation be paid to the owner in order to indemnify him for his loss.

In the period from 1790 to 1870, the judiciary ascended to a major role in this nation. This is evident in the power it exercised with respect to property rights. By the beginning of this period, the federal government and most of the states had ratified constitutions containing due process or law of the land or takings clauses. However, in numerous instances, the interested parties had to await judicial determination of their constitutionality. There was almost always serious controversy between the regulators and the regulated. Overall, hundreds of judges adjudicated hundreds of property rights cases. As reported in Chapter 4, Sections II, III, and IV, the U.S. Supreme Court and judges in every state that was part of the union in 1860 (with the exception of South Carolina) held unlawful the taking of property that was not accompanied by the payment of compensation for the harm sustained by the owner. While the judges differed in certain respects—an inevitable outcome considering the large number of judges and cases involved—the judiciary in effect assured owners that their properties were protected from confiscation or unreasonable regulations. This period constituted a remarkable achievement for property rights. These rights were now enforceable throughout the land and were no longer merely secured by parchment. In the absence of this judicial monitoring, the enormous bene-

fits of private ownership to the U.S. economy and to the people's well-being would have been considerably diminished.

The South Carolina exception to the above generalization related only to roads. Its courts held that the state constitution did not require payment of compensation to a landowner whose land was taken for a public road because reserving part of one's land for this public use was an obligation of ownership. Elsewhere there was general agreement that a taking of property for any public use required payment of compensation; however, the states differed about three related matters. First, they disagreed about whether consequential damages affected a taking requiring compensation. My research indicates that most of the states that considered this issue approved the award of consequential damages. The U.S. Supreme Court sustained this position in the early 1870s. Second, they disagreed about whether a dedication of a private road squared with the constitutional takings requirement that the purpose of an eminent domain action must advance a public and not a private interest. Third, they disagreed in determining whether the value of the benefits obtained by an owner as a result of the taking should be deducted from the amount of the damages he sustained by condemnation.

The almost total unanimity that prevailed both in the federal and state courts through the early 1870s with respect to the protection of property rights is indeed remarkable. The jurisprudence of our founding generation and their close descendants deserves our close attention, for it underscores the centrality of property rights to our system of self-government. This great insight of our ancestors and of their English forebears is largely responsible for both our incomparable abundance and the preservation of our liberty.

Notes

Chapter 1. Introduction

1. Massachusetts, Connecticut, and Rhode Island did not ratify the Bill of Rights until 1941. Eleven states ratified it effective December 15, 1791.
2. Slaughterhouse Cases, 83 U.S. 36 (1872) (Bradley, J., dissenting).
3. Hurtando v. California, 110 U.S. 516, 539 (1884) (Harlan, J., dissenting).
4. GORDON S. WOOD, THE CREATION OF THE AMERICAN REPUBLIC, 1776–1787, at 10 (1969).
5. FEDERALIST NO. 80, 478 (A. Hamilton). (All citations of THE FEDERALIST PAPERS herein refer to the Clinton Rossiter edition of 1961.)
6. 3 M. FARRAND, THE RECORDS OF THE FEDERAL CONVENTION OF 1787, at 435 (rev. ed. 1937).
7. CONG. GLOBE, 39th Cong., 1st Sess. 1089 (1866).
8. CONG. GLOBE, 39th Cong., 1st Sess. 2765 (1866).

Chapter 2. The Rights of Englishmen

1. CHARLES H. MCILWAIN, CONSTITUTIONALISM ANCIENT AND MODERN 86 (1947).
2. Samuel Thorne, *What Magna Carta Was,* in THE GREAT CHARTER 3, 11 (Samuel Thorne et al. eds., 1965).
3. Black's Law Dictionary defines "amercement" as "a pecuniary penalty, in the nature of a fine, imposed upon a person for some fault or misconduct, he being in mercy of his offence." BLACK'S LAW DICTIONARY 175 (5th ed. 1979).
4. 2 DAVID HUME, THE HISTORY OF ENGLAND 1–15 (1778); GEORGE M. TREVELYAN, A SHORTENED HISTORY OF ENGLAND 128–35 (1944); J. UNGARD and H. BELLOC, THE HISTORY OF ENGLAND 326–76 (1912); and GOLDWYN SMITH, A HISTORY OF ENGLAND 75–81 (3d ed. 1966).
5. ARTHUR R. HOGUE, ORIGINS OF THE COMMON LAW 112 (1966). Hogue identifies 18 chapters of King John's Magna Carta as relating to rights in land.

6. TREVELYAN, *supra* note 4, at 132.
7. Wynehamer v. People, 13 N.Y. 378, 433 (1856) (Selden, J.).
8. MCILWAIN, *supra* note 1.
9. HOGUE, *supra* note 5, at 113.
10. 1 HUME, THE HISTORY OF ENGLAND, 487–88.
11. *See supra* note 4.
12. Coke *cited at* 1 BLACKSTONE, COMMENTARIES 124.
13. 1 BLACKSTONE, COMMENTARIES 123–24.
14. *See* HOGUE, *supra* note 5, at 79–80.
15. In his commentary on this chapter, Coke reports about a royal charter granted to Southhampton under which this town was the sole port of entry for the importation of Malmefeyes wines. This royal charter was to be enforced by a fine of triple the amount of customs upon localities that violated this rule. In challenges to this rule, Coke writes, the judges held that it was an invalid "restraint of the subject, against the laws and statutes of the realm." 2 COKE, INSTITUTES 61.
16. Edward S. Corwin, *"The Higher Law" Background of American Constitutional Law,* 42 HARV. L. REV. 365, 394, 395 (1928). Coke writes that "the power and jurisdiction of . . . Parliament . . . is so transcendent and absolute . . . it cannot be confined either for causes or persons within any bounds." 4 COKE, INSTITUTES 36. This assertion is inconsistent with the views he expressed in *Dr. Bonham's Case,* that certain common law principles were superior to the statutory authority of Parliament. In America, however, Coke was noted for the position he took on this issue in *Dr. Bonham's Case. See* CALVIN R. MASSEY, SILENT RIGHTS 226–27 n. 17 (1995). Corwin explains the inconsistency as due to Coke's concern being primarily political, to curb the royalty. "So precedent and authority . . . must be bent to the selected end." Corwin at 366.
17. Corwin, *supra* note 16, at 379.
18. Brockelbank, *The Role of Due Process in American Constitutional Law,* 39 CORNELL L.Q. 516, 562 (1954).
19. Roscoe Pound, *Liberty of Contract,* 18 YALE L. REV. 454, 459 (1908–1909).
20. 1 COKE, INSTITUTES 81.
21. *Id.* at 12.
22. 2 COKE, INSTITUTES 45.
23. *Id.* at 45–46.
24. *Id.* at 46.
25. *Id.* at 50.
26. *Id.*
27. 2 COKE, INSTITUTES 51.
28. 4 COKE, INSTITUTES 41.
29. 2 COKE, INSTITUTES 292.
30. BMW of North America, Inc. v. Gore, 517 U.S. 558 (1996) (Breyer, J., concurring). The United States Supreme Court held that failure to disclose the severity of a penalty violated the due process clause of the Fourteenth Amendment.
31. J. W. GOUGH, FUNDAMENTAL LAW IN ENGLISH CONSTITUTIONAL HISTORY 64 (1955).
32. 2 COKE, INSTITUTES 46.
33. *Id.*
34. *Id.* at 47.

35. *Id.*
36. *Id.*
37. *See* WILLIAM LETWIN, LAW AND ECONOMIC POLICY IN AMERICA 18–32 (1965).
38. For examples of such interpretation of due process *see* ROBERT H. BORK, THE TEMPTING OF AMERICA, 223–40 (1990) and William Letwin, *The Economic Policy of the Constitution,* in LIBERTY, PROPERTY, AND THE FOUNDATION OF THE AMERICAN CONSTITUTION 122–24 (Ellen Frankel Paul and Howard Dickman eds., 1989).
39. *See generally* Wynehamer v. People, 13 N.Y. 378, 433 (1856).
40. Dr. Bonham's Case, 77 Eng. Rep. 646 (K.B. 1610).
41. Edward S. Corwin, *The Natural Law and Constitutional Law,* in 2 UNIVERSITY OF NOTRE DAME NATURAL LAW INSTITUTE PROCEEDINGS 47, 55 (E. F. Barrett ed., 1936).
42. *Id.* at 56–57. The case was Robin v. Hardaway, Jeff, 109 (Va. 1772).
43. John Locke, *Second Treatise* § 222, in LOCKE, TWO TREATISES OF GOVERNMENT (Peter Laslett ed., 1960).
44. 1 BLACKSTONE, COMMENTARIES. *But see* notes 143 and 144 *infra* for an indication that Blackstone believed that judges had powers to reform legislation in some situations.
45. *Id.* at 140.
46. *See* note 40 *supra.*
47. Theodore Plucknett, *Bonham's Case and Judicial Review,* 40 HARVARD L. REV. 30 (1926).
48. *Id.* Plucknett does not provide a citation for *Cessavit* 42. He refers to it as an anonymous case printed by Fitzherbert from an unedited year book. *Id.* at 35. Plucknett cited numerous instances when courts from the middle of the fourteenth century through Coke's day either ignored statutes of Parliament or disregarded their plain meaning.
49. *See* 3 BLACKSTONE, COMMENTARIES, 232–33.
50. *Id.* The earlier case is Copper v. Gederings, 3 Edw. II 105 (1310).
51. HERBERT BROOM, SELECTION OF LEGAL MAXIMS 116 (5th ed., 1874); and GOUGH, note 31 *supra,* at 33. John Locke wrote that "it is unreasonable for men to be judges in their own cases, that self love will make men partial to themselves and their friends." Locke, *supra* note 43, at § 13.
52. COKE, LITTLETON § 212; *see* BROOM, *supra* note 51, at 121.
53. *See* notes 28 and 29 *supra* and *accompanying text.*
54. 2 COKE, INSTITUTES 50, 51, 74. *See* 4 COKE, INSTITUTES 41.
55. *See* BERNARD H. SIEGAN, ECONOMIC LIBERTIES AND THE CONSTITUTION 200–202 (1980).
56. Davenant v. Hurdis, 72 Eng. Rep. 769 (K.B. 1598).
57. Coke referred to *Davenant* in his interpretation of the admonition of Chapter 29 of the Magna Carta (that no freeman shall "be disseised of his liberties"). He asserted that the *Davenant* ruling signifies the freedoms that the people of England have, and that the ordinance was against the "liberty of the subject." 2 COKE, INSTITUTES 48.
58. Darcy v. Allen, 77 Eng. Rep. 1260 (K.B. 1602).
59. 2 COKE, INSTITUTES 47.
60. *See* LETWIN, *supra* note 38.

61. In 1624, Parliament enacted the Statute of Monopolies, drafted principally by Coke, which terminated the power of the monarchy and Parliament to grant private monopolies. However, the act reserved to Parliament the power to grant certain exclusive privileges and contained a considerable number of exceptions, among which was the continuance of the power of cities, boroughs, guilds, and chartered trading organizations to exercise many of their monopoly powers. *See* MALAMENT *infra* note 77 and LETWIN *supra* note 38. Political expediency, that is, the need to accommodate special interests, seems to explain the failure of the statute to be more inclusive.

62. Slaughterhouse Cases, 83 U.S. 36 (1872). This case will be discussed fully in Chapter 5.

63. Justice Field believed that the Fourteenth Amendment's privileges or immunities clause protected liberties that monopolies destroy. The position that monopolies and combinations in restraint of trade were unlawful under the common law was widely held among jurists and legal commentators in the latter part of the nineteenth century, including Senator John Sherman, principal author of the Sherman anti-trust law. *See generally* LETWIN, *supra* note 38.

64. Case of Tailors of Ipswich, 77 Eng. Rep. 1218 (K.B. 1614).

65. Tooley's Case, 80 Eng. Rep. 1055 (K.B. 1613).

66. Rogers v. Parrey, 80 Eng. Rep. 1012 (K.B. 1613).

67. Case of the King's Prerogative in Saltpeter, 77 Eng. Rep. 1295 (1606).

68. 1 BLACKSTONE, COMMENTARIES 232.

69. A. V. DICEY, INTRODUCTION TO THE STUDY OF THE LAW OF THE CONSTITUTION 282 (8th ed., 1915).

70. William B. Stoebuck, *A General Theory of Eminent Domain,* 47 WASHINGTON L. REV. 553, 562–63 (1972).

71. For example, Justice Blackmun (dissenting in the *Lucas* case) cites only *Saltpeter* to support the statement that regulation in the colonial period "could even go so far as to deny all productive use of the property to the owner if, as Coke himself stated, the regulation 'extends to the public benefit . . . for this is for the public, and every one hath benefit by it.' " Blackmun obtains the language that he quotes, from the book called TAKING ISSUE, by F. BOSSELMAN, D. CALLIES, and J. BANTA 80–81 (1913). However, the quotation relates solely to the king's prerogative and has no relation to the compensation issue. Lucas v. South Carolina Coastal Commission, 112 S.Ct. 2886, 2914 (1992) (Blackmun, J., dissenting).

72. Case of the Isle of Ely, 77 Eng. Rep. 1139 (1610).

73. 12 Coke 63 (c. 1600).

74. The rule was later applied to events of actual necessity brought about by great calamities endangering health and safety. Thus, in *Lucas v. South Carolina Coastal Council* (1992), Justice Antonin Scalia referred to "cases of actual necessity" as exceptions to property rights restraints (in addition to control of nuisances) that were required to prevent, for example, the spreading of a fire, or to forestall other grave threats to the lives and property of others. 112 S.Ct. at 2900, note 16.

75. 145 Eng. Rep. 267 (Exch. 1606).

76. 2 COKE, INSTITUTES 63.

77. Barbara Malament, *The "Economic Liberalism" of Sir Edward Coke,* 76 YALE L.J. 1321, 1357 (1967).

78. D. BOORSTIN, THE MYSTERIOUS SCIENCE OF THE LAW 3 (1941) (quoting C. WARREN, HISTORY OF THE AMERICAN BAR 187 [1911]).

79. DAVID A. LOCKMILLER, WILLIAM BLACKSTONE 174 (1938).

80. THE AMERICAN REVOLUTION 1763–1783, A BICENTENNIAL COLLECTION 152, 154 (R. B. Morris ed., 1970).

81. HAMMOND'S BLACKSTONE, I, IX.

82. JONES' BLACKSTONE, I, III–IV. *See* LOCKMILLER, *supra* note 79, at 180–81.

83. Justice Anthony Kennedy, in Alden v. Maine, 119 S.Ct. 2240 (1999).

84. 1 BLACKSTONE, COMMENTARIES, 72, 73, note t.

85. Thomas C. Grey, *Origins of the Unwritten Constitution: Fundamental Law in American Revolutionary Thought,* 30 STANFORD L. REV. 843, 859 (1978) (citing C. ROSSITER, SEEDTIME OF THE REPUBLIC 356, 367–68 [1953]).

86. HOGUE, *supra* note 5, at 205.

87. 4 BLACKSTONE, COMMENTARIES 417.

88. 1 BLACKSTONE, COMMENTARIES 120.

89. *Id.* at 45.

90. *Id.* at 46.

91. *See* SIEGAN, *supra* note 55, at 67–82.

92. Calder v. Bull, 3 U.S. 386 (1798).

93. *See* SIEGAN *supra* note 55, at 204–22.

94. 1 BLACKSTONE, COMMENTARIES 134.

95. *Id.* at 134–35.

96. *Id.* at 135.

97. *Id.*

98. Murray's Lessee v. Hoboken Land and Improvement Co., 59 U.S. 272 (1856).

99. 3 BLACKSTONE, COMMENTARIES 209–10.

100. *Id.* at 217–18.

101. *Id.*

102. *Id.* at 220. Blackstone's definition of nuisance is currently not applicable in the United States. The contemporary test imposes liability only if, after a weighing of the harms and benefits, the gravity of the harm to the plaintiff is found to outweigh the social usefulness of the defendant's activity. PROSSER, TORTS 581 (4th ed.).

103. "But the injuries to the rights of property can scarcely be committed by the crown without the intervention of its officers, for whom the law in matters of right entertains no respect or delicacy, but furnishes various methods of detecting the errors and misconduct of those agents, by whom the king has been deceived, and induced to do a temporary injustice." 3 BLACKSTONE, COMMENTARIES 255. Blackstone thus explains the limitations upon the rule that the king can do no wrong.

104. Merritt v. Parker, 1 Coxe L.Rep. 460 (New Jersey 1795).

105. *Id.* at 463, 465.

106. Gardner v. Village of Newburgh, 2 Johns. Ch. 162 (N.Y. 1816).

107. *Id.* at 167.

108. *Id.*

109. Fench v. Resbridger, 2 Vern. 390 (1700).
110. Bush v. Western, Prec. Ch. 529 (1720).
111. *Gardner*, 2 Johns Ch. at 162, 164.
112. 3 J. STORY, COMMENTARIES ON THE CONSTITUTION OF THE UNITED STATES 661 (1833).
113. Yates v. Milwaukee, 70 U.S. 497 (1870).
114. Pumpelly v. Green Bay Co., 80 U.S. 166 (1871).
115. *See* State v. Dawson, 3 Hill 100 (1836).
116. *See* note 46 *supra* and *accompanying text*.
117. HUGO GROTIUS, DE JURE BELLI ET PACIS, bk. VIII, ch. 14, § 7 (1625).
118. SAMUEL PUFENDORF, DE OFFICIO HOMINES ET CIVIS, tit. II, ch. 15, § 4 (1695). Similar refrains can be found in VATTEL, LE DROIT DES GENS, bk. I, ch. 20, § 244 (1758); BYNKERSHOEK, QUAESTIONEM JURIS PUBLICI LIBRI DUO, 218 (1737); BURLAMAQUI, PRINCIPLES OF NATURAL AND POLITICAL LAW, pt. III, ch. 5, § 25 (1747); and MONTESQUIEU, SPIRIT OF THE LAWS, bk. 26, XV (1748). *See* ELLEN FRANKEL PAUL, PROPERTY RIGHTS AND EMINENT DOMAIN 72–80 (1987).
119. PUFENDORF, DE JURE NATURAE ET GENTIUM 1285 (1672).
120. First English v. County of Los Angeles, 482 U.S. 304 (1987).
121. *See* Zinermon v. Burch, 494 U.S. 113 (1990).
122. 1 BLACKSTONE, COMMENTARIES 85–86.
123. *Id*. at 44.
124. *Id*. at 125.
125. *Id*. at 44.
126. Cleburne v. Cleburne Living Center, Inc., 437 U.S. 432, 452 (1985).
127. Hurtado v. California, 110 U.S. 516, 535–36 (1884).
128. 2 COKE, INSTITUTES 45–46.
129. As previously noted, Blackstone explains that the property right is protected "unless declared to be forfeited by the judgment of his peers or the law of the land." The word "forfeited" has a specific legal meaning. Blackstone devotes a chapter in his *Commentaries* to explaining "forfeiture," which he states

> is a punishment annexed by law to some illegal act, or negligence, in the owner of lands, tenements, or hereditaments; whereby he loses all his interest therein, and they go to the party injured, as a recompense for the wrong which either he alone, or the public together with himself, has sustained. (2 BLACKSTONE 267)

In Blackstone's time, forfeiture applied only to certain offenses and was frequently implemented by a reversion of property to the Crown. Forfeiture statutes also authorized the power of levying fines. The offenses which induced a forfeiture of lands and tenements to the Crown were principally, in Blackstone's time, treason, felony, misprision of treason, praemunire, and various assaults. These laws did not relate to or involve the purchase, use, or commercial transfer of property. Forfeiture was a form of punishment, and was not intended for application by the legislature to solve or remedy social or economic problems involving the use or disposition of property.

130. 1 COKE, INSTITUTES ch. 1, §1.
131. Each wrote major publications. *See* EMERICH E VATTEL, THE LAW OF NATIONS (1760); CORNELIUS BYNKERSHOEK, DE DOMINIO MARIS (1702); and MONTESQUIEU, THE SPIRIT OF THE LAWS (1750).
132. 1 BLACKSTONE, COMMENTARIES 121–22.
133. *Id.*
134. *Id.* at 122.
135. LETTERS AND OTHER WRITINGS OF JAMES MADISON, FOURTH PRESIDENT OF THE UNITED STATES 478–79 (1867).
136. Dolan v. City of Tigard, 114 S.Ct. 2309 (1994).
137. DOUGLAS W. KMIEC and STEPHEN B. PRESSER, THE AMERICAN CONSTITUTIONAL ORDER 90 (1998).
138. 1 BLACKSTONE, COMMENTARIES 41.
139. *Id.* at 91.
140. *See* DOUGLAS W. KMIEC and STEPHEN B. PRESSER, THE HISTORY, PHILOSOPHY AND STRUCTURE OF THE AMERICAN CONSTITUTION 126 (1998).
141. 1 BLACKSTONE, COMMENTARIES 91.
142. *Id.*
143. 1 BLACKSTONE, COMMENTARIES 87–88.
144. *Id.* at 87–92.
145. To pass constitutional muster, a land-use regulation must substantially advance legitimate state interests and not deny an owner economically viable use of his land. Agins v. Tiburon, 447 U.S. 255, 260 (1980).
146. *See* SIEGAN, *supra* note 55, at 111–14.
147. BERNARD BAILYN, THE IDEOLOGIAL ORIGINS OF THE AMERICAN REVOLUTION 27 (1967).
148. CARL L. BECKER, THE DECLARATION OF INDEPENDENCE 27 (1959).
149. FORREST MCDONALD, NOVUS ORDO SECLORUM 60 (1985).
150. LOCKE, *supra* note 43, § 124.
151. *Id.* at § 137.
152. *Id.* at § 138. Locke did not require actual consent of the owner and accepted instead tacit consent (*id.* at § 119), a position which is inconsistent with the idea of a limited government. Tacit consent is something implied, understood, or inferred. Because it cannot be identified with a specific person expressing consent, it enables others to make the decision, thus enlarging the power of government.
153. *Id.* at § 140.
154. *Id.* at § 222.
155. Stoebuck, *supra* note 70, at 585.
156. LOCKE, *supra* note 43, § 131.
157. *Id.* at § 119.
158. *Id.* at § 142.
159. *Id.* at § 199.
160. *Id.* at § 202.
161. *Id.* at § 122–28.
162. *See* GORDON WOOD, THE CREATION OF THE AMERICAN REPUBLIC 9–13 (1969); and Gary J. Schmitt and Robert H. Webking, *Revolutionaries, Antifederalists, and Fed-*

eralists: Comments on Gordon Wood's Understanding of the American Founding, 9 THE POLITICAL SCIENCE REVIEWER 195 (1979).

163. BAILYN, *supra* note 147.

164. 7 FEDERAL AND STATE CONSTITUTIONS, COLONIAL CHARTERS AND OTHER ORGANIC LAWS 3788 (F. Thorpe ed., 1909).

165. Grey, *supra* note 85, at 866 (citing Thorpe ed., *supra* note 164); Saenz v. Roe, 1999 WL 303745, pg. 18, n. 2 (Thomas, J., dissenting).

166. *See* People v. Croswell, 3 John. 337, 344 (1804). The statement is by Hamilton as attorney for the defendant.

167. Wheaton v. Peters, 33 U.S. 591, 658 (1834).

168. MCDONALD, *supra* note 149, at 12–13.

169. *See* Wheaton v. Peters, 33 U.S. at 591.

170. J. STORY, COMMENTARIES § 165.

171. *Declaration and Resolves of the First Continental Congress,* Oct. 14, 1774, in THE MAKING OF THE AMERICAN REPUBLIC, THE GREAT DOCUMENTS 1774–1789, 1–5 (Charles Callan Tansill ed., 1972).

172. 1 JAMES KENT, COMMENTARIES ON AMERICAN LAW 315–16 (Da Capo Press 1971).

173. MERRILL D. PETERSON, THOMAS JEFFERSON AND THE NEW NATION 90 (1970).

174. *See* I and II THE FEDERAL AND STATE CONSTITUTIONS, COLONIAL CHARTERS AND OTHER ORGANIC LAWS (Ben Perley Poore comp., 2d ed., 1878).

175. Tansill, *supra* note 171, at 47–54.

176. PAUL JOHNSON, A HISTORY OF THE AMERICAN PEOPLE 85–86 (1997).

177. 3 WILLIAM TEMPLE FRANKLIN, MEMOIRS OF THE LIFE AND WRITINGS OF BENJAMIN FRANKLIN 262–63 (1818).

178. WILLIAM B. SCOTT, IN PURSUIT OF HAPPINESS 14–15 (1977).

179. JOHNSON, *supra* note 176, at 94.

180. CHESTER WHITNEY WRIGHT, ECONOMIC HISTORY OF THE UNITED STATES 169 (1948). Wright also attributes the colonists' economic success to the fact that most of those who migrated to the colonies sought freedom from religious, political, and economic oppression, and thus were a select group of active, ambitious, and liberty-loving people.

181. ADAM SMITH, THE WEALTH OF NATIONS 73, 347 (Modern Library 1937).

182. WRIGHT, *supra* note 180, at 188.

183. CHARLES GROVE HAINES, THE AMERICAN DOCTRINE OF JUDICIAL SUPREMACY 89–112 (1959).

184. 2 WILLIAM W. CROSSKEY, POLITICS AND THE CONSTITUTION 938–45 (1953).

185. HAINES, *supra* note 183, at 209–10.

186. SCOTT, *supra* note 178, at 12 (citing WILLIAM BRADFORD, OF PLYMOUTH PLANTATION: 1620–1647, 120 [Morrison ed., 1952]).

187. *Id.* at 13–14.

188. 21 JOURNAL OF THE CONTINENTAL CONGRESS 569 (1908).

189. ROBERT F. SCHUETTINGER and EAMMON F. BUTLER, FORTY CENTURIES OF WAGE AND PRICE CONTROLS 41–42 (1979).

190. Alan Reynolds, *A History Lesson on Inflation,* in FIRST NATIONAL BANK OF CHICAGO WORLD REPORT (July 1976).

191. PELATIAH WEBSTER, POLITICAL ESSAYS 65–66 (Philadelphia 1791).

192. SCHUETTINGER and BUTLER, *supra* note 189, at 40.

193. 1 WILLIAM D. GRAMPP, ECONOMIC LIBERALISM 109 (Random House 1965).

194. *See* WOOD, *supra* note 162, at 68–69.

195. *Id.* and *see* William Michael Treanor, *The Origins and Original Significance of the Just Compensation Clause,* 94 YALE L.J. 694, 699–701 (1985).

196. *See* Stanley N. Katz, *Thomas Jefferson and the Right to Property in Revolutionary America,* 19 J. L. & ECON. 467, 474–76, 479–88 (1976).

197. *See* Letter from James Madison to Thomas Jefferson (Oct. 24, 1787), *in* 10 THE PAPERS OF JAMES MADISON 206–19 (R. A. Rutland ed., 1977).

198. FEDERALIST NO. 10, at 84 (Madison).

199. SCOTT, *supra* note 178, at 45.

Chapter 3. Interpreting the Constitution and the Bill of Rights

1. FEDERALIST NO. 22, at 143–45 (A. Hamilton). (All citations of THE FEDERALIST PAPERS herein refer to the Clinton Rossiter edition of 1961.)

2. Chief Justice Hughes, in Home Building and Loan Assn. v. J. Blaisdell, 290 U.S. 398, 427 (1934).

3. 25 THE PAPERS OF ALEXANDER HAMILTON 479 (H. Syrett ed., 1977).

4. J. MAIN, THE ANTIFEDERALISTS: CRITICS OF THE CONSTITUTION, 1781–1788, at 26 (1961).

5. Dam, *The Legal Tender Cases,* 1981 SUP. CT. REV. 367, 383 (1981).

6. *Id.* at 383–84. CHESTER WHITNEY WRIGHT, ECONOMIC HISTORY OF THE UNITED STATES 179–85, 191–92 (2nd ed., 1949).

7. S. MORRISON, THE OXFORD HISTORY OF THE AMERICAN PEOPLE 302 (1965).

8. *See generally* FORREST MCDONALD, NOVUS ORDO SECLORUM, chaps. 1 and 2 (1985).

9. MORRISON, *supra* note 7, at 302–3.

10. Isaac Kramnick, *Editor's Introduction,* in THE FEDERALIST PAPERS 28 (Penguin Classics 1987).

11. 1 THE ADAMS-JEFFERSON LETTERS 264 (Lester Capon ed., 1959).

12. 2 PAGE SMITH, JOHN ADAMS 693, 694 (1962).

13. *Id.* at 694.

14. 10 JAMES MADISON PAPERS 209 (William T. Hutchinson et al. eds., 1962).

15. 1 A. BEVERIDGE, THE LIFE OF JOHN MARSHALL 416–17 (1916).

16. Ogden v. Saunders, 25 U.S. 213, 354–55 (1827) (Marshall, C. J., dissenting).

17. Madison, in THE MAKING OF THE AMERICAN REPUBLIC: THE GREAT DOCUMENTS, 1774–1789, at 162 (C. Tansill ed., 1972).

18. Quoted in Kramnick, *supra* note 10, at 27.

19. 1 BEVERIDGE, *supra* note 15, at 242.

20. A Letter of Marque and Reprisal is an authorization by government to a private citizen to capture and confiscate the ships of another nation.

21. 3 THE RECORDS OF THE FEDERAL CONVENTION OF 1787, at 435 (Max Farrand ed., 1911).

22. 1 ANNALS OF CONGRESS 455 (Joseph Gales ed., 1789).
23. GORDON S. WOOD, THE CREATION OF THE AMERICAN REPUBLIC, 1776–1787, at 538 (1969).
24. Address by James Wilson in 1787, in 1 B. SCHWARTZ, THE BILL OF RIGHTS: A DOCUMENTARY HISTORY 429 (1971).
25. FEDERALIST NO. 84, at 513 (A. Hamilton).
26. *See* Chapter 2, Section IX above.
27. FEDERALIST NO. 45, at 292 (J. Madison).
28. FEDERALIST NO. 39, at 245 (J. Madison).
29. HERBERT STORING, WHAT THE ANTI-FEDERALISTS WERE FOR 5 (1981).
30. *See* Calder v. Bull and Wilkinson v. Leland, discussed below in Chapter 4, Section IV.
31. Chancellor Kent, in Dash v. Van Kleeck, 7 Johns Rep. 476 (1811).
32. J. A. C. Grant, *Our Common Law Constitution,* 40 BOSTON L. REV. 1, 19 (1960).
33. FEDERALIST NO. 84, at 513–14 (A. Hamilton).
34. PENNSYLVANIA AND THE FEDERAL CONSTITUTION, 1787–1788, at 308–9 (J. McMaster and F. Stone eds., 1888).
35. Calder v. Bull, 3 U.S. 386 (1798).
36. *See* BERNARD H. SIEGAN, ECONOMIC LIBERTIES AND THE CONSTITUTION 67 (1980).
37. *See* Fletcher v. Peck, 10 U.S. 87, 138 (1810).
38. FEDERALIST NO. 44, at 282–83 (J. Madison).
39. SAUL PADOVER, THE COMPLETE MADISON 268 (1953).
40. FEDERALIST NO. 84, at 515 (A. Hamilton).
41. FEDERALIST NO. 10, at 84 (J. Madison). Charles F. Hobson, however, suggests that Madison may have been influenced by the relative stability of Virginia, the largest and most populous of the American states. Charles F. Hobson, *Republicanism, Commerce, and Private Rights: Madison's Path to the Constitutional Convention of 1787,* at 95, in LIBERTY, PROPERTY AND THE FOUNDATIONS OF THE AMERICAN CONSTITUTION (Paul and Dickman eds., 1989).
42. PADOVER, *supra* note 39, at 4.
43. Douglas Adair, *James Madison,* in FAME AND THE FOUNDING FATHERS (Trevor Colbourn ed., 1974).
44. JOSEPH J. ELLIS, AMERICAN SPHINX: THE CHARACTER OF THOMAS JEFFERSON 98 (1997). *See* Adair, *supra* note 43.
45. DREW MCCOY, THE LAST OF THE FATHERS, 43 n. 7 (1989).
46. *See* Adair, *supra* note 43, at 132–51.
47. MCDONALD, *supra* note 8, at 7.
48. Adair, *supra* note 43.
49. 1 DAVID HUME, HISTORY OF ENGLAND 445 (1776).
50. *See* ELLEN FRANKEL PAUL, PROPERTY RIGHTS AND EMINENT DOMAIN 248–49 (1987).
51. EUGENE ROTWEIN, DAVID HUME WRITINGS ON ECONOMICS 216–17 (1970).
52. *Id.* at 5.
53. 2 HUME, ESSAYS 273 (T. Green and T. Grose eds., 1889).
54. DAVID HUME, *Of Justice,* in 4 THE PHILOSOPHICAL WORKS 453 (1882).

55. DAVID HUME, WRITINGS ON ECONOMICS ixxix–ixxx (Eugene Rotwein ed., 1970).
56. E. G. WEST, ADAM SMITH: THE MAN AND HIS WORKS (1969).
57. JACK N. RAKOVE, ORIGINAL MEANINGS 40 (1997).
58. *Id*. at 41.
59. *See* FEDERALIST NO. 10, at 83–84 (J. Madison).
60. LETTERS AND OTHER WRITINGS OF JAMES MADISON 325–26 (1865).
61. FEDERALIST NO. 10, at 81 (J. Madison).
62. FEDERALIST NO. 62, at 381 (J. Madison).
63. JAMES BUCHANAN and GORDON TULLOCK, THE CALCULUS OF CONSENT 283 (1962).
64. PADOVER, *supra* note 39, at 267.
65. *Id*. at 267–69.
66. 1 THE RECORDS OF THE FEDERAL CONVENTION OF 1787, at 422–23 (Max Farrand ed., 1911). (Hereafter referred to as FARRAND'S RECORDS.)
67. PADOVER, *supra* note 39, at 269.
68. IRVING BRANT, JAMES MADISON, FATHER OF THE CONSTITUTION 174 (1950), quoted in Joseph L. Sax, *Takings and the Police Power,* 74 YALE L.J. 36, 58 (1964).
69. Judge Richard Posner, in Jackson v. City of Joliet, 715 F.2d 1200, 1203 (7th Cir. 1983).
70. MONTESQUIEU, THE SPIRIT OF LAWS, Book 11, Chap. 6 (1748).
71. 1 BLACKSTONE, COMMENTARIES 151.
72. *See* Chapter 3, Section II.
73. FEDERALIST NOS. 47–51.
74. FEDERALIST NO. 47, at 301 (J. Madison).
75. *Id*.
76. *Id*.
77. FEDERALIST NO. 51, at 320 (J. Madison).
78. *Id*. at 321–22.
79. *Id*.
80. FEDERALIST NO. 48, at 309 (J. Madison).
81. FARRAND'S RECORDS, *supra* note 66, at 74.
82. Letter from James Madison to Thomas Jefferson (Oct. 17, 1788), *in* 1 BERNARD SCHWARTZ, THE BILL OF RIGHTS: A DOCUMENTARY HISTORY 616 (1971).
83. FEDERALIST NO. 10, AT 79 (J. MADISON).
84. THOMAS JEFFERSON, NOTES ON THE STATE OF VIRGINIA 157–58 (Ford ed., 1894). *See* FEDERALIST NO. 48, at 310–11 (J. Madison).
85. 3 JOHN C. HAMILTON, HISTORY OF THE REPUBLIC OF THE UNITED STATES 34 (1859), quoting Alexander Hamilton.
86. FEDERALIST NO. 57, at 350 (J. Madison).
87. FEDERALIST NO. 51, at 322 (J. Madison).
88. GERHARD CASPER, SEPARATING POWER 22 (1997), citing WILLIAM B. GWYN, MEANING OF THE SEPARATION OF POWERS 128 (1965).
89. FEDERALIST NO. 47, at 302 (J. Madison).
90. *See* Mistretta v. United States, 488 U.S. 361 (1989) (Scalia, J., dissenting).
91. I.N.S. v. Chadha, 462 U.S. 919 (1983).

92. 1 THE FOUNDERS' CONSTITUTION 323 (Philip B. Kurland and Ralph Lerner eds., 1987).

93. 1 FARRAND'S RECORDS, *supra* note 66, at 512.

94. *Id.* at 51.

95. FEDERALIST NO. 6, at 56–57 (A. Hamilton).

96. FEDERALIST NO. 78, at 466 (A. Hamilton), quoting MONTESQUIEU, SPIRIT OF LAWS 181 (1748).

97. *See generally* BERNARD H. SIEGAN, THE SUPREME COURT'S CONSTITUTION: AN INQUIRY INTO JUDICIAL REVIEW AND ITS IMPACT ON SOCIETY (1987).

98. FEDERALIST NO. 51, at 323 (J. Madison).

99. *Debates of the Federal Convention of 1787,* as reported by James Madison, in THE MAKING OF THE AMERICAN REPUBLIC 174–78 (Charles Callan Tansill ed., 1972).

100. 10 JAMES MADISON, PAPERS 209 (William T. Hutchinson et al. eds., 1962).

101. IRVING BRANT, THE FOURTH PRESIDENT: THE LIFE AND TIMES OF JAMES MADISON 186 (1970).

102. BERNARD H. SIEGAN, ECONOMIC LIBERTIES AND THE CONSTITUTION 100 (1980).

103. FEDERALIST NO. 33, at 204 (A. Hamilton).

104. SIEGAN, *supra* note 97, at 23–25.

105. *Id.* at 9–10.

106. FEDERALIST NO. 44, 285 (J. Madison).

107. *See* EDWARD BARRETT and WILLIAM COHEN, CONSTITUTIONAL LAW, CASES AND MATERIALS 167 (7th ed., 1985).

108. *See* DREW R. MCCOY, THE LAST OF THE FATHERS 80–81 (1989).

109. FEDERALIST NO. 81, at 483 (A. Hamilton).

110. ANNALS OF CONGRESS 432, 439 (1789–1790).

111. 3 DEBATES OF THE SEVERAL STATE CONSTITUTIONAL CONVENTIONS ON THE ADOPTION OF THE FEDERAL CONSTITUTION 487 (J. Elliot ed., 1836). (Hereafter referred to as ELLIOT'S DEBATES.)

112. THOMAS JEFFERSON, NOTES ON THE STATE OF VIRGINIA 221–22 (William Peden ed., 1787). *See* FEDERALIST NO. 49, at 313 (J. Madison).

113. McCulloch v. Maryland, 17 U.S. 316 (1819).

114. MCCOY, *supra* note 108, at 116–17.

115. *Id.* 69–72.

116. FEDERALIST NO. 78, at 469–70 (A. Hamilton).

117. *Id.*

118. *See* Chapter 2, Section IV.

119. 2 ELLIOT'S DEBATES, *supra* note 111, at 348.

120. Alexander Hamilton, *The Farmer Refuted, &c.,* in 1 THE PAPERS OF ALEXANDER HAMILTON 81, 122 (Harold C. Syrett and J. Cooke eds., 1961).

121. BENJAMIN F. WRIGHT, JR., THE CONTRACT CLAUSE OF THE CONSTITUTION 22 (1938) (opinion of Hamilton). The opinion related to the matter subsequently litigated in Fletcher v. Peck, 10 U.S. (6 Cranch) 87 (1810).

122. FEDERALIST NO. 78, at 468–69 (A. Hamilton).

123. The comment is attributed to Robert Yates, who wrote articles opposing the proposed constitution under the name of Brutus. *See* JACKSON TURNER MAIN, THE ANTIFEDERALISTS, CRITICS OF THE CONSTITUTION 125–26 (1961).

124. Dred Scott v. Sanford, 60 U.S. (19 How.) 393 (1857).

125. CONG. GLOBE, 39th Cong., 1st Sess. 2765 (1866).

126. ROBERT H. BORK, SLOUCHING TOWARDS GOMORRAH 117 (1996).

127. Ex Parte McCardle, 74 U.S. 506 (1868).

128. Marbury v. Madison, 5 U.S. (1 Cranch) 137, 177 (1803). See discussion of this case in Chapter 4, Section III.

129. Calder v. Bull, 3 U.S. 386, 388–89 (1798). See discussion of this case in Chapter 4, Section III.

130. Edward S. Corwin, *A Basic Doctrine of American Law,* 12 MICHIGAN L. REV. 247, 253 (1914).

131. *Id.* at 252.

132. PADOVER, *supra* note 39, at 267.

133. FEDERALIST NO. 79, at 472 (A. Hamilton).

134. 2 JOSEPH STORY, COMMENTARIES ON THE CONSTITUTION § 1790 (1833).

135. "The principle established by the Magna Carta and thus basic to the common law and later to the Constitution was the identification of liberty and property. Ownership of property was evidence of liberty. In solemn ceremony, it was there decreed that neither the King nor government could take property except *per legem terrae.* . . . To the framers, identifying property with freedom meant that if you could own property, you were free." Norman Karlin, *Back to the Future: From Nollan to Lochner,* 17 SW. U. L. REV. 627, 637–38 (1988) (footnotes omitted).

136. CHARLES GROVE HAINES, THE AMERICAN DOCTRINE OF JUDICIAL SUPREMACY 209–10 (1959).

137. 1 FARRAND'S RECORDS, *supra* note 66, at 533–34.

138. Vanhorne's Lessee v. Dorrance, 2 U.S. 304, 310 (1795).

139. James Wilson, *Lectures on Law (1790–91),* in 2 WORKS OF JAMES WILSON 718–19 (Robert G. McCloskey ed., 1967).

140. *Id.*

141. *Id.* at 4–14, 43, 300–331, 711–79. *See* WILLIAM B. SCOTT, IN PURSUIT OF HAPPINESS 116 (1977).

142. 1 FARRAND'S RECORDS, *supra* note 66, at 533–34, 541–42, 469–70, 528, 542; 2 FARRAND'S RECORDS, at 202.

143. ROBERT A. HENDRICKSON, THE RISE AND FALL OF ALEXANDER HAMILTON 214 (1985).

144. 1 FARRAND'S RECORDS, *supra* note 66, at 450.

145. J. W. GOUGH, FUNDAMENTAL LAW IN ENGLISH CONSTITUTIONAL HISTORY 54 (1955).

146. Pursuant to U.S. Constitution, Article V.

147. *See* D. FARBER and S. SHERRY, A HISTORY OF THE AMERICAN CONSTITUTION 226 (1990); and Tansill, *supra* note 17, at 1009–59.

148. FEDERALIST NO. 84, at 513 (A. Hamilton).

149. 2 ELLIOT'S DEBATES, *supra* note 111, at 424.

150. FARBER and SHERRY, *supra* note 147, at 224.

151. *Id.*

152. 1 THE DEBATES AND PROCEEDINGS IN THE CONGRESS OF THE UNITED STATES 439 (J. Gales and W. Seaton eds., 1834).

153. *Id.* at 435.
154. U.S. Constitution, Amendment IX.
155. Tansill, *supra* note 17, at 1027–33.
156. *Id.* at 1052–59 and 1034–44.
157. 4 THE PAPERS OF ALEXANDER HAMILTON 35 (H. Syrett and J. Cooke eds., 1962). (Emphasis is in the original.)
158. *See* Douglas Laycock, *Due Process and the Separation of Powers: The Effort to Make the Due Process Clause Nonjusticiable,* 64 TEX. L. REV. 875, 891 (1982); *see* Robert F. Riggs, *Substantive Due Process in 1791,* WISC. L. REV. 941, 989–90 (1990).
159. Syrett and Cooke, *supra* note 157, at 35.
160. THE BILL OF RIGHTS AND THE STATES 362 (P. T. Conley and J. P. Kaminski eds., 1992).
161. 1 ANNALS OF CONGRESS 431–32 (J. Gales ed., 1834).
162. 1 BLACKSTONE, COMMENTARIES 135.
163. Chicago, B. & Q. R. Co. v. Chicago, 166 U.S. 226 (1897).
164. Calder v. Bull, 3 U.S. 386 (1798).
165. Norman v. Heist, 5 Watts and Serg 193 (1843). Another reason why, prior to the framing of the Bill of Rights, only the Northwest Ordinance and the constitutions of Vermont and Massachusetts contained taking clauses is that until then confiscation of property was a relatively infrequent event. According to law professor Stoebuck, in the English colonies, the payment of compensation for eminent domain acquisitions was well established and extensively practiced at and before the American Revolution. He writes that a similar policy prevailed in England during the seventeenth and eighteenth centuries: "Examination of the Declaration of Independence and ten other important Revolutionary documents revealed that, while the British were scoundrels in a thousand ways, they never abused eminent domain. They surely would have been accused of it if they had." William B. Stoebuck, *A General Theory of Eminent Domain,* 47 WASHINGTON L. REV. 579, 594 (1972).
166. Powers v. Bergen, 6 N.Y. 358, 367 (1852). *See* Taylor v. Porter, 4 Hill 140 (1843).
167. 1 ANNALS OF CONGRESS 431–32 (J. Gales ed., 1834).
168. Tansill, *supra* note 17, at 47–54.
169. *See* William Michael Treanor, *The Origins and Original Significance of the Just Compensation Clause of the Fifth Amendment,* 49 YALE L.J. 694, 702–8 (1985).
170. Vermont Constitution of 1777, Chapter 1, Article 1, and Chapter 2; and Massachusetts Constitution of 1780, Part I, Article X.
171. *See* WILLIAM MICHAEL TREANOR, THE ORIGINAL UNDERSTANDING OF THE TAKINGS CLAUSE 2 (1998).
172. Stoebuck, *supra* note 165, at 580.
173. *Id.* at 579–81.
174. Armstrong v. United States, 364 U.S. 40, 49 (1960).
175. 4 BLACKSTONE, COMMENTARIES 230.
176. The most famous cases are Pumpelly v. Green Bay and Mississippi Canal Co., 180 U.S. 166 (1871), discussed in Chapter 4, Section IV; Gardner v. Newburgh, 2 Johns Ch. 162 (1816), discussed in Chapter 4, Section II; and Sinnickson v. Johnson, 17 N.J.L. 129 (1839), discussed in Chapter 4, Section II.
177. 2 BLACKSTONE, COMMENTARIES 2.

178. 1 BLACKSTONE, COMMENTARIES 134.
179. 3 BLACKSTONE, COMMENTARIES 145.
180. Pennsylvania Coal Co. v. Mahon, 260 U.S. 393 (1922).
181. Lucas v. South Carolina Coastal Council, 505 U.S. 1003 (1992).
182. 1 COKE, INSTITUTES, Ch. 1, § 1.
183. The U.S. Supreme Court has ruled that a taking of property occurs when a regulation denies an owner all economically beneficial or productive use of the land. *See* Lucas, *supra* note 181.
184. Stoebuck, *supra* note 165, at 553, 583.
185. Parham v. Justices, 9 Ga. 341, 348 (1851).
186. *See* John F. Hart, *Colonial Land Use Law and Its Significance for Modern Takings Doctrine,* 109 HARVARD L. REV. 1252 (1996).
187. Gary Lawson, *The Bill of Rights as an Exclamation Point,* 33 UNIV. OF RICHMOND L. REV. 518 (1999).
188. *See* Section IV *infra.*
189. Dred Scott v. Sandford, 60 U.S. 393 (1856). *See* the discussion of slavery in THOMAS G. WEST, VINDICATING THE FRAMERS, Ch. 1 (1997). West states that every leading member of the Constitutional Convention of 1787 acknowledged that slavery was wrong. For another explanation why the Constitution does not impose the takings clause in the states, *see* Mitchell M. McConnell, *Contract Rights and Property Rights on Liberty,* in Paul and Dickman, *supra* note 41.
190. DANIEL A. FARBER, WILLIAM W. ESKRIDGE, JR., and PHILIP P. FRICKEY, CONSTITUTIONAL LAW 431 (2d ed., 1998).

Chapter 4. Judicial Interpretations of Property Rights Prior to the Fourteenth Amendment

1. FRED BOSSELMAN ET AL., THE TAKING ISSUE (1973); William Michael Treanor, *The Origins and Original Significance of the Just Compensation Clause of the Fifth Amendment,* 94 YALE L.J. 694 (1985); Joseph Sax, *Takings and the Police Power,* 74 YALE L.J. 36 (1964); and MORTON HORWITZ, THE TRANSFORMATION OF AMERICAN LAW, 1780–1860 (1977).
2. BOSSELMAN ET AL., *supra* note 1, at v.
3. 2 ALEXIS DE TOCQUEVILLE, DEMOCRACY IN AMERICA 272 (Rep. 1965).
4. Ex parte Dorsey, 7 Port. 293 (1838).
5. Sadler v. Langham, and Moore v. Wright and Rice, 34 Ala. 311 (1859).
6. Ex parte Martin, 13 Ark. 198 (1853).
7. The San Francisco, Alameda and Stockton Railroad Company v. Caldwell, 31 Cal. 368 (1866).
8. Samuel J. Sherman v. D.S.K. Buick and John Carrick, 32 Cal. 241 (1867).
9. Bernard S. Fox v. The Western Pacific Railroad Company, 51 Cal. 538 (1867).
10. Enfield Toll Bridge Co. v. Connecticut River Co., 7 Conn. 28 (1828).
11. Hooker v. New Haven and Northampton Company, 10 Conn. 146 (1841).
12. Woodruff v. Neal, 28 Conn. 165 (1859).
13. *Id.*

14. John Whiteman's Ex'x v. The Wilmington and Susquehanna Rail Road Company, 5 Del. 514 (1839).
15. In the matter of a return of a private road on the petition of George Hickman, 4 Del 580 (1847).
16. Bradford v. Cole, 8 Fla. 263 (1959).
17. Young v. McKenzie, Harrison and others, 3 Ga. 31, 44 (1847).
18. Parkam v. The Justices, 9 Ga. 341 (1851).
19. Peoria & Rock Island R.R. Co. v. Bryant, 57 Ill. 473 (1870).
20. St. Louis, Vandalia & Terre Haute R.R. Co. v. Mollet, 59 Ill. 235 (1871).
21. Cook v. South Park Commissioners, 61 Ill. 115 (1871).
22. Rubottom v. M'Clure, 4 Blackf. 505 (1838).
23. McIntire v. The State, 5 Blackf. 384 (1840).
24. Indiana Central Railroad Company v. Hunter, 8 Ind. 74 (1856).
25. The Trustees of the Wabash and Erie Canal v. Spears, 16 Ind. 441 (1861).
26. The Norristown Turnpike Company v. Burket, 26 Ind. 53 (1866).
27. Grant v. City of Davenport, 18 Iowa 179 (1865).
28. Morford v. Unger, 8 Iowa 82 (Ia. 1859).
29. Henry v. Dubuque & Pacific Railroad Company, 10 Iowa 540 (1860).
30. Gaines v. Buford, 31 Ky. 481 (1833).
31. Transylvania University v. Lexington, 42 Ky. 25 (1842).
32. Cheany v. Hooser, 48 Ky. 330 (1848).
33. City of Covington v. Southgate, 54 Ky. 491 (1854).
34. Mabire v. Canal Bank, 11 La. 83 (1837).
35. Lee v. Pembroke Iron Company, 57 Me. 481 (1867).
36. Comins v. Bradbury, 10 Me. 447 (1833).
37. Lewis v. Webb, 3 Me. 326 (1825).
38. Durham v. Lewiston, 4 Me. 140 (1825).
39. Saco v. Wentworth, 30 Me. 165 (1853).
40. *Id.* at 170.
41. Regents of the University of Maryland v. Williams, 9 G. & J. 365 (1838).
42. Harness v. The Chesapeake and Ohio Canal Company, 1 Md. Ch. 248 (1848).
43. Austin v. Murray, 16 Pick 121 (Mass. 1834).
44. Patterson v. City of Boston, 37 Mass. 159 (1838).
45. Parker v. Boston and Maine Railroad, 57 Mass. 107 (1849).
46. Commonwealth v. Coombs, 2 Mass. 489 (1807).
47. Commonwealth v. Justices of Middlesex, 9 Mass. 388 (1812).
48. Perley v. Chandler, 6 Mass. 454 (1810).
49. Brown v. Worcester, 79 Mass. 31 (1859).
50. Old Colony & Fall River Railroad Co. v. County of Plymouth, 80 Mass. 155 (1859).
51. Hazen v. The Essex Co., 12 Cush. 475 (1853).
52. Holden v. James, 11 Mass. 396 (1814).
53. Piquet, Appellant, 5 Pick. 65 (1827).
54. Avery v. Fox, 2 F. Cas. 245 No. 674 (C.C.W.D. Mich. 1868).
55. Ames v. The Port Huron Log Driving and Booming Co., 11 Mich. 139 (1863).
56. Parsons v. Russell, 11 Mich. 113 (1863).

57. Gray v. First Division, St. Paul and Pacific R.R. Co., 13 Minn. 311 (1860).
58. Winona & St. Peter Railroad Company v. Denmon, 10 Minn. 208 (1865).
59. Landford v. County of Ramsey, 16 Minn. 375 (1871).
60. Griffin v. Mixon, 38 Miss. 424 (1860).
61. Thompson v. The Grand Gulf Railroad and Banking Company, 4 Miss. 240 (1839).
62. Isom v. The Mississippi Central Railroad Co., 36 Miss. 300 (1858).
63. Wells v. City of Weston, 27 Mo. 385 (1856).
64. The Proprietors of the Piscataqua Bridge v. The New Hampshire Bridge, 7 N.H. 35 (1834).
65. Petition of the Mount Washington Road Co., 35 N.H. 134 (1857).
66. Company v. Fernald, 47 N.H. 444 (1867).
67. Eaton v. Boston C. & M. Railroad, 51 N.H. 504 (1872).
68. Bonaparte v. Camden & A.R. Co., 3 F.Cas. 821 (No. 1617) (D. N.J. 1830).
69. Sinnickson v. Johnson, 17 N.J.L. 129 (1839).
70. Glover v. Powell, 2 Stock. 211 (N.J. Ch. 1854).
71. 2 KENT, COMMENTARIES 13 (1826).
72. *Id.* at note 6.
73. *Id.* at 339.
74. *Id.* at 199.
75. Dash v. Van Kleeck, 7 Johns. Rep. 476 (1811).
76. Gardner v. Trustees of the Village of Newburgh, 2 Johns. Ch. 162 (1816).
77. People v. Platt, 17 Johns. Rep. 195 (N.Y. Sup. Ct. 1819).
78. Canal Fund v. Kempshall, 26 Wend. 404 (N.Y. 1841).
79. Rogers v. Bradshaw, 20 Johns. 735 (N.Y. 1823).
80. Taylor v. Porter, 4 Hill 140 N.Y. (1843).
81. *Id.* at 144.
82. MORTON J. HORWITZ, THE TRANSFORMATION OF AMERICAN LAW, 1780–1860, at 260, 346 n. 7 (1977).
83. Lucas v. South Carolina Coastal Council, 115 S.Ct. 2886, 2903 (1992) (Kennedy, J., concurring).
84. *See generally* BERNARD H. SIEGAN, PROPERTY AND FREEDOM: THE CONSTITUTION, THE COURTS, AND LAND-USE REGULATION, Chs. 1, 7 (1997).
85. Embury v. Conner, 3 N.Y. 511 (1850).
86. Powers v. Bergen, 6 N.Y. 358 (1852).
87. *Id.* at 367.
88. Westervelt v. Gregg, 12 N.Y. 202 (1854).
89. Wynehamer v. People, 13 N.Y. 378 (1856).
90. *Id.* at 392.
91. *Id.* at 416.
92. *Id.* at 432.
93. Edward Corwin, *The Doctrine of Due Process of Law Before the Civil War (Pt. 1)* 24 HARVARD L. REV. 460, 467–68 (1917).
94. EDWARD CORWIN, LIBERTY AGAINST GOVERNMENT 114–15 (1948).
95. University of North Carolina v. Foy and Bishop, 5 N.C. (1 Mur.) 58 (1805).
96. *Id.* at 88.
97. Hoke v. Henderson, 15 N.C. 1 (1833).

98. *Id.* at 13–14.
99. State v. Glen, 52 N.C. 321 (1859).
100. Railroad Co. v. Davis, 19 N.C. 451 (1837).
101. Gavit v. Chambers and Coats, 3 Ohio 495 (1828).
102. Cooper v. Williams, 5 Ohio 391 (1832).
103. Walker v. Board of Public Works, 16 Ohio 540 (1847).
104. The Oregon Central R. R. Co. v. Wait, 3 Or. 428 (1869).
105. 3 Or. 99 (1869).
106. McMasters v. Commonwealth of Pennsylvania, 111 Watts 292 (1834).
107. Norman v. Heist, 5 Watts & Serg., 193 (1843).
108. *Id.* at 195.
109. Clark v. Peckham, 10 R.I. 35 (1871).
110. Ham v. McClaws, 1 Bay 93 (1789).
111. Bowman v. Middleton, 1 Bay 252 (1792).
112. Zylstra v. Corporation of Charleston, 1 Bay 382 (1794).
113. *Id.* at 390–91.
114. *Id.* at 397.
115. Lindsay v. East Bay Street Commissioners, 2 Bay 38 (1796).
116. State v. Dawson, 3 Hill 100 (1836).
117. Woodfolk v. Nashville & Chattanooga Railroad Company, 32 Tenn. 422 (1852).
118. Red River Bridge Company v. Mayor and Alderman of Clarksville, 33 Tenn. 176 (1853).
119. Vanzant v. Waddel, 2 Yerg. 260 (1829).
120. *Id.* at 269.
121. Bank of the State v. Cooper, 2 Yerg. 600 (1831).
122. *Id.* at 606.
123. Jones' Heirs v. Perry, 10 Yerg. 59 (1836).
124. *Id.* at 71.
125. Wally's Heirs v. Nancy Kennedy, 2 Yerg. 554 (1831).
126. Budd v. The State, 22 Tenn. 483 (1842).
127. Watkins v. Walker County, 18 Tex. 585 (1857).
128. Miller v. Burch, 32 Tex. 208 (1869).
129. Janes v. Reynolds' Adm'rs, 2 Tex. 250 (1847).
130. Livermore v. Town of Jamaica, 23 Vt. 361 (1851).
131. Joseph Hatch, et al. v. Vermont Central Raiload Company, 25 Vt. 49 (1852).
132. The rule was different in Mississippi. *See* Ison v. Mississippi Central Railroad Company, discussed above under the Mississippi subsection.
133. Crenshaw v. State River Company, 6 Rand. 245 (Va. 1828).
134. Thien v. Voegtlander, 3 Wisc. 461 (1854).
135. Newell v. Smith, 15 Wis. 101 (1862).
136. Norton v. Peck, 3 Wis. 714 (1854).
137. Shepardson v. The Milwaukee and Beloit Railroad Company, 6 Wis. 605 (1857).
138. Ford v. The Chicago and Northwestern Railroad Company, 14 Wis. 609 (1861).
139. Osborn v. Hart, 24 Wis. 89 (1869).
140. Lucas v. South Carolina Coastal Council, 112 S.Ct. 2886, 2914 (1992) (Blackmun, J., dissenting).

141. *See* Michael Giorgino, A Critique of Justice Blackmun's Dissent in the Lucas Case (1999) (unpublished manuscript, on file with the University of San Diego Law School).

142. Case of the King's Prerogative in Saltpeter, 12 Co.Rep. 12–13 (1606).

143. *Lucas,* 112 S.Ct. at 2914–15, citing BOSSELMAN ET AL., *supra* note 1, at 80–81.

144. *Lucas,* 112 S.Ct. at 2915.

145. *Id.,* citing M'Clenachan v. Curwin, 3 Yeates 362, 373 (Pa. 1802).

146. *M'Clenachan,* 3 Yeates at 370.

147. *Id.* at 374.

148. *Lucas,* 112 S.Ct. at 2915, citing HORWITZ, *supra* note 1, at 65, quoting Commonwealth v. Fisher, 1 Pen. & W. 462, 465 (Pa. 1830).

149. *Fisher,* 1 Pen. & W. at 465.

150. Lindsay v. Commissioners, 2 Bay 38, 56 (1796).

151. *Lucas,* 112 S.Ct. at 2915, citing Lindsay v. Commissioners, 2 S.C.L. 38, 49 (1796).

152. State v. Dawson, 3 Hill 100, 107 (1836) (Richardson, J., dissenting).

153. Smith v. City of Greenville, 229 S.C. 252 (1956).

154. *Lucas,* 112 S.Ct. at 2916.

155. *Id.* at 2915, quoting Siegel, *Understanding the Nineteenth Century Contract Clause: The Role of the Property-Privilege Distinction and "Takings" Clause Jurisprudence,* 60 S. CAL. L. REV. 1, 76 (1986).

156. Callender v. Marsh, 1 Pick. 418, 430 (1823).

157. *Id.* at 431.

158. *Id.* at 432.

159. *Lucas,* 112 S.Ct. at 2915.

160. *Id.,* quoting Coates v. City of New York, 7 Cow. 585 (N.Y. 1827).

161. *Coates,* 7 Cow. at 585.

162. *Lucas,* 112 S.Ct. at n. 24.

163. *Id.,* citing Coates, *supra* note 160, at 605.

164. Coates, *supra* note 160, at 606.

165. Brick Presbyterian Church v. City of New York, 5 Cow. 538 (N.Y. 1826).

166. Commonwealth v. Tewksbury, 11 Metc. 55, 59 (Mass. 1846).

167. *Lucas,* 112 S.Ct. at 2915.

168. *Id.,* citing Tewksbury, *supra* note 166, at 57.

169. Tewksbury, *supra* note 166, at 58–59.

170. *Id.*

171. *Lucas,* 112 S.Ct. at 2916, quoting Commonwealth v. Alger, 7 Cush 53, 104 (Mass. 1851).

172. *Alger,* 7 Cush at 102.

173. *Id.* at 104.

174. State v. Paul, 5 R.I. 185 (1858).

175. *Id.* at 191–92.

176. *Lucas,* 112 S.Ct. at 2916.

177. Meritt v. Parker, 1 Coxe 460, 463–65 (1795). Justice Blackmun referred to the 1972 case of Just v. Marinette County, 56 Wisc.2d (1972) to illustrate that some recent cases protect natural uses. I have not commented on this opinion or other post-1900 opinions because they have no relevance to early United States property rights jurisprudence, which was the major concern of his discussion.

178. *Gardner,* 2 Johns. Ch. at 332, 334, discussed in Section II *infra.*
179. Commonwealth v. Parks, 155 Mass. 531 (1892).
180. *Id.* at 532.
181. *Id.* at 533.
182. *Id.*
183. Pennsylvania Coal v. Mahon, 43 S.Ct. 158 (1922).
184. *Id.* at 160.
185. *Lucas,* 112 S.Ct. at 2916.
186. Marbury v. Madison, 5 U.S. 137 (1803).
187. Calder v. Bull, 3 U.S. 386 (1798).
188. *Id.* at 387.
189. *Id.* at 388.
190. 3 JOSEPH STORY, COMMENTARIES ON THE CONSTITUTION OF THE UNITED STATES 661 (1970).
191. Terrett v. Taylor, 13 U.S. 43 (1815).
192. Wilkinson v. Leland, 27 U.S. 627 (1829).
193. *Id.* at 657.
194. Gelpcke v. Dubuque, 68 U.S. 175 (1864).
195. Fletcher v. Peck, 10 U.S. 87 (1810).
196. *Id.* at 135.
197. *Id.* at 139.
198. *See* Chapter 3, Section VII *infra.*
199. Bank of Columbia v. Okely, 17 U.S. 235 (1819).
200. *Id.* at 244.
201. Corfield v. Coryell, 4 Wash. C.C. 371 (1823), Fed. Cas. No. 3, 230.
202. Paul v. Virginia, 75 U.S. 168, 180 (1868).
203. Murray's Lessee v. Hoboken Land and Improvement Company, 59 U.S. 272 (1855).
204. *Id.* at 276.
205. *Id.*
206. *Id.* at 280.
207. Greene v. Briggs, 10 F. Cas. 1135 (Cir. Ct., Rhode Island 1852).
208. *Id.* at 1140.
209. Dred Scott v. Sandford, 60 U.S. 393 (1856).
210. Bloomer v. McQuewan, 55 U.S. 539 (1853).
211. Yates v. Milwaukee, 295 U.S. 497 (1870).
212. Hepburn v. Griswold, 75 U.S. 603 (1870).
213. Knox v. Lee, 79 U.S. 457 (1871).
214. Pumpelly v. Green Bay Co., 80 U.S. 166 (1871).
215. The U.S. Supreme Court did not adjudicate this case under the due process clause of the Fourteenth Amendment. Acknowledging that the case only related to the takings provision of the Wisconsin Constitution, the opinion said that the Wisconsin provision is "almost identical in language" to the Fifth Amendment's takings provision:

> Indeed this limitation of the exercise of the right of eminent domain is so essentially a part of American constitutional law that it is believed that no State

is now without it, and the only question that we are to consider is whether the injury to plaintiff's property, as set forth in his declaration, is within its protection. (80 U.S. 166 at 177)

However, the Green Bay Company asserted a federal connection. It claimed that under federal legislation the river bordering the Pumpelly land was to be forever preserved as a navigable stream and adjoining land burdened with an easement in favor of maintaining the river in this condition. The U.S. Supreme Court rejected this claim.

216. *Id.* at 177–78.
217. *Id.* at 180–81.
218. *Id.* at 181.
219. *See* Loretto v. Teleprompter Manhattan CATV Corp., 458 U.S. 419 (1982).
220. Howard Jay Graham, *Procedure to Substance—Extra-Judicial Rise of Due Process, 1830–1860,* 40 CALIFORNIA L. REV. 483, 484 (1952).
221. *Id.* at 484–88.
222. *See* Chapter 5 *infra.*
223. *Murray's Lessee,* 59 U.S. at 276.
224. Pennsylvania Coal Co. v. Mahon, 260 U.S. 393 (1922).
225. Kris W. Kobach, *The Origins of Regulatory Takings: Setting the Record Straight,* 1966 UTAH L. REV. 1211.
226. Charles Warren, *The New Liberty Under the Fourteenth Amendment,* 39 HARVARD L. REV. 431, 443 (1926).
227. Edward S. Corwin, *The Doctrine of Due Process of Law Before the Civil War (Pt. 2),* 24 HARVARD L. REV. 460–71 (1911).
228. Beebe v. State, 6 Ind. 501 (1855).
229. Jackson v. State, 19 Ind. 312 (1862).
230. Mugler v. Kansas, 123 U.S. 623 (1887).
231. *See* State v. Paul, *supra* note 174.
232. *See* definition and discussion of common-law nuisances in Chapter 6, Section IV *infra.*
233. *Mugler,* 123 U.S. at 663, citing Barbier v. Connolly, 113 U.S. 27, 31 (1884).
234. Wilkinson v. Leland, 27 U.S. 627, 657 (1829).
235. License cases, 46 U.S. 504 (1847).
236. *See* Commonwealth v. Algers, 61 Mass. 53 at 85 (1851).
237. KENT, *supra* note 71, at 441 n. 2.
238. THOMAS M. COOLEY, A TREATISE ON THE CONSTITUTIONAL LIMITATIONS 353–54 (1868).
239. *Wynehamer,* 13 N.Y. at 439.
240. Gitlow v. New York, 268 U.S. 652 (1925).
241. *Id.* at 668, 669.
242. Brandenberg v. Ohio, 395 U.S. 444 (1969).
243. 198 U.S. 45, 57–58. While the *Lochner* decision has been reversed, this kind of test is applied currently in property cases, as will be explained in Chapter 6. *See* BERNARD SIEGAN, ECONOMIC LIBERTIES AND THE CONSTITUTION (1981) for a discussion of the Supreme Court's liberty-of-contract jurisprudence.

244. 1 RODNEY A. SMOLLA, SMOLLA AND NIMMER ON FREEDOM OF SPEECH § 10:11, at 10–15 (3d ed., 1996).

245. THEODORE SEDGWICK, CONSTRUCTION OF STATUTORY AND CONSTITUTIONAL LAW 144 (2d ed., 1874).

246. *See* Section IV *infra* of this chapter.

247. *See* Jeffrey Rosen, *Class Legislation, Public Choice, and the Structural Constitution,* 21 HARVARD J. OF LAW AND PUBLIC POLICY 181 (1997).

248. Brandenburg v. Ohio, 395 U.S. 444 (1969).

249. Mississippi University for Women v. Hogan, 418 U.S. 718 (1982).

250. Romer v. Evans, 517 U.S. 620, 633 (1996).

251. City of Richmond v. Croson, 488 U.S. 469 (1989).

252. *Lucas,* 112 S.Ct. at 2886.

253. Keystone Bituminous Coal Assn. v. De Benedictis, 107 S.Ct. 1232 (1987) (Rehnquist, J., dissenting).

254. Lochner, *supra* note 243. The majority actually believed that "the real object and purpose was simply to regulate the hours of labor between the master and his employees . . . in a private business, not dangerous . . . in any substantive degree to the health of the employees." While the measure was extolled as highly benevolent because it substantially cut the bakers' long working hours, it also had a debilitating impact on their wages, which would be reduced commensurate with the reduction in working hours. Many bakery workers may have been pleased by a lessening of working hours; perhaps just as many were distressed by the legislative imposition of what amounts to a curb on wages. To be sure, under the statute a worker could obtain a part-time job in addition to his regular job to compensate for his loss of income, but obtaining such work would be uncertain and fitting it into a worker's daily schedule would be difficult.

255. GERALD GUNTHER and KATHLEEN M. SULLIVAN, CONSTITUTIONAL LAW 468 (1998 Supplement).

256. Coppage v. Kansas, 236 U.S. 1 (1915).

257. Alan J. Meese, *Will, Judgment, and Economic Liberty: Mr. Justice Souter and the Mistranslation of the Due Process Clause,* 41 WILLIAM AND MARY L. REV. 3, 36 (1999) citing SIEGAN, *supra* note 243, at 116.

Chapter 5. The Due Process Clause of the Fourteenth Amendment

1. Chicago, B & Q. R.R. Co. v. Chicago, 166 U.S. 581 (1897).

2. *See generally* BERNARD H. SIEGAN, PROPERTY AND FREEDOM: THE CONSTITUTION, THE COURTS, AND LAND-USE REGULATION (1997).

3. Saenz v. Roe, 119 S.Ct. 1518 (1999).

4. CONG. GLOBE, 39th Cong., 1st Sess. 1089 (1866).

5. *Id.* at 2765.

6. *See generally* Charles Fairman, *Does the Fourteenth Amendment Incorporate the Bill of Rights? The Original Understanding,* 2 STAN. L. REV. 5 (1949).

7. Murray's Lessee v. Hoboken Land and Improvement Company, 59 U.S. 272

(1856). Summary process usually relates to a proceeding for determining liability without any or most requirements of a judicial proceeding.

8. While the Court's reference in the case is to "process," the decision is equally relevant to substantive matters, as is evidenced by the substantive due process rulings the Court cites. *See* note 9 *infra*.

9. Hoke v. Henderson, 15 N.C. 1 (1833); Taylor v. Porter, 4 Hill 140 (1843); Van Zandt v. Waddel, 2 Yerger 260 (1829); State Bank v. Cooper, 2 Yerger 600 (1831); Jones Heirs v. Perry, 10 Yerger 59 (1836); and Greene v. Briggs, 10 F. Cas. 1135 (Cir. Ct. Rhode Island 1852). The Supreme Court, per Justice Curtis, cited the foregoing cases after explaining that due process "generally implies and includes . . . regular allegations, opportunity to answer, and trial according to some settled course of judicial proceedings." *Murray's Lessee,* 59 U.S. at 280.

10. In *Murray's Lessee*, Justice Curtis cites Coke's *Institutes* to support his interpretation of due process (2 INSTITUTES 47, 50). On page 47, Coke writes about the king authorizing a corporation to confiscate cloth under certain circumstances, a power that the English court found to be against the law of the land because "no forfeiture can grow by letters patents" (*id*. at 47). Coke also notes here that no man can be barred from having the benefits of the law or from his livelihood without answer, which means not without a fair trial. He additionally states that "no man may be taken, imprisoned or put out of his freehold without process of the law," and defines "law of the land" as requiring the adoption of laws that "extend to all," meaning that laws should be general and not special in their impact (*id*. at 50).

11. *See* notes 6, 7, and 8 *infra*. and *accompanying texts*.

12. Adamson v. California, 332 U.S. 4674 (1947) (Black, J., dissenting).

13. CONG. GLOBE, 35th Cong., 2d Sess. 983 (1859).

14. *Id*. at 985.

15. CONG. GLOBE, 34th Cong., 3d Sess. App. 140 (1857).

16. CONG. GLOBE, 39th Cong., 1st Sess. 1094 (1866).

17. Much of the material that follows has appeared in greater detail in other of my publications: ECONOMIC LIBERTIES AND THE CONSTITUTION (1980); THE SUPREME COURT'S CONSTITUTION (1987); and PROPERTY AND FREEDOM (1997).

18. CONG. GLOBE, 39th Cong., 1st Sess. 414 (1866).

19. *Id*.

20. Corfield v. Coryell, 6 F.Cas. 546 (C.C.E.D. Pa. 1823) (No. 3,230).

21. CONG. GLOBE, 39th Cong., 1st Sess. 476 (1866).

22. *Id*.

23. *Id*. at 1117–19.

24. *Id*. at 1117–18.

25. *Id*. at 1117.

26. *Id*. at 1118–19.

27. *Id*. at 474.

28. *Id*. at 1118.

29. *Id*.

30. *Id*. at 1292.

31. *Id*. at 504.

32. *Id.* at 601, 1155.
33. *Id.* at 1785, 3034.
34. J. TENBROEK, EQUAL UNDER LAW 118 (1969). *See also* H. J. GRAHAM, EVERYMAN'S CONSTITUTION 168–71 (1968).
35. TENBROEK, *supra* note 34, at 138 n. 2, 142 n. 7, sets forth these examples:

> The call for the Macedon antislavery convention of 8–10 June 1847 provided that
>
> 1. The true foundation of civil government is the equal, natural and inalienable right of *all men*—and the moral obligation, resting on the entire community to secure the free exercise of those rights, including life, liberty, and pursuit of happiness, to each individual in his person and his property, and in their management.
> 3. The sole and indispensable business of civil government is to secure and preserve the natural and equal rights of all men unimpaired, to prevent and redress, violations of original rights. And the benefits of government are not purchased by giving up any portion of our natural rights for protection of the rest.
> 5. All monopolies, class legislations, and exclusive privileges are unequal, unjust, morally wrong, and subversive of the ends of civil government.
> 6. The primary and essential rights of humanity are, the right to occupy a portion of the earth's surface. . . .
> 9. The right of self-ownership includes, of necessity, the right of each individual to the direction and to the products of his own skill and industry, and the disposal of those products, by barter or sale, in any portion of the earth where a purchaser can be found. These original and natural rights, civil government may neither infringe or impair; and all commercial restrictions therefore (except the wise and needful prohibition of immoral and criminal traffic, which no man has a natural right to engage in) are unjust and oppressive.
> 10. "A tariff for the protection of one particular branch of industry, so far as it reaches its end, is an unjust tax upon one portion of the community for the benefit of another. . . ."

At the Honeoye Liberty Mass Meeting, held December 29, 1846 through January 1, 1847, a declaration of sentiments was unanimously adopted containing similar assertions and it also included the following: "The rightful power of all legislation is to declare and enforce our natural rights and duties and take none of them from us. . . . The idea is quite unfounded, that, on entering society, we give up any natural right." *Id.* at 142 n. 7.

36. CONG. GLOBE, 39th Cong., 1st Sess. 475 (1866).
37. *Id.* at 504.
38. *Id.* at 1151.
39. *Id.* at 1833.
40. *Id.* at 1159.
41. *Id.* at 1160, 1759.

42. *Id.* at 1124. Some commentators have asserted that the extent of the oppression of blacks was exaggerated. *See* H. FLACK, THE ADOPTION OF THE FOURTEENTH AMENDMENT 96 (1908); and Bickel, *The Original Understanding and the Segregation Decision*, 69 HARV. L. REV. 1, 13 (1955).
43. Dred Scott v. Sandford, 60 U.S. 393 (1856).
44. CONG. GLOBE, 39th Cong., 1st Sess. 1088–89 (1866).
45. *Id.* at 1089.
46. *Id.* at 1292.
47. *Id.*
48. *Id.* at 1090.
49. John Locke, *Second Treatise* § 54, in LOCKE, TWO TREATISES OF GOVERNMENT (Peter Laslett ed., 1960).
50. *See* Chapter 4 *infra.*
51. B. B. KENDRICK, THE JOURNAL OF THE JOINT COMMITTEE OF FIFTEEN ON RECONSTRUCTION 85 (1914).
52. CONG. GLOBE, 39th Cong., 1st Sess. 1366, 1413, 1291 (1866).
53. *Id.* at 1291.
54. *Id.* at 1065.
55. *Id.*
56. *Id.* at 1089.
57. *Id.* at 1063.
58. *See id.* at 1064.
59. *Id.* at 2765–66.
60. *Id.* at 2766.
61. CONG. GLOBE, 42d Cong., 1st Sess. App. 81, 83–85 (1871).
62. *Id.* at 2459.
63. CONG. GLOBE, 39th Cong., 2d Sess. 984 (1859).
64. H. J. GRAHAM, *supra* note 34, at 465–66.
65. CONG. GLOBE, 39th Cong., 1st Sess. 2542 (1866).
66. CONG. GLOBE, 34th Cong., 3d Sess. App. 136 (1857).
67. CONG. GLOBE, 39th Cong., 1st Sess. 3543 (1866).
68. *Id.* at 2465.
69. *Id.* at 2502.
70. *Id.* at 2539.
71. *Id.* at 2510.
72. *Id.* at 2535.
73. *Id.* at 2538.
74. *Id.* at 1054.
75. *Id.* at 1291.
76. CONG. GLOBE, 34th Cong., 3d Sess. App. 256 (1857).
77. CONG. GLOBE, 39th Cong., 1st Sess. 2961, 2510 (1866).
78. *Id.* at 1063.
79. TENBROEK, *supra* note 34, at 119–22; GRAHAM, *supra* note 34, at 242–65. Concerning the early abolitionist arguments that would later be advanced under due process concept, *see* A. L. HIGGINBOTHAM, JR., IN THE MATTER OF COLOR, 329–32 (1978).
80. GRAHAM, *supra* note 34, at 250. "Over the next thirty years [from 1834], due

process as a substantive conception, became part of the constitutional stock in trade of abolitionism." TENBROEK, *supra* note 34, at 121. "In comparison with the concept of equal protection of the law, the due process clause was of secondary importance to the abolitionists. It did, however, reach a full development, and by virtue of its emphasis in the party platforms, a widespread usage and popular understanding." *Id*. at 119–20.

81. TENBROEK, *supra* note 34, at 139. The Liberty Party was formed in 1840 and it was dedicated to antislavery. In 1844, its presidential candidate received 60,000 votes. It continued to be strong in local elections in 1846, but united in 1848 with the antislavery Whigs and Democrats to form the Free Soil Party. THE COLUMBIA ENCYCLOPEDIA 1213 (1963).

82. TENBROEK, *supra* note 34, at 140–41, nn. 3 and 4. The Free Soil Party came into existence during 1847–48 and polled 300,000 votes. Its 1852 candidate for president received over 150,000 votes. It was absorbed into the new Republican Party in 1854. THE COLUMBIA ENCYCLOPEDIA, *supra* note 81, at 767.

83. TENBROEK, *supra* note 34, at 141, nn. 5 and 6.

84. GRAHAM, *supra* note 34, at 80.

85. *Id*. at 83–88.

86. *Id*. at 81.

Chapter 6. The Privileges or Immunities Clause of the Fourteenth Amendment

1. Saenz v. Roe, 119 S.Ct. 1518 (1999) (Thomas, J., dissenting).

2. 7 FEDERAL AND STATE CONSTITUTIONS, COLONIAL CHARTERS AND OTHER ORGANIC LAWS 3788 (F. Thorpe ed., 1909).

3. 3 *id*. at 1839.

4. 1 *id*. at 533.

5. 3 *id*. at 1857.

6. 3 *id*. at 1635.

7. 3 *id*. at 1682.

8. 5 *id*. at 2747.

9. 6 *id*. at 3220.

10. 2 *id*. at 773.

11. PROLOGUE TO REVOLUTION: SOURCES AND DOCUMENTS ON THE STAMP ACT CRISIS 56 (E. Morgan ed., 1959).

12. NEIL H. COGAN, CONTEXTS OF THE CONSTITUTION 24 (1999).

13. Morgan, *supra* note 11, at 47–48.

14. 1774 Statement of Violation of Rights, *in* 1 JOURNAL OF THE CONTINENTAL CONGRESS 68 (1904).

15. Corfield v. Coryell, 6 Fed.Cas. 546 (No. 230) (C.C.E.D. Pa. 1823).

16. Articles of Confederation, March 1, 1781, *reprinted in* THE MAKING OF THE AMERICAN REPUBLIC 27–37 (Charles Callan Tansill ed., 1972).

17. FEDERALIST NO. 80, at 478 (A. Hamilton). (All citations of THE FEDERALIST PAPERS herein refer to the Clinton Rossiter edition of 1961.)

18. Campbell v. Morris, 3 Harr. and McHen. 535 (1797).

19. Douglas, Admin. v. Stephens, 1 Del. Ch. 465 (1821).

20. Corfield v. Coryell, 4 Wash. C.C. 371 (1823).

21. Chester James Antieau, *Paul's Perverted Privileges or the True Meaning of the Privileges and Immunities Clause of Article Four,* 9 WILLIAM AND MARY L. REV. 1, 12 (1967). "Every scholar and every court paid homage to its fundamental right interpretation of the clause." *Id*. at 12.

22. Lynch v. Clarke, 1 Sandford's Chancery Reports 683, 645 (1844).

23. 9 Johns, Cas. 507 (1812).

24. Antieau, *supra* note 21, at 12–14, 18–21.

25. CONG. GLOBE, 39th Cong., 1st Sess. 474–75 (1866).

26. *Id*. at 1757.

27. *Id*. at 1115–19.

28. *Id*.

29. CONG. GLOBE, 35th Cong., 2d Sess. 981 (1859).

30. *Id*. at 985.

31. *Id*. at 2765–66.

32. *Id*. at 2961.

33. *Id*. at App. 219.

34. *Id*. at 3031, 3034–35.

35. *Id*. at 240.

36. *Id*. at 3039.

37. *Id*. at 3041.

38. J. TENBROEK, EQUAL UNDER THE LAW 122–31 (1969).

39. CONG. GLOBE, 39th Cong., 1st Sess. 1679–81 (1866).

40. *Id*. at 1832.

41. *Id*.

42. *Id*.

43. *Id*. at 1123–25.

44. *Id*. at 2502.

45. *Id*. at 1267.

46. *Id*.

47. *Id*. at 601.

48. *Id*. at 1268.

49. *Id*. at 597.

50. *Id*. at 599.

51. *Id*. at 1293–94.

52. *Id*. at 1154.

53. *Id*. at 1782.

54. *Id*. at 111.

55. *Quoted in* TENBROEK, *supra* note 38, at 185–86.

56. CONG. GLOBE, 39th Cong., 1st Sess. 1054 (1866).

57. *Id*. at 1057–59.

58. *Id*. at 1066.

59. *Id*. at 1263.

60. *Id*. at 1265.

61. *Id*. at 1268.

62. *Id.* at 1151.
63. *Id.* at 1088.
64. Paul v. Virginia, 75 U.S. 168 (1868).
65. Slaughterhouse Cases, 83 U.S. 36 (1872).
66. However, in 1871, the Supreme Court decided Ward v. Maryland, 79 U.S. 430 (1871), in which it held that a nonresident is entitled to privileges and immunities as defined by the common law, and not by the state of sojourn.
67. *See* Antieau, *supra* note 21, at 22–25.
68. *Saenz,* 119 S.Ct. at 1537.
69. CHARLES FAIRMAN, RECONSTRUCTION AND REUNION, 1864–88, at 1354 (1971).
70. Most of the rights enumerated in the Bill of Rights are now regarded as incorporated in the due process clause of the Fourteenth Amendment.
71. Bartemeyer v. Iowa, 85 U.S. 129 (1873).
72. Hepburn v. Griswold, 75 U.S. 603 (1870).
73. Knox v. Lee, 79 U.S. 457 (1871).
74. Butchers Union Co. v. Crescent Co., 111 U.S. 746 (1884).
75. Allgeyer v. Louisiana, 165 U.S. 578 (1897).
76. *See generally* BERNARD H. SIEGAN, ECONOMIC LIBERTIES AND THE CONSTITUTION (1980).
77. Colgate v. Harvey, 296 U.S. 404 (1935).
78. Madden v. Kentucky, 309 U.S. 83 (1940).
79. United States v. Carolene Products Co., 304 U.S. 144 (1938).
80. Edwards v. California, 314 U.S. 160 (1941).
81. Shapiro v. Thompson, 394 U.S. 618 (1969).
82. San Antonio Independent School District v. Rodriguez, 411 U.S. 1, 20 (1973).
83. Dandridge v. Williams, 397 U.S. 471, 487 (1970).
84. Jackson v. City of Joliet, 715 F.2d 1200, 1203 (7th Cir. 1983).
85. Maher v. Roe, 432 U.S. 464 (1977).
86. Plessy v. Ferguson, 163 U.S. 537 (1896).
87. *See* note 79 *supra.*
88. Barron v. Baltimore, 22 U.S. 243, 250 (1833).
89. Adamson v. California, 332 U.S. 46, 74–75 (1948) (Black, J., dissenting).
90. ROBERT G. MCCLOSKY, PRINCIPLES, POWERS, AND VALUES 11 (Donald Giannella ed., 1965).
91. *See* Hurtado v. California, 110 U.S. 518 (1884), Minneapolis v. St. Louis R.R. Co. v. Bombolis, 241 U.S. 211 (1965), and Twining v. New Jersey, 211 U.S. 78 (1946).
92. AKHIL REED AMAR, THE BILL OF RIGHTS 219 (1998).
93. 2 COKE, INSTITUTES 50, 47.
94. *Id.* at 51.
95. Poe v. Ullman, 467 U.S. 497, 541 (1961) (Harlan, J., dissenting.)
96. Ogden v. Saunders, 25 U.S. 213, 356 (1827) (Marshall, C.J., dissenting).
97. 3 JOSEPH STORY, COMMENTARIES ON THE CONSTITUTION OF THE UNITED STATES 661 (1833).

Index

Index of Cases

About the Author

Bernard H. Siegan is Distinguished Professor of Law at the University of San Diego School of Law, where he has taught since 1975. He received his J.D. from the University of Chicago Law School in 1949. He is the author of *Land Use without Zoning* (1972), *Economic Liberties and the Constitution* (1980), *The Supreme Court's Constitution: An Inquiry into Judicial Review and Its Impact on Society* (1987), *Drafting a Constitution for a Nation or Republic Emerging into Freedom* (1992), and *Property and Freedom* (1997).

DATE DUE

About the Author

Rosemarie Skaine, M.A., Sociology, is an author who lives in Cedar Falls, Iowa. She has published eleven books: *Women of Afghanistan in the Post-Taliban Era* (McFarland, 2008); *Women Political Leaders in Africa* (McFarland, 2008); *Female Suicide Bombers* (McFarland, 2006); *Female Genital Mutilation: Legal, Cultural and Medical Issues* (McFarland, 2005); *The Cuban Family: Custom and Change in an Era of Hardship* (McFarland, 2004); *Paternity and American Law* (McFarland, 2003); *The Women of Afghanistan Under the Taliban* (McFarland, 2002); *Women College Basketball Coaches* (McFarland, 2001); *A Man of the Twentieth Century: Recollections of Warren V. Keller, A Nebraskan, as told to Rosemarie Keller Skaine and James C. Skaine* (Castle Publishing, 1999); *Women at War: Gender Issues of Americans in Combat* (McFarland, 1999); and *Power and Gender: Issues in Sexual Dominance and Harassment* (McFarland, 1996).

Skaine's special awards include: Grand Island Senior High School Hall of Honor inductee (2009); The Gustavus Myers Center Award for the Study of Human Rights in North America (1997) for her outstanding work on intolerance in North America in her book, *Power and Gender: Issues in Sexual Dominance and Harassment* (McFarland & Co., Inc., Publishers, 1996). Since 2006, Skaine has been included in Marquis *Who's Who in the World*, *Who's Who in America*, and *Who's Who of American Women*.